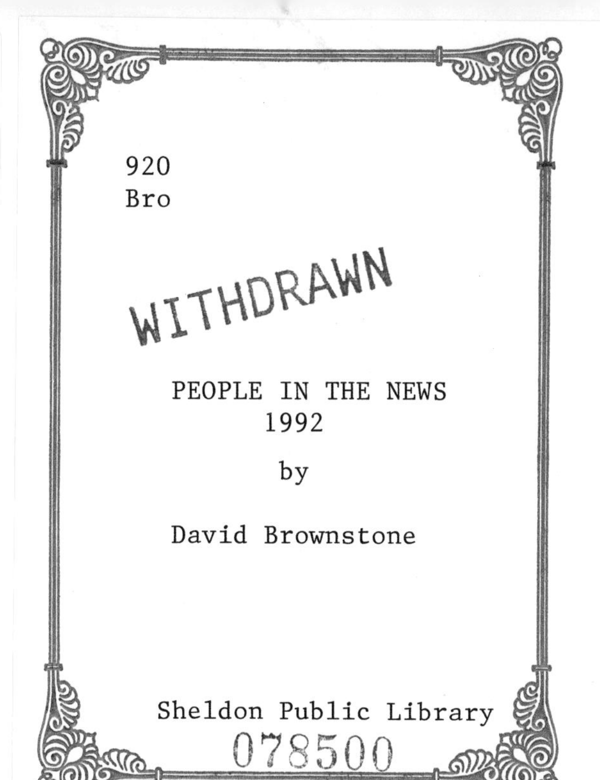

PEOPLE IN THE NEWS
1992

by

David Brownstone

People in the News 1992

People in the News 1992

David Brownstone

Irene Franck

MACMILLAN PUBLISHING COMPANY
NEW YORK
Maxwell Macmillan Canada
TORONTO
Maxwell Macmillan International
NEW YORK OXFORD SINGAPORE SYDNEY

Acknowledgments for illustrative materials are on pp. 383–385, which shall be considered a continuation of the copyright page.

Macmillan Publishing Company
866 Third Avenue
New York, NY 10022

Maxwell Macmillan Canada, Inc.
1200 Eglinton Avenue East, Suite 200
Don Mills, Ontario M3C 3N1

Macmillan Publishing Company is part of the Maxwell Communication Group of Companies

Printed in the United States of America

printing number

1 2 3 4 5 6 7 8 9 10

Library of Congress Cataloging-in-Publication Data
The Library of Congress has catalogued this serial as follows:

Brownstone, David M.
People in the news / David Brownstone Irene Franck.
p. Cm.
Includes bibliographical references and index.
Summary: Presents clear, up-to-date biographical information on a wide selection of the most newsworthy people in the world.

Annual
Begin with issue for 1991.

TSSN 1062-2713
1. Celebrities—Biography. 2. Biography—20th century. [1. Celebrities. 2. Biography.] I. Franck, Irene M. II. Title.
CT120.B76 1991
920—dc20

91-14962
CIP

The paper used in this publication meets the minimum requirements of American National Standard for Information Sciences—Permanence of Paper for Printed Library Materials. ANSI Z39.48–1984 ∞ ™

Contents

Preface

In this second annual edition of **People in the News,** we have again developed current profiles of a wide selection of the world's most newsworthy people, in each profile first stressing 1991 activities, then presenting a concise biography, and then backing each entry with further reading for those who want to dig deeper into current and past histories. These are the world's key political leaders and trendsetters—the presidents, prime ministers, generals, musicians, film stars, directors, scientists, doctors, business leaders, spies, criminals, victims, writers, judges, and the rest who are the main stuff of day-to-day reportage on screen and in print throughout the year.

People in the News is approximately 20 percent larger his year than last, as we have made some of the entries a bit longer, cited more "further reading" materials for the obituary entries, and added a cumulative alphabetical index that covers both editions. That cumulative index is an indispensable addition to the work, making it always possible to reach quickly and easily into the whole set of people covered in any edition of **People in the News.** Please note that, in this edition, the index by occupation has also been made cumulative.

We should note that approximately 75–80 percent of the material in this edition of **People in the News** is completely new, even though the majority of the entries cover people previously profiled. That will always be so, and stems from the nature of the work, for in each such entry material from the previous year has been merged into the biographies, leaving room for the entirely new material comprising the current and usually largest portion of the entry. Entries on living people are current to year's end, and sometimes later. So are the suggestions for further reading, which have also been updated, with newer bibliographic citations added and older ones dropped.

This edition of **People in the News** covers a little under 700 people in all, including nearly 200 key obituaries. As will also always be the case, we have added many newsworthy people, this year approximately 100, and dropped a similar number, some of whom will be back in future editions, as their newsmaking activities warrant.

Our thanks to Philip Friedman, president and publisher of Macmillan's Reference Division, and to managing editor Michael Sander and his assistant, Elena Vega, who have so capably seen this book through the publishing process. We also thank the staff of the Chappaqua Library—Director Mark Hasskarl; the expert reference staff, including Martha Alcott, Teresa Cullen, Carolyn Jones, Paula Peyraud, Mary Platt, and Alice Smith; and the ever-helpful circulation staff, including Marilyn Coleman, Lois Siwicki, and Jane McKean–and their colleagues throughout the northeastern library network, who have once again been so helpful in fulfilling our research needs. Our thanks also to our expert photo researchers: Susan Hormuth, visual resources consultant, and Joan Carroll of Wide World Photos.

David Brownstone
Irene Franck
Chappaqua, New York

People in the News 1992

Abbott, Berenice (1898–1991) Long a leading U.S. photographer, Abbott "discovered" French photographer Eugene Atget while studying with Man Ray in Paris in the late 1920s. She and Ray preserved thousands of Atget's pictures; at Atget's death in 1928, Abbott bought 8,000 of his prints and 1,500 glass plate negatives. She brought them to the United States in 1929 and became Atget's foremost champion for the next four decades, ultimately donating his body of work to the Museum of Modern Art and seeing him recognized as one of the great figures in the history of photography. She later popularized the works of several other photographers and rediscovered the work of Lewis Hine. From 1929 to 1939, she lived in and photographed New York City, creating her main work; in 1939 she published *Changing New York*. Much of her later work was in scientific photography. In 1989 she published *Berenice Abbott, Photographer: A Modern Vision*. (d. Monson, Maine; December 9, 1991)

FURTHER READING

Obituary. *New York Times*, Dec. 11, 1991.
Obituary. *The Times* (of London), Dec. 14, 1991.
Berenice Abbott. Julia Van Haften. Aperture, 1989.
"The black and white of. . . ." Edie Clark. *Yankee*, Dec. 1988.
"No more softball." Bonnie Barrett Stretch. *ARTnews*, Oct. 1988.
"A great age." *Life*, Fall 1988.
Berenice Abbott: An American Photographer. Hank O'Neal and John Canaday. University of Washington Press, 1982; McGraw-Hill, 1982.

Abdul, Paula (1962–) Paula Abdul rode the top of the pop charts again in 1991. Her new album *Spellbound* was an immediate success on its late May release, as were its first two singles releases: "Rush Rush" topped *Billboard*'s pop singles charts for six weeks, to mid-July; then in September, "The Promise of a New Day" hit number one. Her current success brought her 1989 album *Forever Your Girl*—which had already sold seven million copies—back onto the record charts, though at a lowly 117. This was despite charges that Abdul's was not the only voice heard as lead singer on the album: Yvette Marine, one of the three credited backup singers, charged that her voice had been electronically combined with Abdul's on at least two songs from the album and filed suit against the record company. Abdul denied the charges.

Abdul spent most of 1991, as well as $1 million, preparing a new, highly elaborate 90-minute, 14-number production—involving a road crew of 90 people and another 100 hired locally at each stop—for her *Under My Spell* tour. After delays, she kicked off her U.S. tour in November in Atlanta. The production was then scheduled to move abroad to Japan, back to Canada, and around the United States in summer 1992. During 1991, Abdul also recorded the song "Goodnight, My Love," as one of several singers contributing to an album *For Our Children* to benefit the Los Angeles-based Pediatric AIDS Foundation. She also continued her choreography, as for Oliver Stone's film *The Doors,* released in early 1991.

Of Syrian, Brazilian, and French-Canadian descent, California-born Abdul studied tap and jazz dancing as a child, performing summers in a traveling group. She began her work as a choreographer during her six-year engagement as one of the Laker Girls, cheerleaders at the Los Angeles Lakers basketball games. In 1984, she also began to choreograph for Michael Jackson and his brothers, then for Janet Jackson and other entertainment figures, including the Pointer Sisters, Eddie Murphy in *Coming to America,* and Tracey Ullman, winning an Emmy for her choreography of the "Tracey Ullman Show." In 1988, her career took an entirely new turn, as her first album, *Forever Your Girl,* hit the top of the best-seller charts, with such hits as "Straight Up," "(It's Just) The Way That You Love Me," "Knocked Out," "Forever Your Girl," "Gold-Hearted," and "Opposites Attract." "Straight Up" was named the most performed song of 1989 by ASCAP (American Society of Composers, Authors and Publishers). Abdul also won a 1990 Emmy for her choreography of the American Music Awards. Her second hit album was *Shut Up and Dance (The Dance Mixes)* (1990). She attended California State University.

FURTHER READING

"Abdul, Paula." *Current Biography,* Sep. 1991.
Magic of Paula Abdul: Straight Up to Spellbound. DEVRA NEWBERGER. *Scholastic, 1991.*
"Janet Jackson and Paula Abdul. . . ." *Jet,* May 7, 1990.
"The many talents of Paula Abdul. . . ." LYNN NORMENT. *Ebony,* May 1990.
"Paula Abdul." *People,* Spring 1990.
"Straight up . . . and up and up." JEANNE PARK. *People,* Mar. 12, 1990.
Paula Abdul: Forever Yours. GRACE CATALANO. New American Library-Dutton, 1990.

Abe, Shintaro (1924–91) A leading Japanese politician, Abe was long a political power in his country. He began his career as a journalist, entering politics in 1957 as private secretary to foreign minister Nobusuke Kishi. In 1958, he was elected to the first of his nine terms in the House of Representatives. He entered the Tadeo Miki cabinet in 1974, as minister of agriculture and forestry, and then held a long series of cabinet and ruling Liberal Democratic Party posts, most notably as foreign minister in the Yasuhiro Nakasone government (1982–86). He had been widely expected to succeed prime minister Noburu Takeshita, but Takeshita and Abe were both deeply involved in the 1989 Recruit stock scandal; Takeshita resigned, and Abe did not stand for prime minister after admitting that he and his wife had received millions of yen in "gifts" from the company. Instead, he supported Toshiki Kaifu and did not serve in the Kaifu cabinet, although continuing to be a powerful political figure. He was survived by his wife and two sons. (d. Tokyo; May 15, 1991)

FURTHER READING

"Japan's lost leader. . . ." *Economist,* May 18, 1991.
Obituary. *New York Times,* May 16, 1991.
Obituary. *The Times* (of London), May 16, 1991.

Aiello, Danny (Danny Louis Aiello, Jr., 1935–) Late-blooming actor Aiello survived a film industry disaster in 1991, when he played a major supporting role as Tommy Five-Tone in the ill-fated Michael Lehmann film *Hudson Hawk,* starring Bruce Willis. The expensive production, expected to be a commercial blockbuster, was anything but, after being panned by most critics.

Aiello starred in several other 1991 films. In Lasse Hallstrom's *Once Around,* he won critical praise paired with Gena Rowlands as Joe and

Marilyn Bella, whose daughter (Holly Hunter) falls in love with the comically unsuitable "older man" (Richard Dreyfuss). In *The Closer,* he played a Los Angeles real estate tycoon, father to his real-life son, Rick Aiello; the two had acted together, though not as father and son, in three other films. Aiello also played opposite Tim Robbins in *Jacob's Ladder,* a psychological thriller about Vietnam veterans that opened in late 1990. Late in 1991, he opened in *29th Street,* playing the father of 1970s New York City $6 million lottery winner Frank Pesce, Jr.; the cast included the real Frank, Jr., now a character actor. Another starring role was in Paul Mazursky's *The Pickle,* a comedy about a film director directing a teenage movie about a flying cucumber. Forthcoming were several other films, including John Mackenzie's *Ruby,* as Jack Ruby, killer of presumed Kennedy assassin Lee Harvey Oswald; and Barry Primus's *Mistress,* with Robert De Niro, Martin Landau, and Eli Wallach.

New York City-born Aiello played modest supporting roles on stage and screen from the early 1970s, appearing in such films as *The Godfather Part II* (1974), *The Front* (1976), *Fort Apache, the Bronx* (1981), and *The Purple Rose of Cairo* (1984), and emerging in substantial roles in the late 1980s, with leads opposite Cher in *Moonstruck* (1987) and Eddie Murphy in *Harlem Nights* (1989). Aiello won a Best Supporting Actor Oscar nomination and Chicago and Los Angeles film critics awards for his role as Sal, the Italian pizza parlor owner in a racially troubled Brooklyn neighborhood, in Spike Lee's *Do the Right Thing* (1989). He married Sandy Cohen in 1955; the couple have four children.

FURTHER READING

"Broadway Danny. . . ." GAVIN SMITH. *Film Comment,* July–Aug. 1991.
"Danny Aiello." LORENZO CARCATERRA. *People,* Feb. 19, 1990.
"His bus came in." MICHAEL NORMAN. *New York Times Magazine,* Jan. 21, 1990.

Akhromeyev, Sergei (1923–91) An early high-ranking casualty of the failed August 1991 right-wing Soviet coup, Akhromeyev reportedly committed suicide on August 24. His reasons for doing so were unclear; some observers felt that he had supported the coup, although not publicly, while others felt that he might have been deeply depressed by the destruction of his life's work, as the Soviet Union began to come apart.

Akhromeyev had spent his whole life in the Soviet army, joining it in 1940, at the age of 17. He joined the Communist Party in 1943. He served as a frontline commander throughout World War II, and moved up during the postwar period, becoming first deputy armed forces chief of staff in 1979, first deputy minister of defense in 1984, and armed forces chief of staff (1984–88). He was also a candidate member of the Communist Party central committee (1981–86). While a key Soviet arms control figure and a declared supporter of some democratic reforms, he was also entirely committed to the Soviet state and ruling party, and resigned his post of chief of staff in 1988 after announced armed forces cuts. He had stayed on as President Gorbachev's chief military adviser, although increasingly critical of what he considered the too-fast pace of change and military cuts. He was survived by his wife, Tamara, and two daughters. (d. Moscow; August 24, 1991)

FURTHER READING

"Death of a soldier." PAULA CHIN et al. *People,* Sep. 16, 1991.
"A communist, a patriot. . . ." WILLIAM J. CROWE. *Time,* Sep. 9, 1991.
Obituary. *The Times* (of London), Aug. 26, 1991.

Obituary. *New York Times,* Aug. 26, 1991.
"A soldier talks peace. . . ." *Time,* Nov. 13, 1989.
"Building trust." *World Press Review,* Oct. 1988.

Alda, Alan (1936–) After over 20 years, Alan Alda returned to the stage in 1991. Far from the tiny New Jersey theater in which he last acted before a live audience in *Luv* in 1969, Alda opened a major London revival of Thornton Wilder's *Our Town* in September 1991, in the key role of the stage manager. Alda and the production garnered respectful notices and satisfying audiences for the limited run through December. Alda said he had missed the highs of stage work and the ability to build a whole performance instead of filming fragments over several weeks—and felt the strain of writing, directing, and acting in his own films. Sticking with the stage for now, he was scheduled to star in Neil Simon's *Jake's Women* on Broadway in spring 1992.

New York-born Alda, the son of actor Robert Alda, appeared on the New York stage from the late 1950s, in such plays as *Purlie Victorious* (1961), *The Owl and the Pussycat* (1964), and *The Apple Tree* (1966). He became a television star in the 1970s, in *The Glass House* (1972), and then as Korean War surgeon Benjamin Franklin "Hawkeye" Pierce, in the long-running series "M*A*S*H" (1972–83). He has also starred in such films as *The Moonshine War* (1970), *California Suite* (1978), *Same Time Next Year* (1978), and *The Seduction of Joe Tynan* (1979), and appeared in many other films, including *Crimes and Misdemeanors* (1989), for which he won the Directors Guild of America's award for best supporting actor. Alda wrote, directed, and starred in the films *The Four Seasons* (1981), *Sweet Liberty* (1986), and *Betsy's Wedding* (1989). He married Arlene Weiss in 1957; the couple have three children. He attended Fordham University.

FURTHER READING

"Alan Alda. . . ." Cliff Jahr. *Ladies Home Journal,* Mar. 1985.
The Last Days of MASH. Arlene Alda and Alan Alda. Unicorn, 1984.
Alan Alda: A Biography. Raymond Strait. St. Martin's, 1983.
Alan Alda: An Unauthorized Biography. Jason Bonderoff. New American Library-Dutton, 1982.

Alexander, Jane (Jane Quigley, 1939–) In 1991, American actress Jane Alexander specialized in biographical portrayals of striking marriages. From December 1990 through April 1991, she starred on Broadway as Joy Davidman, an American admirer and later wife of reclusive Oxford don and writer C. S. Lewis, played by British actor Nigel Hawthorne, in *Shadowlands,* the story of their brief time together before her death of cancer. Then in July, she starred opposite Christopher Plummer in the American Playhouse telefilm *A Marriage: Georgia O'Keeffe and Alfred Stieglitz,* directed by her real-life husband Edward Sherin. Alexander won considerable praise as the enormously talented, fiercely independent artist O'Keeffe, in her 30-year-long relationship with the older Stieglitz, a highly influential photographer and her mentor, before they embarked on a passionate and stormy marriage. It was something of a dream role for Alexander, who had long admired the woman, her work, and her life; in 1980, she had the rare privilege of a meeting with the intensely private O'Keeffe, then 93 years old. Six years later, after O'Keeffe's death, Alexander tried unsuccessfully to obtain financing for a feature film about her.

Alexander played in regional theatre in the

mid-1960s. She emerged as a major dramatic actress on Broadway in 1968, in her Tony-winning role opposite James Earl Jones in *The Great White Hope.* Some of her most notable stage roles were in *6 Rms Riv Vu* (1972), *Find Your Way Home* (1974), *The Heiress* (1976), *First Monday in October* (1978), *Hedda Gabler* (1981), *Old Times* (1984), and *Night of the Iguana* (1988). On screen, she was nominated for a Best Actress Oscar for the film version of *The Great White Hope* (1970), and she also appeared in such films as *All the President's Men* (1976), *Kramer vs. Kramer* (1979), *Testament* (1983), and *Glory* (1989). She has also made several telefilms, most notably *Eleanor and Franklin* (1976) as a classic Eleanor Roosevelt, *Playing For Time* (1980), and *Calamity Jane* (1984). Alexander attended Sarah Lawrence College and the University of Edinburgh. She has been married twice, to Edwin Sherin since 1975, and has one child.

FURTHER READING

"Liz and Jane. . . ." BILL DAVIDSON. *TV Guide,* Apr. 20, 1985.
"Jane Alexander launching. . . ." JIM ROBBINS. *Variety,* Jan. 30, 1985.

Alexander, Lamar (Andrew Lamar Alexander, Jr., 1940–) In December 1990, President George Bush appointed lawyer and former Tennessee Republican governor Alexander to the post of U.S. secretary of education, replacing Lauro Cavazos. In his first year, Alexander focused on the Bush administration's national campaign for "Choice," which would involve some form of federal funding of tuition grants for parents to use in choosing their children's schools. If widely adopted, the technique would radically restructure American education. It might also be used to provide government aid for religious schools, if the Supreme Court were to rule that such aid was not in violation of the Constitution's separation of church and state. During 1991, the administration proposed a very modest total of $230 million for state Choice experiments, with the proposal encountering immediate sharp opposition in the Democratic Party-dominated Congress, especially on the religious school funding issue. Critics also charged that Choice would result in the segregation of poor and minority children from more affluent White children. Alexander continued to express support for such relatively inexpensive reforms as improved teacher training and additional adult education.

Tennessee-born Alexander began his career as an assistant to U.S. Senator Howard S. Baker (1967–69), and briefly during 1969 worked in the White House, doing Congressional liaison. He practiced law in Tennessee during the 1970s, made an unsuccessful gubernatorial run in 1974, and won next time around, serving as state governor from 1979 to 1987. He also served a term as chairman of the National Governors Association (1985–86), and then was president of the University of Tennessee (1988–91). His 1940 B.A. was from Vanderbilt University, his 1965 LL.D. from New York University. In addition to some works on Tennessee, he has published *Steps Along the Way: A Governor's Scrapbook* (1986) and *Six Months Off: An American Family's Australian Adventure* (1988). He and his wife, Honey, have four children.

FURTHER READING

"Lamar Alexander's. . . ." SUSAN CHIRA. *New York Times Magazine,* Nov. 24, 1991.
"George Bush's point man." SAM ALLIS. *Time,* Sep. 16, 1991.
"Alexander, Andrew Lamar, Jr." *Current Biography,* July 1991.
"Meet the Tennessee 'sparkplug.' " ANITA MERINA. *NEA Today,* May–June 1991.

Alia, Ramiz (1925–) At the beginning of 1991, Albania was the last hard-line communist state in Europe. But popular unrest and calls for democracy continued to grow; even Albania could not be cut off from the rest of the world indefinitely.

On March 1, the Communist Party "won" the parliamentary elections, though many believed democratic opposition charges of vote rigging and intimidation. As anti-government actions continued, Alia directed new elections; the Communist Party won again, and anti-government actions intensified. On April 1, Alia was reelected to the presidency, and immediately quit the Communist Party, as directed by the new Albanian constitution. On May 15, an effective general strike stopped most economic activity; it was followed by civil unrest, and on June 4 the communist government resigned. Alia then appointed Albania's first noncommunist modern government in 47 years, led by former communist Ylli Bufi.

Change had come but the process of democratic changeover had not yet been completed—and Albanians faced a bleak future, with one of the weakest economies in Europe. Albanians fled as soon as they could, 18,000 of them to Italy in August, only to be deported back to Albania later in the month. Alia continued to lead the country, but no one could predict for how long.

Born of a Muslim family, Alia as a teenager joined the anti-German Albanian communist partisans led by Enver Hoxha during World War II, and joined the Communist Party in 1943, when he was 18. He became a member of his party's Central Committee in 1948, at 23, and was a non-voting member of its Politburo in 1956. From 1960, he was a key aide to dictator Hoxha, deeply involved in the 1960 break with the Soviet Union and the long-term hard-line anti-Soviet relationship with Maoist China that followed. He became president in 1982 and leader of the Communist Party in 1985, after Hoxha's death. His wife, Semirani Xhurani, died in 1986.

FURTHER READING

"Alia, Ramiz." *Current Biography,* Jan. 1991.
"Leaping to freedom. . . ." SAM SEIBERT. *Newsweek,* July 16, 1990.
"Tirana too?" *Economist,* July 7, 1990.
"Fortress Albania." STAFFAN BRUUN. *World Press Review,* May 1990.

Allen, Irwin (1916–91) Best known for producing his 1970s disaster movie successes, *The Poseidon Adventure* (1972) and *The Towering Inferno* (1974), veteran producer Allen began as a New York journalist, moved to Hollywood in the late 1930s as an editor, and there began his long broadcasting and film career as a radio producer and director. He moved into film production in the late 1940s and won a 1953 Oscar for the documentary *The Sea Around Us,* which he produced and directed. He moved into science fiction in the 1960s, with *The Lost World* (1960) and *Voyage to the Bottom of the Sea* (1961); he produced and directed both. The latter generated the 1964–68 television series; he also produced the series "Lost in Space" (1965–68), "The Time Tunnel" (1965–68), "Land of the Giants" (1968–70), and "The Swiss Family Robinson" (1975–76). He continued to work in feature films and television until the early 1980s. He was survived by his wife, singer and actress Sheila Mathews. (d. Santa Monica, California; November 2, 1991)

FURTHER READING

Obituary. *Variety,* Nov. 11, 1991.
Obituary. *The Times* (of London), Nov. 4, 1991.

Allen, Woody (Allen Stewart Konigsberg, 1935–) Director-writer-actor Allen moved to a new home in 1991—at least temporarily. He had made his last 11 films at Orion Pictures, but that studio was so financially strapped that in autumn 1991 it was forced to hold up release of several already completed movies for lack of money to publicize them. Among these was Allen's latest movie *Shadows and Fog.* As a result, Allen's next film—the *Woody Allen Fall Project '91,* scheduled for 1992—was being made with TriStar Pictures.

As an actor, Allen starred in early 1991 opposite Bette Midler in Paul Mazursky's *Scenes from a Mall,* about the daylong marital wrangle of an affluent Los Angeles couple in an upscale shopping center. Critical and audience response was less than overwhelming, but the film proved popular in the video rental market. At the 1991 Academy Awards, Allen's script for *Alice* (1990) was nominated as best original screenplay, but he won no awards. In a surprising change of pace, Allen also wrote and directed several television commercials for COOP, an Italian supermarket chain.

A New Yorker, Allen emerged as a leading television comedy writer in the late 1950s, and during the 1960s also worked in cabaret and theater, beginning a long series of hit films as the writer and star of *What's New Pussycat?* (1965). He then became one of the leading filmmakers of the 1970s and 1980s, with such films as his Oscar-winning *Annie Hall* (1977), *Manhattan* (1979), *Hannah and Her Sisters* (1984), and *Crimes and Misdemeanors* (1989). Allen attended City College and New York University. He was formerly married to Louise Lasser. He and Mia Farrow have two children.

FURTHER READING

"Woody Allen. . . ." Eric Lax. *Vogue,* May 1991.
"Woody & Mia. . . ." Eric Lax. *New York Times Magazine,* Feb. 24, 1991.
Woody Allen: A Biography, Eric Lax. Knopf, 1991.
Woody Allen Encyclopedia. Mark A. Altman. Movie Publications, 1991.
Woody Allen: His Films and Career. Douglas Brode. Carol, 1991.
Loser Take All: The Comic Art of Woody Allen, expanded ed. Maurice Yacowar. Continuum, 1991.
Woody Allen. Graham McCann. Basil Blackwell, 1990.
Love, Sex, Death, and the Meaning of Life: The Films of Woody Allen, rev. ed. Foster Hirsch. Limelight, 1990.
Woody Allen on Location. T. De Navacelle. Morrow, 1987.
Woody Allen. Nancy Pogel. G. K. Hall, 1987.

Alley, Kirstie (1955–) Kirstie Alley was honored by her peers in 1991, winning an Emmy and a Golden Globe as the best leading actress in a comedy series, for her work as Rebecca Howe in the long-running and often top-rated television show series "Cheers," opposite Ted Danson as bartender Sam Malone. One of the main plot hinges in their series in the 1992–93 season—its tenth and possibly its last—was the possibility of Sam and Rebecca having a baby. Alley's work in *Look Who's Talking Too* (1990), sequel to her earlier film success, won fewer plaudits. Though commercially successful, it came nowhere near the blockbuster status of the original, either in its general release or in video rentals in mid-1991. With her growing celebrity, Alley was tapped for hosting and presenting honors at several award affairs, including the "first annual" moviegoer Movie Awards, which she co-hosted with Robert Townsend on CBS in January 1991.

Kansas-born Alley worked as an interior decorator before taking up an acting career in the early 1980s. Her most notable early work was her role as Lieutenant Saavik in *Star Trek II: The Wrath of Khan* (1982), which was followed by supporting roles in several other theater and television films. She made her major breakthrough in 1987, when she joined the cast of "Cheers." Her film breakthrough came opposite John Travolta in the comedy *Look Who's Talking* (1989). She went on to star in the 1990 film comedies *Madhouse* and *Sibling Rivalry*. Alley attended Kansas State University. She is married to actor Parker Stevenson.

FURTHER READING

"What's hot. . . ." Kathleen Neumeyer et al. *Ladies Home Journal,* Oct. 1991.
"Feisty, funny Kirstie Alley." Gregg Kilday. *Cosmopolitan,* Dec. 1990.
"The tears behind the Cheers." J. D. Reed. *People,* Oct. 29, 1990.
"Kirstie Alley." Richard Blaine. *Good Housekeeping,* Mar. 1990.
"Chez Alley." Fred Robbins. *Saturday Evening Post,* Jan.–Feb. 1990.

Altman, Robert (1925–) Director-producer-writer Altman returned to the center of filmdom in 1991, shooting *The Player,* his first big-budget Hollywood picture in 18 years, since *The Long Goodbye* (1973). The satirical thriller, based on Michael Tolkin's 1988 novel, is set in the cynical, in this case literally murderous, world of a major Hollywood studio. Tim Robbins is a Machiavellian studio executive, who goes after Greta Scacchi, his victim's former girlfriend, with Whoopi Goldberg as a homicide detective. Altman has once again cast a large number of stars and well-known supporting players, many for the film-within-the-film, including (in alphabetical order) Rosanna Arquette, Harry Belafonte, Cher, James Coburn, Brad Davis, Peter Falk, Louise Fletcher, Peter Gallagher, Henry Gibson, Elliott Gould, Joel Grey, Buck Henry, Anjelica Houston, Jack Lemmon, Marlee Matlin, Andie MacDowell, Malcolm McDowell, Nick Nolte, Burt Reynolds,

Julia Roberts, Mimi Rogers, Susan Sarandon, Rod Steiger, Dean Stockwell, Lily Tomlin, Robert Wagner, Fred Ward, and Bruce Willis. Altman's son Steve is art director on the film. Altman's next scheduled project is *L.A. Short Cuts,* an ensemble work with intertwined story lines in the *Nashville* mold, based on a series of short stories by the late Raymond Carver.

Altman directed in television and films from the late 1950s, emerging as a major film director in the 1970s, with such films as *M*A*S*H* (1970), *Brewster McCloud* (1971), *McCabe and Mrs. Miller* (1972), *California Split* (1974), *Nashville* (1975), and *Buffalo Bill and the Indians* (1976). He received best picture and best director nominations for *M*A*S*H* and *Nashville.* But his film career sagged as the American film industry moved toward the theater of spectacle and away from his kind of social commentary. During the 1980s, he directed a variety of films, plays, and telefilms, most notably *Come Back to the Five and Dime, Jimmy Dean, Jimmy Dean* (1982), *Streamers* (1983), *Vincent and Theo* (1990), and (with Garry Trudeau) the innovative pseudo-documentary series, *Tanner* (1988), in which Michael Murphy played a presidential candidate. Altman has been married three times and has five children. He attended the University of Missouri.

FURTHER READING

"Altman '91." Beverly Walker. *Film Comment,* Jan.–Feb. 1991.

Robert Altman's America. Helene Keyssar. Oxford University Press, 1991.

Robert Altman: Jumping off the Cliff. Patrick McGilligan. St. Martin's, 1989.

Alzado, Lyle Martin (1949–) Noted football star Alzado sparked a national controversy in 1991 over the use of steroids and human growth hormone by athletes to build muscle mass and performance. Stricken with central nervous system lymphoma, a deadly and inoperable form of cancer, he blamed his own long-term use of steroids during his college and professional careers, feeling that the steroids had suppressed his immune system. He also reported that he had switched to human growth hormone during his aborted 1990 comeback because it was not detectable by the tests to reveal steroid use. He called for greatly increased efforts to abolish the use of steroids and human growth hormones, calling anti-steroid programs in the National Football League (NFL) and other sports far too minimal and ineffective. The NFL denied that its program was inadequate but called for a general tightening up of such programs. Whether Alzado's charges were scientifically justified remains an open question, as there is little research evidence on the effect of long-term steroid and human growth hormone use on the human immune system.

New York City-born Alzado was one of the leading professional football players of the 1970s and 1980s. After receiving his B.A. from Yankton College in 1971, he played with the Denver Broncos for eight years (1971–79). In 1975, he received the Earl Harman award as outstanding Denver Broncos defensive lineman and in 1977 he was an All-Pro defensive lineman, American Football Conference defensive player of the year, and National Football League man of the year. He went on to play for the Cleveland Browns (1979–82) and Los Angeles Raiders (1982–85), helping win the Raiders Super Bowl XVIII national championship in 1983. He has since appeared in several movies. He attempted a comeback in 1990 but was forced to withdraw because of injuries. With Doug Moe, he wrote *Still Hungry: The Autobiography of Lyle Alzado* (1985). Alzado is married to model Kathy Davis; he has one son from a previous marriage.

FURTHER READING

"Fourth down and long. . . ." Wayne Edwards. *People,* July 29, 1991.

"A doctor's warning ignored." Shelley Smith. *Sports Illustrated,* July 8, 1991.

"Lyle Alzado. . . ." Shelley Smith. *Sports Illustrated,* July 2, 1990.

Anderson, Terry: See **Lebanon Hostages**

Andreotti, Giulio (1919–) The five-party Italian coalition government led by Christian Democratic Party Premier Andreotti ended on March 29, 1991, after the Socialist Party withdrew. As a practical matter, Andreotti remained

in power, and on April 17 formed and led a new four-party coalition, which did not include the Republicans, members of the previous coalition. His new government was the 50th since World War II; his party had been part of all 50. The politics of drift continued in Italy; on August 5, the four parties in the coalition agreed to defer argument on many major questions and to keep the coalition together until the scheduled spring 1992 general elections. The huge Italian government deficit, at the center of Italy's ongoing financial crisis, continued to grow faster than projected; the 1992 budget, adopted at the last possible moment on September 30, 1991, once again predicted gains in this area, through acceleration of privatization (the sale of state assets), cuts in the national health service, a low level of government employee wage increases, and more efficient tax collection—all goals present in previous budgets.

Andreotti continued to place much of his emphasis and hope on the integration of Italy into the European Community, and the European economic and political union. During 1991, he supported the Allied effort in the Gulf War, sending token forces and supporting the European Community position. His government also voted a $50 million aid package to Albania, emerging with great difficulty from communism, although Italy was less than welcoming to thousands of Albanian refugees.

Rome-born Andreotti began his long political career just after World War II. He entered the Italian parliament in 1947 and was parliamentary chairman of the Christian Democratic Party from 1954 to 1972. He has held many cabinet posts from the 1950s through the early 1990s, and has been prime minister seven times in three periods (1972–73, 1976–79, and 1989–). When out of office, he has been a leading Italian journalist; a new book, *The U.S.A. up Close: From the Atlantic Pact to Bush,* is scheduled for 1992 U.S. publication. He attended the University of Rome. Andreotti married Livia Danese in 1945; the couple have four children.

FURTHER READING

"Andreotti, Italian Prime Minister." *Business Week,* Dec. 24, 1990.

Andrew Albert Christian Edward (1960–) and **Sarah Margaret Ferguson** (1959–), **the Duke and Duchess of York.** Prince Andrew is the third child and second son of Britain's Queen Elizabeth II. He is a Royal Navy helicopter pilot and flight instructor, and a photographer who has published and exhibited his work. The former Sarah Ferguson, known as "Fergie" in the media, worked in publishing before her marriage. In 1986, the couple married; from then on, they became worldwide media-created celebrities; 1991 marked their

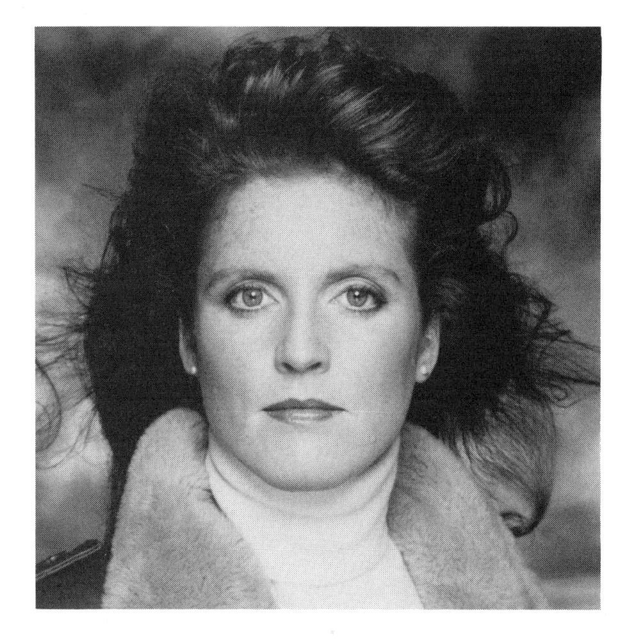

fifth year in the spotlight, with great media attention continuing to be paid to every aspect of Fergie's life and life-style, from the way she wears her hair to her purchase of an article of apparel. The royal couple spend much of their public time in ceremonial appearances and must otherwise pay a great deal of attention to avoiding the media—although in September 1990, their invitation of a photographer into their home and the subsequent informal pictures caught much attention. After one of the most highly publicized pregnancies in recent history, she gave birth to their second daughter, Eugenie, on March 23, 1990; their older daughter is Beatrice. In September 1991, Andrew and Sarah went to New York City, sponsored by the British-American Chamber of Commerce; she visited various charitable institutions, including Harlem's Hale House. With Benita Stoney, Sarah wrote *Victoria and Albert: A Family Life at Osborne House* (1991), about the royal figures and their house on the Isle of Wight; royalties for the book go to the Prince Andrew Charitable Trust. In 1989, she wrote a children's book, *Budgie the Little Helicopter*. The Duke of York is a serving naval officer and attended the Royal Naval College, seeing active service in the Falklands War. The Duchess of York attended secretarial college.

FURTHER READING

"Royalty most raucous. . . ." ADAM HELLKNER et al. *Ladies Home Journal,* Aug. 1991.

"How this sweet little girl. . . ." INGRID SEWARD. *Good Housekeeping,* May 1991.

"Dallas at the palace? . . ." J. D. REED, *People,* Mar. 11, 1991.

Two Royal Women: The Public and Private Lives of Fergie and Di. NORMAN KING. Knightsbridge, 1991.

The Princess and the Duchess: A Behind the Scenes Biography of the Princess of Wales and the Duchess of York. JANE ARTHUR. State Mutual, 1990.

The Private Lives of Britain's Royal Women: Their Passions and Power. UNITY HALL. Contemporary, 1990.

"Fergie at 30." INGRID SEWARD. *Woman's Day,* Oct. 24, 1989.

The Princess and Duchess. JOSEPHINE FAIRLEY. St. Martin's, 1989.

Duchess: An Intimate Portrait of Sarah, Duchess of York. ANDREW MORTON. Contemporary, 1989.

"Andrew, Duke of York." *Current Biography,* Mar. 1987.

"Sarah, Duchess of York." *Current Biography,* Mar. 1987.

Sarah Ferguson: The Royal Redhead. DAVID BANKS. Dillon, 1987.

Their Royal Highnesses the Duke and Duchess of York. CHRISTOPHER WARWICK and VALERIE GARNER. Salem House, 1986.

Annenberg, Walter Hubert (1908–)

In March 1991, philanthropist and former publisher Annenberg made a bequest of his collection of more than 50 French impressionist and post-impressionist paintings, valued at more than $1 billion, to New York's Metropolitan Museum of Art. The works had been on tour for the previous year, at a number of U.S. museums, with the Met finally winning the informal competition for the collection, which includes such major works as Picasso's "Au Lapin Agile," Van Gogh's "Vase of Roses," and Gaugin's "The Siesta," along with other works by Cezanne, Van Gogh, Renoir, Picasso, Degas, Manet, Monet, Toulouse-Lautrec, Gaugin, Seurat, Matisse, Braque, Vuillard, and Bonnard. Annenberg's 1991 gifts also included $60 million to the Corporation for Public Broadcasting (CPB), to help to develop math and science education programs for elementary and secondary students, and $10 million to the Los Angeles County Museum of Art.

Milwaukee-born Annenberg is the son of publisher M. L. (Moe) Annenberg, who founded Triangle Publications, the large publishing company that Walter Annenberg built into an even larger communications empire. He is also a very active Republican Party fundraiser and contributor. An intimate friend of presidents Nixon and Reagan, Annenberg was U.S. ambassador to Britain (1967–75). He is also a major philanthropist, most notably as the founder of the Annenberg School of Communications at the University of Pennsylvania. After selling his interest in Triangle Publications to Rupert Murdoch for approximately $3 billion, he further developed his philanthropic interests. Annenberg attended the University of Pennsylvania and its Wharton School. He has been married twice and has one child.

FURTHER READING

"Walter Annenberg. . . ." *Connoisseur,* Feb. 1991.
"Strength of vision." HUNTER DROHOJOWSKA. *Harper's Bazaar,* Apr. 1989.
The Annenbergs: The Salvaging of a Tainted Empire. JOHN COONEY. Simon & Schuster, 1982.

Antall, József (1932–) Hungarian premier Antall continued to face west during 1991, looking forward to close economic ties and probable future membership in the European Community (EC). An indication of some of the difficulties ahead came in early September, when an EC agreement that would have opened Western markets to Hungarian, Czech, and Polish meat imports was upset by French farm owner protests; but on September 30, quotas for meat from the three countries were raised and they were able to sell some of their meat abroad, their Soviet markets having dried up for lack of Soviet ability to purchase.

Antall also continued to bury the remains of Hungarian and Eastern European communism. In April, the Hungarian parliament voted partial compensation for land seized after 1949, during the communist period. In May, Antall attended the ceremonial reburial of noted anticommunist figure Cardinal Jozsef Mindszenty, who had died in Austria in 1975. On June 19, 1991, the last Soviet troops left Hungary. On June 28, a Budapest meeting of Eastern European leaders disbanded the multinational Council for Mutual Economic Assistance (Comecon), a Soviet economic control instrument. On July 1, a Prague meeting of Eastern European leaders, attended by Antall, disbanded the Warsaw Pact, the last remaining instrument of Soviet military control.

Antall was active in the right-of-center Smallholders Party before the 1947 communist takeover, was mostly out of politics until 1956, and was arrested after joining the failed Hungarian revolution against Soviet domination. He stayed in Hungary after the revolution and was barred from travel abroad until 1973. A historian, he led the Hungarian Democratic Forum to electoral victory in April 1990, and on May 3 became the premier of Hungary, succeeding Socialist Miklos Nemeth. He earned his doctorate at Budapest's Eokvos University.

FURTHER READING

"Antall, Jozsef, Jr." *Current Biography,* Sept. 1990.

Aquino, Corazon (Maria Corazon Cojuangco Aquino, 1933–) Although such basic problems as massive population increases, unemployment in the 20–25 percent range, and deepening poverty continued to develop under the surface of Philippine political life in 1991, President Aquino did to some extent consolidate her government. In October 1990, her armed forces had put down a seventh armed revolt against her government, but no further armed revolt came. In September, Communist rebel armed forces offered a ceasefire in their portion of the long civil war, and there was hope that peace negotiations might begin.

In a gesture of reconciliation—and perhaps in an effort to regain some of an estimated $5 billion of assets abroad—Aquino in the summer of 1991 lifted a ban on the return of Imelda Marcos to the Philippines, also allowing the return of the body of Ferdinand Marcos for burial in his home province. Imelda Marcos returned to face multiple criminal and civil charges on November 4.

Aquino lost a long fight to keep the U.S. naval base at Subic Bay when the Philippine Senate refused to ratify an agreement to renew the lease, on October 2 announcing plans for a three-year staged pullout of U.S. forces. The June volcanic eruptions at Mt. Pinatubo had so badly damaged the U.S. Clark Field air force base that it was never reopened.

In 1980, Corazon Aquino went into exile with her husband, opposition leader Benigno Aquino. On their return to the Philippines in 1983, he was assassinated by agents of then-dictator Ferdinand Marcos. She took her husband's place as head of the Liberal Party and three years later, in 1986, swept Marcos from power and into exile in the elections and following series of events that became the Philippine Revolution. She then introduced a new democratic constitution and government, and has since survived seven right-wing coup attempts and a continuing left-wing insurrection. Corazon Cojuangco and Benigno Aquino were married in 1954 and had five children. She attended New York's Mount St. Vincent College.

FURTHER READING

"Aquino may yet. . . ." DENIS MURPHY. *National Catholic Reporter,* Feb. 8, 1991.

"Cory Aquino. . . ." DENIS MURPHY. *America,* Apr. 21, 1990.

Corazon Aquino: Leader of the Philippines. JAMES HASKINS. Enslow, 1988.

Corazon Aquino. LUCY KOMISAR. Braziller, 1987.

Picture Life of Corazon Aquino. MARGARET M. SCARIANO. Watts, 1987.

Corazon Aquino: The Miracle of a President. CECILIA K. GULLAS. Cultural House, 1987.

Arafat, Yasir (1929–) The Palestine Liberation Organization (PLO) chairman suffered a major defeat early in 1991. He had very publicly backed the Iraqi side during the Persian Gulf crisis that developed into the Persian Gulf War, and in the process he alienated many of his Arab allies. In the aftermath of the lost war, his prestige plummeted throughout the Arab world, as did his bargaining position in the long Arab-Israeli conflict. Nor did his former allies forget; the PLO lost all of the formerly very substantial financial support supplied by Saudi Arabia, Kuwait, and other Arab donors, as well as practical support supplied by several other Arab states. In early July, in a probably related set of operations, Lebanese troops dislodged PLO forces from positions at their main Lebanese base at Sidon; on July 4, Arafat agreed to a surrender at Sidon, with PLO guerrillas turning over their bases and weapons to the Lebanese. In August, the PLO made yet another error of the same kind, when many of its leaders hailed what turned out to be the aborted Soviet right-wing coup.

His position greatly weakened, Arafat made a series of conciliatory moves later in 1991, including expulsion of hard-line terrorist leader Abu Abbas from the PLO executive committee. Arafat also strongly supported PLO endorsement of the Middle East peace talks, and although easily frozen out of the talks, recouped some of his former negotiating strength when the Palestinian representatives made it clear that they were representing the PLO.

Jerusalem-born Arafat was a founder of Al Fatah in 1956 and of its guerrilla army in 1959. He has headed the PLO and been the top leader of the Palestinian national movement since 1969. He suffered major personal defeats when his forces were expelled from Jordan in 1970–71, and from Lebanon in 1983. In the mid-1980s, he moved toward negotiation and publicly renounced terrorism, appearing for a time all but overwhelmed by the more extreme terrorist elements within his own movement. In late 1988, he forced Palestine National Council and PLO acceptance of key United Nations resolutions 242 and 338. On November 15, 1988, he issued a Palestinian declaration of independence, and the proclaimed Palestinian state has since been recognized by more than 50 countries. Arafat attended Cairo University and was an engineer before becoming a full-time political leader.

FURTHER READING

"Yasir Arafat. . . ." *Time,* Oct. 21, 1991.

Behind the Myth: Yasser Arafat and the Palestinian Revolution. ANDREW GOWERS and TONY WALKER. Interlink, 1991.

Arafat and the Palestine Liberation Organization. DIANA REISCHE. Watts, 1991.
Arafat: In the Eyes of the Beholder. JANET WALLACH and JOHN WALLACH. Carol, 1990; Prima, 1991.
Arafat: A Political Biography. ALAN HART. Indiana University Press, 1989.

Aristide, Jean-Bertrand (1953–) On December 17, 1990, the Reverend Aristide, a left socialist Roman Catholic priest, was elected president of Haiti in his country's first democratic election. Aristide won close to 70 percent of the vote, in an election monitored by a 33-member observers' group, led by former U.S. president Jimmy Carter. Aristide, a Catholic liberation theologian long hailed by the Haitian poor, campaigned on an anti-United States, anti-foreign aid program, calling for the prosecution and destruction of the repressive Tonton Macoutes organization, which had flourished during the hated 29-year Duvalier dictatorship while Haiti became the poorest country in the Americas.

With army support, Aristide survived a quick January coup attempt led by former interior minister Roger Lafontant, who was sentenced to life imprisonment and later assassinated. Aristide also made good his campaign promise to attack the Macoutes, prosecuting many, and replacing Macoutes throughout the government and army, as well as replacing older with younger officers. But Haiti continued to be poor, and Aristide's attempts to do without foreign aid had little early success. During his first year in office, he turned to U.S. and other foreign aid sources repeatedly, including the International Monetary Fund and the European Community.

On September 29 and 30, an army coup toppled Aristide in spite of his continuing popular support. There were street demonstrations in Haiti that took some hundreds of lives and demonstrations in Haitian communities abroad and at the United Nations, but to no avail; the army quickly and easily took and held power. Aristide fled to Venezuela, and a three-general junta took charge, led by Aristide appointee General Raoul Cedras. On October 8, Supreme Court Justice Joseph Nerette was installed as interim president. The United States, Britain, France, the Organization of American States, the United Nations, and the European Community all expressed disapproval and took economic action against the new government, but no military action against it was seriously contemplated. Aristide continued to call for his reinstatement from abroad, while the military tightened its hold on Haiti and the exodus of the "boat people," illegal immigrants trying to reach the United States, once again began.

Haiti-born Aristide, an orphan, was raised by the Catholic Salesian order, was ordained a Catholic priest in 1982, and soon became a leading and much-admired worker among the poor in his very poor country. At the same time, he became a leader in the fight against Duvalier and the Tonton Macoutes, and for Haitian democracy, surviving several attempts on his life. One of the young priests who brought liberation theology to Latin America, he was a source of great discomfort to conservative Catholic leaders and was expelled from the Salesian order in 1986. In 1987, a massive popular street protest stopped Church hierarchy attempts to transfer Aristide out of Haiti.

FURTHER READING

"Interview with. . . ." BISHOP EMERSON J. MOORE. *America,* Oct 12, 1991.
"President Jean Bertrand Aristide." ANNE-CHRISTINE D'ADESKY. *Interview,* Oct. 1991.
"The oppositionist. . . ." AMY WILENTZ. *New Republic,* Oct. 28, 1991.
" 'I am president of Haiti.' " *Time,* Oct. 14, 1991.
"Haitian priest-president. . . ." THOMAS HARTMAN. *National Catholic Reporter,* May 17, 1991.
"Aristide, Jean-Bertrand." *Current Biography,* May 1991.

"Haiti takes a new turn. . . ." CAROLE CLEAVER. *New Leader,* Jan. 14, 1991.
"An avalanche for democracy. . . ." GUY GARCIA. *Time,* Dec. 31, 1990.

Arnett, Peter (1934–) Cable News Network (CNN) reporter Arnett arrived in Baghdad four days before the Allied bombing of the city began in the Persian Gulf War. On the night of January 16, 1991, he, CNN anchor Bernard Shaw, and reporter John Holliman—on an open telephone line to CNN headquarters in Atlanta—reported live the first massive Allied air attacks on Baghdad, from the ninth floor of the Al Rasheed hotel. It was one of the high spots of 20th-century journalism, in a century that had already seen more than its share of wars and other catastrophes. Shaw, Holliman, and scores of other Western reporters were evacuated; Arnett stayed on in Baghdad, his reports now heavily censored. He was later criticized by some, who felt that he had in the later period reported essentially what the Iraqis wanted him to report, but such criticism in no way diminished the extraordinary accomplishment of those early days in Baghdad, while the whole world listened. Forthcoming was a book on journalism and his 30-year-long career as a correspondent, due in 1993, which reportedly commanded an advance of more than $1 million.

New Zealand-born Arnett began his long career in journalism as a young reporter in a series of jobs in New Zealand and Australia during the 1950s, in the late 1950s reporting from Indonesia, Laos, and other southeast Asian countries. He became an Associated Press (AP) reporter in Saigon in 1962 and spent the next eight years covering the developing Vietnam War, often from a position highly critical of American involvement and behavior; perhaps his most famous quote was that of the American officer who he reported had said: "It was necessary to destroy the village to save it." He won a 1966 Pulitzer Prize. Arnett went to Washington in 1970 and returned to Vietnam for the AP in 1972 and again in 1975, covering the end of the war. He left the AP for CNN in 1981, covering the White House for the network. But he soon went back to the wars for CNN, covering the civil wars in Afghanistan and El Salvador as well as several other insurrections, and also in such key spots as Moscow and Israel. While in Vietnam, Arnett married; later divorced, he has two children.

FURTHER READING

"Arnett, Peter." *Current Biography,* Nov. 1991.
"Peter Arnett." *People,* Summer 1991.
"If there's a war. . . ." WILLIAM PROCHNAU. *New York Times Magazine,* Mar. 3, 1991.
"Peter Arnett, from Baghdad. . . ." TONY CLIFTON. *Newsweek,* Feb. 11, 1991.
"Living life to the fullest–in Baghdad." SOPHFRONIA SCOTT. *Time,* Feb. 4, 1991.
"As bombs fell. . . ." SUSAN SCHINDEHETTE. *People,* Feb. 4, 1991.

Arnold, Roseanne Barr (1952–) Roseanne changed her name in June 1991, from Barr to Arnold, when she renewed marriage vows with second husband Tom Arnold; at the same time, he was converting to Judaism. In a series of interviews, she described her new inner peace and serenity, while vowing to retain and even intensify her aggressive, caustic humor in her stand-up routine, as on her mid-1991 road tour, her February 1991 "Saturday Night Live" guest shot, and her January 1991 HBO special.

But her self-described personal transformation did not keep her out of the courts. The year saw a series of lawsuits and highly publicized charges and countercharges involving Roseanne Arnold, including a new lawsuit involving the *National Enquirer;* a continuing palimony suit being pursued by her first husband, William

Pentland; and financial disputes involving her former agents and producers.

During the 1990–91 season, "Roseanne" was still in the top ten, and often the top five, but was not so strong in the ratings as in previous years; and both the show and its stars were passed over at Emmy nomination time. In the 1991–92 season, Roseanne and Tom Arnold became co-executive producers of the show. In April 1991 she appeared with other stars in the environmental documentary *A User's Guide to Planet Earth.* In November, she starred in her first telefilm, *Backfield in Motion,* as widow Nancy Seaver, who organizes a mothers-and-sons football game; husband Tom played her on-screen love interest. The animated series "Little Rosey," based on the Roseanne character, lasted only through the 1990–91 season; "The Rosey and Buddy Show," based on Roseanne and Tom Arnold, was scheduled to debut in 1992. In September, speaking to an incest survivors' group, Arnold went public with charges that she had been sexually abused as a child, a charge her parents denied.

Salt Lake City-born Barr began her career as a stand-up comedian in variety in the late 1970s. A decade later, she emerged as the star of the very popular television series "Roseanne" (1988–), which was at or near the top of the ratings during most of 1989–91. Propelled by her personal style, she also emerged as a major celebrity. In 1989, she starred in her first feature film, *She-Devil* (1989), and also published *Roseanne: My Life as a Woman* and *Stand Up!* She has been married twice and has four children, one of whom she bore as a teenager and gave up for adoption.

FURTHER READING

"A star cries incest. . . ." Vickie Bane. *People,* Oct. 1991.
"Roseanne bares all!. . . ." Ryan Murphy. *Advocate,* Mar. 12, 1991.
"Roseanne sings. . . ." Jobeth McDaniel. *Ladies Home Journal,* Jan. 1991.
"The wretched. . . ." Barbara Ehrenreich. *New Republic,* Apr. 2, 1990.
"Roseanne unchained." Jim Jerome. *People,* Oct. 9, 1989.
"The real Roseanne." Kathryn Casey. *Ladies Home Journal,* Sep. 1989.
"Barr, Roseanne." *Current Biography,* May 1989.

Arrau, Claudio (1903–91) Born in Chillán, Chile, Arrau was a child prodigy, who made his debut in Chile at the age of five, won a scholarship to the Berlin Conservatory in 1912, there studying with Martin Krause, and made his European debut in Berlin at the age of 11 in 1914. He based himself in Germany until 1940, touring throughout the world and teaching at the Berlin Conservatory (1924–40). He then returned to Chile and in 1941 settled in the United States, while continuing to tour the world for five more decades. Arrau was a major figure on the world musical scene for almost 80 years, perhaps most notably for his performances of the 32 Beethoven sonatas, but also in a very wide range that included Chopin, Liszt, Mozart, and Schoenberg, among others. He refused to play in Chile during the Pinochet regime, playing instead for Amnesty International in 1977, and returning after 17 years to play in Santiago in 1984. He was married to the singer Ruth Schneider, who died in 1989. He was survived by two children. (d. Mürzzuschlag, Austria; June 9, 1991)

FURTHER READING

"In memoriam." Stephen D. Chakwin, Jr. *American Record Guide,* Sep.–Oct. 1991.
Obituary. *Current Biography,* Aug. 1991.
Obituary. *Variety,* June 17, 1991.
"Where is Orpheus now?" *Economist,* June 15, 1991.
Obituary. *The Times* (of London), June 11, 1991.
Obituary. *New York Times,* June 10, 1991.
"Arrau, Claudio." *Current Biography,* Nov. 1986.

Arrupe, Pedro (1907–91) Bilbao-born Arrupe, a Basque, studied medicine before joining the Society of Jesus in 1927; he was ordained a Catholic priest in 1936. He was sent to Japan in 1938, and became a parish priest, remaining in Japan through World War II. He was one of the first into Hiroshima after the 1945 atom bombing of the city. He rose in the Jesuit order, becoming the order's provincial superior in Japan in 1958 and head of the Society of Jesus in 1965, while at the same time writing a wide range of works that included eight books in Japanese. As head of the order, he participated in the substantial changes that rocked the order and the Catholic Church from the mid-1960s, following the great impact of Vatican II, and including the historic Jesuit turn toward the problems of the poor. He and his order were sharply criticized by Pope John Paul II in 1979; Arrupe offered to resign in 1980, but was asked to stay on in his position. He resigned in 1983 because of ill health. His *Recollections and Reflections of Pedro Arrupe* appeared in 1986. (d. Rome, Italy; February 5, 1991)

FURTHER READING

Obituary. *Current Biography,* Apr. 1991.
"In the footsteps of Micah. . . ." JON SOBRINO. *Commonweal,* Mar. 22, 1991.
America, Feb. 16, 1991. (Special issue on Arrupe)
"Pedro Arrupe. . . ." PETER HEBBLETHWAITE. *National Catholic Reporter,* Feb. 15, 1991.
Obituary. *The Times* (of London), Feb. 7, 1991.
Obituary. *New York Times,* Feb. 6, 1991.

Arthur, Jean (Gladys Georgianna Greene, 1905–91) Born in New York City, Arthur worked as a model and on stage before her silent film debut in 1923. She graduated to leads in the late 1920s and emerged as a major star in the mid-1930s, beginning with her role opposite Edward G. Robinson in *The Whole Town's Talking.* She is best known for her starring roles in three classic Frank Capra films: *Mr. Deeds Goes to Town* (1936), *You Can't Take It with You* (1938), and *Mr. Smith Goes to Washington* (1939). She also starred in such films as *The Plainsman* (1937), *The Talk of the Town* (1942), *The More the Merrier* (1943), *A Foreign Affair* (1948), and the classic western *Shane* (1953). She starred on Broadway in *Peter Pan* (1950) and on television in "The Jean Arthur Show" (1956). She was twice married, to photographer Julian Anker and to producer Frank Ross, and had no children. (d. Carmel, California; June 19, 1991)

FURTHER READING

Obituary. *Current Biography,* Aug. 1991.
Obituary. *Variety,* June 24, 1991.
Obituary. *The Times* (of London), June 22, 1991.
Obituary. *New York Times,* June 20, 1991.

Ashcroft, Peggy (Edith Margaret Emily Ashcroft, 1907–91) One of the greatest actresses of the 20th-century theater, Ashcroft made her debut in 1926 at the Birmingham Repertory in *Dear Brutus,* opposite Ralph Richardson. She went on to star in a wide range of major roles before World War II, perhaps most notably as Desdemona to Paul Robeson's *Othello* (1930) and in John Gielgud's extraordinary *Romeo and Juliet* (1935), in which she played Juliet to Gielgud and Laurence Olivier, who alternated as Romeo and Mercutio. Both roles were early in a career that was to include many centrally important classic and modern roles, from the early 1950s often with the English Stage Company, the Royal Shakespeare Company, and the National Theatre. Ashcroft made her New York debut in 1937, as Lise in *High Tor.* She also played in several films, beginning with *The Wandering Jew* (1933) and *The Thirty-Nine Steps* (1935). Very late in her career, she won a Best Supporting Actress Academy Award for *A Passage to India* (1984), and in 1984 also played Barbie in television's *The Jewel in the Crown.* Ashcroft was a social activist for six decades, campaigning on such issues as nuclear disarmament and equal rights for women. She was married three times, to theater director Theodore Komarisjevsky, Rupert Hart-Davis, and Jeremy Hutchinson. She was survived by a daughter and a son. (d. London, England; June 14, 1991)

FURTHER READING

Obituary. *Current Biography,* Aug. 1991.
Obituary. *Variety,* June 17, 1991.
Obituary. *The Times* (of London), June 15, 1991.
Obituary. *New York Times,* June 15, 1991.
Peggy Ashcroft. MICHAEL BILLINGTON. Trafalgar Square, 1990.
Ashcroft. ROBERT TANITCH. Trafalgar Square, 1988.
"Ashcroft, Peggy." *Current Biography,* Jan. 1987.

These Our Actors: Theatre Acting of Peggy Ashcroft, John Gielgud, Laurence Olivier, Ralph Richardson. RICHARD FINDLATER. Trafalgar Square, 1984.

Ashman, Howard (1950–91) Baltimore-born Ashman was best known for the long-running musical *Little Shop of Horrors,* which ran for five years (1982–87) off-Broadway; he wrote the book and lyrics in collaboration with Alan Menken, who wrote the music. Ashman also produced the play, as artistic director of the WPA Theater. The play received the Best Musical New York Drama Critics Circle Award for 1982–83 and was adapted into the 1986 Frank Oz film. Ashman's work also included such musicals as *Dreamstuff,* based on *The Tempest* (1976; with Menken); *God Bless You, Mr. Rosewater* (1979; with Menken), and *Smile* (1986; with Marvin Hamlisch). For his work on the animated film *Beauty and the Beast* (1991), Ashman received two posthumous Oscars, shared with composer Alan Menken, for original score and for the title song. His career was cut short by acquired immune deficiency syndrome (AIDS); he was survived by his companion, William Lauch; his sister; and his mother. (d. New York City; March 14, 1991)

FURTHER READING

Obituary. *Variety,* Mar. 18, 1991.
Obituary. *New York Times,* Mar. 15, 1991.

Aspin, Les (1938–) Chairman of the U.S. House of Representatives Armed Services Committee, Aspin was before the Persian Gulf War a leading Democratic proponent of large armed forces cuts. In the period just before the war, he was hesitant, supporting the Bush administration buildup in the Gulf while also calling for time to let sanctions work. When war was imminent, he joined the minority of House Democrats who voted for the January 12th war resolution, and fully supported the war when it came. After the war, he soon reverted to his previous position, in April 1991 attacking the Bush administration version of the Strategic Defense Initiative (SDI), and in August and September urging that $1 billion be diverted from the U.S. military to buy food and medicine for the Soviet Union. By the autumn of 1991, Aspin was urging defense budget cuts below those provided by the 1990 White House–Congress budget agreement. During 1991 he published *The Aspin Papers: Sanctions, Diplomacy and War in the Persian Gulf.*

Milwaukee-born Aspin was chairman of President John F. Kennedy's Council of Economic Advisors in 1963. In that year, he moved into his long career as a leading Wisconsin Democratic congressman, with powerful influence on military appropriations through his House committee memberships. His B.A. was from Yale University, his M.A. from Oxford University, and his Ph.D. from the Massachusetts Institute of Technology.

FURTHER READING

"The real Les Aspin story." DAVID BROOKS and PETER OSTERLUND. *National Review,* Dec. 19, 1986.
"Aspin, Les(lie, Jr.)". *Current Biography,* Feb. 1986.

Assad, Hafez al- (1928–) The end of the Cold War and the Allied victory in the Persian Gulf War greatly altered alliances and possibilities in the Middle East; the Iraqi threat was diminished, Middle East peace talks were beginning, the Soviet Union could no longer be relied on for arms and supplies, and Syrian President Assad reached for a new U.S.-Syrian relationship.

Assad strongly supported the Allied side in the Gulf War, sending frontline troops that took part in the ground offensive, operation Desert Storm. He also sharply braked anti-Western terrorist operations based in Syria, during and after the war, and at the same time broke with the discredited Palestine Liberation Organization (PLO), which had supported the Iraqi side in the war.

In May, he and Lebanese President Elias Hrawl signed a bilateral pact codifying the special position of Syria in Lebanon; in July, Assad acquiesced to successful Lebanese Army attacks on PLO bases in Sidon, which ended with the surrender of the bases and their heavy weapons, a major military setback for the PLO. At the same time, throughout the year, he cooperated with U.S. Secretary of State James Baker in efforts to free the Lebanon hostages, and in Baker's attempts, finally successful, to set up what became the Madrid Middle East peace conference. Late in the year, still pursuing the American relationship, he quickly agreed to a second round of peace talks, to be held in Washington.

Assad began his political and military career as a Baath Party activist and air force officer. He became an air force general after the 1963 Baathist coup, and air force commander in chief and minister of defense in 1966. He took power in 1970 and was named president of Syria in 1971. During the Cold War, he was closely allied with and his armed forces were supplied by the Soviet Union. His forces were badly defeated by Israel in the fourth Arab-Israeli (Yom Kippur) war of 1973. Since 1976, his forces have partially occupied Lebanon, although they were defeated again by the Israelis in Lebanon in 1976. During the Iran-Iraq war of the 1980s, he supported Iran against Iraq, a long-term enemy. Assad is married and has five children. He attended Syria's armed forces colleges.

FURTHER READING

"When Shamir blinked. . . ." ELIAHU SALPETER. *New Leader,* Aug. 12, 1991.
" 'It's now up to the Israelis'. . ." LALLY WEYMOUTH. *Newsweek,* Aug. 5, 1991.
"Trouble in Damascus." ALAN COWELL. *New York Times Magazine,* Apr. 1, 1990.
Hafez al-Assad. MATTHEW GORDON. Chelsea House, 1989.

Atwater, Lee (1951–91) Atlanta-born Republican Party political strategist Atwater began his career as an intern to U.S. senator Strom Thurmond; while still in college he led the College Republican organization. He directed the Thurmond re-election campaign in 1978, managed the South Carolina Ronald Reagan campaign in 1980, and in 1984 was a key figure in Reagan's successful re-election bid. He moved into national prominence as the highly controversial and very effective manager of the George Bush 1988 presidential campaign. After the election, Bush named him Republican Party chairman. Throughout his career, Atwater practiced "negative" campaign tactics that sought to polarize the electorate along racial lines to the advantage of his candidate. The most notable example of this was the successful Bush campaign attack on Michael Dukakis as being "soft" on Willie Horton, a Black convicted murderer who raped a woman while on parole from a Massachusetts prison. As Republican Party chairman Atwater caused charges of homosexuality to be leveled against Democratic leader Thomas Foley, charges Bush later repudiated. Atwater resigned his post in 1990, after falling ill with a brain tumor, and in his final months of life apologized to some of those who had been his targets, including Michael Dukakis. Privately, Atwater was an avid blues fan and player. He was survived by his wife and three daughters. (d. Washington, D.C.; March 29, 1991)

FURTHER READING

"Lee Atwater's last campaign." TODD BREWSTER. *Reader's Digest,* June, 1991.
Obituary. *Current Biography,* May, 1991.
Obituary. *National Review,* Apr. 29, 1991.
"Blues for Lee. . . ." SIDNEY BLUMENTHAL. *New Republic,* Apr. 22, 1991.
"B.B. King mourns. . . ." *Jet,* Apr. 15, 1991.
"Political lessons." KENNETH T. WALSH. *U.S. News & World Report,* Apr. 8, 1991.
Obituary. *The Times* (of London), Mar. 30, 1991.
Obituary. *New York Times,* Mar. 30, 1991.
"Atwater, Lee." *Current Biography,* June, 1989.

Atwood, Margaret (1939–) Ottawa-born Atwood, for two decades a major voice in Canadian literature, in 1991 published *Wilderness Tips,* a highly regarded book of short stories in Canadian settings that once again brought her international attention. At the same time, an earlier work, *The Handmaid's Tale* (1986), was finding very wide popular audiences in its 1990 film adaptation, as it moved from theatrical film showings to home screens. More than *Wilder-*

ness Tips, the earlier book expressed Atwood's lifelong feminist concerns, set as it is in a poisoned, partly destroyed world in which the remaining fertile women are turned into baby machines for the new order, run by right-wing fundamentalists. In 1991, Atwood also published a children's work on environmental concerns, *For the Birds,* illustrated by John Bianchi.

Atwood is a versatile poet, novelist, short story writer, essayist, and editor, whose other works include *The Edible Woman* (1969), *Surfacing* (1973), *Life Before Man* (1979), *Murder in the Dark* (1983), and *Cat's Eye* (1989). She is married to Graeme Gibson; the couple have one child. She attended the University of Toronto and Harvard University.

FURTHER READING

Margaret Atwood: Conversations. EARL G. INGERSOLL, ed. Ontario Review Press, 1991.

Margaret Atwood: A Reference Guide. JUDITH McCOMBS and CAROL L. PALMER. G. K. Hall, 1991.

"Witch craft. . . ." CAMILLE PERI. *Mother Jones,* Apr. 1989.

"Reflected in. . . ." KIM HUBBARD. *People,* Mar. 6, 1989.

Margaret Atwood. JEROME H. ROSENBERG. G. K. Hall, 1984.

Aung San Suu Kyi, Daw (1945–) Burmese democratic political leader Aung San Suu Kyi, under house arrest and held incommunicado by her country's military dictatorship for over two years, was in October awarded the 1991 Nobel Peace Prize. On December 10, her 18-year-old son accepted the prize for her. The same month saw U.S. publication of her book *Freedom from Fear and Other Writings,* edited by her husband, Michael Aris.

Rangoon-born Aung San Suu Kyi is the daughter of the founder of modern Burma (now Myanmar), Aung San (1914–47), who became Burma's first prime minister in 1947 and was assassinated on July 19, 1947. She grew up in Burma, leaving her country in 1960 when her mother became Burmese ambassador to India. She was educated in India and at Oxford University. She married archeologist Michael Aris in 1972; they have two sons. She lived with her husband and children in Oxford until 1988, during those years publishing a biography of her father, *Aung San* (1984); she then returned to Burma to nurse her sick mother, who died later in 1988.

Although her reasons for returning to Burma had nothing to do with politics, she arrived during a revolutionary period, often called the Burmese Spring, with hundreds of thousands involved in massive street demonstrations against the 26-year-old military dictatorship of army leader Ne Win. She soon became a leader of the democratic opposition, heading the nonviolent National League for Democracy, and was in 1988 placed under house arrest and forbidden to run for office.

Ne Win resigned in July 1988 but remained in control of the army, while demonstrations continued. A democratic government briefly ruled in August and September, but was overthrown by the September army coup in which thousands were killed. The military dictatorship that then took over Burma was led by General Saw Maung.

Aung San Suu Kyi, once again under house arrest, stayed on in Burma to lead the democratic opposition to the military dictatorship. When the military, facing powerful democratic opposition, promised and held democratic elections in May 1990, her party swept the election. The military then refused to honor the election results and tightened its control, publicly attacking her for marrying a foreigner and at the same time trying to convince her to leave the country by making the terms of her imprisonment more difficult and keeping her family from visiting her.

FURTHER READING

"The wages of courage." *People,* Oct. 28, 1991.

Aycbourn, Alan (1939–) British playwright-director Ayckbourn describes himself as a "one-a-year man," normally designating one month a year for writing a new play. While he refines the new play at his theater in Scarborough, the previous play is getting ready to run on London's West End, generally then joining the long line of Ayckbourn plays in the repertory—43 at last count, which have been translated into 35 languages in over 50 countries. The 1991 West End entry was the *Revenger's Comedies* (1989), actually a pair of plays about two people who meet while both are attempting suicide by jumping off a bridge and decide to solve their problems by each killing off the bane of the other's life. Debuting in May 1991 at Scarborough was *Wildest Dreams,* about a group of misfits who find themselves "taken over" by a set of personalities they initially adopted as a weekly game. Another new play, *Body Language,* centers on two women—a hefty journalist and a curvaceous model—who lose their heads in a helicopter accident, to have them reattached to the wrong bodies by an incompetent doctor. Clearly, Ayckbourn's comedy has gone, as one London critic put it, "from tasteful beige to completely black."

Meanwhile, previous plays continue to percolate throughout the world. For example, Ayckbourn's *Absent Friends* (1974), in which a casual reunion leads to realization of wasted lives, had a belated New York debut in February 1991 at New York's Manhattan Theatre Club, which planned a 1992 production of *A Small Family Business.* His *Hencefoward . . .* (1987), which had its U.S. premiere in Houston in 1989, was given a major production at the Los Angeles Mark Taper Forum in November 1991; the comedy of morals is set in a claustrophobic apartment in an urban wasteland, inhabited by a terrorized composer and his literally robotic housewife. Increasingly interested in writing "family shows" for children, Ayckbourn hopes to take his Scarborough company to the International Theater Festival of Chicago in summer 1992, to perform two of his children's plays. Ayckbourn was named the third Professor of Contemporary Theatre at Oxford University, following Stephen Sondheim and Ian McKellen, for the year 1992; the professorship was endowed by Cameron Mackintosh, producer of such hits as *Cats, Les Misérables,* and *Phantom of the Opera.*

Ayckbourn is an extraordinarily productive playwright, whose comedies of middle-class British life began with *The Square Cat* (1959) and his first hit, *Relatively Speaking* (1965), and include such works as *How the Other Half Loves* (1969), *Family Circles* (1970), *The Norman Conquests* (1973; actually three plays about the same events), *Intimate Exchanges* (1982; eight plays), and a children's play, *Invisible Friends* (1989). Ayckbourn directed plays at the British Broadcasting Corporation (BBC) from 1964 to 1969 and then, except for two years in the 1980s as a director at London's National Theatre, has from 1971 based himself in northern England's Scarborough, as artistic director of the small Stephen Joseph Theatre in the Round. He married Christine Helen Roland in 1959; they had two sons before separating.

FURTHER READING

"Bard of the British bourgeoisie." MEL GUSSOW. *New York Times Magazine,* Jan. 28, 1990.

Alan Ayckbourn, 2nd ed. MICHAEL BILLINGTON. St. Martin's, 1990.

"The swan of Scarborough." *Economist,* Aug. 19, 1989.

File on Ayckbourn. MALCOLM PAGE and SIMON TRUSSLER, eds. Heinemann, 1989.

Conversations with Ayckbourn. IAN WATSON. Faber & Faber, 1989; Humanities, 1981.

Alan Ayckbourn. SIDNEY H. WHITE. G. K. Hall, 1984.

Aykroyd, Dan (Daniel Edward Aykroyd, 1952–) Aykroyd made his directorial debut in early 1991 with *Nothing but Trouble;* he also wrote the screenplay and played two roles, opposite Chevy Chase, John Candy, and Demi Moore. Aykroyd the actor won praise for his performance, but Aykroyd the writer and director fared less well, some reviewers expressing disappointment at what they saw as the waste of Aykroyd's considerable dramatic and comedic talents.

These were on view in Howard Zieff's *My Girl,* which premiered in November 1991, with Aykroyd as a widowed funeral director, father of newcomer Anna Chlumsky in the title role, in a cast that also includes Jamie Lee Curtis and

Macaulay Culkin. Aykroyd also appeared on television in August 1991 with Kirk Douglas and his son Eric Douglas in *Yellow*, a World War I story for HBO's "Tales from the Crypt." Late in 1991 he joined the cast of Richard Attenborough's massive ($40 million) forthcoming film biography, *Charlie,* starring Robert Downey, Jr., as Chaplin. Another project in progress was *This Is My Life,* co-written and directed by Nora Ephron. Also to come was a starring role in the Phil Alden Robinson film *Sneakers,* opposite Robert Redford and Sidney Poitier.

Canadian-born Aykroyd became a star in television comedy as one of the original members of the "Saturday Night Live" troupe (1975–79); he also wrote for the show. He and John Belushi created The Blues Brothers for the show, then starred in the film, *The Blues Brothers* (1980), which Aykroyd wrote. He went on to star in many other films, including *Neighbors* (1981), *Trading Places* (1983), *Ghostbusters* (1984), *Spies Like Us* (1985), *Dragnet* (1987), *The Great Outdoors* (1988), *My Stepmother Is an Alien* (1988), *Ghostbusters II* (1989), and *Loose Cannons* (1990). He won an Oscar nomination for best supporting actor as the son in *Driving Miss Daisy* (1989). He attended Ottawa's Carleton College. He has been married twice and has three children.

FURTHER READING

"A haunted humorist. . . ." BRIAN JOHNSON. *Maclean's,* June 26, 1989.

Aylwin Azócar, Patricio (1919–) Chilean President Aylwin continued during 1991 to restore Chilean democracy and to uncover and deal with the aftermath of the long Pinochet dictatorship. Inaugurated on March 11, 1990, he had freed many of Chile's political prisoners on March 12, and in April he had set up a national commission to study and report on the human rights violations of the Pinochet government, alleged to have tortured tens of thousands and murdered thousands of Chileans in its 16 years of power. On March 4, 1991, the committee reported that over 2,000 cases of murder, disappearance, and torture had occurred during the Pinochet years, including the long-charged murder of folksinger Victor Jara and 1976 car bombing murders in Washington, D.C., of former cabinet minister Orlando Letelier and Ronni Moffitt. Pinochet, the army, and the Supreme Court rejected the report. Ultimately, Cuban hitman Virgilio Paz Romero pleaded guilty to the Letelier-Moffitt murders, and in September was sentenced to 12 years in prison by a U.S. court in Washington, D.C.

Along similar lines, the Chilean government on February 2, 1991, ordered an investigation of charges against and dissolution of Dignity Colony in the Andean foothills 250 miles south of Santiago. The 37,000-acre colony contained a population of approximately 300 German immigrants, was set up essentially as a separate state within Chile, and had long been accused by human rights organizations of being a former secret police installation during the Pinochet regime. Meanwhile, the Aylwin government continued the long, long process of uncovering the mass graves of the victims of the dictatorship.

In the new climate of democracy, the largest of the country's fighting revolutionary organizations, the Manuel Rodriguez Patriotic Front, on May 31 laid down its arms and entered electoral politics as the Manuel Rodriguez Patriotic Movement, though a splinter group broke off and announced its intention to keep on fighting. On the economic side, the debt reduction program begun in 1990 resulted in the June 27, 1991 U.S.-Chile debt reduction agreement, while attempts continued to bring down Chile's inflation rate, reported to have been over 27 percent in 1990.

Aylwin, a lawyer and Christian Democrat, became a senator in 1965 and leader of his party in 1973. He opposed the socialist Allende government in the early 1970s. In the early years he did not openly oppose the Pinochet dictatorship but did join other lawyers in defending some of those imprisoned by the government, and later more openly opposed military rule. Aylwin led the democratic coalition that replaced military dictator Augusto Pinochet Ugarte. He was elected to the Chilean presidency in December 1989. He married Leonor Oyarzun in 1948; the couple have five children.

FURTHER READING

"Chile's uncommon way." JONATHAN KANDELL. *Town & Country,* Oct. 1991.

"Aylwin Azocar, Patricio." *Current Biography,* Aug. 1990.

Aziz, Tariq (Michael Yuhanna, 1936–) As Iraq's foreign minister, Aziz became a well-known figure during the run-up to the Persian Gulf War, as he attempted with very little success to defend Saddam Hussein's conquest of Kuwait. He and U.S. Secretary of State James Baker were the central figures in the flurry of unsuccessful diplomatic initiatives that preceded the January 17, 1991, opening of the Allied air war against Iraq. Aziz appeared as a main figure again, once the war was lost, in a prolonged attempt to use Soviet mediation as a means of securing easier surrender terms and perhaps to save face. He did not succeed, ultimately agreeing to United Nations demands. Aziz was replaced by Ahmed Hussein as foreign minister on March 24, remaining deputy premier, in that position continuing to speak for Iraq from time to time.

For Aziz, defense of an Iraqi attack on one of its neighbors was a familiar role. He had similarly defended the Iraqi invasion of Iran in 1980, claiming Iranian provocation, and had then become Iraq's chief spokesperson and negotiator in Iraq's years-long attempt to find some way out of what until very near the end was a losing war.

Aziz is one of the few Christians in the largely Muslim Iraqi leadership. He attended Baghdad University and was a journalist before the Baath Party coup of 1968. Long an associate of Saddam Hussein, he became a key media specialist for Hussein after the 1970 coup that brought Hussein to power. He was Minister of Information (1974–77) and has been a member of Hussein's small inner group, the Revolutionary Command Council, since 1977. He became a deputy prime minister in 1979.

FURTHER READING

"Tariq Aziz. . . ." PETER HEBBLETHWAITE. *National Catholic Reporter,* Dec. 14, 1990.

B

Baker, James (James Addison Baker, III, 1930–) U.S. Secretary of State Baker was a key player on the international stage during the first three years of the Bush administration. Although active throughout the world, he was particularly visible in two foreign policy areas. The first was the long, highly successful set of negotiations with the Soviet Union that ultimately ended the Cold War, opened up a new period in Soviet-American relations, freed Eastern Europe, united Germany, freed the Baltic States, and resulted in the first real and substantial gains in the long search for arms control and nuclear disarmament. With peace, and with the direct intervention of George Bush and Mikhail Gorbachev acting together as peacemakers, Baker was also able to play a major role in moving toward settlement of long-standing continuing conflicts in Nicaragua, Cambodia, South Africa, Angola, Mozambique, Namibia, Ethiopia, and disputes in several other countries moved swiftly toward resolution.

Even in the Middle East, the graveyard of so many earlier peace initiatives, Baker was able to make some progress. In November 1991, with joint American-Soviet sponsorship and a great deal of nonstop Baker diplomacy, the Madrid Middle East peace talks started, the parties sitting down together to talk about peace for the first time since the Arab-Israeli wars began.

Houston-born Baker, a lawyer, has long been a personal friend and political ally of George Bush; their alliance goes back to the early 1970s, a period in which both men moved from Texas Republican politics onto the national scene. Baker was an under secretary of commerce (1975–76), was active in the Ford campaign of 1976, and in 1979–80 managed the Bush presidential nomination campaign, from which Bush emerged as Ronald Reagan's vice president. Baker went into the Reagan administration, too, in the central role of White House chief of staff. In 1985, he switched jobs with Treasury Secretary Donald Regan, and was treasury secretary from 1985 to 1988. He went on to manage the successful 1988 Bush presidential campaign and then became secretary of state in the new Bush administration. His B.A. was from Princeton University, in

1952, and his LL.B. from the University of Texas, in 1957. He married Susan Garrett in 1973; they have eight children.

FURTHER READING

"The tactician." JOHN NEWHOUSE. *New Yorker,* May 7, 1990.

"James Baker. . . ." ROWLAND EVANS and ROBERT NOVAK. *Reader's Digest,* Nov. 1989.

Bakhtiar, Shapour (1914–91) The former premier of Iran was assassinated at his home outside Paris on August 8, 1991. Born in Iran, Bakhtiar spent much of his youth in France and was educated at the Sorbonne. He fought on the Republican side during the Spanish Civil War, with the French army in 1940, and with the French resistance during World War II. He returned to Iran in 1946 and spent four years in the labor ministry. But he also in 1946 joined the left-leaning National Front party, led by Mohammed Mossadeq. Bakhtiar lost his government job in 1950, but joined the new Mossadeq government as labor minister in1951 and played a major role in nationalizing the oil industry. He was jailed after the military coup that toppled that government in 1953, and spent the next 26 years in opposition to the Shah's government, much of that time underground and for a total of six years in prison. In 1979, with the Shah's government failing, he turned to Bakhtiar, who became Iran's first liberal premier in a quarter of a century, on condition that the Shah leave Iran. That accomplished, Bakhtiar attempted to introduce major reforms, but these lasted only 37 days, then to be swept away by a coalition of Islamic fundamentalists and left revolutionaries, led by Ayatollah Ruhollah Khomeini. Bakhtiar fled, was sentenced to death in absentia, and was granted asylum in France in May, 1979, founding the National Resistance Movement. He spent the next 12 years in France; heavily guarded by his own bodyguards and by French police, he survived at least two assassination attempts before the one that succeeded. He was survived by his second wife, two daughters, and two sons.

FURTHER READING

"Murder, they wrote. . . ." LOUISE LIEF. *U.S. News & World Report,* Dec. 16, 1991.

Obituary. *The Times* (of London), Aug. 9, 1991.

Obituary. *New York Times,* Aug. 9, 1991.

Baldwin, Alec (Alexander Rae Baldwin III, 1958–) After his starring role as CIA agent Jack Ryan in *The Hunt for Red October* (1990), new film star Baldwin was slated to play the role in a sequel, *Patriot Games.* But Baldwin rejected the multimillion dollar project in favor of a starring role on Broadway as Stanley Kowalski in a forthcoming spring 1992 revival of Tennessee Williams' *A Streetcar Named Desire,* opposite Jessica Lange, Amy Madigan, and Timothy Carhart.

In 1991, Baldwin starred opposite Kim Basinger (with whom he was romantically linked) in the poorly received film *The Marrying Man.* Jerry Rees directed; the original screenplay was written by Neil Simon. Forthcoming was a starring role in the Norman Rene film of Craig Lucas's *Prelude to a Kiss,* recreating the role he originated at New York's Circle Repertory Company, in a cast that includes Meg Ryan, Kathy Bates, Ned Beatty, and Patty Duke. Also to come was a role in David Mamet's film adaptation of his play *Glengarry Glen Ross,* directed by James Foley, in a cast that includes Al Pacino, Jack Lemmon, Alan Arkin, Jonathan Pryce, Kevin Spacey, and Ed Harris.

Long Island-born Baldwin starred in the television series "Knots Landing," and in the New York theater in such plays as *Serious Money* and *Prelude to a Kiss,* for which he won an Obie award. He became a film star in the late 1980s, in such films as *She's Having a Baby* (1988), *Beetlejuice* (1988), *Married to the Mob* (1988). *Talk Radio* (1988), and *Working Girl* (1988), making his major breakthrough in *The Hunt for Red October* (1990). His films also include *Miami Blues* (1990) and *Alice* (1990). He attended George Washington University (1976–79), and studied theater at New York University and the Lee Strasberg Institute (1979–80).

FURTHER READING

"Kim and Alec. . . ." ELIZABETH SPORKIN. *People,* Apr. 22, 1991.

"Not just another hunk." CATHLEEN MCGUIGAN. *Newsweek,* Apr. 23, 1990.

"The hunk from 'Hunt.' " PETER TRAVERS. *Rolling Stone,* Apr. 5, 1990.

"Smart Alec." STEPHANIE MANSFIELD. *GQ–Gentlemen's Quarterly,* Feb. 1990.

Baldwin, Hanson Weightman (1903–91) Journalist and military historian Baldwin began his career in 1927 as a reporter for the *Baltimore Sun,* moving to the *New York Times* in 1929. He became military analyst for the *Times* in 1936 and won a 1943 Pulitzer Prize for his reporting from Guadalcanal and other Pacific war sites; later in the war he covered the Allied invasions of North Africa and Europe. During the postwar period, he became a leading Cold War "hawk," strongly advocating U.S. superiority in the atomic arms race and U.S. ties with authoritarian regimes abroad in pursuit of Cold War aims. When the Vietnam War came, he very strongly supported the war, urging its expansion. Baldwin wrote dozens of books and hundreds of articles on a wide range of military and related matters. He was survived by his wife, Helen, and two daughters. (d. Roxbury, Connecticut; November 13, 1991)

FURTHER READING

Obituary. *New York Times,* Nov. 13, 1991.

Ball, William (1931–91) Chicago-born Ball worked as an actor and set designer in regional theater during the 1950s, making his New York directorial breakthrough off-Broadway with Chekhov's *Ivanov,* winning the 1958 Obie and the Drama Desk awards. He went on to a considerable range of other works through the mid-1960s, winning further off-Broadway awards for *Under Milk Wood* (1959) and *Six Characters in Search of an Author* (1962). He founded the American Conservatory Theater (ACT) in Pittsburgh in 1965, and moved it to San Francisco in 1967. There it became a leading regional theater and theater school, operating two playhouses, training a substantial number of theater people, and sending touring companies to several American cities, Japan, and the Soviet Union. Ball's company received a 1979 Tony Award for repertory and training. He left the ACT in 1986, following a dispute with his board of directors and later returned to acting and directing, also attempting to develop screen projects. He wrote *A Sense of Direction: Some Observations on the Art of Directing* (1984). He is survived by his mother, a sister, and two brothers (d. San Francisco; July 30, 1991)

FURTHER READING

Obituary. *Current Biography,* Oct. 1991.
Obituary. *Variety,* Aug. 5, 1991.
Obituary. *New York Times,* Aug. 2, 1991.

Baltimore, David (1938–) A leading U.S. microbiologist and academic, Baltimore won the 1975 Nobel Prize in physiology or medicine. His scientific status lent great importance to his defense of his colleague, Dr. Theresa Imanishi-Karl, as one of the most notable scientific scandals of the modern period unfolded. In 1986, young Massachusetts Institute of Technology researcher Margot O'Toole was fired for charging that Imanishi-Karl had fabricated the research for a key article that had been signed by Baltimore and others. Baltimore and the others, who were never accused of faking the data or of knowing that it had been faked, strongly defended Imanishi-Karl and continued to do so in the years that followed, although evidence began to pile up that the data had been falsified. Baltimore called the investigation a witch-hunt and conducted a national campaign against it. Finally, after a long National Institutes of Health (NIH) investigation, three congressional hearings, and the involvement of the Secret Service, the NIH concluded that the data had indeed been falsified. On March 20, 1991, Baltimore finally agreed to ask that the article be retracted, dropped his defense of Imanishi-Karl, and apologized to O'Toole. The charges against Imanishi-

Karl faced a further long period of investigation. On December 2, 1991, Baltimore resigned from his Rockefeller University presidency.

New York City-born Baltimore has won many awards in addition to the Nobel. He sits on several boards of directors and is a frequent contributor to scientific and medical journals. He began his academic career as a research associate at the Salk Institute (1965–68) and occupied a series of increasingly prestigious positions at the Massachusetts Institute of Technology (1968–90), last as director of the Whitehead Institute of Biomedical Research (1982–90). He became president of Rockefeller University in 1990. His 1960 B.A. was from Swarthmore and his 1964 Ph.D. from Rockefeller University. He is married to the former Alice S. Huang; they have one daughter.

FURTHER READING

"David Baltimore. . . ." ALISON BASS. *Technology Review,* Oct. 1986.

Barbie, Klaus (1913–91) born in Bad Godesburg, Germany, Barbie joined the Hitler Youth in the early 1920s and was for the rest of his life a Nazi. He joined the SS (*Schutzstaffel,* or Blackshirts) in 1935, and was an SS second lieutenant in the Netherlands early in World War II. He soon became a Gestapo (Nazi secret police) officer, rising to become head of the Gestapo section headquartered in Lyon, France. There, throughout the balance of the war he committed the acts that won him the well-deserved title "The Butcher of Lyon," becoming directly responsible for the murder and torture of tens of thousands; most estimates run from 10,000 to 25,000, though some are higher. Among them were Jean Moulin and other leaders of his Resistance group, all but one murdered by the Gestapo.

Barbie survived after the war and in 1947 became a paid informer of U.S. Army intelligence, which hid his existence from French intelligence. In 1951, probably with American help and using false papers, he emigrated to Bolivia as Klaus Altmann, with his wife and two children. There, protected by the military dictatorship, he went into business successfully and even traveled freely to the United States and Europe. He later moved to Peru.

In 1971, he was located in Peru by Nazi hunters Beate and Serge Karsfield. Barbie fled to safety in Bolivia, still a wholly unrepentant Nazi, who admitted his identity but claimed that he was only carrying out his duties. In 1983, a long struggle to extradite him ended when a newly installed civilian government extradited him from Bolivia to France. There, after many delays, he was sentenced to life imprisonment for his war crimes on July 4, 1987. He was survived by a daughter. (d. Lyon; September 25, 1991)

FURTHER READING

Obituary. *The Times* (of London), Sep. 27, 1991.
Obituary. *New York Times,* Sep. 26, 1991.
Nazi War Criminals. Elaine Landau. Watts, 1990.
Hotel Terminus: The Life and Times of Klaus Barbie. MARCEL OPHULS. Simon & Schuster, 1990.
The Trial of Klaus Barbie. Le Monde. Harvest, 1988.
"A verdict on the butcher. . . ." WILLIAM DOWELL. *Time,* July 13, 1987.
"Standing up for Barbie." MARY MCIVER. *Maclean's,* May 25, 1987.
"The Barbie file." TED MORGAN. *New York Times Magazine,* May 10, 1987.
Klaus Barbie: The Untold Story. LADISLAS DE HOYOS. McGraw-Hill, 1985.
Unhealed Wounds: France and the Klaus Barbie Affair. ERNA PARIS. Grove Weidenfeld, 1985.
Klaus Barbie: The Butcher of Lyons. TOM BOWER. Pantheon, 1983.
Klaus Barbie and the United States Government. . . . ALLAN A. RYAN, JR., U.S. Department of Justice Staff. Greenwood, 1984.
The Nazi Legacy: Klaus Barbie and the International Fascist Connection. NEAL ASCHERSON et al. Holt, 1984.
Klaus Barbie: The Shocking Story. . . . ERHARD DABRINGHAUS. Acropolis, 1984.
Confession of Klaus Barbie. . . . ROBERT WILSON. Left Bank, 1984.

Bardeen, John (1908–91) Wisconsin-born Bardeen, an electrical engineer and physicist, won two Nobel Prizes in physics. The 1956 prize, shared with Walter Brittain and William Shockley, was for their 1947 creation of the transistor, so central to the electronic revolution of the latter half of the 20th century. The second Nobel, awarded to Bardeen in 1972, was for his theoretical work on superconductivity, developed together with Leon Cooper and John Schrieffer as the BCS theory. Bardeen worked briefly as a geophysicist before joining the Harvard faculty in 1935. He taught at the University of Minnesota from 1938 to 1941; during World War II was a physicist at the U.S. naval ordnance laboratory (1941–45); did his work on transistors while employed at the Bell Telephone Laboratory from 1945 to 1951; and was a professor of electrical energy and engineering at the University of Illinois from 1951 to 1975, continuing on as a professor emeritus. He was survived by his wife, the former Jane Maxwell, a daughter, and two sons. (d. Boston; January 30, 1991)

FURTHER READING

Obituary. *Current Biography,* Apr. 1991.
Obituary. *The Times* (of London), Feb. 1, 1991.
Obituary. *New York Times,* Jan. 31, 1991.
"John Bardeen. . . ." *Life,* Fall 1990.
Portraits of Success: Impressions of Silicon Valley Pioneers. Carolyn Caddes. Tioga, 1986.

Barnet, Charlie (1913–91) New York City-born Barnet, a jazz saxophonist and bandleader, began his professional career in his mid-teens; at 16, he was a cruise ship band member, and formed his first big band in 1933, booked at New York's Paramount Hotel. He continued to lead bands through the 1930s; very notably, he hired Black and White musicians without discrimination, at a time of segregation in American popular music. In 1934, he was the first white bandleader to play Harlem's Apollo Theater. In the early 1940s, Lena Horne joined his band; it became a show business legend that on tour Barnet forced segregated hotels to offer her lodging by threatening to pull the whole band out of the hotel if she could not stay there.

Musically, Barnet was much influenced by Duke Ellington and Count Basie, especially using many Ellington scores; as an instrumentalist, he was deeply appreciative of Coleman Hawkins and Johnny Hodges. His first major hit came in 1939, with the million-copy "Cherokee," which was followed by such hits as "Redskin Rhumba," "Pompton Turnpike," and the million-copy "Skyliner." His 1984 autobiography, with Stanley Dance, was *Those Swinging Years.* He was survived by his wife of 33 years, Betty, the last of what were variously reported to have been 6 to 11 wives, and a son, Charles Barnet, Jr.

FURTHER READING

Obituary. *Variety,* Sep. 16, 1991.
Obituary. *The Times* (of London), Sep. 9, 1991.
Obituary. *New York Times,* Sep. 6, 1991.

Barr, Roseanne: See **Arnold, Roseanne Barr**

Barry, Marion Shepilov, Jr. (1936–) Although former Washington, D.C., mayor Barry had in 1990 been convicted on cocaine-possession charges and had not run for a fourth mayoral term because of the conviction, he was still a major figure to many of his former constituents. After leaving office on January 1, 1991, he came close to being offered a teaching job in the Criminal Justice Department of the University of the District of Columbia, but the planned offer was canceled after powerful faculty and media opposition developed; instead, the department chairman was relieved of his administrative responsibilities.

For much of the rest of 1991, Barry fought an unsuccessful set of legal actions aimed at negating his conviction and sentencing, but in mid-July the U.S. Court of Appeals affirmed his conviction. On September 16 a three-judge federal appeals court criticized Judge Thomas Penfield Jackson for speaking at Harvard Law School about the case, but also left Jackson on the case. The next day, September 27, Jackson again sentenced Barry to six months in prison. Barry began his prison term on October 26.

Mississippi-born Barry was active in the civil rights movement of the 1960s, and moved into Washington, D.C., politics in the early 1970s, as a member of the school board and then in 1976 of the city council. He began his long, highly controversial tenure as mayor of Washington in 1979. His B.S. was from Lemoyne College, in 1958; his M.S. was from Fisk University, in 1960. He married Effi Barry in 1978; they have one child.

FURTHER READING

"Barry and his city. . . ." JEFFERSON MORLEY. *Nation,* Feb. 19, 1990.

The Mayor Who Stayed Too Long: The Story of Marion S. Barry. JONATHAN I. AGRONSKY. British American, 1990.

"A bright, broken promise." MICHAEL RILEY. *Time,* June 26, 1989.

"Washington's mayor. . . . MONTGOMERY BROWER. *People,* Jan. 16, 1989.

Baryshnikov, Mikhail (1948–) Premier dancer Baryshnikov continued his post-American Ballet Theater work with the White Oak Dance Project, a dance company that he co-founded with ultra-modern dancer-choregographer Mark Morris in the fall of 1990. The 11-member company began a 15-city tour in July 1991, with performances at the Wolf Trap Farm Park in Vienna, Virginia, and visited the West Coast for the first time. In October, Baryshnikov danced Martha Graham's "El Penitente," giving what one reviewer called "one of the best performances of his entire career," despite knee trouble, to open her dance troupe's first season after her death on April 1.

In September 1991, Baryshnikov opened on screen in Nicholas Meyer's post-Cold War spy story *Company Business,* playing former Soviet mole Pyotr Grushenko who—after the failure of an exchange to return him—goes on the run with CIA agent Sam Boyd (Gene Hackman). Earlier in 1991, he had opened as Cesar in *The Cabinet of Dr. Ramirez,* a highly experimental first film written and directed by theater director Peter Sellars.

Russian-born Baryshnikov was well on his way to becoming a world figure in ballet when he defected to the West in 1974, after five years as a leading dancer with the Kirov Ballet (1967–74). The promise came to pass: In the years that followed, he danced as a leading guest artist with most of the world's great ballet companies and was artistic director of the American Ballet Theatre (1980–89). His work included the creation of leads in such new ballets as *Vestris* (1965), *Hamlet* (1970), *Santa Fe Saga* (1978), and *Rhapsody* (1980); the choreography of new versions of *The Nutcracker* (1976), *Don Quixote* (1978), and *Cinderella* (1984); and appearances in several films, including *White Nights* (1985) and *The Dancers* (1987). After abruptly leaving the American Ballet Theater late in 1989, he and Morris founded the White Oak Dance Project. On Broadway, Baryshnikov appeared as Gregor Samsa in a stage version of Franz Kafka's *Metamorphosis* (1989). With Peter Anastos, he wrote *The Swan Prince* (1987).

FURTHER READING

"Misha's moment. . . ." ELIZABETH KAYE. *Connoisseur,* Nov. 1991.

"And now, superstar? . . ." IRIS M. FANGER. *World Monitor,* June 1991.

Mikhail Baryshnikov. BRUCE GLASSMAN. Silver Burdett, 1991.

"Baryshnikov. . . ." DEBORAH JOWITT. *Dance Magazine,* Jan. 1990.

"Baryshnikov's transformation. . . ." JACK KROLL. *Newsweek,* Mar. 20, 1989.

"The next stage." PATRICIA CORBETT. *Connoisseur,* Jan. 1989.

Misha!: The Mikhail Baryshnikov Story. BARBARA ARIA. St. Martin's, 1989.

Basinger, Kim (1953–) Co-stars in Jerry Rees's *The Marrying Man,* Kim Basinger and Alec Baldwin turned an on-screen romance into an off-screen one. In the Neil Simon comedy set in the late 1940s and 1950s, they are Las Vegas lounge singer Vicki Anderson and toothpaste heir Charley Pearl, who pair and split over eight years. The movie was not very well received by most critics, audiences were modest, and the film arrived on television before the end of 1991.

Forthcoming were two other projects: *Cool*

World, directed by Ralph Bakshi and co-starring Gabriel Byrne; and *Final Analysis,* directed by Phil Joanou, with a cast that includes Richard Gere, Uma Thurman, and Eric Roberts. Scheduled to star in *Boxing Helena,* Basinger left the cast, citing the old standby "creative differences."

Georgia-born Basinger worked as a New York model in the mid-1970s, then moved into television, most notably in *Katie—Portrait of a Centerfold* (1978), and in the 1979 remake of *From Here to Eternity.* On screen, she starred in *Hard Country* (1980) and *The Man Who Loved Women* (1983), and became one of Hollywood's leading sex symbols of the 1980s as Domino in Sean Connery's last James Bond film *Never Say Never Again* (1983) and opposite Mickey Rourke in *9½ Weeks* (1986). She also starred in *The Natural* (1984), *Fool for Love* (1985), and *Batman* (1989). Basinger attended New York's Neighborhood Playhouse. She was formerly married.

FURTHER READING

"Kim up close. . . ." Jonathan Van Meter. *Vogue,* May 1991.
"Kim and Alec. . . ." Elizabeth Sporkin. *People,* Apr. 22, 1991.
"Basinger, Kim." *Current Biography,* Feb. 1990.

Bates, Alan (1934–) In Udayan Prasad's *101 Boulevard Haussmann,* which aired on television's Arts and Entertainment channel in November 1991, British star Bates played nervous, asthmatic French novelist Marcel Proust, cossetted and to some extent trapped in his cork-lined study by his protectors, and fixed on a young man in the string quartet giving a private recital. The London Film Festival in November brought *Secret Friends,* a film directed by Dennis Potter from his own novel *Ticket to Ride,* in which Bates starred as John, an illustrator who dreams of murdering his wife Helen (Gina Bellman). Bates also starred in the Andrew Piddington film *Shuttlecock,* as James Prentis, a World War II British spy who decides to tell his story 20 years later in Portugal. Meanwhile, wider audiences saw him as Claudius in Franco Zeffirelli's film version of *Hamlet* (1990; released in video in 1991).

Bates became a star in Harold Pinter's *The Caretaker* (1960; and the 1964 film version). He went on to such plays as *Butley* (1972; he won a Tony), *Otherwise Engaged* (1975), *A Patriot for Me* (1983), and *Ivanov* (1989). He has appeared in such films as *A Kind of Loving* (1962), *King of Hearts* (1966), *Far from the Madding Crowd* (1967), *A Day in the Death of Joe Egg* (1972), *In Celebration* (1974), *An Unmarried Woman* (1977), *Nijinsky* (1979), *The Return of the Soldier* (1982), and *A Prayer for the Dying* (1987), and in such telefilms as *An Englishman Abroad* (1983) and *Pack of Lies* (1987). Bates attended the Royal Academy of Dramatic Arts. He married Victoria Ward in 1970; they have two children.

FURTHER READING

"Alan Bates returns. . . ." Carol Lawson. *New York Times,* Dec. 30, 1983.

Bates, Kathy (1948–) Time after time, Kathy Bates saw parts she originated on stage go to more "glamorous" actresses on screen. But that all seemed to change with her Oscar- and Golden-Globe-winning performance in Rob Reiner's film of Stephen King's *Misery* (1990), as Annie Wilkes, the psychopathic fan who traps a novelist (James Caan).

Even before winning her 1991 Oscar, she had moved into leading roles in several films, starring opposite Tom Berenger and Daryl Hannah in Hector Babenco's *At Play in the Fields of the Lord,* based on Peter Matthiessen's novel, and opposite Jessica Tandy in John Avnet's film

Fried Green Tomatoes, which opened to critical acclaim late in 1991.

Forthcoming were starring roles as Elsa Barlow (a role she had played onstage) in Athol Fugard's *The Road to Mecca;* in Norman Rene's *Prelude to a Kiss,* the film version of Craig Lucas's 1990 play; and opposite Tandy, Shirley MacLaine, and Marcello Mastroianni in *Used People.*

Memphis-born Bates began her acting career in New York in 1970, often working in children's and regional theater, with occasional small film roles, as in Milos Forman's *Taking Off* (1971) and Dustin Hoffman's *Straight Time* (1978), and guest spots on television series and telefilms. Her first lead was in the off-Broadway play *Vanities* (1976), and she originated the role of Lenny McGrath in Beth Henley's Pulitzer Prize-winning play *Crimes of the Heart* (1979) at its Louisville debut, but her breakout role was as the suicidal Jessie Cates in Marsha Norman's Pulitzer Prize-winning *'Night Mother* (1983), for which she won the Outer Critics Circle Award and a Tony nomination. This was followed by a string of leading stage roles, including *Come Back to the Five and Dime, Jimmy Dean, Jimmy Dean* (1982) and *Frankie and Johnny in the Claire de Lune* (1987) for which she won an Obie Award, and supporting roles on film, after her 1985 move to Los Angeles, as in *Arthur 2 on the Rocks* (1988) and *Dick Tracy* (1990). Bates graduated from Southern Methodist University in Dallas. In 1991, Bates married long time companion, actor Tony Campisi.

FURTHER READING

"Bates, Kathy." *Current Biography,* Sep. 1991.
"Kathy Bates." Michael Lassell and Timothy Greenfield-Sanders. *Interview,* Aug. 1991.
" 'I never was an ingenue.' " David Sacks. *New York Times Magazine,* Jan. 27. 1991.
"Wallowing in Misery. . . ." Mary H. J. Farrell. *People,* Dec. 24, 1990.

Baulieu, Etienne-Emile (1926–) French biochemist Baulieu, one of the world's leading endocrinologists, is the inventor of RU 486, the so-called abortion pill, and has since its invention in the late 1970s led the worldwide campaign to introduce the pill, against the opposition of anti-abortion campaigners.

Pro-RU 486 forces won a major victory in July 1991, when Britain approved the use of the pill in National Health Service hospitals carrying out abortions. Use of the pill was limited in France, however, after the first death in approximately 60,000 abortions was reported; those over 35 and regular smokers of any age were barred from using the pill. In the United States, the Bush administration continued to oppose introduction of RU 486, although pressure grew to permit its use. The first major breakthrough came when the New Hampshire legislature in May 1991 approved testing of the pill as part of the process of securing Food and Drug Administration approval of the drug for U.S. use; several other states were moving toward similar actions. A powerful financial boost was provided in October when feminist Peg Yorkin donated $10 million to the Feminist Majority Foundation, the money earmarked for a pro-RU 486 campaign.

Baulieu continued to campaign for RU 486, while at the same time continuing to express regret that the long argument would harm research into several other promising medical uses of the drug. Late in 1991, he published the book *The Abortion Pill,* co-authored with Mort Rosenblum, in which he reviewed his work with RU-486 and argued that the pill provided a safe, effective, and affordable means of abortion.

Baulieu received his medical degree from the University of Paris in 1955, and taught medicine at Reims, Rouen, the University of Paris, and Columbia University during the 1950s and early 1960s. In 1963, he became director of a hormonal research unit of the French National Institute of Health and Medical Research (Inserm), and founded the International Society for Research in the Biology of Reproduction in 1967. He led the research group that developed the abortion pill RU 486 in the late 1970s. He also led the successful campaign that forced the French government to order production and distribution of the pill in France. Baulieu married Yolande Compagnon in 1947; they have three children.

FURTHER READING

Interview. *Omni,* Sep. 1991.

Beatty, Warren (Warren Beaty, 1937–) Warren Beatty's new movie brought him a new love in 1991. In the title role of Barry Levinson's *Bugsy,* Beatty played the flamboyant, womanizing 1940s mobster Bugsy Siegel, who created the

Las Vegas gambling-entertainment industry in the Nevada desert. While working on the film, Beatty met and soon became inseparable from actress Annette Bening. In July Beatty and Bening announced through his publicist that they were expecting a child early in 1992. The child, a daughter named Kathlyn Bening Beatty, was born in January 1992. The couple married privately, at an undisclosed date and location. The film opened in December, to great critical acclaim; Beatty, the film, and director Barry Levinson were strong candidates for 1992 Oscars.

Beatty had previously been romantically linked with a parade of Hollywood actresses (often co-stars), including Diane Keaton, Leslie Caron, Julie Christie, and Madonna. Normally averse to publicity, Beatty insisted that ex-companion Madonna remove from her concert film *Truth or Dare* (1991) some segments involving him, notably a telephone conversation that he did not know was being taped.

Virginia-born Beatty, the brother of actress Shirley MacLaine, acted in television and theater from the late 1950s, moving into films in the early 1960s. He starred in *Splendor in the Grass* (1961), but his breakthrough role was that of Clyde Barrow in *Bonnie and Clyde* (1961). He produced that film, and went on to produce and star in such films as *McCabe and Mrs. Miller* (1971) and *Heaven Can Wait* (1978), which he also wrote. His most substantial work, so far, has been the epic film *Reds* (1981); he produced, directed, co-wrote, starred as John Reed, and won a Best Director Oscar for the film. In 1987, he starred in the disastrous *Ishtar.* In 1990, he directed and produced *Dick Tracy.* Beatty attended the Stella Adler theater school. (For photo, see **Bening, Annette.**)

FURTHER READING

"The Warren report. . . ." NORMAN MAILER. *Vanity Fair,* Nov. 1991.
The Films of Warren Beatty. LAWRENCE J. QUIRK. Carol, 1990.
Actors: A Celebration. RITA GAM. St. Martin's, 1988.
Warren Beatty and Desert Eyes: A Life and a Story. DAVID THOMSON. Doubleday, 1987.

Bell, James "Cool Papa" (1903–91) Alabama-born Bell, an African-American, was one of the greatest athletes ever to play baseball. An extraordinary star in the segregated Negro leagues, his career spanned 25 seasons, 20 of them in the United States and 5 in Latin America. He began his career in 1922, as an outfielder for the St. Louis Stars, that year hitting .417; his average during the 20 American seasons was between .330 and .340, a period in which he stole over 170 bases. After his 1946 retirement, he worked for 21 years as a custodian at the St. Louis City Hall. In a long overdue recognition of his place in the history of baseball, he was in 1974 elected to the Baseball Hall of Fame. (d. St. Louis; March 7, 1991)

FURTHER READING

" 'Cool Papa' Bell. . . ." *Jet,* Mar. 25, 1991.
"A loss for baseball." RICHARD DEMAK. *Sports Illustrated,* Mar. 18, 1991.
Obituary. *New York Times,* Mar. 9, 1991.

Bellamy, Ralph Rexford (1904–91) Best known by far for his Tony-winning portrayal of Franklin D. Roosevelt on stage in *Sunrise at Campobello* (1958) and on screen in the 1960 film version of the play, Bellamy was one of the leading character actors of the American stage and screen. His career spanned seven decades, starting with bit parts in silent films and touring in repertory in the 1920s. He played second leads in scores of such Hollywood films as *The Awful Truth* (1937), *Carefree* (1938), and *His Girl Friday* (1940), and starred in the four "Ellery Queen" films (1940–41) before going back into the theater. Bellamy emerged as a leading player on the New York stage in *Tomorrow the World* (1943), *State of the Union* (1945), and *Detective Story* (1950). His later work included many further films and much work in television; one of his late roles was as Franklin D. Roosevelt again, in the 1983 miniseries "The Winds of War." He was a founding member of the Screen Actors Guild and was president of Actors' Equity from 1952 to 1964. He was survived by his fourth wife, Alice Murphy, and by a daughter, a son, and a sister. (d. Los Angeles; November 29, 1991)

FURTHER READING

Obituary. *The Times* (of London), Dec. 2, 1991.
Obituary. *Variety,* Dec. 2, 1991.
Obituary. *New York Times,* Nov. 30, 1991.

Annette Bening and Warren Beatty.

Bening, Annette (1958–) Bening's recent acting career has been described as a Hollywood comet. For her performance as con artist's girlfriend Myra Langtry in *The Grifters* (1990), she won an Oscar nomination and the National Society of Film Critics nod as best supporting actress. Bening also played a notable cameo in Mike Nichols's *Postcards from the Edge* (1990), as the actress who loves sex for the "endolphins."

In 1991, Bening starred opposite Harrison Ford in another Nichols film, *Regarding Henry,* as Sara Turner, an attorney's wife who suddenly must face life with an injured man who does not even remember her. She also starred as the wife of a blacklisted writer (Robert De Niro) in Irwin Winkler's McCarthy-era film *Guilty by Suspicion.* In December, she scored a success as Virginia Hill in *Bugsy,* Barry Levinson's film about the 1940s Las Vegas gangster Bugsy Siegel, played by Warren Beatty. In July Beatty and Bening—who had met on the set—announced that they were expecting a child early in 1992. Because of the pregnancy, Bening dropped out of her scheduled role as Catwoman in the forthcoming *Batman,* being replaced by Michelle Pfeiffer. The child, a daughter named Kathlyn Bening Beatty, was born in January 1992. The couple maried privately at an undisclosed date and location.

Born in Kansas, Bening was raised in San Diego and attended San Diego's Mesa College and San Francisco State University. She spent five years at San Francisco's American Conservatory Theater (ACT)—first as student, then company member—and a season at the Denver Theater Center, before coming to New York and winning the lead in Tina Howe's *Coastal Disturbances,* garnering a Tony nomination in 1987 on its move to Broadway. She had brief roles in John Hughes's film *The Great Outdoors* (1988), and on Broadway in Michael Weller's *Spoils of War* (1988), before being signed for her breakthrough role in *Valmont* (1988). Bening was previously married to actor Steve White.

FURTHER READING

"Annette Bening. . . ." *Cosmopolitan,* Dec. 1991.
"Oh, oh Annette." Ben Brantley and Helmut Newton. *Vanity Fair,* Aug. 1991.
"Regarding Annette." Christopher Connelly and Timothy White. *Premiere.* July 1991.
"Annette Bening." Graham Fuller. *Interview,* May 1991.

Berg, Jack "Kid" (Judah Benjamin, 1909–91) Born in London's East End, the child of Russian Jewish immigrants, Berg made his debut as a professional boxer in 1924, beginning a long career that ended in 1945. He became a great celebrity in Britain and the United States after defeating "Kid" Chocolate before a sold-out New York Polo Grounds crowd in June 1930. That was also the year he became the world junior welterweight champion, defeating Mushy Callahan to win the title. He made nine successful title defenses before losing to Tony Canzoneri in 1931. Berg was also British lightweight champion from 1934 to 1936. He later worked as a stuntman and actor in Hollywood. He was married twice, and was survived by his second wife, Mora, and one daughter (d. April 22, 1991)

FURTHER READING

Jack Kid Berg: The Whitechapel Windmill. John Harding and Jack Berg. Parkwest Publications, 1992.
Obituary. *The Times* (of London), Apr. 23, 1991.

Bergen, Candice (1946–) After the 1990–91 television season's most discussed cliffhanger, Bergen returned as the title character in "Murphy Brown" in September to record-setting high ratings for the opening night of a new television season. Fans had learned in spring 1991 that 42-year-old Murphy was pregnant—or at least had showed positive on a home pregnancy test—but had to wait all summer to learn whether it was so and who the father was: Murphy's ex-husband Jake, played by Robin Thomas. Many were surprised to find that Murphy was keeping the baby, and without marrying Jake, who left the series for the Amazon, or going through with a "shotgun marriage" to a younger man, as part of her boss's proposed "damage control."

Although many television "insiders" felt that the continuing pregnancy story could mean lower ratings, the show continued to enjoy excellent ratings through year's end; the 1991–92 series was scheduled to end with the baby's birth on the show's finale (and 100th episode) in May 1992. Television audiences continued to respond to a show that deliberately blurs the distinction between fact and fiction, with real-life news celebrities appearing in guest spots on the show and episodes modeled on actual events in the world of broadcast journalism.

Apart from a posthumous Guest Actress award for Colleen Dewhurst, who played Murphy's mother, Bergen and her fellow players—Pat Corley, Faith Ford, Charles Kimbrough, Robert Pastorelli, Joe Regalbuto, and Grant Shaud—were Emmy-less in 1991. However, Bergen was named top network television performer by her peers in the Friars Club.

Daughter of famed ventriloquist Edgar Bergen, the creator of Charlie McCarthy, California-born Bergen is a star in her own right, with a long series of major roles in such films as *Carnal Knowledge* (1971), *Starting Over* (1979), *Rich and Famous* (1981), and *Gandhi* (1982). In 1988, she began a whole new aspect of her career, playing the lead (reportedly modeled on Diane Sawyer, among others) in television's "Murphy Brown." She won two consecutive Best Actress in a Comedy Emmys (1989 and 1990), and the show won a Best Comedy Series Emmy in 1990. She has also written and photographed articles for several major magazines, and wrote the autobiographical *Knock Wood* (1984). Bergen is married to film director Louis Malle and has one daughter. She attended the University of Pennsylvania.

FURTHER READING

"Murphy's laws. . . ." Jim Jerome. *People,* Dec. 2, 1991.
"Candice Bergen. . . ." Maureen Dowd. *McCall's,* Oct. 1991.
"Candid Candice." Linda Ellerbee and Michael J. Bandler. *Ladies Home Journal,* June 1990.
"Playboy interview. . . ." David Sheff. *Playboy,* Dec. 1989.
"Candice Bergen. . . ." Michael Segell. *Cosmopolitan,* Nov. 1989.

Bergman, Ingmar (1918–) Though most widely known for his screen work, Bergman has recently focused on stage work with the Royal Dramatic Theater of Stockholm. International audiences had a chance to see the results in mid-1991, when Bergman brought three of his Swedish-language productions to the Brooklyn Academy of Music (BAM), as part of the New York International Festival of the Arts: August Strindberg's *Miss Julie,* Eugene O'Neill's *Long Day's Journey into Night,* and Henrick Ibsen's *A Doll's House.* Though very different plays, all three were widely praised for the strength and uniqueness of the director's vision.

Bergman's lifetime achievement was honored in late 1991 by the Japanese Art Association, whose prizes were established two years earlier to honor artists whose works do not fall in the categories of the Nobel Prize. Bergman also wrote Billy August's epic television series and film, *The Good Will,* scheduled for release in late 1991, and was working on the next installment of his autobiography, the forthcoming *Pictures,* a sequel to *The Magic Lantern* (1987).

The Swedish director, writer, and producer is a central figure in world film history and at the same time a major figure in the Swedish theater. From the mid-1950s, he created a series of film masterworks that have been tremendously important to all who followed, including such classics as *Smiles of a Summer Night* (1955), *Wild Strawberries* (1957), *The Magician* (1958), *The Virgin Spring* (1960), *Through a Glass Darkly* (1961), *Scenes from a Marriage* (1974), *Fanny and Alexander* (1982), *After the Rehearsal* (1984), and *Good Intentions* (1989). In March 1990, he received the D. W. Griffith award from the Directors Guild of America, for lifetime contribution to film. Bergman attended Stockholm University. He has been married six times and has eight children. His son, Daniel Bergman, is also a film director; his sister, Margareta Bergman, is a novelist.

FURTHER READING

The Poet at the Piano: Portraits of Writers, Filmmakers, and Performers at Work. MICHIKO KAKUTANI. Random, 1988.
Ingmar Bergman: A Guide to References and Resources. BIRGITTA STEEN. G. K. Hall, 1987.
"Ingmar Bergman. . . ." MICHIKO KAKUTANI. *New York Times Magazine,* June 26, 1983.
"God, sex and. . . ." RICHARD CORLISS and WILLIAM WOLF. *Film Comment,* May–June 1983.
Talking with Ingmar Bergman. G. WILLIAM JONES, ed. SMU Press, 1983.
Ingmar Bergman, LISE-LONE MARKER and FREDERICK J. MARKER. Cambridge University Press, 1982.
Ingmar Bergman: A Critical Biography. PETER COWIE. Macmillan, 1982.

Bermudez Varela, Enrique (1932–91) Former Nicaraguan Contra commander Bermudez was assassinated in Managua on February 16, 1991. A career officer in the Nicaraguan army, Bermudez received his military training in Nicaragua, Panama, and the United States. He was with the Organization of American States (OAS) peacekeeping forces that replaced U.S. forces after the 1965–66 U.S. intervention in the Dominican Republic, and was a Nicaraguan military attache in Washington during the 1979 Sandinista insurrection in Nicaragua, which toppled the Anastasio Somoza government. Opposing the Sandinistas, he was in 1981 an organizer of the Nicaraguan Democratic Force, soon becoming commander of the guerrilla forces known as the Contras. After Violeta Chamorro was elected president of Nicaragua in February, 1990, Bermudez returned home, then participating in the series of postwar agreements that followed, including the demobilization of Contra forces. He was survived by his wife, Elsa, and three children. (d. Managua, Nicaragua; February 16, 1991)

FURTHER READING

"Murder in Managua." JAMES LEMOYNE. *New Republic,* Mar. 18, 1991.
Obituary. *The Times* (of London), Feb. 23, 1991.

Bertolucci, Bernardo (1940–) It was off with the new and on with the old in 1991 for Italian filmmaker Bertolucci. *The Sheltering Sky,* his version of Paul Bowles's novel, starring Debra Winger and John Malkovich, released late in 1990, won mixed reviews and only modest audiences, disappearing rather quickly. However, his 1976 classic, *1990,* was restored to its full length of 5 hours and 11 minutes—it had been cut by over an hour for its original U.S. release—and was re-released to considerable acclaim in theaters in several American cities and also on cable. The restoration had been done under the eye of the original cinematographer, Vittorio Storaro (who also shot *The Sheltering Sky*) and included a new soundtrack in Dolby stereo. Some expressed unhappiness that the restored film was the English-language version, not the original Italian version with English subtitles. However, the original film was an international co-production, with players such as Robert De Niro, Gérard Depardieu, Burt Lancaster, Donald Sutherland, Dominique Sanda, Sterling Hayden, Alida Valli, and Laura Betti speaking in their own languages, and then being dubbed, into either Italian or English, as appropriate. Bertolucci's next project was scheduled to be a film biography, *Buddha.* A Hong Kong company had sued for an injunction to prevent the making of the film, but in a London court in late 1990 he won the right to proceed.

Parma-born Bertolucci has long been one of the leading directors of the Italian cinema. He was an assistant director on Pier Paolo Pasolini's *Accatone* (1961), and then set off on his own, with *The Grim Reaper* (1962). In 1964 came the well-received *Before the Revolution,* and in 1970 *The Spider's Strategem* and the classic *The Conformist.* Marlon Brando starred in Bertolucci's *Last Tango in Paris* (1972); the film, sexually explicit for a mainstream film of its time, created a worldwide controversy over its alleged pornography. His films also include *Luna* (1979), *Tragedy of a Ridiculous Man* (1982), and *The Last Emperor* (1987), for which he won a Best Director Oscar, one of nine Oscars won by the film. Bertolucci is married to filmmaker Clare Peploe, sister of screenwriter Mark Peploe, who adapted *The Sheltering Sky.*

FURTHER READING

"Love and sand. . . ." ROBERT GERBER. *Interview,* Jan. 1991.
"Last tango in Tangier." BOB SPITZ. *New York Times Magazine,* May 20, 1990.
"Hollywood continues. . . ." LAWRENCE COHN. *Variety,* Oct. 25, 1989.

Bernardo Bertolucci. Robert P. Kolker. Oxford University Press, 1985.

Bessmertnykh, Aleksandr Alessandrovich (1933–) Named Soviet foreign minister by Mikhail Gorbachev in January 1991, career diplomat Bessmertnykh played a major role in seeing through the series of agreements that ended the more than four decades-long U.S.-U.S.S.R. Cold War, including the historic agreement to cut for the first time stockpiles of long-range strategic nuclear weapons and the agreement to cut conventional forces in Europe. He also played a substantial role during the Persian Gulf crisis and war, officially supporting Allied aims while questioning the need to actually go to war, and after the Iraqi defeat unsuccessfully attempting to soften Allied peace terms.

During the failed August Soviet right-wing coup attempt, Bessmertnykh disappeared from public view, as did very many other Soviet officials. He reappeared at an August 21 press conference, to tell a very skeptical press that he had been ill during the three days of the coup. He was fired by Mikhail Gorbachev on August 23, and was replaced by Boris Pankin, a diplomat who had spoken out against the coup while it was in progress.

Siberian-born Bessmertnykh spent his entire career as a professional diplomat, much of it in the United States. He was attached to the United Nations secretariat in the 1960s, and then to the U.S. Soviet embassy (1970–83). From 1988 to 1990, he was a first deputy foreign minister, responsible for the Middle East and North America, and in 1990 became Soviet ambassador to the United States. He is a graduate of the Moscow State Institute of International Relations. He is married to his second wife, Maria Vladimirova, and has two children.

FURTHER READING

"Bessmertnykh, Aleksandr Aleksandrovich." *Current Biography,* June 1991.

Bhutto, Benazir (1943–) In the first full year after her dismissal as prime minister of Pakistan, Benazir Bhutto continued to be at great personal risk. So was her husband, Asif Ali Zardari, still in prison on criminal charges that could lead to his execution, although four key witnesses against him withdrew their testimony in March 1991, claiming that it had been forced by the government. Although still herself facing charges of abuse of power while in office, and with the whole world mindful of the fate of her father at the hands of the same military, Bhutto continued and strengthened her role as leader of the united opposition to Pakistan's military-dominated government. On August 4, 1991, in protest against the arrest of an estimated 5,000 members of her party, Bhutto went on a brief hunger strike. The conservative government of Pakistan continued to move to the right, in May once again establishing strict observance of Islamic law as the law of the land.

Bhutto and her mother, Nusrat Bhutto, were under house arrest in Pakistan from 1977 to 1984, after the coup that deposed her father. She left Pakistan in 1984, returned for the funeral of her brother in 1985, and was rearrested and expelled from her country. She returned again in 1986 as head of the Pakistan People's Party and led the opposition to the government.

After the death of military dictator Zia Ul-Haq in an August 1988 plane crash, Bhutto was elected prime minister of Pakistan in the free election of December 2, 1988. She was the second Bhutto to become prime minister. Her father, Zulfikar Ali Bhutto, had been Pakistani prime minister from 1972 to 1977; he was executed in 1979 by Zia's military government.

In office, Benazir Bhutto was hailed as one of the world's leading women; but at home, she faced increasing opposition from the Pakistani army and fundamentalist religious leaders. On August 6, 1990, she was removed from office by President Ishak Khan, acting with the support of the military; she was charged with corruption, her husband and many supporters were arrested, and she was forbidden to leave the country. She and her party were defeated in the October 24, 1990, elections, which she called fraud-ridden.

Bhutto attended Harvard University and Lady Margaret Hall, Oxford University. In 1989 she published *Daughter of Destiny: An Autobiography.* She married Asif Ali Zardari in 1987; they have two children.

FURTHER READING

Benazir Bhutto. Diane Sansevere-Dreher. Bantam, 1991.

Benazir Bhutto. Katherine M. Doherty and Craig A. Doherty. Watts, 1990.
From Prison to Prime Minister: A Biography of Benazir Bhutto. Libby Hughes. Dillon, 1990.
Women and Politics in Islam: The Trial of Benazir Bhutto. Rafig Zakaria. New Horizons, 1990.
"Dynasty's daughter." Tariq Ali. *Interview,* Feb. 1989.

Biden, Joseph Robinette, Jr. (1942–) The highly visible chairman of the Senate Judiciary Committee was very much in the news during 1991, most notably as presiding senator at the nomination hearings of Judge Clarence Thomas to the U.S. Supreme Court. These hearings culminated in the extraordinary spectacle of the Anita Faye Hill–Clarence Thomas confrontation over sexual harassment charges before a worldwide television audience. Biden was widely criticized during and after those hearings for insensitivity to women's equality and freedom questions; ironically, he was a key sponsor of the landmark Violence Against Women Act.

The Thomas confirmation hearings had been for several reasons conducted in a rather low key, and Thomas was able to avoid or refuse to discuss most substantive questions. That low-key approach—perhaps indeed coupled with insensitivity on the sexual harassment issue—may very well have contributed to the failure of the Democratic majority to take seriously Professor Anita Faye Hill's sensational charges against Judge Clarence Thomas when they were made to Senate committee staff members in early September. But in October, when Professor Hill went public with her charges, Senator Biden and his colleagues were forced to take her very seriously indeed, and the public and quite historic October 6–15 Hill–Thomas confrontation was the result. No one was to come out of those hearings unscathed, including Senator Biden.

During 1991, Biden was also a key figure in the development of anti-crime legislation, as sponsor and chief Democratic negotiator of what became the Senate anti-crime bill. He also voted against the Persian Gulf War resolution and played an active role in the Senate Foreign Relations Committee.

After briefly practicing law in Delaware, Biden became a Democratic senator from that state in 1972, later moving into a key position as head of the Senate Judiciary Committee. In 1986, he played a major role in the rejection of President Reagan's nomination of Robert Bork to the Supreme Court. He was a leading candidate for the 1988 Democratic presidential nomination, but withdrew after allegations that he had plagiarized some of the material in his campaign speeches from the speeches of British Labor leader Neil Kinnock. In early 1990, he survived two brain operations, both for aneurysms, then resumed his Senate career. Pennsylvania-born Biden, a four-term senator, was previously married to Neilia Hunter, and married Jill Tracy Jacobs in 1977; he has had four children, including two sons from his first marriage, who survived the 1972 automobile accident that killed their mother and infant sister. He received his A.B. from the University of Delaware, and his J.D. from Syracuse University.

FURTHER READING

"Biden is also reborn." Margaret Carlson. *Time,* Sep. 12, 1988.
"The fall of a contender." Marci McDonald. *Maclean's,* Oct. 5, 1987.
"Joe Biden. . . ." Gary Smith. *Life,* Oct. 1987.
"Biden's familiar quotations. . . ." Walter Shapiro. *Time,* Sep. 28, 1987.
"Biden, Joseph (Robinette), Jr." *Current Biography,* Jan. 1987.

Bigart, Homer William (1907–91) Pennsylvania-born Bigart was one of the leading journalists of his generation, the winner of two Pulitzer Prizes (1946, 1951) and a wide range of other awards. He began his career in

1929, as a copy boy on the *New York Herald Tribune,* became a general assignment reporter for the newspaper in 1933, and entered the international arena as a war correspondent in 1942. A leading World War II reporter, he covered the war in Europe from the Blitz through German capitulation, and then moved to the Pacific theater to cover the Japanese defeat, being one of the first correspondents into Hiroshima after the atom bombing of the city. In the decades that followed, he covered the Korean War, the Vietnam War, and a very wide range of national and international events, from the long series of Arab-Israeli wars to the convulsions that rocked the United States during the 1960s. He left the *Herald Tribune* for the *New York Times* in 1955, retiring in 1972. He was married three times, and was survived by his second wife, author Else Holmelund Minarik, a sister, and a stepdaughter. (d. Portsmouth, New Hampshire; April 16, 1991)

FURTHER READING

Obituary. *Current Biography,* July 1991.
Obituary. *U.S. News & World Report,* Apr. 29, 1991.
Obituary. *New York Times,* Apr. 17, 1991.

Blackmun, Harry Andrew (1908–)
"Concern for a woman's existing or potential offspring historically has been the excuse for denying women equal employment opportunities. . . . We do no more than hold that the Pregnancy Discrimination Act means what it says."—from Justice Blackmun's March 20, 1991, opinion in *United Automobile Workers v. Johnson Controls Inc.,* a landmark women's rights case. Blackmun, writing for a 6–3 majority, held that employers could not ban pregnant women from jobs potentially dangerous to their unborn children; it was a rare instance of his liberal views prevailing in an increasingly conservative Court.

During the 1990–91 term, he also wrote the March 4, 1991, 7–1 majority opinion in *Pacific Mutual Life Insurance Co. v. Haslip,* holding that it was unconstitutional for courts to restrict punitive damages awarded by juries in civil cases, although states could do so by law.

Blackmun joined Justice Kennedy's June 3, 1991, majority opinion in *Edmonson v. Leesville Concrete Co.,* barring exclusion of jurors in civil cases because of race, following earlier bans on exclusion because of race in criminal cases. He joined Kennedy again on June 20, in *Masson v. New Yorker Magazine Inc.,* holding that invented or materially altered quotes attributed to a public figure could be libelous. On the same day, he joined Justice Stevens in two cases holding that the federal Voting Rights Act, prohibiting discriminatory voting practices or election district abuses, applied to elected judges, who were "representatives" within the meaning of the law.

But Blackmun was seldom with the conservative majority: In the critically important May 23, 1991, *Rust v. Sullivan* decision, the Court voted 5–4 to uphold federal regulations banning federally funded family planning clinics from offering abortion counseling. Blackmun, who had written the majority opinion in the landmark *Roe v. Wade* case, dissented.

He also voted with the liberal minority on several other key cases. *Board of Education of Oklahoma City v. Dowell* eased conditions for the lifting of court supervision of segregated school districts, even when the net results of all efforts to desegregate schools had been the re-creation of single-race schools, reflecting local housing patterns. *Arizona v. Fulminante* held that coerced or involuntary confession in a criminal case could be a "harmless error" if conviction would have resulted without it; the decision reversed *Chapman v. California* (1967), holding that such a confession was always grounds for acquittal. *County of Riverside, California v.*

McLaughlin held that those arrested without warrants could be held up to 48 hours while a judge decided if there was probably cause for the arrest. *Cohen v. Cowles Media* held that a breach of a promise of confidentiality made to a news source was not protected by the First Amendment as against a suit for damages caused by the breach. *Barnes v. Glen Theater* upheld an Indiana state law banning nude dancing, and was widely viewed as opening the way to local censorship of arts. *Florida v. Bostick* held that police could board buses and search passengers' luggage, with their permission. *Coleman v. Thompson* greatly restricted the use of habeas corpus writs by state prisoners who have exhausted state appeals to challenge constitutionality of their convictions, reversing the 1963 *Fay v. Noia* decision. *Harmelin v. Michigan* held that a Michigan law requiring a life sentence without the possibility of parole for possession of 650 grams (1.5 pounds) of cocaine did not violate the cruel and unusual punishment prohibition of Eighth Amendment, although the federal law was much less stringent. And *Payne v. Tennessee* allowed "victim impact" evidence to be presented by the prosecution during the sentencing phase of criminal case, thereby reversing 1987 and 1989 cases that had decided the opposite, generating a very sharp response from the Court's diminishing liberal minority.

Nashville-born Blackmun practiced and taught law in Minneapolis during the 1930s and 1940s, and was then counsel to the Mayo Clinic (1950–59). He was named to the 8th Circuit of the U.S. Court of Appeals in 1959 and was appointed by President Richard Nixon to the Supreme Court in 1970. His course in the liberal Warren Court of the time was thought to be moderately conservative, but in later years Blackmun's unwavering commitment to what were seen by most as a set of liberal positions on civil and personal rights placed him with the liberal minority in a more conservative Court. His B.A. and LL.B. were from Harvard, in 1929 and 1932. He married Dorothy Clark in 1941; they have three children.

FURTHER READING

"A new day in court." Lauren Tarshis and James Earl Hardy. *Scholastic Update,* Nov. 1, 1991.

"What they say it is. . . ." *Time,* July 6, 1987.

Bly, Robert Elwood (1926–)

Minnesota-born Bly, a poet, editor, and translator, emerged as a national figure in an entirely different context during 1991. With his book, *Iron John: A Book About Men* (1990), he became the philosophical leader of a new "men's movement," and his book was at the top of the best-seller lists for much of 1991. In his book, in many media appearances, such as his widely seen televised interviews with Bill Moyers and at men's encounter groups throughout the United States, Bly stressed what he felt was a new kind of male liberation. For Bly, this process enabled men to free the "inner warrior" said to be repressed within, as a way to maturing into a whole person, in an industrial world featuring a compulsory education system and largely female teachers, which he felt had destroyed preindustrial father-son relationships. Discussions also centered on such matters as the need for nonfamily male mentors, the historic role of initiation rites in several societies, and Bly's interpretation of some Jungian theoretical constructs. Encounter group sessions feature mythological stories and group exercises such as shouting or grunting together, a sort of group approximation of primal scream, in attempts to liberate the "king" and "wild man" said to be buried inside each man.

Bly's published works in 1991 include *Jumping Out of Bed* and *Remembering James Wright.* Among publications due in 1992 were *What Have I Ever Lost by Dying?, Angels of Pompeii* (with

Stephen Brigidi), and *The Rag and Bone Shop of the Heart: Poems for Men* (edited with James Hillman and Michael Meade). Also forthcoming was a new play for children, *Tattercoats.*

Bly's B.A. was from Harvard, in 1950, his M.A. from the University of Iowa in 1956. He has published numerous works of poetry, winning the 1968 National Book Award for his poetry, as well as translation and critical works. His recent works include *The Moon on a Fencepost* (1988), *A Little Book on the Human Shadow* (1988), *Point Reyes Poems* (1989), *The Apple Found in the Plowing* (1989), and *American Poetry: Wildness and Domesticity* (1990). He has been married twice, last to Ruth Ray, and has four children.

FURTHER READING

"Robert Bly, wild thing." Charles Gaines. *Esquire,* Oct. 1991.
"The child is. . . ." Lance Morrow. *Time,* Aug. 19, 1991.
"Drums, sweat and tears. . . ." Jerry Adler. *Newsweek,* June 24, 1991.
"Masculinity's champion. . . ." Art Levine. *U.S. News & World Report,* Apr. 8, 1991.
The Incorporative Consciousness of Robert Bly. Victoria F. Harris. Southern Illinois University Press, 1991.
Robert Bly: A Primary and Secondary Bibliography. William H. Roberson and Barbara Lee, eds. Scarecrow, 1986.
Robert Bly. Richard P. Sugg. Macmillan, 1986.
Understanding Robert Bly. William V. Davis. University of South Carolina Press, 1989.

Bolling, Richard (1916–91) New York City-born Bolling won a Bronze Star in the Pacific theater during World War II, and after the war became national vice chairman of the American Veterans Committee. He was also a leader of Americans for Democratic Action (ADA). He began his long congressional career by winning a House seat as a liberal Democrat from Missouri, in the 1948 campaign that brought Harry Truman to the presidency. Bolling served 17 terms in the House, retiring in 1982. Throughout that long period he became an increasingly powerful Democratic leader, though always falling just short of winning the Speaker's chair. He was a long-term member of the Rules Committee and used his position to foster civil rights legislation and a long liberal agenda, with particular success in the 1960s. He was survived by his wife, Nona, a daughter, and two stepsons. (d. Washington, D.C.; April 21, 1991)

FURTHER READING

Obituary. *Current Biography,* July 1991.
Obituary. *New York Times,* Apr. 23, 1991.

Boskin, Michael Jay (1945–) To the chairman of President Bush's Council of Economic Advisors fell the unenviable tasks of claiming that the quite obviously out-of-control U.S. budget deficit was under control, and then denying the very existence of the patently obvious recession that would not go away. Michael Boskin did the first in 1990; his initial annual economic report, given in February 1990, made a series of rather optimistic predictions, among them that the federal deficit would be paid off by the mid-1990s. But the deficit continued to soar throughout the first three years of the Bush presidency, registering an unprecedented $260 billion increase in 1991, and no solution or even improvement was in sight at the end of the year.

Boskin steadfastly denied the existence of a recession throughout 1990, while unemployment figures rose, the savings and loan and bank crises grew, and consumer confidence fell so seriously that even lower interest rates failed to stimulate a badly sagging American economy. Finally, on January 2, 1991, Boskin and the Bush administration admitted that a recession had begun, placing its start in the last quarter of 1990. Boskin's second annual economic report, issued on February 12,1991, described the recession as a temporary lag in the growth of a healthy economy, and predicted a quick return to prosperity. At the same time, Boskin, speaking for the administration, attempted to blame the recession on too-restrictive Federal Reserve credit policies and called for further steps to make credit easier and cheaper to obtain.

For the rest of 1991, Boskin sounded the same themes, again and again claiming that the recession was temporary and not very deep, as unemployment figures soared, unemployment benefits began to run out for many, interest rate manipulation failed, and consumer confidence plummeted even further. In December, he called the "recovery" "sluggish," and predicted a turn toward recovery in the spring of 1992.

New York-born Boskin taught economics at California's Stanford University for almost two decades and was director of Stanford's Center for Economic Policy Research (1986–1989), before going to Washington as chairman of the Council of Economic Advisors. His B.A., M.A, and Ph.D. were from the University of California at Berkeley in 1967, 1968, and 1971. He married Chris Dornin in 1981.

FURTHER READING

"Mr. Bush's forecaster. . . ." THOMAS G. DONLAN. *Barron's,* Nov. 12, 1990.
"Free markets. . . ." *Challenge,* May–June, 1990.
"Boskin, Michael Jay." *Current Biography,* Sep. 1989.

Botha, Roelof Frederik (Pik) (1932–) South African foreign minister, after State President Frederik W. De Klerk the second most powerful leader of the ruling National Party, Botha maintained his role as his government's chief international spokesperson during 1991, though in vastly changed circumstances. As the process of reconciliation began in South Africa, previously isolated Botha found himself rejoining the world community. The year saw the redevelopment of trade and political relations with many African nations, with some, like Kenya and Zimbabwe, going beyond the limited recommendations of the June 1991 meeting of the Organization of African Unity (OAU). South Africa came forward, too: On June 27, it finally announced willingness to sign the 1968 Nuclear Nonproliferation Treaty and to permit international inspection of its nuclear facilities. Then, in quick succession came two central changes: On July 9, the 21-year-old Olympic boycott was lifted, and on July 10, the United States sanctions were lifted, paving the way for widespread reacceptance of South Africa into the world community.

But the shadow of the long, complex set of wars and civil wars in southern Africa still pursued Botha. On July 19, the South African government admitted that it had made substantial payments to Inkatha, the Zulu-dominated organization at virtual civil war with the African National Congress; part of the admission, which created a national scandal, was that Botha had authorized some of the Inkatha payments. On July 25, Botha admitted that the payments had been part of a pattern; the South African government had also contributed more than $35 million to seven Namibian parties before the 1989 Namibian elections, a charge long denied by the South Africans.

Botha, a lawyer, has spent his whole career in South African government service. He joined the foreign service in 1953 and held a long series of diplomatic and legal posts at home and in Europe during the 1950s and 1960s. He was elected to parliament in 1970, serving until 1974. He was South African ambassador to the United Nations (1974–77), and to the United States as well (1975–77). He went home to become South African foreign minister in 1977, and was his government's chief international spokesperson during its long fight to maintain and deepen the apartheid system. He failed in his February 1989 bid to succeed president Pieter William Botha as National Party leader, and stayed on as foreign secretary in the new De Klerk government, becoming a key negotiator in the long African National Congress–government talks that resulted in the August 7, 1990, ceasefire. Botha attended the University of Pretoria. He married Helen Bosman in 1953; they have four children.

FURTHER READING

"Giving as good as he got." *Time,* Nov. 21, 1988.

Boutros Ghali, Boutros (1922–) On January 1, 1992, Egyptian diplomat and lawyer Boutros Ghali began his five-year term as the sixth United Nations secretary general, following Javier Pérez de Cuéllar, whose second five-year term expired on December 31, 1991. Boutros Ghali had campaigned long and hard for the job: An experienced mediator who played a significant role in negotiating the1978 Camp David Accords and the 1979 Egypt-Israel peace treaty, he was thought by many to be a logical choice to continue the expanded worldwide UN mediating role developed so successfully by Pérez de Cuéllar. His early commitments included continuing such tasks as trying to bring the Yugoslavian and Somalian civil wars to an end and carrying through the Cambodian peace

accords, as well as a planned reorganization of UN secretariat.

Cairo-born Boutros Ghali attended Cairo University and the University of Paris. He was a professor of international law and head of the political science department at Cairo University and has long been active in international law, political studies, and human rights organizations. He was Egypt's minister of state for foreign affairs (1977–91) and became deputy prime minister in 1991.

FURTHER READING

"Hello, Ghali." *Nation,* Dec. 16, 1991.
"A man for all nations." BONNIE ANGELO. *Time,* Dec, 2, 1991.

Bowie, David (David Robert Jones, 1947–) At the time of his 1990 *Sound and Vision* tour, rock star Bowie said he was finished with his personal oldies and would now move on. That is just what he did in his new album *Tin Machine II,* released in September 1991: Moving away from Bowie's previous topicality, the album focuses on private questions of love and loss, in such songs as "Baby Universal," "Goodbye Mr. Ed," "Betty Wrong," "You Belong in Rock-and-Roll," "One Shot," "If There Is Something," "Shopping for Girls," "Amlapura," and "A Big Hurt." In the United States, a considerable fuss erupted about the original album's jacket cover, featuring four classic Greek sculptures of nude men—what some dubbed a "kouros line." U.S. record dealers forced a redesign of the cover, with the statues' genitals airbrushed out. In August, the video for the single "One Shot" became the first ever to premiere on the Sony Video I Jumbo Vision in New York City's Times Square. Bowie and the Tin Machine began a British tour in November 1991. On hearing that he was among the 15 nominees for induction into the Rock and Roll Hall of Fame in 1991, Bowie asked that his name be removed from consideration, saying "I know my own worth. I don't need a medal." Bowie the actor will also appear in the forthcoming film *The Linguine Incident.*

Bowie became a leading rock singer and songwriter in 1969, with publication of his first song, "Space Oddity," followed by such albums as *The Man Who Sold the World* (1970), *Hunky Dory* (1971), *The Rise and Fall of Ziggy Stardust and the Spiders from Mars* (1972), *Pin Ups* (1973), *Young Americans* (1975), *Lodger* (1979), *Let's Dance* (1983), *Tin Machine* (1989), *Sound + Vision* (1989), and the retrospective *Changesbowie* (1990), which added 7 songs and 27 minutes to the original 1976 *Changesonebowie* album. As an actor, Bowie also starred as the alien in the film *The Man Who Fell to Earth* (1976), and appeared in such films as *Merry Christmas, Mr. Lawrence* (1983) and *The Last Temptation of Christ* (1988), and on Broadway in *The Elephant Man* (1980). Among his written works are *David Bowie in His Own Words* (1981), *David Bowie: Tonight* (1984), and *David Bowie Anthology* (1985). Bowie was formerly married, and has one child.

FURTHER READING

"Bowie." GLEN O'BRIEN. *Interview,* May 1990.
Alias David Bowie. PETER GILLMAN and LENI GILLMAN. Holt, 1987.
Stardust: The David Bowie Story. TONY ZANETTA and HENRY EDWARDS. McGraw-Hill, 1986.
Bowie. Jerry Hopkins. Macmillan, 1986.

Bowman, Patricia (1961–) Ms. Bowman accused medical student William Kennedy Smith, a nephew of Senator Edward Kennedy, of raping her at the Kennedy family estate at Palm

Beach, Florida, on March 30, 1991, initiating a case that received enormous media attention for much of the rest of the year. Although she did not directly charge Edward Kennedy with involvement in any way, his presence on the grounds and the fact that he had had a drink with the alleged victim and her alleged attacker before she was invited out to the estate was enough to draw massive media attack. A related dispute, over whether Ms. Bowman should have been publicly named in the media, was also a source of much public discussion, as was a continuing debate about whether Smith and Kennedy had been too considerately treated by the local police.

The trial, when it came, was almost an anticlimax, although it received enormous media attention. After a 10-day trial, which included testimony by Smith, Bowman, Kennedy, several other witnesses and nonwitnesses, and several experts, on December 11, 1991, the jury took 77 minutes to acquit Smith on all counts. Ms. Bowman, who had testified with her face shielded from the television cameras, later identified herself in a nationally televised interview with Diane Sawyer on "Prime Time Live."

Patricia Bowman attended Palm Beach Community College. She is a single mother with one daughter.

FURTHER READING

"A face and a name." AMY BERNSTEIN. *U.S. News & World Report,* Dec. 30, 1991.
"The trial you won't see." DAVID KAPLAN. *Newsweek,* Dec. 16, 1991.

Box, Muriel Baker (1905–91) A major figure in British films in the two decades following World War II, Muriel Baker began her film career in 1927, as a script typist for director Anthony Asquith, and wrote her first filmscript in 1935 for *Alibi Inn.* She and Sidney Box married in 1935; in the next decade they collaborated on scores of one-act plays, and during World War II, on many short nonfiction films. Their first full-length fiction screenplay was *The Seventh Veil* (1945), which Sidney Box produced. That screenplay won an Academy Award, and their screenplays for such movies as *Holiday Camp* (1947) and *Christopher Columbus* (1949) were also well received. She later directed such films as *The Happy Family* (1952), *Street Corner* (1953), *Simon and Laura* (1945), *The Truth About Women* (1958; she also produced), and her last film *Rattle of a Single Man* (1964). She and Sidney Box divorced in 1969; she later married Lord Gardiner. Box was an active feminist, and a founder of the Femina Press. She was survived by a daughter, Leonora. (d. May 18, 1991).

FURTHER READING

Obituary. *The Times* (of London), May 22, 1991.

Boyle, Andrew Philip (1919–91) Dundee-born Boyle, an intelligence officer, writer, and broadcaster, served with British military intelligence in East Asia during World War II. After the war, he began his long association with the British Broadcasting Corporation (BBC), working in radio news. In 1965, he produced what became the very popular news program "The World at One," and in 1970 became news and current affairs head at BBC Scotland.

Boyle was also a biographer, from 1955 writing several popular biographies of British public figures; his biography of politician Brendan Bracken won a 1974 Whitbread award. He became a well-known figure with publication of *The Climate of Treason* (1979; in the United States published as *The Fourth Man*), in which he exposed the presence of a "fourth man," in the Soviet spy ring that included Kim Philby, Guy Burgess, and Donald MacLean. The investigation that followed made public the name of Anthony Blunt, British art historian, museum director, and art adviser to the royal family, who had been knighted in 1956. Blunt had been found out by British intelligence in 1964, cooperated, and was then pardoned. After Blunt's 1979 exposure, his honors were revoked, though his work in art history continued. Boyle later charged that there had been many other spies and defectors in the British intelligence establishment, but no further major exposés were forthcoming. He was survived by his wife, Eleanor, a daughter, and a son.

FURTHER READING

Obituary. *New York Times,* Apr. 25, 1991.
Obituary. *The Times* (of London), Apr. 24, 1991.

Brady, James (1944–) and **Sarah Kemp Brady** (1942–) Sarah and James Brady scored a victory in spring 1991, with House of Representatives passage of the Brady Handgun Violence Prevention Act, nicknamed the Brady Bill. James Brady was president Ronald Reagan's press secretary; he was seriously wounded during John Hinckley's March 31, 1981, presidential assassination attempt, shot with a cheap $29 handgun, and remains partially paralyzed. After the incident, Sarah Kemp Brady, his wife, became an extraordinarily effective crusader for gun control, her work continuing and expanding throughout the 1980s and into the 1990s. She is chairman of Handgun Control, Inc.

James Brady continued to be presidential press secretary during the Reagan years, and spoke little on the subject of gun control until after the 1988 elections. But starting in 1989, he came forward very strongly, in congressional testimony, public statements, and as sponsor of the Brady Bill, calling for a seven-day waiting period before the purchase of handguns. In March 1991, former President Reagan reversed his earlier anti-gun control position to press for passage of the Brady Bill; he was later joined by former President Richard Nixon, and ultimately by George Bush, modifying his own anti-gun control position. Ultimately, a series of compromises made the Brady Bill part of the 1991 Crime Bill, which called for a five-day waiting period before handgun purchase. But in late November President Bush threatened to veto the Crime Bill, calling it too "soft" on criminals in some respects, and Democratic congressional leaders, without enough votes to overturn a veto, dropped the bill from further consideration, killing the prospect of any gun control in 1991. The year also saw the June 16 premier of the HBO telefilm biography *The James Brady Story,* starring Beau Bridges in the title role, opposite Joan Allen as Sarah Brady.

Grand Rapids-born James Brady practiced law in Michigan (1969–77) and was a U.S. attorney in western Michigan (1977–81) before becoming presidential press secretary. He attended the University of Western Michigan and Notre Dame. Sarah Kemp Brady is an experienced political professional, who worked for the Republican Congressional Committee in the late 1960s and then was an administrative assistant to two Republican congressmen (1970–74) and an administrator with the Republican National Committee (1974–78). James and Sarah Brady have one son; Brady also has a daughter from a previous marriage.

FURTHER READING

"Brady, James C." *Current Biography,* Oct. 1991.
Thumbs Up: The Jim Brady Story. MOLLIE DICKENSON. Morrow, 1987.

Brady, Nicholas Frederick (1930–) Treasury Secretary Brady, a close personal friend of President Bush, continued to face huge, worsening domestic and international financial crises during 1991, and some new problems as well. During 1991, some of the new needs he faced were produced by diplomatic triumphs; these especially included the need to help the Soviet Union and the newly freed nations of

Eastern Europe through the economic crises that came with the systemic breakdown that accompanied the end of the Soviet empire. In August and September 1991, he pressed the International Monetary Fund to speed the flow of experts to the Soviet Union, at the same time urging increased direct U.S. financial aid. During the Persian Gulf War, he also played a major role in securing Allied contributions to help the United States pay for the cost of U.S. engagement.

Brady's key international debt initiative came in March 1989; this Brady Plan called for the first time for voluntary forgiveness of a portion of international debts by private U.S. banks, in return for debtor-nation internal actions aimed at better ability to repay the new balances. In essence it recognized the fact that much of what was owed was not likely to be repaid, and attempted to restimulate U.S. foreign trade with debtor countries, which had in some instances dragged to a near-halt. Through 1991 the plan had met mixed results, with adoption in amended form by several countries and some progress in Brazil-American debt renegotiation.

At home, however, nothing went very well as it became clear that the cost of the savings and loan bailout would approach and possibly even exceed $200 billion and was likely to be joined by a massive bank bailout. The bond market scandals of late 1991 joined the earlier junk bond scandals, while the traditionally quite safe insurance industry lost much of its apparent safety due to reckless investment practices and a collapse in the U.S. real estate industry. Also, the federal deficit continued to grow and grow, defying so-far entirely inadequate administration and congressional efforts to bring it under control.

Brady went to Washington after a long career in investment banking. He spent 28 years with Dillon, Read, ultimately becoming its chief executive officer and chairman, and leaving to become a U.S. senatorial appointee from his home state of New Jersey in 1982. He was chairman of the Purolator Company (1983–88), leaving the business world again in 1989, to become treasury secretary in the Bush administration. His B.A. was from Yale, in 1952, his M.B.A. from Harvard, in 1954. Brady married Katherine Douglas in 1952; the couple have three children.

FURTHER READING

"Who is Nick Brady? . . ." LOUIS S. RICHMAN. *Fortune,* May 22, 1989.

Branagh, Kenneth (1960–) British actor-director Branagh produced another tour de force in 1991 with his first American film, the 1940s-style *Dead Again,* which he directed, with himself and his wife, Emma Thompson, both starring in double roles. On its August opening in 1991 in the United States, the twisty romantic mystery—described by one review as "spiritually sired by Alfred Hitchcock out of Shirley MacLaine"—garnered strong reviews and became a surprise hit, even topping the box office on Labor Day weekend. It fared less well at the hands of British reviewers but still exhibited strong pull for audiences around the world.

Meanwhile, Branagh's stage work continued; with Peter Egan he co-directed Pam Gems's version of *Uncle Vanya* for his Renaissance Theatre Company's United Kingdom tour in summer 1991. After that, Branagh announced that he planned to take the rest of the year off, before starting to film a Shakespeare comedy—though he declined to say which one.

Belfast-born Branagh was one of the most promising theater people to come out of the 1980s. After attending the Royal Academy of

Dramatic Art (RADA), Branagh debuted in London in *Another Country,* then quickly became a notable Shakespearean actor, starring on stage as *Hamlet* and *Henry V* (at age 23) and directing and producing *Romeo and Juliet,* all in Britain. In 1987, he starred in the highly regarded television series *The Fortunes of War,* co-starring Thompson, and the film *A Month in the Country.* After a notable split with the Royal Shakespeare Company, he founded the Renaissance Theatre Company in 1987, and two years later brought to the United States stage productions of Shakespeare's *Midsummer Night's Dream* and *King Lear,* and Ibsen's *Ghosts,* starring in the latter two; *Ghosts* also appeared on television. In 1989, he also made his directorial debut and starred in a new film version of Shakespeare's *Henry V;* he won the Directors Guild of America's D. W. Griffith Award for best director, the movie was named the British Film Institute's best film, and both he and the film gained Oscar nominations. Branagh published an autobiography, *Beginning,* in 1990, at age 28; he had earlier written and produced a play, *Public Enemy.* He married Emma Thompson in 1989.

FURTHER READING

"Vaulting ambition. . . ." F. X. Feeney. *American Film,* Sep.–Oct. 1991.
"Branagh . . ." *Cosmopolitan,* Oct. 1991.
"Stratford on Sunset. . . ." Johanna Schneller. *GQ–Gentlemen's Quarterly,* Sep. 1991.
"Renaissance man." Georgina Howell *Vogue,* Sep. 1991.
"L. A. bard." *Esquire,* Sep. 1991.
"The man who would be king. . . ." Kim Hubbard. *People,* Feb. 12, 1990.
"A rising star enlivens Shakespeare." Gary Arnold. *Insight,* Jan. 15, 1990.

Brando, Marlon (Marlon Brando, Jr., 1924–) The intensely private Brando, who has rarely even granted interviews, agreed in 1991 to write his autobiography. In March, after spirited competition among publishers, Random House announced that they had acquired the world rights to the work for a seven-figure sum, believed to be $3.5 million. In a written statement, Brando commented that "recent events in my life have convinced me of the usefulness of retracing my steps."

Two weeks earlier, Brando had made an emotional appeal in court for his 32-year-old son, Christian, charged with the shooting death of Dag Drollet, lover of Christian's half-sister, Cheyenne. The killing had reportedly occurred during an argument at the family home over Drollet's beating of the pregnant Cheyenne. Christian pleaded guilty to voluntary manslaughter, and was sentenced to a 10-year prison term.

Marlon Brando's send-up of his *Godfather* role was widely seen in 1991, as *The Freshman* (1990) moved strongly into the video rental market and onto television screens. A younger Brando also appeared on televison in late 1991, in *Hearts of Darkness: A Filmmaker's Apocalypse,* about the making of Francis Ford Coppola's controversial Vietnam epic *Apocalypse Now* (1979). Shot by Coppola's wife, Eleanor, the documentary includes interviews with some of the principals, including Brando, who played the key role of Colonel Kurtz. Late in 1991 it was announced that Brando would appear as the Grand Inquisitor Tomas de Torquemada in the forthcoming movie *Christopher Columbus: The Discovery.*

Omaha-born Brando is one of the leading stage and screen actors of his time. In 1947, he created the role of Stanley Kowalski in Tennessee Williams's *A Streetcar Named Desire* (recreated in the 1951 film). This major breakthrough role also signaled the arrival of "method" acting, the enormously influential American version of the Stanislavski school, as taught at New York's Actors Studio. Brando's first Best Actor Oscar was for his film role in *On the Waterfront* (1951), his second for creation of another landmark role, that of Vito Corleone in *The Godfather* (1972). He also starred in such films as *Julius Caesar* (1953), *One-Eyed Jacks* (1961), *Last Tango in Paris* (1972), and after some years of seclusion *The Dry White Season* (1989). He has been married to Anna Kashfi and Movita. He has six children.

FURTHER READING

"Runnin' into Marlon." William A. Wellman, Jr. *Film Comment,* July–Aug. 1991.
Brando: A Life in Our Times. Richard Schickel. Macmillan, 1991.
"Marlon Brando. . . ." *Life,* Fall 1990.
"Brando." Mark Kram. *Esquire,* Nov. 1989.
Brando: The Unauthorized Biography. Charles Higham. NAL-Dutton, 1987.

Brando: A Biography in Photographs. CHRISTOPHER NICKENS. Doubleday, 1987.
Marlon Brando: The Only Contender. GARY CAREY. St. Martin's, 1985.

Bridges, Beau (Lloyd Vernet Bridges III, 1941–) Ten years after the event, Beau Bridges remade history, when he recreated the near-fatal shooting of press secretary James Brady during the attempted assassination of President Reagan in 1981. The HBO drama, *Without Warning: The James Brady Story,* based on Mollie Dickenson's *Thumbs Up,* debuted in June 1991, with Bridges opposite Joan Allen as Brady's wife, Sarah. In preparation for the role, Bridges went with Brady to the Washington Hilton, site of the shooting, and to the White House, where President Bush and his own press secretary, Marlin Fitzwater, gave them a private tour. Bridges was highly praised for his performance as the severely wounded and partly paralyzed Brady. In December, Bridges also starred in Diane Keaton's television film *Wildflower,* set in the South during the Great Depression. Forthcoming were starring roles in Arthur Hiller's *Married to It,* an ensemble film about the marital troubles and adjustments of three couples, and Aaron Norris's film *Sidekicks.*

As a child, Beau Bridges appeared in such films as *Force of Evil* (1948) and *The Red Pony* (1949). From his late teens, he emerged as a Hollywood star, in such films as *Gaily Gaily* (1969), *The Landlord* (1970), *Lovin' Molly* (1974), *The Other Side of the Mountain* (1975), *Norma Rae* (1979), *Heart Like a Wheel* (1983), *The Iron Triangle* (1989), and *The Fabulous Baker Boys* (1989), and in such telefilms as *The Child Stealer* (1979), *The Runner Stumbles* (1979), *Witness for the Prosecution* (1984), *Space* (1985), and *Women and Men: Stories of Seduction* (1989). Los Angeles-born Bridges is the son of actor Lloyd Bridges and the brother of actor Jeff Bridges, his co-star in *Baker Boys.* He attended the University of California at Los An- [illegible] After an earlier divorce, Bridges remar- [illegible] has four children.

[illegible]DING

[illegible]ows guns. . . ." TOM GLIATTO. [illegible]1.
[illegible]KAREN DE WITT. *New York* [illegible]

Bridges, Jeff (1949–) Jeff Bridges won both critical acclaim and box-office success for his role opposite Robin Williams in Terry Gilliam's *The Fisher King.* In this modern-day fable set in New York City, an independent-style film turned into a major release largely by the performance of its stars, Bridges plays Jack Lucas, a cynical radio personality who seeks redemption through homeless idiosyncratic visionary Parry (Williams). The film was the official U.S. entry at the Venice International Film Festival in September.

In 1991 Bridges was also seen anew in his career-making, Oscar-nominated role of Duane Jackson in *The Last Picture Show,* re-edited (with scenes not in the original) by director Peter Bogdanovich for release on laser disc. The sequel, *Texasville* (1990), with Bridges as a 30-years-older Duane Jackson in midlife crisis, appeared on television and in video stores, with the two films often renting together. Bridges also appeared on televison in April on the environmental documentary *A User's Guide to Planet Earth,* along with other stars such as Roseanne Barr and Richard Chamberlain. In autumn 1991, Bridges was in Seattle, shooting Martin Bell's *American Heart,* as a recently released convict shaping a relationship with his son.

Los Angeles-born Bridges is one of the leading American film actors of the last two decades, in such films as *The Last Picture Show* (1971), *Hearts of the West* (1975), *Starman* (1984), *Tucker* (1989) in the title role, and *The Fabulous Baker Boys* (1989) opposite his brother, Beau Bridges. Jeff and Beau Bridges are the sons of actor Lloyd Bridges; Jeff played his first screen role at the age of eight in his father's television series, "Sea Hunt." He is married to photographer Susan Geston; they have three children.

FURTHER READING

"Jeff Bridges." TIM CAHILL. *Esquire,* Oct. 1991.
"Jeff Bridges." JOHN CLARK. *Premiere,* May 1991.
"Bridges, Jeff." *Current Biography,* Mar. 1991.
"Lone star Bridges," MARTHA FRANKEL. *American Film,* Oct. 1990.

Brodsky, Iosif (Joseph) Alexandrovich (1940–) On May 10, 1991, Leningrad-born Brodsky became the fifth United States Poet Laureate, succeeding Mark Strand, who returned to teaching. Among the

previous poet laureates were Robert Penn Warren, Richard Wilbur, and Howard Nemerov. A new work of poetry, *Nazidanie,* is scheduled for 1992 publication.

Brodsky was a teenage dissenting poet in the Soviet Union in the mid-1950s and soon became a major voice in the protest movement of that time. He was imprisoned in Siberia for 18 months (1964–65), and emigrated to the United States in 1972. A world literary figure, he was awarded the 1987 Nobel Prize for Literature. His works include *A Christmas Ballad* (1962), *Elegy for John Donne* (1963), *Isaac and Abraham* (1963), *Verses on the Death of T. S. Eliot* (1965), *Verses and Poems* (1965), *Song Without Music* (1969), *A Stop in the Desert: Verses and Poems* (1970), *Selected Poems,* (1973), *A Part of Speech* (1980), *History of the Twentieth Century* (1986), *To Urania* (1988), *Marbles: A Play in Three Acts* (1989), and many essays, including those collected in *Less Than One* (1986). He was educated in the Soviet Union, leaving high school in 1956. He has one son.

FURTHER READING

"From Russia with poetry." HELLE BERING-JENSEN. *Insight,* June 24, 1991.

"Let them read Proust." *Economist,* Oct. 13, 1990.

Joseph Brodsky: A Poet for Our Time. VALENTINA POLUKHINA. Cambridge University Press, 1989.

"A cat and a half." MICHAEL TIGHE. *Interview,* Dec. 1988.

"A writer who would not be kept down." ANDREW D. BASIAGO. *America,* Apr. 2, 1988.

Brokaw, Tom (Thomas John Brokaw, 1940–) In the network nightly news ratings race, news anchor Brokaw and NBC remained behind ABC in 1991, well behind during the Persian Gulf War and the attempted Soviet coup, but at times moved slightly ahead of CBS. Brokaw and the "NBC Nightly News" were also time-shifted in September from their traditional 7 PM slot to 6:30 PM in major markets, a move ABC and CBS had previously made. Like his ABC and CBS counterparts, Brokaw stayed in New York during the Persian Gulf War, and unlike ABC and CBS he did not go to Madrid for the opening of the Middle East peace conference in October, but he did travel to Moscow in July to cover the Bush-Gorbachev summit, there interviewing then-out-of-office Soviet Foreign Minister Eduard Shevardnadze.

Brokaw's Sunday night half-hour news show "Exposé," which debuted in January 1991, did not fare well in the ratings. Worse, some stories were sharply criticized for tabloid-style audience-grabbing tactics, most notably in a May 1991 program on Virginia Senator Charles Robb, which one reviewer called an out-and-out smear. The series was ended in November, with Brokaw scheduled in 1992 to anchor "Brokaw Reports," a series of prime time programs on issues and challenges facing the country during the election year. In line with its decade-long cutback in election coverage, NBC announced in August that Brokaw would be covering the 1992 presidential conventions on PBS, not NBC, which plans to carry money-spinning entertainment shows during the first two hours of the conventions' evening sessions (except for major breaking stories).

South Dakota-born Brokaw began his long career in broadcasting in 1962, and anchored news shows in Atlanta and Los Angeles during the mid-1960s, before becoming NBC White House correspondent in 1973. He became a nationally known figure as the host of the "Today" show (1976–82), and has anchored the "NBC Nightly News" since 1982, as one of the key American news broadcasters of the modern period. His B.A. was from the University of South Dakota. He married Meredith Lynn Auld in 1962; the couple have three children.

FURTHER READING

"50/50: Happy Birthday. . . ." JOHANNA ELM. *TV Guide,* Feb. 3, 1990.

Anchors: Brokaw, Jennings, Rather and the Evening News. ROBERT GOLDBERG and GERALD J. GOLDBERG. Carol, 1990.
"NBC's power-Brokaw. . . ." JOHN LIPPMAN. *Variety,* Aug. 3, 1988.
"Tom Brokaw. . . ." JAMES KAPLAN. *Vogue,* Apr. 1988.

Brown, Ron (Ronald Harmon Brown, 1941–) Democratic National Committee chairman Brown spent much of 1991 trying to rebuild his badly damaged party after the landslide 1988 Michael Dukakis loss to George Bush. For the first three quarters of 1991, his efforts were greatly hampered by the widely held view that George Bush was unbeatable in 1992. Even some previously "safe" constituencies seemed at great risk: On June 13 and 14, Brown held a meeting of key fundraisers and candidates at Pamela Harriman's Middleburg, Virginia home; four months later, Harriman, furious at the conduct of the Democratic members of the Senate Judiciary Committee during the Anita Faye Hill–Clarence Thomas confrontation, broke off fundraising for the Democratic National Committee.

But in the autumn and early winter of 1991, the deepening American recession that George Bush could not wave away as well as associated health care concerns provided the Democrats with central issues, which they set out to exploit as they went into the 1992 presidential campaign and moved toward New York City and the 1992 Democratic National Convention.

Born in Washington, D.C., Brown began his career as a Washington "insider" soon after his graduation from the St. John's University School of Law in 1970. He worked in a series of increasingly responsible posts at the National Urban League (1971–79); was counsel for the Senate Judiciary Committee in 1980; worked in the 1979–80 presidential campaign of Senator Edward Kennedy, remaining with him in 1981; and was a partner in Patton, Boggs & Blow (1981–89). He worked with the Democratic National Committee from 1981. He was Jesse Jackson's 1988 Democratic Convention manager, a Dukakis political adviser during the 1988 presidential campaign, and in February 1989 became the trailblazing first Black Democratic National Committee chairman. Brown's B.A. was from Middlebury College, in 1962, and his 1970 J.D. was from St. John's. He married Alma Arrington in 1962; the couple have two children.

FURTHER READING

"From two new party chairmen. . . ." *American Visions,* June 1989.
"Brown, Ronald Harmon." *Current Biography,* July 1989.
"Ron Brown. . . ." *Ebony,* May 1989.
"Running as his own man." WALTER ISSACSON. *Time,* Jan. 30, 1989.

Brown, Virginia Mae (1923–91) West Virginia-born Brown piled up a series of "firsts" during her long career in state and national government. A lawyer, she began her career as a law clerk to the West Virginia attorney general (1947–49). She was the first woman to be West Virginia assistant attorney general (1952–61), the state's first woman insurance commissioner (1961–62), and the first woman member of the state's Public Service Commission (1961–62). She became the first woman member of the federal Interstate Commerce Commission (ICC) in 1964, commission vice chairman in 1968, and chaired the commission in 1969, becoming the first woman to head an independent federal agency. She left the ICC in 1979 and returned to West Virginia, becoming an administrative law judge for the federal Department of Labor and the Social Security Administration. She was once married, and was survived by two daughters and a sister. (d. Charleston, West Virginia; February 24, 1991).

FURTHER READING

Obituary. *Current Biography,* May 1991.
Obituary. *New York Times,* Feb. 27, 1991.

Browne, Coral (Coral Edith Brown, 1913–91) Melbourne-born Browne made her stage debut in her native Australia at the age of 17, and in 1934 arrived in London. Her first major success was as Maggie Cutler in *The Man Who Came to Dinner* (1941); it was followed by a long series of London stage roles, and during the 1950s by a strong move into the classics, which included a notable Lady Macbeth at the Old Vic in 1956, Gertrude to Michael Redgrave's *Hamlet* in a 1958 Soviet tour, and the title role in Shaw's

Mrs. Warren's Profession for the National Theatre in 1970. She made her film debut in 1935, and appeared in such films as *Auntie Mame* (1958), *The Roman Spring of Mrs. Stone* (1961), *The Killing of Sister George* (1968), *The Ruling Class* (1972), *Theatre of Blood* (1973), and *Dreamchild* (1986). In 1983, she appeared on television as herself, opposite Alan Bates as Guy Burgess, in *An Englishman Abroad,* based on an incident that had occurred during the 1958 Soviet tour of *Hamlet.* She was married twice, first to Philip Pearman and then to actor Vincent Price, who was her sole survivor. (d. Los Angeles: May 29, 1991).

FURTHER READING

Obituary. *Current Biography,* July 1991.
Obituary. *Variety,* June 3, 1991.
Obituary. *The Times* (of London), May 31, 1991.
Obituary. *New York Times,* May 31, 1991.

Buckley, William: See **Lebanon Hostages**

Burch, Dean (1927–91) Oklahoma-born Burch graduated from the University of Arizona Law School in 1953, and developed his career in that state, moving from there onto the national scene. He was an assistant state (Arizona) attorney general (1953–54), legislative and administrative assistant to senator Barry Goldwater (1955–59), deputy director of the Goldwater presidential campaign committee (1963–64), and chairman of the Republican National Committee (1964–65). He was named chairman of the Federal Communications Commission (FCC) by President Richard M. Nixon in 1969, resigning in 1974, and was Nixon's White House political counselor in the months before the Nixon resignation. He was also President Gerald Ford's White House political counselor in 1975, then resigning to practice law in Washington until 1987, when he became director general of Intelstat, the worldwide multinational communications network. He was survived by his wife, Patricia, two daughters, and a son. (d. Potomac, Maryland; August 4, 1991)

FURTHER READING

Obituary. *Variety,* Aug. 12, 1991.
Obituary. *Variety,* Aug. 5, 1991.
Obituary. *New York Times,* Aug. 5, 1991.

Burnett, Carol (1936–) Carol Burnett returned to her old home at CBS for the 1991–92 season. Her half-hour comedy-variety series "Carol & Company" had debuted successfully in September 1990 on NBC, but the network rejected her notion to expand the show to a one-hour, revue-style weekly series. So she went back to CBS—and back to Stage 33, where her original comedy-variety series had been made—for her new hour-long variety series "The Carol Burnett Show," which debuted in November 1991. Forthcoming was a starring role in *Noises Off,* Peter Bogdanovich's film version of Michael Frayn's stage farce about a down-at-the-heels theater company on a provincial tour.

San Antonio-born Burnett became a highly regarded television comedian in the early 1960s and was the enormously popular star of her own "The Carol Burnett Show" (1967–79). Through the early 1980s, she also appeared in several plays, including *Plaza Suite* (1970) and *I Do, I Do* (1973) on Broadway, and in such films as *Pete 'n' Tillie* (1972), *A Wedding* (1977), and *Annie* (1982), then falling into a difficult period through the 1980s. She began what became a major comeback with the Christmas 1989 television special *Julie and Carol,* shared with Julie Andrews; her "Carol & Company" (1990–91) followed. In 1986, she published the autobiographical *One More Time.* Burnett attended the University of California at Los Angeles. She was formerly married to Joseph Hamilton and has three children.

FURTHER READING

"Burnett, Carol." Current Biography, Nov. 1990.
"Carol Burnett comes home." ERIC SHERMAN. *Ladies Home Journal,* Sep. 1990.
"Carol Burnett. . . ." MARK MORRISON. *Woman's Day,* Aug. 7, 1990.
"Carol Burnett is a legend. . . ." CHARLES BUSCH. *Interview,* Mar. 1990.
Laughing Till It Hurts. J. RANDY TARBORELLI. Morrow, 1988.
Carol Burnett: The Sound of Laughter. JAMES HOWE. Viking Penguin, 1987.

Carol Burnett. CAROLINE LATHAM. New American Library-Dutton, 1986.

Busch, Niven (1903–91) New York City-born Busch, began his career as a journalist, working for *Time* magazine in the mid-1920s while also contributing articles to the *New Yorker, McClure's,* and other magazines. He went to Hollywood as a screenwriter in 1931, producing his first screenplay for the Howard Hawks film *The Crowd Roars* (1932). He went on to write or co-author original stories or screenplays for such films as *Babbitt* (1934), *In Old Chicago* (1938; Oscar nomination for original story), *The Westerner* (1940), *The Postman Always Rings Twice* (1946), *Pursued* (1947), and *The Furies* (1950). Busch wrote 13 novels, many of them adapted into films; his first novel was *The Carrington Incident* (1939). His best-known work was the novel *Duel in the Sun* (1944), which became the basis of King Vidor's 1947 classic film Western. His novel *They Dream of Home* was the basis of the Edward Dmytryk film *Till the End of Time* (1946), and his novel *The Furies* became the basis of the 1950 Anthony Mann film, starring Walter Huston and Barbara Stanwyck. He was married to the actress Teresa Wright from 1942 to 1952. He was survived by his wife, Suzanne, two daughters, five sons, a sister, a stepdaughter, and two stepsons.

FURTHER READING

Obituary. *Variety,* Sep. 2, 1991.
Obituary. *The Times* (of London), Aug. 28, 1991.
Obituary. *New York Times,* Aug. 27, 1991.
"Niven Busch: Sportsman." DAVID THOMSON. *Film Comment,* Aug. 1985.

Bush, Barbara Pierce (1925–) In one of the more highly publicized sledding accidents in recent history, U.S. First Lady Barbara Bush broke a bone in her right leg after running into a tree at Camp David on January 13, 1991. She recovered without complications and was able to attend the historic Moscow Summit in late July. The publicity surrounding her accident was inevitable; those who live in the White House expect that kind of attention, and she had earlier encountered the same kind of publicity in connection with the radiation treatments on her

swollen eyes, the result of Graves's disease, a thyroid disorder.

Far from shrinking away from publicity, Barbara Bush has used it to promote literacy and spur the fight against cancer, both causes she was involved in long before her husband became president. Her second dog's-eye look at Washington life, this time through the eyes of Millie, the family's springer spaniel, was *Millie's Book: As Dictated to Barbara Bush* (1990). It became a 1990–91 best-seller, generating royalties of over $1 million, all going to the nonprofit Barbara Bush Foundation for Family Literacy.

On the political side, she strongly supported George Bush's coming second-term candidacy, denounced Kitty Kelley's unauthorized biography of Nancy Reagan, sent public personal regards to Raisa Gorbachev after the Gorbachevs survived the failed August Soviet coup, and did the round of appearances and interviews that are part of the First Lady's role.

Barbara Pierce married George Bush in 1945. The couple have five living children—George, John, Neil, Marvin, and Dorothy; their second child, Robyn, died of leukemia in 1953 at the age of three. She attended Smith College. She continues to be active in a wide range of voluntary organizations. Since 1983, she has been a trustee of the Morehouse School of Medicine. Her earlier book was *C. Fred's Story* (1984).

FURTHER READING

Barbara Bush. DIANE SANSEVERE-DREHER. Bantam, 1991.

Barbara Bush. KAREN B. SPIES. Macmillan, 1991.
Barbara Bush: First Lady. ROSE BLUE and CORRINE J. NADEN. Enslow, 1991.
First Ladies: The Saga of the Presidents' Wives and Their Power. CARL S. ANTHONY. Morrow, 1991.
Barbara Bush. ARLEEN HEISS. Chelsea House, 1991.
"Barbara Bush. . . ." CINDY ADAMS. *Ladies Home Journal,* Nov. 1990.
"In the eye of the storm." PAULA CHIN. *People,* Oct. 1, 1990.
"The hidden life. . . . KENNETH T. WALSH. *U.S. News & World Report,* May 28, 1990.
Barbara Bush: First Lady of Literacy. JUNE BEHRENS. Childrens, 1990.
Simply Barbara Bush: A Portrait of America's Candid First Lady. DONNIE RADCLIFFE. Warner, 1990.
"Bush, Barbara Pierce." *Current Biography,* Oct. 1989.

Bush, George (George Herbert Walker Bush, 1924–) The quick and decisive U.S. and Allied victory over Iraq in the Persian Gulf War was also a major personal victory for George Bush, for it was accompanied by very few U.S. casualties (although the number of Iraqi casualties was enormous). The long, debilitating war feared by so many, filled with pictures of body bags containing the bodies of young Americans, did not come to pass. It was not a repeat of the Vietnam War, Saddam Hussein had been contained (though he still ruled Iraq), the industrial world's main oil supply had been secured, and the United States had a new and more powerful role to play in the Middle East.

The war was followed by the July 1991 Moscow Summit, where Presidents Gorbachev and Bush signed the START agreement, limiting long-range strategic weapons, and also agreed to co-sponsor Middle East peace talks. With the winning of the Gulf War and these further triumphs, George Bush's popularity at home soared, with a 90 percent approval rating reported during the immediate post–Gulf War period.

After the failed August Soviet coup came further steps toward peace. On September 27,1991, Bush announced major unilateral atomic weapons cuts and a standdown of strike force units that had been on continuous alert for over four decades. The Soviet Union responded favorably, and the world moved measurably away from the brink of atomic catastrophe. In late October, Israeli-Arab peace talks began in Madrid, the first such efforts since the beginning of the Arab-Israeli wars more than 40 years before.

But all was not well at home, and George Bush's triumphs abroad were paralleled by deep, serious, and growing American problems. The savings and loan crisis was joined by developing commercial bank and insurance industry crises, along with recurrent large financial scandals, as the financial excesses of the 1980s came to light. The national debt continued its enormous and rapid growth, exposing as shams a series of painfully arrived at federal budget compromises. And a deep recession came, in the United States and throughout much of the world, as international financial and trading continued on their anarchic path. With increasing layoffs, unemployment benefits ran out, the number of people on welfare and homeless rose, and the already huge gap between interest paid on savings and that charged on lendings widened even further. Consumer confidence faltered so badly that even the standard remedy of interest manipulation failed. Near the end of 1991, George Bush's popularity was seriously faltering in spite of the international triumphs that had earlier characterized his administration.

On the personal side, President Bush was on May 4, 1991, hospitalized with atrial fibrillation (a quick, irregular heartbeat). He was diagnosed with Graves's Disease, which caused a mild hyperthryroid condition that triggered the heart irregularity. The condition responded to medication and he soon returned to relatively normal activities, though somewhat less than the very athletic life he had previously led. His January collapse at a Tokyo state dinner, attributed to the flu, generated new fears about the state of his health.

George Bush defeated Michael Dukakis in the bitterly contested 1988 presidential race, becoming the 41st president of the United States in 1989, the climax of a political career that began in Texas in the early 1960s. He had grown up in a Republican Party family, the son of Connecticut senator Prescott Bush. He left New England to enter the oil business in Texas in the early 1950s, in 1953 co-founding the Zapata Petroleum Company and in 1956 becoming president and then board chairman of the Zapata Off Shore Company. He was an unsuccessful Republican senatorial candidate from Texas in 1964 but won a House seat in 1966, moving to Washington as a Houston congressman for two terms (1967–71). In 1970, he made another unsuccessful run for the Senate on the Republican ticket.

Bush was United States ambassador to the United Nations during the waning days of the Vietnam War (1971–72), and then Republican National Committee chairman (1973–74). He was the chief American liaison officer in Peking (1974–76), returning to Washington as head of the Central Intelligence Agency (CIA) (1976–77). He made an unsuccessful Republican presidential nomination run in 1980 but withdrew in favor of Ronald Reagan, subsequently becoming Reagan's two-term vice president. He served in those eight years in a largely ceremonial and standby fashion, as have most vice presidents. He then succeeded Reagan as president.

The early Bush years saw a series of major international triumphs as the Cold War ended and the Soviet empire collapsed. First came the quick and easy invasion of Panama that toppled the Noriega dictatorship. Then came a series of major Soviet-American peace moves, with planned troop pullbacks and real progress on arms control and the ending of a whole series of regional conflicts that had for decades been spurred by Soviet and American sponsorship of the combatants. With both countries acting in concert as peacemakers and with the direct intervention of George Bush and Mikhail Gorbachev, the continuing conflicts in Nicaragua, Cambodia, Angola, Mozambique, Namibia, Ethiopia, and several other countries moved swiftly toward resolution.

The president's B.A. was from Yale in 1948. A navy pilot in World War II, he married Barbara Pierce in 1945. Their five children are George, John, Neil, Marvin, and Dorothy; their second child, Robyn, died of leukemia at age three. During the 1988 presidential campaign, Bush published two books, *Man of Integrity* (with Doug Wead) and *Looking Forward: The George Bush Story* (with Victor Gold).

FURTHER READING

"How his days. . . ." KENNETH T. WALSH. *U.S. News & World Report,* June 3, 1991.

"George Bush. . . ." RICHARD BEM CRAMER. *Esquire,* June 1991.

"The surprising. . . ." LALLY WEYMOUTH. *M Inc.,* May 1991.

"Bull moose. . . ." SIDNEY BLUMENTHAL. *New Republic,* Jan. 7, 1991.

George Bush: His World War Two Years. ROBERT B. STINNETT. Pictorial History, 1991.

George Bush. KAREN B. SPIES. Macmillan, 1991.

The Postmodern President: George Bush Meets the World, 2nd ed. RICHARD ROSE. Chatham House, 1991.

Flight of the Avenger: George Bush at War and in Love. JOSEPH HYAMS. Harcourt Brace, 1991.

"Men of the year." DAN GOODGAME et al. *Time,* Jan. 7, 1991.

"Commander. . . ." KENNETH WALSH. *U.S. News & World Report,* Dec. 31, 1990.

George Bush: An Intimate Portrait. FITZHUGH GREEN. Hippocrene, 1990.

Our Forty-First President: George Bush. Scholastic, 1989.

George Bush: The Story of Our Forty-First President. Dell, 1989.

George Bush: Forty-First President of the United States. JUNE BEHRENS. Childrens, 1989.

Picture Life of George Bush. RON SCHNEIDERMAN. Watts, 1989.

Butcher, Susan (1955–) Four-time winner and defending champion Susan Butcher was in the lead at the midway point in Alaska's 1,163-mile Anchorage-Nome Iditarod Trail Sled Dog Race, but in the end failed in her 1991 bid to retain her title. Winner of the race for a record fifth time was Rick Swenson, who said he had to take advantage of the weather, knowing that Butcher had a larger, faster team. Swenson and Martin Buser pushed on through a life-threatening blizzard; Butcher and two others turned back in the storm while others were caught en route, with one later found sheltering in a snow cave and another losing his dogs. Butcher eventually came in third out of the 75 mushers in the field. In November 1991, Butcher visited Washington, D.C., to receive one of the Lab School's Washington Awards, to high achieving individuals who have had to fight learning disabilities. Unable for some months to reach Butcher by telephone or mail to invite her to the awards, the school had faxed their invitation to a nearby kennel, whose staff pinned it to Butcher's tent in the woods.

Massachusetts-born Butcher and her husband, lawyer Dave Monson, live and breed sled dogs at Trail Breaker Kennel, in Eureka, Alaska. She arrived in Alaska by way of two years spent in Colorado, and in 1977 moved to Eureka and founded her kennels. That year, she first attracted media attention, dog sledding to the top of Mount McKinley. During the late 1980s and early 1990s, she became a symbol of endurance and accomplishment for women throughout the world, as a leading figure in what had before been viewed as a "man's" sport. In March 1990, Butcher set a new course record of 11 days, 1 hour, and 53 minutes in winning the 18th Iditarod; it was her fourth win in five years.

FURTHER READING

"Butcher, Susan." *Current Biography,* June 1991.
"The dogged pursuit of excellence. . . ." Sonja Steptoe. *Sports Illustrated,* Feb. 11, 1991.

Buthelezi, Mangosuthu Gatsha

(1928–) Zulu leader Buthelezi maintained his political strength during 1991, forcing Nelson Mandela and the African National Congress (ANC) to recognize the independent status of the Zulu-dominated and Buthelezi-led Inkatha Freedom Party. Buthelezi met with Mandela and President Frederik W. De Klerk repeatedly, as the Inkatha-ANC civil war grew and spread throughout the country. As Inkatha strength grew, so did Buthelezi's status at home and abroad. On June 20, he met with President George Bush in Washington, and on July 10 with British foreign secretary Douglas Hurd in South Africa; Hurd met separately with De Klerk and Mandela, thereby according all three major status.

Inkatha's increasing strength was not diminished even after at least partial confirmation of repeated ANC claims that South African security forces were arming and supplying Inkatha. On July 19, the South African government admitted that it had made substantial payments to Inkatha. The admissions created a national scandal and eventually forced the demotion of the Law and Order and Defense ministers, though De Klerk remained in office. On September 14, Buthelezi, Mandela, and De Klerk signed a new peace pact, aimed at ending the civil war; but it was signed with unchecked Zulu demonstrations continuing and with Buthelezi voicing open skepticism as to its effectiveness. Inkatha seemed quite willing to continue as before.

Buthelezi became chief of the Buthelezi tribe in 1963, succeeding his father, Mathole Buthelezi. He was a Zulu administrator for two decades, becoming chief minister of the KwaZulu in 1976. As the long fight for South African democracy developed during the 1970s and 1980s, he emerged as the main spokesperson and leader of the Zulus and a third force in South African politics, for he negotiated with the White South African government on behalf of the Zulus and often opposed the African National Congress. His followers, organized into the Inkatha movement, carried those disagreements into anti-ANC street fighting throughout the 1980s. Buthelezi emerged as a powerful independent force in South African politics during 1990, as negotiations over the future of the country began between the De Klerk government and the ANC, led by newly freed Nelson Mandela, which had tried to bypass Buthelezi but found itself engaged in a hot and growing civil war.

Buthelezi married Irene Audrey Thandekile Mzila in 1952; they have seven children. He attended Adams College and Fort-Hare University.

FURTHER READING

"The chief steps forward. . . ." Christopher S. Waren. *New York Times Magazine,* Feb. 17, 1991.
Gatsha Buthelezi: Chief with a Double Agenda. Mzala. Humanities, 1988.
An Appetite for Power: Buthelezi's Inkatha and South Africa. Gerhard Mare and Georgina Hamilton. Indiana University Press, 1988.
"The chief." Michael Massing. *New York Review of Books,* Feb. 12, 1987.
"Buthelezi, Gatsha Mangosuthu." *Current Biography,* Oct. 1986.

Caan, James (1939–) Jump-started by his performance in *Misery* (1990), Caan's career moved back into high gear with Mark Rydell's musical *For the Boys*. Caan as Eddie Sparks and Bette Midler as Dixie Leonard are a U.S.O. song-and-dance team whose lives and relationship are followed over five decades, from the early days of World War II. Unfortunately, reviews were mixed and the movie did not have the hoped-for box-office success. Among Caan's forthcoming projects were *Honeymoon in Vegas,* written and directed by Andrew Bergman, and *The Dark Backward,* directed and written by Adam Rifkin. Caan and his wife Ingrid Hajek had a son, Alexander, in April 1991.

New York City-born Caan played in New York theater and television in the early 1960s and emerged as a major player in the early 1970s with his notable television lead in *Brian's Song* (1971). This was followed by his star-making role in *The Godfather* (1972), in which he created the classic "tough guy" role of Sonny Corleone. He went on to such films as *Cinderella Liberty* (1974), *Funny Lady* (1975), *Rollerball* (1975), *A Bridge Too Far* (1977), *Chapter Two* (1979), *Hide in Plain Sight* (1980; he also directed), and *Kiss Me Goodbye* (1982). He retired from filmmaking during the mid-1980s, returning in *Gardens of Stone* (1987) and *Alien Nation* (1988). Caan attended Michigan State University, Hofstra College, and New York's Neighborhood Playhouse. He has been married three times, since 1990 to Ingrid Hajek, and has four children, one of them adopted.

FURTHER READING

"Raising Caan." AL REINERT. *Premiere,* Dec. 1991.

Caine, Michael (Maurice Joseph Micklewhite, 1933–) Though he had been living for several years in his native Britain and had sold his Beverly Hills home in 1987, Caine returned to Hollywood in 1991, buying another Beverly Hills residence. During the spring, he was shooting *Noises Off,* Peter Bogdanovich's film version of Michael Frayn's stage farce about a down-at-the-heels theater company on a provincial tour, appearing with Carol Burnett, John Ritter, Julie Hagerty, Christopher Reeve, Denholm Elliott, and Mark Linn-Baker; the film was scheduled for early 1992 release. October 1991 saw the release in letter-box-style video form of John Huston's classic 1975 film, *The Man Who Would Be King,* with Caine and Sean Connery as rogue soldiers in Rudyard Kipling's tale of late 19th-century Britons in India and points north. During 1991, Caine was also involved in developing several new film projects, including *Living Evidence,* co-starring Klaus Maria Brandauer and directed by John Irvin; *Blue Ice,* a thriller directed by Roger Spottiswood, to be shot in Britain in 1992; and *Bullseye,* a British heist movie co-starring Roger Moore and directed by Michael Winner.

London-born Caine has been a durable, versatile film star since the mid-1960s, beginning with such films as *Zulu* (1964), *The Ipcress File* (1965), *Alfie* (1966), *The Wrong Box* (1966), *Gambit* (1966), and *Funeral in Berlin* (1966). His work also includes such films as *Sleuth* (1973), *The Wilby Conspiracy* (1975), *California Suite* (1978), *Educating Rita* (1982), *The Holcraft Covenant* (1985), *Hannah and Her Sisters* (1986; he won a Best Supporting Actor Oscar), *Dirty Rotten Scoundrels* (1988), *To Kill a Priest* (1989), *Mr. Destiny* (1990), and *A Shock to the System* (1990). In 1989, he also published a book, *Acting in Film: An Actor's Take on Movie Making,* based on his one-hour BBC special on movie acting. Also for television, he did *Jekyll & Hyde* (1990). His earlier written works include *Michael Caine's Moving Picture Show* (1989). Formerly married to Patricia Haines, he married Shakira Khatoon Baksh in 1973. He has two children.

FURTHER READING

"The extraordinary. . . ." John Culhane. *Reader's Digest,* Nov. 1991.
"Michael Caine. . . ." John Ennis. *Reader's Digest* (Canadian), Dec. 1988.
"Caine, Michael." *Current Biography,* Jan. 1988.

Candy, John (John Franklin Candy, 1950–) Candy continued his winning—and very busy—ways in 1991. Early in the year he arrived on screen in *Nothing but Trouble,* written and directed by Dan Aykroyd, who also starred, with Chevy Chase and Demi Moore; Candy played Aykroyd's daughter. In May Candy opened in Chris Columbus's bittersweet comedy *Only the Lonely,* as a Chicago cop in love with shy mortician Ally Sheedy, but dominated by his possessive mother, Maureen O'Hara. In August Candy opened in *Delirious,* playing a daytime soap opera scriptwriter who finds himself in the middle of one of his own stories. In December, he was seen in a cameo role in Oliver Stone's *JFK.* Forthcoming projects included *Once Upon a Crime,* directed by Eugene Levy, with a cast including Jim Belushi, Cybill Shepherd, Sean Young, and Giancarlo Giannini. Candy and fellow Canadian Wayne Gretzky also became part-owners of the Toronto Argonauts, in the Canadian Football League.

Toronto-born Candy began his career as a comedian in Canadian cabaret and films, joined Chicago's Second City group in 1972, and worked with Second City groups in Toronto and Los Angeles during the rest of the 1970s, becoming a television star in the SCTV comedy show, spun off from the groups. He became a leading film comedian in such movies as *1941* (1979), *The Blues Brothers* (1980), *Stripes* (1982), *Vacation* (1983), *Splash* (1984), *Brewster's Millions* (1985), *Volunteers* (1985), *Summer Rental* (1985), *Little Shop of Horrors* (1986), *Planes, Trains and Automobiles* (1987), *The Great Outdoors* (1988), and *Uncle Buck* (1989). Candy attended Toronto's Centennial College (1969–71). He married Rosemary Margaret Hobor in 1979; they have two children.

FURTHER READING

"Candy, John." *Current Biography,* Feb. 1990.
"20 Questions. . . ." *Playboy,* Aug. 1989.

Capra, Frank (1897–1991) Born in Palermo, Italy, Capra emigrated to Los Angeles at the age of six. Working every step of the way, be became a graduate chemical engineer in 1918 but never worked at that profession, instead in 1922 finding his way into the movies as the director of a one-reeler. During the 1920s, he learned his trade in a wide range of jobs, and in the late 1920s directed several feature films. His career blossomed in the early 1930s with such films as *Platinum Blonde* (1931), *The Bitter Tea of General Yen* (1933), and *Lady for a Day* (1933; it won his first Oscar nomination). With his first classic comedy, *It Happened One Night* (1934), starring Claudette Colbert and Clark Gable, he hit his full stride; he won a Best Director Oscar, and Oscars also were awarded to the film, Colbert, and Gable. Capra then emerged as a major figure of Hollywood's Golden Age, his classic late-1930s and 1940s comedy-dramas developing sentimental, enormously popular themes that exalted common decency and entirely suited a nation going through the Great Depression and World War II. His second Best Director Oscar came for *Mr. Deeds Goes to Town* (1936), and his third for *You Can't Take It with You* (1938), which also won a Best Film Oscar. In 1937, he directed the classic *Lost Horizon,* his Great Depression escape film. He returned to populist themes in *Meet John Doe* (1941), and in 1946 created yet another populist classic, *It's a Won-*

derful Life, a James Stewart vehicle that is still one of the most popular of American Christmas films. His last classic work was the Spencer Tracy-Katharine Hepburn film *State of the Union* (1950). During World War II, he was a much-decorated maker of propaganda films; his *Prelude to War* (1942) won a Best Documentary Film Oscar. His last film was a remake of *Lady for a Day,* titled *A Pocketful of Miracles* (1961); he spent the next three decades as a much-honored American legend. He wrote an autobiography, *The Name Above the Title* (1971). He was survived by a daughter and two sons.

FURTHER READING

Frank Capra: The Catastrophe of Success. Joseph McBride. Simon & Schuster, 1992.
Obituary. *Current Biography,* Oct. 1991.
"The Catholic imagination of. . . ." Richard A. Blake. *America,* Sep. 21, 1991.
"Capra's Catholicism. . . ." Stephen Scharper. *National Catholic Reporter,* Sep. 20, 1991.
"More than a heart warmer. . . ." Richard Schickel. *Time,* Sep. 16, 1991.
"It was a wonderful life." Mark Goodman. *People,* Sep. 16, 1991.
"Capra scorn." Miriam Horn. *U.S. News & World Report,* Sep. 16, 1991.
Obituary. *Variety,* Sep. 9, 1991.
Obituary. *The Times* (of London), Sep. 5, 1991.
Obituary. *New York Times,* Sep. 4, 1991.
Italian and Irish Filmmakers in America: Ford, Capra, Coppola and Scorsese. Lee Lourdeaux. Temple University Press, 1990.
American Madness: The Life of Frank Capra. Joseph McBride. Knopf, 1989.
Frank Capra: A Guide to References and Resources. Charles Wolfe. G. K. Hall, 1987.
Great American Film Directors. Dian G. Smith. Messner, 1987.
American Vision: The Films of Frank Capra. Ray Carney. Cambridge University Press, 1986.

Capriati, Jennifer (1976–) Not yet old enough to vote, drink, or drive the BMW her success had brought her, 15-year-old Capriati was nevertheless a big-league tennis player in 1991. In July, at Wimbledon, she had a stunning win over defending champion Martina Navratilova, becoming the youngest player ever to reach the Wimbledon finals, before herself losing to Gabriela Sabatini. In July at the Pathmark Tennis Classic and in August at the Mazda Tennis Classic she defeated another not-quite-as-young wunderkind, Monica Seles, then ranked number one women's tennis player in the world. She also defeated Seles in the much-publicized July exhibition match at Mahwah, New Jersey, that cost Seles $20,000 and her place at the 1992 Olympics. Then in September at the U.S. Open, Capriati defeated defending champion Sabatini in straight sets and came within a match point of winning in the semifinals against Seles. Capriati came out on top at the Player's Challenge, in Toronto in August. During 1991 Capriati rose to number six in the world and hoped to rise higher, with the aid of Pavel Slozil, who had earlier coached Steffi Graf into the number one spot. She also took some time out from the pro tour to attend high school, traveling with a tutor while on the circuit.

Capriati was trained for tennis from the age of four, first by her father Stefano Capriati, and then by Florida tennis professional Jimmy Evert, father of tennis star Chris Evert. She began winning junior tennis championships at the age of 12. At 13, she won junior titles at the U.S. and French Open tournaments. In 1990, then barely 14 and still an eighth-grade student at the Saddlebrook Tennis Academy, she turned professional.

FURTHER READING

"Learn from the game's. . . ." Tim Gullikson et al. *Tennis,* Dec. 1991.
"But seriously folks. . . ." Cindy Schmerler. *World Tennis,* June 1991.
Jennifer Capriati. Mikki Morrissette. Little, Brown, 1991.
Jennifer Capriati. Ellen E. White. Scholastic, 1991.
"Tennis' new legend. . . ." Dave Scheiber. *Saturday Evening Post,* July–Aug. 1990.

Carey, Mariah (1970–) Singer-composer Carey won a 1991 Grammy award as the best new artist of 1990 and a second 1991 Grammy for top female pop vocal for her hit single "Vision of Love." She had also been nominated for top album, top record, and top song. Carey won several other awards during 1991 as well, including *Billboard's* top artist of the year award and three Soul Train awards. Carey had burst onto the popular music scene in 1990, with her first album *Mariah Carey,* which sold well over 4 million copies; was number one on the *Billboard* chart for five months; and generated a series of hit singles, most notably "Vision of Love." Her song "Someday" was also a 1991 number one single. Her second album, *Emotions,* was released in September 1991.

Long Island-born Carey left high school to live and work in New York City in 1987. She worked as a waitress and backup singer before signing her first recording contract, with Columbia Records.

FURTHER READING

"Pop meteor. . . ." CHRIS SMITH. *New York,* Sep. 23, 1991.
"Mariah Carey tells why. . . ." *Jet,* Mar. 4, 1991.
"Careerwise or couchwise. . . ." *People Weekly,* Jan. 28, 1991.
"Building the perfect diva." ROB TANNENBAUM, *Rolling Stone,* Aug. 23, 1990.
"Pop's new vision." CHRIS SMITH. *New York,* May 28, 1990.
"In person. . . ." *Seventeen,* Oct. 1990.

Carradine, Keith Ian (1949–) Carradine went from Hollywood character actor to Broadway star in May 1991, playing the rope-twirling, wise-cracking title character in Tommy Tune's new musical *The Will Rogers Follies,* a performance that won him a Tony nomination. Meanwhile, films shot earlier appeared. May brought *The Ballad of the Sad Cafe,* the film based on Edward Albee's stage adaptation of Carson McCullers's novel; Carradine won praise as Vanessa Redgrave's malevolent estranged husband Marvin Macy, though the film itself was not well reviewed. In June, Carradine appeared in a television thriller, *Payoff,* directed by Stuart Cooper, opposite Kim Greist, Harry Dean Stanton, John Saxon, and Robert Harper. August saw Carradine in the title role of Roberto Faenza's *The Bachelor,* set in pre–World War I Europe, in a cast that included Miranda Richardson, Max von Sydow, Kristin Scott-Thomas, and Sarah-Jane Fenton. In September, Carradine participated in a fund-raising concert to help save the opera house in Telluride, Colorado, hoping (as co-founder of the Sheridan Arts Foundation) to transform it into an experimental theatre.

California-born Carradine made his film debut in *A Gunfight* (1970), and went on to such films as *McCabe and Mrs. Miller* (1971), *Emperor of the North* (1972), *Thieves Like Us* (1973), *Nashville* (1975), *The Duellists* (1976), *Pretty Baby* (1977), *Lumiere* (1976), *Welcome to L.A.* (1977), *Old Boyfriends* (1979), *An Almost Perfect Affair* (1979), *The Long Riders* (1980), *Southern Comfort* (1981), *Choose Me* (1983), *Maria's Lovers* (1983), *Blackout* (1985), *Half a Lifetime* (1986), *The Moderns* (1988), *Backfire* (1987), and *Cold Feet* (1989). His theater appearances include *Hair* (1969–70) and *Foxfire* (1982–83). He has also appeared often in television, in such works as *A Rumour of War* (1981), *Chiefs* (1983), *Half a Lifetime* (1986), *Eye on the Sparrow* (1987), *Murder Ordained* (1987), and *The Forgotten* (1989), and *Judgment* (1990). He won an Oscar as composer of the song "I'm Easy," which he introduced in *Nashville.* The son of actor John Carradine and the brother of actors David and Robert Carradine, Carradine attended Colorado State University. He is married to Sandra Will; they have two children. He is also the father of actress Martha Plimpton.

FURTHER READING

"Roping in the raves." MARK GOODMAN and TOBY KAHN. *People,* Sep. 30, 1991.
"Carradine, Keith." *Current Biography,* Aug. 1991.
"Ballad of a quiet man. . . ." WOLF SCHNEIDER. *American Film,* Apr. 1991.

Carter, Jimmy (James Earl Carter, Jr., 1924–) During 1991, former President Jimmy Carter continued to play a considerable elder statesman's role in international affairs and, late in the year, expanded his role to include a major new initiative within the United States. He also continued publicly to state his views on

the issues of the day, as in January 1991, when he opposed the Middle East policies of President George Bush, favoring a Middle East peace conference that would attempt to bring peace before the coming major war broke out and warning of the long-term dangers stemming from such a war.

Carter was again active in what has become his long-established mediator's role. He had in 1989 played a major role in mediating the end of the Nicaraguan Civil War; in 1991, he mediated Contra-Sandinista talks on key economic issues. In 1990, he had gone to Africa, unsuccessfully playing a mediator's role in Ethiopia and the Sudan; in 1991, he far more successfully led an observer's team into the October Zambian elections, helping to guarantee the historic, peaceful election of Frederick Chiluba and the retirement of founding father Kenneth Kaunda. In December 1990, his 33-member observation team had observed and helped guarantee the peaceful election of Jean-Bertrand Aristide to the Haitian presidency; later, when Aristide was overthrown by the Haitian military, Carter joined the worldwide protest. For his role as an advocate of peaceful conflict resolution, Carter was awarded the $100,000 1991 Onassis International Prize for Man and Society.

On October 25, 1991, Carter turned his attention once again to domestic problems, announcing that he would be developing a program to help solve the problems faced by poor people in his home state's capital city, Atlanta, Georgia, such as "teen pregnancy, crack babies, drug addiction, juvenile delinquency, school dropouts, homelessness, unemployment, divided families." In 1991, he also published *America On My Mind.*

The former president was touched by adverse publicity, though in no way implicated, by the massive Bank of Credit and Commerce International (BCCI) scandal, when it was disclosed that Global 2000, a charitable organization he sponsored, had received donations of $8 million from the scandal-ridden bank.

As with all former presidents, he was also touched by the echoes of historic events that occurred during his presidency, as when an autobiography by exiled Iranian President Abolhassan Bani-Sadr and other books charged that during the 1980 presidential campaign Ronald Reagan had made a deal with the Iranian government to stall the release of the Iran hostages until after the presidential election. Carter joined former hostages in calling for investigation of the charge, Reagan denied them, and Congress in early August 1991 set up an investigation.

Georgia-born Carter became the 39th president of the United States in 1977, the climax of a political career that began with his four years in the Georgia Senate (1963–67). He went on to become governor of Georgia (1971–75), emerged as the surprise "outsider" winner of the Democratic presidential nomination after a long series of primary campaigns, and defeated incumbent Gerald Ford in the 1976 presidential race. His earlier career included seven years as a naval officer (1946–53) and ten years as a successful Georgia farmer and businessman in Plains, Georgia.

Jimmy Carter's very difficult presidential term was dominated by largely adverse foreign affairs matters, including the Arab oil embargo of the mid-1970s, the Iran hostage crisis that began in late 1979 and colored the rest of his presidency, and the worsening Soviet-American relations that began with the Soviet invasion of Afghanistan and resulted in the American boycott of the 1980 Moscow Olympics. His major accomplishment was the 1978 Camp David Accords, which paved the way for the 1979 Egyptian-Israeli peace treaty.

He married Rosalynn Smith in 1946; the couple have four children. After he left office, they collaborated in writing *Everything to Gain: Making the Most of the Rest of Your Life* (1988).

FURTHER READING

"Jimmy Carter." ROBERT N. HOFFMAN. *Workbench,* Nov. 1991.
"The Carter connection. . . ." DEBBIE S. MILLER. *Wilderness,* Winter 1990.
"Hail to the ex-chief. . . ." STANLEY CLOUD. *Time,* Sep. 11, 1989.
Jimmy Carter. ED SLAVIN. Chelsea House, 1989.
The President Builds a House: The Work of Habitat for Humanity. TOM SHACHTMAN. Simon & Schuster, 1989.

Castro Ruz, Fidel (1926–) For a few days in August 1991, it seemed possible that Soviet-Cuban relations might reverse, with the accession of hard line Soviet leaders during the abortive August coup. But with the failure of the coup, it became clear that very little could be expected from the Soviet Union, and hard times continued in Cuba, even though Soviet-Cuban trade, cut off in January, had resumed on a limited barter basis in the spring of 1991. Castro appealed for economic aid at the July Ibero-American summit meeting, and limited diplomatic relations were restored with Colombia and Chile. But he was still a hard-line communist, rejecting Latin-American and Spanish pressure for democracy in Cuba, supporting Iraq in the Gulf War, and continuing to abuse human rights in his country. He also rejected the United Nations Commission on Human Rights decision to send a human rights monitor to Cuba. Castro's Cuba remained isolated, its relations with Europe greatly damaged, its Soviet aid gone, its Soviet troops soon to follow, and no improvement of U.S.-Cuban relations in sight.

Castro has been a key figure in world politics since taking power in Cuba in 1959 after leading the successful revolution against the government of Fulgencio Batista. He survived the U.S.-backed Bay of Pigs invasion of 1961 and also the Soviet missile withdrawal, after the 1962 Cuban Missile Crisis came very close to igniting World War III, remaining in power as a Soviet ally and economic dependent through the late 1980s. Castro has played a major role in supplying and training leftist revolutionaries throughout Latin America, and sent tens of thousands of troops to Angola and Ethiopia in the late 1970s. Withdrawal of those forces was agreed upon only in the late 1980s, under pressure from the Soviet Union. He attended the University of Havana, and practiced law in Havana before beginning his political career. He is married to Mirta Diaz-Bilart, and has one son.

FURTHER READING

"Maximum leader." GEORGIE ANNE GEYER. *American Heritage,* Nov. 1991.
"The last Communist." GEORGIE ANNE GEYER. *Reader's Digest* (Canadian), July 1991.
"The last communist." MARK FALCOFF. *Commentary,* June 1991.
"Guerrilla Prince. . . ." ARTURO CRUZ, JR. et al. *New Republic,* Apr. 22, 1991.
"Low fidelity. . .." CHARLES LANE. *New Republic,* Jan. 7, 1991.
Guerrilla Prince: The Real Story of the Rise and Fall of Fidel Castro. GEORGIE A. GEYER. Little, Brown, 1991.
Fidel Castro. JUDITH BENTLEY. Messner, 1991.
Castro's Cuba, Cuba's Fidel. LEE LOCKWOOD. Westview, 1990.
Fidel: A Critical Portrait. TAD SZULC. Avon, 1987.
Fidel Castro. JOHN VAIL. Chelsea House, 1986.

Caulfield, Joan (Beatrice Joan Caulfield, 1922–91) New Jersey-born Caulfield was a model and stage actress in the early 1940s, most notably on Broadway in *Kiss and Tell* (1943). She made her film debut in *Duffy's Tavern* (1943), followed by starring roles in such films as *Blue Skies* (1946), opposite Bing Crosby; *Monsieur Beaucaire* (1946), opposite Bob Hope; and *Dear Ruth* (1947), opposite William Holden. She also appeared in such films as *The Unsuspected* (1947), *Petty Girl* (1950), and *The Rains of Ranchipur* (1955), although limiting her screen roles after her marriage to film producer Frank Ross in 1950. She starred in the television series "My Favorite Husband" (1953–57) and "Sally" (1957–58). She was twice married and divorced, and was survived by two sons and two sisters. (d. Los Angeles; June 18, 1991)

FURTHER READING

Obituary. *New York Times,* June 20, 1991.
Obituary. *Current Biography,* Aug. 1991.

Chaikin, Sol Chick (1918–91) New York City-born Chaikin became an organizer for the International Ladies Garment Workers Union (ILGWU) in 1940, the same year that he graduated from Brooklyn Law School. After Air Force service during World War II, he rejoined the staff of the union, until 1959 holding a wide range of organizing positions. He became assistant director of the Northeast Department in 1959, an international vice president in 1965, general secretary and treasurer in 1973, and was president of the union from 1975–86. He was also a vice president and executive council member of the A.F.L.–C.I.O. In 1980 he published *A Labor Viewpoint.* He was president of New York's Javits Convention Center in 1989–90. He was survived by his wife, the former Rosalind Bryan, a daughter, and three sons. (d. New York City; April 1, 1991)

FURTHER READING

Obituary. *Current Biography,* June 1991.
Obituary. *New York Times,* Apr. 3, 1991.

Chamberlain, Richard (George Richard Chamberlain, 1935–) Since the demise of his most recent television series "Island Son" (1989–90), Chamberlain has primarily been seen in single-spot television movies and specials, remaining what one journalist dubbed him: "king of the sweeps." In March 1991 he starred in Glenn Jordan's television film *Aftermath: A Test of Love,* about the trauma and recovery of a child physically and emotionally damaged during the course of a holdup. In May he appeared in a notable television remake, the classic mid-American thriller, *Night of the Hunter.* The 1955 original had been a Robert Mitchum vehicle directed by Charles Laughton; in David Greene's telefilm, Chamberlain took the Mitchum role as the psychotic "Preacher" Harry Powell, tracking down two innocent children—a departure for Chamberlain after decades of playing caring heroes. He also appeared in ABC's environmental documentary, *A User's Guide to Planet Earth,* in April, hosted by Tom Selleck.

Los Angeles-born Chamberlain's first major role was a long run as television's "Dr. Kildare" (1961–66). He went on to star in such productions as *Centennial* (1978), *Shogun* (1980), *The Thorn Birds* (1985), *Wallenberg: A Hero's Story* (1985), and *Dream West* (1986). He also played in many action-adventure films, including *The Three Musketeers* (1974), *The Four Musketeers* (1974), *The Slipper and the Rose* (1977), *King Solomon's Mines* (1985), *Allan Quartermain and the Lost City of Gold* (1988), and *The Return of the Musketeers* (1989). Chamberlain attended the Los Angeles Conservatory of Music and studied acting with Jeff Corey.

FURTHER READING

Richard Chamberlain: An Actor's Life. BARBARA SIEGEL and SCOTT SIEGEL. St. Martin's. 1989.
Richard Chamberlain: An Unauthorized Biography. JEFFREY RYDER. Dell, 1988.
"Chamberlain, Richard." *Current Biography,* Nov. 1987.

Chamorro, Violeta (Violeta Barrios de Chamorro, 1939–) Nicaraguan President Chamorro faced severe economic and related political problems in 1991. The long Sandinista-Contra civil war had left the country effectively bankrupt, in debt to several countries of the former communist bloc, and suffering from a huge and accelerating ratc of inflation that made almost impossible a real start toward economic recovery. At the same time, in the aftermath of the civil war many Sandinistas remained in possession of confiscated property, which they refused to surrender, and although the Contras had largely laid down their arms after the war, frequent armed Contra-Sandinista confrontations over property issues continued to occur throughout the country. In the northwest, many Contras rearmed themselves in response to Sandinista attacks, while Contra attacks on Sandinistas were also reported.

Chamorro's response to the country's economic problems included a March-April economic recovery plan that included a major reevaluation of the cordoba, the basic unit of currency, and large wage and price adjustments. She also gained more economic aid from abroad, most notably from Germany, along with debt-interest relief from Czechoslovakia. On the political side, she continued the task of reconciliation, though with considerable difficulty, as armed clashes continued. On September 11, she vetoed legislation canceling gifts of property made to themselves by members of the outgoing Sandinista government, all of it confiscated by that government while in power; she labeled that legislation unconstitutional, and declared herself opposed to the confiscations.

Chamorro became the elected president of Nicaragua on February 25, 1990, after Sandinista leader Daniel Ortega had quite surprisingly agreed to a free election and to honor the election results. Her election was the start of a new chapter in a story that began on January 10, 1978, when her husband, crusading newspaper editor Pedro Joaquin Chamorro Cardenal, a leading opponent of the dictator Anastasio Somoza Debayle, was murdered on a street in Managua. That murder made him a martyr and helped trigger the series of events that led to the Sandinista revolution and the overthrow of Somoza.

Violeta Chamorro was a member of the first Sandinista government but withdrew within a year, when she saw the Sandinistas moving toward a dictatorship of their own, and took her husband's place as the crusading editor of *La Prensa,* in opposition to Sandinista attacks on freedom. Then came ten years of civil war between Contra and Sandinista forces, with the United States helping the Contras, and Cuba and the Soviet Union helping the Sandinistas. In her first year as president of a free Nicaragua, she successfully reached agreements to disarm the former combatants, guaranteeing the freedom that she and her husband had fought for, and trying to set her very poor and damaged country on the road to economic recovery.

Violeta Barrios and Pedro Chamorro had four children. Carlos Fernando and Claudia became highly placed Sandinistas, while Pedro Joaquin became a Contra leader and Cristiana an editor of *La Prensa.*

FURTHER READING

"The woman who. . . ." TREVOR ARMBRISTER. *Reader's Digest* (Canadian), Feb. 1991.
"Flowers for Violeta." DENNIS COVINGTON. *Vogue,* Aug. 1990.
"Chamorro, Violeta Barrios de." *Current Biography,* June 1990.
"A defiant widow. . . ." RON ARIAS. *People,* Mar. 19, 1990.
"A family affair. . . ." D'ARCY JENISH. *Maclean's,* Mar. 12, 1990.
"Chamorro: More than just a name?" John Moody. *Time,* Mar. 12, 1990.
Life Stories of the Nicaraguan Revolution. DENIS L. HEYCK. Routledge Chapman & Hall, 1990.
Nicaragua Divided: La Prensa and the Chamorro Legacy. PATRICIA T. EDMISTEN. University Presses of Florida, 1990.

Chandler, A. B. (Happy) (Albert Benjamin Chandler, 1898–1991) Kentucky-born Chandler, a lawyer, built a long political career in his native state and then moved into the national arena. He was a Kentucky state senator (1929–33), lieutenant governor (1931–35), governor (1935–39), and a U.S. senator from Kentucky (1940–45). He resigned from the Senate in 1945 to become commissioner of baseball (1945–51), succeeding Kenesaw Mountain Landis. As commissioner, he pushed through Branch Rickey's historic decision to desegregate the national game by bringing Jackie Robinson to the Brooklyn Dodgers in 1947. Returning to Kentucky, he served a second gubernatorial term (1955–59). He was survived by his wife, Mildred, two daughters, two sons, and a sister. (d. Versailles, Kentucky; June 18, 1991)

FURTHER READING

Obituary. *Current Biography,* Aug. 1991.
"Happy life. . . ." *Sporting News,* June 24, 1991.
"A man of character. . . ." WILLIAM F. REED. *Sports Illustrated,* June 24, 1991.
Obituary. *New York Times,* June 19, 1991.

Chang Min-Chueh (1908–91) Born at Taiyuan, China, Chang was a leading biologist who studied and taught in China in the 1930s, taught and conducted research at Cambridge University (1941–45), and began his long tenure as a leading reproductive biologist at the Worcester Foundation in 1945, becoming principal scientist emeritus at the foundation after his 1982 retirement. During the late 1940s and 1950s, Dr. Chang, Dr. Gregory G. Pincus, and Dr. John Rock worked with steroids and progesterone to develop the ovulation-preventing oral contraceptive pill, which came to market as Enovid in 1960; "the pill" immediately became a worldwide family planning tool and a key element in the sexual revolution then under way. Chang was also a leading figure in the development of in vitro fertilization, the outside-the-body fertilization technique that produces "test tube" babies. He was survived by his wife, Isabelle, two daughters, and a son. (d. Worcester, Massachusetts; June 5, 1991)

FURTHER READING

Obituary. *The Times* (of London), June 14, 1991.
Obituary. *New York Times,* June 7, 1991.

Chaplin, Oona O'Neill (1926–91) Bermuda-born Chaplin was the daughter of playwright Eugene O'Neill and his second wife, Agnes Boulton. After their divorce, when she was two years old, she lived with her mother and was educated in New York. At 17, while still in high school and headed for an acting career, she met Charles Chaplin, then 54 and a world figure. The two fell in love and were married at Santa Barbara, California, in 1943; she was 18 years old. Her father denounced the marriage to Chaplin and entirely broke off relations with his daughter afterward. Other viewers-with-alarm pointed to Chaplin's two previous broken marriages to very young women, and to the Joan Barry paternity suit, then in process. But the marriage lasted until his death parted them in 1977, and without a hint of the turbulence that had marked his earlier relationships.

From the mid-1940s through the early 1950s, as the McCarthy period developed in the United States, Charles Chaplin was under severe attack for his liberal sympathies by the witch-hunters of the day, although they did not go so far as to force Chaplin, the world's leading comedian, to appear before a congressional committee. Instead, they forced him out of the United States in September 1952, refusing him reentry into the United States after he, Oona, and four of their children had gone to London for the premiere of *Limelight*. They did not return, instead settling in Switzerland. Oona O'Neill Chaplin then publicly adopted British citizenship. After Chaplin's death, she returned to New York for a time but continued to live mainly at their home at Vevey sur Corsier in Vaud, Switzerland. She and Charles Chaplin had eight children, several of them actors: Geraldine, Michael, Josephine, Victoria, Eugene, Jane, Annette, and Christopher. (d. Vaud, Switzerland; September 26, 1991)

FURTHER READING

Obituary. *Variety*, Oct. 7, 1991.
Obituary. *The Times* (of London), Sep. 28, 1991.

Charles Philip Arthur George, the Prince of Wales (1948–) The Prince of Wales is the oldest son of Elizabeth II and Prince Philip, and heir to the British throne. As such, he is, like the other British "royals," the object of enormous worldwide media attention, directed at every aspect of his personal life. For example, during 1991, on the occasion of his tenth anniversary, the media went on at great length about rumors that his marriage to the Princess of Wales, the former Diana Spencer, was in great difficulty. The media also devoted much coverage to an injury suffered while playing polo, which kept him from the game for a month during June and July, and to his large number of ceremonial visits in Britain and many other countries. But the Prince of Wales is also a very serious environmental activist who has spoken out on ecological issues for many years; for example, his 1991 schedule included a five-day visit to Brazil in April and serious discussions with Brazilian President Fernando Collor de Mello about the future of the Amazon basin and talks about other worldwide ecological issues. It also included a joint discussion of those issues with Collor and U.S. Environmental Protection Agency administrator William K. Reilly, with some attention directed to the forthcoming Earth Summit, to be held in Rio de Janiero in 1992.

Beyond his ecological interests, the Prince of Wales is also a highly visible critic of modern architecture. Major objects of his attack have included such massive buildings as Britain's National Theatre, National Gallery, and National Library. In 1991, he resigned as president of the patrons of the Museums of Scotland, opposing the prize-winning modernist design of the new Edinburgh Museum. During 1991, he published *The Prince of Wales' Watercolours*; forthcoming was *Highgrove: Portrait of an Estate* (1993).

Prince Charles attended Trinity College, Cambridge, and the University College of Wales. He married Lady Diana Spencer in 1981; the couple have two children: William Arthur Philip, born June 21, 1982; and Henry Charles Albert David, born September 15, 1984. His books include *A Vision of Britain* (1989) and *The Old Man of Lochnagar* (1980).

FURTHER READING

"Windsor knot. . . ." CHRISTOPHER HITCHENS. *New York Times Magazine,* May 12, 1991.
"Diana and Charles. . . ." ANTHONY HOLDEN. *McCall's,* June 1991.
Charles and Diana: The Tenth Anniversary. BRIAN HOEY. Studio Books, 1991.
"Charles III–in waiting. . . ." ANTHONY HOLDEN. *Maclean's,* Nov. 14, 1988.
"Prince Charles; a dangerous age." BRAD DARRACH. *People,* Oct. 31, 1988.
"Prince Charles. . . ." PETER DAVIS. *Esquire,* Apr. 1988.
The Picture Life of Charles and Diana. HENRY RASOF. Watts, 1988.

Chase, Chevy (Cornelius Crane Chase, 1943–) Chase was in trouble again in 1991: *Nothing but Trouble,* a film written and directed by Dan Aykroyd. Chase and Demi Moore are Wall Street types adrift in an Atlantic coast village ruled by the bizarre Aykroyd and his daughter (yes, daughter) John Candy. Forthcoming was John Carpenter's black comedy *Memoirs of an Invisible Man* about a Wall Streeter who is made invisible after an industrial accident and is hunted by the CIA; Chase co-produced the film, which also starred Daryl Hannah, Sam Neill, Michael McKean, and Patricia Heston.

In February 1991, Chase was also one of almost 100 celebrities who made a record and video, *Voices That Care,* in support of Allied troops in the Persian Gulf. He was also among the celebrities, such as Bill Cosby, Reggie Jackson, and Michael Landon, who helped Boys Town to publicize a 24-hour national hot line for troubled young people.

New York City-born Chase was a comedy writer and off-Broadway comedian in cabaret in the late 1960s and early 1970s, emerging in the mid-1970s as a nationally recognized television comedian as a member of "Saturday Night Live" troupe. In the late 1970s, he also became a leading film comedian, in such movies as *Foul Play* (1978), *Oh Heavenly Dog* (1980), *Caddyshack* (1980; and the 1988 sequel), *Modern Problems* (1981), *Deal of the Century* (1983), *Fletch* (1985; and the 1988 and 1989 sequels), *Spies Like Us* (1985), *Three Amigos* (1986), *Funny Farm* (1988), and *National Lampoon's Christmas Vacation* (1989). Chase has been married three times, and has three children.

FURTHER READING

"Playboy interview. . . ." JOHN BLUMENTHAL. *Playboy,* June 1988.

Cheney, Dick (Richard Bruce Cheney, 1941–) U.S. Defense Secretary Cheney played a major role in the preparation and prosecution of the Persian Gulf War. He was highly visible from August 1990 through the end of the war, traveling again and again to what became the theater of war and conducting a series of joint press conferences with Generals Colin Powell and Norman Schwarzkopf to build popular support for the war, while at the same time carefully managing the news and limiting possibly embarrassing free press involvement. It was Cheney who carried out the previously prepared air war attack timetable after President Bush had made the decision to go to war on January 16, 1991; and it was Cheney and Powell who conducted the first wartime press conference on January 17. The Cheney-Powell collaboration continued throughout the war and into the post-war period of disengagement; it was Cheney who announced the troop-return schedule, and both welcomed American prisoners of war (POWs) home after the war.

During the war, and afterward, Cheney also continued to implement the long-term military winding down plans that accompanied the end of the Cold War. Although the process slowed considerably during the Gulf War, the modest base closings, armed forces reductions, and project cuts announced in June 1990 continued. He canceled the hugely expensive A-12 Stealth attack plane program in January 1991, introduced a six-year military budget-cutting plan in February, and went forward to specific major U.S. military base closing and personnel cut announcements in the spring and summer. But he strongly resisted the massive additional cuts proposed by many congressional Democrats after the failed August Soviet coup, voicing concern about future Soviet stability.

Nebraska-born Cheney is a long-term Washington "insider," who worked in several Washington administrative positions during the 1970s, ultimately becoming a White House assistant of President Gerald Ford (1975–77). He became a Republican congressman from Wyoming in 1979, and during the 1980s became a leading House Republican. He became defense secretary in early 1989, after the John Tower nomination had been rejected in a long, bitter Senate fight. His B.A. and M.A. were from the University of Wyoming, in 1965 and 1966. He married Lynne Anne Vincent in 1964; they have two children.

FURTHER READING

"Cheney for the defense." Rowland Evans et al. *Reader's Digest,* Dec. 1991.
"Five who fit the bill. . . ." *Time,* May 20, 1991.
"Cracking the whip. . . ." Michael R. Gordon. *New York Times Magazine,* Jan. 27, 1991.
"Cheney, Richard Bruce." *Current Biography,* Aug. 1989.

Cher (Cherilyn LaPiere Sarkisian, 1946–) Cher the pop icon was in the ascendancy in 1991, over Cher the serious actress—a label she rejects. Early in 1991, she had a high-rated *Las Vegas Special* on CBS. In February for MTV's VH-1 network, she made a two-hour television and radio special, *Cher's Video Canteen,* for U.S. soldiers stationed in Saudi Arabia—though in deference to their host country, her costumes were played down. She introduced videos by artists such as Bonnie Raitt, Bruce Springsteen, Paul Simon, the Rolling Stones, and the Traveling Wilburys; reminisced about the musicians; and showed off a montage of her own videos, including "The Shoop Shoop Song" from her movie *Mermaids* (1990).

Summer 1991 saw a new record, *Love Hurts,* with accompanying music videos. Cher also continued to appear live, as in her late 1991 Atlantic City show, and on television talk shows. Other projects included an exercise video *CherFitness,* a book *Forever Fit* (1991), and a cameo appearance in Robert Altman's forthcoming Hollywood satire *The Player.* Cher also continued her work as honorary chairwoman of the Children's Craniofacial Association, a connection springing from her 1985 movie *Mask* about a disfigured child.

California-born Cher became a popular singer in the mid-1960s, teamed with her first husband, Sonny Bono, as Sonny and Cher. On her own from the late 1970s, she emerged as a star entertainer and recording artist, and as one of the leading celebrities of the 1980s. She turned to acting in Robert Altman's New York stage production of *Come Back to the Five and Dime, Jimmy Dean, Jimmy Dean* in 1981, and then emerged as a leading dramatic actress, whose notable body of work includes *Silkwood* (1983), *The Witches of Eastwick* (1987), her Oscar-winning lead in *Moonstruck* (1987), and *Mermaids* (1990). In addition to Bono, she was formerly married to Gregg Allman, and has two children.

FURTHER READING

Totally Uninhibited: The Life & Wild Times of Cher. Lawrence J. Quirk. Morrow, 1991.
"Cher." *Current Biography,* June 1991.
"Cher today. . . ." Jim Jerome. *People,* Jan. 21, 1991.
"Cher the unstoppable." Cliff Jahr. *Ladies Home Journal,* Nov. 1990.
Cher. J. Randy Tarraborrelli. St. Martin's, 1986.

Chissanó, Joaquim Alberto (1939–) Mozambique President Chissanó in 1991 continued his efforts to end his country's long civil war and to develop a democratic and constitutional government. But ending the war proved difficult; sporadic fighting continued even as his government moved toward new peace talks with the rebel Mozambique National Resistance (Renamo) and simultaneously began to prepare for democratic elections. The process was not helped by stories of a July Renamo massacre that reportedly took the lives of more than 1,000 villagers in northern Mozambique. As the civil war continued, electoral plans stalled as well, depending in part on the terms of a peace agreement, although the Chissanó government did announce nonspecific plans to go ahead with the elections even in the absence of a peace agreement. Meanwhile, Mozambique's people continued to wait for peace and to suffer in the aftermath of the long, bloody civil war, which had taken an estimated one million lives, many from famine and famine-induced disease.

Chissanó has spent his whole career as a Mozambiquan revolutionary and then government official. After holding several responsible posts in the Mozambique National Liberation Front (Frelimo) during the long war against the Portuguese colonizers of his country, he was foreign minister of newly independent, one-party, Marxist Mozambique (1975–86), and succeeded Samora Machel as president in 1986. In 1989, he began to move his party away from Marxism and one-party rule, toward multiparty democracy, a market-driven economy, and a peaceful reconciliation with the Renamo insurgents. He was helped greatly by the withdrawal of South African support for Renamo, as part of the general settlement of hostilities in southern Africa, by the heads of several neighboring Black frontline governments, and by American and Soviet support for new peace initiatives. In July 1990 Chissanó declared that his government would give up its one-party rule and participate in free elections, and on November 3, 1990 a new democratic constitution was adopted. Mozambique now awaits peace and concrete moves to establish democracy. Chissanó is married to Marcelina Rafael Chissanó; they have four children.

FURTHER READING

"Chissanó, Joachim Alberto." *Current Biography,* Nov. 1990.

Chung, Connie (Constance Yu-hwa Chung, 1946–) CBS newscaster Chung reduced her work and travel schedule even further in 1991 so that she could concentrate on having a baby. She had already in 1990 scaled down her successful weekly news-and-feature program to a series of occasional specials, under the title *Face to Face with Connie Chung.* But in April 1991, production on the specials was suspended at her request. She did, however, return in December in a full-hour show with Earvin (Magic) Johnson, his first prime-time interview since he announced he was infected with the human immunodeficiency virus (HIV), the virus that causes AIDS (acquired immune deficiency syndrome). In line with her reduced work load, Chung took a pay cut from an estimated $1.8 million a year to about $1 million. She continued serving as weekend anchor on the "CBS Evening News" and filling in occasionally on CBS morning news programs. Attention continued to be focused on Chung partly because her dilemma is shared by many women in her generation, who have focused on achieving career success at the expense of some personal choices. In early 1991, the American Women in Radio and Television commended *Face to Face with Connie Chung* for its effective portrayal of women's changing roles in society.

Born in Washington, D.C., Chung is a leading broadcast journalist and Asian-American, who began her broadcasting career in 1969, as a Washington-area television reporter, and moved through a series of increasingly responsible and highly visible jobs in the next two decades, including seven years (1976–83) anchoring KNXT in Los Angeles and a series of anchor assignments with NBC (1983–89), before moving to CBS. Her B.S. was from the University of Maryland, in 1969. She is married to television talk-show host Maury Povich.

FURTHER READING

"Waking up. . . ." SUSAN SCHINDEHETTE. *People,* Aug. 20, 1990.
"Chung, Connie." *Current Biography,* July 1989.

Cicippio, Joseph: See **Lebanon Hostages**

Clark, Gene (Harold Eugene Clark, 1944–91) Missouri-born Clark, a classic folk-rock guitarist, singer, and composer, was a member of the New Christy Minstrels in the early 1960s. With Chris Hillman, Roger McGuinn, David Crosby, and Michael Clarke, he was in 1964 a founder of the seminal folk-rock group, the Byrds. Their first hit was a remake of Bob Dylan's "Mr. Tambourine Man," a top hit in 1965, the year of its issue. Clark wrote several of the Byrds's most popular songs, including "Eight Mile High" and "I'd Feel a Whole Lot Better." He left the Byrds in 1966, partnered with Doug Dillard in the late 1960s, and then was largely a solo performer, although he later worked with McGuinn and Hillman. His last album was *So Rebellious a Love* (1987). He was survived by two sons. (d. Los Angeles; May 24, 1991)

FURTHER READING

"Gene Clark dies. . . ." David Fricke. *Rolling Stone,* July 11, 1991.
Obituary. *The Times* (of London), June 27, 1991.
Obituary. *New York Times,* June 26, 1991.
Obituary. *Variety,* June 3, 1991.

Clay, Andrew Dice (Andrew Silverstein, 1957–) Somebody out there likes Andrew Dice Clay. The controversial comedian has alienated a large part of the American population with his foul-mouthed, virulent attacks on women, homosexuals, physically disabled people, the elderly, Blacks, Asians, other ethnic minorities, and a wide range of other victims. Some performers have refused to appear on the same program with him, most notably regular Nora Dunn and guest singer Sinead O'Connor on the May 1990 "Saturday Night Live"; some prominent comedians, such as Robin Williams, have publicly attacked his bigotry; MTV has barred him from their channel because of his obscenities at the 1989 video awards; in 1991, the Portland, Oregon, city council went so far as to write an open letter to ticket holders, urging them not to attend a Clay show. Reviewers slashed his movie *The Adventures of Ford Fairlane* (1990), and at Hollywood's 1991 Golden Raspberry Awards it was named worst movie and Clay the worst actor. The film did so badly at the box office, after an initial surge, that 20th Century Fox dropped its plans to release *The Andrew Dice Clay Concert Movie,* the film of a performance at New York's Madison Square Garden.

Yet when *Ford Fairlane* was released on video in January 1991, it quickly jumped into the top ten on the video rental charts. Clay's concert film was finally released by Carolco in May 1991, under the title of *Dice Rules,* though the original theater chain dropped the film; the soundtrack was released by Def-American Records, which handles several other highly controversial performers. Some have suggested that Clay's act is a kind of pornography; in any case, he seems to maintain a hard-core audience.

A stand-up comedian, Clay has worked in cabaret since the late 1980s. Billed as Andrew Clay, he appeared as a continuing character in the television series "Crime Story" (1986–88). He was formerly married.

FURTHER READING

"Critics load the dice. . . ." Daniel Wattenberg. *Insight,* Sep. 10, 1990.
"Andrew Dice Clay. . . ." Andrew Abrahams. *People,* May 28, 1990.
"20 questions. . . ." David Rensin. *Playboy,* Jan. 1990.

Clayton, Buck (Wilbur Dorsey Clayton, 1911–91) Classic jazz trumpeter, composer, and arranger Clayton began his career with his father's church orchestra in Parsons, Kansas. He played professionally in California in the early

1930s, there forming his first jazz band. He played in China with Teddy Weatherford's band (1934–36), and then joined Count Basie's band in 1936. From 1936 until his army service began in 1943, he was one of the band's stars; in the same period he often accompanied Billie Holliday and memorably recorded with the Kansas City Six and Kansas City Seven. In this period, his arranging skills began to emerge. After the war, he resumed his career, touring widely in Europe and America, with his own and other groups, and most notably recording the Columbia Records "Buck Clayton Jam-session" discs. Physical problems forced him to give up playing in 1969, but he continued to compose and arrange, and in the mid-1980s he once again formed his own big band. His autobiography is *Buck Clayton's Jazz World* (1986). He was survived by his wife, Patricia, a daughter, and a sister. (d. New York City; December 8, 1991)

FURTHER READING

Obituary. *Variety,* Dec. 16, 1991.
Obituary. *The Times* (of London), Dec. 13, 1991.
Obituary. *New York Times,* Dec. 12, 1991.
"Buck Clayton." DAVE HELLAND. *Down Beat,* Sep. 1989.
Goin' to Kansas City. NATHAN W. PEARSON, JR. University of Illinois Press, 1987.

Clifford, Clark McAdams (1906–) In the course of 46 years spent in Washington, Clifford became the consummate "insider," a key adviser to three presidents, and a former secretary of defense. In 1991, at the age of 84, he became a central figure in the Bank of Credit and Commerce International (BCCI) affair, one of the most highly publicized bank scandals of the century; though not accused of wrongdoing, his involvement was such as to greatly damage his previously excellent reputation.

Senator John Kerry encountered BCCI while investigating international drug trading in 1987 as chairman of the Senate Foreign Relations subcommittee on Terrorism, Narcotics, and International Operations. In 1988, he discovered the $20 million BCCI account of Panama's General Manuel Noriega. Ultimately, BCCI was revealed to have been involved in bribery, larceny, conspiracy to illegally acquire interests in other financial institutions, money laundering, the funding of illegal arms dealing, and a host of other illegal activities.

In 1990, Kerry discovered ties between BCCI and its secretly owned Washington-area First American Bankshares. Clifford had been chairman of First American since 1982; Clifford's law partner, Robert Altman, had been president of the bank. Both resigned their positions on August 13, under great pressure, after having denied all knowledge that BCCI had secretly bought a controlling interest in First American. BCCI, by then a $20 billion international bank, had at that time been the center of an enormous scandal for many months, culminating in the July 5 closing down of BCCI operations in seven countries, with losses to depositors and investors estimated at more than $5 billion.

Clifford made his first public appearance on September 11, 1991, before the House Banking Committee. He and Altman stated that they had been innocent dupes who had not known that BCCI owned First American Bankshares. Their denials were greeted with extreme skepticism by the members of House committee and the media, which by then had followed and detailed some the multiple relationships between both men, American Bankshares, and BCCI. The worldwide investigation of BCCI proceeded, although some journalists accused the U.S. Justice Department, which had been investigating BCCI at least since 1988, of dragging its feet, and publicly wondered if that might be due to alleged relationships between the Central Intelligence Agency (CIA) or some of its operatives, and BCCI.

Kansas-born Clifford began his long career in St. Louis, practicing law there (1928–43). He became a White House naval aide in 1945 and quickly became a key political adviser to fellow Missourian Harry S. Truman, who was the first of the several Democratic presidents who came to rely on his advice. He was a special counsel to Truman (1946–50) and to presidents John F. Kennedy and Lyndon Johnson until becoming secretary of defense in 1968–69. After his years in government, he stayed in Washington, becoming one of the country's most powerful, politically connected Washington "insiders." He became board chairman of Washington-based First American Bankshares in 1982. His LL.B. was from Washington University, in St. Louis. He is married to the former Margery Pepperell Kimball; they have three daughters.

FURTHER READING

"A matter of influence. . . ." EVAN THOMAS. *Newsweek,* May 20, 1991.
"All the presidents' man." *M Inc.,* Mar. 1991.

Clinton, Bill (William Jefferson Blythe IV, 1946–) Arkansas governor Clinton entered the Democratic presidential nomination race on October 3, 1991, sounding the same themes he had been developing as chairman of the middle-of-the-road Democratic Leadership Council since 1990. Running as a centrist trying to gain the votes of the "forgotten middle class," Clinton appealed to those in his party who felt that the Democratic Party had been losing ground because of its populist image, and that to win Presidency the "middle" of the electorate had to be won. At the same time, he tried to appeal to traditional party supporters, favoring national health insurance and outlawing the practice of hiring permanent replacement workers in strike situations. He also said that he was for education, against welfare cheating, and for child-support laws. At year end, Clinton was generally viewed as one of the frontrunners for the 1992 Democratic nomination.

Arkansas-born Clinton taught law at the University of Arkansas Law School and was in private practice (1973–76) before entering politics in 1977 as state attorney general, a position he held until he became governor at 32. He was governor from 1979 to 1981, and again since 1983. His B.S. was from Georgetown in 1968, his J.D. from Yale in 1973. He was a Rhodes Scholar at Oxford (1968–70). Born three months after his father's death, he later took his stepfather's surname. Clinton is married to attorney Hillary Rodham Clinton, board chairman of the Children's Defense Fund; they have one child.

FURTHER READING

"Bill Clinton: Front-runner. . . ." MARGARET CARLSON. *Time,* Dec. 30, 1991.
"Slick Willy. . . ." MORTON KONDRACKE. *New Republic,* Oct. 21, 1991.
"Man-child. . . ." DONALD BAER. *U.S. News & World Report,* Oct. 14, 1991.
"Not so thoroughly moderate. . . ." BILL WHALEN. *Insight,* Sep. 9, 1991.
"Arkansas traveler." JOE KLEIN. *New York,* Aug. 12, 1991.
"An interview with. . . ." FRANK NEWMAN. *Change,* Mar.–Apr. 1990.
"Clinton, Bill." *Current Biography,* Apr. 1988.
Laboratories of Democracy. DAVID OSBORNE. *Harvard Business,* 1988.

Close, Glenn (1947–) American actress Close was seen in two very different roles in 1991: one as an early 1900s pioneer woman, the second as a worldly opera diva. The first was her February title role as the New England spinster who answers an advertisement for a mail-order bride to a Kansas man (Christopher Walken) with two children in Hallmark Hall of Fame's high-rated television special, *Sarah, Plain and Tall.*

In the fall of 1991, Close opened as Swedish opera singer Karin Anderson in Istvan Szabó's film *Meeting Venus,* about the trials and tribulations of a Parisian production of *Tannhäuser.* In both the film and the opera-within-the-film, she and Jay O. Sanders were the only Americans; the rest—and thereby hang many of the wild confusions—were an international, multilingual group. In mid-summer, Close was in Hollywood starring with Laura Dern and Woody Harrelson in the premiere of a new play by Lisa-Maria Radano, directed by James L. Brooks, called *Brooklyn Laundry.* She also appeared in a cameo as a male sailor in Steven Spielberg's updating of the Peter Pan tale, *Hook.* Forthcoming in early 1992 was a staring role opposite Gene Hackman and Richard Dreyfuss on Broadway in *Death and the Maiden.*

Connecticut-born Close, on stage from the

early 1970s, emerged as a stage and screen star in the 1980s, winning a Tony for her Broadway role in *The Real Thing* (1984) and playing leads in such films as *The World According to Garp* (1982), *The Big Chill* (1983), *The Natural* (1984), *Fatal Attraction* (1987), *Dangerous Liaisons* (1988), *Reversal of Fortune* (1990), and *Hamlet* (1990). Her B.A. was from the College of William and Mary, in 1974. She was previously married to Cabot Wade and James Marlas, and has one child.

FURTHER READING

"Glenn Close." FRANK SPOTNITZ. *American Film,* Nov.–Dec. 1991.
"Getting Close. . . ." STEPHEN FARBER. *Connoisseur,* Aug. 1991.
"Glenn gets close." CLIFF JAHR. *Ladies Home Journal,* Jan. 1991.

Collett, Alec: See **Lebanon Hostages**

Collins, LeRoy (1909–91) Tallahassee-born Collins built a long political career in his native state. A lawyer, he won a seat in the Florida House of Representatives in 1934 and was elected to the state senate in 1940. After serving in the Navy during World War II, he returned to the state senate (1946–54) and won his first gubernatorial race in 1954. During his six years as governor, he took what was then believed in the South to be a moderate and even liberal position on segregation, officially endorsing the color line but by 1957 openly seeing the end of segregation as inevitable, and by 1960 taking anti-segregation positions. He was chairman of the 1960 Democratic National Convention. During the 1960s, he was president of the National Association of Broadcasters (1961–64), director of the Community Relations Service of the Department of Commerce (1964–65), and Under Secretary of Commerce in the Johnson administration (1965–66), then returning to Florida to practice law. He edited (with Charles U. Smith) *The Civil Rights Movement in Florida and the United States: Historical and Contemporary Perspectives* (1989). He was survived by his wife, the former Mary Call Darby, three daughters, and a son. (d. Tallahassee, Florida; March 12, 1991)

FURTHER READING

Obituary. *Current Biography,* May 1991.
Obituary. *New York Times,* Mar. 13, 1991.
Governor Leroy Collins of Florida: Spokesman of the New South. THOMAS R. WAGY. University of Alabama Press, 1985.

Collins, Phil (1951–) The word for Collins in 1991 was "Paradise." His "Another Day in Paradise," a song about homelessness, won the Grammy for best single record of the year; Collins, the song, and the album in which it originally appeared, *. . . But Seriously* (1989), had also received seven other nominations, including best album, songwriter, engineered recording, pop vocal, music video (short and long form), producer, and pop instrumental (for "Saturday Night and Sunday Morning"). "Paradise" was also named the most peformed song of 1990 by the American Society of Composers, Authors and Publishers, and Collins was named songwriter of the year by the British Performing Right Society. "Paradise" also appeared on Collins's follow-up record *Serious Hits . . . Live!*, released late in 1990. Late in 1991, Collins appeared on screen as Inspector Good in a cameo in Steven Spielberg's Peter Pan update, *Hook.*

London-born Collins joined the rock band Genesis in 1971, as the group's drummer and became lead singer in 1975, recording such albums as *And Then There Were Three* (1978), *Abacab* (1981), and *Genesis* (1983). He emerged as a major rock soloist in the 1980s, starting with the album *Face Value* (1981) and going on to the album *No Jacket Required* (1985), with its Grammy-winning "Against All Odds." He starred in the film *Buster* (1988), co-writing the Grammy-winning "Two Hearts." He has been married twice, last to Jill Collins in 1984, and has three children.

FURTHER READING

Genesis of Phil Collins. SCOTT NANCE. Movie Publications Services, 1991.
Phil Collins. TOBY GOLDSTEIN. Ballantine, 1987.
"Collins, Phil." *Current Biography,* Nov. 1986.
The Phil Collins Story. JOHNNY WALLER. H. Leonard, 1986.
Phil Collins. PHILIP KAMIN. H. Leonard, 1985.

Collor de Mello, Fernando Affonso

(1949–) As the worldwide 1990–91 recession deepened and his country slid into an extremely dangerous combination of recession and worsening inflation, Brazilian President Collor de Mello made major but not greatly successful attempts to stem the tide of adverse events. On January 31, his economics minister, Zelia Cardosa de Mello, announced a "shock" program to stop inflation, which included a package of wage and price increases and subsequent freezes, to go into effect on February 2, after a one-day February 1 bank holiday. But the plan did not work; on May 8, Cardosa resigned, along with most of Collor's other economic advisers. She was succeeded by United Nations ambassador Marcilio Marques Moreira, who announced that he would attempt to conclude another rescheduling of Brazil's huge debt interest repayments, re-establish damaged international financial community ties, and fight inflation, all with Collor's approval but without any new plans.

On the environmental front, Collor made some progress, announcing new preserves for the threatened Yanomani people of the Amazon basin, several debt-for-nature swaps and continuing limits on mining in the basin. He also sharply attacked U.S. environmental policies in a September 23, 1991, speech to the United Nations General Assembly as part of the run-up to the June 1992 Earth Summit meeting, to be hosted by Brazil.

Collor de Mello spent the early part of his career in his family's communications companies, becoming their president in 1978. He moved into politics in 1979, as the military government-appointed mayor of Maceió, in the state of Alagoas. He was elected to the federal legislature from Alagoas in 1982 and became governor of the state in 1986. He founded Brazil's Reconstruction Party in 1989 and was elected to the presidency in December 1989 with a program that stressed the importance of encouraging private enterprise, paying Brazil's huge international debts, and cutting social welfare programs. He took office in March 1990, succeeding José Sarney Costa. He attended the University of Brasilia. He was formerly married to Lilibeth Monteiro de Carvalho, is married to Rosane Malta, and has two children.

FURTHER READING

"The man and the moment. . . ." *Economist,* Dec. 7, 1991.
"Collor de Mello, Fernando Affonso." *Current Biography,* Mar. 1990.
"Putting his best foot forward. . . ." Michael S. Serrill. *Time,* Jan. 1, 1990.

Connery, Sean

(Thomas Connery, 1930–) For Connery, the old became new again in 1991. John Huston's classic film from a Kipling tale, *The Man Who Would Be King* (1975), starring Connery and Michael Caine as rogue soldiers in India and points north, was released for the first time on video, in letter-box-style format. *The Russia House* (1990), in which he starred with Michelle Pfeiffer, also received new life; it fared poorly at the box office in general release but quickly jumped into the top ten when released for video rental in August 1991.

In mid-1991, Connery appeared in an unbilled scene-stealing cameo as Richard the Lionheart in the worldwide hit *Robin Hood: Prince of Thieves,* starring Kevin Costner. Connery turned executive producer for *Medicine Man,* a love story set in the Amazon rain forest and involving the search for a rare cancer-curing plant. Directed by John McTiernan and starring Connery and Lorraine Bracco, the film was shot in Mexico—some of it actually in treetops, with wires and harnesses—in the spring of 1991 and was released in early 1992. *Highlander II: The Quickening,* a sequel to the 1986 time-traveling adventure, shot in Argentina in late 1990 by Connery and Christopher Lambert, opened in late 1991 to generally poor reviews.

Connery spoke out for Scottish nationalism in 1991, narrating a 5-minute political advertisement for the Scottish Nationalist Party, urging that his fellow Scots support the movement to break their economic and political ties with the rest of the United Kingdom.

Edinburgh-born Connery was on stage and screen in small roles during the 1950s and early 1960s; he became an instant star as sex-symbol James Bond in *Dr. No* (1962), and went on to become a worldwide celebrity in six more James Bond films: *From Russia With Love* (1963), *Goldfinger* (1964), *Thunderball* (1965), *You Only Live Twice* (1967), *Diamonds are Forever* (1971), and *Never Say Never Again* (1983). But he soon became far more than a sex symbol, showing himself to be a strong and flexible actor, in such films as *A Fine Madness* (1966), *The Molly Maguires* (1970), *The Wind and the Lion* (1975), *The Man Who Would Be King* (1975), *Robin and Marian* (1976), *Cuba* (1979), *The Untouchables* (1986; winning a Best Supporting Actor Oscar), *The Name of the Rose* (1987), *Indiana Jones and the Last Crusade* (1989), *Family Business* (1989), and *The Hunt for Red October* (1990). Connery has been married twice and has one child, the actor Jason Connery.

FURTHER READING

The Films of Sean Connery. Robert Sellers. St. Martin's, 1991.

"A man called Connery." Susan Schindehette. *People,* Dec. 18, 1989.

"Sean Connery. . . ." John Culhane. *Reader's Digest,* Aug. 1989.

"Connery. . . ." Ben Fong-Torres. *American Film,* May 1989.

Sean Connery. Michael F. Callan. Scarborough House, 1985.

Sean Connery: A Biography. Kenneth Passingham. St. Martin's, 1983.

Connick, Harry, Jr. (1967–) Harry Connick has a mission: to put the "big band sound in everyone's ears." That's how he put it in the liner notes to his album *Blue Light, Red Light* (1991), a collection of original big-band-style songs, four written by Connick himself and all arranged and orchestrated by him for the 17-piece Harry

Connick, Jr., Orchestra. Reviewed as his most successful album yet, the record debuted promisingly in autumn 1991, quickly bringing to four the number of records Connick had on *Billboard*'s chart of the top 200 albums. The other three were *20* (1988), *When Harry Met Sally . . .* (1989), and *We Are in Love* (1990); he won Grammy awards for best male jazz vocals in 1990 and 1991 for the last two.

Connick was also seen on screen in 1991 in Jodie Foster's *Little Man Tate,* playing Eddie, the college student who teaches child prodigy Fred Tate how to play pool. April saw the release of *Swinging Out Live,* a video of a Connick performance in Dallas, filmed during his 1990 tour and featuring the 1930s and 1940s big-band songs that have become his trademark—and that cause some to liken him to a young Frank Sinatra. Connick also sang "The Bare Necessities" as one of several singers doing classic Disney songs on the recording and video release *Simply Mad About the Mouse.*

New Orleans-born jazz and pop singer, songwriter, and pianist Connick studied with James Booker III and Ellis Marsalis (head of the Marsalis jazz clan) in his hometown while still in high school, and at the same time received much of his practical training playing the piano in French Quarter jazz clubs. Arriving in New York City at age 18, he attended the Manhattan School of Music, and, with door-opening help from Wynton Marsalis, cut his first jazz record, *Harry Connick, Jr.* (1987). A year later, at age

20, he cut his second record *20* (1988). Then came his breakthrough soundtrack contributions to the film *When Harry Met Sally . . .* (1989), followed in 1990 by *Lofty's Roach Soufﬂe,* a piano trio album, and *We Are in Love.* He made his film debut in *Memphis Belle* (1990).

FURTHER READING

"Connick, Harry, Jr." *Current Biography,* Nov. 1990.

"Harry's double take." Becca Pulliam. *Down Beat,* Oct. 1990.

"The entertainer. . . ." Rob Tannenbaum. *Rolling Stone,* Mar. 23, 1989.

Connors, Jimmy (James Scott Connors; 1952–) The old man of tennis confounded the experts—and gave heart to all "30-somethings"—by reaching the semifinals of his 21st U.S. Open in the week of his 39th birthday, in September 1991. Connors won five straight victories, including extremely close, hard-fought matches with Aaron Krickstein, Patrick McEnroe, and Paul Haarhuis (after which he sometimes needed intravenous rehydration), before finally being stopped in straight sets in the semifinals by 21-year-old Jim Courier. The spectacle caught the attention of millions, including many who are not normally tennis lovers; Ted Koppel even devoted an episode of *Nightline* to the phenomenon. During the two-week tournament, Connors jumped from 174th to 66th in the Association of Tennis Professionals (ATP) Tour rankings.

The unseeded Connors had been coming back from a 14-month layoff because of a career-threatening wrist injury that required surgery, in addition to late-1989 foot surgery, and he been much employed in the NBC television booth commenting on other tennis players' performances. At the French Open in early June 1991, which he entered ranked 324th in the world, he had become a folk hero for battling 19-year-old American star Michael Chang to a standoff in their third-round match before he had to withdraw in the fifth set because of back spasms and dehydration. Later in June, he entered his 20th Wimbledon as a wild card; in his 100th Wimbledon match—a men's record—he defeated Krickstein in straight sets before himself being ousted.

An All-American in 1971, the year he was NCAA single champion, Connors turned professional in 1972 and was named player of the year in 1974. He was number one in the men's world rankings for a record 159 weeks—from July 29, 1974, to August 16, 1977—and also holds the all-time record for number of tournaments won, at 109. He has had eight Grand Slam singles wins: the Australian Open (1974), Wimbledon twice (1974, 1982), and the U.S. Open five times (1974, 1976, 1978, 1982, 1983). Among his doubles titles are two Grand Slams: Wimbledon (1974) and the U.S. Open (1975), both with Ilie Nastase. With Robert J. LaMarch, he wrote *Jimmy Connors: How to Play Tougher Tennis* and *Winning Tennis My Way* (both 1986). Connors attended the University of California at Los Angeles. He is married to Patti McGuire; they have one son.

FURTHER READING

"Ten living legends. . . ." Steve Wulf. *Sports Illustrated,* Dec. 23, 1991.

"Jimbo, part X. . . ." Mike Lupica. *Esquire,* Sep. 1991.

"He's baaack! . . ." Cindy Schmerler. *World Tennis,* June 1991.

"Jimmy Connors. . . ." Mark Preston. *Tennis,* May 1991.

Conte, Silvio O. (1921–91) Pittsfield-born Conte, a lawyer, served in the Seabees during World War II and began his long career as a liberal Republican with his election to the Massachusetts state senate in 1950. He served in the state senate until winning the first of his 17 terms in the federal House of Representatives in 1958. The only Republican in the Massachusetts congressional delegation, he became a very powerful liberal voice in the House, at first supporting intervention in Vietnam and then opposing the war's continuance, very early sponsoring AIDS research, and later becoming one of only three House Republicans to oppose the Persian Gulf War resolution. He was survived by his wife, Corinne, three daughters, and a son. (d. Bethesda, Maryland; February 8, 1991)

FURTHER READING

Obituary. *New York Times,* Feb. 10, 1991.

Cooper, John Sherman (1901–91) Kentucky-born Cooper, a lawyer, began his long political career in 1927, with his election to the Kentucky legislature. From 1930 to 1938, he served as a county judge, then as a circuit judge in Kentucky in 1946, resigning to win election to his first term in the U.S. Senate, filling out the unexpired term of Happy Chandler, who had resigned to become commissioner of baseball. He served in the Senate from 1946 to 1948, and became a United Nations delegate in 1949. He was elected to fill out a second unexpired Senate term from 1952 to 1955, then becoming U.S. ambassador to India and Nepal. In 1957, he was elected to the Senate to fill out another unexpired term, this time replacing Alben Barkley, who died in office; Cooper served in the Senate until 1973. A liberal, he took a wholly independent course in the Senate, as when he denounced the witch-hunts conducted by Senator Joseph McCarthy in the 1950s, and joined Democrat Frank Church in opposing the Cambodian intervention, in the Cooper-Church Amendment, and leading the fight to prohibit the use of U.S. troops in Laos and Thiland. After leaving the Senate, he was the first U.S. ambassador to the German Democratic Republic (1974–76). He later practiced law in Washington. He was survived by a brother and a niece. (d. Washington, D.C.; February 21, 1991)

FURTHER READING

Obituary. *Current Biography,* Apr. 1991.
Obituary. *New York Times,* Feb. 23, 1991.
Senator John Sherman Cooper: Consummate Statesman. Clarice J. Mitchner. Ayer, 1985.

Coppola, Carmine (1911–91) A composer and flutist, Coppola was a flutist for several symphony orchestras during the 1940s and became first flutist with Arturo Toscanini's NBC Symphony Orchestra in 1951. He also was a conductor for several Broadway musicals. He moved to Hollywood to join his son, Francis Ford Coppola, in the mid-1960s, and scored several minor films; his first major film was *Finian's Rainbow* (1968), directed by his son. He also scored several other films, including *The Godfather, Part II* (1974), for which he won an Academy Award, and *Apocalypse Now* (1979), both also directed by his son. In 1981, he wrote a new score to accompany the restored classic Abel Gance silent film *Napoleon* and conducted the symphony orchestra that played his score at the 1981 Radio City Music Hall premiere of the restored film. He was survived by his wife, Italia; a daughter, actress Talia Shire; and two sons, director Francis Ford Coppola and screenwriter and teacher August Coppola. (d. Northridge, California; April 26, 1991)

FURTHER READING

Obituary. *Variety,* May 5, 1991.
Obituary. *New York Times,* Apr. 28, 1991.

Coppola, Francis Ford (1939–) The past dominated the present for Coppola in 1991. *The Godfather, Part III,* released at the end of 1991, stood deep in the shadows of his previous Oscar-winning *Godfather* films. Critical reaction was mixed and it had a respectable, but not smashing, box office. The film won several Oscar nominations, including for best picture, director, supporting actor (Andy Garcia), song ("Promise Me You'll Remember," co-written by Coppola's father, Carmine Coppola, who died in April 1991), editing, and cinematography (Gordon Willis), but won none. By late 1991, *Part III* was released on video, with nine minutes of footage restored.

Coppola was the unwitting star and his wife Eleanor the director in the wrenching feature-length documentary film *Hearts of Darkness: A*

Filmmaker's Apocalypse (1991), a unique film journal of Coppola's making of the classic—and classically troubled—film *Apocalypse Now* (1979), involving contemporary footage of principals such as Marlon Brando, Robert Duvall, Dennis Hopper, and Martin Sheen, as well as intimate tapes from Coppola himself. The film was widely seen on cable television and won the best documentary award at the Montreal International Festival of New Cinema and Video in October.

As for the future, Coppola was set to revive the tradition of live original dramas for CBS television, producing occasional programs starting in the spring of 1992 under the title *Playhouse 90's,* the title paying homage to the 1950s CBS series. Forthcoming in 1992 was *Bram Stoker's "Dracula,"* based on the original 1897 Bram Stoker novel. Through his Zoetrope Production studios, Coppola was also acting as co-executive producer for *Wind,* a film shot in Australia about the America's Cup race.

Detroit-born Coppola is best known by far for two films: the Oscar-winning *The Godfather* (1972; he directed and co-wrote the screenplay) and the Oscar-winning *The Godfather, Part II* (1974; he directed, produced, and wrote the screenplay), for which he won Best Director and Best Screenplay Oscars. Together, these Sicilian-American Mafia stories are one of the greatest achievements of the American cinema; Coppola also combined them, with additional material, into a "novel for television" that some observers thought superior to the individual films. Although he created many other films, including the notable *Apocalypse Now* (1979), *Peggy Sue Got Married* (1986), and *Tucker: The Man and His Dream* (1988), nothing else ever came close to duplicating the achievement of his massive Godfather films. Coppola's B.A. was from Hofstra University in 1958, his M.A. in cinema from UCLA in 1968. He married Eleanor Neil, and has had three children, one of whom died in a boating accident in 1986. Actress Talia Shire is Coppola's sister.

FURTHER READING

"Coppola, Francis Ford." *Current Biography,* July 1991.

"Francis Ford Coppola." DAVID BRESKIN. *Rolling Stone,* Feb. 7, 1991.

Coppola. PETER COWIE. Macmillan, 1990.

On the Edge: The Life and Times of Francis Coppola. MICHAEL GOODWIN and NAOMI WISE. Morrow, 1989.

Francis Ford Coppola. JEAN-PAUL CHAILLET and ELIZABETH VINCENT. St. Martin's, 1985.

Cosby, Bill (1937–) Superstar comedian Bill Cosby prepared to move on in 1991. His "The Cosby Show" was still in the top ten television shows, continued to be first in its time period, and is reportedly the most profitable show in television history; but it had dropped to fifth place among all television shows, from second place in 1990–91 and first place for five years before that. Cosby has said that the 1991–92 season would be his last as Cliff Huxtable. Cosby is scheduled to move to CBS in the fall of 1992, with a revival of the old Groucho Marx comedy-quiz show "You Bet Your Life"; Cosby is to produce and star in the show, appearing five nights a week in the early evening.

For the year 1991 Cosby was also knocked from the number one spot on *Forbes* magazine's list of the highest-paid entertainers, pushed to number two by the New Kids on the Block—although his 1990–91 earnings were estimated at $113 million. In 1991, he published another book, *Childhood.* Personally, he continued a wide variety of activities reflecting his strong social concerns.

Philadelphia-born Cosby became a television star and pioneering Black performing artist in the thriller "I Spy" (1965–68), and went on to star in his own "The Bill Cosby Show" (1969–71), which later had a second life (1972–73). He also became a leading solo comedy performer and recording artist as well as starring in several films, including *Uptown Saturday Night* (1974), *Let's Do It Again* (1975), *Mother, Jugs and Speed* (1976), and *Ghost Dad* (1989). In 1984, with his long-running family situation comedy "The Cosby Show" he became one of the leading performers in American television, and with that also a leading celebrity. His books include *The Wit and Wisdom of Fat Albert* (1973), *Fatherhood* (1986), *Time Flies* (1987), and *Love and Marriage* (1989). Cosby attended Temple University; his M.A. and Ed.D. were from the University of Massachusetts, in 1972 and 1977. He married Camille Hanks in 1964; they have five children.

FURTHER READING

"Bill Cosby. . . ." MICHAEL BOURNE. *Down Beat,* Sep. 1991.
"Cosby talks." BOB THOMAS. *Good Housekeeping,* Feb. 1991.
Bill Cosby: The Changing Black Image. ROBERT ROSENBERG. Millbrook, 1991.
Cosby. RONALD L. SMITH. St. Martin's, 1987.
Bill Cosby: Family Funny Man. LARRY KETTELKAMP. Messner, 1987.
Bill Cosby: Superstar. PATRICIA S. MARTIN. Rourke, 1987.
Cosby. RONALD L. SMITH. St. Martin's, 1986.
The Picture Life of Bill Cosby. BARBARA JOHNSTON ADAMS. Watts, 1986.

Costner, Kevin (1955–) No doubt about it: 1991 was Kevin Costner's year. His *Dances with Wolves* (1990), an epic about the relationship between idealistic cavalry officer Lt. John Dunbar (played by Costner) and the Sioux tribes of the post–Civil War West, swept the Academy Awards in March, winning 7 Oscars overall, from among 12 nominations, including best picture and adapted screenplay; Costner won a Best Director Oscar in his directorial debut. He also won the best director award of the Directors Guild of America, and Golden Globes for best picture and director. The film was released on video in autumn 1991. A book by Costner followed: *Dances with Wolves: The Illustrated Story of the Epic Film* (1991).

Kevin Costner (left) and Jay O. Sanders.

In June, Costner opened in the title role of *Robin Hood: Prince of Thieves.* Though reviewers criticized his American-not-English accent and style, the film became an enormous hit not only in the United States but worldwide, from Japan to Australia, with *Dances With Wolves* making Costner suddenly a top international superstar.

Meanwhile Costner himself had moved on to play New Orleans District Attorney Jim Garrison in Oliver Stone's *JFK,* who with investigators such as Lou Ivon (Jay O. Sanders) explores conspiracy theories about the assassination of President John F. Kennedy. The cast also included such established stars as Sissy Spacek, Tommy Lee Jones, Gary Oldman, and numerous stellar cameos. Publicity and controversy swirled around the picture for months and it was one of the most-awaited pictures of 1991, opening strongly the week before Christmas.

Forthcoming was a starring role as a Secret Service agent in *The Bodyguard,* assigned to protect a celebrity actress and singer, played by

Whitney Houston. Later in 1991, Costner was executive producer of a new movie, *China Moon,* starring Ed Harris.

California-born Costner emerged as a film star in the mid-1980s, in *Silverado* (1985), *The Untouchables* (1987), *No Way Out* (1987), and *Bull Durham* (1988), and the very popular *Field of Dreams* (1989). He attended California State University. He is married to Cindy Silva; the couple have three children.

FURTHER READING

"Into the woods. . . ." STEPHANIE MANSFIELD. *GQ–Gentlemen's Quarterly,* July 1991.
"Safe sex symbol. . . ." BARBARA LIPPERT. *M Inc.,* June 1991.
"Kevin Costner. . . ." SALLY OGLE DAVIS. *Ladies Home Journal,* Apr. 1991.
"Kevin Costner." FRED SCHRUERS. *Rolling Stone,* Nov. 29, 1990.
"Pack leader. . . ." MARJORIE ROSEN. *People,* Nov. 19, 1990.
"Dancing with the wolves." FRED SCHRUERS. *Premiere,* Oct. 1990.
"Costner, Kevin." *Current Biography,* June 1990.

Cousteau, Jacques-Yves (1910–) In 1991, the celebrated French marine explorer and inventor scored a major victory in his long fight against the commercial exploitation of Antarctica, viewed by Cousteau and other environmentalists as a world heritage area. The specific battle was the worldwide fight against the Wellington Convention, an international agreement signed at Wellington, New Zealand, in June 1988, that would have allowed oil drilling and mining in Antarctica. Before the Wellington Convention, drilling activity had been barred by the 37-nation 1961 Antarctic Treaty. Cousteau, then nearing 80, traveled the world to fight ceaselessly against the Convention and for a proposal that would have recognized Antarctica and its seas as an international nature preserve. His moral authority was such that he was able almost singlehandedly to change the course of world events. France began the shift, reversing its support of the treaty, as did several other nations, and in April 1991, 38 nations proposed a 50-year moratorium on Antarctic mineral extraction. The United States, which had at first opposed the moratorium, in July reversed its position to one of support.

Cousteau has been one of the leading marine explorers and environmentalists of the 20th century. In 1943, he was one of the inventors of the Aqualung, now called scuba gear, and from the late 1940s tested and further developed the bathysphere, now the chief vehicle for underwater exploration. He co-authored such very influential books as *The Silent World* (1952) and *The Living Sea* (1962); the former was the basis of his 1956 Oscar-winning documentary film. He has also made many films for television, including the tremendously popular series "The World of Jacques Cousteau" (1966–68), and "The Underwater World of Jacques Cousteau" (1968–76). In 1973, he founded the Virginia-based Cousteau Society to further marine research. Cousteau attended the Best Naval Academy. In 1937, he married Simone Melchior, who accompanied him on his expeditions for four decades; she died on December 2, 1990. The couple had two children.

FURTHER READING

"Jacques Cousteau." BAHGAT ELNADI et al. *UNESCO Courier,* Nov. 1991.
Jacques Cousteau: A Biography. MARGARET DAVIDSON. Scholastic, 1991.
Great Lives: Nature and the Environment. DORIS FABER and HAROLD FABER. Macmillan, 1991.
"Cousteau. . . ." ROBERT H. BOYLE. *Sports Illustrated,* Apr. 30, 1990.
Cousteau: The Captain and His World. RICHARD MUNSON. Paragon, 1989.
Cousteau: An Unauthorized Biography. AXEL MADSEN. Beaufort, 1987.

Cranston, Alan (1914–) California Senator Cranston's fourth and final term in office was blighted by his involvement in the Keating Lincoln Savings and Loan Association case, which brought charges that he and four other senators (the "Keating Five") unethically intervened with federal bank regulators on behalf of the Lincoln Savings and Loan Association of Irvine, California, controlled by Charles H. Keating, Jr. The bank was in 1989 taken over by federal banking authorities in a bailout carrying an estimated cost of at least $2 billion.

After 14 months of hearings, the Senate Ethics Committee on February 27, 1991, stated that Cranston "may have engaged in improper conduct that may reflect upon the Senate." The committee found that four specific contacts had been made on behalf of Keating by Cranston or his staff with the Federal Home Loan Bank Board from April 1987 through April 1989, "in close connection with the solicitation or receipt of contributions." Cranston was found to have received $39,000 in direct campaign contributions from Keating and his associates, while Keating also gave $850,000 to political groups founded or controlled by Cranston and $85,000 to the California Democratic Party. The other four senators were also criticized, though less severely. In July, committee special counsel Robert S. Bennett recommended that Cranston be censured by the full Senate, but for several months the committee report was not sent to the full Senate, as committee members disagreed on whether the report had been too severe regarding Cranston. In an unsuccessful attempt to speed committee action, Senator Jesse Helms leaked an Ethics Committee report on the case. On November 20, the Ethics Committee voted to reprimand Cranston but to take the matter no further.

Senator Cranston continued to function on a wide range of issues, perhaps most notably as a member of the Senate Judiciary Committee during the Judge Clarence Thomas Supreme Court nomination proceedings, with their Anita Faye Hill–Clarence Thomas confrontation. He voted against the Thomas nomination.

Palo Alto-born Cranston was a foreign correspondent in the late 1930s, and a real estate executive after World War II. He was California state controller (1959–67), and made his first successful run for the Senate in 1968. He was Senate Democratic Whip (1977–89), was during his final term chairman of the Veterans Affairs Committee, and is a member of the Banking and Foreign Relations committees. In November 1990, he announced that he had prostate cancer and would therefore not seek re-election as Senate Democratic whip or in 1992 to Congress. Cranston attended Pomona College and the University of Mexico, receiving his B.A. from Standord University in 1936. He has had two children.

FURTHER READING

"Alan Cranston. . . ." LESLIE KAUFMAN. *California,* Sep. 1991.
"Cranston wiggling." WESTON KOSOVA. *New Republic,* Mar. 19, 1990.
"Seven sorry senators. . . ." MARGARET CARLSON. *Time,* Jan. 8, 1990.

Cristiani Burchard, Alfredo (1948–)
Cristiani, the president of El Salvador, scored a major triumph at the end of 1991, when peace talks conducted under United Nation auspices with the country's five main revolutionary organizations resulted in a ceasefire and peace agreement in his country's 12-year-long civil war. The main remaining question was whether Cristiani would be able to bring along fully the Salvadoran armed forces and possibly dissident members of his own party, especially those who had been responsible for the formation and operation of the right-wing death squads that had committed so many extra-legal murders during the long war.

Those basic questions remained alive even after the precedent-setting September 28 conviction of two army officers in the military death squad murders of six Jesuit priests and two women bystanders in November 1989; the murders had stirred international condemnation. The acquittals of seven others accused, and the military-led demonstrations following the convictions, again raised serious questions about Cristiani's ability to control his army and party. Salvadoran peace accords were finally signed in January 1992.

Cristiani was an executive in his family's companies before going into politics in the early 1980s. In 1985, he became leader of the right-wing Nationalist Republican Alliance Party (ARENA), succeeding Robert D'Aubisson, under whose leadership ARENA had been widely accused of being implicated in the mass killings perpetrated by Salvadoran death squads. Cristiani was seen as a more moderate business-interests leader and won a clear majority of those voting in the 1989 presidential elections, although the elections were boycotted by several armed revolutionary organizations. He attended Georgetown University and is married to Margarita Cristiani.

FURTHER READING

"Delicate peace. . . ." *American Legion Magazine,* July 1991.
"At home with President Cristiani." *America,* Dec. 8, 1990.
"Cristiani, Alfredo." *Current Biography,* Jan. 1990.

Cronyn, Hume (Hume Blake, 1911–) Distinguished actor Cronyn looked back in 1991 in his memoir *A Terrible Liar,* reviewing his life from his privileged childhood in Canada through his theatrical career, much of it in tandem with his wife, actress Jessica Tandy. Going only to 1966, the autobiography was favorably reviewed as "candid and witty" and refreshingly full of entertaining stories, not mean-spirited gossip.

In January 1991, Cronyn won an ACE (cable television's version of the Emmy) as best actor in a cable movie for his performance opposite Vincent Gardenia in *Age-Old Friends* (1989). The same role had brought him his first Emmy in 1990, as best actor in a miniseries or special; his daughter Tandy Cronyn also appeared in the film. In late 1991, Cronyn starred with Fred Savage (of "The Wonder Years") in CBS's *Christmas on Division Street,* a story about the friendship between an affluent suburban boy and an elderly homeless man.

Ontario-born Cronyn has been on stage professionally for 60 years, in character roles from the 1930s and in leading roles from the 1950s. His long, celebrated partnership with Jessica Tandy has included co-starring roles in *The Fourposter* (1951), *A Delicate Balance* (1966), *The Gin Game* (1977), and *Foxfire* (1982). He won a Tony for his Polonius in *Hamlet* (1964). He made his screen debut in *Shadow of a Doubt* (1943) and went on to play strong character roles in such films as *The Seventh Cross* (1944), *Lifeboat* (1944), *Sunrise at Campobello* (1960), *The World According to Garp* (1982), and *Cocoon* (1985). Cronyn attended Ridley University, McGill University, and the New York School of Drama. He and Jessica Tandy have been married since 1942 and have three children.

FURTHER READING

"He drives Miss Daisy. . . ." Eve Drobot. *Saturday Night,* Oct. 1991.
"Doyen of theater. . . ." Helle Bering-Jensen. *Insight,* Oct. 21, 1991.
"Two lives, one ambition. . . ." Gerald Clarke. *Time,* Apr. 2, 1990.
"Happily ever after." Jeanne Marie Laskas. *Life,* Apr. 1990.
"Cronyn, Hume." *Current Biography,* June 1988.

Cruise, Tom (Thomas Cruise Mapother IV, 1962–) On Christmas Eve 1990, superstar Cruise achieved a Hollywood rarity—a secret wedding—slipping the media net to a rented home in Colorado, where he married Australian actress Nicole Kidman, whom he had met on the set of *Days of Thunder* (1990). The two journeyed to Australia in August 1991 to meet her family. After shooting *Billy Bathgate,* Kidman joined Cruise for Ron Howard's film about an Irish couple who fall in love during the 1840s potato famine and emigrate to America, shooting in mid-1991 in Montana and Ireland. For the film—tentatively titled *Far and Away* and scheduled for 1992 release—both had to brush up on their Irish brogues, with the help of dialect

coaches and tapes. Along with James Stewart and Lauren Bacall, Cruise was honored with a 1991 American Cinema Award for distinguished achievement in film. Late in 1991, Cruise was in Washington, D.C., shooting Rob Reiner's *A Few Good Men,* scripted by Aaron Sorkin from his own play; the cast includes Jack Nicholson, Demi Moore, Kevin Bacon, Kiefer Sutherland, and Kevin Pollak.

Born in Syracuse, New York, Cruise became very popular in the early 1980s in such films as *Risky Business* (1983), *All the Right Moves* (1983), *Legend* (1984), *Top Gun* (1986), *The Color of Money* (1986), *Rain Man* (1988), and *Days of Thunder* (1990). He won an Oscar nomination for his portrayal of disabled Vietnam War veteran Ron Kovic in Oliver Stone's *Born on the Fourth of July* (1989). He was married to Mimi Rogers (1987–90); he married Nicole Kidman in 1990.

FURTHER READING

"From here to maturity. . . ." *Seventeen,* July 1991.
"A Cruise in outer space. . . ." JAN GOLAB. *California,* June 1991.
"Burn a little rubber. . . ." JEANNIE PARK. *People,* July 23, 1990.
"What's driving. . . ." JEANNE MARIE LASKAS. *Life,* June 1990.
"Cruise at the crossroads." TRIP GABRIEL. *Rolling Stone,* Jan. 11, 1990.
"Playboy interview. . . ." ROBERT SCHEER. *Playboy,* Jan. 1990.
Top Gun: The Films of Tom Cruise. ED GROSS. Pioneer, 1990.
Tom Cruise. JOLENE ANTHONY. St. Martin's, 1988.

Crystal, Billy (1947–) It was another very good year for Billy Crystal. He once again had an audience of over one billion people, when he returned as host of the 63rd annual Academy Awards show in March 1991, work that later won him an Emmy for Individual Performance, Variety or Music Program. Crystal also won four awards, including best comedy special, from the National Academy of Cable Programming for HBO's *Billy Crystal: Midnight Train to Moscow* (1990); and with his colleagues Whoopi Goldberg and Robin Williams, the Norma Zarky Humanitarian Award, given at the annual Women in Film ceremony, for their annual *Comic Relief,* which raises funds for the homeless.

June saw the debut of one of mid-1991's few hit films: Ron Underwood's *City Slickers,* produced by and starring Crystal, who had plugged the movie at the Academy Awards by making his entrance on a horse. In this comedy about mid-life crises worked out on a dude ranch, Crystal plays advertising salesman Mitch Robbins, who with his friends Phil Berquist (Daniel Stern) and Ed Furillo (Bruno Kirby) goes on a cattle drive. Still focusing on mid-life crises, Crystal turned co-writer, co-executive producer, and general inspiration of a new six-part half-hour comedy series for HBO, *Sessions,* starring Michael McKean as lawyer Dan Carver and Elliott Gould as his therapist, Dr. Bookman, with their weekly encounters supplying the plot lines for the series; Carver's daughter is Crystal's own 18-year-old daughter. Forthcoming in 1992 is *Mr. Saturday Night,* with Crystal again writing, producing, and starring—but this time also directing.

New York-born Crystal worked as a comedian in cabaret in the mid-1970s and moved into television in the long-running "Soap" (1977–81), which was followed by the short-lived "The Billy Crystal Hour" (1982). He was well received as a continuing character in the 1984–85 season of "Saturday Night Live," and has also appeared in several telefilms. He began playing film leads in the late 1980s, in *Running Scared* (1986), *Throw Momma From the Train* (1987), *Memories of Me* (1988), and *When Harry Met Sally . . .* (1989), for which he and co-star Meg Ryan won American

Comedy Awards. He also shared a 1990 Emmy for Best Variety or Musical Show. With Dick Schaap, he wrote *Absolutely Mahvelous* (1986). Crystal attended Nassau Community College and New York University. He is married to Janice Crystal; the couple have two children.

FURTHER READING

"Cover Q&A." FRANK SANELLO. *Los Angeles,* Sep. 1991.
"Billy Crystal. . . ." BARBARA GERBASI. *McCall's,* July 1991.
"Crystal, Billy." *Current Biography,* Feb. 1987.

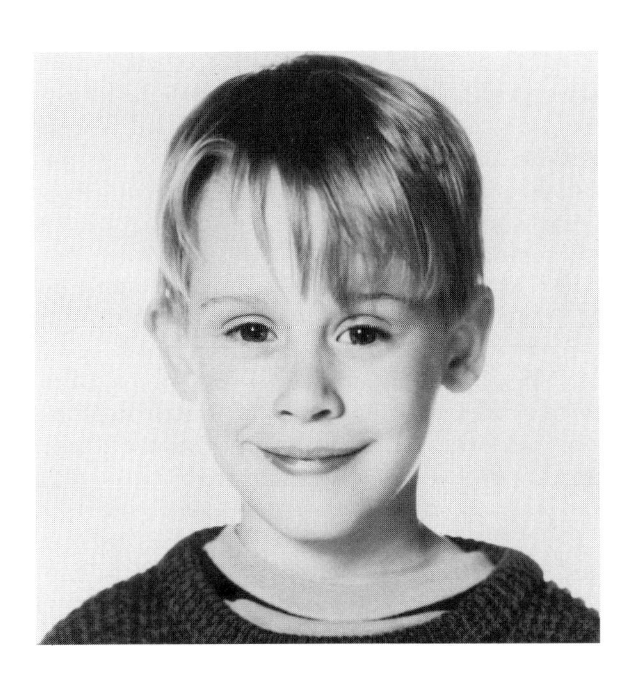

Culkin, Macaulay (1980–) Macaulay Culkin—Mack to his friends—emerged as a leading child actor playing Kevin McCallister in Chris Columbus's enormously successful movie *Home Alone* (1990), in which he bested two adult burglars with a series of highly innovative moves. Along with the American Comedy Awards' nod to Culkin as best movie actor, the film brought him numerous other projects. In 1991, also with Columbus, he played brother to his real-life brother Kieran (*Home Alone*'s cousin Fuller) in *Only the Lonely.* In *My Girl,* under Howard Zieff's direction, he was Thomas J., best friend of newcomer Anna Chlumsky, opposite Dan Aykroyd and Jamie Lee Curtis. Film insiders wondered whether his death in the film would traumatize his fans, especially children.

Late in 1991 Culkin and director Columbus were hard at work on a sequel, *Home Alone 2: Lost in New York,* co-starring Joe Pesci and Daniel Stern. Also forthcoming was *The Good Son,* a psychological thriller about two young boys, an orphan and his cousin, who turns out to be psychotic.

On stage in New York, Culkin performed in a September reading of a new Keith Reddin play *Sam I Am.* He also appeared on Michael Jackson's new video for the song "Black or White"; joined Arnold Schwarzenegger at the White House for the President's Council on Physical Fitness and Sports; presented an Oscar at the Academy Awards; and was national spokesman for the Marine Corps Reserve Toys for Tots program.

Culkin began his career at age four, acting in off-Broadway plays and later appearing as a featured dancer in the New York City Ballet's annual *The Nutcracker* at Lincoln Center. His films include *Rocket Gibraltar* (1988) as Burt Lancaster's grandson, *See You in the Morning* (1989), *Uncle Buck* (1989) as John Candy's nephew, and *Jacob's Ladder* (1990). Culkin comes from a theatrical family, brought onto the stage (along with his four brothers and two sisters) by his father, actor Christopher (Kit) Culkin, now his children's theatrical manager; actress Bonnie Bedelia is his aunt.

FURTHER READING

"Baby, it's you." ZOE F. CARTER. *Premiere,* Nov. 1991.
"Macaulay Culkin." KAREN JAEHNE and KAREN KUEHN. *Interview,* July 1991.
"Macaulay Culkin. . . ." ERIC SHERMAN. *Ladies Home Journal,* May 1991.
"The kid who. . . ." MAYNARD GOOD STODDARD. *Saturday Evening Post,* Apr. 1991.
"Running away. . . ." TOM GLIATTO. *People,* Dec. 17, 1990.

Cuomo, Mario Matthew (1932–) New York's governor Cuomo, a leading Democratic liberal, was during 1991 viewed as a prime contender for the 1992 Democratic presidential nomination—if he chose to run. He had refused to run in 1988, and in May 1991 declared again that he would not run for the presidency; but late in 1991 he seemed to reconsider the matter very seriously, especially in light of President Bush's waning popularity in the face of a deep-

ening recession that could no longer be ignored by the ruling Republicans. Ultimately, however, he once again announced that he would not run in 1992.

Like George Bush, and like all of the nation's governors, Cuomo and New York State faced massive economic problems during the early 1990s. In March, his state awash in red ink and facing an estimated $6 billion state deficit, he proposed a state budget that carried major tax increases and massive state spending cuts that would force tens of thousands of layoffs of state and local employees. An unusually long deadlock followed, with a budget achieved on June 4 followed by Cuomo vetoes of almost $1 billion in spending increases. The state fiscal crisis had not been resolved at year's end.

New York-born Cuomo moved into politics after two decades as a practicing lawyer and law teacher. He was New York secretary of state (1975–79), lieutenant governor (1979–82), and became his party's candidate and then governor in 1983 after defeating then-New York City mayor Ed Koch in a hotly contested primary campaign. He wrote of the gubernatorial contest in his *Diaries of Mario M. Cuomo: The Campaign for Governor* (1984). As governor, he became a powerful Democratic Party leader. Since his keynote address to the 1984 Democratic national convention, he has been thought to be a leading contender for the American presidency, even though he is a much-attacked Catholic liberal who has refused to modify his pro-choice views and whom one Catholic cleric stated "was in serious risk of going to hell" because of his pro-choice stand, in spite of Cardinal O'Connor's later-denied threat of excommunication. Cuomo has also declined to reverse his long-standing opposition to the death penalty. His B.A. was from St. John's College, in 1953, his LL.B. from St. John's University. He is married to the former Matilda Raffa; they have five children.

FURTHER READING

"Mario's calling." Jacob Weisberg. *New Republic,* Dec. 2, 1991.
"Cuomo's hologram. . . ." Joe Klein. *New York,* Oct. 7, 1991.
"The state of the governor. . . ." Elizabeth Kolbert. *New York Times Magazine,* Feb. 10, 1991.
"Mario the fire god." Richard Brookhiser. *National Review,* May 28, 1990.
"Message for Mario. . . ." Magie Mahar. *Barron's,* Mar. 12, 1990.
"Mario the magician. . . ." Joe Klein. *New York,* Feb. 5, 1990.
"Can Mario run?" Martin Schram. *Washingtonian,* Jan. 1990.
Mario Cuomo: A Biography. Robert S. McElvaine. Macmillan, 1988.

Curtis, Ken (Ken Gates, 1916–91) Colorado-born Curtis, a songwriter, singer, and actor, began his career as a singer with NBC Radio in Los Angeles in 1938, and then replaced Frank Sinatra as a singer with Tommy Dorsey's band. After World War II military service, he resumed his career, starring as a singing cowboy in several films and as a member of the Sons of the Pioneers, a singing group that included Roy Rogers. He also played nonsinging character roles in many films, including such John Ford classics as *Rio Grande* (1950), *The Searchers* (1956), and *Cheyenne Autumn* (1964). Curtis is best known by far for his role as Festus in television's "Gunsmoke," a role he played from 1963 to 1975. He was survived by his wife, Torie, and two children. (d. Fresno, California; April 27, 1991)

FURTHER READING

Obituary. *Variety,* May 6, 1991.
Obituary. *New York Times,* May 1, 1991.

D

Dahmer, Jeffrey L. (1960–) Mass murderer Jeffrey Dahmer is society's nightmare come true. In May 1991, his Milwaukee neighbors called the police because a dazed, naked, bleeding young man was in the street outside Dahmer's apartment. But when the police came, they believed Dahmer's story that he and Konerak Sinthasomphone had had a lovers' quarrel, so the young man was left in the custody of Dahmer, who then murdered him. The police officers were later suspended during an investigation of their behavior that day. On July 22, a handcuffed man fled Dahmer's apartment and found police who would listen to his story. Investigating officers entering Dahmer's apartment for the first time found the remains of 11 of Dahmer's victims. He then confessed to 17 murders, going back to 1978, when he was still living in his parents' home in Ohio, just after his high school graduation. Most of the murders were of men with whom he had sex; he then drugged, killed, and dismembered his victims. On September 10, 1991, Dahmer pleaded not guilty to 15 murder charges, despite his previous confessions, and later changed his plea to insanity.

Born in Bath Township, Ohio, near Akron, Dahmer briefly attended Ohio State University and served for three years in the U.S. army before moving to Milwaukee in the early 1980s. His army discharge involved drug or alcohol abuse. In 1986, he was sentenced to a year in jail for child molestation.

FURTHER READING

"Dahmer's inferno." Brian Masters. *Vanity Fair,* Nov. 1991.

"The door of evil. . . ." Paula Chin. *People,* Aug. 12, 1991.

Milwaukee Massacre: Jeffrey Dahmer and the Milwaukee Murders. Robert Dvorchak. Dell, 1991.

Massacre in Milwaukee: The Macabre Case of Jeffrey Dahmer. Richard W. Jaeger et al. *Wisconsin State Journal,* 1991.

Step into My Parlor, the Jeffrey Dahmer Story: A Detailed Look Inside Milwaukee's House of Horror. Ed Baumann. Bonus Books, 1991.

Dalai Lama (Tenzin Gyatso, 1935–) After 32 years in exile, the Dalai Lama, exiled religious and political ruler of Tibet and the spiritual leader of an estimated 6 million Buddhists throughout the world, continued to campaign for Tibetan independence, and during 1991, in considerably changed circumstances. With liberalization in the Soviet Union came freedom of worship in the Soviet Union and Mongolia, and with the breakup of the Soviet Union came much Chinese government concern about the situation in Tibet, which had continued to be an occupied country rather than being entirely absorbed as a Chinese province, as claimed by China. Growing American support for Tibetan independence was a further source of Chinese concern, as was the Dalai Lama's great and growing prestige throughout the world, which had been enhanced by his 1989 Nobel Peace Prize.

The Dalai Lama continued to travel widely during 1991 from his base in northern India, at Dharamsala. One of his most significant journeys was his first visit, in September, to a newly free Mongolia, with religious ceremonies involving tens of thousands of Mongolian Buddhists. The implications of his visit were quite clear to Chinese government officials, in control of what had been Inner Mongolia and Sinkiang, flanking occupied Tibet.

The Dalai Lama also made two very significant visits to the United States in the spring and autumn. In April, he made a U.S. national tour, ending in Washington, D.C., with an informal address to members of Congress in the Capitol rotunda, a Senate resolution condemning Chinese actions in Tibet, and a meeting with President George Bush—all of which worsened already strained Chinese-American relations and greatly encouraged the Tibetan independence movement.

In October, he toured the United States again; one of those who met and toured with him was the actor Richard Gere, founder and chairman of Tibet House and a sponsor of 62 Tibet-related events organized into the International Year of Tibet. During his tour, at a Yale University speech, the Dalai Lama stepped up the pressure on the Chinese, declaring himself ready to return to Tibet; Chinese premier Li Peng, harassed by Tibetan exiles during his autumn visit to India, responded that he was willing to talk with the Dalai Lama about anything but Tibetan independence, a position echoed by other Chinese government officials. So it stood as 1991 ended.

With Robert A. Thurman, he has written *The Politics of Enlightenment: A Handbook for the Cool Revolution,* scheduled for 1992 publication.

Tenzin Gyatso was born to a Tibetan rural family in 1935. He became the Dalai Lama formally in 1940, although Tibet was ruled by a regency until 1950, when he took power. He fled Llasa in 1950, after attempted Tibetan resistance to the Chinese, but returned to a nine-year relationship with the Chinese (1950–59). He fled Tibet after the failed 1959 Tibetan insurrection against Chinese rule, then leading the Tibetan exile community in northern India while continuing to be a world religious figure. His works include *My Land and People* (1962), *The Opening of the Wisdom Eye* (1963), *The Buddhism of Tibet and the Opening of the Middle Way* (1975), *Kindness, Charity, and Insight* (1984), *A Human Approach to World Peace* (1984), *The Bodhgaya Interviews* (1988; edited by Jose Ignacio), *Five Point Peace Plan for Tibet* (1988), *Oceans of Wisdom: Guidelines for Living* (1980), *The Dalai Lama at Harvard: Lectures on the Buddhist Path to Peace* (1989; with Jeffrey Hopkins), *Tibet the Sacred Realm* (1990), *The Nobel Peace Prize and the Dalai Lama* (1990; with Sidney Piburn), and *Freedom in Exile: The Autobiography of the Dalai Lama* (1990).

FURTHER READING

"Hello Dalai. . . ." Jim Holt. *New Republic,* Nov. 11, 1991.

"Lost horizons." Jonathan Mirsky. *New York Review of Books,* Dec. 20, 1990.
"A god-king in exile." *Maclean's,* Oct. 15, 1990.
"The days of a holy man." Lynn Rosellini. *U.S. News & World Report,* Oct. 29, 1990.
"A biography of His Holiness. . . ." Tynley Nyandak. *Catholic World,* May–June 1990.
Great Ocean: An Authorized Biography of the Buddhist Monk Tenzin Gyatso His Holiness the Fourteenth Dalai Lama. Roger Hicks and Ngakpa Chogyam. Viking Penguin, 1990.
The Dalai Lama: The Leader of the Exiled People of Tibet and Tireless Worker for World Peace. Christopher Gibb. Gareth Stevens, 1990.
The Dalai Lama: A Policy of Kindness. Sidney D. Piburn. Snow Lion, 1990.
The Dalai Lama: A Biography. Claude D. Levenson. Unwin Hyman, 1989.
A Long Look Homeward: Interview with Dalai Lama of Tibet. G. H. Mulern. State Mutual Books, 1988.
The Last Dalai Lama: A Biography. Michael H. Goodman. Shambhala, 1986.
Ocean of Wisdom: The Life of Dalai Lama. P. N. Chopra. South Asia Books, 1986.

Dalton, Timothy (1946–) Though he did not open in a new James Bond film in 1991, Dalton was still seen in the role, as his films were widely played on television and circulated on videotape. In April 1990, he had even won unspecified libel damages from *Globe* magazine for suggesting that he was to be dropped from future Bond films. Dalton played a very different role in *The Rocketeer,* as Nazi villain Neville Sinclair in the comic-book-style action film set in 1938 Hollywood, directed by Joe Johnston and also starring Bill Campbell, Jennifer Connelly, Alan Arkin, and Paul Sorvino. The film opened with great fanfare in June 1991, but neither reviews nor audiences favored the film and it became one of a series of summer failures. On stage, however, Dalton and Whoopi Goldberg played to turn-away crowds as one of the notable rotating sequence of pairs in the Beverly Hills production of A. R. Gurney's two-character *Love Letters* in summer 1991.

Wales-born Dalton made his stage debut in 1966, in British regional theater. His screen debut came in 1968, as Philip II in *The Lion in Winter.* He went on to star as Heathcliff in a 1970 remake of *Wuthering Heights,* and appeared in such films as *Mary, Queen of Scots* (1971), *Permission to Kill* (1975), *Agatha* (1979), *Sextette* (1978), *Flash Gordon* (1980), *Chanel Solitaire* (1981), and *The Doctor and the Devils* (1985), and starred in the 15th and 16th Bond films, *The Living Daylights* (1987) and *Licence to Kill* (1989). He has also continued to appear on stage and has played in several television films. Dalton attended the Royal Academy of Dramatic Art.

FURTHER READING

"Dalton, Timothy." *Current Biography,* May 1988.
"What's hot in hunks." Eric Sherman. *Ladies Home Journal,* Aug. 1987.
"Meet the new Bond. . . ." Gerri Hirshey. *Rolling Stone,* July 16, 1987.

Daly, John (1966–) Daly zoomed out of obscurity in his first year as a professional golfer to win the 73rd Professional Golfers Association (PGA) Championship at the Crooked Stick Golf Club in Carmel, Indiana, in September 1991—not by a whisker, but by three strokes. In the end, he was 12 under par for the event, which he had dominated almost from the start, on a course he had never seen before, much less played. A crowd-pleasing underdog, known for his spectacular long-distance drives, Daly was the last player entered into the tournament, having originally been ninth alternate; when a player dropped out, Daly drove more than seven hours from Memphis for the tournament, arriving without even time for a practice round and working with someone else's caddy. After his win, Daly was swamped with attention—interviews, letters, endorsements, appearances. A country song, "Long John Daly," even appeared on the music charts. Though nearly broke a few months before the tournament, he donated $30,000 of his $230,000 first prize to fund a scholarship in the name of Thomas Weaver, a spectator killed by lightning during the championship.

Born and raised in Arkansas, Daly is a self-taught golfer, inspired by golf great Jack Nicklaus, whom he acknowledged on winning by shouting jubilantly into the microphone, "I love you, Jack!" Before joining the PGA tour, he had played on the Ben Hogan circuit, a "minor league" developmental tour, where his biggest victory was the Utah Open. His highest previous finish on the PGA Tour was third at Chattanooga, and he had earned only $33,000 up to then, missing the cut on his previous two tournaments. He attended the University of Arkansas. Previously divorced, Daly was engaged to hotel executive Bettye Fulford.

FURTHER READING

"Full blast." DAVE KINDRED. *Golf,* Nov. 1991.
"A real long shot." MIKE PURKEY. *Golf,* Oct. 1991.

Daly, John Charles (1914–91) An American born in Johannesburg, Daly worked as a reporter and news analyst for CBS from 1937 to 1949 and as White House reporter from 1937 to 1941. He moved to ABC in 1949 and was ABC news, special events, and public affairs vice president from 1953 to 1960. He was best known by far as the moderator of television's long-running "What's My Line" (1950–67), with panelists Benett Cerf, Dorothy Kilgallen, and Arlene Francis, and a fourth celebrity guest panelist. After leaving ABC, he was briefly director of the Voice of America (1967–68). He was survived by his wife, Virginia, a daughter, and two sons. (d. Chevy Chase, Maryland; February 25, 1991)

FURTHER READING

Obituary. *Current Biography,* May, 1991.
Obituary. *Variety,* Mar. 4, 1991.
Obituary. *New York Times,* Feb. 27, 1991.

Daly, Tyne (1947–) Fresh from her Broadway triumph in *Gypsy,* Tyne Daly was back on television in 1991. In February she starred in the television movie *The Last to Go* as the middle-aged wife and mother of three, whose surgeon-husband of 22 years abandons her for a young nurse. December saw her in *Face of a Stranger,* playing a homeless woman befriended by a society matron (Gena Rowlands). Daly also appeared in two television series guest spots. On the NBC series "Wings," she was a rich woman who causes havoc trying to buy friendship; it was the first time she had ever worked professionally with her brother, Timothy Daly. Then she visited "The Trials of Rosie O'Neill," appearing with her former "Cagney and Lacey" partner, Sharon Gless, the two playing high school classmates at their 25th reunion. In November 1991 it was announced that Daly would open at California's Long Beach Civic Light Opera in February 1992 in *Ballroom,* a musical about an older couple's romance in a Manhattan public dance hall, based on the television movie *Queen of the Stardust Ballroom.*

Daly appeared in supporting stage and screen roles throughout the 1970s; she emerged as a television star as Mary Beth Lacey opposite Sharon Gless in the long-running "Cagney and Lacey" (1982–88; she won Emmys in 1983, 1984, and 1988). In 1987, she starred in the film *Kids Like These,* directed by her husband, Georg Stanford Brown. In 1989, she starred on Broadway as Rose in the hit revival of the musical, *Gypsy,* and in 1990 won a Best Actress in a Musical Tony for the role. Daughter of actor James Daly and sister of actor Timothy Daly, she attended Brandeis University and the American Music and Drama Academy. Daly and Brown have three children; they filed for divorce in 1990.

FURTHER READING

"Tyne Daly. . . ." LESLIE BENNETTS. *McCall's,* Apr. 1990.

Danson, Ted (1947–) Danson was at the top of the television heap in 1991. In its ninth season (1990–91), his "Cheers" was for the first time the top-rated television show, a spot it maintained as the show's tenth and possibly final season opened in fall 1991. And Danson himself was again honored by his peers. For his work as bartender Sam Malone, he was named best male television performer at the American Comedy Awards; won best comedy actor honors at the Golden Globes, as did co-star Kirstie Alley (as Rebecca Howe) and "Cheers" itself; and was nominated for an Emmy. One of the main plot hinges of the 1991–92 season involved Sam and Rebecca's plans to have a baby. *Three Men and a Little Lady* (1990), in which Danson co-starred with Steve Guttenberg and Tom Selleck, became a popular video rental release in 1991.

Danson also continued his environmental activities, especially through the American Oceans Campaign, an organization founded by Danson and his wife, which often draws on celebrities to support environmental action. Danson was also producer for an environmentally oriented movie, and for the television series *Down Home,* starring Judith Ivey, which premiered in spring 1991.

Danson worked in the New York theater and in television in the early 1970s, beginning his film career with *The Onion Field* (1979), followed by such films as *Body Heat* (1981), *Creepshow* (1983), *Just Between Friends* (1986), *Three Men and a Baby* (1987), *Cousins* (1989), and *Dad* (1990). In 1982, he became a star of the long-running television series "Cheers," and won a 1990 Emmy as Best Actor in a Comedy Series. His large body of television work also includes the Emmy-winning *Something About Amelia* (1984) and the telefilm *When the Bough Breaks* (1986). Danson attended Stanford University and Carnegie-Mellon University. Previously divorced, he is married to Casey Danson and has two children.

FURTHER READING

"Three men and. . . ." JEFF ROVIN. *Ladies Home Journal,* Dec. 1990.
"Danson, Ted." *Current Biography,* Oct. 1990.

Dante, Nicholas (Conrado Morales, 1949–91) A dancer and writer, Dante told what was in large part his own story and the stories of those closest to him when he and James Kirkwood co-authored the long-running Broadway musical *A Chorus Line,* for which they won a Pulitzer Prize and a Tony award. The show, conceived, directed, and choreographed by Michael Bennett, ran for 15 years, from its opening at the New York Shakespeare Festival's Public Theater in 1975 until its 1990 closing. The play was set around the auditions for a Broadway musical, in which the players told their own stories; Dante's story was that of a young, poor, cast-out New York gay. He began his dancing career early, working in several Broadway shows and in cabaret before beginning his writing career with *A Chorus Line.* His later work included *Jolson Tonight* and several unproduced plays and screenplays. Dante, a victim of AIDS (acquired immune deficiency syndrome), was survived by his mother, Mary Morales, a niece, and a nephew. (d. New York City; May 21, 1991)

FURTHER READING

Obituary. *Variety,* May 27, 1991.
Obituary. *New York Times,* May 22, 1991.

Darman, Richard Gordon (1943–) Darman's White House Office of Management and Budget once again fulfilled its major responsibility in early 1991, providing the figures for President Bush's fiscal 1992 federal budget, presented to Congress on February 4—and once again Darman was sharply criticized by congressional Democrats and by many private economists as presenting overly optimistic estimates, aimed at hiding the real size of the anticipated budget deficit. As he had done in previous years, Darman defended his budget estimates as quite realistic.

In May 1991, Darman revised his 1991 budget deficit estimates from $318 billion to below $300 billion, still much higher than ever before in American history. In late July, Darman sharply raised the disputed fiscal 1992 budget deficit estimate, from $280.9 billion to 348.3 billion, an increase of $67.4 billion, or 24 percent.

North Carolina-born Darman is a long-term Washington "insider," who emerged as a key figure in the 1980s, as a Reagan White House assistant (1981–85) and deputy Treasury secretary (1985–87). He left Washington to become managing director of the Shearson Lehman Hutton investment banking firm (1987–88), and returned as Bush administration director of the Office of Management and Budget in 1989. Darman's B.A. and M.B.A. were from Harvard. He married Kathleen Emmet in 1967; they have two children.

FURTHER READING

"Dead wrong again. . . ." WARREN T. BROOKES et al. *National Review,* Oct. 7, 1991.
"Beasts of the beltway. . . ." FRED BARNES. *New Republic,* Dec. 24, 1990.
"Darman, Richard Gordon." *Current Biography,* May 1989.

Davis, Brad (1949–91) Tallahassee-born Davis is best known for his starring role as the young American imprisoned for drug-running in Turkey, in Alan Parker's film *Midnight Express* (1978). He also played a small but notable role as American Olympic runner Jackson Scholz in *Chariots of Fire* (1981), the title role of Rainer Werner Fassbinder's *Querelle* (1983), and in such later films as *Heart* (1987), *Rosalie Goes Shopping* (1989), and *Hangfire* (1991). He also played in a wide range of television roles, perhaps most notably as Robert Kennedy in the miniseries *Robert Kennedy and His Times,* and with Sally Field and Joanne Woodward in *Sybil* (1976).

On stage, Davis scored a major success at the New York Shakespeare Festival's Public Theater in 1985 starring in *The Normal Heart,* a play by Larry Kramer that was one of the earliest works to take up openly and seriously the impact of AIDS (acquired immune deficiency syndrome) on the lives of those afflicted by the disease. As his wife, casting director Susan Bluestein, revealed after his death, that was the year he learned that he was an AIDS victim. Sure that if he was known to have AIDS he would no longer get work in films, he kept his illness secret from all but his wife and close friends, and then was able to continue his work. Late in his illness, bitterly angry at film industry indifference to people with AIDS, he developed a book proposal, discussing his six years of secrecy; his wife released his unfinished work after his death, as he had desired. He was survived by his wife and daughter. (d. Los Angeles; September 8, 1991)

FURTHER READING

"When midnight comes. . . ." TIM ALLIS et al. *People,* Sep. 23, 1991.
Obituary. *Variety,* Sep. 16, 1991.
Obituary. *The Times* (of London), Sep. 11, 1991.
Obituary. *New York Times,* Sep. 10, 1991.

Davis, Geena (Virginia Elizabeth Davis, 1957–) After years of rising success and critical acclaim for performances in flaky roles, Geena Davis had a major box-office success in 1991, playing Thelma to Susan Sarandon's Louise in Ridley Scott's surprise hit *Thelma and Louise,* about two women on an initially innocent trip becoming feminist vigilantes in a role-reversing female-buddy action movie. During 1991 Davis was shooting a new film, Penny Marshall's *A League of Their Own,* about an all-female baseball league. Also forthcoming was a starring role opposite Dustin Hoffman in the Stephen Frears film *Hero.* In 1991, Davis founded a small actor-based company, Genial Pictures, on the lot of 20th Century Fox, which has first crack at any new project developed by the company.

Massachusetts-born Davis made her film debut in *Tootsie* (1982), and went on to appear in such films as *Fletch* (1985), *Transylvania 6–5000* (1985), *The Fly* (1986), *Beetlejuice* (1988), *The Accidental Tourist* (1988; she won a Best Supporting Actress Academy Award), *Earth Girls Are Easy* (1989), and *Quick Change* (1990). Her television appearances include the series "Buffalo Bill" (1983–84) and "Sara" (1985), and the telefilm *Secret Weapons* (1985). She graduated from Boston University. She married actor Jeff Goldblum in 1987; they divorced in 1991.

FURTHER READING

"Davis, Geena." *Current Biography,* Oct. 1991.
"Ridin' shotgun. . . ." Jim Jerome. *People,* June 24, 1991.
"Straight shooter." Joe Rhodes. *Harper's Bazaar,* May 1991.
"20 Questions. . . ." David Rensin. *Playboy,* Oct. 1989.
"Geena Davis." Tina Johnson. *Harper's Bazaar,* Sep. 1989.

Davis, Miles Dewey, Jr. (1926–91) Illinois-born Davis, a leading jazz trumpeter and bandleader, grew up in East St. Louis, began his long career as a trumpeter while still in high school, and went east to study at New York's Juilliard School in 1944. But it was jazz that drew him: He left Juilliard after a few months, and from 1945 played and helped originate bop in the band of his friend and mentor Charlie Parker. He toured with Billy Eckstine's band in 1947, and formed his own first band in 1948, a nine-member group that included saxophonist Gerry Mulligan. He won a long fight against drug addiction in the early 1950s, and in 1955 formed the celebrated Miles Davis Quintet, with saxophonist John Coltrane, pianist Red Garland, drummer Philly Joe Jones, and bassist Paul Chambers; later they were joined by saxophonist Cannonball (Julian) Adderley. With a varying group of members, the band played a powerful role in the development of jazz throughout the 1950s and 1960s, playing bop, cool jazz, chamber jazz, bebop, hard bop, and in the late 1960s moving into rock-and-roll. His career declined in the early 1970s, and he went into virtual retirement from 1975 to 1980, returning to play on a limited basis during the 1980s. Some of his best-known albums were *Kind of Blue* (1959), *Miles in the Sky* (1968), *Bitches Brew* (1979), and *The Man with the Horn* (1982). Among his written works are *Miles: The Autobiography* (1989; with Quincy Troupe) and *The Art of Miles Davis* (1991). He was married three times, last to actress Cicely Tyson, and is survived by a daughter, three sons, a sister, and two brothers. (d. Santa Monica, California; September 28, 1991)

FURTHER READING

Obituary. Robert Palmer. *Rolling Stone,* Nov. 14, 1991.
"Prince of darkness." Gene Santoro. *Nation,* Nov. 11, 1991.
"The Prince of Darkness. . . ." Frank McConnell. *Commonweal,* Oct. 25, 1991.
"Miles Davis remembered. . . ." *Jet,* Oct. 14, 1991.
" 'Miles followed his heart.' " Donna Foote. *Newsweek,* Oct. 14, 1991.
"Miles bows out." Steve Dougherty et al. *People,* Oct. 14, 1991.
Obituary. *Variety,* Oct. 7, 1991.
Obituary. *The Times* (of London), Sep. 30, 1991.
Obituary. *New York Times,* Sep. 29, 1991.
Miles Davis. Barry McRae. Seven Hills, 1991.
Milestones I: The Music and Times of Miles Davis to 1960; Milestones Two . . . since 1960. Jack Chambers. University of Toronto Press, 1983, 1985; Morrow, both 1985.
Miles Davis: A Biography. Ian Carr. Morrow, 1984.
Miles Davis. Michael James. A. S. Barnes, 1982.
Miles Davis: A Critical Biography. Ian Carr. Morrow, 1982.
Round About Midnight: A Portrait of Miles Davis. Eric Nisenson. Doubleday, 1982.

Davis, Ossie (1917–) Davis scored a television success as Ponder Blue, whose barbecue stand serves as a meeting place for the extraordinary ensemble of characters in the television series "Evening Shade," including Burt Reynolds, Elizabeth Ashley, Charles Durning, Marilu Henner, Hal Holbrook, and Michael Jeter, among others. The show returned for its second season in fall 1991. On film, the veteran actor and his wife, actress Ruby Dee, played key roles in Spike Lee's interracial love story, *Jungle Fever* (1991), as the Reverend and Mrs. Purify, the tradition-minded parents of Flipper Purify (Wesley Snipes), a married Black architect who falls in love with his Italian-American

secretary. Forthcoming was a starring role in Rowdy Herrington's *Gladiator,* about corruption in the world of underground amateur boxing. As a writer, Davis wrote a play, *Sybil,* and a children's book about the Reverend Martin Luther King, Jr., to be published in 1992.

Georgia-born Davis has been on stage for over 50 years, as actor, writer, director, and producer, and one of the leading Black theater figures of his time. He is best known for his portrayal of the Walter Lee Younger role in *A Raisin in the Sun* (1959), opposite Dee as Ruth Younger; and for his play *Purlie Victorious* (1961: and the 1963 film version, titled *Gone Are the Days*), in which he created the title role. He has also directed such films as *Cotton Comes to Harlem* (1970) and *Black Girl* (1972), and has acted in scores of films and telefilms, including his notable *The Emperor Jones* (1955), *Harry and Son* (1983), and *Do the Right Thing* (1989). Davis appeared in continuing roles in the television series "B. L. Stryker" (1989–90) and "Evening Shade" (1990–). He and Dee also appeared in the radio series, the "Ossie Davis and Ruby Dee Story Hour" (1974–78). His written works include *Langston: A Play* (1982) and *Escape to Freedom: A Play About Young Frederick Douglass* (1989). Davis attended Howard University from 1935 to 1938. He and Dee married in 1948; the couple, who have worked together in the theater and as social activists ever since, have three children, one of whom is actor-playwright Guy Davis.

FURTHER READING

"Ossie Davis and . . ." JOYCE WANSLEY. *People Weekly,* Mar. 23, 1981.

Dee, Ruby (Ruby Ann Wallace, 1924–) Dee was honored by her peers in 1991. In August she was awarded an Emmy as Best Supporting Actress in a Mini-Series or Special for her performance as James Garner's tart-tongued, independent housekeeper on Hallmark Hall of Fame's *Decoration Day* (1990). In June 1991 she was honored, along with Penny Marshall, Jessica Tandy, and Liv Ullman, at the 15th annual Women in Film Crystal Awards for those who have helped expand the role of women in the entertainment industry.

Dee and her husband, Ossie Davis, played key roles in Spike Lee's interracial love story, *Jungle Fever* (1991), as the Reverend and Mrs. Purify, the tradition-minded parents of Flipper Purify (Wesley Snipes), a married Black architect who falls in love with his Italian-American secretary. Dee also published a children's book, *The Tower to Heaven* (1991); appeared on stage in *The Disappearance* at Brown University in spring 1991; and served as narrator for the documentary video *Lady Day: The Many Faces of Billie Holiday* (1991).

Cleveland-born Dee began her five-decades-long career in 1941, with the American Negro Theatre. Some of her most notable stage roles were in *Anna Lucasta* (1946); opposite Davis in

Jeb (1946); as Ruth Younger, again opposite Davis, in *Raisin in the Sun* (1959; she also appeared in the 1961 screen version); and again opposite Davis in *Purlie Victorious* (1961; both appeared in the 1963 film, titled *Gone Are the Days*); and in *Boesman and Lena* (1970), *Wedding Band* (1972), and in several classic roles at the Stratford American Shakespeare Festival. Among her other films are *The Balcony* (1963), *Buck and the Preacher* (1972), and *Do the Right Thing* (1989). Dee has also often appeared on radio and television, perhaps most notably in the radio series, the "Ossie Davis and Ruby Dee Story Hour" (1974–78), which she also coproduced, and in an American Playhouse production on Zora Neale Hurston (1990), writing, narrating, and starring in the title role. She has written a volume of poetry, *Glowchild* (1972), children's books such as *Two Ways to Count to Ten* (1988), and a wide range of short stories and essays. Dee's B.A. was from New York's Hunter College, in 1945. She married Davis in 1948; the couple have three children, one of whom is actor-playwright Guy Davis.

FURTHER READING

"Ossie Davis and . . ." JOYCE WANSLEY. *People Weekly,* Mar. 23, 1981.

de Castries, Christian de la Croix

(1902–91) Paris-born de Castries, son of a French military family, was a young cavalry officer during the mid-1920s, but left the peacetime army to become an international horse jumping champion in the 1930s; he won the world show jumping championship in Paris in 1933. He returned to the army in 1940, was taken prisoner by the Germans, escaped from a prison camp in 1941, and fought in Italy and on the western front from 1943 to 1945, rising to the rank of major. He was a much decorated and three times wounded lieutenant colonel during the 1946–54 Indochinese war of independence. In December 1953, he was named French commander at Dien Bien Phu, a heavily fortified Laos-Vietnam border town with a French garrison of 16,000. The French had seriously underestimated the size and armament of the North Vietnamese army. Moving from guerrilla to positional siege tactics, a 40,000-strong North Vietnamese force, with heavy artillery, surrounded the French, cut off all sources of supply, and from March to May 1954 besieged the town and cut its garrison to pieces while de Castries refused to surrender and the world watched the end of French rule in Indochina. On April 24, de Castries was made a general and, because of his role in the siege, became a great French war hero. He surrendered the remaining 10,000 men of his force on May 17 and was himself a prisoner for four months. An estimated 4,000 men of his force survived captivity. He was survived by his wife, Jacqueline, who was a nurse in Hanoi during the Dien Bien Phu siege, and one daughter. (date and place of death not announced)

FURTHER READING

Obituary. *The Times* (of London), Aug. 1, 1991.
Obituary. *New York Times,* July 31, 1991.

DeConcini, Dennis (1937–) For three-time U.S. Democratic Arizona senator DeConcini, 1991 brought the end of his long involvement in the Keating Lincoln Savings and Loan Association case, which brought charges that he and four other senators (the "Keating Five") unethically intervened with federal bank regulators on behalf of the Lincoln Savings and Loan Association of Irvine, California, controlled by Charles H. Keating, Jr. The bank was in 1989 taken over by federal banking authorities in a bailout carrying an estimated cost of at least $2 billion.

On February 27, 1991, after 14 months of hearings, the Ethics Committee decided to drop the case against DeConcini with a mild rebuke concerning his appearance of misconduct. He called the committee's decision "full exoneration," and continued on with his long Senate career. Later in the year, as a member of the Senate Judiciary Committee, he found himself evaluating serious allegations made against others before a worldwide television audience in the hearings on the Judge Clarence Thomas Supreme Court nomination, with its extraordinary Anita Faye Hill–Clarence Thomas confrontation; and in the hearings on the nomination of Robert Gates to be Central Intelligence Agency (CIA) director. In both instances, he voted for confirmation.

Tucson-born DeConcini practiced law in Tucson before going into local politics; he was a county attorney before his first election to the Senate in 1976. He serves on several Senate committees, including the influential appropriations and judiciary committees. His B.A. and LL.B were from the University of Arizona, in 1959 and 1963. He married Susan Margaret Hurley in 1959; the couple have three children.

FURTHER READING

"Seven sorry senators. . . ." MARGARET CARLSON. *Time*, Jan. 8, 1990.

De Klerk, Frederik Willem (1936–) During his second full year in office South African President De Klerk persevered in his attempt to transform South Africa into a multiracial constitutional democracy, by dismantling the apartheid system and bringing South Africa back into the world community. It was not an easy year. Although he had freed Nelson Mandela and other political prisoners and in August 1990 negotiated the historic ceasefire with the African National Congress (ANC), he faced powerful White conservative opposition and an escalating civil war between the ANC and the largely Zulu Inkatha movement, led by Gatsha Buthelezi. Throughout the year, De Klerk attempted with little success to mediate the Inkatha-ANC civil war. His position was greatly undermined when on July 19 he was forced to admit that his government had made substantial payments to Inkatha and his own security forces had aided Buthelezi's movement. The admissions created a national scandal and eventually forced him to demote Law and Order minister Adriaan Vlok and Defense minister Maagnus Malan, though he himself was not forced out of office. In September, De Klerk managed to negotiate a peace pact, signed by himself, Buthelezi, and Mandela, but Buthelezi immediately expressed doubt that the pact would work, and clashes continued. De Klerk also faced considerable economic problems, as South Africa's economy had been damaged by the long period of unrest and international sanctions and was now also affected by the 1990–91 worldwide recession.

The year was historic for South Africa in many ways. It saw the De Klerk-initiated repeal of several basic apartheid laws, among them the 1913 and 1936 Land Acts, the 1950 segregated Population Registration, and the 1966 Group Areas Act. It also saw the beginning of very limited school desegregation. President De Klerk also moved toward even more basic reforms. On September 4, he outlined the main features of a proposed new constitution, which would establish the right of all South Africans to vote and would restructure the country's government at all levels; his proposals served as a basis for continuing government-ANC constitutional negotiations.

On the international scene, De Klerk scored major successes, most notably with the July 9 lifting of the 21-year-old Olympic boycott against South African participation and the July 10 lifting of United States sanctions against South Africa, paving the way for widespread reacceptance of South Africa into the world community. He also re-established trade relations with many African states. In June, he visited President Moi of Kenya, another historic step in the normalization process.

De Klerk practiced law in the 1960s and early 1970s and was elected to the national assembly in 1972. He became Transvaal leader of the ruling National Party in 1982. He held several cabinet posts from the mid-1970s, was education minister in the government of Pieter Willem Botha, and succeeded Botha as head of the National Party in February 1989. Botha resigned as president in August; De Klerk became acting president and was named to a full five-year presidential term in September, bringing with him a new spirit of reconciliation between the races. In October 1989, De Klerk released eight long-term political prisoners, including Walter Sisulu of the ANC, six other ANC leaders, and Jafta Masemola of the Pan Africanist Congress. On February 2, 1990, he legalized the ANC and several other outlawed organizations, and on February 11 freed ANC leader Nelson Mandela, opening a new chapter in South African history. On August 7, 1990, the ANC agreed to a full ceasefire, bringing 30 years of guerrilla war to an end. The government in turn agreed to free many more political prisoners, allow many exiles to return home freely, and relax several repressive laws; it lived up to its promises.

Frederik De Klerk attended Potchefstroom University. He married Marike Willemse in 1959; the couple have three children.

FURTHER READING

"The mandate for. . . ." ARNAUD DE BORCHGRAVE. *Insight,* July 2, 1990.
"After apartheid. . . ." COLIN VALE and R. W. JOHNSON. *National Review,* Oct. 15, 1990.
"The authoritarian center. . . ." SANFORD J. UNGAR. *New Republic,* Oct. 1, 1990.
"de Klerk, Frederik Willem." *Current Biography,* Feb. 1990.

Delacorte, George Thomas, Jr. (1893–1991) New York City-born Delacorte founded the Dell Publishing Company in 1921 and became a major pulp magazine and comic book publisher during the interwar period; his comic book characters included many Walt Disney creations as well as Bugs Bunny and Woody Woodpecker. After World War II, Dell became a major paperback publisher and in 1963 added Delacorte Press, a hardcover publisher. Delacorte sold his company to Doubleday in 1976. He made a considerable number of philanthropic contributions to his home city, including Central Park's Delacorte Theater, the Delacorte Center for Magazine Journalism at Columbia University, and several well-known statues, fountains, and other monuments in Central Park. He was survived by his second wife, Valerie, three daughters, two sons, a sister, and a brother. (d. New York City; May 4, 1991)

FURTHER READING

Obituary. *Current Biography,* July 1991.
Obituary. *Variety,* May 13, 1991.
Obituary. *New York Times,* May 5, 1991.

Demetrios I (Dimitri Papadopouluos, 1914–91) Ecumenical Patriarch of Constantinople (now Istanbul), Demetrios I was the spiritual leader of an estimated 250–300 million Eastern Orthodox Christians, approximately 5 million of them in the United States, organized into several different and independent churches, though all describing themselves as Eastern Orthodox. As Patriarch, he was the Eastern Orthodox Church's equivalent of the Catholic Pope, reflecting the split between the two branches of Christianity that occurred in the 11th century A.D. Unlike the Pope, who is the church leader for Roman Catholics, the Patriarch acts as a spiritual leader, since Eastern Orthodox churches are self-governing.

Dimitri Papadopouluos graduated from theological school at Halki in 1937 and was a deacon and preacher in Turkey and Greece before his ordination as a priest in 1942. From 1945 to 1950, he worked in Tehran, Iran. He became a bishop in 1964 and in 1972 was elected to the Patriarchy by the Holy Synod of his church, after the two strongest candidates for the post were vetoed by the Turkish government. In 1980, he was visited by Pope John Paul II and the two leaders began an unprecedented dialogue on doctrinal differences. In the late 1980s, Demetrios made a series of groundbreaking visits around the world, to the Soviet Union, Greece, and Britain. In 1990 he came to the United States where he met with President George Bush and presided over a Washington, D.C., meeting of Orthodox Church leaders. (d. Istanbul, Turkey; October 2, 1991)

FURTHER READING

Obituary. *The Times* (of London), Oct. 4, 1991.
Obituary. *New York Times,* Oct. 3, 1991.

Demme, Jonathan (1944–) Demme scored a major breakthrough in 1991 with his highly acclaimed film *The Silence of the Lambs,* starring Jodie Foster as FBI agent Clarice Starling, opposite Anthony Hopkins as imprisoned psychopathic killer Dr. Hannibal Lecter, whom Starling consults in prison for help in finding a psychopathic killer still at large. Demme directed from Ted Tally's screenplay, based on the Thomas Harris novel. The film, a major artistic and commercial success, was particularly notable in a period when serious drama was largely being shunned by Hollywood. At year's end, Demme was selected best director of 1991 by the New York Critics Circle, which also selected the work best film, Foster best actress, and Hopkins best actor. The film and those who made it had also by then received several Golden Globe nominations, and were thought strong contenders for Academy Awards.

Long Island-born Demme began his film career in the late 1960s, as a writer in the publicity departments of several film companies and *Film Daily,* and as a producer of television commercials. He co-wrote and co-produced several Roger Corman films in the early 1970s and made his feature film directorial debut with *Caged Heat* (1974). He went on to direct such films as *Crazy Mama* (1975), *Melvin and Howard* (1980), *Swing Shift* (1984), *Something Wild* (1986), *Swimming to Cambodia* (1987), *Married to the Mob* (1988), and *Miami Blues* (1990). He attended the University of Florida. He is married to Joanne Howard; they have one child.

FURTHER READING

"Heavy estrogen." GARY INDIANA. *Interview,* Feb. 1991.

"Identity check." GAVIN SMITH. *Film Comment,* Jan.–Feb. 1991.

Deng Xiaoping (T'eng Hsiao-ping, 1904–) Although reportedly ill, making very few public appearances, and holding no major positions in the Chinese Communist Party or the Chinese government, Deng is still widely viewed as the undisputed leader of his country. During 1991, he faced several very substantial continuing problems—economic and political, domestic and foreign. To the north, along the whole long Soviet-Chinese border, the "prison house of nations" was disintegrating as Soviet communism died. In the wake of the abortive August coup in the Soviet Union, Chinese communist fears of democratic contamination reportedly ran very high; at the same time China provided asylum for some Soviet conservatives, including those fleeing from prosecution.

There were also severe economic problems at home, as reported by Premier Li Peng to the March 1991 National Peoples Congress meeting in Beijing—the same problems that had beset Deng as he moved China in the moderate, market-oriented direction that had characterized the 1980s, at the same time generating the move to political liberalization that had ended with the 1989 Tienanmen Square massacre. As newly conservative China moved back toward an unworkable centralized command economy, economic problems once more multiplied, and in 1991 Deng and Li Peng again attempted to moderate their course somewhat in the direction of private trade while continuing the sharp repression of democracy—in essence trying to go in two directions at the same time as the Chinese economy and government continued to drift.

Abroad, the Chinese tried to repair some of the damage done to China's relations with the Western world, as the government attempted to foster trade links and cultivated a moderate image in such international matters as the Persian Gulf crisis. However, the Chinese reacted adversely to Western attempts to raise questions of human rights abuse, rejecting the comments of British Prime Minister John Major during his September visit to China, and of U.S. Secretary of State James Baker during his November visit.

On November 6, 1989, Deng formally left his last major position, that of head of the Central Military Commission of the Chinese Communist Party. He had been known as a political and economic moderate during much of the previous 40 years of communist power in China; now, he was equally well known as the political conservative who at first resisted the use of force during the student demonstrations of 1989, but then agreed to what became the Tienanmen Square massacre of June 4, 1989.

Deng joined the Communist Party of China in the 1920s while a student in France. He fought through the whole length of the Chinese Civil War (1927–49), and is a survivor of the 1934 Long March. During communist ascendancy, he became a major moderate leader, was purged twice (1973 and 1976), and survived to become the primary leader of Chinese communism. Deng attended the French School in Chongqing, studied in France during the 1920s, and attended Moscow's Far Eastern University. He married Cho Lin; the couple had five children.

FURTHER READING

China Under Deng Xiaoping: Political and Economic Reform. DAVID WEN-WEI CHANG. St. Martin's, 1991.

Politics of Disillusionment: The Chinese Communist

Party Under Deng Xiaoping, 1978–1989. Hsi-Sheng Ch'i. M. E. Sharpe, 1991.
"Rise of a perfect apparatchik. . . ." William R. Doerner. *Time,* July 10, 1989.
"An unlikely 'emperor.'" Mary Nemeth and Louise Doder. *Maclean's,* May 29, 1989.
Deng Xiaoping. Uli Franz. Harcourt Brace, 1988.

De Niro, Robert (1945–) De Niro struck fear into the hearts of moviegoers with his portrayal of the viciously vengeful, psychotic, slicked-down, pumped-up, heavily tattooed ex-con Max Cady in *Cape Fear* (1991), the role originated by Robert Mitchum in 1962 but given a significantly darker twist under director Martin Scorsese. De Niro's performance in the film was so impressive that it was credited with sparking increased public interest in his other recent movies, which immediately picked up business in the video rental markets. These showed typical De Niro excellence and variety. Ron Howard's *Backdraft* (1991) was about a family of Chicago firefighters. In Irwin Winkler's *Guilty by Suspicion* (1991), he was David Merrill, a Hollywood writer blacklisted during the McCarthy era; the cast included Annette Bening as his wife Ruth, Sam Wanamaker (himself blacklisted then), and Martin Scorsese in a rare acting appearance. Another strong De Niro title was *GoodFellas* (1990), which was at or near the top of the video rental charts during 1991. For *Awakenings* (1990), De Niro won the best actor award of the New York Film Critics Circle (for both *Awakenings* and *GoodFellas*) and the National Board of Review (the latter shared with Robin Williams) as well as an Oscar nomination. Other honors came his way, too: In 1991, De Niro was named a Commander of Arts and Letters by France for his lifetime achievement; the Friars Club named him 1991's best film performer; and the Museum of the Moving Image held a tribute in his honor in March.

Meanwhile, De Niro was filming opposite Jessica Lange in a noir-style thriller, *Night and the City,* another remake (of Jules Dassin's 1950 film), this one directed by Irwin Winkler, about an attorney entangled as a boxing promoter. Also forthcoming were *This Boy's Life,* a film based on Tobias Wolff's 1950s autobiographical novel; and John MacNaughton's *Mad Dog and Glory,* produced by Scorsese. De Niro was executive producing and playing a cameo in Barry Primus's *Mistress,* a dark-if-not-black comedy about some former Hollywood stars whose desperate attempt to make a film is complicated by their mistresses' attempts to get the plum roles. De Niro was acting as co-producer for Michael Apted's film *Thunderheart,* a murder mystery set on an Indian reservation. De Niro's TriBeCa Film Center project in lower Manhattan continues to grow, as well; in 1991 he purchased land nearby on which he wants to build a performing arts center.

New York-born De Niro became one of the leading actors of the American cinema in the mid-1970s, beginning with his strong supporting roles in *Bang the Drum Slowly* (1973) and *Mean Streets* (1973), and as the young Vito Corleone in *The Godfather, Part II* (1974), for which he won a Best Supporting Actor Oscar. He went on to star in *Taxi Driver* (1976), *The Deer Hunter* (1978), and *Raging Bull* (1980), for which he won a Best Actor Oscar. In the 1980s, he starred in such films as *Once Upon a Time in America* (1984), *Brazil* (1985), *Midnight Run* (1988), *We're No Angels* (1989), and *Stanley and Iris* (1989). He began the 1990s on two very high notes, in *GoodFellas* (1990) and *Awakenings* (1990). He was previously married and has two children.

FURTHER READING

"Awake and sing." Fred Schruers. *Premiere,* Jan. 1991.
"De Niro. . . ." *Video Review,* Mar. 1989.
Robert De Niro: The Hero Behind the Mask. Keith McKay. St. Martin's, 1986.

Depardieu, Gérard (1948–) Long-time French star Gérard Depardieu became an international superstar in 1990 and 1991, with some widely varied successes. In his first English-language (though certainly French-accented) film, *Green Card,* he plays George, a French musician who wants to work in the United States and contracts a marriage of convenience with Brontë (Andie MacDowell). After its Christmas 1990 opening, the film won wide audiences and brought Depardieu a Golden Globe as the year's best comic actor. Earlier in 1990, he had played the title role in *Cyrano de Bergerac,* the performance winning him the best actor award in the Cannes Film Festival, the D. W. Griffith Award of the National Board of Review, and an Oscar nomination. Though in French with subtitles, *Cyrano* later became a U.S. video-rental success, largely because of Depardieu's new-found American celebrity. Also in 1990 he had appeared on American screens in *Camille Claudel* as sculptor Auguste Rodin and in Bertrand Blier's *Too Beautiful for You* as a happily married car dealer inexplicably in love with his frumpy secretary.

In 1991 Depardieu starred in Claude Berri's film *Uranus,* as Watrin Leopold, a French schoolteacher who consents to the hiding of a Nazi collaborator in 1945. The film takes up the now-familiar moral themes stemming from the collaboration of some and the resistance of others to the Nazi World War II occupiers of France, so deeply explored by Marcel Ophul in his landmark documentary *The Sorrow and the Pity* (1970). Also in 1991 Depardieu was once again seen as Olmo, when Bernardo Bertolucci's *1900* was for the first time released in its restored uncut version. Late in the year, Depardieu was shooting a new film by Ridley Scott, playing the title role in *Christopher Columbus.* To be released was an environmentally oriented film, *Welcome to Veraz,* directed by Xavier Castano and shot in southern France in late 1990, also starring Kirk Douglas.

The seeming anthithesis of a romantic star, with his chunky physique, skewed nose, and lantern jaw, French-born Depardieu burst on the French film scene as an amoral *Easy Rider*-style juvenile delinquent in *Going Places* (1974) and then emerged as a leading French actor of the 1970s and 1980s, making over 60 films. These included *Stavisky* (1974), *1900* (1976), *Get Out Your Handkerchiefs* (1978), *The Last Metro* (1980; he won a César award as best French actor), *My American Uncle* (1980), *Danton* (1982), *The Return of Martin Guerre* (1982), *Tartuffe* (1984), and *Jean de Florette* (1986). He also became a substantial theater actor in France, and has appeared on television. He is married to the actress, singer, and songwriter Elisabeth Guignot; they have one daughter and one son.

FURTHER READING

"Gerard Depardieu. . . ." TOM CONROY. *Rolling Stone,* Mar. 7, 1991.
"Gerard Depardieu. . . ." JEANNIE PARK. *People,* Feb. 4, 1991.
"Life in a big glass. . . ." RICHARD CORLISS. *Time,* Feb. 4, 1991.
"Deciphering Depardieu." PAUL CHUTKOW. *Vogue,* Dec. 1990.
"Gerard Depardieu." STEPHEN O'SHEA and BRIGETTE LACOMBE. *Interview,* Dec. 1990.
"Depardieu, Gerard." *Current Biography,* Oct. 1987.

DeVito, Danny (Daniel Michael DeVito, 1944–) Danny DeVito embodied the acquisitive ethic as corporate takeover financier Lawrence Garfield, better known as Larry the Liquidator, in Norman Jewison's film *Other People's Money* (adapted from Jerry Sterner's 1987 play), opposite Gregory Peck as the raided old-line Rhode Island mill owner and Penelope Ann Miller as Peck's lawyer, who falls for the predatory Larry. DeVito was praised for the swagger and zest he brought to the film, which quickly became number one at the box office after its October release. During 1991 DeVito was relishing another villain's role, that of the Penguin in *Batman Returns,* scheduled for 1992 release.

DeVito's *The War of the Roses* (1989), which he directed and in which he starred with Michael Douglas and Kathleen Turner as the warring spouses of the title, was released on laser disc in a special collector's edition, including not only the movie as originally seen in the theater, but also DeVito's "free-wheeling narration" and 30 minutes' worth of scenes cut from the released film. Forthcoming was a starring role in Marshall Herskovitz's *Jack the Bear* in which DeVito plays the newly widowed father of two young boys who moves to California and becomes a late-night television horror film host. As director, he was in late 1991 shooting the biographical film *Hoffa,* starring Jack Nicholson in the title role.

New Jersey-born DeVito was a New York stage actor before making his main career in Hollywood. He appeared in such off-Broadway productions as *The Man with a Flower in His Mouth* (1969) and *One Flew over the Cuckoo's Nest* (1971), recreating his role in the 1975 film version, and went on to such films as *Car Wash* (1976), and *Goin' South* (1978). Then came his role as Louie DePalma in the long-running television series "Taxi Driver" (1978–83), for which he won a 1981 Emmy, and roles in such films as

Terms of Endearment (1983), *Romancing the Stone* (1984), *Jewel of the Nile* (1985), and *Ruthless People* (1986). He had starring roles in *Tin Men* (1987), *Throw Momma from the Train* (1987; he also directed), and *Twins* (1988). In 1989, he directed *The War of the Roses*. DeVito is married to actress Rhea Perlman and has three children.

FURTHER READING

"Danny DeVito. . . ." MICHAEL J. BANDLER. *Ladies Home Journal*, Jan. 1990.
"Funny as hell." ROBERT SEIDENBERG. *American Film*, Sep. 1989.
"DeVito, Danny." *Current Biography*, Feb. 1988.

Dewhurst, Colleen (1926–91) Though born in Montreal, Dewhurst grew up in the United States. On stage from 1946, she played in small roles until her breakthrough as Kate in a New York Shakespeare Festival production of *The Taming of the Shrew* (1956). She went on to become one of the leading stars of the American theater, winning her first Tony as Mary Follet in Tad Mosel's *All the Way Home* (1960) and her second as Josie Hogan in Eugene O'Neill's *A Moon for the Misbegotten* (1973). A memorable interpreter of O'Neill, she made many other notable appearances, as in *Desire Under the Elms* (1963), *Mourning Becomes Electra* (1973), and *A Long Day's Journey into Night* (1988). She also played in many strong supporting roles in films and television, and is probably best known for her role in the miniseries *Anne of Green Gables* (1986) and for three seasons as Murphy's mother in the series "Murphy Brown" (1989–91), for which she won a 1991 Emmy. Dewhurst was two-term president of Actor's Equity (1985–91). She was married three times, to actor James Vickery and twice to actor George C. Scott. She was survived by two sons, one of them actor Campbell Scott. (d. South Salem, New York; August 22, 1991)

FURTHER READING

Obituary. *Current Biography*, Oct. 1991.
"Brava, Colleen." MARK GOODMAN. *People*, Sep. 9, 1991.
Obituary. *Variety*, Aug. 26, 1991.
Obituary. *The Times* (of London), Aug. 26, 1991.
Obituary. *New York Times*, Aug. 24, 1991.

Diana, Princess of Wales (Diana Frances Spencer, 1961–) Diana Spencer married Charles, Prince of Wales, heir to the British throne, in July 1981, in a ceremony watched worldwide by hundreds of millions of viewers; in 1991, on their tenth anniversary, the pageant was rerun on television. Ten years later, the couple continue to be great celebrities; like the other "royals," they are followed everywhere by the media, who chronicle and photograph every public and some private moves. Their focus during 1991 was on the private life of the royal couple, with boundless speculation about the future of their marriage and such matters as his alleged attention to other women, her solo ceremonial visits at home and abroad, and the possibility that one of them will leave the other. Much ink was also spilled about relations and presumed strains between Diana and other members of the royal family, including Queen Elizabeth II, Charles's mother, and Sarah, Duchess of York, nicknamed "Fergie," wife of Charles's brother, Prince Andrew.

The couple have two children: William Arthur Philip, born June 21, 1982; and Henry Charles Albert David, born September 15, 1984.

FURTHER READING

The Definitive Diana: An Intimate Look at the Princess of Wales from A to Z. SALLY MOORE. Contemporary, 1991.
Charles and Diana: The Tenth Anniversary. BRIAN HOEY. Studio Books, 1991.

Two Royal Women: The Public and Private Lives of Fergie and Di. NORMAN KING. Knightsbridge, 1991.
"A royal star shines. . . ." MARTHA DUFFY. *Time,* July 29, 1991.
"Three decades of Di." *People,* July 1, 1991.
"Diana . . ." SUSIE PEARSON. *Ladies Home Journal,* June 1991.
"Diana and Charles. . . ." ANTHONY HOLDEN. *McCall's,* June 1991.
" 'Don't worry about me. . . .' " ANDREW MORTON. *Good Housekeeping,* Apr. 1991.
Princess Diana: A Book of Questions and Answers for Children. VICTORIA G. NESNICK. M. Evans, 1989.
Diana: An Intimate Portrait. INGRID SEWARD. Contemporary, 1988.
The Picture Life of Charles and Diana. HENRY RASOF. Watts, 1988.

Dillon, Matt (1964–) Dillon's major role of 1991 was that of the charming psychopath Jonathan Corliss, in the film thriller *A Kiss Before Dying,* directed and scripted by James Dearden, based on the Ira Levin novel. In this remake of the 1956 Robert Wagner and Joanne Woodward film, Corliss murders his girlfriend and marries her twin sister (a double role for Sean Young) in his bid for the money and power of her father (Max von Sydow). Unfortunately, neither critics nor audiences were much taken with the film, released in April. Dillon did, however, win praise for his work as a rising 1939 boxer battling his impatient wife (Kyra Sedgwick) in *Return to Kansas City,* one of three short television films that appeared on HBO in August under the title *Women and Men: In Love There Are No Rules.* Future projects included a starring role in the film *The Boxer and the Blonde,* directed by Andy Wolk.

Born in New Rochelle, New York, Dillon began his movie career as a teenager, in *Over the Edge* (1979), quickly followed by *Little Darlings* (1980), which established him as a leading teenage Hollywood star. During the 1980s, he starred in such films as *My Bodyguard* (1980), *Liar's Moon* (1982), *Tex* (1982), *The Outsiders* (1983), *Rumblefish* (1983), *The Flamingo Kid* (1984), *Native Son* (1986), *Kansas* (1988), *Drugstore Cowboy* (1989), and *Bloodhounds of Broadway* (1989). Actor Kevin Dillon is his younger brother.

FURTHER READING

"From here to maturity. . . ." *Seventeen,* July 1991.
"Matt Dillon." BRENDON LEMON. *Interview,* Apr. 1991.
"The Dillon papers. . . ." BRET EASTON ELLIS. *American Film,* Feb. 1991.
The Matt Dillon Scrap Book. CHERYL MEAD. St. Martin's, 1984.

Dinkins, David Norman (1927–) In 1991, New York City's historic first African-American mayor found himself facing the same kinds of huge, extremely difficult economic and human problems that had confronted all recent mayors. If anything, his problems were worse, for the physical city continued to deteriorate; its bridges, tunnels, water supply system, utility lines, environmental support systems—in short, its whole physical infrastructure—were rapidly falling apart, while tax monies, federal support, and state support diminished. Dinkins in 1991 found himself spending most of his time in an unsuccessful effort to make New York City work: while cutting essential city jobs and vitally needed school, library, and other social service budgets, he was at the same time generating huge tax increases.

On January 2, Mayor Dinkins made a settlement with the city's unions and the next day announced that deficits would be far higher than expected in fiscal 1992, up from a projected \$1.6 billion to \$1.8–\$2.1 billion. By May, the 1992 deficit was being projected at \$3.5 billion; Dinkins then proposed a budget with \$1 billion in new taxes, 20,000 layoffs, and \$2 billion in spending cuts. Finally, on June 30, only hours before the 1991 fiscal year ended, a budget compromise was reached; the next day it was repudiated by many New York City politicians and union leaders.

Dinkins had taken office calling for racial and ethnic conciliation in a badly divided city, and 1991 saw limited progress in that direction. The Bensonhurst and Central Park Jogger cases ended, and peacefully, and few major confrontations occurred. The worst racial incident was in Crown Heights Brooklyn, where African-American anti-Jewish riots started after an automobile accident in which a car driven by a Hassidic Jew killed an African-American child. The rioters murdered a visiting Jewish student. Mayor Dinkins went to the scene, his presence and that of other community leaders and large numbers of police helping eventually to end the riots.

New Jersey-born Dinkins practiced law and politics in New York City from the mid-1950s. He was elected to the State Assembly in 1965 and served in several appointive posts, withdrawing from a deputy's mayor's position in 1973, at least partly because he had failed to file tax returns for several years. He was city clerk (1975–85), and then the elected borough president of Manhattan (1985–88). He became the historic first African-American mayor of New York City in 1989 after defeating incumbent mayor Edward Koch in the 1989 Democratic mayoral primary and Republican Rudolph Giuliani in the general election. Dinkins attended Howard University and Brooklyn Law School. He married Joyce Burrows in 1953; the couple have two children.

FURTHER READING

Changing New York City Politics. ASHER ARIAN et al. Routledge, 1991.

"Mayor Dinkins. . . ." SAM ROBERTS. *New York Times Magazine,* Apr. 7, 1991.

"Being there." MARIE BRENNER. *Vanity Fair,* Jan. 1991.

"Dinkins, David Norman." *Current Biography,* Mar. 1990.

Dixon Kelly, Sharon Pratt (1944–) Washington, D.C., mayor Dixon, who changed her name to Kelly after her December 1991 marriage to James R. Kelly III, is the first elected African-American woman mayor of a major city. She was sworn in on January 2, 1991, succeed-

ing former Washington, D.C., mayor Marion Barry, who had in 1990 been convicted on cocaine possession charges and had not run for a fourth mayoral term.

In November 1990, Kelly won a landslide 86 percent of the vote, running on a platform that included developing a model progressive educational system, more economic power for African-Americans and Hispanics, no new taxes, no cuts in vital services, and cuts in unnecessary and unproductive staff jobs. By the end of her first year in office, however, Kelly was spending much of her time dealing with the multiple problems faced by all other mayors of big American cities, governing in an extremely adverse economic climate. During her first few very promising months in office, she substantially cut the $300 million deficit she had inherited and won $100 million in new funding from a previously resistant Congress. But by year's end, she was encountering substantial difficulty in going forward. She had indeed cut some vital services, most notably drug-treatment programs. She had not yet come even close to renewing the top layer of city government, leaving approximately half of Barry's appointees in place and also leaving many key jobs unfilled. She had so far laid off far fewer than an anticipated 2,000 middle managers. Her uncertain and vital relationship with the D.C. City Council was at great risk. And she had even run into a minor but nationwide storm on April 9 by favoring disciplinary spanking by teachers in schools, with major educational organizations condemning her position. She later stated that it had been only her personal position and not a proposal that Washington schools adopt the previously prohibited practice.

A third-generation Washingtonian, Kelly graduated from Howard University Law School in 1968. Three years later, after bearing two children, she joined her father's general practice law firm. In 1972 she began teaching public interest law at the innovative Antioch Law School in Washington. From 1976 she worked at the Potomac Electric Power Company (PEPCO) as a corporate lawyer, becoming vice president for consumer affairs. While still at PEPCO, she was elected D.C.'s delegate to the Democratic National Committee in 1977, and in 1984 became the first Black and first woman to be treasurer of the Democratic National Committee. She was formerly married to Arrington L. Dixon, chairman of the D.C. City Council under then-mayor Marion Barry. They had two daughters.

FURTHER READING

"Trust me." HARRY JAFFE et al. *Washingtonian,* May 1991.
"Sharon Dixon. . . ." GLORIA BORGER. *U.S. News & World Report,* Dec. 31, 1990.

Doctorow, E. L. (Edgar Lawrence Doctorow, 1931–) Another of Doctorow's very popular and highly literate novels sought even wider audiences in its film adaptation during 1991. *Billy Bathgate* (1989), the Prohibition-era story of a teenager who witnesses the rise and fall of New York mobster Dutch Schultz, was a very successful and highly regarded best-seller, winning the 1990 National Book Critics' Circle Award and the PEN/Faulkner Award, but just missing out on the Pulitzer Prize. The film version was directed by Robert Benton, its screenplay written by Tom Stoppard, and starred Dustin Hoffman as Dutch Schultz. Over budget and behind schedule, the film ultimately opened in November 1991, and was not very well received by either audiences or reviewers, several critics feeling the screen version had lost the novel's resonance and richness of language.

New York-born Doctorow worked in publishing in the 1960s during the early stages of his writing career, and later held several university teaching positions. He became recognized as a major author in the 1970s, with his novels *The Book of Daniel* (1971) and *Ragtime* (1975). In the 1980s, he published *Loon Lake* (1980), *Lives of the Poets* (1984), and the American Book Award-winning *World's Fair* (1985). Doctorow's B.A. was from Kenyon College, in 1952. He married Helen Setzer in 1954; the couple have three children.

FURTHER READING

"The audacious lure. . . ." ALVIN SANOFF. *U.S. News & World Report,* Mar. 6, 1989.
Writers at Work: The Paris Review Interviews. GEORGE PLIMPTON, ed. Viking Penguin, 1988.

Dole, Elizabeth Hanford (1936–) Long one of the most highly visible women in American public life, Dole had spent almost two years as George Bush's almost invisible Secretary of Labor before in 1991 emerging once again, this time as president of the American Red Cross. Her first gesture after taking office on February 4 was to announce that she would forego her $200,000 annual salary for her first year in office.

As always the Red Cross was deeply involved in world relief efforts, during 1991 very notably in the wake of the Persian Gulf War; in mid-March Dole traveled with relief supplies worth $1 million to Kuwait City, where she met with Red Cross workers and the U.S. military. The American Red Cross continued to send relief workers to Kuwait, Iraq, and to Kurdish refugees in the aftermath of the war. In her capacity as American Red Cross president, Dole was active in major fund-raising activities throughout the year as well as in disaster and war relief, as in the Bangladesh cyclone and Ethiopian civil war relief campaigns. She also announced a complete overhaul of the American Red Cross blood program to "address the problem of AIDS in the blood supply," with efforts focused on new computer and laboratory testing systems, to eliminate continuing problems in the testing and distribution of blood.

North Carolina-born Dole is a long-term Washington "insider" who came to the capital as a Democrat in the late 1960s and stayed to serve in the administrations of four Republican presidents. She was Ronald Reagan's secretary of transportation (1983–87), and campaigned for her husband, Senate Minority Leader Robert Dole, in his unsuccessful run for the 1988 Republican presidential nomination. Afterward, she was seriously discussed as a possible vice presidential running mate for George Bush. In December 1988, she was named secretary of labor in the incoming Bush administration, serving until October 1990 when she accepted the presidency of the American Red Cross. Dole's B.A. was from Duke in 1958, her M.A. from Harvard in 1960, and her J.D. from Harvard in 1965. Elizabeth Hanford married Bob Dole in 1975; together they published *Doles: Unlimited Partners* (1988).

FURTHER READING

Elizabeth Dole: Public Servant. CAROLYN MULFORD. Enslow, 1992.

"Out to make a difference." ANNE GOWEN. *Insight,* Oct. 28, 1991.

"Dole on a roll. . . ." BILL HEWITT. *People,* June 24, 1991.

Dole, Bob (Robert Joseph Dole; 1923–) After voicing some early misgivings on quick U.S. military action in the Persian Gulf crisis that ultimately became the Persian Gulf War, Dole—the senior Senator from Kansas and Republican Senate minority leader—in January led the winning Senate fight to support the Gulf War resolution. In this, he was once again supporting his party and president, even after losing the ex-

traordinarily bitter 1988 presidential primary fight to George Bush. As he had done in 1990, however, he also continued to play an independent role, in January reacting to Soviet military moves in the Baltic states by urging a slowdown in rapprochement with the Soviet Union, and specifically a suspension of agricultural credits. Later, as the extent of the Soviet changes became apparent, he reversed that position, favoring granting the credits, and in July met with Boris Yeltsin in Washington. But on the key issues of the year, he led Senate Republicans in straightforward support of the administration.

Kansas-born Dole has spent three decades in Washington, starting with the first of his four congressional terms (1961–69). A leading Republican, he has served in the Senate since 1969, and has been Senate Republican leader since 1985. He was chairman of the Republican National Committee (1971–73), and his party's unsuccessful vice presidential candidate in 1976. He made unsuccessful runs for the Republican presidential nomination in 1980 and 1988. His B.A. and LL.B. were from Washburn Municipal University at Topeka. Robert Dole married American Red Cross president and former Secretary of Labor Elizabeth Hanford Dole in 1975; together they published *Doles: Unlimited Partners* (1988).

FURTHER READING

"The two Bobs." WILLIAM MCGURN. *National Review,* Dec. 2, 1991.

Bob Dole: American Political Phoenix. STANLEY G. HILTON. Contemporary, 1988.

Dos Santos, José Eduardo (1942–) Thirty years of revolution and civil war ended in Angola in May 1991. On May 1, the Angolan government and the National Union for the Total Independence of Angola (UNITA) signed an agreement to end their 16 years of civil war, with fighting to end by May 15. The agreement provided for multiparty free elections, to take place in 1992, and a merger of ground forces. Contrary to some expectations, the truce held. On May 25, Cuban forces completed their pullout from Angola. On May 31, Angolan president Dos Santos, the chairman of the Popular Movement for the Liberation of Angola (MPLA), and UNITA leader Jonas Savimbi formally signed the peace agreement, which had been achieved with the help of the Soviet Union and the United States, formerly key suppliers and sponsors of the two sides in the long civil war.

For Dos Santos, it was the end of two consecutive wars that had occupied his entire adult life. He had been an activist in the MPLA since he joined it in 1961. He went into exile that year and became president of the MPLA youth organization. From 1963 to 1970, he was educated in the Soviet Union, as a petroleum engineer and telecommunications specialist, the latter skills being used when he returned to the Angolan war of independence in 1970. He became a member of the MPLA central committee in 1974, was foreign minister of the new Soviet-backed MPLA Angolan government in 1975, and held several cabinet-level posts during the next four years, as the civil war continued. After the death of President Augustinho Neto, Dos Santos became Angolan president, commander in chief, and head of the MPLA.

FURTHER READING

"Angola to pursue. . . ." *Washington Post,* June 30, 1987.

Douglas, John: See **Lebanon Hostages**

Douglas, Kirk (Issur Danielovich Demsky, 1916–) March 1991 was a very good month for Douglas. After surviving a February helicopter-plane crash that killed two men and injured two others, including the pilot of the helicopter in which he was traveling, Douglas was honored with the American Film Institute's 19th annual Life Achievement Award; the tribute aired on CBS in May. In late March, Douglas hosted a "reunion reception" for cast members of the 1960 film *Spartacus,* including Tony Curtis and Jean Simmons; the film—directed by Stanley Kubrick, but produced by and starring Douglas—was re-released theatrically later in the spring, not only restored but also containing five minutes of previously censored material. Also in March, Douglas was honored with the Writer's Guild of America's Robert Meltzer Award, recognizing his role in helping to end blacklisting in Hollywood—which included his insistence that the then-blacklisted Dalton Trumbo receive on-screen credit for *Spartacus.* While Douglas was still in the hospital in February, he and his wife Anne were given the American Friends of the Hebrew University's Scopus Award for their lifelong contributions to the arts and for their humanitarian work. The couple contributed $500,000 to the building campaign of the Los Angeles Mission.

In August, Douglas appeared with his son Eric Douglas as a father and son in the final show of the HBO series "Tales from the Crypt," also starring Dan Aykroyd. On the big screen, he also appeared in John Landis's *Oscar,* as the father of Angelo (Snaps) Provolone (Sylvester Stallone), with a notably vigorous and comic deathbed scene. Among his forthcoming projects was an environmentally oriented film, *Welcome to Veraz,* directed by Xavier Castano and shot in southern France in late 1990, also starring Gérard Depardieu; and *The Secret* for CBS, in which he plays the grandfather of a nine-year-old boy with dyslexia. With his writer's hat on, Douglas spent much of 1991 finishing his second novel and preparing to write a third.

Born "a ragman's son" in Amsterdam, New York, Douglas, the father of actor-producer Michael Douglas, has been a Hollywood star for over four decades, ever since his role in *Champion* (1949). In the peak years of his film career, he starred in *The Glass Menagerie* (1950), as Van Gogh in *Lust for Life* (1956), and in such diverse films as *Gunfight at the O.K. Corral* (1957), *Paths of Glory* (1959), *Lonely Are the Brave* (1962), and *Seven Days in May* (1964), the last three produced by his own production company, Bryna. He also wrote the bestselling autobiography *The Ragman's Son* (1988) and the novel *Dance with the Devil* (1990). Douglas's B.A. was from St. Lawrence University, in 1938. He studied at the American Academy of Dramatic Arts, from 1939 to 1941. After an earlier marriage to Diana Dill, he married Anne Buydens in 1954; he has four children.

FURTHER READING

Films of Kirk Douglas. Tony Thomas. Carol, 1991.
"A man cut for the screen. . . ." Frank Thompson. *American Film,* Mar. 1991.

Douglas, Michael (Michael Kirk Douglas, 1944–) Actor-producer Douglas was in the midst of a hot controversy in 1991. The San Francisco production of the film *Basic Instinct* was the target of numerous demonstrations, protests, and vandalism from gay and lesbian activists, who criticized the psychological thriller for negative depiction of lesbians. In the film, scheduled for 1992 release, Douglas plays an unstable, drug-addicted cop who falls in love with one of several lesbian murder suspects, a bisexual female novelist. In May, during the shooting, Douglas dropped out as master of ceremonies for an AIDS (acquired immune deficiency syndrome) fund-raising auction, fearing that protests would disrupt the project; Douglas personally contributed $5,000 and offered for auction lunch for four on the *Basic Instinct* movie set.

The War of the Roses (1989), starring Douglas and Kathleen Turner, was released on laser disc in 1991, with lively commentary by director Danny DeVito and 30 minutes' worth of deliciously vicious scenes cut from the theatrical version. Scheduled for early 1992 release was David Seltzer's *Shining Through,* a romantic spy thriller set in Berlin and London during World War II, with Melanie Griffith, Liam Neeson, John Gielgud, and Joely Richardson.

Son of actor Kirk Douglas, Michael Douglas first became a star in the television series "The Streets of San Francisco" (1972–75), paired with Karl Malden. Moving into films, he produced the Oscar-winning *One Flew over the Cuckoo's Nest* (1975) and the notable nuclear-accident film *The China Syndrome* (1979). He produced and starred in such films as *Romancing the Stone* (1984), *Jewel of the Nile* (1985), and *The War of the Roses* (1989), all three with Kathleen Turner, and also starred in such films as *A Chorus Line* (1985), *Fatal Attraction* (1987), *Wall Street* (1987; he won a Best Actor Oscar and Golden Globe Award), and *Black Rain* (1989). Douglas's B.A. was from the University of California, in 1967. He married Diandra Mornell Luker in 1977; the couple have one son.

FURTHER READING

"Business as usual." David Thomson. *Film Comment,* Jan.–Feb., 1990.
"A prince. . . ." Linda Blandford. *New York Times Magazine,* Dec. 3, 1989.

Dreyfuss, Richard (Richard Stephan Dreyfuss, 1947–) Veteran actor Dreyfuss continued to display his very wide range during 1991. In Lasse Hallstrom's film *Once Around,* he played the rich "older man" Sam Sharpe, who falls in love with Holly Hunter, then proceeds to disrupt her Italian-American family. In Frank Oz's *What About Bob?* he played psychiatrist Leo Marvin, followed to his summer retreat by a new patient, Bob Wiley (Bill Murray), who to Dreyfuss's dismay becomes part of the family and ruins his holiday. In February, Dreyfuss debuted as the Player King (replacing Sean Connery, who dropped out with throat problems), leader of a troupe of traveling players, in Tom Stoppard's film version of his 1965 play *Rosencrantz and Guildenstern Are Dead,* with Gary Oldman and

Tim Roth, respectively, playing the characters from Shakespeare's *Hamlet.*

In a very different vein, Dreyfuss co-produced and starred in the HBO telefilm *Prisoner of Honor,* playing not Alfred Dreyfus (believed to have been a distant relation) but Colonel George Picquart, a 19th-century anti-Semite who nevertheless risks his reputation to demand justice after discovering that the French army has used Dreyfus as a Jewish scapegoat in a treason trial. Dreyfuss also appeared in Sherry Gershon Gottlieb's oral history of Vietnam War draft resisters, *Hell No, We Won't Go!* (1991), and talked about applying for conscientious objector status. In 1992 it was on to Broadway opposite Gene Hackman and Glenn Close in *Death and the Maiden.*

New York-born Dreyfuss became a leading film star of the 1970s, with his roles in *American Graffiti* (1973), *The Apprenticeship of Duddy Kravitz* (1974), *Jaws* (1975), *Close Encounters of the Third Kind* (1977), and *The Goodbye Girl* (1977), for which he won a Best Actor Oscar. He went on to star in such films as *Whose Life Is It Anyway?* (1981), *Down and Out in Beverly Hills* (1986), *Tin Men* (1987), and *Always* (1989). Dreyfuss attended San Fernando Valley State College (1965–67). He is married to Jeramie Rain; the couple have three children.

FURTHER READING

"Against all odds." SUSAN SCHINDEHETTE. *People,* Mar. 4, 1991.
"Richard Dreyfuss. . . ." DIGBY DIEHL. *Cosmopolitan,* Nov. 1990.

Ducroux, Etienne (1899–1991) One of the greatest 20th-century teachers of mime, Ducroux was also an accomplished actor and a leading mime of the French theater. He began his career in 1923, as an actor in Paris, in Jacques Copeau's experimental company and went on to play in 65 plays and 35 films, including Marcel Carné's classic *Les Enfants du Paradis* (*Children of Paradise,* 1945). He began to work in mime in 1928, opened his centrally important school of mime in Paris in 1940, and worked wholly in mime from 1946. Ducroux taught three generations of mimes, including Marcel Marceau and hundreds of others; he also taught many actors the principles of mime, at his school and as a guest teacher in theater schools all over the world. He was survived by his wife, Suzanne, and a son. (d. Paris, France; March 12, 1991)

FURTHER READING

Obituary. *New York Times,* Mar. 21, 1991.

Duke, David Ernest (1950–) On November 18, 1991, Louisiana voters resoundingly defeated ex-Ku Klux Klan leader and ex-Nazi David Duke, running for governor as a Republican, electing the Democratic candidate, former governor Edwin W. Edwards, by a margin of 22 percent, with 61 percent for Edwards and 39 percent for Duke. Duke had insisted during his campaign that he had changed and that he no longer held his racist and anti-Semitic views, but a wide range of voters did not believe him. Many also feared for their economic futures if Duke were to be elected, as business and convention leaders warned that their state would be shunned by business groups and vacationers if Duke were to be elected.

Duke had attracted national interest with his upset second-place win in the October 19, 1991, Louisiana gubernatorial contest. Edwards and Duke then went into the November 16 run-off election. Duke, who ran an only very slightly veiled racist campaign, full of code words attacking African-Americans, was publicly disowned by the Republican Party, and specifically by President George Bush, who stated during the campaign that if he lived in Louisiana he would vote for the Democrat Edwards. On December 4, Duke announced that he would run for the Republican presidential nomination in the 1992 elections.

Duke was associated with the Ku Klux Klan from his youth; he joined the Klan while still in high school and was active in it throughout the late 1960s and 1970s, becoming Grand Wizard of the Louisiana Knights of the Ku Klux Klan after the 1975 murder of his Klan leader, James Lindsay. He was also openly associated with American Nazi movements, becoming a follower of Nazi leader George Lincoln Rockwell while a college student in the late 1960s.

In the late 1970s, he moved from the raw, open bigotry that had until then characterized his career toward the more sanitized racism that marked his later political development, in an attempt to appeal to the White middle class. He continued that approach after he had officially left the Klan in 1979, then forming the National Association for the Advancement of White People. He was elected as a Republican to the Louisiana legislature in 1989 although he had been denounced by the Republican Party. In 1990, he was defeated in a bid for the United States Senate by three-time Democratic Senator J. Bennett Johnston. Duke attended Louisiana State University. He was once married and has two children.

FURTHER READING

"Deconstructing Duke. . . ." JOE KLEIN. *New York,* Dec. 2, 1991.
"The hazards of Duke. . . ." JOHN MAGINNIS. *New Republic,* Nov. 25, 1991.
"The real. . . ." BILL TURQUE. *Newsweek,* Nov. 18, 1991.
"An ex-Klansman. . . ." BILL HEWITT et al. *People,* Nov. 18, 1991.
"Hate with a pretty face." JULIA REED. *Vogue,* Nov. 1991.
David Duke: Evolution of a Klansman. MICHAEL ZATARAIN. Pelican, 1990.

Dunaway, Faye (Dorothy Faye Dunaway, 1941–) In TBS's five-part, ten-hour epic miniseries *Voice of the Planet,* Dunaway was the disembodied voice of Gaia, the mother goddess of the Earth, who leads author-ecologist William Planter (played by William Shatner) on a tour through time and space, from the first appearance of life on Earth to today's toxic pollution and extinctions around the world, in what some have described as a love story between the two: Nature and humankind. Then—as a very different kind of mother—Dunaway appeared as the fairy godmother and manager of the rock-hero (Johnny Depp) in Tom Petty's new video *Into the Great White Open.*

Among her forthcoming projects was Lina Wertmuller's *Crystal or Ash, Fire or Wind, as Long as It's Love,* in which she vies with Nastassia Kinski for Rutger Hauer, unaware that he has AIDS (acquired immune deficiency syndrome); *The Arrowtooth Waltz,* directed and scripted by Emir Kusturica; and Bruce Wagner's *Force Majeure,* directed and scripted by Wagner from his own novel about Hollywood studios, agents, and aspiring actors.

Florida-born Dunaway became a film star in 1967, with her portrayal of 1930s midwestern outlaw Bonnie Parker in *Bonnie and Clyde.* She went on to become a leading Hollywood star, in such films as *The Thomas Crown Affair* (1968), *Chinatown* (1974), and *Network* (1976), for which she won a Best Actress Oscar. Her credits include *Mommie Dearest* (1981), in which she played Joan Crawford, a role she describes as "career suicide," *Barfly* (1987), and *The Handmaid's Tale* (1990). On television, she appeared as revivalist preacher Aimee Semple McPherson in *The Disappearance of Aimee* (1976) and in the title role of *Evita Peron* (1982); in 1990 she produced and starred in the cable telefilms *Cold Sassy Tree* and *Silhouette.* Dunaway attended Boston University. She was formerly married to Peter Wolf, is married to Terrence O'Neill, and has one child.

FURTHER READING

"Faye Dunaway." TINA JOHNSON. *Harper's Bazaar,* Sep. 1989.
Faye Dunaway. ALLAN HUNTER. St. Martin's, 1986.

Dunnock, Mildred (1900–91) Baltimore-born Dunnock made her Broadway debut in *Life Begins* (1932), scored her first major theater triumph as Welsh schoolteacher Miss Ronberry in Emlyn Williams's *The Corn Is Green* (1940), and went on to play in scores of plays and films for the next five decades. She is best known for her creation of Linda Loman, opposite Lee J. Cobb as Willy Loman in Arthur Miller's *Death of a Salesman* (1945), and won an Academy Award nomination for the role in the 1951 film, opposite Fredric March. She joined Cobb again in the 1966 television version. She won a second Academy Award nomination for *Baby Doll* (1956). On Broadway, Dunnock also created such roles as Lavinia in Lillian Hellman's *Another Part of the Forest* (1946) and Big Mama in Tennessee Williams's *Cat on a Hot Tin Roof* (1955). From 1950, she appeared in a wide range of television roles. She was survived by her husband, Keith Urmy, and a daughter, Linda McGuire. (d. Martha's Vineyard, Massachusetts; July 5, 1991)

FURTHER READING

Obituary. *Current Biography,* Sep. 1991.
Obituary. *Variety,* July 15, 1991.

Obituary. *The Times* (of London), July 11, 1991.
Obituary. *New York Times,* June 22, 1991.

Durning, Charles (1923–) Veteran character actor Durning won a 1991 Golden Globe award as best supporting actor in a series, miniseries, or motion picture for his role as Rose Fitzgerald Kennedy's father, "Honey Fitz," in television's *The Kennedys of Massachusetts* (1990). On television, he also appeared as a regular during the 1991–92 season in the television series "Evening Shade" in a cast led by Burt Reynolds, Elizabeth Ashley, and Ossie Davis. On moving picture theater screens, and later in the year on home screens, he appeared as the Chicago police lieutenant in *V. I. Warshawski* in a cast led by Kathleen Turner and Jay O. Sanders. The wide-ranging actor was also the voice of Grandpa Yook in TNT's television version of Dr. Seuss' *The Butter Battle Book.* Throughout his career a leading stage player, Durning in 1991 portrayed Norman Thayer, Jr., in *On Golden Pond* at the Long Beach Civic Light Opera's Center Theater. He also became artistic director of the newly formed Second Avenue Productions.

Durning has been a strong character actor for over 30 years, creating a wide range of notable roles on stage, screen, and television. In the theater he memorably played the governor in *Best Little Whorehouse in Texas* and won a Best Featured Actor in a Play Tony for his role as Big Daddy in the 1990 Broadway revival of Tennessee Williams's *Cat on a Hot Tin Roof.* On film, he was unforgettable as Jessica Lange's father and Dustin Hoffman's would-be suitor in *Tootsie* (1982). Among his other films are *The Sting* (1973), *Mass Appeal* (1984), *The Rosary Murders* (1987), *Far North* (1988), and *Dick Tracy* (1990). Durning married Mary Ann Amelio in 1974. He was born in Highland Falls, New York, and attended New York University and Columbia.

FURTHER READING

"Playing a fiery big daddy. . . ." Toby Kahn. *People,* June 4, 1990.

Durocher, Leo (1905–91) Massachusetts-born Durocher became a national figure during almost 50 years in baseball, as a player, coach, manager, and commentator. His "Nice guys finish last" comment was widely and by some very approvingly quoted for decades, although modern American sports attitudes have changed and the phrase is no longer very widely or at least openly used. Known as "Lippy" or "Leo the Lip," Durocher joined the New York Yankees as a shortstop in 1928 and played with the Cincinnati Reds from 1930 to 1933 and the St. Louis Cardinals from 1933 to 1938. He joined the Brooklyn Dodgers in 1938 and became the team's manager in 1939, soon becoming a national celebrity as the tough-talking, umpire-baiting, always in trouble figure who turned around the previously hapless Dodgers. His team won the National League pennant in 1941, to be beaten by the Yankees in the World Series. He was suspended from baseball in 1947, largely for having contacts with known gamblers, though also for many headline-getting minor infractions of baseball rules. He managed the New York Giants from 1948 to 1955, his teams winning pennants in 1951 and 1954, and the 1954 World Series. He worked as a baseball commentator and as an entertainer in the late 1950s, was a coach with the Houston Astros from 1961 to 1964, managed the Chicago Cubs from 1966 to 1972 and the Astros briefly from 1972 to 1973, then retiring. His autobiography was titled *Nice Guys Finish Last* (1975) (d. Palm Springs, California; October 7, 1991)

FURTHER READING

"One for the hall. . . ." Bob Verdi. *Sporting News,* Oct. 21, 1991.
"Lip service. . . ." Robert W. Creamer. *Sports Illustrated,* Oct. 21, 1991.
Obituary. *New York Times,* Oct. 8, 1991.

Duvall, Robert (1931–) The celebrated actor continued to play major character leads in 1991, in some of the year's most artistically interesting new and forthcoming films. One such was *Stalin,* which began shooting in Moscow in the fall of 1991, after the aborted right-wing August coup had for a time threatened to destroy the project. In his HBO film, Duvall stars as Stalin opposite Maximilian Schell as Lenin; one of the Moscow locations was Lenin's original office, now a museum inside the former Supreme Soviet building. Another Duvall project was Luis Penzo's forthcoming film *The Plague*, based on the Albert Camus novel, with a cast that also includes William Hurt, Raul Julia, and Victoria Tennant.

In 1991 Duvall starred in the very well received Martha Coolidge film *Rambling Rose*; Duvall is the father of the Southern middle-class family that takes in a highly sexually charged, straightforward, poor girl, played by Laura Dern, in a cast that includes Diane Ladd and Lukas Haas. He also starred opposite James Earl Jones as planter Soll Gautier in Peter Masterson's film *Convicts,* adapted by Horton Foote from his own play, set on a sugar plantation staffed by convict labor on the Texas Gulf Coast, on Christmas Eve 1902.

San Diego-born Duvall was recognized as a powerful supporting actor in such films as *To Kill a Mockingbird* (1963), *True Grit* (1969), *M*A*S*H* (1970), the first two *Godfather* films (1972, 1974), *Network* (1976), and *Apocalypse Now* (1979). He went on to win a Best Actor Oscar for his lead in *Tender Mercies* (1983) while continuing to play strong supporting roles and sometimes leads in such films as *Colors* (1988), *Days of Thunder* (1990), and *The Handmaid's Tale* (1990). On television, he played Dwight D. Eisenhower in the miniseries *Ike* (1979). A graduate of Principia College, Duvall is married to Gail Youngs.

FURTHER READING

"Robert Duvall." Laura Dern. *Interview,* Oct. 1991.
Robert Duvall: Hollywood Maverick. Judith Slawson. St. Martin's, 1985.

Dyer-Bennett, Richard (1913–91) The celebrated 20th-century "minstrel," as Dyer-Bennett preferred to be called, was a concert folk singer and composer whose works and presence made a major contribution to recognition of the folk song as part of Anglo-American classical music. He was a scholar of folk music, as well, who rediscovered folk songs going back to early Anglo-Saxon, Scandinavian, and Norman roots, which he introduced into the modern folk repertoire. He was a folk performer in New York cabaret in the early 1940s, made a major breakthrough in solo concert at Town Hall in 1944, and under the aegis of Sol Hurok toured widely for three decades, becoming a very popular broadcasting and recording artist. He also wrote in his field and taught at the Stony Brook campus of the State University of New York. He was survived by his wife, Malvene Ipcar, four daughters, a sister, and a brother. (d. Monterey, Massachusetts; December 15, 1991)

FURTHER READING

Obituary. *New York Times,* Dec. 16, 1991.

Dylan, Bob (Robert Alan Zimmerman, 1941–) Without doing any new recording at all, Dylan became one of the most talked about recording artists of 1991. It happened with the release by Columbia of Dylan's *The Bootleg Series, Volumes 1–3 (Rare and Unreleased) 1961–91,* a three-CD boxed set carrying 58 Dylan tracks, approximately a quarter of which had never before been released on records. Some, like "Farewell, Angelina," recorded by Joan Baez, had long been sung by other performers, while other tracks were different versions of familiar Dylan songs. During 1991, Dylan provided a memorable performance moment at the 33rd Grammy awards presentation, with his rendition of "Masters of War" on the February 20 telecast. He also received a Lifetime Achievement Grammy. A second memorable performance was "This Old Man," recorded on the benefit album *For Our Children* for the Pediatric AIDS Foundation. The year of Dylan's 50th birthday also saw a spate of new biographies and reference books about him.

Duluth-born Dylan was one of the leading counterculture figures of the early 1960s, an enormously popular folk-rock singer and composer known to millions for many of his own songs, such as "The Times They are A-Changin" (1963) and "Blowin' in the Wind" (1963). Later in the 1960s and through the 1970s and 1980s, he was much more a rock than a folk-rock musician; although he continued to be a very popular figure in concert and on records, his impact was greatest in the early years when he burst on the scene as a 1960s emblem of protest. Dylan made a substantial comeback on records and in performance, starting in 1989, with his album *Oh Mercy* and a world tour. In 1990, his new album *Under the Red Sky,* was very well received, as was his second *Traveling Wilburys* album, made with George Harrison, Tom Petty, Jeff Lynne, and Roy Orbison. Dylan attended the University of Minnesota in 1960.

FURTHER READING

"Dylan, Bob." *Current Biography,* Oct. 1991.

"Bob Dylan. . . ." Tom Piazza. *New York Times Book Review,* May 26, 1991.

"Forever young. . . ." Marc Eliot. *California,* June 1991.

"Subterranean half-century blues." *Economist,* May 25, 1991.

Bob Dylan Behind the Shades. Clinton Heylin. Summit, 1991.

Wanted Man: In Search of Bob Dylan. John Bauldie, ed. Carol, 1991.

Dylan Companion: A Collection of Essential Writing About Bob Dylan. Elizabeth Thomson. Delacorte, 1991.

Bob Dylan: Portraits from the Singer's Early Years. Daniel Kramer. Carol, 1991.

Bob Dylan, Performing Artist: The Early Years 1960–1973. Paul Williams. Underwood-Miller, 1991.

Positively Bob Dylan: A Thirty-Year Discography, Concert and Recording Session Guide, 1960–1989. Michael Krogsgaard. Popular Culture, 1991.

Bob Dylan: American Poet and Singer: An Annotated Bibliography and Study Guide of Sources and Background Materials, 1961–1991. Richard D. Wissolik et al., eds. Eadmer, 1991.

Dylan: A Biography. Bob Spitz. McGraw-Hill, 1989.

Death of a Rebel. Marc Eliot. Watts, 1989.

E

Eastwood, Clint (1930–) Eastwood's major art film, *White Hunter, Black Heart,* in which he played an obsessive John Huston-like director on location in Africa, was not very well received, critically or commercially, on its 1990 debut, and the lack of audience interest carried over to its 1991 video rentals. But his more familiar police movie, *The Rookie,* co-starring Charlie Sheen, did very well on home screens, although it too had audience problems in theatrical release. Forthcoming was another familiar kind of Eastwood film, this one the story of William Munny, an outlaw who has gone straight and who briefly becomes a bounty hunter to pursue a murderer who has murdered a prostitute. Morgan Freeman co-stars as Eastwood's gunman buddy, Gene Hackman as a sheriff.

San Francisco-born Eastwood was a star in television as the lead in the western series "Rawhide" (1958–65). He pursued the same western themes in the Italian-made Sergio Leone "spaghetti westerns" that made him a worldwide star, the first being *A Fistful of Dollars* (1967). He then went on to become one of the most durable of all international action film stars, and beginning with *Play Misty For Me* (1971), directed, produced, and starred in many of his films. These included *Honkytonk Man* (1982), *Bird* (1988; about jazz great Charlie Parker), *White Hunter, Black Heart* (1990), and *The Rookie* (1990). Eastwood attended Los Angeles City College. He is divorced and has one son, Kyle, who appeared in *Honkytonk Man.*

FURTHER READING

Clint Eastwood: Malpaso. Fuensanta Plaza. Ex Libris (CA), 1991.
"The man who would be Huston." Graham Fuller. *Interview,* Oct. 1990.
"Clint Eastwood. . . ." *Film Quarterly,* Spring 1989.
"Eastwood, Clint." *Current Biography,* Mar. 1989.
The Films of Clint Eastwood. Boris Zmijewsky and Lee Pfeiffer. Carol, 1988.
Clint Eastwood. Jeffrey Ryder. Dell, 1987.
Clint Eastwood. Francois Guerif. St. Martin's, 1986.

Edberg, Stefan (1966–) Quiet man Edberg pulled his game together to become world champion, being named top male tennis player of 1991 by the International Tennis Federation. He struggled early in the year and won only one of the four Grand Slam tournaments, but it was one that had eluded him in the past: the U.S. Open, where in 1990 he had ignominiously exited in the first round. In 1991, he overcame his past "U.S. Open phobia" to defeat Jim Courier (to whom he had earlier lost in the quarterfinals at the French Open, and who had himself unseated the crowd's favorite, Jimmy Connors), doing so in straight sets. It was Edberg's fifth Grand Slam victory, and pushed him to number one in the world rankings, from the number two spot. In 1991, Edberg also won five other tournaments, more than any other tennis player on the men's side. An unusual situation occurred at Wimbledon, where he was defending champion:

Edberg was eliminated in the semifinals by eventual winner Michael Stich without ever having his service broken when, after winning the first set, he lost three straight tiebreakers.

Swedish-born Edberg emerged as a winner with the Junior Grand Slam 1983 and went on to a series of victories in tournaments around the world, his major wins including the Australian Open in 1986 and 1987, and Wimbledon in 1988 and 1990. Noted for his relentless full-court pressure, and strong volley, overhead smash, and backhand, Edberg has also had great success as a doubles player, teamed with Anders Jarryd, winning the Masters and the French Open in 1986, and the Australian and U.S. Opens in 1987. Engaged to Annette Olson, he makes his home in London.

FURTHER READING

"A stand-up guy. . . ." Franz Lidz. *Sports Illustrated,* June 24, 1991.

"Stefan Edberg. . . ." Kim Cunningham. *World Tennis,* Oct. 1988.

Elizabeth II (Elizabeth Alexandra Mary, 1926–) "As a nation we are rightly proud of our armed forces. That pride has been fully justified by their conduct in the Gulf War so far. As they, with our allies, face a fresh and yet sterner challenge, I hope that we can unite in praying that their success will be as swift as it is certain, and that it may be achieved with as small a cost to human life and suffering as possible. Then may the true reward of their courage be granted a just and lasting peace." So spoke Elizabeth II, Queen of the United Kingdom of Great Britain and Northern Ireland, in her February 24, 1991, wartime address to the nation after the start of the Allied ground offensive in the Persian Gulf War; it was the first such wartime address in her 39-year-reign. In war, her largely ceremonial role becomes historically resonant, as did that of her father, King George VI, during World War II.

Beyond that, her 65th year was indeed a ceremonial one, some of the most visible ceremonies occurring during her visit to the United States in May 1991. These included an address to Congress, the knighting of General H. Norman Schwarzkopf, and visits to Florida, Texas, and Kentucky. Affirming Britain's continuing world role, she received Group of Seven leaders George Bush, François Mitterrand, Giulio Andreotti, Toshiki Kaifu, John Major, Helmut Kohl, and Brian Mulroney at Buckingham Palace in mid-July. One out-of-the-ordinary visit was to Northern Ireland on July 31; it was her first such visit since 1977.

Elizabeth II is the daughter of George VI and Elizabeth Angela Marguerite, the Queen Mother. She succeeded her father to the throne in 1952, also becoming head of the British Commonwealth. She married Philip Mountbatten in 1947, and is the mother of Prince Charles (1948–), Princess Anne (1956–), Prince Andrew (1960–), and Prince Edward (1964–).

FURTHER READING

"Windsor knot. . . ." Christopher Hitchens. *New York Times Magazine,* May 12, 1991.

"The princess bride. . . ." Roland Flamini. *People,* May 20, 1991.

Sovereign: Elizabeth II and the Windsor Dynasty. Roland Flamini. Delacorte, 1991.

Royal Sisters. Anne Edwards. Morrow, 1990.

The Queen: The Life of Elizabeth II. Elizabeth Longford. Ballantine, 1984.

Emerson, Thomas Irwin (1907–91) New Jersey-born Emerson, a leading constitutional lawyer, was in private practice in the early 1930s, most notably as part of the defense team in a key civil rights case, that of the "Scottsboro Boys." He was a federal government lawyer from

1933 to 1945, holding major positions with the National Recovery Administration (1933–34), National Labor Relations Board (1934–36), Social Security Board (1936–37), and several other federal agencies and departments, including the Office of Price Administration, Office of Economic Stabilization, and Office of War Mobilization and Reconversion during and just after World War II. In 1946, he became a professor at Yale Law School where he spent the rest of his career. Emerson became one of the most notable civil liberties lawyers of the century and was a prolific author on free expression and other Bill of Rights matters. In 1965, he successfully argued *Griswold v. Connecticut* before the Supreme Court; the landmark case overturned a state law banning the sale of contraceptives and was part of the line of cases that included *Roe v. Wade.* He was also president of the National Lawyers Guild in 1950–51; his *Government Power and Social Change: Memoirs of a New Deal Lawyer* appeared in 1990. He was survived by his wife, formerly Ruth Calvin, a daughter, three sons, and three brothers. (d. New Haven, Connecticut; June 19, 1991)

FURTHER READING

Obituary. *Nation,* July 29, 1991.
Obituary. *New York Times,* June 22, 1991.

Engle, Paul Hamilton (1908–91) Iowa-born Engle, a poet, writer, editor, and teacher, graduated from the University of Iowa in 1932 and returned in 1937 to teach English at the university after postgraduate work at Columbia and as a Rhodes Scholar at Oxford. *American Child,* the first of his many poetry collections, was published in 1945. His work also included many reviews and essays. Continuing to teach at Iowa, he was best known by far as co-founder in 1967 of the university's International Writing Program, which attracted many distinguished writers to its faculty and more than 800 writers. Co-director of the program was the Chinese writer Hualing Nieh, who became his second wife. He and his wife retired in 1987, though continuing to write. He was survived by his wife, two daughters, two stepdaughters, and a sister. (d. Chicago, Illinois; March 22, 1991)

FURTHER READING

Obituary. *Current Biography,* May 1991.
Obituary. *New York Times,* Mar. 24, 1991.

Ewing, Patrick (1962–) Journalists called it "L'Affaire Patrick." Ewing's 10-year contract with basketball's New York Knicks contained a clause that allowed Ewing to become an unrestricted free agent in 1992 after his sixth season if he was not among the four highest-paid players in the National Basketball Association (NBA) on June 1, 1991. He claimed that he was not and was a free agent; the Knicks claimed that he was, and under contract to them. The dispute went to arbitration in July, and the arbitrator ruled that Ewing was indeed one of the four highest-paid basketball players. But the Knicks renegotiated Ewing's contract anyway, and in November he became the highest-paid player in all team sports, with a new average annual salary of $5.5 million on a contract extension amounting to $33 million over the next six years. Ewing had turned down the same offer in May in his bid to become a free agent. Responding to Ewing's underlying desire to be on a winning team, the Knicks also brought in championship coach Pat Riley and overhauled the rest of the team. Early results were favorable. By January, midway through the 1991–92 season, the Knicks were leading their division. In August 1991, Ewing accepted an invitation to play on the U.S. basketball team at the 1992 Olympics, the first to allow NBA players; when still in college, he had played on the gold-medal-winning 1984 U.S. Olympic team. He was the starting center on the 1991 Eastern NBA All-Star team.

Jamaica-born Ewing is one of the leading centers in modern basketball, a fact that became apparent while he was still a college player at Georgetown University. After his 1985 graduation from Georgetown, Ewing joined the New York Knicks, beginning a career that would in the next six years take him to six all-star games (1986, 1987, 1988, 1989, 1990, and 1991, in the latter two as starting center) and international celebrity, even without a longed-for national championship. Ewing is married and has one child.

FURTHER READING

"Ewing, Patrick." *Current Biography,* May 1991.
"Patrick Ewing." SPIKE LEE. *Interview,* May 1990.
Patrick Ewing. MATTHEW NEWMAN. Macmillan, 1986.

Eyen, Tom (1941–91) Ohio-born Eyen studied acting in New York City and worked as a press agent while beginning his playwrighting career. During the 1960s, he was a prolific playwright; most of his 35 plays of the period were produced off-off-Broadway in such experimental theatres as La Mama and by his own Theater of the Eye company. They had considerable shock value in their time for their nudity and language, although the main body of his work satirized exploitation works aimed at achieving just that sort of impact. His best-known work and first major success was *The Dirtiest Show in Town* (1970). His greatest success came with the Broadway musical *Dreamgirls* (1981); he wrote the book and lyrics, winning a Tony for the book and sharing a Grammy for the best cast album. Eyen also wrote for television. He was survived by his mother, two sisters, and three brothers. (d. Palm Beach, Florida; May 26, 1991)

FURTHER READING

Obituary. *Variety,* June 3, 1991.
Obituary. *New York Times,* May 28, 1991.

F

Fahd, Ibn Abd al-Aziz Al Saud (1923–) With the advent of the Persian Gulf crisis, the Saudi Arabian king generated a series of sharp policy changes, greatly affecting Saudi relations with its neighbors and the balance of forces in the Middle East. He had previously tried to take a peacemaker's role, but the August 2, 1990, Iraqi invasion of Kuwait changed everything; now he directly faced powerful Iraqi forces, with Saudi forces wholly inadequate to check an invasion.

Fahd invited American troops into Saudi Arabia on August 6. From then on he actively participated in the Allied buildup and the Persian Gulf War, with Saudi air and ground forces fully engaged in the air war and then in operation Desert Storm. With his Gulf allies, Fahd cut off aid to the Palestine Liberation Organization (PLO) and Jordan, identifying both as Iraqi allies. Fahd also announced postwar plans to take a far greater role in regional affairs, to continue the U.S. alliance, and to modernize and greatly expand Saudi armed forces.

At home, Fahd resisted growing calls for a softening of his very conservative, authoritarian Islamic rule, with liberals in December 1990 and conservatives in May 1991 calling for different sets of reforms. In mid-November 1991 he promised to set up a consultative body and introduce written laws, an assurance that was met with general skepticism, as similar past promises had not resulted in significant changes. International organizations continued to criticize his government for human rights violations.

Riyadh-born Fahd is the son of King Abdul al-Aziz Ibn Saud. He succeeded to the throne in 1982 after the death of his half-brother Khalid. He had previously been a member of the Saudi delegation to the San Francisco founding meeting of the United Nations in 1945, education minister in 1953, interior minister (1962–75), and a deputy prime minister (1962–82); he became prime minister as well as king in 1982. He had been named crown prince in 1975 after the assassination of King Faisal.

FURTHER READING

"King Fahd's big gamble. . . ." Peter Theroux. *Vanity Fair,* Apr. 1991.
"Who's sitting pretty. . . ." *Business Week,* Mar. 11, 1991.
"Lifting the veil. . . ." Lisa Beyer. *Time,* Sep. 24, 1990.
"An exquisite balancing act. . . ." George J. Church. *Time,* Sep. 24, 1990.
King Fahd and Saudi Arabia's Great Evolution. Nasser I. Rashid and Esber I. Shaheen. International Institute of Technology, 1987.

Fairbank, John King (1907–91) South Dakota-born Fairbank graduated from Harvard University in 1929 and began his lifelong association with East Asia as an Oxford University Rhodes Scholar in Peking in 1929, there teaching and traveling widely. He taught East Asian history at Harvard from 1936. He was attached to the Office of Strategic Services (OSS) during World War II, serving in China. Immediately after the war he was in China as director of the U.S. Information Service. He returned to Harvard in 1946. The first of his many books was *The United States and China* (1948). Two major works, both with Edwin Reischauer, were *East Asia, the Great Tradition* and *East Asia, the Modern Transformation.*

During the late 1940s and early 1950s witch-hunts of the McCarthy period, Fairbank, who favored American recognition of Communist China, was attacked by McCarthy and others as pro-communist. He survived the attack to join President Richard Nixon's "opening to China" trip in 1972, being credited even by conservative Republicans as a key figure in Chinese-American relations. Fairbank was head of the East Asian Research Center at Harvard from 1955 to 1973. He retired from his teaching position at Harvard in 1977 but continued to write and lecture extensively. Among his later works were *Chinabound: A Fifty Year Memoir* (1982), *China Watch* (1987), and his final book, *China: A New History,* finished shortly before his death. He was survived by his wife, Wilma, and two daughters. (d. Cambridge, Massachusetts; September 14, 1991)

FURTHER READING

Obituary. *The Times* (of London), Sep. 20, 1991.
Obituary. *New York Times,* Sep. 16, 1991.
John King Fairbank and the American Understanding of Modern China. Paul M. Evans. Blackwell, 1987.

Faldo, Nick (1957–) In April 1991, British golfer Faldo had the chance to do what no one had ever done before: win the Masters three straight years. But after his 1989 and 1990 wins, Faldo went through the whole of 1991 without a major win, in mid-year dropping out of the number one position in the world rankings, replaced by fellow British golfer Ian Woosnam. With that and his reserved, sometimes brusque personal style, Faldo took considerable heat from the press, especially in Britain—he was playing too much golf, or too little; he was musclebound, or carrying too much weight; and the like. To many of his fellow golfers, however, Faldo ranks among the best.

Faldo was also embarrassed and apologetic over remarks credited to him in a *Sports Illustrated* interview that were critical of other golfers, though he noted that in many instances he was responding to comments made by the interviewer. A different side showed in his Nick Faldo Charity Fund, which benefits various organizations, and his Nick Faldo Golf Centers in England that, while profit-making ventures, also provide free or low-cost instruction to children, especially those from inner cities.

Faldo became a leading junior British golfer in the mid-1970s and turned professional in 1976. He was voted best new British golfer of the year in 1977 and went on to build a solid, unspectacular career; he emerged as a major figure a decade later, after rebuilding his entire game in 1985. His wins include the 1987 British Open, the 1988 and 1989 French Opens, the 1989 and 1990 Masters, and a second British Open in 1990—a stunning win by five strokes with a record-setting 18 strokes under par. Faldo attended the University of Houston. He is married and has two children. (For photo, see **Woosnam, Ian.**)

FURTHER READING

"Nick Faldo." *Sporting News,* Apr. 15, 1991.
"Do you know me? . . ." Rick Reilly. *Sports Illustrated,* Apr. 8, 1991.
"What's next for Nick?" Michael McDonnell. *Golf,* Feb. 1991.

Falk, Peter (1927–) "Columbo" was still going strong in 1991, and with it Falk, who has for worldwide audiences become identified as the rumpled, raincoat-wearing, cigar-smoking, seemingly naive, actually crafty, enormously popular detective. An Emmy-winner in 1990, Falk was again nominated in 1991, but this year the Emmy went to James Earl Jones, in the title role of "Gabriel's Fire." As Falk's show entered its 20th year, it was guaranteed at least two more years of life, with a two-season commitment from ABC. The 1991–92 "Columbo" season opened on December 15, 1991, with the two-hour *Columbo: Death Hits the Jackpot,* guest-starring Rip Torn as the villain of the piece. Forthcoming was an appearance in Robert Altman's film *The Player,* in a cast that features many leading film players.

New York-born Falk won a Tony for his role in *The Prisoner of Second Avenue* (1971) and has appeared in many other plays and films, including the films *A Woman Under the Influence* (1976), *Murder by Death* (1976), *The Brink's Job* (1978), *The In-Laws* (1979), *Cookie* (1989), and *Tune in Tomorrow* (1990). But in public acclaim, no other role matches that of the detective series "Columbo" (1971–78), which was revived as part of the "ABC Mystery Movies" series in 1988. Falk lost his right eye to surgery for a malignant tumor at the age of 3. His B.A. was from the New School of Social Research in 1951; his M.P.A. from Syracuse University in 1953. He was formerly married to Alyce Mayo, with whom he had two daughters, and later married Shera Danese.

FURTHER READING

"A wrinkle in time." Tim Allis et al. *People,* Dec. 16, 1991.
The Columbo Phile: A Casebook. Mark Dawidziak. Mysterious Press, 1989.

Farrow, Mia (Mia Villiers Farrow, 1945–) After her highly regarded starring role in Woody Allen's *Alice,* Farrow starred once again opposite Allen in *Shadows and Fog,* written, directed, and co-produced by Allen. But her long run of major Woody Allen films was interrupted in 1991–92; *Shadows and Fog* was one of several "big" and many commercially "smaller" films thrown into a kind of limbo late in 1991 by the financial problems of Orion Pictures, and late in 1991 it was still forthcoming; a March 1992 release date was later announced. Also forthcoming was another starring role opposite Allen, in the film tentatively titled *Woody Allen Fall Project '91*; here, too, Allen wrote, directed, and co-produced, assembling a cast that included Juliette Lewis, Judy Davis, and Liam Neeson.

Los Angeles-born Farrow became a star in television as Alison Mackenzie in "Peyton Place" (1964–66). On screen, she appeared in *Rosemary's Baby* (1968), *John and Mary* (1969), *The Great Gatsby* (1973), *Death on the Nile* (1978), *Zelig* (1983), *Broadway Danny Rose* (1984), *Hannah and Her Sisters* (1986), *Radio Days* (1987), *Crimes and Misdemeanors* (1989), and *Alice* (1990). She also had several leading stage roles in Britain during the mid-1970s as a member of the Royal Shakespeare Company. The daughter of actress Maureen O'Sullivan and director John Farrow, she has been married twice, to Frank Sinatra and Andre Previn; Woody Allen is her longtime companion. Farrow has nine children, five of them adopted Vietnamese.

FURTHER READING

"Woody and Mia. . . ." Eric Lax. *New York Times Magazine,* Feb. 24, 1991.
Mia: The Life of Mia Farrow. Edward Z. Epstein. Delacorte, 1991.
Mia Farrow: Flower Child, Madonna, Muse. Sam Rubin and Richard Taylor. St. Martin's, 1989.

Field, Sally (1946–) Field took center stage in 1991 in Michael Hoffman's film *Soapdish* as Celeste Talbert, a slipping soap opera star whose professional and personal lives become unsettled when an old flame (Kevin Kline) and an ingenue (Elisabeth Shue) are brought into the cast of her long-running series, "The Sun Also Sets." Something of a family affair, since Field's husband Alan Griesman co-produced with Aaron Spelling, the comedy premiered lavishly in May, and Field won praise for her performance; but the film did not have the hoped-for box-office or critical success.

Field ran into political problems when she opened in January 1991 in Brian Gilbert's fact-based film *Not Without My Daughter.* She portrayed Betty Mahmoody, a Michigan woman married to an Iranian-born physician, who accompanies him to fundamentalist Iran in 1984 on what was supposedly a visit, finds herself held hostage, and must fight desperately to leave and take her daughter back home with her. Some reviewers criticized the film as negative and anti-Islamic. While making the film, Field received threats and was obliged to have a personal security guard. Wearing a different hat, Field acted as co-producer with Kevin McCormick for *Dying Young,* a 1991 film starring Campbell Scott as a cancer patient and Julia Roberts as his nurse.

Pasadena-born Field became a star in two television series, "Gidget" (1965–66) and "The Flying Nun" (1967–70), and also appeared in the series "The Girl with Something Extra" (1973). She later emerged as a major dramatic actress, winning Best Actress Oscars for *Norma Rae* (1979) and *Places in the Heart* (1984), and appearing in such films and telefilms as *The Way West* (1967), *Sybil* (1976; she won an Emmy), *Smokey and the Bandit* (1977), *Hooper* (1978), *The End* (1978), *Absence of Malice* (1981), *Murphy's Romance* (1985; she was also executive producer), and *Steel Magnolias* (1989). Field attended the Actor's Studio. Griesman is her second husband; she has three children.

FURTHER READING

"Queen for a decade." Marc Eliot. *California,* Sep. 1991.
"She likes herself! . . ." Elizabeth Sporkin. *People,* July 8, 1991.
"The perils of being perky." Maureen Dowd. *McCall's,* July 1991.
"Sally Field. . . ." Michael J. Bandler. *Ladies Home Journal,* Feb. 1990.
Sweethearts of Sixties TV. Ronald L. Smith. St. Martin, 1989.
Sally Field. Jason Bonderoff. St. Martin's, 1987.

Finkelstein, Louis (1895–1991) As head of the Jewish Theological Seminary from 1940 to 1972, Dr. Finkelstein became a key figure in Conservative Judaism in a period that after World War II saw the development of that movement into the largest of the three branches of American Judaism. Ordained in 1919, he joined the faculty of the seminary in 1920 and during the interwar period served in serveral teaching capacities. After becoming the seminary's leader he developed into a major force, establishing several related institutes, building personal and institutional relationships with many world figures of all faiths, and representing his community on many national and international bodies. Finkelstein was also a prolific scholar, writer, and editor. He later became chancellor emeritus of the seminary. He was survived by three children. (d. New York City; November 29, 1991)

FURTHER READING

Obituary. *New York Times,* Nov. 30, 1991.

Finley, Karen (1956–) During 1991, there were several developments in the National Endowment for the Arts (NEA) censorship case that had blown up around performance artist Finley and three other artists denied NEA grants in 1990. On January 5, 1991, the NEA essentially reversed its position, granting $35,000 to two New York theaters for production of new Finley and Holly Hughes works. But Finley, Holly Hughes, John Fleck, and Tim Miller continued to pursue the case of the "NEA Four." The federal government denied that any political considerations had been involved, but government documents—released in September 1991 as part of the disclosure process in a Los Angeles lawsuit filed on behalf of the artists by the National Campaign for Freedom of Expression, the Center for Constitutional Rights, and the American Civil Liberties Union—revealed that NEA chairman Frohnmayer had indeed cited political considerations in refusing the grants. In November 1991, Frohnmayer held a press conference to announce that the NEA was making 1992 grants to Holly Hughes and Tim Miller; in his statement, he strongly supported freedom of expression.

Finley, who grew up in Chicago and Evanston, Illinois, attended the Art Institute of Chicago and the San Francisco Art Institute. Her *Shock Treatment* (1990) contains the text of some of her controversial performances, among other writings. She was formerly married.

FURTHER READING

"Blood and chocolate. . . ." Luc Sante. *New Republic,* Oct. 15, 1990.
"Karen Finley. . . ." Richard Schechner. *Drama Review,* Spring 1988.

Finney, Albert (1936–) Finney focused on film again in 1991; the celebrated British actor during 1991 starred as innkeeper Maurice Allington facing a ghost in the television film *The Green Man,* based on a 1969 Kingsley Amis novel, in a cast that included Michael Hordern, Linda Marlowe, and Sarah Berger. Forthcoming was a starring role in Gillies McKinnon's film *The Playboys,* set in modern Ireland, which was filmed in Ireland in the summer and fall of 1991. In the work written by Shane Connaughton, Finney plays Hegarty, a village police officer, opposite Robin Wright as a single mother and Aidan Quinn as a member of a traveling theater troupe. Also forthcoming was a starring role opposite Jill Clayburgh in Bruce Beresford's film *Rich in Love,* in a cast that includes Piper Laurie, Suzy Amis, and Kyle MacLachlan.

Born in Lancashire, Finney has been a major figure in the British theater for 30 years, beginning with his appearance as *Billy Liar* (1960). He went on to star in such plays as *Luther* (1961), *A Day in the Death of Joe Egg* (1967), *Krapp's Last Tape* (1973), and in a wide range of classic works including his National Theatre *Macbeth* (1978). At the same time, he became a film star as *Tom Jones* (1963), as Hercule Poirot in *Murder on the Orient Express* (1974), and in such films as *Gumshoe* (1972), *Annie* (1982), *Under the Volcano* (1984), *Orphans* (1987), and *Miller's Crossing* (1990). In 1990, he made a highly acclaimed appearance on the London stage in Ronald Harwood's *Another Time.* Finney attended the Royal Academy of Dramatic Art. He has been married to Jane Wenham and Anouk Aimée, and has one child.

FURTHER READING

" 'The opportunity. . . .' " ALVIN SANOFF. *U.S. News & World Report,* Dec. 14, 1987.

Fish, Hamilton (1888–1991) Born in Garrison, New York, Fish became a major figure in U.S. politics, as were his father and grandfather. He began his political career with his 1912 election to the New York State Assembly on Theodore Roosevelt's Bull Moose Party ticket. He commanded Black troops of the 369th infantry—the so-called "Harlem Hellfighters"—in combat during World War I, winning a Silver Star and a Croix de Guerre. Fish won a congressional seat in 1920 and became one of the most powerful congressional Republicans of the interwar period, ultimately sitting on both the Rules and Foreign Affairs committees. A leading conservative, he sharply opposed Franklin Delano Roosevelt's New Deal and Roosevelt's anti-Nazi foreign policy. He was a leading isolationist during the run-up to World War II, and during the late 1930s was identified—rightly or wrongly—as pro-Nazi. He was made especially vulnerable by his August 14, 1939, tea with German foreign minister Von Ribbentrop, at a castle near Salzburg, and his acceptance of Nazi air transport to Oslo. After December 7, 1941, he unreservedly supported the American war effort and was re-elected to Congress in 1942. But his career did not survive the 1944 election; he did not again seek office and was entirely dropped by the leaders of his party. He later wrote and lectured; his *Hamilton Fish: Memoir of an American Patriot* appeared in 1991. He was married four times and was survived by his wife, Lydia, and two children: a son, Congressman Hamilton Fish, Jr., and a daughter, Elizabeth S. Pyne. (d. Cold Spring, New York; January 18, 1991)

FURTHER READING

Obituary. *American Legion Magazine,* Apr. 1991.
Obituary. *Current Biography,* Mar. 1991.
Obituary. WILLIAM F. BUCKLEY, JR. *National Review,* Feb. 11, 1991.
Obituary. *New York Times,* Jan. 1991.

Fisher, Carrie (Carrie Frances Fisher, 1956–) As *Postcards from the Edge* moved from theatrical release to great popularity in home video distribution, Fisher moved toward television, too. Through her company, Deliquesce Inc., she was to produce a new CBS television comedy series tentatively titled "Esme's Little Nap," in which her mother, Debbie Reynolds, was to play a grandmother. But at the end of 1991 the project seemed to be on hold, although CBS called it still forthcoming.

On screen, Fisher starred in May 1991 in the Ate De Jong comedy *Drop Dead Fred,* in a cast that included Phoebe Cates, Rik Mayall, Marsha Mason, and Tim Matheson; the film was not very well received, critically or commercially. She also appeared as Betsy Faye in the Michael Hoffman film comedy *Soapdish,* along with Sally

Field, Kevin Kline, Whoopi Goldberg, and Robert Downey, Jr.

Los Angeles-born Fisher played her first starring role as Princess Leia in *Star Wars* (1977) and its sequels, *The Empire Strikes Back* (1980) and *Return of the Jedi* (1983). Her films also include *Hannah and Her Sisters* (1986) and *When Harry Met Sally . . .* (1989), and television's *Sweet Revenge* (1990). The daughter of stars Debbie Reynolds and Eddie Fisher, she adapted her semi-autobiographical 1987 novel *Postcards from the Edge* into the hit 1990 film, with Shirley MacLaine and Meryl Streep playing Hollywood mother and daughter. In 1990 she published another novel, *Surrender the Pink*. Fisher attended London's Central School of Speech and Drama. She was briefly married to singer and songwriter Paul Simon (1983–84).

FURTHER READING

"Fisher, Carrie." *Current Biography,* Feb. 1991.
"A spy in her own house. . . ." CARL WAYNE ARRINGTON. *Time,* Oct. 15, 1990.
"Postcards from the top." JOANNE KAUFMAN. *Ladies Home Journal,* Sep. 1990.
"Straight up with a twist." TIM APPELO. *Savvy Woman,* Sep. 1990.
"Carrie Fisher." LISA LIEBMANN. *Interview,* Sep. 1990.

Fitzwater, Marlin (Max Marlin Fitzwater, 1942–) White House press secretary Fitzwater has become a very familiar face on the television screen, informing, explaining, and discussing Bush administration viewpoints on the full range of national concerns. During 1991, he issued statements on such diverse matters as the progress of the Persian Gulf War, post-coup events in the Soviet Union, and the Wichita anti-abortion protests, which occurred in his home state.

Kansas-born Fitzwater is a long-term Washington "insider," a writer and public relations professional who worked for the Department of Transportation, Environmental Protection Agency, and the Treasury before becoming deputy press secretary to the president in the mid-1980s. He was press secretary to Vice President George Bush (1985–87), became President Ronald Reagan's press secretary in 1987, and stayed on in the White House as press secretary to President Bush. Fitzwater's B.S. was from Kansas State University, in 1965. He has four children.

FURTHER READING

"As the Gulf war rages. . . ." PAULA CHIN. *People,* Feb. 11, 1991.
"Fitzwater, Max Marlin." *Current Biography,* May 1988.

Fodor, Eugene (1905–91) An editor and publisher born in Léva, Hungary, Fodor studied in France, worked as an interpreter for a French shipping line, and began his career by writing travel articles for his employer and as a free-lancer. He moved to London in 1934; his first book was *1936 on the Continent*. He followed it with *Europe 1937,* very popular in the United States on publication in 1938, the year he emigrated across the Atlantic. During World War II, he became a captain of U.S. intelligence. In 1950, he began the long series of Fodor's Modern Guides that made his a familiar name all over the world. Fodor denied charges that he and some of his travel writers were Central Intelligence Agency (CIA) operatives during the Cold War, though he did state that he had on some occasions cooperated with the CIA during his years as a travel publisher. He was survived by his wife, formerly Vlasta Zobel. (d. Torrington, Connecticut; February 18, 1991)

FURTHER READING

Obituary. AMY BERNSTEIN. *U.S. News & World Report,* Mar. 4, 1991.
Obituary. *The Times* (of London), Feb. 20, 1991.
Obituary. *New York Times,* Feb. 20, 1991.

Foley, Thomas Stephen (1929–) Although Speaker of the House Foley had generally supported the U.S. military buildup in the Pesian Gulf during the run-up to the Gulf War, he spoke against the resolution during the January 12 House debate, while imposing no Democratic Party discipline and urging all Representatives to vote with their consciences rather than their parties. He then fully supported the war.

Soon afterward, normal political life resumed and Foley, as a chief spokesman for his party, sharply criticized the administration, especially on the domestic economic issues so damaging to the Republican Party later in 1991. In July, Foley called Bush's opposition to a five cents per gallon increase in the federal gasoline tax "mindless" and "partisan and political." In August, Foley began the process that in November resulted in unemployment benefits extension. Also that month he announced the formal opening of the "October Surprise" probe of allegations that William Casey, who had headed the 1980 Republican presidential campaign, had conspired with Iranian officials to delay Iran hostage releases until after the 1980 election.

Foley also moved to save some of the much-tarnished reputation of Congress. In late September, after the General Accounting Office had reported that House members had bounced 8,331 checks in a one-year period and the story hit the media, he ruled that the House of Representatives Bank would stop covering member overdrafts. On October 3, he announced that the House bank would be closed by year's end. And on October 8, he ended the practice of traffic-ticket fixing for members.

Spokane-born Foley practiced law and was Washington state assistant attorney general before going to Washington, D.C., as a lawyer in 1961. A liberal Democrat, he entered the House in 1965, and in 25 uninterrupted years rose to become chairman of the House Democratic Caucus in 1976, majority whip in 1981, and majority leader in 1987. He was elected 49th Speaker of the House on June 6, 1989, replacing James C. Wright, who had resigned while facing charges of ethics violations. Foley's B.A. and LL.B. were from the University of Washington, in 1951 and 1957. He married Heather Strachan in 1968; she is one of his key congressional aides.

FURTHER READING

"Mr. Nice Guy. . . ." BILL WHALEN. *Insight,* Aug. 19, 1991.
"Hill potatoes. . . ." FRED BARNES. *New Republic,* May 20, 1991.
"Foley's law." MICHAEL ORESKES. *New York Times Magazine,* Nov. 11, 1990.
"Foley, Thomas Stephen." *Current Biography,* Sep. 1989.

Fonda, Jane (1937–) Actress and businesswoman Fonda moved in rather a new set of directions during 1991, essentially relocating from California to Atlanta, Georgia, headquarters city of Ted Turner's many companies. Signaling the change was her April 1991 closure of Jane Fonda's Workout, the Beverly Hills studio that was the start of what became her chain of bodybuilding shops, all accompanied by her best-selling workout books, the latest of which— *Jane Fonda's New Pregnancy Workout and Total Birth Program* (written by Femmy DeLyser)— was published in 1991.

Fonda and Turner were married on December 21, 1991, at the Turner ranch near Capps, Florida; the wedding party was small, totaling a reported 30. Media interest was intense, but no massive media presence was permitted, though hovering news helicopters recorded the event. Although Fonda was not visibly active on stage, screen, or television during 1991, many observers felt that her alliance with media owner Turner would likely result in substantial new Fonda projects in the arts.

New York City-born Fonda appeared on the New York stage and in supporting film roles in the early 1960s, in the mid-1960s starring in such film comedies as *Cat Ballou* (1965), *Any Wednesday* (1966), and *Barefoot in the Park* (1967), and also in the science fiction film *Barbarella* (1968), directed by her first husband, Roger Vadim. She then emerged as a major film star, in drama and comedy, with such films as *They Shoot Horses, Don't They* (1969), her Oscar-winning role in *Klute* (1970), *A Doll's House* (1973), *Fun with Dick and Jane* (1976), *Julia* (1977), her second Oscar-winning role in *Coming Home* (1978), *California Suite* (1978), *The China Syndrome* (1979), *The Electric Horseman* (1979), *Nine to Five* (1980), *On Golden Pond* (1981), *Agnes of God* (1985), *The Morning After* (1986), *Stanley and Iris* (1989), and *Old Gringo* (1990). She also wrote several widely circulated exercise books, starting with *Jane Fonda's Workout Book* (1981). Fonda attended Vassar College. Her previous marriages were to Vadim and to social activist Tom Hayden. The daughter of actor Henry Fonda and the sister of actor Peter Fonda, she has two children.

FURTHER READING

"Jane and Ted's excellent adventure. . . ." JERRY ADLER. *Esquire,* Feb. 1991.
Jane Fonda: Political Activism. RUSSELL SHORTO. Millbrook, 1991.
Jane Fonda: An Intimate Biography. BILL DAVIDSON. NAL-Dutton, 1990.
Citizen Jane: The Turbulent Life of Jane Fonda. CHRISTOPHER ANDERSEN. Holt, 1990.
The Post-Feminist Hollywood Actress: Biographies and Filmographies of Stars Born after 1939. KERRY SEGRAVE and LINDA MARTIN. McFarland, 1990.
Fonda: Her Life in Pictures. JAMES SPADA. Doubleday, 1985.
Jane Fonda: More Than a Movie Star. ELLEN ERLANGER. Lerner, 1984.
Jane Fonda: Heroine for Our Time. THOMAS KIERNAN. Berkley, 1983.

Fonteyn, Margot (Peggy Hookam, 1919–91) Born at Reigate, Surrey, England, Fonteyn spent much of her youth abroad, following her engineer father; her most notable early teacher was George Goncharov in Shanghai. She began her very long career by joining the Vic-Wells ballet school and company in 1934. She moved into leading roles a year later, after Alicia Markova left the company, dancing many classic leads and originating roles in several Frederick Ashton ballets, including *Le Baiser de la Fée* (1935) and *Apparitions* (1936), at the start of her long association with Ashton. By the early 1940s, she was the company's prima ballerina; by 1948, when the company became the Sadler's Wells, she was Britain's leading international ballerina, a status confirmed when the company became the Royal Ballet in 1956.

Throughout her career, Fonteyn continued to originate new roles, for Ashton, Roland Petit, John Cranko, Ninette de Valois, and many others. In 1962, she began her long and celebrated stage partnership with Rudolph Nureyev, which ended only with her retirement in 1979. Fonteyn married Panamanian diplomat Robert de Arias in 1955 and lived in Panama for much of her later life, though continuing her dancing career. Arias was crippled during a 1964 assassination attempt, and died in 1989. Her written works include *Margot Fonteyn: Autobiography* (1976) and several books on ballet, including *The Magic of Dance* (1982), *Pavlova: Self-Portrait of a Dancer* (1984), and several works for students. She was survived by a brother, two stepdaughters, and a stepson. (d. Panama City, Panama; February 31, 1991)

FURTHER READING

"Remembering Fonteyn and Graham." LAURA JACOBS. *New Leader,* Apr. 8, 1991.
"Remembering Margot Fonteyn." PETER BRINSON. *Dance Magazine,* May 1991.
Obituary. *Current Biography,* Apr. 1991.
Obituary. *National Review,* Mar. 18, 1991.
"For 40 years prima ballerina. . . ." *People,* Mar. 11, 1991.
Obituary. *U.S. News & World Report,* Mar. 4, 1991.
"Sleeping beauty. . . ." LAURA SHAPIRO. *Newsweek,* Mar. 4, 1991.
Obituary. *Variety,* Feb. 25, 1991.
Obituary. *The Times* (of London), Feb. 22, 1991.
Obituary. *New York Times,* Feb. 22, 1991.
Margot Fonteyn. ANNE SEBBA. Julia Macrae Blackbird Books, 1983.

Ford, Gerald Rudolph, Jr. (1913–) Former President Ford continued to play a largely ceremonial role in 1991, symbolizing political stability and the long tradition of peaceful and democratic continuity that for many in other countries is such an attractive part of the American experience. At the Ford presidential museum in Grand Rapids, Michigan, he and former West German chancellor Helmut Schmidt dedicated a piece of the former Berlin Wall. On November 4, he and Betty Ford were present at the opening of the Reagan presidential library at Simi Valley, California, joining all the other living ex-presidents and their wives.

Omaha-born Ford, then vice president, became the 38th president of the United States in August 1974 on the resignation of Richard Nixon, who faced impeachment because of his complicity in the Watergate affair. A month later, Ford pardoned Nixon. A year earlier, Ford had been appointed by Nixon to replace Vice President Spiro Agnew, who had resigned under fire.

The Ford presidency was relatively uneventful, seeming especially so after the turbulence of the 1960s, the Vietnam War, and the shock of Watergate. That incident did enable Ford to curb the excesses of the Central Intelligence Agency (CIA) and other national security organizations, however; beyond that, he began little new legislation, attempted with little success to mediate continuing Middle East crises, and furthered American relations with China. Ford defeated Ronald Reagan's bid for the Republican presidential nomination but was himself defeated by Jimmy Carter in the 1976 presidential election. He wrote of his life and experiences in *A Time to Heal: The Autobiography of Gerald R. Ford* (1979).

Earlier, Ford had been an All-American college football player, a naval officer in World War II, and a lawyer in Grand Rapids (1941–49). He went to Washington as a congressman in 1949, and became minority leader of the House (1965–73). His B.A. was from the University of Michigan in 1935, his LL.B. from Yale in 1941. Ford married Elizabeth Bloomer in 1948; they have four children.

FURTHER READING

Farewell to the Chief: Former Presidents in American Public Life. Richard N. Smith and Timothy Walch, eds. High Plains, 1990.
Gerald R. Ford's Date with Destiny: A Political Biography. Edward L. Schapsmeier and Frederick H. Schapsmeier. P. Lang, 1989.
"Former presidents reflect. . . ." Michael Delon. *USA Today,* Nov. 1988.
Gerald R. Ford: President. Sallie Randolph. Walker, 1987.

Ford, Harrison (1942–) The creator of Han Solo and Indiana Jones continued to display a far wider range than was evident in his two extraordinarily successful action-adventure series. In 1991, he starred opposite Annette Bening as Henry, the abrasive, successful New York lawyer who becomes an amnesiac after a head wound and then finds a better self in Mike Nichols's film *Regarding Henry.* Forthcoming was another blockbuster action-adventure role, as the Central Intelligence Agency (CIA) analyst-hero in the Philip Noyce film *Patriot Games,* based on the Tom Clancy novel, a sequel to his *The Hunt for Red October.* Ford, who took the role after Alec Baldwin withdrew for a stage role, will star opposite Anne Archer as his wife, in a cast that includes Thora Birch, Sean Bean, and Patrick Bergin. *Patriot Games* is the first of a three-film commitment with Paramount Pictures. Also forthcoming was a starring role in Harold Becker's film *Night Ride Down.*

Chicago-born Ford played largely in supporting roles, working part-time as a carpenter, for a decade before breaking through as Han Solo in *Star Wars* (1977) to become a leading movie star.

He completed the Star Wars trilogy with *The Empire Strikes Back* (1980) and *Return of the Jedi* (1983), meanwhile doing the blockbuster Indiana Jones trilogy: *Raiders of the Lost Ark* (1981), *Indiana Jones and the Temple of Doom* (1984), and *Indiana Jones and the Last Crusade* (1989). Among his other films are *Witness* (1985), *The Mosquito Coast* (1986), *Working Girl* (1988), and *Presumed Innocent* (1990). Ford attended Ripon College. He has been married twice and has two children.

FURTHER READING

"Harrison Ford. . . ." NATALIE GITTELSON. *McCall's*, June 1991.
The Films of Harrison Ford. ED GROSS. Pioneer Books, 1990.
Harrison Ford. MINTY CLINCH. Trafalgar Square, 1988.
Harrison Ford. TOLEDO VARE. St. Martin's, 1988.

Ford, Tennessee Ernie (Ernest Jennings Ford, 1919–91) Best known by far for his signature song "Sixteen Tons" (1956), country singer Ford began his career in 1930 as a disk jockey in his hometown of Bristol, Tennessee. After World War II service, he resumed his radio career. In 1948, he signed his first recording contract, with Capitol Records, and in the next several years emerged as a star recording artist, with such songs as "Mule Train" (1949), "Ballad of Davy Crockett" (1955), and then "Sixteen Tons." He also became a television star, with three very popular shows (1955–57; 1956–61; and 1962–65). In the same period, he became a leading gospel singer, remaining so long after his career as a popular country singer had waned. One notable late-career tour came in 1974, when he led the first American popular music group through what was then the Soviet Union. He was survived by his second wife, Beverly, a daughter, and two sons. (d. Reston, Virginia; October 17, 1991)

FURTHER READING

"Bless his pea-pickin' heart." MARK GOODMAN. *People*, Nov. 4, 1991.
Obituary. *U.S. News & World Report*, Oct. 28, 1991.
Obituary. *Variety*, Oct. 21, 1991.
Obituary. *The Times* (of London), Oct. 19, 1991.
Obituary. *New York Times*, Oct. 18, 1991.

Foreman, Dave (David Foreman, 1947–) The trial of environmental activist Dave Foreman and four other activists began on June 10, 1991, in a federal district court at Prescott, Arizona. All were accused of a January 1989 conspiracy to damage transmission towers and power lines feeding the Rocky Flats, Diablo Canyon, and Palo Verde nuclear plants, though they were not charged with actually having carried out the allegedly planned sabotage. Their defense contended that the charges were part of a federal government plot to "get" Foreman, a founder of Earth First! On August 14, a plea bargain was announced that for Foreman meant pleading guilty to one felony count of conspiracy, with sentencing to be suspended for five years and then negotiated. The judge took the plea bargain under consideration.

In the summer of 1991, Foreman broke with Earth First! A long-time conservative, he sharply disagreed with what he felt was a group move toward action on left-leaning social and political causes rather than on straightforward nature conservation. He did not, however, move away from recommending the "eco-guerrilla" tactics he had popularized, most of them also called "monkeywrenching." Additionally, he published the autobiographical *Confessions of an Eco-Warrior* (1991).

Foreman moved from political conservatism to radical activism early in his career. He chaired the Young Americans for Freedom chapter and campaigned for Barry Goldwater in college, but then in the early 1970s became a lobbyist for the Wilderness Society. In 1978, losing faith in the democratic political process, he and three friends—Mike Roselle, Bart Koehler, and Howie Wolke—founded Earth First!, an activist environmentalist organization that urged sabotage and other acts of guerrilla violence in what they saw as the unending battle to save the environment. His book *Ecodefense: A Field Guide to Monkeywrenching* (1985; 2nd ed., 1987) is the "bible" of the Earth First! movement. Foreman attended the University of New Mexico. He has been married twice, since 1986 to Nancy Morton.

FURTHER READING

"Court Jester. . . ." BILL MCKIBBEN. *Mother Jones*, 1991.
Defending the Earth: A Dialog Between Murray Bookchin and Dave Foreman. South End, 1991.

"Protector or provocateur? . . ." DOUGLAS S. LOONEY. *Sports Illustrated,* May 27, 1991.
"Ecoterrorist seeks. . . ." VALERIE RICHARDSON et al. *Insight,* Mar. 25, 1991.
"Earth First! What next?" STEPHEN TALBOT. *Mother Jones,* Nov.–Dec. 1990.
"Eco-warrior Dave Foreman. . . ." SUSAN REED. *People,* Apr. 16, 1990.
"Dave Foreman! . . ." CHARLES BOWDEN. *BUZZWORM: The Environmental Journal,* Mar.–Apr. 1990.

Forman, Milos (1932–) Forman's film *Valmont* opened to critical acclaim in Britain in November 1991, two years after its original release. In 1989, the film had opened in the United States and France to mixed reviews, after the year-earlier success of *Dangerous Liaisons,* based on the same novel. Forman's film died commercially, and during 1991 he was still making a comeback. Forthcoming was his film *Hell Camp,* reportedly a romantic comedy about an American businessman out of work in Japan who becomes a sumo wrestler; it was scheduled for 1992 release. Active in worldwide film art matters, Forman in 1991 joined other film figures in supporting the proposed U.S. Film Disclosure Act of 1991, which would require warning labels on films regarding such alterations as colorization, which they sharply opposed.

Forman was one of Czechoslovakia's leading film directors in the mid-1960s, with such films as *Black Peter* (1964), *The Knave of Spades* (1965), *A Blonde in Love* (1965), and *A Fireman's Ball* (1968). He fled to the West after the 1968 invasion of Czechoslovakia and settled in the United States. There he won directing Oscars for *One Flew over the Cuckoo's Nest* (1975) and *Amadeus* (1983), also directing such films as *Taking Off* (1971), *Hair* (1979), *Ragtime* (1981), and *Valmont* (1989).

FURTHER READING

"Hollywood continues. . . ." LAWRENCE COHN. *Variety,* Oct. 25, 1989.
Milos Forman: A Bio-Bibliography. THOMAS J. SLATER. Greenwood, 1987.

Foster, Jodie (Alicia Christian Foster, 1962–) Still emerging as a major film figure, Foster in February 1991 starred as Federal Bureau of Investigation (F.B.I.) agent Clarice Starling, seeking insight from imprisoned serial killer Dr. Hannibal Lecter, played by Anthony Hopkins in Jonathan Demme's *The Silence of the Lambs.* Foster, Hopkins, Demme, and the film were all highly acclaimed, and the powerful drama became a worldwide hit. It was at year's end on everyone's list of top films, and in late December 1991 became the first film ever to sweep the New York Film Critics Circle awards, winning best picture, director, actor, and actress.

Jodie Foster and Anthony Hopkins (in background).

Foster went on to score another major coup with the October 1991 release of her directorial debut, the feature film *Little Man Tate.* It is the story of Fred Tate, a gifted seven-year-old, played by Adam Hann-Byrd; Foster herself played Dede Tate, his bartender mother, opposite Dianne Wiest's Dr. Jane Grierson, a psychologist who wants to take Fred off to college and intellectual stimulation. The low-budget film was very well received and became an artistic and commercial hit. Forthcoming for Foster was an acting role in Woody Allen's *Shadows and Fog,* its release delayed until 1992. In development for Foster as both star and director was *The Dinosaur Man,* based on Dr. Susan Baur's work with schizophrenics.

Los Angeles-born Foster was a leading child actor in television, beginning with "Mayberry R.F.D." in 1969. In her early teens, she played major roles in such films as *Alice Doesn't Live Here Any More* (1975) and *Taxi Driver* (1976). She then made the often extremely difficult transition to adult roles, in such films as *The Hotel*

New Hampshire (1984), *Five Corners* (1986), and most notably *The Accused* (1988), for which she won a Best Actress Oscar. Her B.A. was from Yale, in 1985.

FURTHER READING

"Burden of the gift." Julie Cameron. *American Film,* Nov.–Dec. 1991.
"Wunderkind." Arion Berger. *Harper's Bazaar,* Nov. 1991.
"Foster child. . ." Tom Gliatto et al. *People,* Nov. 18, 1991.
"Jodie Foster." Ingrid Sischy. *Interview,* Oct. 1991.
"What's driving Miss Jodie?" Michael Segell. *Redbook,* Nov. 1991.
"Jodie Foster." Phillip Zonkel. *Seventeen,* Oct. 1991.
"A screen gem turns director." Richard Corliss. *Time,* Oct. 14, 1991.
"Jodie Foster. . . ." Brian D. Johnson. *Maclean's,* Sep. 16, 1991.
"Jodie Foster." Geari Hirshey. *Rolling Stone,* Mar. 21, 1991.
"Yet again. . . ." Tracy Young. *Vogue,* Feb. 1991.
"Child of the movies." Jonathan Van Meter. *New York Times Magazine,* Jan. 6, 1991.

Fox, Michael J. (1961–) In *The Hard Way,* which opened in March 1991, Fox starred as a movie star determined to learn enough to get a tough cop's role, opposite James Woods as the tough cop he is studying; the cast included Annabella Sciorra, Stephen Lang, and Penny Marshall. Fox also starred in Michael Caton-Jones's *Doc Hollywood,* as young plastic surgeon Ben Stone, bound from Washington, D.C., to Beverly Hills to make his fortune. Instead, he finds himself in a South Carolina town in need of a doctor and ultimately decides to stay. Fox's *Back to the Future* films continued to appeal on the home screen, and a new animated children's television version was introduced in autumn 1991.

Vancouver-born Fox became a popular television player as the conservative young son in the series "Family Ties" (1982–89), and a film star in the teenage fantasy-comedies *Back to the Future* (1985), *Back to the Future II* (1989), and *Back to the Future Part III* (1990). He also starred in the highly regarded *Casualties of War* (1989). He married Tracy Pollan in 1988; they have one child.

FURTHER READING

"Walking tall with. . . ." Chris Chase. *Cosmopolitan,* Apr. 1991.
"The new age of. . . ." Paul Dougherty. *California,* Mar. 1991.
Secret of Michael J. Fox's Success. Edward Gross. Movie Publications Services, 1990.
"Getting back to his future." Michael Alexander. *People,* Dec. 4, 1989.
Michael J. Fox Scrapbook. Mimi Kasbah. Ballantine, 1987.
Michael J. Fox. Keith E. Greenberg. Lerner, 1986.

Foxx, Redd (John Elroy Sanford, 1922–91) Popular African-American comedian Foxx began his career as a variety performer in Black vaudeville in the late 1930s. He found no opportunities in Hollywood in the early 1950s because of his race; his treatment in this period and on other occasions was a source of lifelong bitterness. He found very large audiences, however, for his "blue" party records of the mid-1950s and thereafter. With the civil rights movement of the 1960s, he began to make a name in television and as a cabaret performer. Then, in 1972, came his quite unexpected breakthrough as the star of the long-running television series "Sanford and Son." He later starred in two less successful television series.

Although during the 1980s Foxx continued to be a very popular performer in cabaret, he ran into financial difficulties, seeking the protection of bankruptcy in 1983. But he could not protect himself from the Internal Revenue Service, which seized much of his property in 1989. His death occurred during a rehearsal of his new television series. He was survived by his third wife, Ka Ha Cho, an adopted daughter, and his mother. (d. Los Angeles; October 11, 1991)

FURTHER READING

"The Redd Foxx that nobody knew." *Jet,* Nov. 4, 1991.
"Redd Foxx exits, laughing." Mark Goodman et al. *People,* Oct. 28, 1991.
Obituary. *Variety,* Oct. 21, 1991.
Obituary. *New York Times,* Oct. 13, 1991.
"Eddie Murphy, Richard Pryor, Redd Foxx. . . ." Walter Leavy. *Ebony,* Jan. 1990.
"Still Foxxy and going strong." Douglas C. Lyons. *Ebony,* June 1988.

Franciscus, James (1934–91) Missouri-born Franciscus began his acting career in the film *Four Boys and a Gun* (1956) and went on to roles in many other films and telefilms. He was by far best known as a television player, beginning with his role in the series "Naked City" (1958). He played the title roles in the "Mr. Novak" series (1963–64), and in the "Mr. Longstreet" series (1971–72) as the blind insurance investigator, as well as a very wide range of continuing and guest television roles. Franciscus also wrote, produced, and appeared in several of his own plays, and during the 1980s he wrote several film and television scripts. He was survived by his second wife, Carla, four daughters, and a brother. (d. Los Angeles; July 8, 1991)

FURTHER READING

"Blue blood, blue ending. . . ." *People,* July 22, 1991.
Obituary. *Variety,* July 15, 1991.
Obituary. *New York Times,* July 10, 1991.

Frank, Barney (1940–) Massachusetts Democratic Congressman Frank, a leading House liberal and openly a homosexual, continued to focus on a wide range of environmental and health issues in 1991, as when in October he led a group of 63 House members in asking the Bush administration to allocate approximately $25 million in special contingency administrative funds to Medicare in order to keep open free 800-number hot lines. Earlier, in January, he had organized a letter signed by more than 50 House members, urging the release of contingency funds to secure prompt payment of Medicare reimbursements.

Frank became involved in a headline-getting situation in August 1989 when a newspaper story charged that he had put a male prostitute on his payroll in 1985 and that the man, Steven L. Gobie, had then run a house of prostitution out of Frank's Washington apartment. On July 25, 1990, after a long investigation, the House of Representatives reprimanded Frank for using his office improperly to help Gobie; at the same time, the House rejected the original charges. Frank was re-elected to the House in November 1990, and during 1991 continued to represent his district in the House effectively. His autobiographical *Frankly Speaking* was scheduled for 1992 publication.

Frank became a Massachusetts state legislator (1972–80) after teaching at Harvard and working as a political assistant in Boston and Washington. He began his congressional career in 1981. His B.A. and J.D. were from Harvard, in 1962 and 1977.

FURTHER READING

"Sodom and begorra." *Boston Magazine,* Nov. 1989.
"In defense of Barney. . . ." MORTON KONDRACKE. *New Republic,* Oct. 9, 1989.
" 'I was emotionally vulnerable'. . . ." ELEANOR CLIFT. *Newsweek,* Sep. 25, 1989.

Freeman, Bud (Lawrence Bud Freeman, 1906–91) Chicago-born Freeman, a tenor saxophonist, began his seven-decades-long musical career in 1922 as a founder of Chicago's Austin High School Gang, a group of high school friends that included cornetist and trumpeter Jimmy McPartland (d. March 13, 1991). Resident at Friars Inn, the group, working with Eddie Condon and other jazz musicians, played a key role in modifying New Orleans jazz, creating the new Chicago style. From the late 1920s through the mid-1930s Freeman worked with Condon in the groups, the Chicagoans and the Chicago Rhythm Kings. He began his recording career at this time, most notably in "The Eel (Home Cooking)" (1933). He then played with several big bands, including those of Paul Whiteman and Benny Goodman, and led his own Summa Cum Laude Orchestra (1939–40).

After leading an army band during World War II, Freeman resumed his performing and recording career, often working with Condon in New York, and touring throughout the world even after he entered his 80s. During the 1960s, he played with the Newport Jazz Festival All-Stars and with the World's Greatest Jazz Band from 1968 to 1974. He lived and worked in Britain in the late 1970s, returning to the United States in 1979. Freeman wrote *You Don't Look Like a Musician* (1974) and *Crazeology: The Autobiography of a Chicago Jazzman as Told to Robert Wolf* (1989). He was survived by a sister. (d. Chicago; March 15, 1991)

FURTHER READING

Obituary. JOHN McDONOUGH. *Down Beat,* June 1991.
Obituary. *New York Times,* Mar. 23, 1991.
Obituary. *The Times* (of London), Mar. 22, 1991.
Voices of the Jazz Age: Profiles of Eight Vintage Jazzmen. CHIP DEFFAA. University of Illinois Press, 1990.

Freeman, Morgan (1938–) Now firmly established in character leads, Freeman in 1991 starred as Azeem in *Robin Hood: Prince of Thieves.* The film, critically panned, was a worldwide hit; directed by Kevin Reynolds, it starred Kevin Costner as Robin. On a considerably more serious note, Freeman in October 1991 narrated the "American Experience" television documentary *The Massachusetts 54th Colored Infantry,* the African-American Union Army regiment celebrated in the film *Glory.* On a similar note, he spoke at the July 4, 1991, opening of the National Civil Rights Museum at Memphis, Tennessee. Forthcoming were starring roles in Clint Eastwood's western *Unforgiven,* opposite Eastwood, Gene Hackman, and Richard Harris; and in John G. Avildsen's *The Power of One,* along with John Gielgud, Stephen Dorff, Armin Mueller-Stahl, and Fay Masterson.

Freeman has spent most of his long career in the theatre, winning a 1978 Tony nomination for his role in *The Mighty Gents,* and appearing in a considerable range of Shakespearean and other classical roles. He emerged as a leading screen and stage player late in his career, beginning with his lead off-Broadway as Hoke Colburn, the Black chauffeur in *Driving Miss Daisy* (1987), and in strong supporting roles in such films as *Street Smart* (1987) and *Clean and Sober* (1988). His major breakthrough came in 1989, with his film re-creation of the *Driving Miss Daisy* role, for which he won a 1990 Oscar nomination. In the same year, he appeared in *Glory* and created the Joe Clark role in *Lean on Me.* In 1990, he appeared as Petruchio opposite Tracey Ullman in the New York production of *The Taming of the Shrew.* He has also appeared as a regular on two television series: public television's children's show "The Electric Company" (1971–76) and for a time in the early 1980s on "Another World," a daytime soap opera.

FURTHER READING

"Freeman, Morgan." *Current Biography,* Feb. 1991.
"In the driver's seat. . . ." JANICE C. SIMPSON. *Time,* Jan. 8, 1990.
"Two for the road." HENRY ALFORD and PAULA BULLWINKEL. *Interview,* Nov. 1989.
"Johnny Handsome. . . ." ROBERT SEIDENBERG. *American Film,* Oct. 1989.

Frisch, Max Rudolph (1911–91) Zurich-born Frisch, a playwright and novelist, began his career in the early 1930s as a free-lance journalist. He studied architecture in the mid-1930s and practiced as an architect until the mid-1950s, at the same time writing such novels as *Jürg Reinhart* (1934), *Santa Cruz* (1940), *When the War Was Over* (1949), *I'm Not Stiller* (1954), *Homo Faber* (1957), *A Wilderness of Mirrors* (1964), and *Man in the Holocene* (1980). As a playwright, he was best known for *The Fire Raisers* (1957), which was staged in New York as *The Firebugs* in 1963. His play *Andorra* (1961) was also staged in New York in 1963. In addition, Frisch wrote several autobiographical works. He was married twice and is survived by two daughters and a son. (d. Zurich, Switzerland; April 4, 1991)

FURTHER READING

Obituary. *Current Biography,* June 1991.
Obituary. *New York Times,* Apr. 5, 1991.
Obituary. *The Times* (of London), Apr. 5, 1991.
Understanding Max Frisch. WULF KOEPKE. University of South Carolina Press, 1990.
Perspectives on Max Frisch. GERHARD F. PROBST and JAY F. BODINE, eds. University Press of Kentucky, 1982.
Max Frisch. CAROL PETERSEN. Continuum, 1980.

Frohnmayer, John Edward (1921–) National Endowment for the Arts (NEA) chairman Frohnmayer continued to be at the center of an ongoing and often stormy tug-of-war dur-

ing 1991, as he had been since his July 1989 appointment by President George Bush. His longest-running controversy began in August 1990, when he canceled grants to four artists, all accused of "obscenity"; these were Karen Finley, Holly Hughes, John Fleck, and Tim Miller, from then on known as the "NEA Four." Frohnmayer went on to deny several more grants and to institute an "anti-obscenity oath," a pledge by those receiving federal grants through the NEA that they would not use the money to create "obscene" art. Joseph Papp of the New York Shakespeare Festival, among others, refused to take offered NEA grants as long as the oath was in effect. Throughout the period, the federal government steadfastly denied that any political considerations were involved in Frohnmayer's actions. But in September 1991, government documents—released as part of the disclosure process in a Los Angeles lawsuit filed on behalf of the artists by the National Campaign for Freedom of Expression, the Center for Constitutional Rights, and the American Civil Liberties Union—revealed that Frohnmayer had indeed cited political considerations in refusing the grants.

In 1991, Frohnmayer began to change some of his positions. In November 1990, after Congress had approved NEA funding, Finley and Hughes received NEA grants without opposition from Frohnmayer, and in December he declared himself unwilling to enforce "decency" restrictions on grants. In March 1991, he put himself solidly behind the very explicit anti-violence film *Poison,* which also explored homosexual themes and which was financed partly by a $25,000 post-production grant from the National Endowment for the Humanities. He was then strongly attacked by such organizations as the Reverend Pat Robertson's Christian Coalition and the Reverend Donald Wildman's American Family Association, which saw the film as homosexual pornography, and on the floor of Congress, charged with being pro-pornography. In November 1991, he held a press conference to announce that the NEA was making grants to Holly Hughes and Tim Miller and strongly supported freedom of expression. The NEA Four lawsuit continued.

Oregon-born Frohnmayer practiced law in Oregon (1972–89). He was also a member of the Oregon Arts Commission (1978–85) and has been a singer and active developer of regional musical groups. His 1964 B.A. was from Stanford University, his 1969 M.A. from the University of Chicago, and his 1972 J.D. from the University of Oregon. He married Leah Thorpe in 1967; they have two children.

FURTHER READING

"Frohnmayer, John Edward." *Current Biography,* Apr. 1990.

Frye, Northrop (Herman Northrop Frye, 1912–91) Born in Sherbrooke, Quebec, Frye was ordained a United Church of Canada priest in 1936 but decided instead to make a career in education. He read English at Oxford, became a member of the English faculty at Victoria College of the University of Toronto in 1939, and spent his entire teaching career at the university. Frye became one of the leading literary critics of the 20th century, beginning with his early 1940s reviews in the *Canadian Forum,* and in such books as *Fearful Symmetry* (1947), his seminal *Anatomy of Criticism* (1957), *Northrop Frye in Modern Criticism* (1966), *T. S. Eliot* (1963), and *On Teaching Literature* (1972). Frye was survived by his second wife, the former Elizabeth Brown. (d. Toronto; January 23, 1991)

FURTHER READING

"The Reverend Doctor Frye." JOHN FRASER. *Saturday Night,* Apr. 1991.

"Frye at the Forum." HILDA KIRKWOOD. *Canadian Forum,* Mar. 1991.
Obituary. *Current Biography,* Mar. 1991.
Obituary. *The Times* (of London), Jan. 26, 1991.
Obituary. *New York Times,* Jan. 25, 1991.
Northrop Frye. IAN BALFOUR. Macmillan, 1988.
Northrop Frye: An Annotated Bibliography of Primary and Secondary Sources. ROBERT D. DENHAM. University of Toronto Press, 1987.
Northrop Frye: A Vision of the New World. DAVID COOK. St. Martin's, 1986.

Fujimori, Alberto (1938–) Peruvian President Fujimori during 1991 faced an intertwined set of problems that had turned into a prolonged national disaster. The Shining Path Maoist guerrilla army continued to gain strength in the Andean provinces and increasingly in other parts of the country, destroying peasant self-defense forces at will and controlling large portions of the countryside. A new revolutionary guerrilla army, the Tupac Amaru Revolutionary Movement, also appeared and gained strength, striking easily in the cities. Simultaneously, a massive cholera epidemic took hold, quickly spreading throughout Peru and then to other Latin American countries; the World Health Organization and other public health authorities warned that the epidemic might well affect over 200 million and kill tens of thousands. At the same time, Peru suffered a major recession that made resistance to revolution and disease far more difficult—and which was caused in part by Fujimori's austerity measures, aimed at controlling ruinous inflation and restoring international credit. Some international credit was restored; Fujimori visited Washington in mid-September 1991, seeking almost $95 million in economic and military aid that had been blocked because of Peruvian human rights abuses. He came away with administration and congressional encouragement on the promised aid, conditional upon Peruvian implementation of promised human rights improvements, and secured State Department release of the funds in July. He also secured an Inter-American Development Bank loan of $425 million for Peru's very damaged economy.

The total situation continued to worsen, however, especially regarding the Shining Path insurgency. It continued to gain strength, and near year's end even threatened the capital and main city, Lima. In response, Fujimori in November issued a series of decrees greatly strengthening direct army control of much of the country. With virtually unlimited new emergency powers, the Peruvian army was expected by many human rights observers to initiate a bloody, ruthless reign of terror; the army and government denied that any such thing was in mind.

Peruvian-born Fujimori, the son of Japanese-Peruvian immigrants, attended La Molina, the National Agrarian University, graduating in 1961, and then taught at the university. His 1969 master's degree was in mathematics, from the University of Wisconsin. He became dean of the science faculty at La Molina in 1984, was principal of the university (1984–89), and was president of the Peruvian National Council of Principals (1987–89). He scored an upset victory over novelist Mario Vargas Llosa in the 1990 presidential election. He married civil engineer Susana Higuchi in 1974; they have four children.

FURTHER READING

"The 'Karate Kid' meets. . . ." TOM VOGEL, JR. *Commonweal,* Jan. 11, 1991.
"Fujimori, Alberto." *Current Biography,* Nov. 1990.
"Fujimori. . . ." JEFFREY KLAIBER. *America,* Sep. 8, 1990.
"Who is Fujimori anyway?" LINDA ROBINSON. *U.S. News & World Report,* Apr. 23, 1990.
"Engulfed by 'the Tsunami'. . . ." FREDERICK UNGEHEUER. *Time,* Apr. 23, 1990.
"The man from nowhere." *Economist,* Apr. 14, 1990.

Gaillard, Slim (Bulee Gaillard, 1916–91) Detroit-born Gaillard, a composer and musician, became a very popular jazz figure in the late 1930s, when he teamed with bassist Slam Stewart in 1938–39 as Slam and Slim. Their earliest and greatest hit was "Flat Foot Floogie" (1938), followed by "Tutti Frutti" and "Cement Mixer." They were a popular radio team on New York's WNEW. Gaillard served in the army air force during World War II, and after the war returned to show business, continuing to compose and perform, and appearing in several films as well. He moved to Britain in 1982, and became a very popular performer once again. A four-part BBC biography of Gaillard was aired in 1989. He was survived by his son, Mark. (d. London, England; February 26, 1991)

FURTHER READING

Obituary. *Down Beat,* May 1991.
Obituary. *New York Times,* Feb. 28, 1991.
Obituary. *The Times* (of London), Feb. 27, 1991.

Gallo, Robert Charles (1937–) The long, often bitter French-American dispute over who had discovered the AIDS (acquired immune deficiency syndrome) virus was apparently settled in 1991. Gallo, head of the U.S. National Cancer Institute's laboratory of tumor cell biology and a leading AIDS researcher at the U.S. National Institutes of Health, and French AIDS researcher Luc Montagnier had been jointly

credited with discovery of the virus, both deriving enormous worldwide prestige and the prospect of Nobel Prizes from the discovery. But Montagnier had long claimed that Gallo did not really discover the virus, instead using samples that Montagnier had sent to him. Both claimed credit for the discovery in 1984, beginning a long controversy that ultimately generated a French lawsuit and a 1987 court settlement, though Montagnier and other French researchers continued to charge Gallo with misappropriation of the French specimens.

In 1991, Montagnier offered a new theory, stating that his laboratory records indicated that

Gallo had been sent a contaminated specimen which then grew to replace the different specimens both had been working on. Gallo seemed tacitly to accept that theory, although continuing to point out that he had specimens from several sources in addition to the French specimen. But the matter was not entirely closed; in October, the National Institutes of Health announced that an investigation of the matter would continue. Gallo has written of his work in *Virus Hunting: Cancer, AIDS, and the Human Retrovirus: A Story of Scientific Discovery* (1991).

Connecticut-born Gallo is one of the world's leading tumor cell biologists. He has been associated with the National Cancer Institute of the National Institutes of Health since 1965, in a series of increasingly responsible positions, and has been head of its tumor cell biology laboratory since 1972. He has also taught courses at Cornell and George Washington University, published numerous scientific works, and received many honors and awards for his work. Gallo's B.A. was from Providence College in 1959; his M.D. was from Jefferson Medical College in 1963. He married Mary Jane Hayes in 1961; they have two children.

FURTHER READING

"AIDS' relentless adversary. . . ." SHANNON BROWNLEE. *U.S. News & World Report,* June 3, 1991.
"Taking credit for AIDS." JUDITH COLP. *Insight,* May 13, 1991.
"Profile: AIDS dispute. . . ." TIM BEARDSLEY. *Scientific American,* Jan. 1991.

Gandhi, Rajiv (1944–91) On May 26, 1991, while on a campaign swing, Gandhi was assassinated. The bombing that ended his life occurred at Sriperumbudur, Tamil Nada, in southern India. He was the son of prime minister Indira Gandhi (1917–84), who had been assassinated by her Sikh bodyguards, and the grandson of India's first prime minister, Jawaharlal Nehru.

Rajiv Gandhi, an engineer and pilot, had little interest in politics in his early years; he entered Indian political life after the 1980 death of his brother Sanjay in an airplane crash, and only in response to his mother's urgent request that he become her political heir. He was elected to parliament in 1981, quickly became a key Congress Party leader and then head of the party in 1983. He succeeded his mother as prime minister on the day of her assassination; he was elected prime minister in the December 1984 elections, leaving office after electoral defeat in 1989. Gandhi was survived by his wife, Sonia, a daughter, Priyanka, and a son, Rahul. (d. Sriperumbudur, Tamil Nadu, India; May 26, 1991)

FURTHER READING

Obituary. *Current Biography,* July 1991.
Maclean's, June 3, 1991. (Three articles)
"Passage from regal India. . . ." EMILY MACFARQUHAR. *U.S. News & World Report,* June 3, 1991.
"Death's return visit. . . ." JAMES WALSH. *Time,* June 3, 1991.
Obituary. *The Times* (of London), May 23, 1991.
Obituary. *New York Times,* May 22, 1991.
Rajiv Gandhi: His Mind and Ideology. ATTAR CHAND. South Asia Books, 1991.
Assassination of Rajiv Gandhi. SHASHIU AHULWALIA. South Asia Books, 1991.
Rajiv Gandhi: Son of Dynasty. NICHOLASON NUGENT. Parkwest, 1991.
Rajiv Gandhi's Worldview. ERIC GONSALVES, ed. Advent (NY), 1990.
Rajiv Gandhi: The Years of Power. KATHLEEN HEALY. Advent (NY), 1989.
India Under Indira and Rajiv Gandhi. JAMES HASKINS. Enslow, 1989.
Rajiv Gandhi: A Political Study. BHABANI S. GUPTA. Advent (NY), 1989.
The New Choices: Thoughts and Ideas of Rajiv Gandhi. NURUL HUDA. South Asia Books, 1989.
Rajiv Gandhi: A Political Study. BHABANI SEN GUPTA. South Asia Books, 1989.

Garcia Marquez, Gabriel (1928–) Colombian writer and Nobel Laureate Garcia Marquez was sporadically working on yet another novel on historical themes during 1991, this one set in Mexico. He also spent a good deal of time in Mexico writing for television, reflecting a relatively new and absorbing interest in the screen forms, expressed in his participation in a new Colombian television news program and in such ceremonial appearances as the opening of the August New York Latino film festival. For his New York appearance, he was granted free entry into the United States under new immigration laws; for 33 years, although entering by special permit, he had been officially barred because of his allegedly left-leaning politics. In politics, Garcia Marquez is an independent, critical of both socialism and capitalism, though he was greatly influenced by Marxism through the early 1960s and is a close personal friend of Cuban leader Fidel Castro.

A leading Latin American novelist, Garcia Marquez won the Nobel Prize for literature in 1982, in recognition of a body of novels and short stories that by then had made him a world figure. These included the novels *One Hundred Years of Solitude* (1967), *Death of a Patriarch* (1975), and *Love in the Time of Cholera* (1984). His most recent major work is the novel, *The General in His Labyrinth* (1989), published in the United States in September 1990. He attended the National University at Bogota. He is married to Mercedes Garcia Marquez; they have two children.

FURTHER READING

"Gabriel Garcia Marquez." MANUEL OSORIO. *UNESCO Courier,* Oct. 1991.
Garcia Marquez: The Man and His Work. GENE H. BELL-VILLADA. University of North Carolina Press, 1990.
"Love and. . . ." TIM MCCARTHY. *National Catholic Reporter,* May 12, 1989.
Gabriel Garcia Marquez. RAYMOND WILLIAMS. G. K. HALL, 1985.

García Robles, Alfonso (1911–91) Born in Zamora, Mexico, García Robles had planned to study for the priesthood but instead ultimately became an international lawyer, beginning his long diplomatic career with two years in Sweden. He returned to Mexico and a post at the Foreign Ministry in 1941. In 1945, he was assigned to the Mexican delegation at the San Francisco founding conference of the United Nations, then serving with the UN Secretariat until 1957. He returned home as director general of the Foreign Ministry and became Mexico's ambassador to Brazil in 1960.

With the Cuban Missile Crisis of October 1962, García Robles became highly sensitized to the danger of humanity-destroying nuclear war and quickly became Latin America's leading anti-nuclear activist. He played a very large role in convincing Mexican president Gustavo Diaz Ordaz to join him in that cause. In 1967 he saw his work bear fruit in the 1967 Treaty of Tlatelolco, in which 14 nations, none of them nuclear powers, renounced nuclear weapons; seven others signed later. García Robles was also a co-author of the 1968 Nuclear Non-Proliferation Treaty. He shared the 1982 Nobel Peace Prize with Alva Myrdal. He was the author of 20 books on international affairs and nuclear disarmament. (d. Mexico City; September 2, 1991)

FURTHER READING

Obituary. *The Times* (of London), Sept. 12, 1991.
Obituary. *New York Times,* Sep. 4, 1991.

Garner, James (James Baumgarner, 1928–) Still working with great success in television, Garner won a 1991 Golden Globe award as best actor in a miniseries or motion picture for his 1990 starring role in the Hallmark Hall of Fame production *Decoration Day.* In September 1991 he inaugurated the new weekly television series "Man of the People," starring as Jim Doyle. A grifter appointed to fill the city council seat of his former wife after her death while in office, the character pursues small-time con games while on the council. Garner also continued occasionally to produce for television, as in his *Mittleman's Hardware* (1991), starring George C. Scott. On September 25, Garner was inducted into the Academy of Television Arts and Sciences Hall of Fame.

Oklahoma-born Garner began his long screen career in the mid-1950s in a small, nonspeaking role in *The Caine Mutiny Court Martial* (1954) and in bit parts in television. He quickly emerged as a major television series star, in the title role of the western "Maverick" (1957–61), and later as private investigator Jim Rockford in "The Rockford Files" (1974–80). His wide range of films included *Sayonara* (1957), *The Great Escape* (1963), *The Americanization of Emily* (1964), *Marlowe* (1969), *They Only Kill Their Masters* (1972), *Victor/Victoria* (1982), and *Sunset* (1987). He also starred in such telefilms as *Promise* (1986), which won five Emmys, including best drama; and *My Name is Bill W* (1989), in the title role as the founder of Alcoholics Anonymous. Garner attended the University of Oklahoma. He married Lois Clarke in 1956; they have three children.

FURTHER READING

"Meet a James Garner. . . ." Mary Murphy. *TV Guide,* Dec. 13, 1986.
"The man is back." Jane Hall. *People,* Apr. 22, 1985.
James Garner: A Biography. Raymond Strait. St. Martin's, 1985.

Garrison, Lloyd (1897–1991) One of the leading civil rights lawyers and liberal figures of his time, Garrison bore part of the name of his celebrated grandfather, abolitionist William Lloyd Garrison, and was the grandson of literary figure Wendell Phillips Garrison. In scope and public service, his career was equally notable: During the 1920s a young, impeccably connected Wall Street lawyer, he in 1924 joined and became very active in the Urban League, beginning a lifelong commitment to the fight against racial discrimination and for equality in his country. He was president of the Urban League from 1947 to 1952. He was also a leader of the American Civil Liberties Union and a Reform Democrat who powerfully influenced the course of New York politics.

Garrison was an expert in bankruptcy fraud, widely consulted throughout the country and by the Hoover administration, which became the first of several federal administrations to employ his talents. During the Roosevelt years, he was from 1932 a professor of law and then dean of the University of Wisconsin Law School. At the same time he was a leading labor law consultant who helped organize the National Labor Relations Board and who often served as a mediator and arbitrator. He returned to his New York law practice in 1945 and in 1947 became a professor of law at New York University Law School.

During the McCarthy period, he defended such witch-hunt targets as playwright Arthur Miller and poet Langston Hughes before the House Un-American Activities Committee, and defended J. Robert Oppenheimer in his celebrated security clearance case before the Atomic Energy Commission. He was a partner in Paul, Weiss, Rifkind, Wharton, and Garrison. He was survived by his wife, the former Ellen Jay, two daughters, and a son. (d. New York City, October 2, 1991)

FURTHER READING

Obituary. *The Times* (of London), Oct. 5, 1991.
Obituary. *New York Times,* Oct. 3, 1991.

Garry, Charles R. (Garabed Robutlay Garabedian, 1909–91) Massachusetts-born Garry, who grew up in California's San Joaquin Valley, was a night law student at San Francisco College of Law when he joined the 1934 San Francisco general strike, his first but far from last labor and left political involvement. He was a lawyer and political activist throughout his working life who became a leading radical defense lawyer in the 1960s, his legal practice having survived his 1957 appearance as an unfriendly witness before the House Un-American Activities Committee. As a defense lawyer for the Black Panthers in the mid-1960s, he defended Huey P. Newton on a murder charge. Newton was ultimately convicted of manslaughter. In the late 1970s, he represented James Jones's Peoples Temple, narrowly escaping the 1978 Guyana mass murders and suicides by fleeing through the jungle. His autobiography was *Streetfighter in the Courtroom* (1977). He was survived by his wife, Louise Evelyn Edgar. (d. Berkeley, California; August 16, 1991)

FURTHER READING

Obituary. *New York Times,* Aug. 18, 1991.

Gates, Daryl F. (1926–) On July 22, 1991, 64-year-old Los Angeles police chief Gates, a veteran of 42 years on the force, announced that he planned to retire from his post in April 1992, if by then his successor had been named. His announcement came under enormous pressure, which began with the brutal beating of Black motorist Rodney G. King by several White Los Angeles police officers on the night of March 3, 1991. Unlike other such incidents in Los Angeles, this one was caught on a videotape by an eyewitness, and the tape was then played again and again to horrified American and worldwide audiences. This time no denial was really possible; the truth of the beating was inescapable.

What happened then was that long-standing charges of a continuing pattern of Los Angeles police brutality directed at Blacks and other minority group members began to be taken far more seriously. Ultimately, several city officials, including Los Angeles mayor Tom Bradley, called on Gates to resign, but neither the mayor nor the city police commission could force him to do so. His announcement came 13 days after an independent commission headed by former Deputy Secretary of State Warren Christopher called for his resignation but suggested that he stay on until his successor was chosen. Later in the year, Gates seemed to waver in his decision to resign, but the search for his successor continued and his resignation was expected, as promised. Gates's B.S. in Public Administration was from the University of Southern California.

FURTHER READING

"Law and disorder in LA." John Gregory Dunne. *New York Review of Books,* Oct. 24, 1991.
"Gates's hell." Frederic Dannen. *Vanity Fair,* Aug. 1991.
"Playboy interview. . . ." Diane K. Shah. *Playboy,* Aug. 1991.
"Gatesgate. . . ." Harold Meyerson. *New Republic,* June 10, 1991.

Gates, Robert Michael (1943–) Gates's nomination to be head of the U.S. Central Intelligence Agency (CIA) was confirmed by the Senate on November 5, 1991, after a nomination process that had lasted almost six months and included a Senate Intelligence Committee investigation and three weeks of hearings. Gates had in 1987 been nominated for the same post by President Ronald Reagan but had withdrawn his name from consideration in the face of very serious charges of complicity in the Iran-Contra affair. Four years later, immediately after the Persian Gulf War, in which he had played a role as White House assistant National Security Advisor under his friend and mentor Brent Scowcroft, it seemed possible to get his nomination through the Senate, although the old Iran-Contra involvement questions remained and were asked once again. The basic question still at issue was whether Gates, then deputy to CIA director William J. Casey, had early knowledge of the secret plan to sell arms to Iran and use the profits of those sales to supply the Nicaraguan Contras. Gates, who became acting CIA director after Casey's death, continued to deny that knowledge, although he did state that he had made some mistakes and had learned from them. During the 1991 hearings, questions were also raised as to whether Gates had slanted intelligence estimates for policy purposes, an allegation he denied. Ultimately, and with the strong support of intelligence committee chairman David Boren, Gates was confirmed.

Born in Wichita, Kansas, Gates is a career intelligence officer. His B.A. was from the College of William and Mary, his M.A. from Indiana University, and his Ph.D. in Russian and Soviet history from Georgetown University. He joined the CIA as an intelligence analyst in 1966 and was assigned to the White House-based National Security Council (1974–79), where he worked for Brent Scowcroft. Gates returned to the CIA in 1979 and rose through a series of administrative positions, becoming deputy director in 1986. He rejoined Scowcroft, then National Security Advisor, as Deputy National Security Advisor, in 1988. Gates has a son and a daughter.

FURTHER READING

"The arrogance of the clerks." Angelo Codevilla. *National Review,* Nov. 4, 1991.
"Toughie, smoothy. . . ." Dan Goodgame. *Time,* May 27, 1991.

Gaviria Trujillo, César (1947–) During 1991, Colombian President Gaviria Trujillo moved to further his developing de facto peace with his country's drug cartels, essentially reversing the anti-drug course and war pursued by his predecessor, Virgilio Barco Vargas. He also moved further to directly bring his country's long civil war to an end, without great success.

On the drug cartel front, Gaviria Trujillo made a series of accommodations with drug cartel leaders, soon ending the virtual civil war between the government and the drug traffickers, although some cartel-ordered assassinations continued. In his administration, extradition to the United States was barred by a constitutional amendment, many previously seized properties were returned to drug cartel leaders, and those leaders became able to plead guilty to a single criminal charge, in essence a kind of mass plea bargain prior to surrender. The most prominent cartel leader to surrender was Pablo Escobar Gaviria, leader of the Medellin drug cartel. He surrendered in June 1991 and was then imprisoned in luxurious circumstances in a "prison" built to his own specifications, from which he continued to operate his drug empire. Gaviria-led Colombia continued to be the world's leading cocaine exporter.

As to the civil war, Gaviria continued to talk with other major guerrilla groups after his success in bringing the M-19 group into peaceful participation in national life, with the inclusion of M-19 leader Antonio Navarro Wolf in his new cabinet. But progress proved far slower with the other revolutionary groups. Peace talks began in June 1991 and continued through the balance of 1991.

An economist, Gaviria entered politics at the age of 27 as mayor of his home town of Pereira. He later served several terms in the national assembly and in 1986 became finance minister in the Barco Vargas government, later serving in other cabinet-level posts. He became campaign manager for Liberal Party presidential candidate Luis Carlos Galan Sarmiento in 1989; after Galan's August assassination, Gaviria became a candidate, was nominated by his party in March 1990, and was elected president of Colombia on May 27, 1990. He attended the University of the Andes.

FURTHER READING

"Gavaria's gamble." James Brooke. *New York Times Magazine,* Oct. 13, 1991.
"Colombia's next president. . . ." Linda Robinson. *U.S. News & World Report,* July 30, 1990.
"Colombia's elections." C. Dominique van de Stadt. *World Press Review,* July 1990.
"President of last resort." *Time,* June 11, 1990.

Gephardt, Richard Andrew (1941–)
House Majority Leader Gephardt, a powerful spokesperson for his party and an early front-runner during the 1988 Democratic presidential primaries, was widely expected to be a 1992 presidential candidate. But on July 17,

1991 he took himself out of the race—though politicians have been known to change their minds on such matters right up to the moment of nomination.

Gephardt opposed the Persian Gulf War resolution, but he supported the war once it began. After the war, as both parties resumed their normal stances, he once again became a leading critic of George Bush and his administration, focusing on such issues as trade policy, in particular Japanese-American trade policy; crime legislation; educational policy; and late in 1991 on the wide range of domestic economic issues that so sharply damaged Bush and the Republican Party as the 1990–91 recession deepened and public confidence disappeared. Gephardt also very strongly urged economic aid to the Soviet Union after the failed right-wing coup.

St. Louis-born Gephardt began his political career as a St. Louis alderman (1971–76) and his congressional career in 1979. His B.S. was from Northwestern University in 1962, his J.D. from the University of Maryland in 1965. He married Jane Ann Byrnes in 1966; they have three children.

FURTHER READING

"Wanted. . . ." Douglas Harbrecht. *Business Week,* Nov. 19, 1990.
"Gephardt speaks for the majority." Bill Whalen. *Insight,* July 3, 1989.
"Man for all seasons. . . ." Morton M. Kondracke. *New Republic,* July 3, 1989.

Gere, Richard (1949–) In *Rhapsody in August* (1991), director Akira Kurosawa cast Gere as the Japanese-American cousin of the Japanese family whose losses in the atom bombing of Nagasaki and subsequent history are the story of the film. Kurosawa's choice not to cast an Asian-American in the role brought some criticism, and some other aspects of the film were controversial; but Gere's work in the role was very well received. Forthcoming were starring roles as a manic-depressive psychiatric patient in Mike Figgis's film *Mr. Jones,* opposite Lena Olin as the psychiatrist who falls in love with him; and opposite Kim Basinger in Phil Joanou's film *Final Analysis.* Long interested in Buddhism and Eastern philosophy, Gere is the founder and chairman of Tibet House. In October 1991, he met the Dalai Lama at Kennedy airport, to begin 62 Tibet-related events organized into the International Year of Tibet.

Philadelphia-born Gere began his theater career in the early 1970s and became a star in such films as *Report to the Commissioner* (1975), *Looking for Mr. Goodbar* (1977), *Yanks* (1979), *An Officer and a Gentleman* (1982), and *Internal Affairs* (1989). After several years in the doldrums, Gere's career received an enormous boost in 1990 from the unexpected popularity of *Pretty Woman,* the Pygmalion-like romantic comedy in which he co-starred with Julia Roberts. He attended the University of Massachusetts. He married model Cindy Crawford late in 1991.

FURTHER READING

"Richard Gere." Maura Moynihan and Andy Warhol. *Interview,* Oct. 1983.
"Richard Gere. . . ." Linda E. Watson. *Teen,* Apr. 1983.
Richard Gere: An Unauthorized Biography. Judith Davis. NAL-Dutton, 1983.

Getz, Stan (1927–91) Philadelphia-born Getz, a jazz saxophonist, made his professional debut at the age of 15 with Jack Teagarden's band; in the 1930s and 1940s, he went on to play with Stan Kenton, Benny Goodman, Jimmy Dorsey, and Woody Herman. In 1948, he recorded a breakthrough solo on Herman's "Early Autumn," then recording and leading bands on his own. Getz encountered serious drug problems in the late 1950s, emigrating to Denmark in 1958. He returned to the United States in 1961, finding commercial success with the album *Focus.* In 1962, he and guitarist Charlie Byrd recorded the *Jazz Samba* album, with its "The Girl from Ipanema." Getz won 11 Grammy awards during his long career. He was survived by two daughters and three sons. (d. Malibu, California; June 4, 1991)

FURTHER READING

"Stan Getz, 1927–'91." John McDonough. *Down Beat,* Sep. 1991.
Obituary. *Current Biography,* Aug. 1991.
"Stan Getz. . . ." Herb Alpert. *Rolling Stone,* Aug. 8, 1991.
Obituary. *Variety,* June 10, 1991.
"Stan Getz. . . ." Joseph Hooper. *New York Times Magazine,* June 9, 1991.
Obituary. *The Times* (of London), June 8, 1991.
Obituary. *New York Times,* June 8, 1991.
Stan Getz. Richard Palmer. Seven Hills, 1991.

Gibson, Mel (1956–) As Gibson's *Hamlet* (1990), with Glenn Close, Paul Scofield, and Alan Bates, moved through its theatrical release and onto home screens, Gibson moved back to his native Australia, fulfilling his promise to take some time off with his family after making four films in a row. Late in 1991, he returned to filmmaking, in the kind of action-adventure movie that has made him a familiar face all over the world. It was to be *Lethal Weapon 3,* a sequel to the two extraordinarily popular *Lethal Weapon* films. The film, directed and co-produced by Richard Donner, starred Gibson and Danny Glover, in a cast that included Rene Russo, Joe Pesci, Steven Kahan, Darlene Love, Traci Wolfe, Damon Hines, Ebonie Smith, and Stuart Wilson.

Born in Peekskill, New York, Gibson emigrated to Australia with his family in 1968. He appeared on stage and screen in Australia from 1977, in South Australian regional theater in the classics, in several television series, and most notably in the film *Tim* (1979). He soon became a popular worldwide film star, in such action films as *Mad Max* (1979) and its two sequels: *The Road Warrior* (1982) and *Mad Max Beyond Thunderdome* (1985); the dramas *Gallipoli* (1981) and *The Year of Living Dangerously* (1983); the *Lethal Weapon* films (1987, 1989), *Bird on a Wire* (1990), and *Air America* (1990). Gibson attended the Australian National Institute of Dramatic Arts. He married Robyn Moore in 1979; they have six children.

FURTHER READING

"Mel-o-drama. . . ." Roy Sekoff. *Seventeen,* Jan. 1991.
"Mel Gibson. . . ." John Lahr. *Cosmopolitan,* Dec. 1990.
"Road worrior. . . ." *Harper's Magazine,* Aug. 1990.
"Talking with Mel Gibson. . . ." Carson Jones. *Redbook,* Aug. 1990.
Mel Gibson: Australia's Restless Superstar. Keith McKay. Doubleday, 1986.
Mel Gibson. David Ragan. Dell, 1985.

Gielgud, John (Arthur John Gielgud, 1904–) In his sixth decade in the theater, the acclaimed British actor continued to display his very wide range. He won the 1991 Emmy as best leading actor in a miniseries or special for his performance as scruffy columnist Haverford Downs in the four-part television miniseries *Summer's Lease,* based on John Mortimer's novel, in which he starred with Susan Fleetwood, Michael Pargiter, Leslie Phillips, Rosemary Leach, and Jeremy Kemp. In *Prospero's Books* (1991), Peter Greenaway's highly visual and unorthodox film version of *The Tempest,* Gielgud had an extraordinary tour de force: as Shakespeare, he played *all* of the main speaking roles for most of the film; other players included Alec Guinness, Ian Richardson, Isabelle Pasco, Erland Josephson, and Michel Piccoli. Gielgud also made a new record, reading Herman Melville's *The Encantadas* to Tobias Picker's music played by the Houston Symphony; and in the summer of 1991 he recorded the book of Genesis for BBC Radio's serialization of the Bible. Forthcoming were roles in David Seltzer's World War II spy thriller *Shining Through,* based on Susan Isaacs's novel and starring Michael Douglas, Melanie Griffith, Liam Neeson, and Joely Richardson, scheduled for early 1992 release; and John Avildsen's *The Power of One,* in a cast that includes Morgan Freeman, Stephen Dorff, Armin Mueller-Stahl, and Fay Masterson.

One of the leading actors of the English-speaking theater for over six decades, London-born Gielgud made his stage debut in 1921. By 1929, he had become a highly regarded Shakespearean actor at the Old Vic, going on to play major roles in Shakespeare for the next half-century, perhaps most notably as *Hamlet.* He directed a legendary 1935 *Romeo and Juliet* in London, alternating with Laurence Olivier in the Mercutio and Romeo roles. Late in his career, he created several modern roles, among others in *Nude With Violin* (1956), *Tiny Alice* (1964), *Home* (1970), and *No Man's Land* (1970). Although Gielgud made his film debut in 1921 and played leads in the films *Secret Agent* (1936) and *Julius Caesar* (1970), he has for most of his career been primarily a theater actor. In recent years, however, he has played numerous strong supporting roles in such films as *Murder on the Orient Express* (1974), *Arthur* (1981; he won a Best Supporting Actor Oscar), and *Chariots of Fire* (1981), and in such television productions as *Brideshead Revisited* (1981) and *War and Remembrance* (1988). Among his writings are *Early Stages: A Theatrical Reminiscence* (1939), *Stage Directions* (1963), *An Actor in His Time* (1981), and *Backward Glances: Times for Reflection and Distinguished Company* 1990).

FURTHER READING

"A man for all seasons. . . ." Gerald C. Lubenow. *Newsweek,* Mar. 21, 1988.

Gillespie, Dizzy (John Birks Gillespie, 1917–) In his 74th year, legendary trumpeter Gillespie paused briefly to have a cataract operation and then moved right back into action on what amounts to his perpetual world tour. His traveling quintet included guitarist Ed Cherry, tenor saxophonist Ron Holloway, drummer Ignacio Berroa, and electric bassist John Lee. During the year, Gillespie played on four continents, as a soloist, with his quintet, and at the head of his United Nations Orchestra. The year 1991 also saw release of the record *Live at the Royal Festival Hall,* taped in London by the orchestra. A second recording was the CD *The Paris All-Stars: Homage to Charlie Parker,* featuring Gillespie and many other classic jazz musicians. In October, Gillespie celebrated his 74th birthday with his third appearance at the ninth annual Floating Jazz Festival aboard the cruise ship *Norway.*

South Carolina-born Gillespie, a trumpeter, composer, arranger, bandleader, and recording artist, became a leading jazz figure in the mid-1940s; in that period, with Charlie Parker and others, he is credited with having originated "bop," also often called "be-bop." Gillespie became a trumpeter in the early 1930s and played with Teddy Hill, Cab Calloway, Benny Carter, Duke Ellington, and others until he formed his first successful band, in 1946. Gillespie composed such jazz and popular standards as "Night in Tunisia" (1942), "Salt Peanuts" (1945), and "Manteca" (1947), and has toured widely and recorded for the past five decades. He has appeared in several films, most recently in the documentary *A Night in Havana* (1990). In 1990, Gillespie received the first Duke Ellington Award, at Washington's Kennedy Center, and a National Medal of the Arts from President George Bush at the White House. An early autobiography was *To Be or Not to Bop: Memoirs of Dizzy Gillespie* (1955; written with Al Fraser). He married Lorraine Wills in 1940.

FURTHER READING

Waiting for Dizzy. GENE LEES. Oxford University Press, 1991.
Dizzy Gillespie. TONY GENTRY. Chelsea House, 1991.
"Dizzy." WHITNEY BALLIETT. *New Yorker*, Sep. 17, 1990.
"Dizzy Gillespie. . . ." JAMES JOYCE IV. *Down Beat*, Aug. 1990.
"Bebop's joyful pop. . . ." TIM POWIS. *Maclean's*, Mar. 20, 1989.
Dizzy Gillespie. BARRY MCRAE. Phaidon Universe, 1989.
Dizzy Gillespie. RAYMOND HORRICKS. Hippocrene, 1984.

Gingrich, Newt (Newton Leroy Gingrich, 1943–) Still the focal point of much enmity from congressional Democrats in the wake of the 1988–90 House ethics scandals, House Republican Whip Gingrich continued to be a chief Republican conservative attack vehicle in 1991. He drew a good deal of attention in February when he sharply criticized House Speaker Thomas Foley's appointments of liberal Democrats to the House Intelligence Committee, implying that they might leak intelligence information. In March, in the wake of the Persian Gulf War, Gingrich was once again sharply critical, this time of those Democratic opponents who had voted against the war resolution, calling on them to admit their mistake publicly. In June, Gingrich attacked the investigative agency of Congress, the General Accounting Office, accusing it of pro-liberal bias. Late in the year, he moved into somewhat more defensive positions, as Democratic attacks on economic issues during the deepening recession began to hurt the Bush administration, and urged the administration to move more swiftly and decisively on bread-and-butter issues.

Pennsylvania-born Gingrich taught at West Georgia College before his election to the House of Representatives in 1979. He drew national attention in 1987 and 1988, as chief accuser of Democratic House Speaker Jim Wright, who ultimately resigned from the House. In August 1989, he urged ethics probes of 17 other congressional Democrats as well. Gingrich himself was accused of earlier ethics violations in April 1989, soon after his March 1989 selection as House Republican Whip, and faced further ethics charges in October; but all charges against him were dropped in March 1990. Gingrich attended Emory and Tulane Universities. In 1984, with David Drake and Marianne Gingrich, he published *Window of Opportunity: A Blueprint for the Future*. He has been married twice and has two children.

FURTHER READING

"A party's Newt testament. . . ." DANIEL WATTENBERG. *Insight*, Nov. 12, 1990.
"Having read George Bush's lips. . . ." BILL HEWITT. *People*, Nov. 12, 1990.
"New Newt news." DAVID BEERS. *Mother Jones*, Feb.–Mar. 1990.
"Master of disaster. . . ." DAVID BEERS. *Mother Jones*, Oct. 1989.
"Gingrich, Newton Leroy." *Current Biography*, July 1989.

Ginzburg, Natalia Levi (1916–91) Ginzburg was one of the leading Italian novelists of the postwar period, and a notable essayist and translator. Born in Palermo, she grew up in Turin, the child of socialist, anti-fascist parents. Her first short story was published in 1934. In 1938, she married Leone Ginzburg, an anti-fascist university professor; together they worked in the newly formed Einaudi publishing firm in Turin in the late 1930s. They were forced by anti-Jewish laws to live in a ghetto area near Rome from 1940 to 1943, a period in which she published her first novel, *The Road to the City*, under a pseudonym because of those laws. An active anti-fascist, Leone Ginzburg was arrested in 1943, imprisoned, and died soon thereafter, probably murdered by his jailers. She returned to Turin after the war and created such novels as *The Dry Heart* (1947), *A Light for Fools* (1952), *Voices in the Evening* (1961), *Family Sayings* (1963), and *No Way* (1973). In her later years, she became a prolific essayist on a wide range of social matters; many of her essays are collected in *Never Must You Ask Me* (1973). Her second marriage was to Gabriele Baldini in 1950; he died in 1969. She is survived by three daughters and a son. (d. Rome; October 8, 1991)

FURTHER READING

Obituary. *The Times* (of London), Oct. 9, 1991.
Obituary. *New York Times,* Oct. 9, 1991.
Natalia Ginzburg: Human Relationships in a Changing World. Alan Bullock. Berg Publications, 1991.
"Ginzburg, Natalia." *Current Biography,* July 1990.

Glass, Philip (1937–) A wide-ranging composer and musician, Glass continued to work in several forms during 1991. He wrote the music for choreographer David Gordon's *The Mysteries, and What's So Funny?,* introduced at the Spoleto Dance Festival, about Marcel Duchamp. He also wrote the music for Joanne Akalaitis's production of Shakespeare's *Henry IV, Parts 1 and 2,* at New York's Public Theater. A third work is Glass's adaptation for the theater of Jean Cocteau's film *Orpheus,* to be presented by the Cambridge American Repertory Theater. Forthcoming was a major work, the new opera *The Voyage,* about Christopher Columbus and the meeting of the cultures of the Old and New Worlds. Commissioned by the Metropolitan Opera for introduction in 1992, the 500th centenary year of the Columbus voyage of discovery, the libretto is by David Hwang. Also forthcoming was another new opera, *The White Raven,* with libretto by Robert Wilson.

In his developing body of work, Baltimore-born Glass has wiped out any "line" that might still be said to exist between modern classical and popular music. He emerged as a leading modern composer in the late 1960s, after a Paris period in which he worked with Ravi Shankar and studied with Nadia Boulanger, then weaving modernist and Indian themes and techniques into his music. He founded the Philip Glass Ensemble in 1968 and became a well-known figure on tour and a popular recording artist in the early 1970s, with such works as *Music in 12 Parts* (1971–74) and *Glassworks* (1982). He also began a major career as a classical composer in the 1970s, with *Einstein On the Beach,* still his best-known classical work, and the other two parts of his celebrated "portrait opera" trilogy: *Akhnaten* (1980) and *Satyagraha* (1985). Among his other operas are *The Civil Wars* (1982–84), *The Making of the Representative for Planet 8* (1988), *One Thousand Airplanes on the Roof* (1988), *Mattogrosso* (1989), and *The Hydrogen Jukebox* (1990). The last was produced in collaboration with poet Allen Ginsberg and visual artist Jerome Sirlin, starting from a cantata based on Ginsberg's anti-war poem, "Wichita Vortex Sutra." In 1987 Glass published the memoir *Music by Philip Glass.* He attended the University of Chicago and the Juilliard School of Music. He was formerly married and has two children.

FURTHER READING

"Philip Glass. . . ." *Connoisseur,* Feb. 1991.
American Music Makers. Janet Nichols. Walker, 1990.
"Glass." Tim Page. *Opera News,* June 1988.

Glenn, John Herschel Jr. (1921–) Senator Glenn, a much decorated World War II and Korean War pilot, was the first American to orbit the Earth, on February 20, 1962, in the Mercury spacecraft *Friendship 7,* a feat that he carries with him throughout his lifetime. In 1991, he saw the end of an episode that had somewhat tarnished some of his later years, his alleged involvement in the Keating Lincoln Savings and Loan Association case, with its charges that he and four other senators (the "Keating Five") unethically intervened with federal bank regulators on behalf of the Lincoln Savings and Loan Association of Irvine, California, controlled by Charles H. Keating, Jr. In 1989, the bank was taken over by federal banking authorities, in a bailout carrying an estimated cost of at least $2 billion. On February 27, 1991, after 14 months of hearings, the Ethics Committee decided to drop the case against Glenn, with only a comment about "exercising poor judgment." In effect, the committee had taken its own counsel's recommendation that the charges against Glenn be dropped for lack of evidence.

During 1991, Glenn continued to deal with a wide range of public issues, perhaps most notably as chairman of the Senate's Governmental Affairs Committee, continuing to expose waste in military spending as when he in January criticized government spending of over $100 million on unnecessary germ warfare weapons defense systems. His July attempt to transfer $118 million earmarked for the nuclear weapons program into nuclear waste cleanup efforts did not pass in the Senate.

Ohio-born Glenn began his flying career as a Marine pilot in 1943. In addition to his wartime experience, he was a leading test pilot, and on July 16, 1957, was the first transcontinental pilot to fly at supersonic speeds. In 1959, he became a Project Mercury astronaut. In 1974, he was elected to the first of his three terms as an Ohio Democratic senator. Glenn's 1962 B.Sc. was from Muskingum College; he had been a student at the college from 1939 to 1942. He also attended naval flight schools. He married Anna Margaret Castor in 1943; they had two children.

FURTHER READING

"John Herschel Glenn, Jr." PATRICIA BARNES-SVARNEY. *Ad Astra,* July–Aug. 1991.
"Seven sorry senators. . . ." MARGARET CARLSON. *Time,* Jan. 8, 1990.
Presidential Odyssey of John Glenn. RICHARD F. FENNO, JR. *Congressional Quarterly,* 1990.
John Glenn: Space Pioneer. ANN ANGEL. Fawcett, 1989.
Famous in America: Jane Fonda, George Wallace, Phyllis Schlafly, John Glenn. PETER N. CARROLL. NAL-Dutton, 1986.
John Glenn: Around the World in Ninety Minutes. PAUL WESTMAN. Dillon, 1980.

Gobel, George (1919–91) Gobel made his debut as a singer and guitarist on radio in his home city of Chicago, and continued to perform on radio and live throughout the 1930s. After army air force service in World War II, he returned to show business in cabaret as a singer, instrumentalist, and comedian. He broke into early television as a repeat guest on "The Garry Moore Show" and other variety shows, and became a major television star in his own "George Gobel Show" (1954–57), receiving a 1954 Emmy award as outstanding new personality of the year, a Peabody award, and several other honors. He also appeared in a number of films and plays. He was a regular guest on the "Hollywood Squares" from 1966 into the 1980s. He was survived by his wife, Alice, two daughters, and a son. (d. Encino, California; February 24, 1991)

FURTHER READING

Obituary. *Current Biography,* Apr. 1991.
"TV's lonesome George. . . ." *People,* Mar. 11, 1991.
Obituary. *Variety,* Mar. 4, 1991.
Obituary. *New York Times,* Feb. 25, 1991.

Goldberg, Whoopi (Caryn Johnson, 1950–) Very popular actress Goldberg won a 1991 Best Supporting Actress Oscar for her role in *Ghost* (1990); and as the film moved from its extraordinarily successful $210-million theatrical run to top place in video rentals, her career went into even higher gear. While that was happening, in May she starred opposite Sally Field and Kevin Kline in the Michael Hoffman film comedy *Soapdish,* and in June opened at the Cannes Film Festival as one of a group of women comedians doing their routines in *Wisecracks.* Forthcoming was a starring role in the film version of the South African musical, *Sarafina!,* to be shot on location in Soweto; an appearance in the Robert Altman film *The Player,* in a multistar cast; and a starring role in Richard Benjamin's *Radio Free Alaska.* She stars too in a

forthcoming Disney film, *Sister Act,* but apparently none too happily: She is quoted as saying at a 1991 Friars Club tribute for Richard Pryor that "working for Disney, I do feel like a nigger again, and I'm not afraid to say it." Goldberg is starting yet another career, as well; in the autumn of 1992, she is scheduled to host and produce "The Whoopi Goldberg Show," a television talk show focusing on one-on-one interviews with leading newsmakers and entertainers. Three comedy specials for HBO are also committed.

New York City-born Goldberg, who had previously worked as a popular cabaret and stage entertainer, emerged as a film star in *The Color Purple* (1985; she received an Oscar nomination), and went on to such films as *Jumpin' Jack Flash* (1986), *Fatal Beauty* (1987), *Burglar* (1988), and *The Long Walk Home* (1990). In 1990, she scored a major success as the Harlem-based Black psychic in the year's surprise top-grossing film, *Ghost,* opposite Patrick Swayze and Demi Moore. She also starred opposite Jean Stapleton in the short-lived television series "Bagdad Cafe" (1990). She had a one-woman show on Broadway in 1984, and toured in a second one-woman show in 1988. Goldberg was previously married and has one child.

FURTHER READING

"Whoopi Goldberg. . . ." *Jet,* Apr. 22, 1991.
"Whoopi Goldberg. . . ." STEPHEN FARBER. *Cosmopolitan,* Mar. 1991.

Goldblum, Jeff (1952–) Demonstrating his great range in yet another character lead, Goldblum starred as the Pianist in Ben Lewin's surreal film comedy *The Favour, the Watch and the Very Big Fish,* which opened at the London Film Festival in November 1991. The cast of the French-British work included Bob Hoskins, Natasha Richardson, and Jean-Pierre Cassel. Forthcoming were starring roles opposite Mimi Rogers in Baz Taylor's *Shooting Elizabeth* and opposite Rosanna Arquette in Paul Mones's *Fathers and Sons.* Goldblum will also appear in the forthcoming Robert Altman film *The Player* in a cast that includes many other stars, including Tim Robbins, Greta Scacchi, Whoopi Goldberg, Anjelica Huston, Julia Roberts, Susan Sarandon, Jack Lemmon, Cher, Rosanna Arquette, Nick Nolte, Mimi Rogers, and Burt Reynolds.

Pittsburgh-born Goldblum played in the New York theater in the early 1970s, most notably in *Two Gentlemen of Verona* (1971). His wide range of films includes *Invasion of the Body Snatchers* (1978), *The Big Chill* (1983), *The Right Stuff* (1983), *Silverado* (1985), *The Fly* (1986), *Beyond Therapy* (1987), *Earth Girls Are Easy* (1989) opposite his then-wife Geena Davis, *Twisted Obsession* (1990), *The Tall Guy* (1990), and *Mr. Frost* (1990). He also appeared in the television series "Tenspeed and Brownshoe" (1980), in the telefilms *The Race for the Double Helix* (1987) as scientist James Watson, and *Framed* (1990). Goldblum attended the Neighborhood Playhouse. He was previously married to actress Geena Davis (1987–91).

FURTHER READING

"Married . . . with chicken." JOHANNA SCHNELLER. *GQ–Gentleman's Quarterly,* June 1989.
"The new Jeff Goldblum. . . ." JACK CURRY. *Cosmopolitan,* May 1987.

Gonzalez Márquez, Felipe (1942–) Spanish Prime Minister Gonzalez, secretary general of the Spanish Socialist Workers Party (PSOE), continued to lead a divided party and

hold power rather shakily in his third term and ninth year in office, while at the same time being increasingly respected abroad. At home, he faced continuing economic problems; focusing on inflation control, his government managed to keep inflation under 7 percent; but a reported unemployment rate of over 15 percent, with foreign workers continuing to arrive in considerable numbers, continued to erode some of the basic support of his party. He introduced a major tax reform law in spring 1991, and simultaneously announced plans to build 400,000 new low-priced housing units, though his method of financing, involving forced low-rate bank mortgages, was widely criticized. He also furthered the integration of Spain into the new Europe that was emerging as the European Community strengthened.

Gonzalez was an early supporter of American action in the Persian Gulf crisis, a course much opposed in traditionally neutralist Spain, and especially so within his own party. In Latin American affairs, Gonzalez undertook a special role, on July 18 and 19 attending the first Ibero-American summit, at Guadalajara, Mexico, and committing himself to try to act as a bridge between the nations of Latin American and those of the new Europe. At the conference, he also continued to press Fidel Castro for democratic reforms in Cuba.

Gonzalez became a member of the then-illegal Spanish Socialist Workers Party in 1964, having been a socialist youth group member since 1962. He rose to become his party's leader and succeeded Adolfo Suarez González as prime minister with his party's victory in the 1982 elections. He was the first socialist prime minister of Spain since the Spanish Civil War; his election signaled the full emergence of a new Spain after the long night of the Franco period. In 1986, he took Spain into the European Common Market. He won a third term in the October 1989 elections, though only by one parliamentary seat; and on review that seat was lost by his party, leaving him without a clear parliamentary majority. Gonzalez attended the Catholic University of Louvaine. He is married to Carmen Romero; they have three children.

FURTHER READING

"For Spain and 'Felipe.' . . ." John Darnton. *New York Times,* June 26, 1984.

Goodman, John (1952–) Roseanne Barr Arnold's television husband continued to star in "Roseanne" during the 1991–92 season, while also appearing in several new and forthcoming feature films. In February, he starred as a Las Vegas entertainer turned into British royalty in the title role of David S. Ward's film comedy *King Ralph;* the cast included Peter O'Toole and John Hurt. The film was badly received, critically and commercially. His next film did far better critically; he played Charlie Meadows opposite John Turturro in the title role in the Coen brothers' *Barton Fink,* one of the hits of the 1991 Cannes Film Festival. Forthcoming was a starring role as Babe Ruth in Arthur Hiller's *The Babe* in a cast that includes Kelly McGillis, Trini Alvarado, and Bruce Boxleitner.

Before his "Roseanne" role catapulted him to stardom, Missouri-born Goodman had played in strong character roles in the theater and in films, on Broadway in such plays as *Loose Ends* (1979) and *Big River* (1985), and in such films as *Eddie Macon's Run* (1983), *True Stories* (1986), *Raising Arizona* (1987), *Sea of Love* (1989), *Always* (1989), and *Stella* (1990). Goodman attended Southwest Missouri State College. He married Anna Elizabeth (Annabeth) Hartzog in 1989; they have one daughter.

FURTHER READING

"John Goodman." Tom Green. *Los Angeles,* Mar. 1991.

"Being the big guy. . . ." PETER DE JONGE. *New York Times Magazine,* Feb. 10, 1991.
"John Goodman. . . ." ERIC SHERMAN. *Ladies Home Journal,* Feb. 1991.
"John Goodman. . . ." FRED ROBBINS. *Woman's Day,* May 1, 1990.
"Everybody's all American. . . ." RICHARD ZOGLIN. *Time,* Feb. 19, 1990.

Gorbachev, Mikhail Sergeyevich (1931–) For a few days in August, all of Mikhail Gorbachev's massive work was threatened. On August 19, his removal from office was announced by a right-wing Communist State of Emergency Committee headed by Vice President Gennadi I. Yanayev, and including such key figures as KGB Chairman Vladimir A. Kryuchkov, Interior Minister Boris L. Pugo, and Defense Minister Dimitri Yazov. Gorbachev, then vacationing in the Crimea with his family, was placed under house arrest. Many of the coup leaders were his own recent appointees, some of them conservatives he had selected over the strong objections of his closest advisers.

While Gorbachev refused to sign away his leadership in the Crimea, Boris Yeltsin led the massive resistance that immediately developed in several major cities, with his supporters holding the White House, the Russian parliament building in Moscow, as massive unarmed crowds gathered to defend it. The resistance was decisively helped by the refusal of key capital military units to move against Yeltsin; indeed, elite paratroops, Afghanistan war veterans, and Soviet armor sent against him all turned themselves to face any attacking force, guaranteeing the safety and quick victory of the resistance. Quick support of the resistance by U.S. President George Bush and British Prime Minister John Major were also reportedly of importance.

On August 21, the aborted coup collapsed. Gorbachev came back to Moscow on August 22, but to a much changed situation, in which Yeltsin was a national hero. It was quickly clear that the attempted coup had engineered precisely its opposite, a second Russian Revolution that was in the process of sweeping away the remnants of Soviet communism—and ultimately swept away the Soviet state itself. On Gorbachev's return from the Crimea, all the coup plotters were arrested, except Pugo, who had already committed suicide; large numbers of key administrators and army leaders were fired and replaced; and the Communist Party was essentially disbanded. Gorbachev wrote of these events in *The August Coup: The Truth and the Lessons* (1991).

But Gorbachev himself did not seize the moment to re-establish his leadership. Yeltsin and other leaders took control of a disintegrating Soviet Union, as Gorbachev's attempts to hold the country together failed. On December 8, 1991, Russian president Yeltsin, Ukrainian president Leonid Kravchuk, and Byelorussian president Stanislav Shushkevich founded a new "Commonwealth of Independent States" and declared the Soviet Union at an end. On December 25, Gorbachev resigned; he was seen throughout the world as still by far the greatest Soviet leader of the 20th century.

Gorbachev's early career proceeded in orthodox Soviet fashion: He joined the Communist Party of the Soviet Union in 1952 and for the next 33 years moved up through the party and government. He became a member of his party's central committee in 1971 and was minister of agriculture (1978–85). In 1985, he became general secretary of the Soviet Communist Party Central Committee and effectively leader of the Soviet Union. In power, he immediately began the process of internal change. His two main slogans were *perestroika,* meaning a massive restructuring of the Soviet economy, away from central planning, bureaucracy, and full state ownership and toward a market economy, private enterprise, and even private ownership of land; and *glasnost,* or "openness," meaning a move toward basic democratic freedoms.

Abroad, Gorbachev also moved very quickly once in power. In a series of meetings with Presidents Ronald Reagan and George Bush, he initiated what became the end of the 45-year-long Cold War, beginning with the 1987 intermediate nuclear forces treaty, the first of a series of major Soviet-American peace moves, with planned troop pullbacks and for the first time in decades real progress on arms control. In the process, he and the American presidents helped to negotiate the end of conflicts in Nicaragua, Cambodia, Angola, Mozambique, Namibia, Ethiopia, and several other countries, both superpowers ending their long sponsorship of opposing parties in many regional conflicts. At the same time, he normalized relations with China, bringing that 30-year-old conflict to an end. And, during the late 1980s, he essentially agreed to set the peoples of Eastern Europe free, encouraging the development of what became independent, non-communist governments in Poland, Czechoslovakia, Hungary, Bulgaria, Romania, and East Germany. The developments in East Germany led directly to the tearing down of the Berlin Wall in the 1990 unification of Germany.

A key figure in modern history, Mikhail Gorbachev made an enormous contribution to world peace and the end of the Cold War, and brought massive and welcome changes to his own country and much of the world. In 1990, Gorbachev was awarded the Nobel Peace Prize. Among his recent works are *Perestroika and Soviet-American Relations* (1990), *At the Summit: A New Start in U.S.-Soviet Relations* (1988), and *Toward a Better World* and *Perestroika: New Thinking for Our Country and the World* (both 1987). Mikhail Gorbachev attended Moscow State University and the Stavropol Agricultural Institute. He and Raisa Maksimova Titorenko married in 1956; they have one child.

FURTHER READING

" 'I want to stay the course.' " JOHN KOHAN et al. *Time,* Dec. 23, 1991.

" 'There is no way.' . . ." MORTIMER B. ZUKERMAN et al. *U.S. News & World Report,* Dec. 2, 1991.

"Red star falling." GAIL SHEEHY. *Vanity Fair,* Dec. 1991.

"The Man Who Changed the World. . . ." TATYANA TOLSTAYA. *New Republic,* May 27, 1991.

"Good-bye Gorbachev?" PAUL KLEBNIKOV. *Forbes,* Apr. 15, 1991.

"Whodunit?" HENDRIK HERTZBERG. *New Republic,* Jan. 21, 1991.

Gorbachev: The Story of a Survivor. NEIL FELSHMAN. St. Martin's, 1991.

Gorbachev and After. STEPHEN WHITE. Cambridge University Press, 1991.

Gorbachev and His Reforms. RICHARD SAKWA. Prentice-Hall, 1991.

Mikhail Gorbachev. MICHEL TATU. Columbia University Press, 1991.

The Impact of Gorbachev. DEREK SPRING, ed. Columbia University Press, 1991.

Mikhail Gorbachev. JEROME MOGA. Bantam, 1991.

What Went Wrong with Perestroika. MARSHALL I. GOLDMAN. Norton, 1991.

The Gorbachev Phenomenon: A Historical Interpretation, rev. ed. MOSHE LEWIN. University of California Press, 1991.

Mikhail Gorbachev. JOHN W. SELFRIDGE. Chelsea House, 1991.

Why Gorbachev Happened: His Triumphs and His Failure. ROBERT G. KAISER. Simon & Schuster, 1991.

Mikhail Gorbachev: Revolutionary for Democracy. ANNA SPROYLE. Gareth Stevens, 1991.

The Man Who Changed the World: The Lives of Mikhail S. Gorbachev. GAIL SHEEHY. HarperCollins, 1990.

Gorbachev: Heretic in the Kremlin. DUSKO DODER and LOUISE BRANSON. Viking Penguin, 1990.

Mikhail Gorbachev: A Leader for Soviet Change. WALTER OLEKSY. Childrens, 1989.

Mikhail Gorbachev: The Soviet Innovator. STEVEN OTFINOSKI. Fawcett, 1989.

Mikhail S. Gorbachev: An Intimate Biography. DONALD MORRISON. New American Library-Dutton, 1988.

Gorbachev, Raisa Maksimova Titorenko (1934–) At 5:00 PM, on August 19, 1991, Raisa and Mikhail Gorbachev, then vacationing in the Crimea, were placed under house arrest by the organizers of the failed right-wing coup that began the second Russian Revolution. What followed were 72 hours of intense pressure, with the coup plotters attempting to talk the Soviet president into signing the country over to them, which he adamantly refused to do. The coup failed, and the Gorbachevs returned to Moscow on August 22, but the strain of the event told on Raisa Gorbachev, who developed severe hypertension, partial loss of the ability to speak, and numbness in one arm, as reported by Mikhail Gorbachev in September. She was later reported to have fully recovered. An autobio-

graphical book, *I Hope,* consisting of a long interview with writer Georgi Pryakhin, was published by HarperCollins in September 1991. By year's end, the Soviet Union was gone and Mikhail Gorbachev had relinquished power, and with it the strain of public life for both Gorbachevs.

Raisa Maksimova Titorenko was born in Stavropol, attended Moscow University and the Stavropol Teachers Training College, and was a teacher in Stavropol when she married Mikhail Gorbachev in 1956. From 1957 to 1961, she was on the staff of the Stavropol Teachers Training Institute. As the wife of Soviet leader Mikhail Gorbachev, she had considerable impact in her own right, speaking out for reform on many of the difficult questions facing the Soviet Union during the Gorbachev era. Although not herself a political leader, she has served in some ways as a model for many Soviet women, her popularity and status being very different from that of previous women in her position, who were seldom seen and never spoke out. Even her clothes and shopping trips while abroad made news in her country, as Soviet women reached out for life-styles already common in most other industrial countries. She made a particularly notable impression in the United States during the June 1990 Washington summit, making highly publicized visits to several American cities and joining Barbara Bush as a commencement speaker at Wellesley College. She and Mikhail Gorbachev have one child.

FURTHER READING

" 'Those days were horrible.' " SUSAN TIFFT. *Time,* Sep. 16, 1991.
"Raisa. . . ." CAITLIN KELLY. *New York Times Book Review,* July 28, 1991.
Raisa Gorbachev. Chelsea House, 1991.
"Gorbachev, Raisa." *Current Biography,* May 1988.

Gordimer, Nadine (1923–) On October 3, 1991, the Swedish Academy of Letters awarded the 1991 Nobel Prize for Literature to South African writer Nadine Gordimer. She was the first woman to win the prize in 25 years, since poet Nelly Sachs in 1966. Quite in line with her lifelong commitment to freedom, her December 9 Nobel acceptance speech in Stockholm defended British author Salman Rushdie, his life threatened by Islamic fundamentalists, and urged United Nations action on his behalf. Her most recent work is *Jump and Other Stories* (1991), a collection of 16 stories, many of them previously published in magazines.

Gordimer has long been a critic of South African racism and of the system of apartheid; she is a founder and active member of the Congress of South African Writers, an organization composed mostly of Black writers and often allied with the African National Congress (ANC), and joined the ANC as soon as it was "unbanned," saying "I'm happy to be a card-carrying member of the ANC." She is also a vice president of International PEN. But although politically ac-

tive, she has often been called the "conscience of South Africa" for a body of work that illuminates the multiple corruptions and injustices at the heart of a racist society through the personal lives and concerns of the people in her stories, rather than as a set of direct political statements. Her novels include *The Lying Days* (1953), *A World of Strangers* (1958), *Occasion for Loving* (1963), *The Late Bourgeois World* (1966), *A Guest of Honour* (1970), *The Conservationist* (1974; for which she shared a Booker Prize), *Burger's Daughter* (1979), *July's People* (1981), *A Sport of Nature* (1987), and *My Son's Story* (1990). She has also published many volumes of short stories from *The Soft Voice of the Serpent* (1953) to *Six Feet of Country* (1986), and several volumes of essays.

Gordimer was born in the Transvaal, the daughter of Jewish immigrants from Latvia and Britain. She published her first short story at the age of 15. She has been married twice and has three children.

FURTHER READING

"Apartheid's daughter." *People,* Oct. 21, 1991.
"The power of a well-told tale." PAUL GRAY et al. *Time,* Oct. 14, 1991.
"Ordinary loves. . . ." LAUREL GRAEBER. *New York Times Book Review,* Oct. 21, 1990.
Conversations with Nadine Gordimer. NANCY TOPPING BAZIN and MARILYN DALLMAN SEYMOUR, eds. 1990.
Nadine Gordimer. JUDIE NEWMAN. Routledge Chapman & Hall, 1988.

Goren, Charles (1901–91) Philadelphia-born Goren, a lawyer, became the world's leading authority on the game of contract bridge during a career that spanned four decades. He worked with auction bridge expert Milton Work in the late 1920s, beginning to publish articles in the early 1930s. He left the practice of law in 1936, the year he published his very successful book *Winning Bridge Made Easy,* and went on to become a widely syndicated bridge columnist, host of the syndicated television program "Championship Bridge," and the author of such books as *Contract Bridge Complete* (1942), *The Standard Book of Bidding* (1944), and *Point-Count Bidding* (1949). Beginning in 1933, Goren became a leading bridge player, as well; he and his long-term bridge partner Helen Sobel won the first of their several U.S. national championships in 1940. He was also a member of the winning American team at the first Bermuda Bowl world championship in 1950. Ultimately, he became informally known as "Mr. Bridge," a title made formal by the American Contract Bridge League in 1973. He was survived by a nephew and two nieces. (d. April 3, 1991; Encino, California)

FURTHER READING

Obituary. *Current Biography,* July 1991.
Obituary. MICHAEL JAFFE. *Sports Illustrated,* Apr. 22, 1991.
Obituary. *Variety,* Apr. 15, 1991.
Obituary. *The Times* (of London), Apr. 13, 1991.
Obituary. *New York Times,* Apr. 12, 1991.

Gossett, Louis, Jr. (1936–) Always bringing something more to his theatrical and television films, Gossett continued to star in drama and action-adventure works during 1991. In a dramatic role, he starred as a war hero trying to clear his electrocuted brother's name in a 30-year-old rape-murder case, in the film *Carolina Skeletons.* In the film *Toy Soldiers,* he was the dean of a boys' school taken over by narco-terrorists. In television's *The Josephine Baker Story,* he played opposite Lynn Whitfield in the title role, in a cast that included David Dukes and Ruben Blades. Forthcoming were *Aces,* a third "Iron Eagle" film, with Gossett in the title role, in another drug-battling film, directed by John Glen; and Michael Ritchie's *Diggstown,* opposite James Woods and Bruce Dern.

After over two decades as a highly regarded character actor in theater, films, and television, Brooklyn-born Gossett won an Emmy for his role as Fiddler in television's *Roots* (1977). He then went on to win a Best Supporting Actor Oscar in *An Officer and a Gentleman* (1982), and to appear in such films as *Iron Eagle* (1985) and *The Principal* (1987). On television, he had the title role in the miniseries *Sadat* (1983); his other telefilms include *A Gathering of Old Men* (1987), *Zora Is My Name!* (1990), *El Diablo* (1990), and *Sudie and Simpson* (1990). Gossett's B.A. was from New York University, in 1959.

FURTHER READING

"Family business. . . ." MARK GOODMAN. *People,* May 6, 1991.
"Gossett, Louis, Jr." *Current Biography,* Nov. 1990.

Gowing, Lawrence (1918–91) A leading British painter and art historian, Gowing's long, multi-faceted career began in the late 1930s, with his association with the Euston Road school, and in particular with his teacher, William Coldstream. He was a conscientious objector during World War II, during the war also beginning to write in art and art history, and to teach, at the Camberwell School of Art. He went on to teach at Kings College, Newcastle on Tyne (1948–58); Chelsea Polytechnic (1958–65); the University of Leeds (1968–75); and as Slade professor at University College, London (1975–85). He was long a trustee of the Tate Gallery and keeper of its British collection for two years (1966–67), in that period very notably organizing the exhibition "Turner: Imagination and Reality" at the Museum of Modern Art. Beginning in 1954, he also organized several landmark Cezanne and Matisse exhibitions. Gowing's books included studies of Vermeer, Cezanne, and Matisse. He continued to paint throughout his life and had a retrospective at the Serpentine Gallery in 1982. He was survived by his third wife, the former Jenny Wallis, and three daughters. (d. London, England; February 5, 1991)

FURTHER READING

Obituary. *The Times* (of London), Feb. 7, 1991.
Obituary. *New York Times,* Feb. 7, 1991.

Graf, Steffi (Stephanie Maria Graf, 1969–) In what some described as the best-played women's Grand Slam final in years, Steffi Graf won her third crown at Wimbledon in July 1991 against Gabriela Sabatini, who had defeated her in their last five matches. Along with victories at Berlin, Hamburg, and San Antonio, the Wimbledon win was part of Graf's fight to regain the number one ranking that she had held for a record 186 consecutive weeks before losing it to Monica Seles in March 1991. In August, when Jennifer Capriati defeated Seles at the Mazda Classic, Graf once again became number one, but fell to second when Seles won the U.S. Open, where Graf was eliminated in the semifinal by veteran Martina Navratilova.

It was all part of Graf's uphill battle to regain her concentration and set aside the personal distractions and physical problems that had haunted her since her most recent Grand Slam title (the Australian Open) in January 1990. These included a broken thumb, recurrent sinus infections, and (after the Wimbledon win) a shoulder injury, as well as a paternity suit against her father, which turned into a media fest. Tennis lovers noted that during 1991 Graf seemed to recover joy in tennis, after some earlier wistful comments looking forward to retirement. In December, Graf was named player of 1991 by the International Tennis Federation.

Graf emerged as a leading under-14 tennis player in the early 1980s, turning professional at 13. She won the German Open in 1986 and from 1987 was the world's dominant tennis player, with a string of 66 consecutive victories. She took the French Open in 1987, becoming World Champion in 1988, the year she won the U.S., Wimbledon, Australian, and French Opens, along with the Olympic championship. She then went on to victory at the U.S., Wimbledon, and German Opens again in 1989, and the Australian Open in 1990. Graf was coached from her earliest years by her father, Peter, and from 1987 by Pavel Slozil.

FURTHER READING

"The spirit of '88." Andrea Leand. *World Tennis,* Feb. 1991.

Steffi Graf. Little, Brown, 1990.
"Serving her country." CURRY KIRKPATRICK. *Sports Illustrated,* June 26, 1989.
"Graf, Steffi." *Current Biography,* Feb. 1989.
Steffi Graf. JUDY MONROE. Crestwood House, 1988.

Graham, Bill (Wolfgang Grajanka, 1931–91) The Berlin-born rock music promoter, who lost his family in the Jewish Holocaust and fled to America at age 13, was a rarity in the early world of rock music—a skilled business manager. He became manager of the San Francisco Mime Troupe in 1964 and became a rock concert organizer-promoter almost by accident, in the course of organizing benefits for the near-bankrupt mime company. He opened San Francisco's former Carousel Ballroom as the Fillmore in 1966 and quickly made it the center of the emerging rock music and countercultural explosion of the time. He went on to open New York's Fillmore East in 1968, and for the next two decades he provided a model that many others in the business of music followed. Graham also organized many massive concerts and tours for social causes, perhaps most notably the 1985 Live Aid concert. He and two others died in a helicopter crash. He was survived by three sons and three sisters. (d. near Vallejo, California; October 25, 1991)

FURTHER READING

"Rock loses its fiercest friend." STEVE DOUGHERTY et al. *People,* Nov. 11, 1991.
Obituary. *Variety,* Nov. 4, 1991.
Obituary. *The Times* (of London), Oct. 28, 1991.
Obituary. *New York Times,* Oct. 27, 1991.
"Bill Graham." TOM TEICHOLZ. *Interview,* Apr. 1986.
"Fire still burns for Bill Graham." LANI SILVER. *Mother Jones,* Jan. 1986.

Graham, Martha (1894–1991) Pennsylvania-born Graham was one of the leading dance figures of the 20th century, a dancer and choreographer who played a major role in creating the modern dance. She began her seven-decades-long career in 1916, enrolling in the Denishawn dance school and company. Leaving the company in 1923, she danced with the Greenwich Village Follies (1923–24), taught dance, gave the first concert of her own works in April 1926, established the Martha Graham School of Contemporary Dance in 1927, and founded her own company in 1929. Graham trained and worked with three generations of American dancers, including Erick Hawkins, Merce Cunningham, Anna Sokolow, Sophie Maslow, and Paul Taylor. A few of the best known of her more than 150 works are *Primitive Mysteries* (1931), *American Document* (1938), *Appalachian Spring* (1944), *Night Journey* (1947), *Clytemnestra* (1958), and *Phaedra* (1962). She continued to choreograph well into her 90s: Her *Maple Leaf Rag* premiered in New York in October 1990. *Blood Memory: An Autobiography* (1991) was published after her death. Graham was once married, to dancer Erick Hawkins. (d. New York City; April 1, 1991) (For photo, see **Madonna.**)

FURTHER READING

"Martha." CHRISTOPHER PORTERFIELD. *People,* Oct. 21, 1991.
"Martha. . . ." ARLENE CROCE. *New Yorker,* Oct. 14, 1991.
"The dancer from the dance." AGNES DE MILLE. *Vanity Fair,* Aug. 1991.
"Martha remembered. . . ." JOSEPH H. MAZO. *Dance,* July 1991.
"Martha Graham. . . ." CAMILLE HARDY. *Dance,* June 1991.
Obituary. *Current Biography,* May 1991.
" 'Graph of the heart.' . . ." LAURA SHAPIRO. *Newsweek,* Apr. 15, 1991.
"The deity of modern dance. . . ." MARTHA DUFFY. *Time,* Apr. 15, 1991.
Obituary. *U.S. News & World Report,* Apr. 15, 1991.
"Martha Graham. . . ." *People,* Apr. 15, 1991.
"Remembering Fonteyn and Graham." LAURA JACOBS. *New Leader,* Apr. 8, 1991.
Obituary. *Variety,* Apr. 8, 1991.
Obituary. *The Times* (of London), Apr. 3, 1991.
Obituary. *New York Times,* Apr. 2, 1991.
Martha: The Life and Work. AGNES DE MILLE. Random, 1991.
"Martha Graham. . . ." *Life,* Fall 1990.
"Bianca Jagger: Martha. . . ." BIANCA JAGGER. *Interview,* May 1990.
Deep Song: The Dance Story of Martha Graham. ERNESTINE STODELLE. Schirmer, 1984.

Grange, Harold (Red) (1903–91) Nicknamed the "Galloping Ghost," Pennsylvania-born Grange and his number 77 became part of football myth at the University of Illinois in the mid-1920s; he burst into public consciousness with a five-touchdown performance against undefeated Michigan in 1924, four of the scores on long runs totaling 265 yards, early in the game. He turned professional in November 1925, generating a highly charged college-professional controversy that ultimately resulted in the college draft system. Grange quickly became one of professional football's early stars, with the Chicago Bears and New York Yankees football teams, retiring from the Bears in 1934. He later briefly coached, tried an acting career, and then became a sports broadcaster for the Bears (1947–61). He was survived by his wife, Margaret. (d. Lake Wales, Florida; January 28, 1991)

FURTHER READING

Obituary. JEFFREY HART. *National Review,* Feb. 25, 1991.
Obituary. *Sports Illustrated,* Feb. 4, 1991.
Obituary. *New York Times,* Jan. 29, 1991.
"Present at the creation. . . ." ERNEST L. CUNEO. *American Scholar,* Aug. 1987.
"Football's first superstar." ROBERT W. PETERSON. *Boys' Life,* Nov. 1985.
The Galloping Ghost: Biography of Harold "Red" Grange, First Football Superstar. IRA MORTON. Crossroads, 1984.

Gray, William H., III (1942–) To the surprise of his colleagues in Congress, Gray left the fast track in 1991. Though only 12 years in office, Gray was the most powerful Black member of Congress, serving as House Majority Whip, the third-ranking Democratic leader; he had been tipped as possibly a future first Black Speaker of the House and perhaps a candidate for national office. But in June 1991, Gray announced that he was resigning his seat to accept the presidency of the United Negro College Fund (UNCF), desiring to "make a more focused contribution and . . . spend more quality time with my family and my church." Some suggested that the move stemmed from frustration over congressional inability to effect meaningful social change. Others cited rumors of the Justice Department's investigation into his finances, denied by Gray and the Justice Department since 1989 but confirmed in December 1991 when a federal grand jury subpoenaed records of Gray's honoraria for speaking engagements, though the nature of the inquiry was unclear. Gray also noted that he is, by background and training, an educator and a minister, so it is natural for him to want to serve in an organization that aims to ease Black students' access to college education, by financially supporting traditionally Black colleges. He began in the post in September 1991.

Born in Baton Rouge, Gray earned a B.A. from Franklin and Marshall College in 1963, an M. Div. from Drew Theological Seminary, and a Th.M. from Princeton Theological Seminary. Ordained as a Baptist minister, he served in various churches in New Jersey and Pennsylvania, notably Philadelphia's Bright Hope Baptist Church, where he served 1963–64 and has been senior minister since 1972. He has also been a lecturer at several colleges in the region. Gray was first elected to represent Pennsylvania's Second District in 1978, became chairman of the House Budget Committee, and was House Majority Whip from 1989. He was also active in the Congressional Black Caucus and was vice chairman of the Democratic Leadership Council. Gray married Andrea Dash in 1971; they have three sons.

FURTHER READING

"Feel the power." MIKE MALLOWE. *Philadelphia Magazine,* Dec. 1989.

"Top of Capitol Hill. . . ." LAURA B. RANDOLPH. *Ebony,* Dec. 1989.
"Gray, William H., 3d." *Current Biography,* Feb. 1988.

Greene, Graham (1904–91) A leading British author of the 20th century, Greene was a prolific writer of novels, short stories, and screenplays as well as a playwright and essayist. Always deeply concerned with questions of belief, he was briefly a Communist while at Oxford, and converted to Catholicism in the mid-1920s. Much of his work was concerned with moral issues, often presented within the context of the thrillers for which he was most widely known, many of them adapted into films. A few of his best known works are *This Gun for Hire* (1936), *Brighton Rock* (1938), *The Confidential Agent* (1939), *The Power and the Glory* (1940), *The Ministry of Fear* (1943), *The Heart of the Matter* (1948), *The Third Man* (1950), *The Quiet American* (1956), *Our Man in Havana* (1958), *A Burnt-Out Case* (1961), and *The Comedians* (1966). He also wrote several plays, most notably *The Living Room* (1953) and *The Potting Shed* (1957), and two autobiographical works, *A Sort of Life* (1971) and *Ways of Escape* (1980). He was survived by a daughter and a son. (d. Vevey, Switzerland; April 3, 1991)

FURTHER READING

Obituary. J. M. CAMERON. *New York Review of Books,* May 30, 1991.
"The end of the case." PETER GLENVILLE. *National Review,* May 27, 1991.
Obituary. *Current Biography,* May 1991.
"A restless traveler. . . ." MARK GOODMAN. *People,* Apr. 22, 1991.
"An Edwardian on the Concorde. . . ." PAUL THEROUX. *New York Times Book Review,* Apr. 21, 1991.
"Map Greeneland. . . ." JACK KROLL. *Newsweek,* Apr. 15, 1991.
"A life on the world's edge. . . ." PAUL GRAY. *Time,* Apr. 15, 1991.
Obituary. DAVID LAWDAY. *U.S. News & World Report,* Apr. 15, 1991.
"The literary consul. . . ." GLEN ALLEN. *Maclean's,* Apr. 15, 1991.
Obituary. *Variety,* Apr. 8, 1991.
Obituary. *The Times* (of London), Apr. 4, 1991.
Obituary. *New York Times,* Apr. 4, 1991.
A Bibliography of Graham Greene. NEIL BRENNAN and A. R. REDWAY. Oxford University Press, 1990.
The Life of Graham Greene, Vol. I: 1904–1939. NORMAN SHERRY. Viking Penguin, 1989.
Graham Greene. NEIL MCEWAN. St. Martin's, 1988.
Graham Greene. A. A. DEVITIS. Macmillan, 1986.

Greenspan, Alan (1926–) Until mid-1991, with the fact of recession long established, Greenspan continued to resist making substantial interest rate cuts or loosening money supplies, despite considerable pressure from both the Democratic and Republican Parties and President George Bush. During the Persian Gulf crisis that developed into the Persian Gulf War, he continued to refrain from action, arguing that oil prices and the cost of the American commitment might affect economic growth, inflation, and recession. Even after beginning to take modest action early in 1991, he continued to downplay the scope and depth of the recession. In January, he said that he saw signs the economy was beginning to stabilize; in February, he saw continuing recession, but felt that it would "bottom out reasonably soon." Speaking at Osaka, Japan, on June 5, he saw evidence that a recovery had started, making interest cuts probably unnecessary; and later in June he said the economy had probably hit bottom. But the recession deepened, and by year's end, with the Bush administration in serious political trouble because of the nonexistent recovery that was in reality a deep recession that would not go away, Greenspan had cut interest rates to levels that had not been seen for 20 years—and was expressing grave doubts about the immediate future of the American economy.

Greenspan, a leading free-market economic conservative, was a key economic consultant to Presidents Nixon and Ford, and was chairman of the national Council of Economic Advisors (1974–76). He moved into the center of national economic activity when he was appointed head of the Federal Reserve System by President Ronald Reagan. He was reappointed to a second term by President Bush in July 1991. A New Yorker, Greenspan received his B.S. in 1948, his M.A. in 1950, and his Ph.D. in 1977, all from New York University.

FURTHER READING

"The politician-economist. . . ." GLORIA BORGER. *U.S. News & World Report,* July 1, 1991.
"Alan Greenspan's. . . ." ROB NORTON. *Fortune,* Apr. 8, 1991.
"Is Alan Greenspan impotent?" ROBIN WRIGHT. *New Republic,* Apr. 9, 1990.
"Greenspan, Alan." *Current Biography,* Jan. 1989.

Griffith, Melanie (1957–) In a considerable change of pace, Griffith in late 1991 opened opposite her husband, Don Johnson, in a mild family drama, *Paradise,* written and directed by Mary Agnes Donoghue. Griffith's most recent work had included two quite adult films, *Pacific Heights* and *The Bonfire of the Vanities,* while Johnson was best known for his role in the fast, violent television series "Miami Vice." Forthcoming was a starring role as a secretly anti-Nazi American working in 1941 Germany, in David Seltzer's World War II spy thriller *Shining Through,* in a cast that includes Michael Douglas, John Gielgud, Liam Neeson, and Joely Richardson. Also forthcoming was a starring role in Sidney Lumet's *Close to Eden.*

New York City-born Griffith got off to a quick start, playing strong young supporting roles in three 1975 films: *Night Moves, The Drowning Pool,* and *Smile,* but then encountered personal and professional problems. She re-emerged as a leading dramatic actress in the mid-1980s, in such films as *Something Wild* (1986), *The Milagro Beanfield War* (1988), and *Stormy Monday* (1988), scored a major hit opposite Harrison Ford in *Working Girl* (1988), winning an Oscar nomination, and followed up with starring roles in *Pacific Heights* (1990) and *The Bonfire of the Vanities* (1990). Griffith and Johnson have one child.

FURTHER READING

"Melanie Griffith. . . ." LAURIE WERNER. *Woman's Day,* Nov. 26, 1991.
"Melanie Griffith." BILL HIGGINS. *Los Angeles Magazine,* Oct. 1991.
"Griffith, Melanie." *Current Biography,* Oct. 1990.
"Melanie mellows out." BONNIE SIEGLER. *Ladies Home Journal,* Oct. 1990.
The New Breed: Actors Coming of Age. KAREN HARDY and KEVIN J. KOFFLER. Holt, 1988.

Guard, Dave (1934–91) Honolulu-born Guard, with Bob Shane and Nick Reynolds, in 1957 founded the Kingston Trio. He had graduated from Stanford with a degree in economics a year earlier; Shane and Reynolds were students at Menlo College. The trio became a hit in the San Francisco Bay area, singing on college campuses and in such cabarets as The Hungry i and The Purple Onion. Soon after, they became an international hit, in 1959 winning a Grammy for their single "Tom Dooley." In 1960, they won a second Grammy, for best folk album. Their most successful album was *The Kingston Trio at the Hungry i* (1960). Enormously popular in the early 1960s, their easygoing folk style was by the mid-1960s superseded by a harder-edged protest style; they disbanded in 1966. Guard, who had left the group in 1961, founded the far less successful Whiskyhill Singers and then moved to Australia, remaining until 1968, there hosting a television show. He also became a record producer and wrote several books, one of them on guitar technique. He was survived by two daughters, a son, and his mother. (d. Rollinsford, New Hampshire; March 22, 1991)

FURTHER READING

Obituary. *The Times* (of London), Apr. 10, 1991.
Obituary. *Variety,* Apr. 1, 1991.
Obituary. *New York Times,* Mar. 24, 1991.

Guare, John (1938–) U.S. playwright Guare's *Six Degrees of Separation* (1990) was critically well received and became a hit of the 1990–91 season, raising many continuing questions of New York racial and class relations, homelessness, Black despair, and liberal guilt. Among its awards were the New York Drama Critics' Circle Award as the best play of the 1990–91 season and the 1991 Dramatists Guild Hull-Warriner Award. In a bizarre development, a New York judge on April 10 ordered con man David Hampton to stay away from Guare; Hampton had threatened Guare's life, demanding payment because the story basis of the play was Hampton's 1983 con, in which he successfully posed as "David Poitier," Sidney Poitier's "son," and ultimately stayed with, borrowed money from, and then robbed his victims. Forthcoming from Guare were a new play, *Four Baboons Adoring the Sun,* and a film comedy, *Stark Truth,* in development with Universal Pictures.

New York City-born Guare wrote the plays *Muzeeka* (1968) and *Cop-out* (1969) before emerging as a major modern playwright with his Tony-winning *House of Blue Leaves* (1971). His later plays included *Landscape of the Body* (1977), *Bosoms and Neglect* (1979), *Lydie Breeze* (1982), and *Moon over Miami* (1988). He scored a huge success with the Broadway production of *Six Degrees of Separation* (1990). Guare received an Oscar nomination for his 1981 *Atlantic City* screenplay. His 1961 B.A. was from Georgetown University and his M.A. from Yale. He is married to Adele Chatfield-Taylor.

FURTHER READING

"Guare, John." *Current Biography,* Aug. 1982.

Gumbel, Bryant Charles (1948–) The status of Bryant Gumbel, and so the future direction of the "Today" show, was in some question during 1991. Gumbel's contract was up for renewal in November, and he and the show were still reeling from the 1989–90 upheavals involving departure of long-time co-anchor Jane Pauley, her replacement by Deborah Norville, the addition of Joe Garagiola as a third co-anchor and Faith Daniels as news reader, Norville's departure on maternity leave, and *her* temporary and then permanent replacement by Katie Couric, with whom Gumbel established an easygoing relationship. Rumors flew as the ratings of the "Today" show zigzagged throughout 1990 and 1991, gradually recovering somewhat during 1991. Some suggested that other networks had made overtures to Gumbel; and at one point *Variety* even reported rumors that Gumbel's anchor spot was being offered to NBC sports anchor Bob Costas. But as 1991 drew to a close, Gumbel signed a new contract for another three years, bringing an end to the rumors—at least temporarily.

During 1991, Gumbel and crew traveled to various places, including Saudi Arabia during the Persian Gulf War, Disneyland in Orlando, Florida, and Hawaii, where they had to shoot the previous day, to have a daylight setting for their show. In one notable interview, actress Robin Givens walked out of the studio when Gumbel brought up the tabloid coverage of her breakup with boxer Mike Tyson.

New Orleans-born Gumbel began his career as a writer and then editor (1971–72) of the magazine *Black Sports.* He moved into broadcasting as a California sportscaster (KNBC, Burbank, 1972–81), and was also a widely known NBC network sportscaster (1975–82), receiving 1976 and 1977 Emmy awards. He became a national figure as co-host of the "Today" show (1982–), a trailblazer as the first Black star of a television morning show. His B.A. was from Bates College, in 1973. He married June Baranco in 1973; they have three children. Sportscaster Greg Gumbel is his brother.

FURTHER READING

"It's brother vs. brother. . . ." Jane Marion. *TV Guide,* July 14, 1990.
"The mourning anchor." Rick Reilly. *Sports Illustrated,* Sep. 26, 1988.
"Today's man. . . ." Sheila Weller. *McCall's,* June, 1987.

Guthrie, A. B. (Alfred Bertram Guthrie, Jr., 1901–91) Indiana-born Guthrie, a leading novelist on Western themes, grew up in Choteau, Montana, and was a longtime newspaper reporter and editor, who worked for 21 years at the *Lexington Leader* in Kentucky. He turned to fiction in 1943, and in 1947 published the very popular *The Big Sky,* which became the 1952 Howard Hawks film. His novel *The Way West*

(1949) won a Pulitzer Prize; it became the 1967 Andrew McLaughlin film. A third novel, *These Thousand Hills* (1956), became the 1959 Richard Fleischer film. He wrote several other novels, some of them mysteries, and *Blue Hen's Chick* (1965), an autobiography. Guthrie won a best screenplay Academy Award for *Shane* (1953), and wrote the screenplay for *The Kentuckian* (1955). He was survived by his second wife, the former Carol Luthin, a daughter, and a son. (d. Choteau, Montana; April 26, 1991)

FURTHER READING

Obituary. *Current Biography,* July 1991.
Obituary. *Variety,* May 6, 1991.
Obituary. *The Times* (of London), Apr. 30, 1991.
Obituary. *New York Times,* Apr. 27, 1991.
Growing up Western. CLARUS BACKES, ed. Knopf, 1990.
"A. B. Guthrie, Jr. . . ." JIM ROBBINS. *American West,* June, 1987.
A. B. Guthrie, Jr. THOMAS W. FORD. Macmillan, 1981.

H

Hackman, Gene (1930–) Always-busy Hackman starred in yet another Central Intelligence Agency (CIA)-related thriller in 1991—but this time he was ex-CIA agent Sam Boyd in Nicholas Meyer's film *Company Business,* a comedy-thriller about post–Cold War spies, in a cast that included Mikhail Baryshnikov, Kurtwood Smith, and Terry O'Quinn. Hackman also starred as old-fashioned liberal lawyer Jedediah Tucker Ward, opposite Mary Elizabeth Mastrantonio as his lawyer daughter, Maggie Ward, in Michael Apted's *Class Action,* in a cast that included Joanna Merlin, Larry Fishburne, Colin Friels, and Donald Moffat. Forthcoming was a starring role in Clint Eastwood's revenge-driven western *Unforgiven,* opposite Eastwood and Morgan Freeman, scheduled for 1992 release. Also forthcoming in 1992 was a starring role on Broadway, opposite Richard Dreyfuss and Glenn Close, in the Ariel Dorfman play *Death and the Maiden,* directed by Mike Nichols.

California-born Hackman became a star in his Best Actor Oscar-winning role as Popeye Doyle in *The French Connection* (1971), a role he repeated in *The French Connection II* (1975). Among his other films are *The Poseidon Adventure* (1972), *The Conversation* (1974), *Night Moves* (1975), the notable *Mississippi Burning* (1988), *The Package* (1989), *Postcards from the Edge* (1990), *Narrow Margin* (1990), and *Loose Cannons* (1990). He was previously married to Faye Maltese and has three children.

FURTHER READING

"Hollywood's uncommon man." MICHAEL NORMAN. *New York Times Magazine,* Mar. 19, 1989.

"Fire this time. . . ." ELIZABETH L. BLAND, et al. *Time,* Jan. 9, 1989.

"The last honest man. . . ." BEVERLY WALKER. *Film Comment,* Nov.–Dec. 1988.

Gene Hackman. ALLAN HUNTER. St. Martin's, 1988.

Hall, Arsenio (1955–) In 1991, Arsenio Hall continued to be one of the hottest late-night talk show hosts around—and to draw some of the hottest talk-show guests. The "Arsenio Hall Show" saw Roseanne Barr's first appearance after changing her name to Roseanne Arnold; "CBS Evening News" anchor Dan Rather, promoting his recent memoirs; a rare appearance by rock star Prince, who normally shuns talk shows; and most notably Earvin "Magic" Johnson's first public interview after his extraordinary news conference announcing that he had been infected with the human immunodeficiency virus (HIV), the virus that causes AIDS (acquired immune deficiency syndrome), with Johnson's dramatic appearance kicking off a major push to educate the public. Lines start to form at dawn for tickets to Hall's show, with fans eager to join in the "Woof! Woof! Woof!" chant that characterizes his audience's enthusiastic responses. Through his own production company, Hall developed a new music-and-dance show, "The Party Machine With Nia Peeples" to follow his own, starting in early 1991; however, it did not fare well in the ratings. He was also still involved in the kinds of lawsuits that seem to surround modern celebrities; among them was a breach-of-contract suit filed by Robert Wachs, his former manager from 1987 to August 1990, seeking 50 percent of Hall's profits from the "Arsenio Hall Show."

Cleveland-born Hall began his career as a stand-up comedian in the late 1970s, and moved to Los Angeles in the early 1980s; his first sustained talk show exposure was on the late-night "Thicke of the Night" (1983); he was also host of "Solid Gold," a rock and roll series. He was a guest host on Fox's "The Late Show" in 1987, and appeared in the film *Coming to America* before breaking through with his "Arsenio Hall Show" in 1989. His B.A. was from Kent State University.

FURTHER READING

"Arsenio Hall talks. . . ." Laura B. Randolph. *Ebony,* Dec. 1990.

"The rise and rise. . . ." Digby Diehl. *Cosmopolitan,* Mar. 1990.

" 'Let's get busy!' . . ." Richard Zoglin. *Time,* Nov. 13, 1989.

"Alone at the top." Patrick Goldstein. *Rolling Stone,* Nov. 2, 1989.

"Late-night cool." Michael Norman. *New York Times Magazine,* Oct. 1, 1989.

"Hall, Arsenio." *Current Biography,* Sep. 1989.

Hall, Peter (Peter Reginald Frederick Hall, 1930–) Celebrated British producer and director Hall directed a very well received 1991 London stage revival of Harold Pinter's *The Homecoming,* with a cast that included Warren Mitchell, Nicholas Woodeson, Douglas Mcferran, and Cherie Lunghi; he had introduced the work in 1965. He also directed Shakespeare's *Twelfth Night* at London's Playhouse Theatre, with Eric Porter, David Ryall, Dinsdale Landen, Richard Garnett, Sara Crowe, and Martin Jarvis in the cast. Julie Walters starred in his London production of *The Rose Tattoo.* The Peter Hall Company staged a London production of *Tartuffe,* while Hall was scheduled to direct Francesca Annis and Martin Shaw in Stephen Poliakoff's *Siena Red.* For television, Hall produced a five-part miniseries, *Camomile Lawn,* based on the Mary Wesley novel, with a cast that included Felicity Kendal, Claire Bloom, and Virginia McKenna. Although he had resigned as artistic director of the Glyndebourne Opera in 1990, Hall continued to be active in opera, with a production of *Peter Grimes* at Munich in late 1991 and a Los Angeles production of *The Magic Flute* scheduled for late 1992.

Hall has been one of the leading directors of the British theater since the mid-1950s; he directed the very notable first English-language production of Samuel Beckett's *Waiting for Godot* in London in 1955 and went on to direct scores of productions of the traditional classics. He introduced such other modern classics as *The Homecoming* (1965; and the 1973 film version), *No Man's Land* (1975), and *Amadeus* (1979, and New York, 1980). He won directing Tonys for *The Homecoming* and *Amadeus.* He was managing director of the Royal Shakespeare Company (1960–68) and co-director of the National Theatre with Laurence Olivier (1973–88). He has directed many operas, most of them at Covent Garden and the Glyndebourne Festival, and also at the Metropolitan Opera and other American houses; he was artistic director of the Glyndebourne Festival Opera (1984–90). He scored two notable trans-Atlantic critical and commercial successes in 1989–90, directing Vanessa Redgrave in Tennessee Williams's *Orpheus Descending* and Dustin Hoffman and Geraldine James in Shakespeare's *The Merchant of Venice;* both also appeared in television adaptations. He published *Peter Hall's Diaries* in 1984. Hall attended St. Catherine's College, Cambridge. He has been married three times and has five children.

FURTHER READING

Peter Hall Directs Anthony and Cleopatra. Tirzah Lowen. *Limelight,* 1991.

"Weldon-Minskoff-Hall heat up. . . ." RICHARD HUMMLER. *Variety,* Oct. 4, 1989.

Hammer (Stanley Kirk Burrell; M. C. Hammer; 1962–) Until 1991, the rap artist had been M. C. Hammer; now he is Hammer, and it is under that name that he released his best-selling 1991 album *Too Legit to Quit.* Hammer and co-producer Felton C. Pilate, II, wrote all but two of the songs in the album, including such notable new songs as the title song, "Brothers Hang On," "Street Soldiers," "Living in a World Like This," "Good to Go," "Lovehold," "This Is the Way We Roll," and "The Addams Groove," a hit song in the smash year-end film *The Addams Family* (1991). "Too Legit to Quit" and "The Addams Groove" also became top-selling singles. Hammer's past work also continued to be enormously popular. *Please Hammer Don't Hurt 'Em* became the best-selling album of 1990, with sales of over 8 million copies, and *Please Hammer Don't Hurt 'Em the Movie* won a 1991 Grammy as the best video of 1990. Hammer also won many other awards, including five of the 18th annual American Music Awards. While continuing to tour, he also appeared in the notable September HBO film *Influences: James Brown and M. C. Hammer,* as well as making his acting debut in an episode of the television series "Amen." On the personal side, he became one of the many public figures who have sued tabloids, initiating a $30 million claim for alleged libel.

Oakland-born Hammer became the Oakland A's batboy in the mid-1970s; he often traveled with the team after he caught the attention of club owner Charles Finley, who saw him doing dance routines in the stadium parking lot. His start as a recording artist came with his own production of some of his songs, with the help of A's players Mike Davis and Dwayne Murphy (with whom he has since had financial disagreements). His first professional album was *Let's Get It Started.* He scored an enormous hit in 1990, with his second album, *Please Hammer Don't Hurt 'Em,* and had several hit singles, including "U Can't Touch This." He became the first major rap artist to make a fully successful crossover to popular music. Hammer also runs his own studio and record company, Bust It Productions. He is married and has one child.

FURTHER READING

"Hammer. . . ." BARBARA BAILEY KELLEY. *California,* June 1991.
"Hammer, M. C." *Current Biography,* Apr. 1991.
"What's next for. . . ." *Jet,* Feb. 18, 1991.
M. C. Hammer and Vanilla Ice. NANCY E. KRULIK. Scholastic, 1991.
"It's Hammer time!" . . ." *Ebony,* Dec. 1990.
"M. C. Hammer says. . . ." CLARENCE WALDRON. *Jet,* Sep. 17, 1990.
"Hammer time. . . ." JEFFREY RESSNER. *Rolling Stone,* Sep. 6, 1990.
"M. C. Hammer. . . ." LISA RUSSELL. *People,* Aug. 6, 1990.

Hanks, Tom (1956–) Although *The Bonfire of the Vanities* was not well received, either critically or in theatrical release, the film did well on home screens in 1991. Also in 1991, Hanks narrated *Radio Flyer,* a story of child abuse; the film was scheduled for early 1992 release. Also forthcoming were Penny Marshall's *A League of Their Own,* about an all-woman baseball team, with a cast that includes Hanks, Geena Davis, Madonna, Lori Petty, Tracy Reiner, Ann Cusack, and Megan Cavanagh; and *Night and the City,* a remake of the 1950 Jules Dassin film, with Hanks as a boxing promoter.

California-born Hanks appeared in the television series "Bosom Buddies" (1980–82), emerged as a film star in the mid-1980s with *Splash* (1984), and went on to star in such films as *Bachelor Party* (1984), *Volunteers* (1985), *The*

Man with One Red Shoe (1985), *The Money Pit* (1986), *Every Time We Say Goodbye* (1986), *Big* (1988), *Punchline* (1988), *Turner and Hooch* (1989), *Joe Versus the Volcano* (1990), and *The Bonfire of the Vanities* (1990). Hanks attended California State University at Sacramento. He is married to Rita Wilson; they have two children.

FURTHER READING

"It's a cool gig." . . ." CAROL TROY. *American Film,* Apr. 1990.
"Tom Hanks." NANCY ANDERSON. *Good Housekeeping,* May 1989.
"Tom Hanks, seriously." CHRISTOPHER CONNELLY. *Premiere,* Apr. 1989.
"Hanks, Tom." *Current Biography,* Apr. 1989.
"Hanks to you." BEVERLY WALKER. *Film Comment,* Mar.–Apr. 1989.
"Playboy interview. . . ." DAVID SHEFF. *Playboy,* Mar. 1989.
Tom Hanks. TRAKIN. St. Martin's, 1987.

Hare, David (1947–) British writer and director Hare introduced a new play in 1991, *Murmering Judges,* which opened in London in October, with a cast that included Robert Patterson, Alphonsia Emmanuel, Keith Allen, Joseph O'Connor, Michael Bryant, and Richard Pasco; it was produced by Richard Eyre. A morality play, the work is about the evils of the British judiciary and prison systems, telling the story of an Irish worker in Britain who takes part in a robbery and is imprisoned for a long term. On a much quieter note, Hare also wrote and directed the film *Heading Home,* starring Joely Richardson as a young librarian in London in the late 1940s, and Gary Oldman and Stephen Dillane as the two men she loves and loses. Hare also published a book of essays, *Writing Left-Handed* (1991).

Hare emerged as a leading British playwright of social protest in the 1970s, with such plays as *Slag* (1970) and *Fanshen* (1975). He went on to write such well-received works as *Plenty* (1978; also the 1985 film adaptation), *A Map of the World* (1982), *Pravda* (1985), *The Secret Rapture* (1988), *Plays and Players* (1988), and *Racing Demon* (1990). He wrote and directed the film *Wetherby* (1984) and also wrote the filmscripts for *Paris By Night* (1988) and *Strapless* (1989). He has written several telefilms. Hare attended Jesus College, Cambridge. He was formerly married and has three children.

FURTHER READING

"Local heroes." MICHAEL BILLINGTON. *Harper's Bazaar,* Oct. 1991.
David Hare. JOAN F. DEAN. G. K. Hall, 1990.
David Hare: Theatricalizing Politics. JUDY L. OLIVA. UMI, 1990.
"Ruffled Hare airs Rich bitch. . . ." RICHARD HUMMLER. *Variety,* Nov. 15, 1989.
"Dramatically speaking." DAVID BAILEY and KATHLEEN TYNAN. *Interview,* Apr. 1989.

Harkin, Thomas Richard (1939–) On September 15, 1991, Iowa Senator Harkin declared himself a candidate for the 1992 Democratic presidential nomination, becoming the third Democrat to announce his candidacy, after former Massachusetts senator Paul Tsongas and Virginia governor L. Douglas Wilder. He positioned himself as a traditional liberal Democrat, for a massive public works program to combat recession and against special privilege, which he identified with George Bush and the Republican Party. At year's end, assisted by a very small staff, he was campaigning in New Hampshire.

Born in Cumming, Iowa, Harkin earned his 1962 B.S. from Iowa State University and his 1972 J.D. from the Catholic University of America. He was a U.S. Navy jet pilot (1962–67). He was a congressional aide (1969–70) and a staff assistant to the House Select Committee on

American Involvement in Southeast Asia (1970–72), then returning to Iowa as a lawyer with the Des Moines Legal Aid Society. Harkin served in the U.S. House of Representatives (1975–85), was then elected to the Senate, and was in 1991 serving in his second term. In 1990, with C. E. Thomas, he published *Five Minutes to Midnight: Why the Nuclear Threat Is Growing Faster Than Ever.* Harkin married Ruth Raduenz in 1968; they have a daughter and a son.

FURTHER READING

"The primal scream. . . ." SIDNEY BLUMENTHAL. *New Republic,* Oct. 21, 1991.
"The no bull campaign." HOWARD FINEMAN. *Newsweek,* Oct. 14, 1991.
"Down-home Democrat. . . ." PAUL CLANCY. *National Catholic Reporter,* Sep. 27, 1991.
"Liberal and proud of it. . . ." ELEANOR CLIFT and JOHN MCCORMICK. *Newsweek,* Aug. 26, 1991.
"GOP dream. . . ." MARK LAWRENCE RAGAN. *Insight,* July 8, 1991.

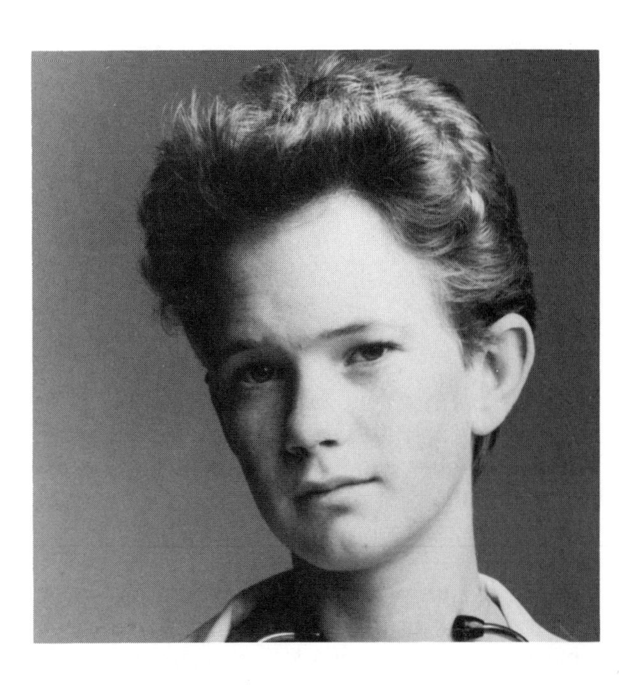

Harris, Neil Patrick (1973–) At age 17, Harris continued to star during the 1991–92 season in the title role of the television series "Doogie Howser, M.D." During the season, the series moved toward a very frank discussion of sexual matters as part of a new national focus on understanding safe sex as an essential part of the fight against the worldwide epidemic of AIDS (acquired immune deficiency syndrome). Harris also starred as the 17-year-old total amnesiac in the fact-based television film *Stranger in the Family,* opposite Teri Garr as his mother.

Since the September 1989 premiere of "Doogie Howser," Harris has starred in the imaginative role of a teenage doctor who graduated from medical school at the age of 14. Harris grew up in the little town of Ruidoso, New Mexico, acted in school productions, and was discovered by playwright Mark Medoff at a summer drama camp. He made his first film, *Clara's Heart,* in 1988, followed by the telefilms *Cold Sassy Tree* (1989) and *Leave Her to Heaven* (1989). He has also appeared in guest roles in several television series.

FURTHER READING

"Neil Patrick Harris. . . ." JOANNE KAUFMAN. *People,* Mar. 19, 1990.
"New teens on the tube." *Teen,* Jan. 1990.

Harrison, George (1943–) Building on the comeback that began in 1987 and continued with the popularity of his new affiliation, the Traveling Wilburys, Harrison in 1991 announced plans to make a comeback as a headliner, beginning with a year-end Japanese tour with Eric Clapton and his band; it would also be Clapton's first professional outing since the March 1991 death of his four-year-old son after a fall from a New York apartment window. Tentative plans to extend the tour throughout the United States and to Europe were also announced. On the personal side, Harrison became one of the many public figures suing supermarket tabloids, filing a defamation of character lawsuit against a tabloid for allegedly portraying him as a Nazi sympathizer.

Liverpool-born Harrison joined the Quarrymen in 1958, as a guitarist, and in 1960, with Paul McCartney, John Lennon, and Pete Best (replaced by Ringo Starr in 1962), formed the Beatles; Harrison was lead guitarist and sometimes a singer. As a member of the group, he helped trigger a revolution in popular music and in the early 1960s emerged as a worldwide celebrity. He also played a special role in helping to bring Indian music into the Western popular music of his time, studying with Indian musician Ravi Shankar, learning the sitar and several other Indian instruments, and introducing Indian strains into the work of the Beatles.

Harrison's main work as a songwriter developed after the Beatles years; he also formed his own film production and rock management companies and was active in organizing Bangladesh relief concerts in 1971. He scored a substantial comeback with the album *Cloud Nine* (1987), and in 1988 was prime mover in the organization of the extraordinary "new" group, the Traveling Wilburys, consisting of Harrison, Bob Dylan, Roy Orbison (until his death), Tom Petty, and Jeff Lynne, all longtime stars. Harrison has been married twice and has one child.

FURTHER READING

Dark Horse: The Private Life of George Harrison. GEOFFREY GIULIANO. NAL-Dutton, 1990.
"Harrison, George." *Current Biography,* Jan. 1989.
"The rise of a craftsman." NICHOLAS JENNINGS. *Maclean's,* Oct. 17, 1988.
"Handmade man." ELAINE DUTKA. *Film Comment,* May–June 1988.
It Was Twenty Years Ago Today. DEREK TAYLOR. Simon & Schuster, 1987.
Yesterday—the Beatles 1963–1965. ROBERT FREEMAN. Holt, 1983.
The Beatles A–Z: John Lennon, Paul McCartney, George Harrison and Ringo Starr. GOLDIE FRIEDE et al. Routledge Chapman & Hall, 1981.

Havel, Vaclav (1936–) After the tumultuous events that brought freedom to Czechoslovakia and much of Eastern Europe, Havel—dissident playwright who became the new Czechoslovak president—emerged as one of the world's most respected leaders. During 1991, he continued to take his small country into a new set of relationships with the West while at the same time burying the last remnants of communism in Czechoslovakia and Eastern Europe. He also strongly supported emerging freedom movements, during 1991 speaking sharply for the rights of the formerly Soviet Baltic states and continuing to press Fidel Castro on democracy and human rights abuse issues.

On June 21, 1991, the last Soviet troops left Czechoslovakia. On June 28, a Budapest meeting of Eastern European leaders disbanded the multinational Council for Mutual Economic Assistance (Comecon), a Soviet economic control instrument. On July 1, Havel hosted a Prague meeting of Eastern European leaders, which disbanded the Warsaw Pact, the last remaining instrument of Soviet military control. Havel opposed and expressed great concern over the August Soviet right-wing coup—and with all the leaders of newly free Eastern Europe expressed enormous relief at the triumph of Soviet democracy. Going forward toward a market economy, Havel's government in January 1991 began to auction off small businesses formerly owned by the state. In February and March, new laws provided for the return of land seized by the communist government between 1948 and 1989, or for the payment of compensation; privatization of large enterprises; and privatization of the communications media, formerly a key instrument of state control.

Havel and Czechoslovakia were not immune to the ethnic tensions that gripped so many other countries of the former Soviet bloc. His government faced renewed demands for Slovak independence, which had started with the transition to democracy in 1989 and had grown into a powerful movement. There were nationalist demonstrations in the Slovak capital of Bratislava on March 11; three days later, Havel was jeered at a public meeting in that city. On March 14, in a nationwide radio address, he called for a referendum on Slovak independence. Havel discussed politics, literature, theater, and autobiographical memories in a series of interviews published as *Disturbing the Peace* (1991).

Havel has been a leading Czech playwright since the early 1960s; such plays as *The Garden Party* (1963) and *The Memorandum* (1967) helped bring about the "Prague Spring" of 1968; they were repressed after the Soviet invasion that destroyed the new Czech government. Havel's plays were banned from the Czech stage for two decades, while he continued to be a leading dissenter. He was a leader of the Charter 77 organization in 1977, was under house arrest (1977–79), in prison (1979–83), and was imprisoned again in early 1989. Then on December 29, 1989, he became interim president, the first non-communist president of his country since 1948. On July 5, 1990, he was re-elected to the presidency for a full two-year term.

In 1964, Havel married Olga Splíchalová, to whom he wrote *Letters to Olga* (1989) from prison. Among his other non-dramatic works were *Vaclav Havel: Or, Living in Truth* (1987) and *Vaclav Havel: Open Letters; Selected Prose 1965–1990* (1990; selected and edited by George Wilson).

FURTHER READING

" 'Uncertain Strength.' . . ." DANA EMINGEROVA et al. *New York Review of Books,* Aug. 15, 1991.

"Havel's choice." STEPHEN SCHIFF. *Vanity Fair.* Aug. 1991.

" 'Parallels with a prison.' . . ." ANDREW NAGORSKI. *Newsweek,* July 22, 1991.

"Vaclav Havel." LINA WERTMULLER et al. *Interview,* May 1991.

Vaclav Havel: The Authorized Biography. EDA KRISEOVA. Atlantic Monthly, 1991.

After the Velvet Revolution: Vaclav Havel and the New Leaders of Czechoslovakia Speak Out. TIM D. WHIPPLE, ed. Freedom House, 1991.

"All the president's plays. . . ." STANISLAW BARANCZAK. *New Republic,* July 23, 1990.

"Metamorphosis in Prague. . . ." LEONID SHINKAREV. *World Press Review,* May 1990.

"The prisoner who. . . ." RICHARD Z. CHESNOFF. *U.S. News & World Report,* Feb. 26, 1990.

"A life like a work of art. . . ." MILAN KUNDERA. *New Republic,* Jan. 29, 1990.

"Life turns upside down. . . ." ANDREA CHAMBERS. *People,* Jan. 22, 1990.

"Prague's choice takes office." MARY NEMETH. *Maclean's,* Jan. 8, 1990.

"Dissident to president. . . ." WILLIAM A. HENRY III. *Time,* Jan. 8, 1990.

Hawke, Bob (Robert James Lee Hawke, 1929–) Like so many other world political leaders, Australian Prime Minister Hawke encountered major economic problems as the world slid further into the deepening 1990–91 recession. As unemployment grew into the 9 to 10 percent range and businesses slowed down and failed, government predictions of an economic turnaround seemed to Australian voters merely hopeful, rather than to be taken seriously. Calls for far more government action to stimulate Australia's sagging economy arose from within Hawke's own Australian Labour Party, as well as from the opposition.

In late May, Hawke's leadership of the Labour Party was challenged by government Treasurer and Deputy Prime Minister Paul Keating, until then thought to be Hawke's logical successor. Hawke won the subsequent contest, and Keating resigned his positions on June 3; but the struggle between their two factions continued throughout the year, with every issue seized as an opportunity for factional fighting. One major battle arose over the proposed 1992 budget, criticized as not providing enough stimulation for the economy, particularly in the area of public works; another battle was over environmental policy issues. At the same time, both factions sharply attacked U.S. and European Community wheat subsidies as damaging the Australian grain industry. On December 19, Keating won the long battle, and Hawke resigned.

Hawke began his long career as a trade unionist in 1958, as an economist with the Australian Council of Trade Unions (ACTU), acting as ACTU's president (1970–80). At the same time, he moved into Labour Party politics, becoming president of his party in 1978 and leader in 1983;

in that year, with party victory, he became prime minister, succeeding John Malcolm Fraser, and served a record-setting four terms, last being elected in March 1990. A moderate socialist, he captured much of the Australian "middle," coming forward with strongly environmentalist and anti-nuclear testing positions. Hawke publicly confessed adultery and heavy drinking during a television broadcast interview in March 1989; the admissions apparently did him no political damage. He attended the University of Western Australia and Oxford University. He married Hazel Masterson in 1956; they have three children.

FURTHER READING

"Australia: When friends desert." *Economist,* Dec. 14, 1991.

Hawn, Goldie (1945–) Durable comedian Hawn starred in 1991 as betrayed wife Adrienne Saunders, who becomes an amateur detective to investigate her husband's extramarital affairs in *Deceived.* The cast included John Heard as her husband, Mary Saunders, and Robin Bartlett; Damon Harris directed. Forthcoming was a starring role in Roger Zemeckis's *Death Becomes Her;* Hawn plays opposite Meryl Streep, Kevin Kline, and Bruce Willis in another triangle story, as an aging actress competing for the affections of her surgeon husband with his former lover. Also to come were *Crisscross,* shot in 1990, with Hawn starring as a dancer who finds that her son is a drug pusher, and *Housesitter,* opposite Steve Martin.

Hawn began her career as a dancer in the mid-1960s and became a star comedian in television in the "dumb blonde" role she created for Rowan and Martin's "Laugh-In" (1968–73). Her film career includes a Best Supporting Actress Oscar in *Cactus Flower* (1969) and starring roles in several popular films, mostly comedies, including *There's a Girl in My Soup* (1970), *Butterflies Are Free* (1972), *The Sugarland Express* (1973), *Shampoo* (1975), *The Duchess and the Dirtwater Fox* (1976), *Private Benjamin* (1980), *Best Friends* (1982), *Swing Shift* (1984), *Overboard* (1987), *Last Wish* (1988), and *Bird on a Wire* (1990). Hawn attended American University. She has been married twice, and has four children.

FURTHER READING

"Goldie Hawn. . . ." Stephen Farber. *Cosmopolitan,* Aug. 1990.
"Pure Goldie." Kristine McKenna. *Harper's Bazaar,* July 1990.
"24-karat Goldie!" Jim Jerome. *People,* June 11, 1990.
Sweethearts of Sixties TV. Ronald L. Smith. St. Martin's, 1989.
Solid Goldie: An Illustrated Biography of Goldie Hawn. Connie Berman. Simon & Schuster, 1981.

Heffer, Eric (1911–91) Hertford-born Heffer became a British woodworkers' union and Labour Party activist in the late 1930s. During the 1940s and early 1950s, he was for some years a communist, and later a founder of the Socialist Workers' Federation. In 1956, he returned to the Labour Party where he spent the rest of his career. His power base was in Liverpool, where he became president of the Trades Council in 1959 and a city councilman in 1960. From 1964 until his death, he was a member of parliament for Liverpool's Walton Division. Heffer took a generally "left" line within his party; he sharply opposed party leadership inquiries and attacks on the Militant Tendency group and left the 1985 Labour Conference on the issue. At the same time, he denounced Stalinism as early as the late 1940s and later supported dissent in the Soviet Union and Eastern Europe. In 1974, he was minister of state in the Department of Industry, in Harold Wilson's Labour government. Heffer's *Never a Yes Man: An Autobiography* was published in 1991. He was survived by his wife, Doris. (d. London, England; May 27, 1991)

FURTHER READING

Obituary. *The Times* (of London), May 28, 1991.

Heinz, John (Henry John Heinz, III, 1938–91) Pittsburgh-born Heinz, an heir to the H. J. Heinz fortune, joined the family company after military service, working in marketing. Becoming active in Republican politics, he made a successful run for a Pittsburgh congressional seat in 1971 and served three terms in the House of Representatives (1972–76). He won a seat in the U.S. Senate in 1976 and was reelected twice. He was midway into his third term when he was killed in an aircraft collision over Lower Merion Township, Pennsylvania. During his legislative career, he was generally regarded as a moderate Republican but was in some ways rather atypical, supporting protectionist trade legislation that favored Pennsylvania's ailing steel and other basic industries, and strongly supporting social welfare legislation that favored the elderly, especially in such areas as health insurance, nursing home standards, and pension plan protection.

Heinz was succeeded by Democrat and political unknown Harrison Wofford, who in a major upset defeated the former U.S. attorney general and Pennsylvania governor, Richard Thornburgh. Wofford ran as a liberal, stressing the kinds of issues that Heinz had so successfully brought forward during his six terms in office.

Heinz's B.A. was from Yale University and his M.B.A. from Harvard University. He was survived by his wife, Maria Simoes-Ferreira, and three children.

FURTHER READING

Obituary. *Current Biography,* May 1991.
"A fiery midair collision. . . ." PAULA CHIN. *People,* Apr. 22, 1991.
"Tragedy strikes twice." *Time,* Apr. 15, 1991.
"Flying into tragedy." BOB LEVIN. *Maclean's,* Apr. 15, 1991.
Obituary. *U.S. News & World Report,* Apr. 15, 1991.
"Sen. John Heinz. . . ." LESLIE WOLLACK. *Nation's Cities Weekly,* Apr. 8, 1991.
Obituary. *New York Times,* Apr. 5, 1991.

Helms, Jesse (1921–) During 1991, North Carolina Republican Senator Helms continued to play a major ultra-conservative role in the Senate, taking as his main field of action such highly controversial issues as censorship and public morality, AIDS (acquired immune deficiency syndrome), and civil rights, far to the right of and often in sharp disagreement with President George Bush. A few of his more notable victories were the July Senate bill establishing criminal penalties for health workers who performed invasive medical procedures while knowing they were infected with the human immunodeficiency virus (HIV); the July appropriations bill amendment establishing prison terms for those convicted of selling what was defined as

child pornography; and in October the blocking of $10 million in funds for adolescent and adult sexual behavior research intended to further the fight against AIDS. A very notable defeat was congressional refusal to renew and extend "anti-obscenity" restrictions on National Endowment for the Arts (NEA) grants. On August 4, 1991, Senator Helms leaked a Senate Ethics Committee report on Senator Alan Cranston and the "Keating Five" case in an attempt to speed Senate censure action on Cranston after the committee had voted to delay its recommendation. Other committee members called his action a violation of committee rules and instituted an investigation of Helms's role in the leak.

North Carolina-born Helms began his senatorial career in 1973, after a career in broadcasting; since 1987, he has been the most senior Republican in the Senate, with memberships on several key committees. He was re-elected in 1990, weathering a powerful challenge by former Charlotte mayor Harvey B. Gantt, made even more notable because Gantt was an African-American candidate facing a highly visible anti-civil rights conservative. Helms attended Wingate College and Wake Forest College. He married Dorothy Jane Coble in 1942; they have three children.

FURTHER READING

"Race-baiting wins again. . . ." LAURENCE I. BARRETT. *Time,* Nov. 19, 1990.
"Republican of fear." SIDNEY BLUMENTHAL. *New Republic,* Nov. 12, 1990.

"Gantt versus. . . ." DOROTHY VIDULICH. *National Catholic Reporter,* Oct. 26, 1990.
"Jesse Helms. . . ." DONALD BAER. *U.S. News & World Report,* May 14, 1990.
"Our most effective. . . ." PAUL WEYRICH. *Conservative Digest,* Jan.–Feb. 1989.
Hard Right: The Rise of Jesse Helms. ERNEST B. FURGURSON. Norton, 1986.

Hennard, George J. (1956–) On October 16, 1991, mass murderer Hennard drove his pickup truck through the window of crowded Luby's restaurant in Killeen, Texas. Getting out of the truck, and using Glock 17 and Ruger 19 semi-automatic pistols, within ten minutes and at short range he killed 22 people, 14 women and 8 men, and wounded at least that many more. Wounded by law officers, he killed himself. The loss of 23 lives made this the worst mass shooting incident ever to have occurred in the United States.

Hennard had no known direct motive for the murders. The son of an army doctor who had been assigned to nearby Fort Hood, his family had moved to the Killeen area in 1974. He had become a merchant seaman in 1971 and spent most of his subsequent working life on the sea. He lost his seaman's license in 1989, after a series of incidents and the emergence of a drug abuse problem, was not able to get his license back, and was unemployed at the time of the shootings.

On October 17, the next day, the U.S. House of Representatives, by a vote of 247–177, refused to ban the sale and ownership of semi-automatic weapons and large ammunition clips. The vote was hailed by the National Rifle Association (NRA) and denounced by those favoring gun control. Representative Chet Edwards of Texas, representing the Killeen area, who had formerly opposed the rejected gun control law, now voted for it, but to no avail.

FURTHER READING

"A Texas massacre." PAULA CHIN et al. *People,* Nov. 4, 1991.

Hepburn, Katharine (1907–) *Me: Stories of My Life,* the long-awaited autobiography by Katharine Hepburn, was published in September 1991, was a main selection of the Book-of-the-Month Club, and almost immediately soared to the top of the best-seller lists. The book did not disappoint: Hepburn seemed to speak quite frankly about her life, views, motives, screen and stage roles, and—perhaps what most readers wanted to see—of her 27-year-long relationship with Spencer Tracy. She was equally candid in several highly publicized and watched interviews, done as part of the publicity effort surrounding book publication, appearing for long interviews on television shows, as in her interview with Barbara Walters on "20/20" and her three-part interview with Katie Couric on the "Today" show.

Hepburn's career spans more than six decades; it began on stage, in 1928, but it is her work as a leading film actress that has made her a world figure. She has won four Best Actress Oscars—more than any other performer—and starred opposite Spencer Tracy in nine classic films. Her first film role was the lead opposite John Barrymore in *Bill of Divorcement* (1934). She went on to win Oscars for *Morning Glory* (1936); opposite Tracy in their last film together, *Guess Who's Coming to Dinner* (1967); *The Lion in Winter* (1968); and *On Golden Pond* (1981). Some of her other most notable films were *Little Women* (1933), *Stage Door* (1937), *Holiday* (1938), *The Philadelphia Story* (1940; also the 1939 Broadway play), *Woman of the Year* (1942), *Keeper of the Flame* (1942), *The Sea of Grass* (1947), *State of the Union* (1948), *Adam's Rib* (1949), *The African Queen* (1951), *Pat and Mike* (1952), *Sum-*

mertime (1955), *Desk Set* (1957), *Suddenly Last Summer* (1959), *Long Day's Journey into Night* (1962), *A Delicate Balance* (1973), and *Rooster Cogburn* (1976). On Broadway, she also played the lead in *Coco* (1969). She was honored for her lifetime achievement at the Kennedy Center in 1990. A previous book was *The Making of "The African Queen": Or How I Went to Africa with Bogart, Bacall and Huston and Almost Lost My Mind* (1987). Hepburn attended Bryn Mawr College. She was formerly married, to Ludlow Ogden Smith; her long personal relationship with Spencer Tracy ended with his death, in 1967.

FURTHER READING

"Kate talks straight." MYRNA BLYTH. *Ladies Home Journal,* Oct. 1991.
"Kate the great." LIZ SMITH. *Vogue,* Sep. 1991.
"Katharine Hepburn." POPE BROCK. *People,* Nov. 5, 1990.
"Katharine Hepburn. . . ." SUSAN WARE. *History Today,* Apr. 1990.
"Katharine Hepburn. . . ." A. SCOTT BERG and JOHN BRYSON. *Architectural Digest,* Apr. 1990.
The Private World of Katharine Hepburn. JOHN BRYSON, Photographer. Little, Brown, 1990.
The Films of Katharine Hepburn, rev. ed. HOMER DICKENS. Carol, 1990.
"Katharine Hepburn at 80." BARBARA LOVENHEIM. *McCall's,* Nov. 1989.
Katharine Hepburn. CAROLINE LATHAM. Chelsea House, 1989.
Young Kate: The Remarkable Hepburns and the Childhood That Shaped an American Legend. CHRISTOPHER ANDERSEN. Holt, 1988.
Tracy and Hepburn. GARSON KANIN. Donald I. Fine, 1988.
A Remarkable Woman: A Biography of Katharine Hepburn. ANN EDWARDS. Morrow, 1985.
Katharine Hepburn. SHERIDAN MORLEY. Little, Brown, 1984; Viking Penguin, 1990.
Katharine Hepburn: A Hollywood Yankee. GARY K. CAREY. DELL, 1984.
Katharine Hepburn. MICHAEL FREEDLAND. Salem House, 1984.
Kate: The Life of Katherine Hepburn. CHARLES HIGHAM. New American Library-Dutton, 1981.

Heston, Charlton (Charles Carter, 1923–) To hundreds of millions of television movie watchers all over the world, Heston is still Ben-Hur, El Cid, and Gordon of Khartoum. In 1991, he was also Sherlock Holmes, appearing out of the London fog in *Crucifer of Blood,* with Richard Johnson as his Watson, in a TNT television production adapted, directed, and produced by his son, Fraser Heston. The Hestons, father and son, had in the same way created a remake of *Treasure Island* in 1990, with Charlton Heston as Long John Silver, as they had the 1987 production of *A Man for All Seasons.* Forthcoming for Heston père was a new feature film, *Solar Crisis,* about a mission to the sun in 2050.

On stage, Heston starred again in the Los Angeles production of A. R. Gurney's *Love Letters,* this time opposite Stephanie Beacham. He also narrated *Opera Stories* on laser disc; was grand marshal of the 60th annual Hollywood Christmas Parade; had sharp public interchanges with those with whom he disagreed on political and social matters; and appeared as presenter and attendee at a wide range of ceremonial functions, as befitted one of Hollywood's elder statespersons.

Illinois-born Heston began his long stage and screen career in the late 1940s; on stage, his work has included three appearances as *Macbeth* (1954, 1959, 1976), and leads in *A Man for All Seasons* (1965 and 1987) and *The Caine Mutiny Court Martial* (1985; he also directed and starred in the 1988 film version). On screen, he has been a star since the early 1950s in such films as *Julius Caesar* (1950 and 1970), *The Greatest Show on Earth* (1952), *The Far Horizons* (1955), *Ben-Hur* (1959), *The Wreck of the Mary Deare* (1959), *El Cid* (1961), *Diamond Head* (1962), *55 Days at Peking* (1962), *The Greatest Story Ever Told* (1965), *Khartoum* (1966), *Planet of the Apes* (1967; and the 1969 sequel), *Soylent Green* (1973), and *Midway* (1975). He has also worked extensively in television. Heston attended Northwestern University. He married Lydia Clark in 1944; the couple have one child, producer-director Fraser.

FURTHER READING

"Charlton Heston." IVOR DAVIS. *Los Angeles Magazine,* Apr. 1988.
"Heston, Charlton." *Current Biography,* July 1986.
Charlton Heston: A Biography. MICHAEL MUNN. St. Martin's, 1986.

Higgins, William: See **Lebanon Hostages**

Hildesheimer, Wolfgang (1916–91) Hamburg-born Hildesheimer, a German Jew, left Germany with his family in 1933 and was educated abroad, ultimately finishing his schooling and settling in Britain. He served in British intelligence in Palestine during World War II, and from 1946 to 1948 was an interpreter at the Nuremberg Nazi war crimes trials. He began his career before World War II as a stage designer and visual artist, and emerged as a prolific and wide-ranging writer in the 1950s, beginning with his short-story collection *Loveless Legends* (1952). Other works are his plays *The Dragon Throne* (1955; based on his 1953 radio play), *The Delay* (1961), and *Mary Stuart* (1981), and the novels *Tynset* (1965) and *Marbot* (1981). In the English-speaking world, he is best known by far for his 1977 biography of Mozart. Hildesheimer did not want to live in Germany after World War II but was very much part of the postwar German-language culture; he settled in Poschiavo, Switzerland, after the Nuremberg trials. He was survived by his wife, Sylvia, and two stepdaughters (d. Poschiavo, Switzerland; August 21, 1991)

FURTHER READING

Obituary. *The Times* (of London), Aug. 27, 1991.
Obituary. *New York Times,* Aug. 22, 1991.

Hill, Anita Faye (1956–) A tenured full professor of law at the University of Oklahoma with an utterly unblemished personal and professional reputation, Anita Faye Hill became the center of a storm of controversy on October 6, 1991, the day that newspaper and broadcast media began to report that she had accused Supreme Court nominee Judge Clarence Thomas of having sexually harassed her from 1981 to 1983, while she was his assistant at the U.S. Department of Education, and then at the U.S. Equal Employment Opportunity Commission, which he then headed. On September 27, after a long confirmation process, the Senate Judiciary Committee had deadlocked 7–7 on the nomination of Judge Thomas to the Supreme Court. Professor Hill's accusations served to re-open Judiciary Committee hearings, which were telecast worldwide.

Because of the impact of her charges on the already highly controversial appointment, their

very specific sexual nature, the raw nerve in American society touched by her open charge of sexual harassment, the countercharges of anti-Black bigotry raised by Justice Thomas (although both Hill and Thomas are African-Americans, and both are political conservatives)—and probably because of the way the members of the Senate committee handled her charges and the total situation—what followed was a riveting, extraordinarily distasteful mud bath that left the reputations of many individual senators and of the U.S. Senate in grave disrepair.

Professor Hill had been approached by Senate staff members on September 3, had told her story, and had requested some degree of anonymity—how much and on what terms still, and probably for decades to come, a matter of dispute. The committee decided not to air her charges publicly, and they were not a significant factor during the long process that led to the 7–7 deadlock. Dissatisfied, Professor Hill "went public" with a press conference on October 7, making very specific and lurid charges against Judge Thomas, who issued a blanket denial the next day, October 8. Now at the center of a storm, the Senate on October 8 postponed its imminent vote on the nomination, and the committee rescheduled hearings, which occurred October 11–13. Professor Hill made her accusations public and was sharply and immediately attacked by the Republican members of the committee, most notably by Senators Arlen Specter, Orrin Hatch, and Alan Simpson. Senator Specter even directly accused her of perjury, a charge that was never pursued. Justice Thomas denied her charges completely and charged the committee with "high-tech lynching." Professor Hill was supported by several highly reputable witnesses, all of whom testified that she had made these charges privately to them years before. Judge Thomas was supported by several highly reputable character witnesses. The hearings adjourned late on Sunday, October 13. Judge Thomas was confirmed by the Senate on Tuesday, October 15, by a vote of 52–48. Professor Hill went home to Oklahoma to teach law.

Anita Faye Hill was born in Morris, Oklahoma, the youngest of 13 children. She attended Lone Tree Baptist Church. She was valedictorian of her class at Morris High School, having been a straight-A student, secretary of the student council, member of the National Honor Society, and member of the Future Homemakers of America and the Pep Club. She attended Oklahoma State University and graduated in 1977 with honors. She attended Yale Law School (1977–80), interning at the Washington, D.C., law firm of Ward, Harkrader, and Ross while in law school, then joining the firm after graduation. She became personal assistant to Clarence Thomas at the Office for Civil Rights of the U.S. Education Department in 1981, and moved with him to the U.S. Equal Employment Opportunity Commission. She left Washington to teach law at Oral Roberts University in 1983. She has taught law at the University of Oklahoma since 1986 and became a tenured full professor in 1990.

FURTHER READING

"She could not keep silent." BILL HEWITT and BETH AUSTIN. *People,* Oct. 28, 1991.
"A question of character." RICHARD LACAYO. *Time,* October 21, 1991.
"An ugly circus." NANCY GIBBS. *Time,* Oct. 21, 1991.
"Thomas and Hill. . . ." ELOISE SALHOLZ. *Newsweek,* Oct. 21, 1991.
"Anatomy of a debacle." DAVID A. KAPLAN. *Newsweek,* Oct. 21, 1991.
"A moment of truth." *Newsweek,* Oct. 21, 1991.
"Judging Thomas." GLORIA BORGER. *U.S. News & World Report,* Oct. 21, 1991.

Hines, Gregory (Gregory Oliver Hines, 1946–) Two Hines films were in theatrical release in 1991. The first was Duncan Gibbons's science fiction thriller *Eve of Destruction;* Hines played Jim McQuade, a troubleshooter searching for a malfunctioning super-android, played by Renee Soutendijk, in a cast that included Michael Greene and Kevin McCarthy. On a quite different theme, Hines starred opposite Robin Givens in the Bill Duke film adapted from the Chester Himes novel, *A Rage in Harlem* (1991); the cast included Zakes Mokae, Danny Glover, and Bajda Djola. A soundtrack album was issued. Hines also starred in the television film *White Lie* as an African-American who sets out to investigate his father's death 20 years earlier in the South and finds continuing deep racism; Annette O'Toole co-starred.

A leader of the tap revival of the 1980s, Hines is a multitalented tap dancer, actor, and variety entertainer. Born in New York City, he was on stage professionally at the age of five with his brother Maurice, touring as the Hines Kids (1949–55), the Hines Brothers (1955–63), and then with their father Maurice as Hines, Hines, and Dad (1963–73). On stage, he won Tony nominations in *Eubie* (1978), *Comin' Uptown* (1980), and *Sophisticated Ladies* (1981), and emerged as a film star in the 1980s, in such movies as *Wolfen* (1981), *The Cotton Club* (1984), *White Nights* (1985), *Running Scared* (1986), *Off Limits* (1988), *Tap* (1989), and *Eve of Destruction* (1990). He also made his directorial debut in 1990 with the independently produced *Gotta Dance.* He has been married twice, last to Pamela Koslow in 1981, and has three children.

FURTHER READING

"Former child stars. . . ." MICHELLE MCCALOPE. *Jet,* Apr. 15, 1991.
"Gregory Hines on. . . ." LAURA B. RANDOLPH. *Ebony,* Jan. 1991.
Black Dance in America: A History Through Its People. JAMES HASKINS. Harper, 1990.
"Hines on tap." SALLY SOMMER. *Dance Magazine,* Dec. 1988.

Hoffman, Dustin (Dustin Lee Hoffman, 1937–) Still at the peak of his long career, Hoffman starred in two major 1991 films. His first role was as Dutch Schultz in the Robert Benton film *Billy Bathgate,* a high-budget blockbuster that had originally been scheduled for summer release, but was delayed again and again for reshooting and recutting. Tom Stoppard wrote the filmscript, based on the

E. L. Doctorow novel; the cast included Nicole Kidman, Loren Dean, and Bruce Willis. When finally released, the film was not very warmly received by critics or public; in commercial terms, it was an expensive failure. His second major 1991 role was as Captain Hook opposite Robin Williams as Peter Pan in Steven Spielberg's Christmas confection *Hook,* which was far better received on all counts. At year's end, Hoffman was shooting the forthcoming Stephen Frears film *Hero.* On the business side, Hoffman in June made a new three-year production agreement with Columbia Pictures and Tri-Star Pictures.

Los Angeles–born Hoffman has been a major film star since his breakthrough role as *The Graduate* (1967), which he followed with such films as *Midnight Cowboy* (1969), *Little Big Man* (1971), *Lenny* (1974), *All the President's Men* (1976), *Marathon Man* (1976), *Kramer vs. Kramer* (1979) winning a Best Actor Oscar, *Tootsie* (1982), *Rain Man* (1988) and a second Best Actor Oscar, *Family Business* (1989), and *Dick Tracy* (1990). On stage he was a notable Willy Loman in the 1984 revival of *Death of a Salesman* (televised in 1985), and in 1990 brought his Shylock from London to Broadway in Peter Hall's production of *The Merchant of Venice.* Hoffman attended Santa Monica City College. He was formerly married to Anne Byrne, married Lisa Gottsegen in 1980, and has five children.

FURTHER READING

"Acting his age. . . ." Mark Rowland. *American Film,* Dec. 1988.
"Rebirth of a salesman." Marie Brenner. *New York,* Mar. 26, 1984.
Dustin Hoffman. Iain Johnstone. Hippocrene, 1984.
Making Tootsie: A Film Study with Dustin Hoffman and Sydney Pollack. Susan Dworkin. Newmarket, 1983.
The Films of Dustin Hoffman. Douglas Brode. Carol, 1983.
Dustin Hoffman: Hollywood's Anti-Hero. Jeff Lenburg. St. Martin's, 1982.

Holyfield, Evander (1962–) In 1991, Evander Holyfield was boxing's world heavyweight champion, with a 26–0 record, but his tenure seemed questionable. He had taken the title from an overweight, out-of-condition James "Buster" Douglas in October 1990. His first title defense was against George Foreman in April 1991; though Holyfield won in a unanimous decision, he was far from overwhelming against the 42-year-old ex-champion. Then in November, Holyfield barely held on against journeyman boxer Bert Cooper, a 22-to-1 underdog with a 26–8 record, fighting on short notice, after Mike Tyson and Francesco Damiani pulled out because of injuries. Holyfield was knocked into the ropes and took a count for the first time in his career, though he eventually won on a technical knockout. Boxing fans were looking forward to a Holyfield-Tyson match in early 1992 (depending on the timing and outcome of Tyson's trial on rape charges) to provide the real test of Holyfield's championship mettle. Whatever the result, *Forbes* magazine reported that Holyfield had clearly dethroned Tyson for the title of highest-paid athlete, with 1991 earnings expected to be about $60 million. Holyfield was also scheduled to appear with several football greats as a prison football team in Paramount's *Necessary Roughness.*

Alabama-born Holyfield won a bronze medal in the 1984 Olympics, and turned professional in 1986. For most of his career, he has been a light-heavyweight, rather than a heavyweight, and became World Boxing Association light-heavyweight world champion in 1986. Holyfield was divorced in 1991 and has four children.

FURTHER READING

"The real deal. . . ." Gary Cartwright. *Texas,* June 1991.
"No joke. . . ." Pat Putnam. *Sports Illustrated,* Apr. 29, 1991.
"Evander Holyfield. . . ." Douglas C. Lyons. *Ebony,* Jan. 1991.
"Evander Holyfield. . . ." *Jet,* Nov. 19, 1990.
"At last!" David Miller. *Sport,* Nov. 1990.

Honda, Soichiro (1906–91) An automobile mechanic who became one of the world's leading industrialists, Honda was from the first a strikingly independent figure whose defiance of Japanese bureaucracy helped him to build his company. He began his career in Tokyo as a 16-year-old apprentice automobile mechanic, opened his own shop six years later, and by the mid-1930s was a racing car builder and driver. After World War II, he emerged as an automobile manufacturer, founding the Honda Motor

Company in 1947; he soon became a major motorcycle manufacturer and entered the export market in 1962. Honda began producing automobiles in 1957, and by 1972, when he retired at the age of 65, the company had become one of Japan's largest auto manufacturers, rivaling Toyota and Nissan. In retirement, Honda focused his attention on the Honda Foundation, its purpose to foster technological innovation, while the company he had founded continued to grow. He was survived by his wife, Sachi, two daughters, and a son. (d. Tenryu, Japan; August 5, 1991)

FURTHER READING

Obituary. *Motor Trend,* Nov. 1991.
Obituary. KEVIN CAMERON. *Cycle World,* Nov. 1991.
Obituary. *U.S. News & World Report,* Aug. 19, 1991.
Obituary. *The Times* (of London), Aug. 6, 1991.
Obituary. *New York Times,* Aug. 6, 1991.
"10 best moguls. . . ." BROCK YATES. *Car and Driver,* Jan. 1988.
"Mr. Iacocca, meet Mr. Honda. . . ." JOEL KOTKIN. *Inc.*, Nov. 1986.
"Auto biographies. . . ." BOB NAGY and JACK R. NERAD. *Motor Trend,* Nov. 1985.

Hooker, John Lee (1917–) Now in his mid-70s and still enjoying his second musical revival, the celebrated blues musician John Lee Hooker issued yet another album in 1991. The September release was *Mr. Lucky,* with "I Cover the Waterfront," a very well received duet between Hooker and Van Morrison, and guest performances by Keith Richards, Johnny Winter, Robert Cray, Albert Collins, Carlos Santana, and Booker T. Jones. Forthcoming was the sound track for a new Dennis Hopper movie, *The Hot Spot,* starring Don Johnson and Virginia Madsen; the soundtrack also featured jazz luminary Miles Davis. Hooker continued to appear in concert and on tour, though on a somewhat more limited basis than in earlier years.

Mississippi-born Hooker became a leading blues musician in the late 1940s, with such songs as "Boogie Chillun" (1948) and "I'm in the Mood" (1951). He was a popular figure during the folk and blues revival of the 1960s, appearing often at the Newport and other jazz festivals and recording scores of albums, such as *The Folklore of John Lee Hooker* (1962) and *The Big Soul of John Lee Hooker* (1964). He enjoyed yet another revival in the late 1980s, on tour again and with such albums as *Jealous* (1986). His album *The Healer* (1989) included a cut with Bonnie Raitt, "I'm in the Mood," which won the 1990 Grammy for best traditional blues recording.

FURTHER READING

John Lee Hooker: The Healer. H. LEONARD, 1991.
"John Lee Hooker. . . ." STEVE DOUGHERTY. *People,* Oct. 29, 1990.
"John Lee Hooker. . . ." JOSEF WOODARD. *Down Beat,* Feb. 1990.
"John Lee Hooker. . . ." JAS OBRECHT. *Guitar Player,* Nov. 1989.

Hopkins, Anthony (1937–) Hopkins caught worldwide attention in 1991 as Hannibal "The Cannibal" Lecter, an imprisoned psychiatrist and serial killer, in the powerful drama and box-office success *The Silence of the Lambs,* directed by Jonathan Demme. Playing opposite Jodie Foster, as novice Federal Bureau of Investigation (F.B.I.) agent Clarice Starling, who seeks his help in identifying and catching another serial killer, Hopkins won the New York Film Critics Circle Award for best actor and was nominated for a 1992 Best Actor Oscar. On the small screen, Hopkins also won praise as Paraguayan doctor and human rights activist Joel Filartiga, seeking the truth about his teenage son's death, playing opposite Norma Aleandro and Ruben Blades, in the HBO telefilm *One Man's War* in April 1991. Late in 1991 he appeared as Errol Wallace in the Australian comedy *Spotswood,* directed by Mark Joffe. In a very different vein, he narrated a television documentary *Top Guns and Toxic Whales: Our Environment.* Forthcoming were starring roles in Geoff Murphy's futuristic thriller *Freejack;* opposite Winona Ryder in Francis Ford Coppola's *Bram Stoker's Dracula;* and a new Merchant-Ivory-Jhabvala collaboration, *Howard's End,* based on the E. M. Forster novel, with a stellar cast that includes Vanessa Redgrave, Emma Thompson, James Wilby, Helena Bonham Carter, Prunella Scales, and Jemma Redgrave.

Wales-born Hopkins played in repertory during the early 1960s; he joined the National Theatre in 1967, the same year that he made his film debut in *The Lion in Winter.* A few of his most notable theater roles were in the title role of *Macbeth* (1972; National Theatre), *Equus* (1974–75; on Broadway), *Pravda* (1985; National Theatre), *King Lear* (1986; National Theatre), and *Anthony and Cleopatra* (1987; title role, National Theatre). He has appeared in such films as *The Looking Glass War* (1967), *A Bridge Too Far* (1976), *Magic* (1978), *The Elephant Man* (1978), *The Bounty* (1984) as Captain Bligh, *84 Charing Cross Road* (1987), and *Desperate Hours* (1989). He has also acted in a wide range of television roles, winning Emmys in *The Lindbergh Kidnapping Case* (1975) and *The Bunker* (1980), and playing such title roles as *Kean* (1980) and *Othello* (1981). Hopkins attended the Welsh College of Music and Drama and the Royal Academy of Dramatic Art. His second wife is the former Jennifer Lynton; he has one daughter. (For photo, see **Foster, Jodie.**)

FURTHER READING

Anthony Hopkins: Too Good to Waste. Quentin Fack. Isis (NY), 1990.

"Anthony Hopkins." David Gritten. *M Inc.,* Aug. 1991.

"Anthony Hopkins." Jim Jerome. *People,* March 4, 1991.

Hoskins, Bob (Robert William Hoskins, 1942–) Once described as a "ferociously gifted actor," Hoskins was much in demand during 1990–91. Late in 1990 he appeared in Richard Benjamin's film *Mermaids* as Lou Landsky, a shoe store owner who wants to settle down with the unorthodox Mrs. Flax, played by Cher. In October 1991, he opened as eccentric private eye and pet shop owner Gus Klein in Wolfgang Petersen's mystery film *Shattered,* with Tom Berenger, Greta Scacchi, Joanne Whalley-Kilmer, and Corbin Bernsen. In Steven Spielberg's major 1991 Christmas movie, *Hook,* his updated retelling of the Peter Pan story, Hoskins was the gleefully villainous Smee. On British radio, Hoskins also played Sancho Panza to Paul Scofield's Don Quixote in April 1991.

Forthcoming at year's end were Andrei Konchalovsky's *The Inner Circle,* about Stalin's world as seen through the eyes of his film projectionist, with Tom Hulce, Lolita Davidovich, and Bess Meyer; and Lindsay Anderson's film version of Anton Chekhov's *The Cherry Orchard,* with Maggie Smith and Alan Bates. Late in 1991, Hoskins was in Pittsburgh shooting Charlie Peters's *Passed Away,* with William Petersen, Pamela Reed, Nancy Travis, Tim Curry, Peter Riegert, and Blair Brown.

From the mid-1980s, Hoskins emerged as a leading British film actor, making his debut in *National Health* (1974) and going on to such movies as *Royal Flash* (1975), *Zulu Dawn* (1980), *The Long Good Friday* (1980), *The Honorary Consul* (1984), *Lassiter* (1984), *The Cotton Club* (1985), *Sweet Liberty* (1986), *Mona Lisa* (1986), *A Prayer for the Dying* (1987), *The Lonely Passion of Judith Hearne* (1988), *Who Framed Roger Rabbit?* (1988), *Heart Condition* (1990), and *Mermaids* (1990). He wrote, directed, and appeared in *The Raggedy Rawney* (1988). He has also appeared often on television, most notably in his powerful lead in *Pennies from Heaven* (1979). His second wife is the former Linda Banwell; he has two daughters and two sons.

FURTHER READING

"Hoskins, Bob." *Current Biography,* Sep. 1990.

"Cockney charisma." William Boyd. *New York Times Magazine,* Dec. 6, 1987.

"Bob Hoskins." *People,* Dec. 22, 1986.

Houston, Whitney (1963–) Houston was tremendously visible early in 1991. Her Super Bowl rendition of "The Star Spangled Banner" became a hit, partly because it came during the patriotic surge generated by the Persian Gulf War; it made her for a little while the equivalent of Kate Smith singing "God Bless America" during World War II. She followed it with another superpatriotic effort, this her April 2 "Welcome Home Heroes with Whitney Houston" concert at the Norfolk, Virginia, Naval Air Station, for service men and women returning from the Gulf War; broadcast by HBO, it was widely simulcast on radio and also generated a hit album. In the same period, her pop single "All the Man That I Need" hit the top of the charts. Houston also continued to tour widely during the year. Forthcoming was a change of pace—a starring role as a celebrity who is being hunted

by an insane fan, opposite Kevin Costner as an ex-Secret Service agent hired to protect her, in the Mick Jackson film *The Bodyguard,* scheduled for 1992 release. Houston is slated to appear in several other films, having in 1990 signed a multi-picture agreement with 20th Century Fox to star in and produce projects through her Nippy Productions, headed by her father, John Houston.

New Jersey–born Houston suddenly emerged as a leading popular singer in the mid-1980s, with her first album, the Grammy-winning *Whitney Houston* (1985), followed by *Whitney* (1986), and with such songs as "Didn't We Almost Have it All," "The Greatest Love of All," and "How Will I Know." In 1990, her single "I'm Your Baby Tonight," from the album of the same name, also hit number one. Houston is the daughter of singer Cissy Houston, and the cousin of singer Aretha Franklin.

FURTHER READING

"Whitney Houston talks. . . ." LYNN NORMENT. *Ebony,* May 1991.
"20 questions. . . ." *Playboy,* May 1991.
"Singer Whitney Houston. . . ." *Jet,* July 16, 1990.
"Whitney Houston." DAVID VAN BIEMA. *Life,* Oct. 1990.
"Whitney Houston." *Harper's Bazaar,* Sep. 1989.
The Picture Life of Whitney Houston. GENE BUSNAR. Watts, 1988.
Whitney Houston. KEITH E. GREENBERG. Lerner, 1988.

Howard, Ron (1954–) Actor-director-producer Howard directed a blockbuster commercial hit in theatrical release during the spring and summer of 1991: the fire disaster movie *Backdraft* with Kurt Russell and William Baldwin as Chicago firefighters Stephen and Brian McCaffrey, carrying on the tradition of their dead firefighting father. The cast includes Robert De Niro as a fire inspector, Donald Sutherland as a pyromaniac arsonist, Rebecca DeMornay, and Jennifer Jason Leigh. Forthcoming was a film tentatively titled *Far and Away,* directed and co-produced by Howard. Tom Cruise and Nicole Kidman star as an Irish couple who fall in love during the 1840s potato famine and emigrate to America, in a cast that includes Robert Prosky, Thomas Gibson, Barbara Babcock, Colm Meaney, Cyril Cusack, and Niall Toibin.

Oklahoma-born Howard was a child star in television, as Opie in "The Andy Griffith Show" (1960–68), and later in "The Smith Family" (1971–72) and "Happy Days" (1974–80). He also appeared in such films as *The Music Man* (1962), *American Graffiti* (1973), and *The Shootist* (1976). As an adult, he directed, and in several instances co-wrote and produced, such films as *Splash* (1984), *Cocoon* (1985), *No Man's Land* (1987), *Clean and Sober* (1988), *Willow* (1988), and *Parenthood* (1989). Howard was also (with Brian Grazer) executive producer and writer of the television series spun off from *Parenthood.*

He attended the University of Southern California. He married Cheryl Alley in 1975; they have five children.

FURTHER READING

"Ron Howard." JOHN CLARK. *Premiere,* Apr. 1991.

Hurt, William (1950–) Still finding serious film roles in a movie world full of special effects and comic strip heroes, Hurt starred in 1991 in Randa Haines's *The Doctor,* an artistically and commercially successful film about a top heart surgeon who learns he has cancer, sees a far more negative side of his own medical establishment than he had ever suspected, and discovers his own humanity. The cast included Christine Lahti, Elizabeth Perkins, Mandy Patinkin, and Adam Arkin. Hurt also starred in *Until the End of the World,* a science fiction espionage thriller directed and co-written by Wim Wenders, with a distinguished international cast that included Solveig Dammartin, Max von Sydow, Jeanne Moreau, and Sam Neill. Forthcoming was another starring role as a doctor, in Luis Puenzo's adaptation of Albert Camus's *The Plague.* In a very notable television appearance, Hurt narrated the documentary *A. Einstein: How I See the World,* a documentary in the Public Broadcasting System "American Masters" series.

On the personal side, the New York Court of Appeals, the state's highest court, ruled in favor of Hurt by refusing to hear an appeal of lower court decisions finding that Hurt and Sandra Jennings did not have a common law marriage, ending a years-long palimony case that had attracted wide attention.

Born in Washington, D.C., Hurt became a leading dramatic actor in the late 1970s, starring in such films as *Body Heat* (1978), *The Big Chill* (1983), *Gorky Park* (1983), *Kiss of the Spider Woman* (1985), for which he won a Best Actor Oscar, *Children of a Lesser God* (1986), *Broadcast News* (1987), *The Accidental Tourist* (1988), and *Alice* (1990). Hurt attended Tufts University and the Juilliard School. He was formerly married to actress Mary Beth Hurt. He married Heidi Henderson in 1989; they have one son. During the 1981–84 relationship between Jennings and Hurt, Jennings bore a son.

FURTHER READING

"The news about. . . ." JANE HALL and BRAD DARRACH. *People,* Feb. 1, 1988.
William Hurt: The Actor and His Work. TOBY GOLDSTEIN. St. Martin's, 1987.
"William Hurt. . . ." JACK KROLL. *Esquire,* Oct. 1986.
"Hurt, William." *Current Biography,* May 1986.

Husàk, Gustav (1913–91) The last communist president of Czechoslovakia, Husàk became a communist in 1933, the same year that he began to study law in his home town of Bratislava, in Slovakia. Husàk became a Slovak leader of his party in the 1930s and was a resistance leader during World War II, who in 1943 became a member of the Slovak party central committee. After the communist takeover of Czechoslovakia in 1948, he became a member of the Czechoslovak party central committee, but was deposed for alleged nationalist views in 1950 and imprisoned (1951–60). "Rehabilitated" in 1963, he was out of power until joining Alexander Dubcek's Prague Spring government as deputy premier in 1968, then also becoming first secretary of the Slovak Communist Party. After the Soviet invasion and reconquest of his country, he became an instrument of Soviet control, becoming first secretary of the Czechoslovak Communist Party (1969–87) and president of Czechoslovakia (1975–89). A conservative, Husàk resisted the reforms of the Gorbachev era, but on December 10, 1989, ultimately gave way, resigning to be replaced by Vaclav Havel. In 1990, he was expelled once again from the Czechoslovak Communist Party but was not prosecuted by the new government. He was twice married, and was survived by a sister. His *Speeches and Writings* was published in 1986. (d. Bratislava, Czechoslovakia; November 18, 1991)

FURTHER READING

Obituary. *New York Times,* Nov. 19, 1991.
Obituary. *The Times* (of London), Nov. 19, 1991.

Hussein I (Hussein ibn Talal, 1935–) As the Persian Gulf crisis developed into the Persian Gulf War, the Jordanian king attempted to adopt a peacemaker's role, entirely unsuccessfully shuttling between the sides as the crisis worsened. As the air war developed, he declared

himself a neutral, vowing to resist incursions into Jordanian air space, while at the same time serving as an overland Iraqi supply source. In his wartime public statements, he supported the Iraqi side, winning great popular support from Jordan's largely Palestinian, pro-Iraqi population, and considerable enmity from the nations allied against Iraq; these included the oil-rich Gulf nations, led by Saudi Arabia, which responded by stopping their subsidies to Jordan. In the wake of the lost war, Jordan and its king were cut off, deeply damaged, and beset by hundreds of thousands of Iraqi refugees, along with hundreds of thousands of Jordanians returning home, many in flight from angry Saudi and Kuwaiti governments. It was thought by some that Jordan's inclusion in the autumn 1991 Middle East peace talks signaled the beginning of a Jordanian return to the regional and international communities.

Hussein became king of Jordan in 1953, succeeding his father, Abdullah Ibn Hussein, himself the son of Hussein Ibn Ali, head of the 1916 Arab revolt against the Turks during World War I, the revolt assisted by British officer T. E. Lawrence (Lawrence of Arabia). For almost four decades, Hussein survived as a moderate in the turbulent politics of the Middle East, although he was drawn into the 1967 Third Arab-Israeli War and lost control over the West Bank and Jerusalem, which Israel has occupied ever since. He gave up all territorial claims to these in 1988, during the Palestinian Intifada, to pave the way for a Palestinian declaration of independence. In 1970, he fought and won a war against the Palestine Liberation Organization (PLO), then headquartered in his country, although by 1990 the relatively large Palestinian population of Jordan strongly influenced his position on the Iraqi invasion of Kuwait, which was supported by most Palestinians. Hussein attended Victoria College and Sandhurst in England. He has been married four times, since 1978 to Lisa Halaby, now Queen Noor; he has 11 children.

FURTHER READING

" 'Trying to catch our breath.' . . ." CHRISTOPHER DICKEY. *Newsweek,* Aug. 19, 1991.
"The great survivor. . . ." JOHN STACKS and DEAN FISCHER. *Time,* July 22, 1991.
"Who's sitting pretty. . . ." *Business Week,* Mar. 11, 1991.
"Speech defect. . . ." MICHAEL KELLY. *New Republic,* Mar. 4, 1991.
"Divided loyalties." JOEL BRINKLEY. *New York Times Magazine,* Dec. 16, 1990.
"Facing a no-win. . . ." DEAN FISCHER and JAMES WILDE. *Time,* Nov. 5, 1990.
"Dangerous crossroads. . . ." *Maclean's,* July 9, 1990.
Hussein of Jordan: From Survivor to Statesman. JAMES LUNT. Morrow, 1989.
King Hussein and the Challenge of Arab Radicalism: Jordan, 1955–1967. URIEL DANN. Oxford University Press, 1989.

Hussein, Saddam (1937–) During the first two months of 1991, Iraq reaped the whirlwind sown by Saddam Hussein's August 1, 1990, invasion of Kuwait. On January 17, 1991, after a huge military buildup, the Allied air war against Iraq began, causing massive destruction throughout Iraq, quickly grounding the Iraqi air force, and blinding the Iraqi military. The attack was accompanied with feints and amphibious exercises in the Gulf, and the turning of the Iraqi military to meet a supposed invasion from that direction. Massive Allied armored forces then deployed west, to prepare the main thrust around the key Iraqi defenses and into northern Kuwait and southern Iraq. During the weeks that followed, the air war destroyed Iraqi ability to resist, and Iraq was not able to change the balance of forces by attacking Israel with Scud missiles; Israel did not enter the war, and U.S.-built Patriot missiles knocked down many Iraqi missiles.

The Allied main armored force struck on February 24 and within three days had met and destroyed the reserve Republican Guard divisions, while direct assaults easily destroyed Iraqi frontline defenses, with Allied frontline armor moving into Kuwait City far more quickly than many had expected. With all of Iraq open to Allied forces, the Iraqis gave up, and the brief war was over. But Saddam Hussein still lived and ruled what was left of Iraq, and some of his forces escaped destruction—enough to allow him to put down a postwar Shiite rebellion in southern Iraq and a postwar Kurdish rebellion in northern Iraq. In the aftermath of the Shiite rebellion, tens of thousands of Shiites were given asylum in Saudi Arabia. In the wake of the Kurdish rebellion, an estimated one million Kurds fled to the Iranian and Turkish borders, ultimately to be protected by Allied and then by United Nations troops. At year's end, Iraq had suffered enormous human and material losses, and Saddam Hussein still ruled Iraq.

Takrit-born Hussein joined the Baath socialist party in 1957, and went into Egyptian exile in 1958 after he took part in the failed attempt to assassinate general Karim Kassem, premier of the Iraqi republic. He returned to Iraq in 1963 after the army coup in which Kassem was killed. Hussein was a leader of the Baath coup of 1968 and took full power in 1971, then surrounding himself with followers from his home village, instituting a reign of terror in his country, and becoming the dictator of Iraq. He also then began to develop a massive "cult of personality" around himself.

In 1980, Hussein's forces attacked Iran, beginning the Iran-Iraq war (1980–88); his forces used large amounts of poison gas against the Iranians, although such chemical warfare has been condemned throughout the world. In the late 1980s, after the 1988 ceasefire with Iran, his forces continued to use poison gas, this time against Iraq's own rebellious Kurdish population, killing thousands of civilians and forcing hundreds of thousands to flee into exile. With the end of the Iran-Iraq war, he emerged as a Middle Eastern strongman. On August 2, 1990, his armies invaded oil-rich Kuwait, which his armies quickly took. He then turned toward far richer Saudi Arabia, either to invade or intimidate, and was met by the U.S.-led multinational response, coupled with UN action, that resulted in sanctions, blockade, and ultimately the Persian Gulf War.

Hussein attended Cairo University and Baghdad's al-Mujstanseriya University. He married Sajidal Khairalla in 1963 and has four children.

FURTHER READING

Saddam Hussein. Nita Renfrew. Chelsea House, 1992.
"How Saddam survived. . . ." Gail Sheehy. *Vanity Fair,* Aug. 1991.
"Getting even." Uriel Dann. *New Republic,* June 3, 1991.
"His war, his peace. . . ." *Economist,* Feb. 23, 1991.
"The man behind. . . ." Paul Gray. *Time,* Feb. 11, 1991.
"Saddam. . . ." Lisa Beyer. *Time,* Jan. 7, 1991.
Saddam Hussein: A Political Biography. Efraim Karsh and Inari Rautsi. Pergamon, 1991.
Outlaw State: Saddam Hussein's Quest for Power and the Gulf Crisis. Elaine Sciolino. Wiley, 1991.
Saddam Hussein: A Political Biography. Efraim Karsh. Free Press, 1991.
Instant Empire: Saddam Hussein's Ambition for Iraq. Simon Henderson. Mercury House, 1991.
"Blood Baath. . . ." David A. Korn. *New Republic,* Oct. 29, 1990.
"Iraq's strongman. . . ." Lauren Tarshis. *Scholastic Update,* Oct. 5, 1990.
"What makes. . . ." Brian Duffy. *U.S. News & World Report,* Sep. 10, 1990.
"Saddam Hussein's. . . ." Louise Lief. *U.S. News & World Report,* Sep. 10, 1990.
"Like a wolf. . . ." J. B. Kelly and Brian Crozier. *National Review,* Sep. 3, 1990.
"Thief of Baghdad. . . ." Fouad Ajami. *New Republic,* Sep. 3, 1990.
"Behind Saddam Hussein's smile. . . ." *People,* Aug. 20, 1990.
"Tyrant of the Gulf." John Bierman. *Maclean's,* Aug. 13, 1990.
"Master of his universe." Otto Friedrich. *Time,* Aug. 13, 1990.
"Resourceful aggressor. . . ." Maggie Mahar. *Barron's,* Aug. 13, 1990.
Saddam Hussein and the Crisis in the Gulf. Judith Miller and Laurie Mylorie. Random, 1990.

Huston, Anjelica (1952–) As *The Grifters* and *The Witches* moved from theatrical release into home video, Huston in 1991 added yet another striking characterization to what has by now become a long list of memorable roles, as Morticia in Barry Sonnenfeld's film version of *The Addams Family,* in a cast that included Raul Julia as Gomez Addams, Christopher Lloyd as Fester, Christina Ricci as Wednesday, Jimmy Workman as Pugsley, Judith Malina as Granny, and Carel Struyken as Lurch. Forthcoming were roles in Nicolas Roeg's film *Two Deaths,* and in the Robert Altman film *The Player,* in a multi-star cast that includes Tim Robbins, Greta Scacchi, Dean Stockwell, Whoopi Goldberg, Marlee Matlin, Andie MacDowell, Julia Roberts, Susan Sarandon, Jack Lemmon, Cher, and Burt Reynolds.

Born in Los Angeles but raised in Ireland, Huston took a critical pounding when her father, actor-director John Huston, cast the 15-year-old in his film, *A Walk with Love and Death* (1967). She retreated from film to the stage, but emerged as a leading dramatic actress in the mid-1980s, winning a Best Supporting Actress Oscar as Maerose Prizzi in John Huston's *Prizzi's Honor* (1985); and starring in *Gardens of Stone* (1987); *The Dead* (1987), with screenplay by brother Tony Huston; *A Handful of Dust* (1988), John Huston's last film; *Enemies, A Love Story* (1989); *Crimes and Misdemeanors* (1989); *The Grifters* (1990); and *The Witches* (1990). In 1990, she ended a 17-year relationship with Jack Nicholson. She is the granddaughter of actor Walter Huston. Huston worked with acting coach Peggy Feury.

FURTHER READING

"Anjelica Huston." SUSAN MORGAN. *Interview,* Dec. 1991.
"Huston Addams." SUSAN MORGAN. *Interview,* July 1991.
"A bit of a coyote. . . ." DAVID THOMSON. *American Film,* Nov. 1990.
"Anjelica Huston. . . ." VICKI WOODS. *Vogue,* Nov. 1990.
"Huston, Anjelica." *Current Biography,* July 1990.
Anjelica Huston: The Lady and the Legacy. MARTHA HARRIS. St. Martin's, 1989.
The Hustons. LAWRENCE GROBEL. Macmillan, 1989.

Hyde White, Wilfred (1903–91) Gloucestershire-born Hyde White, a very durable supporting actor, made his stage debut in stock, in 1922, and his London debut in *Beggar on Horseback,* in 1925. He went on to five decades of character roles, on stage and screen. His most notable roles came rather late in his career. On stage these included 1951 appearances with Laurence Olivier's company in *Caesar and Cleopatra* and *Anthony and Cleopatra,* and as Jimmy Broadbent in *The Reluctant Debutante* (1955); he won a Tony nomination for the role in 1956 and was nominated again for *The Jockey Club Stakes* (1972). His most substantial screen role was that of Colonel Pickering in the film version of *My Fair Lady* (1964). He also appeared in a wide range of other films, including *Rembrandt* (1936), *The Third Man* (1949), *The Browning Version* (1950), *Outcast of the Islands* (1952), and *Ten Little Indians* (1966). He also appeared on television in several continuing series roles. He moved to southern California in 1960. He was survived by his second wife, the former Ethel Drew, a daughter, and two sons. (d. Los Angeles; May 6, 1991)

FURTHER READING

Obituary. *Variety,* May 13, 1991.
Obituary. *The Times* (of London), May 8, 1991.
Obituary. *New York Times,* May 7, 1991.

I

Iacocca, Lee (Lido Anthony Iacocca, 1924–) In a year of massive losses for the Big Three U.S. automobile manufacturers—General Motors, Ford, Chrysler—Chrysler chairman Iacocca fought hard to keep his company afloat. Despite continuing losses, he was in March able to secure $1.75 billion in replacement lines of credit; although these were smaller than Chrysler's previous lines of credit, the company was also able in mid-year to improve somewhat its internal cash generation. In a move jarring to stockholders, Chrysler substantially reduced dividends in 1991.

All three automobile company heads met with President George Bush on March 21 to discuss the plight of the American auto industry. Bush rejected Iacocca's suggestion that Japanese automobile competition in the United States be restricted by law, though pressure to restrict Japanese imports and goods made by Japanese plants functioning in the United States continued to grow throughout the year, as the deepening recession brought severe hardship to U.S. workers and Japanese home market restrictions remained very effectively in force.

On the personal side, Iacocca was one of those who refused an offer of appointment to the unexpired senate term of the late Senator John Heinz. The seat went to Harrison Wofford, who ultimately defeated former Pennsylvania governor and U.S. attorney general Richard Thornburgh in the upset November 4 special election.

Iacocca began his long career with the Ford Motor Company in 1946; he rose to the presidency of the Ford division in 1970, leaving in 1978 to become the highly visible president and chief operating officer of Chrysler. He saved Chrysler from looming bankruptcy with the help of a massive federal "bailout" and went on to become a leading figure in American industry. During the mid-1980s, Iacocca was the prime mover in the restoration of the Statue of Liberty and the reclamation of Ellis Island. The former immigration station opened as a museum of American immigration and a national shrine on September 9, 1990. Iacocca was an honored guest, although he had by then been partially pushed aside for political reasons by the Bush administration. He published two bestselling autobiographical works, *Iacocca: An Autobiography* (1986; with William Novak) and *Talking Straight* (1989). Pennsylvania-born Iacocca received his B.S. from Lehigh University, in 1945, and his M.E. from Princeton, in 1946. He married Mary McCleary in 1956; they had two children.

FURTHER READING

"U.S. needs a 'game plan.'" *Design News,* June 3, 1991.
"Playboy interview. . . ." PETER ROSS RANGE. *Playboy,* Jan. 1991.
Lee Iacocca: Chrysler's Good Fortune. DAVID R. COLLINS. Garrett, 1991.
"Iacocca talks. . . ." ALEX TAYLOR III. *Fortune,* Feb. 12, 1990.
"Iacocca, Lee Anthony." *Current Biography,* Oct. 1988.
Standing up for America: A Biography of Lee Iacocca. PATRICIA HADDOCK. Dillon, 1987.
The Unknown Iacocca. PETER WYDEN. Morrow, 1987.

Iliescu, Ion (1930–) Romanian President Iliescu faced a developing economic crisis in 1991 as well as widespread public perception that he and other key government officials were communist holdovers who had little real interest in developing a democratic Romania. Such charges seemed to have some basis in reality; after Iliescu's election to the presidency on May 20, 1990, opposition groups protesting the organization and conduct of the elections were beaten and dispersed by thousands of coal miners armed with clubs, at Iliescu's urging. In 1991, Iliescu and Prime Minister Petre Roman attempted to move in the direction of a market economy, in April and May introducing a series of austerity measures in return for International Monetary Fund credits and other international guarantees amounting to more than $1 billion. Romania also lifted foreign exchange restrictions and made a series of moves aimed at encouraging foreign investment.

Iliescu has been associated with the Romanian Communist Party ever since joining its youth organization in 1944. He rose swiftly in the party hierarchy until the early 1970s, becoming a member of his party's central committee in 1967 and youth minister in 1967–72. But then he fell into disfavor with dictator Nicolae Ceausescu, was sidetracked and demoted; he was head of a state-run publishing house in 1989, when Ceausescu fell. In that fall, Iliescu rose, on December 22, 1989, emerging as a member of the revolutionary council, the National Salvation Front. On December 23, as president of the Front, he announced the arrest of Nicolae and Elena Ceausescu, who were executed on December 25. On December 26, Iliescu was named provisional president of Romania. He attended the Bucharest Polytechnical Institute and Moscow University, and is married to Elena Iliescu.

FURTHER READING

"Iliescu, Ion." *Current Biography,* June 1990.
"Between revolutions. . . ." VLADIMIR TISMANEANU. *New Republic,* Apr. 23, 1990.

Irons, Jeremy (1948–) Celebrated British actor Irons won a 1991 Best Actor Oscar for his 1990 portrayal of Claus von Bulow in *Reversal of Fortune;* it was one of several such honors for the role. His next film was Steven Soderbergh's *Kafka* (1991), set in Prague in 1919; Irons starred as an amateur detective searching for a lost friend, who instead finds an oppressive, murderous bureaucracy. The cast included Theresa Russell, Ian Holm, Alec Guinness, Joel Grey, Jeroen Krabbé, Armin Mueller-Stahl, and Brian Glover. Forthcoming was Stephen Gyllenhaal's *Waterland,* based on the Graham Swift novel; Irons and his wife, Sinead Cusack, star as a childless British couple who emigrate to America in search of a new life. Irons and Julie Andrews were the co-presenters of the 1991 Tony Awards.

Irons emerged as a screen and stage star in the early 1980s. In 1981, he created the Charles Ryder role in *Brideshead Revisited,* the celebrated television miniseries adaptation of the Evelyn Waugh novel. In the same year, he played opposite Meryl Streep in *The French Lieutenant's Woman.* He went on to star in such films as *Moonlighting* (1982), *Betrayal* (1983), *The Wild Duck* (1983), *Swann in Love* (1984), *The Mission* (1986), *Dead Ringers* (1989), *Frankenstein Unbound* (1989), and *A Chorus of Disapproval* (1989). He won a Best Actor Tony for *The Real Thing* (1984). He and Sinead Cusack have two children.

FURTHER READING

"Metamorphosis man." HARLAN KENNEDY. *American Film,* Nov.–Dec. 1991.

"Claus encounters." ELLEN STERN. *GQ—Gentlemen's Quarterly,* Nov. 1990.
"Irons." DAVID DENICOLO. *Interview,* June 1990.
Actors: A Celebration. RITA GAM. St. Martin's, 1988.

Irwin, James Benson (1930–91) Pittsburgh-born Irwin, a U.S. air force pilot who became an astronaut, went to the moon on July 15, 1971, as a crew member of the Apollo 15 mission. He and Colonel David Scott became the seventh and eighth persons to walk on the moon, and the first two to travel any substantial distance on its surface, going several miles in the Lunar Rover. Their achievement was somewhat marred at the time, as they had taken along several hundred envelopes to hand cancel and stamp on the moon, for sale as collector's items on their return, a scheme that misfired. Irwin, who went through a religious conversion while on the moon, retired after his return and founded the High Flight Foundation, an evangelical organization; under its aegis he lectured and traveled widely. He also led two expeditions to Turkey's Mount Ararat in an unsuccessful search for Noah's Ark, and published *Destination: Moon* (1989) for children, as well as several religious books. He was survived by his wife Mary Ellen, three daughters, two sons, his mother, and a brother. (d. Glenwood Springs, Colorado; August 8, 1991)

FURTHER READING

Obituary. *The Times* (of London), Aug. 10, 1991.
Obituary. *New York Times,* Aug. 10, 1991.
"Footprints on the moon. . . ." DOUGLAS MACKINNON and JOSEPH BALDANZA. *American History Illustrated,* Summer 1989.

Ismail, Raghib Ramadan (Rocket) (1969–) They call him the Rocket because of the way he speeds down the football field. When exciting wide receiver and kick-return specialist Raghib Ismail skipped his senior year at Notre Dame to enter the April 1991 National Football League draft, he was widely considered to be the number one player picked. But before the draft, Ismail "defected" from the NFL, announcing that he would sign with the Toronto Argonauts of the Canadian Football League (CFL), a team owned by Bruce McNall, hockey star Wayne

Gretzky, and actor John Candy. The highly lucrative contract was reportedly for $26.2 million, with $18.2 million guaranteed, making him the highest-paid professional football player in history. The Argonauts may well feel they got their money's worth. In his first year, Ismail withstood initial pre-season media criticism to energize the CFL, and in November led his team to the Grey Cup, in the championship game returning one kickoff 87 yards for a touchdown and gaining 167 yards on other returns—and not surprisingly being named the game's most valuable player. During 1991 Ismail indicated that he might play just two years in the CFL and then switch to the NFL, presumably with the Los Angeles Raiders, who chose his rights in the fourth round in the April NFL draft.

Raised in Newark, New Jersey, and Wilkes-Barre, Pennsylvania, Ismail received his nickname in high school for his powerful bursts of speed. Over his three-year career at Notre Dame, he averaged an astonishing 62 yards on the 17 touchdowns he scored and was a two-time all-American. In his final season, when he was runner-up for the Heisman Trophy, he had a team-high 32 receptions, for an average 21.9 yards, and two touchdowns.

FURTHER READING

"Rocket's red glare. . . ." BRUCE WALLACE. *Maclean's,* May 6, 1991.
"Raghib Ismail." *Sporting News,* Apr. 29, 1991.
"The rocket man." CRAIG ELLENPORT. *Sport,* Nov. 1990.

"The light and the lightning." RALPH WILEY. *Sports Illustrated,* Sep. 25, 1989.

Ivory, James Francis (1928–) After two films set in the contemporary United States, the celebrated film director Ivory returned to more familiar ground during 1991. His new film was *Howard's End,* based on E. M. Forster's 1910 novel and set in an English country house of that name in class-dominated Edwardian Britain just before the Great War that was to sweep away so much of that life-style. The screenplay is by Ruth Prawer Jhabvala, so often Ivory's collaborator; the cast includes Anthony Hopkins, Vanessa Redgrave, Emma Thompson, James Wilby, Helena Bonham Carter, Prunella Scales, Joseph Bennett, Adrian Ross Magenty, Jemma Redgrave, and Sam West. The film, clearly intended to be an important segment of Ivory's main work, was scheduled to have its world premiere in early February 1992 aboard the *MS Nieuw Amsterdam* at the second annual Floating Film Festival.

California-born Ivory began his long, fruitful collaboration with producer Ismail Merchant and Jahbvala in the early 1960s with such films as *Shakespeare Wallah* (1965), *Bombay Talkie* (1970), and *Autobiography of a Princess* (1975), all of them largely set in India. His later films included *The Europeans* (1979), *Heat and Dust* (1983), *A Room with a View* (1986), *Maurice* (1987), *Slaves of New York* (1989), and *Mr. and Mrs. Bridge* (1990). Ivory's B.F.A. was from the University of Oregon, in 1951, his M.A. from the University of Southern California.

FURTHER READING

Films of Merchant Ivory. ROBERT E. LONG. Abrams, 1991.
"Mr. and Mrs. Bridge." GRAHAM FULLER. *Interview,* Nov. 1990.
"The Raj duet. . . ." DINITIA SMITH. *New York,* Oct.5, 1987.
"Merchant and Ivory." *American Film,* Jan.–Feb. 1987.

J

Jackson, Glenda (1936–) In what may be her valedictory year in theater and films, the extraordinary British actress, twice an Oscar winner, starred during 1991 in a Glasgow production of Eugene O'Neill's *Mourning Becomes Electra.* In December, she was seen in the United States as Bernarda Alba in the television version of Gabriel Garcia Lorca's *The House of Bernarda Alba,* opposite Joan Plowright; this revival of the play had been a London stage hit on its initial presentation in 1986. Jackson also starred opposite Denholm Elliott in the television film *A Murder of Quality,* based on an early John Le Carré novel.

Jackson's major focus continued to be the upcoming British general election. In 1990, she announced her intention to run for Parliament, as Labour Party candidate for Hampstead, in London, and stated that, if she won, she would give up acting for a full-time career in politics. A Labour Party member since her teens and a powerful critic of Conservative Party policies, Jackson won the Labour selection poll for the Hampstead seat over three other women candidates, with 60 percent of the vote, and moved directly into the early stages of her campaign. She also began her emergence as a key figure in her party and in British politics, with a major speech at the October 1991 Labour Party National Conference, sharply attacking the ruling Conservative Party for its neglect of Britain's state-funded education system. At year's end, she seemed a very strong candidate.

Jackson made her stage debut in 1957. She joined the Royal Shakespeare Company in 1964 and that year emerged as a powerful dramatic actress, as Charlotte Corday in *Marat/Sade,* a role she recreated on Broadway in 1965 and in the 1966 film. She went on to become a very notable stage and screen star, on stage as Ophelia in *Hamlet* (1965), Masha in *The Three Sisters* (1967), as *Hedda Gabler* (1975), and as poet Stevie Smith in *Stevie* (1977; and in the 1977 film), and in such plays as *Rose* (1980), *Strange Interlude* (1984), *Macbeth* (1988), and in Los Angeles in late 1989 in Edward Albee's production of his own *Who's Afraid of Virginia Woolf.* On screen, she was a notable Elizabeth I in the television miniseries *Elizabeth R* (1971), won Best Actress Oscars for *Women in Love* (1969) and *A Touch of Class* (1973), and also starred in such films as *Sunday Bloody Sunday* (1971), *The Abbess of Crewe* (1976), *The Return of the Soldier* (1982), *Turtle Diary* (1985), and *The Rainbow* (1989). Jackson attended the Royal Academy of Dramatic Art. She was formerly married and has one child.

FURTHER READING

"Labour pains. . . ." Christopher Silvester. *Connoisseur,* July 1991.
"With more than a touch. . . ." Andrea Chambers. *People,* Mar. 18, 1985.
Glenda Jackson: A Study in Fire and Ice. Ian Woodward. St. Martin's, 1985.
Glenda Jackson. David Nathan. Hippocrene, 1984.

Jackson, Janet (1966–) Janet Jackson, sister of Michael Jackson, continued to emerge as a major popular singer on her own during 1991. Her enormously successful 1989 album, *Rhythm Nation: 1814,* ultimately generated four number one pop singles. In January 1991, her "Love Will Never Do (Without You)" became number one pop single. Later in the year, she received an MTV Video Music Award for the video version of the hit. In March 1991, she signed a three-album, $40 million agreement with Virgin Records, becoming one of the highest paid of the world's performing artists. (Her brother Michael was soon to sign an even larger agreement, with a $65 million guarantee that could ultimately reach the $1 billion range.) Her next album, the first under her new agreement, was due in 1992.

Jackson, a rather shy, soft-spoken young woman with strong social service views, in March 1991 received the Starlight Foundation Humanitarian Award. In November, she received a National Association for the Advancement of Colored People (NAACP) special Image Award for her work and financial contributions, such as a $500,000 donation to the United Negro College Fund in January 1991.

Jackson appeared as a child with her brothers, then the Jackson Five. She made three albums in the early 1980s: *Janet Jackson* (1982), *Dream Street* (1984), and *Control* (1986); the last introduced several hit singles and suggested the major career that would blossom a few years later. She scored a major success in 1989 with the hit album *Rhythm Nation: 1814*. Singer and dancer Jackson began her first concert tour on March 1, 1990, in Miami, and from there went on to tour the United States, Japan, and Europe. She was formerly married.

FURTHER READING

"Jackson, Janet." *Current Biography,* June 1991.
"Former child stars. . . ." MICHELLE MCCALOPE. *Jet,* Apr. 15, 1991.
La Toya: Growing up in the Jackson Family. LA TOYA JACKSON and PATRICIA ROMANOWSKI. NAL-Dutton, 1991.
"Janet Jackson and Paula Abdul. . . ." JET, May 7, 1990.
"Free at last." ANTHONY DECURTIS. *Rolling Stone,* Feb. 22, 1990.
"Janet Jackson. . . ." ROBERT E. JOHNSON. *Ebony,* Feb. 1990.
My Family, The Jacksons. KATHERINE JACKSON. St. Martin's, 1990.
Janet Jackson. D. L. MABERY. Lerner, 1988.
Janet Jackson: In Control. NANCY ROBISON. Dillon, 1987.

Jackson, Jesse Louis (1941–) Twice a presidential candidate, Jesse Jackson emerged from the 1988 campaign and his electrifying address to the 1988 Democratic convention as the leading African-American political figure of his day. But political movements are volatile, new leaders with sharply defined political bases can rise, and the media spotlight can shift away when a political leader is not tied to breaking issues. In 1991 Jackson continued to be a major African-American and Democratic Party liberal leader—but it was still something of an in-between year for him.

Jackson strongly opposed the Gulf War, leading rallies against the war in Washington and other cities, and traveling widely to speak and organize anti-war opposition. At the same time, early in the year, he took office on January 2 as one of the new Washington, D.C., "shadow" senators, the other being Florence Pendleton; both then began the very serious task of lobbying for Washington, D.C., statehood, and for a series of other wants, as well. They were only "shadow" senators, though, unable to enter the Senate floor during sessions or become involved in Senate business.

Although Jackson was not invited to the May 6–7 first national convention of the conservative Democratic Leadership Council, many Democratic presidential candidates and potential candidates attended the June Washington, D.C., convention of Jackson's Rainbow Coalition, attesting to Jackson's continuing potency within the Democratic Party. As expected, he announced in November that he would not seek the Democratic nomination in 1992. Much of his activity in 1991 was as a political talk show host and widely traveled speaker.

Long active in the civil rights movement, Jackson directed the Southern Christian Leadership Operation Breadbasket (1967–71), and in 1971 founded Operation PUSH (People United to Save Humanity), and later the Rainbow Coalition. He made an unsuccessful bid for the Democratic presidential nomination in 1984, but emerged as a major figure. In 1988, he published *A Time to Speak: The Autobiography of the Reverend Jesse Jackson.*

South Carolina–born Jackson received his B.A. from North Carolina Agricultural and Technical University, in 1964. After postgraduate work at the Chicago Theological Seminary, he became a Baptist minister, in 1968. He married Jacqueline Brown in 1964; the couple have five children.

FURTHER READING

I Am Somebody!: A Biography of Jesse Jackson. JAMES HASKINS. Enslow, 1992.

Keep Hope Alive: Super Tuesday and Jesse Jackson's 1988 Campaign for the Presidency. PENN KIMBALL. Joint Center for Political Studies, 1992.

"From Jim Crow. . . ." MARILYN BERLIN SNELL. *New Perspectives,* Summer 1991.

Jesse Jackson and Political Power. TERESA CELSI. Millbrook, 1991.

Jesse Jackson. ROBERT JAKOUBEK. Chelsea House, 1991.

Jesse Jackson: A Biography. PATRICIA C. MCKISSACK. Scholastic, 1991.

Jesse Jackson: Still Fighting for the Dream. BRANDA WILKINSON. Silver Burdett, 1990.

The Jackson Phenomenon: The Man, the Power, and the Message. ELIZABETH O. COULTON. Doubleday, 1989.

Jesse Jackson: A Voice for Change. STEVE OFFINOSKI. Fawcett, 1989.

Jesse Jackson. ANNA KOSOF. Watts, 1987.

Up with Hope: A Biography of Jesse Jackson. DOROTHY CHAPLIK. Dillon, 1986.

Jackson, Michael Joseph (1958–) A new Michael Jackson album is a major event; so is a new Michael Jackson recording agreement—and 1991 saw both. First came the agreement: On March 20, Jackson and Sony announced an agreement under which Jackson would create a new record label, Nation Records, and do six new albums for Epic, a Sony subsidiary. He would also create feature films, theatrical shorts, and television programming, and would star in his first feature film, to be produced by Columbia, a Sony subsidiary. Sony reportedly guaranteed Jackson at least $65 million, with the possibility of up to $1 billion in total income from the agreement.

His new album, *Dangerous,* was released in November, accompanied by a huge advertising campaign. It was preceded by an 11-minute video version of the album's first song, "Black and White." The final four minutes of the video, featuring scenes of sexual moves and violence, were criticized by many, including the Fox Network, which had broadcast it; Jackson immediately self-censored the video, cutting out the offending section for further broadcasts. The album, which also featured such songs as "Drive Me Wild," "Jam," "In the Closet," and "Heal the World," was not well received by many critics, nor was it immediately the anticipated commercial blockbuster. Personally, Jackson was host for Elizabeth Taylor's October wedding to Larry Fortensky; not only was the elaborate affair held on Jackson's California ranch but he also gave the bride away.

Indiana-born Jackson began his extraordinary career in 1969, as the 11-year-old lead singer of his family singing group, the Jackson Five. He became a leading popular soloist in the late 1970s, with such albums as *Off the Wall* (1979), *Thriller* (1982), which sold over four million copies, *Bad* (1987), and such singles as "I Can't Stop Loving You," along with many popular videos. He starred opposite Diana Ross in the film version of *The Wiz* (1978), and in *Moonwalker* (1988).

FURTHER READING

" 'Dangerous' album proves. . . ." *Jet,* Dec. 2, 1991.
"Former child stars. . . ." MICHELLE MCCALOPE. *Jet,* Apr. 15, 1991.
"Madonna and Michael." STEVE DOUGHERTY. *People,* Apr. 15, 1991.
Michael Jackson: The Magic and the Madness. J. RANDY TARABORRELLI. Carol, 1991.
La Toya: Growing up in the Jackson Family. LA TOYA JACKSON and PATRICIA ROMANOWSKI. NAL-Dutton, 1991.
Michael Jackson: A Life in Music. HAL SCHUSTER. Movie Publications, 1990.
My Family, the Jacksons. KATHERINE JACKSON. St. Martin's, 1990.
Sequins and Shades: The Michael Jackson Reference Guide. CAROL TERRY. Popular Culture, 1989.
Moonwalk. MICHAEL JACKSON. Doubleday, 1988; Writers Digest, 1989.
Michael Jackson Electrifying. GREG QUILL. Barrons, 1988.
The Michael Jackson Story. NELSON GEORGE. Dell, 1987.
Trapped: Michael Jackson and the Crossover Dream. DAVE MARSH. BANTAM, 1985.
About Michael Jackson. JAMES HASKINS. Enslow, 1985.

Jagger, Dean (1903–91) Ohio-born Jagger was briefly a teacher before beginning his long career as a character actor. He was on stage from the mid-1920s, and on Broadway in the 1930s. The major part of his career was in film; he made his screen debut in 1929, in *The Woman from Hell,* and went on to such films as *People Will Talk* (1935), *Brigham Young–Frontiersman* (1940) in the title role, *Western Union* (1941), *Twelve O'Clock High* (1950; winning a Best Supporting Actor Oscar), *Executive Suite* (1953), *White Christmas* (1953), *Elmer Gantry* (1960), *Firecreek* (1968), and *Alligator* (1980). He also appeared on television, most notably in the "Mr. Novak" series (1963–64). He was married three times, and was survived by his third wife, Etta, a daugher, two stepsons, and a sister. (d. Santa Monica, California; February, 5, 1991)

FURTHER READING

Obituary. *Variety,* Feb. 11, 1991.
Obituary. *New York Times,* Feb. 6, 1991.

Jagger, Mick (Michael Philip Jagger, 1941–) Jagger and the Rolling Stones made a sharp political statement early in 1991, in the form of the anti-Persian Gulf War single "High Wire," a condemnation of the widescale Middle East arms dealing they felt had so greatly contributed to the war. Jagger began writing the song in December, before the air war began, finished it while the hot war was in progress, and introduced it in early March, to much criticism from war supporters. April saw the introduction of a new Stones album, *Flashpoint;* it included two new songs—"High Wire" and "Sex Drive"—and 14 songs recorded during the Stones' 1989–90 "Steel Wheels" tour. The tour also generated the concert film *The Rolling Stones at the Max,* using a film projection process (IMAX) that presents the Stones on a 56-foot-high screen. Forthcoming was a starring role in Geoff Murphy's science fiction film *Freejack,* with Jagger playing Vacenkak, a villainous bounty hunter. In January 1992, Jagger and his wife, Jerry Hall, had a third child, a daughter, Georgia May Ayeesha.

Jagger was in 1962 the chief organizer of the Rolling Stones; he and Keith Richards were the group's main songwriters, and Jagger was its leading performer, playing the role of an angry, deeply alienated, uncontrollably violent, mythic sexual figure, as a model for the scores of other such rock and popular music figures that would follow in the next three decades. Such albums as *The Rolling Stones* (1964; and two 1965 sequels), *Aftermath* (1966), and *Their Satanic Majesties*

Request (1967), coupled with their worldwide tours, established them as one of the leading popular musical groups of the century. In 1969, after a murder by their Hell's Angels security guards at an Altamont, California, Stones concert, the group toned down their image somewhat. Although they continued to tour and record throughout the 1980s, their popularity lessened after the mid-1970s. Yet their very successful 1989–90 world tour showed that the 28-year-old rock group still had enormous vitality and drawing power. Jagger has appeared in such films as *Ned Kelly* (1969), and in the film of the Altamont concert, *Gimme Shelter* (1972). He has also done several solo recordings. Jagger attended the London School of Economics. He was married to Bianca Jagger (Bianca Pérez Morena de Macîas) from 1971 to 1979, and married his longtime companion, model Jerry Hall, in 1990. Jagger has five children, the three youngest with Hall.

FURTHER READING

Time Is on My Side: The Rolling Stones Day-by-Day, 1962–1984. ALAN STEWART and CATHY SANFORD. Popular Culture, 1992.
The Rolling Stones' Rock and Roll Circus. MIKE RANDOLPH. Chronicle Books, 1991.
Rolling Stones Images. DAVID FRICKE. Simon & Schuster, 1991.
Blown Away: The Rolling Stones and the Death of the Sixties. A. E. HOTCHNER. Simon & Schuster, 1990.
The Pictorial History of the Rolling Stones. MARIE CAHILL. BDD Promo Books, 1990.
Rolling Stones Complete Recording Sessions. MARTIN ELLIOTT. Borgo Press/Sterling 1990.
The Rolling Stones Chronicle. MASSIMO BONANNO. Holt, 1990.
The Rolling Stones. TIM DOWLEY. Seven Hills, 1989.
It's Only Rock 'n' Roll: My On-the-Road Adventures with the Rolling Stones. CHET FLIPPO. St. Martin's, 1989.
The Life and Good Times of the Rolling Stones. PHILIP NORMAN. Outlet, 1989.
The Rolling Stone Interviews: The 1980s. St. Martin's, 1989.
Uncle Joe's Record Guide: The Rolling Stones. JOE BENSON. J. Benson, 1987.
Written in My Soul: Rock's Great Songwriters . . . Talk About Creating Their Music. BILL FLANAGAN. Contemporary, 1986.
Yesterday's Papers: The Rolling Stones in Print, 1963–1984. JESSICA MACPHAIL. Popular Culture, 1986.
The True Adventures of the Rolling Stones. STANLEY BOOTH. Random, 1985.
The Rolling Stones: The Early Years. DEZO HOFFMAN. McGraw-Hill, 1985.
The Rolling Stones. ROBERT A. HEINLEIN. Ballantine, 1985.
Heart of Stone: The Definitive Rolling Stones Discography, 1962–1983. FELIX AEPPLI. Popular Culture, 1985.

Jamison, Judith (1944–) In her second full year as artistic director of the Alvin Ailey American Dance Theater, dancer-choreographer Jamison continued to present Ailey's now-classic works, and further developed the work of carrying African-American modern dance to wide popular audiences. At the same time, she began to develop the company along her own lines. In December, she choreographed a new work, *Rift,* with score by Nona Herdryx; Sarita Allen and Dwight Rhoden danced the leading roles. Jamison also took steps to provide more money for the always fragile company, initiating a strong fund-raising effort and beginning the company's yearly five-week residency in Baltimore. She also started a company summer dance camp for young people of talent but small means.

Philadelphia-born Jamison made her debut in 1965 with the American Ballet Theater. She danced with the Alvin Ailey company in 1965, and rejoined it as the company's leading dancer (1967–80), in that period becoming one of the world's first-rank dancers, with special emphasis on her work on African-American themes. In 1980, she left the company, starred on Broadway in *Sophisticated Ladies* (1980), and spent most of the 1980s as guest dancer and choreographer with several American ballet companies. She founded the Jamison Project in 1988, but after Ailey's death returned to take his place as artistic director of the theater.

FURTHER READING

"Arts. . . ." VALERIE GLADSTONE. *Ms.,* Nov.–Dec. 1991.
"Carrying on the legacy. . . ." JANICE C. SIMPSON. *Time,* July 15, 1991.
"Judith Jamison. . . ." Ebony, Dec. 1990.
Black Dance in America: A History Through Its People. JAMES HASKINS. Harper, 1990.
Judith Jamison: Aspects of a Dancer. OLGA MAYNARD. Doubleday, 1982.

Jennings, Peter Charles (1938–) News anchor Jennings's background as a foreign correspondent helped him to remain ahead in ABC's nightly news ratings race with CBS and NBC, significantly so during the Persian Gulf War, when he anchored ABC's ongoing news coverage. In January, he also hosted a special, *Line in the Sand: War or Peace,* and—in a notable addition to the war's coverage—a 90-minute Saturday-morning television special, *War in the Gulf: Answering Children's Questions,* in which he and a panel of military experts and correspondents answered questions from children in the studio and around the country. Jennings also provided the introduction to a video program, *Schwarzkopf: How the War Was Won,* released in March.

In the year's other major news arena, Jennings pulled off two notable coups. Anchoring from Moscow during the Bush-Gorbachev summit in July, he had an exclusive one-on-one television interview with Soviet Premier Gorbachev, in the unusual venue of the Kremlin gardens. Then in September, after the failure of the August coup, Jennings hosted another first: Gorbachev and Russian President Boris Yeltsin in a live, satellite-feed talk show, answering questions from people all around the United States. Jennings did, however, get caught by a hoax, in November airing a story that proved to be false, about the cash-starved Soviet Union proposing to sell Lenin's preserved corpse.

Closer to home, Jennings took *World News Tonight* to Ohio in June, for a notable series of programs focusing on the problem of American children in poverty; he returned to the subject again and again during the balance of the year, often in the "American Agenda" section of his newscast. He also continued his occasional series of news specials, "Peter Jennings Reporting," as in "From the Heart of Harlem," in which he examined the plight of the cash-strapped Dance Theater of Harlem.

Toronto-born Jennings worked in Canadian broadcasting before joining ABC News in 1964. During the next two decades, much of that time spent abroad, he rose to become chief London correspondent for ABC, in 1983 became the anchor of "World News Tonight," and with Dan Rather at CBS and Tom Brokaw at NBC is one of the three key American interpreters of the world news. Jennings attended Carleton University, and his LL.D. is from Rider College. Twice divorced, he is married to writer Kati Marton; he has two children.

FURTHER READING

"How 'Stanley Stunning.' . . ." ALAN EBERT. *Good Housekeeping,* Apr. 1991.

Anchors: Brokaw, Jennings, Rather and the Evening News. ROBERT GOLDBERG and GERALD J. GOLDBERG. Carol, 1990.

"The kiss of the anchor man." E. JEAN CARROLL. *Playboy,* Dec. 1990.

"Peter Jennings gets no self-respect." ELIZABETH KAYE. *Esquire,* Sep. 1989.

"The A-B-Cs of Peter Jennings." NORMAN ATKINS. *Rolling Stone,* May 4, 1989.

Jiang Qing (Chiang Ch'ing or Luan Shumeng; stage name, Lan P'ing; 1914–91) On stage professionally as a teenager in Shandong and then in Beijing, Jiang Qing developed a modest stage and screen career from the late 1920s through the late 1930s. She met Mao Zedong in Yenan in 1938; their subsequent relationship scandalized many in the Chinese Communist Party, as Mao was then still married to his second wife. Jiang became his third wife in the early 1940s, and was a minor figure in Chinese political life until the mid-1960s. She then emerged as a major force in China's Cultural Revolution, leading much of the attack against her country's cultural and intellectual leaders and initiating the massive destruction of artworks and institutions characteristic of the period. Mao died in 1976; shortly afterward Jiang, Zhang Chunqiao, Wang Hongwen, and Yao Wenhuan were charged with trying to take power in China, arrested, and ultimately brought to trial as the Gang of Four. In 1981, Jiang was sentenced to death, then reprieved and sentenced to life imprisonment. On June 4, 1991, the Chinese government announced that Jiang Qing had committed suicide on May 14, 1991; no specifics were provided. She was survived by one daughter.

FURTHER READING

Obituary. *Variety,* June 10, 1991.
"A widow dies in China." SIDNEY URQUHART. *Time,* June 10, 1991.
Obituary. *New York Times,* June 5, 1991.

John Paul II, Pope (Karol Wojtyla, 1920–) Holding the line on his strongly conservative positions, Pope John Paul II during 1991 continued to focus on such matters as abortion, resistance to liberalization of the Catholic Church, and the spread of Church doctrine in the world's poorer countries and in newly free Eastern Europe and the Soviet Union. On January 22, his eighth encyclical called for Roman Catholic missionary activity throughout the world, including those Islamic countries forbidding other religious teachings. On May 2, his ninth encyclical endorsed the efficacy of the free market over the economic concepts of communism, but at the same time warned against gross consumerism and urged the rightness of social justice in satisfaction of human needs. His views were published in a new work *The Pope Speaks to the American Church: John Paul II's Homilies, Speeches, and Letters to Catholics* (1992).

The Pope visited Poland June 1–9, 1991; there he strongly condemned abortion, legal in Poland, and likened abortion to the Nazi Holocaust, a comparison criticized by some Jewish leaders. He visited Poland again August 13–16, and was the first Pope to visit Hungary, August 16–20. There he met with Hungarian Jews and issued an August 18, 1991, statement deploring anti-Semitism. While in Hungary, he spoke in support of the national aspirations of Yugoslavian Croats, in the dispute that would flare into the Yugoslavian Civil War.

He visited Brazil October 12–21, calling for Catholic resistance to the evangelical Protestants winning over hundreds of thousands of Brazilian and other Latin American Catholics every year. He also called for land distribution reform, while stopping short of radical land reform and repeating his long-standing opposition to liberation theology. In his October 20 address at Salvador, Brazil, he included a plea to stop those Brazilians who were murdering abandoned children and poverty-stricken street children engaged in begging and petty crime.

John Paul II is the first Pope of Polish origin, and the first non-Italian Pope in the last four centuries. He was ordained as a Catholic priest in 1946, and then moved steadily upward in the Polish Catholic Church, becoming a professor of theology in the 1950s, and ultimately archbishop of Crakow (1963–78). He became a Cardinal in 1967, and then Pope in 1978. He has been largely a very conservative Pope, strongly opposing abortion and strongly discouraging liberal social action on the part of the priesthood. He attended Cracow's Jagellonian University and Rome's Angelicum.

FURTHER READING

Covenant of Love: Pope John Paul II on Sexuality, Marriage, and Family in the Modern World. RICHARD M. HOGAN and JOHN M. LEVOIR. Ignatius, 1992.
"Thoughts on a Slav pope. . . ." PETER HEBBLETHWAITE. *National Catholic Reporter,* June 21, 1991.
The Keys of This Blood: Pope John Paul II vs. Russia and the West for Control of the New World Order. MALACHI MARTIN. Simon & Schuster, 1991.
The Making of an Economic Vision: John Paul II's on Social Concern. OLIVER F. WILLIAMS and JOHN W. HOUCK, eds. University Press of America, 1991.
John Paul the Second on Science and Religion: Reflections on the New View from Rome. ROBERT J. RUSSELL et al., eds. University of Notre Dame Press, 1991.
Portrait of John Paul II. ANDRE FROSSARD. Ignatius, 1990.
Pope John Paul II: Pilgrim of Peace. POPE JOHN PAUL II. Crown, 1987.
Pope John Paul II: The People's Pope. GEORGE SULLIVAN. Walker, 1984.
Pope John Paul II. MIECZYSLAW MALINSKI. Doubleday, 1982.
Pope John Paul II: An Authorized Biography. LORD LONGFORD. Morrow, 1962.

Johnson, Earvin (Magic), Jr. (1959–) A great career ended in 1991 and an uncertain future began for basketball superstar Earvin "Magic" Johnson. At the beginning of the 1991–92 season, Johnson learned that he was infected with human immunodeficiency virus (HIV), the virus that causes AIDS (acquired immune deficiency syndrome). With enormous strength and courage, he immediately went public, on November 7th announcing his retirement from professional basketball and his commitment to educating others about the dangers of unsafe sex. He began his campaign that very week, on the "Arsenio Hall Show," and was soon appointed by President Bush to the National Commission on AIDS. He also signed with Random House to do three books, two on his life and career, with co-authors William Novak and Roy S. Johnson, respectively, and the third on responsible sexual behavior, to be written with former U.S. Surgeon General C. Everett Koop, scheduled for spring 1992; royalties will go to his newly formed AIDS research and education foundation. Johnson's stance won him strong public support, which many hoped would help change public attitudes toward those infected with the deadly virus. The advertisers with whom Johnson has been associated were initially very supportive; their long-term response remained to be gauged. In September, Johnson had married Earletha (Cookie) Kelly; she tested negative for HIV.

Earlier, during the 1990–91 season, Johnson had broken Oscar Robertson's National Basketball Association (NBA) assists record with his 9,888th assist, by season's end building that record to 9,921. In May, he led his Los Angeles Lakers unexpectedly past the Portland Trailblazers and into the championship finals, where they were stopped by the Chicago Bulls, in a series many treated as a matchup between basketball greats Johnson and Michael Jordan. In September 1991, Johnson was invited to play on the U.S. basketball team for the 1992 Olympics; at year's end he was still planning to play. In January 1992, two months after his retirement, Johnson was among the leaders in the fans' voting for the 1992 NBA All-Star game. He did play, and was selected the game's Most Valuable Player. He continued to be a "cheerleader" on the Lakers' sidelines, and asserted his determination to remain involved in basketball, perhaps as an owner.

Michigan-born Johnson attended Michigan State University, leading his team to the 1979 NCAA championship. In his 12 seasons, he led the Los Angeles Lakers to the NBA finals nine times for five NBA titles (1980, 1982, 1985, 1987, 1988); was picked Most Valuable Player (MVP) in the playoffs three times (1980, 1982, 1987); and was named the league's MVP three times (1987, 1989, 1990). Twelve times an NBA All-Star, he was selected MVP for the first time in the 1990 All-Star Game. Overall, Johnson amassed 17,239 points in 874 games, for an average of 19.7 a game; took down 6,376 rebounds; and had 1,698 steals, second only to Maurice Cheeks's 2,197. With his friend and rival, Larry Bird, and later with Jordan as well, Johnson dominated the game of basketball in the 1980s. More than that, he revolutionized the way the game was played, being the first large player—at 6′9″—to dominate as a point guard, with his astonishing versatility and skill, and with his magnetic personality, helping to make basketball popular worldwide. Johnson has also been a leader in establishing summer all-star games and other fund-raising events to benefit inner-city and minority youth: Over the last six seasons, in exhibition games at Los Angeles's Forum alone, he raised $6.5 million for the United Negro College Fund. He has written two previous autobiographical works, *Magic* (1983; with Richard Levin) and *Magic's Touch* (1989; with Roy S. Johnson). He is married to retailer Earletha (Cookie) Kelly, who manages their Los Angeles sporting goods store, Magic 32. He has a son, Andre Mitchell.

FURTHER READING

"Magic Johnson's. . . ." *Jet,* Nov. 25, 1991.
"Magic Johnson. . . ." *Jet,* Nov. 25, 1991.
"It was Magic. . . ." PAUL ATTNER. *Sporting News,* Nov. 18, 1991.
"Tragic Magic. . . ." JAMES DEACON. *Maclean's,* Nov. 18, 1991.
"Unforgettable." JACK MCCALLUM. *Sports Illustrated,* Nov. 18, 1991.
"Show of shows . . ." JACK MCCALLUM. *Sports Illustrated,* June 10, 1991.
"The wonderful world of. . . ." SAM BLAIR. *Boys' Life,* Feb. 1991.
Magic Johnson. Scholastic, 1991.
"Magic's kingdom. . . ." RICHARD HOFFER. *Sports Illustrated,* Dec. 3, 1990.
"The Sport athlete of the decade. . . ." *Sport,* Oct. 1989.
The Sports Great Magic Johnson. JAMES HASKINS. Enslow, 1989.
Magic Johnson. MICHAEL E. GOODMAN. Crestwood, 1988.
Magic Johnson Larry Bird. BRUCE WEBER. Avon, 1986.

Jones, James Earl (1931–) Celebrated actor James Earl Jones, who in 1990 created the ex-cop/ex-convict turned investigator hero of television's "Gabriel's Fire," won a 1991 Emmy as best lead actor in a drama series for the role. But although the series was artistically successful, it was less so commercially. For 1991–92 it was renamed "Pros and Cons" and somewhat refocused to include comedy, with Richard Crenna added as Jones's new detective partner. At year's end, the changes had not materially helped the show's ratings, but neither had they damaged Jones's portrayal, head and shoulders above much of what was to be found in network television. Jones also won a 1991 Emmy as best supporting actor in a miniseries or special for his role in TNT's "Heat Wave" (1990), set in the 1965 Los Angeles Watts riots. His work in television continued to include a wide range of commercials and narrations, perhaps the most notable being his April narration of the TBS documentary *Portrait of Castro's Cuba.* In December, Jones starred as Ben Johnson opposite Robert Duvall as planter Soll Gautier in Peter Masterson's film *Convicts,* adapted by Horton Foote from his own one-act play. The drama takes place on a sugar plantation staffed by convict labor on the Texas Gulf Coast, on Christmas Eve, 1902.

Mississippi-born Jones has been a leading figure in the American theater since his starring role as Black heavyweight champion Jack Jefferson (inspired by the real-life Jack Johnson) in *The Great White Hope* (1968; on film 1970). A classical actor of enormous range, he is highly regarded for such roles as *Macbeth* (1962), *King Lear* (1973), Hickey in *The Iceman Cometh* (1973), *Othello* (1982), and his starring role in *Fences* (1988), for which he won a Tony. He was the voice of Darth Vader in *Star Wars* (1977), portrayed Alex Haley in television's *Roots II* (1979), and played major roles in such films as *Gardens of Stone* (1987), *Field of Dreams* (1989), and *The Hunt for Red October* (1990). Jones's B.A. was from the University of Michigan, in 1957. He married Cecilia Hart in 1982. He is the son of actor Robert Earl Jones.

FURTHER READING

"The struggle to be. . . ." MICHELLE GREEN. *Saturday Review,* Feb. 1982.

Jones, Quincy (Quincy Delight Jones, Jr., 1933–) "Pray for peace on earth and when we get peace on earth, let's take care of the earth." That was legendary pop music figure Quincy Jones, at the 33rd annual Grammy Awards ceremony, held in New York City on February 20, 1991. Jones won all six Grammy awards for his album *Back on the Block;* they made him the most honored pop artist in the history of the

Grammys, with a total of 25 Grammys during his long career. The highest previous pop total was amassed by Henry Mancini, with 20 Grammys. Only conductor and pianist Georg Solti has won more, totaling 28 Grammys for classical music. Jones's 1991 Grammys were for best album of the year, best producer, best rap performance by a duo or group, best jazz fusion performance, best instrumental arrangement, and best instrumental arrangement accompanying a vocal. In a considerable change of pace, Jones appeared late in the year in a cameo role in Steven Spielberg's big Christmas film *Hook,* a modern version of J. M. Barrie's *Peter Pan* tale, which starred Robin Williams, Dustin Hoffman, and Julia Roberts. Jones, who in 1990 had sold half of his Quincy Jones Entertainment and Quincy Jones Broadcasting companies to Time-Warner for an estimated $30 million, continued to be active in social causes and to produce the syndicated series hosted by Jesse Jackson. During 1991, he was also writing his autobiography.

Chicago-born Jones has had a long and varied career, which in four decades has included working as a trumpeter and arranger with Lionel Hampton and Dizzy Gillespie in the mid-1950s; as an arranger for many of the leading singers of the 1950s and 1960s; in the 1960s as music director and producer for Mercury Records; and as composer and conductor of many film scores. From 1969, he was a prolific recording artist, with such albums as *Walking in Space* (1969), *Smackwater Jack* (1971), and *Mellow Madness* (1975). He was most notably producer of the Michael Jackson records *Off the Wall* (1980) and *Thriller* (1982). His 1989 album *Back on the Block,* sold over a million copies. His documentary *Listen Up: The Lives of Quincy Jones* was widely distributed in 1990. Jones attended the Berkeley College of Music and the Boston Conservatory. He was formerly married and has five children.

FURTHER READING

"The piano next door. . . ." *Economist,* July 20, 1991.
"On Q." Diane K. Shah. *New York Times Magazine,* Nov. 18, 1990.
"Quincy Jones." Steve Dougherty. *People,* Oct. 15, 1990.
"Story of Q." Brendan Lemon. *Interview,* Sep. 1990.
"Playboy interview. . . ." Alex Haley. *Playboy,* July 1990.
"Quincy Jones." Eliot Tiegel. *Stereo Review,* June 1990.
"After 40 years. . . ." Aldore Collier. *Ebony,* Apr. 1990.
"Back on the block. . . ." Robert L. Doerschuk. *Interview,* Jan. 1990.
"Herbie and Quincy. . . ." Josef Woodard. *Down Beat,* Jan. 1990.
Quincy Jones. Raymond Horricks. Hippocrene, 1986.

Jordan, Michael (1963–) In 1991, Michael "Air" Jordan won it all. In the National Basketball Association (NBA) Eastern Conference finals, Jordan and his Chicago Bulls knocked off the Detroit Pistons, defending champions for the two previous seasons. Then in the championship finals, they defeated the Los Angeles Lakers, five-time champions in the 1980s, in a 4–1 series billed as a classic contest between basketball greats: Jordan and Earvin (Magic) Johnson. Jordan was named Most Valuable Player for both the regular 1990–91 season and the playoffs, and was also the league's scoring leader for the fifth time, averaging 31.5 points a game. But the key to the Bulls' first championship was Jordan's working with the other players in a team effort. As the 1991–92 season started, Jordan and the Bulls picked up where they left off, playing early-season games with the crispness and skill of playoff contests and racking up a league-leading won-lost record.

During 1991, Jordan was named to the U.S. basketball team for the 1992 Olympics, the first to allow NBA players. He at first declined the invitation, but later—presumably because of public outcry—accepted it. He had played on the 1984 gold-medal-winning U.S. Olympic team. Jordan also continued active as an amateur golfer.

Jordan is one of the leading basketball players of the late 1980s and early 1990s. He starred at the University of North Carolina before turning professional in 1984, when he immediately emerged as a star for the Bulls. He was rookie of the year in the 1984–85 season and the NBA's Most Valuable Player and best defensive player in the 1987–88 season. He and his wife Juanita have two sons, the second born on Christmas Eve, 1991.

FURTHER READING

The Jordan Rules: The Inside Story of a Turbulent Season with Michael Jordan and the Chicago Bulls. Sam Smith. Simon & Schuster, 1992.

Taking to the Air: The Rise of Michael Jordan. Jim Naughton. Warner, 1992.

"Ten living legends. . . ." Steve Wulf. *Sports Illustrated,* Dec. 23, 1991.

"For all his fame. . . ." Curry Kirkpatrick. *Sports Illustrated,* Dec. 23, 1991.

"Michael Jordan. . . ." Jack McCallum. *Sports Illustrated,* Dec. 23, 1991.

"In pursuit of. . . ." Jeff Weinstock. *Sport,* Dec. 1991.

"Show of shows. . . ." Jack McCallum. *Sports Illustrated,* June 10, 1991.

"Michael Jordan. . . ." *Jet,* Apr. 29, 1991.

"Michael Jordan. . . ." Bruce Shlain. *Sport,* Jan. 1991.

"Air to the throne." George Castle. *Sport,* Jan. 1991.

Michael Jordan. Scholastic, 1991.

Michael Jordan: A Biography. Bill Gutman. Pocketbook, 1991.

"Michael Jordan, king of style." Bruce Shlain. *Sport,* Jan. 1991.

"Michael Jordan leaps. . . ." John Edgar Wideman. *Esquire,* Nov. 1990.

Michael Jordan. Little, Brown, 1990.

Michael Jordan: Gentleman Superstar. Gene L. Martin. Tudor, 1988.

Michael Jordan, Basketball's Soaring Star. Paul J. Deegan. Lerner, 1988.

Michael Jordan. Mitchell Krugel. St. Martin's, 1988.

Michael Jordan. Dan McCune. Crestwood, 1988.

Kaganovich, Lazar Moisevich (1893–1991) One of the last of the Old Bolsheviks, Kaganovich joined Lenin's Bolshevik wing of the Russian socialist movement before World War I, while still a young tannery worker in Kiev before and during the war; exiled in 1915, he escaped and returned to Kiev. He headed the Belorussian communist organization late in 1917, and led the successful Bolshevik organization among Czarist frontline troops. He commanded Red Army units and was then a political commissar during the Russian Civil War. He became a member of the Communist Party Central Committee in 1924, and was party head in the Ukraine from 1925 to 1928. During the 1920s, he became a trusted aide and troubleshooter for Joseph Stalin, then consolidating his hold on the Soviet Union. From 1930 to 1935, Kaganovich headed the Moscow Communist Party organization, and from 1934 was head of the Party Control Commission, taking a major role in the Great Purge (1934–39) that killed hundreds of thousands of his own old friends and comrades throughout the Soviet Union, some of the tens of millions who perished during the Stalin years. Kaganovich was one of the few Jews in high positions to keep their power during the Stalin years. After Stalin's death, in 1953, Kaganovich stayed in power for four years; part of the group that opposed Nikita Khrushchev, he was removed from all key posts in 1957 and lived the rest of his life in obscurity. (d. Moscow; July 23, 1991)

FURTHER READING

Obituary. *Current Biography,* Sep. 1991.
Obituary. *National Review,* Aug. 26, 1991.
Obituary. *New York Times,* July 29, 1991.
Obituary. *The Times* (of London), July 27, 1991.
The Wolf of the Kremlin. Stuart Kahan. Morrow, 1987.

Kaifu, Toshiki (1931–) On October 4, 1991, Prime Minister Kaifu announced he would not seek re-election, after his reform proposals were rejected by his own Liberal Democratic

Party (LDP). He was succeeded by the powerful longtime party leader Kiichi Miyazawa, who had in 1988 resigned his position as finance minister after his implication in the financial scandals that had forced the resignation of Prime Minister Noburo Takeshita and many others in his government. Kaifu had been selected by the LDP as one of the few "clean" candidates available after the scandals had compromised much of the party's leadership, succeeding Sosuko Uno, who lasted two months before being forced to resign because of a sex scandal. Kaifu's inability to win approval of his reform program clearly indicated that Japan's leading politicians now felt that it was safe to re-assume power openly, after enough of the heat generated by the multiple scandals had died down.

During his period in office, Kaifu continued to negotiate the difficult issue of Japanese–United States trade imbalances, to the continuing great advantage of Japan. But at home he encountered growing economic problems, as the Japanese stock market fell sharply, Japanese banks curtailed loans abroad, and the Japanese real estate market faltered, mirroring a worldwide trend.

A career politician, Kaifu entered the Japanese parliament in 1960 after working in political staff jobs. He had several cabinet-level positions before becoming prime minister. Kaifu graduated from Tokyo's Waseta University. He is married to Sachiyo Kaifu and has two children.

FURTHER READING

"Who's sitting pretty. . . ." *Business Week,* Mar. 11, 1991.
"Kaifu, Toshiki." *Current Biography,* June 1990.

Kaye, Sylvia Fine (1913–91) Composer, lyricist, and producer Kaye wrote much of her work for her husband, Danny Kaye (1913–87); they met while doing summer theater in the late 1930s and their earliest Broadway show, *The Straw Hat Revue,* was produced in 1940, the year they married. They worked together for four decades, he performing and she writing the words and music of over 100 of the complex, comic songs that became his trademark in such films as *Up in Arms* (1944) and *Knock On Wood* (1954); she also produced several of his films and had a hand in the production of all. A leading film producer, Kaye won Oscar nominations for *The Moon Is Blue* (1955) and *The Five Pennies* (1959). In the 1970s, she moved into television, producing and teaching musical comedy, and won a Peabody award for the miniseries *Musical Comedy Tonight.* She was survived by a daughter and a sister. (d. New York City; October 28, 1991)

FURTHER READING

Obituary. *Variety,* Nov. 5, 1991.
Obituary. *The Times* (of London), Nov. 4, 1991.
Obituary. *New York Times,* Oct. 29, 1991.

Keating, Charles Humphrey, III (1923–) On December 3, 1991, a state court jury in Los Angeles, California, found financier Keating guilty of 17 counts of securities fraud, the charges stemming from the sale of American Continental Corporation bonds through branches of the subsequently failed Lincoln Savings and Loan Association, both organizations that Keating controlled. On December 12, Keating and four associates were indicted on a 77-count set of federal charges in the Lincoln Savings and Loan Association case. The long and complicated financial collapse and its aftermath had reached into the United States Senate, generating the case of "Keating Five" which was finally resolved in February 1991 with a Senate Ethics Committee reprimand of Senator Alan Cranston, and minor criticism of senators Dennis DeConcini, John Glenn, Donald W. Riegle, Jr., and John McCain.

Keating emerged as a corporate takeover figure in the late 1970s, as executive vice president of the Cincinnati-based American Financial Corporation. He bought control of the Lincoln Savings Bank, in Irvine, California, in 1984 for $51 million and began the process of building it into a $6 billion bank. It was heavily invested in junk bonds and heavily committed to what turned out to be very weak real estate loans, many of them to American Continental Corporation. Faced with opposition from the Federal Home Loan Bank Board, Keating engaged in a long-running battle with regulators, which included substantial contributions to many key

Washington and state politicians and set the stage for the investigations of the "Keating Five." Lincoln was taken over by federal bank regulators on April 14, 1990, as the national savings and loan crisis developed; the cost of the government bailout was estimated to be well over $2 billion. Keating was from the early 1970s also a substantial Cincinnati-based antipornography contributor; he founded an antipornography organization in the 1950s and was a member of the 1969–70 Presidential Commission on Obscenity and Pornography.

Keating attended the University of Cincinnati and was a star swimmer, becoming 1946 national collegiate breaststroke champion. He married Mary Elaine Fette in 1941; they have six children.

FURTHER READING

"Mr. S & L faces the music." KATHLEEN KERWIN. *Business Week,* Nov. 25, 1991.
"The great banks robbery. . . ." JAMES K. GLASSMAN. *New Republic,* Oct. 8, 1990.
"Dirty bookkeeping. . . ." DAVID CORN. *New Republic,* Apr. 2, 1990.
"Money talks. . . ." MARGARET CARLSON. *Time,* Apr. 9, 1990.
"The man who shot Lincoln Savings." PHIL GARLINGTON. *California,* Mar. 1990.
"Seven sorry senators. . . ." MARGARET CARLSON. *Time,* Jan. 8, 1990.
The Greatest-Ever Bank Robbery: The Collapse of the Savings and Loan Industry. MARTIN MAYER. Macmillan, 1990.

Keaton, Diane (1946–) In her first major commercial role in three years, Keaton in 1991 starred in Charles Shyer's remake of Vincente Minnelli's 1950 *Father of the Bride.* Keaton as mother recreated the Joan Bennett role, Steve Martin as father the Spencer Tracy role, and Kimberly Williams was the bride, in the Elizabeth Taylor role. The film was a commercial success, though some critics felt that its 1950s suburban life-style concerns were not very well translated into the concerns of 1991 audiences, making what had been a strong film into an empty nostalgia piece. After directing shorter works for television in 1990, Keaton took a major step in 1991, directing *Wildflower,* her first full-length television film, set in 1930s Georgia and starring Patricia Arquette and Reese Witherspoon; it appeared in early December.

California-born Keaton made the transition from the New York theater to Hollywood in Woody Allen's *Play It Again Sam,* starring opposite Allen on Broadway in 1971 and again in the 1972 film version. She was Michael Corleone's wife in the classic *Godfather* films (1972, 1974), won a Best Actress Oscar for Allen's *Annie Hall* (1977), and also starred in his *Interiors* (1978) and *Manhattan* (1979). She went on to star in such films as *Reds* (1981), *The Little Drummer Girl* (1984), *Crimes of the Heart* (1986), *Radio Days* (1987), *The Godfather, Part III* (1990), reprising her Kay Corleone role, and *The Lemon Sisters* (1990). She was a student at New York's Neighborhood Playhouse in 1968.

FURTHER READING

Diane Keaton: The Story of the Real Annie Hall. JONATHAN MOOR. St. Martin's, 1989; G. K. Hall, 1991.
"Hotel 'Heaven.' . . ." MARLAINE GLICKSMAN. *Film Comment,* Mar.–Apr. 1987.
"Knockin' on heaven's door. . . ." DAVID EDELSTEIN. *Rolling Stone,* May 7, 1987.
"Diane Keaton." GERALD L'ECUYER. *Interview,* Jan. 1987.

Keaton, Michael (Michael Douglas, 1951–) In September 1991, Batman began his return, as *Batman II* went into production. The original *Batman,* with Keaton in the starring role, was the top-grossing film of 1989, ultimately taking in over $400 million worldwide and selling a reported 13 million videocassettes. *Batman II* again stars Keaton in the title role and is again directed by Tim Burton; the cast includes Michele Pfeiffer as Catwoman, Danny DeVito as the Penguin, Christopher Walken, Michael Gough, Pat Hingle, Marlon Wayans, and Michael Murphy. During 1991, Keaton starred as New York detective Artie Lewis in *One Good Cop;* Heywood Gould wrote and directed. Keaton was also highly visible on home screens, as his 1990 *Pacific Heights* became a top television rental.

Pittsburgh-born Keaton began his career as a comedian with the Los Angeles Second City group, appeared in television from the mid-1970s, and played in such films as *Night Shift* (1982), *Mr. Mom* (1983), and *Touch and Go* (1987). He emerged as a star in the film drama *Clean and Sober* (1988), and in the title role of

Batman (1989), followed by *The Dream Team* (1989). Keaton attended Kent State University. He married Caroline McWilliams in 1982; the couple have one child.

FURTHER READING

"Michael Keaton. . . ." DIGBY DIEHL. *Cosmopolitan,* Nov. 1991.
"Batman and the new world order." CAROL CALDWELL. *Esquire,* June 1991.
"Batguy." TERRI MINSKY. *Premiere,* July 1989.

Keillor, Garrison (1942–) Folksy humorist Keillor suddenly seemed to be everywhere. He had moved from Minnesota, site of his fictional Lake Wobegon, "the town that time forgot," to New York City in the late 1980s; fruits of that move were found in *Local Man Moves to City* (1991), an audiotape by Keillor and company, including a typical collection of radio monologues and diverting songs, but now from an outsider with a love-hate relationship to his new home, New York. The year also saw Keillor's first novel, *WLT: A Radio Romance* (1991), set in and around Minneapolis radio station WLT (With Lettuce and Tomato), run by the Soderbjerg brothers, Ray and Roy, and focusing on young Frank White. The work was simultaneously released on audiotape. In November 1991, Keillor was seen in *Garrison Keillor's Home,* the first of three television specials for the Public Broadcasting Company, simulcast on radio; he acknowledged it as an oddity, a kind of "cinemá verité radio," being a videotaped radio show rather than specifically crafted for television. Meanwhile, Keillor continued the widely carried weekly radio broadcast of his "American Radio Company." In December 1991, he also hosted a live two-hour broadcast from Red Cloud, Nebraska, to honor writer Willa Cather's birth there in 1873.

Minnesota-born Keillor was creator, writer, and announcer of the enormously popular radio show "A Prairie Home Companion," which he hosted for 13 years (1974–87). After moving briefly to Denmark, Keillor settled in New York City, where he began a new show,"American Radio Company." His written works include *Happy to Be Here* (1982); *Lake Wobegon Days* (1985), which in its audio form received a 1987 Grammy for best non-musical recording; *Leaving Home* (1987); and *We Are Still Married* (1989). Keillor's B.A. was from the University of Minnesota in 1966. He married Ulla Skaeverd in 1985; he has one son and three stepchildren.

FURTHER READING

"Garrison Keillor. . . ." PAUL ALEXANDER. *M Inc.,* Oct. 1991.
"Still mad." CHUCK BENDA. *MPLS-St. Paul,* Jan. 1991.
Garrison Keillor: A Voice of America. JUDITH Y. LEE. University Press of Mississippi, 1991.

Kelley, Kitty (1942–) Kelley, who has achieved considerable commercial success as the author of "unauthorized" biographies, in April 1991 published *Nancy Reagan: The Unauthorized Biography.* In it, she dwelled at length on Nancy Reagan's allegedly massive influence on the conduct of the Ronald Reagan presidency and on many other items detrimental to the reputations of Nancy and Ronald Reagan. Both denied her allegations, as did many who were close to the Reagans during the White House years. The book became a massive best-seller, and book and author both were the beneficiaries of extensive media attention, while foes and friends of the Reagans conducted an acrimonious short-lived debate about the truth or falsity of the trivia discussed in the work. Kelley was herself the target of an unfriendly 1991 biography: *Poison Pen: The Unauthorized Biography of Kitty*

Kelley, by George Carpozi, Jr. Forthcoming was Kelley's syndicated talk show. In December 1991, she was reportedly working on yet another unauthorized biography; its subject had not been disclosed.

Kelley began her career in journalism in the late 1960s as a press assistant to Senator Eugene McCarthy (1966–69), worked at the *Washington Post* (1969–71), and was an editor of the *Washingtonian* (1971–73); then she became a free-lance writer, contributing articles to many magazines. Her published books include *The Glamour Spas* (1975) and three other highly controversial biographies: *Jackie Oh!* (1978), a biography of Jacqueline Kennedy Onassis; *Elizabeth Taylor: The Last Star* (1981); and *His Way: The Unauthorized Biography of Frank Sinatra* (1986). The Sinatra biography generated a highly publicized lawsuit, which Sinatra lost. Kelley's B.A. was from the University of Washington.

FURTHER READING

Poison Pen: The Unauthorized Biography of Kitty Kelley. George Carpozi, Jr. Barricade Books, 1991.
"Kitty Kelley. . . ." Maureen Dowd. *Vogue,* May 1991.
"Meow, meow. . . ." Michelle Green. *People,* Apr. 29, 1991.
"The scoop on. . . ." Cathleen McGuigan. *Newsweek,* Apr. 22, 1991.
"Wretched excess." Jonathan Alter. *Newsweek,* Apr. 22, 1991.
"Meeeow! . . ." Jesse Birnbaum. *Time,* Apr. 22, 1991.
"The First Lady and the Slasher. . . ." Richard Zoglin. *Time,* Apr. 22, 1991.
"The hairdo with anxiety. . . ." Eleanor Clift. *Newsweek,* Apr. 15, 1991.

Kelso, Louis Orth (1913–91) Denver-born Kelso, a lawyer, practiced and taught law from 1938 to 1970, with a break for World War II service. During the 1950s, he was the chief developer of the Employee Stock Ownership Plan (ESOP), which sought to stimulate collective employee ownership of companies. He and Mortimer Adler co-authored *The Capitalist Manifesto* (1958) and *The New Capitalists* (1960), while he and Patricia Hetter co-authored *The Two-Factor Theory: The Economics of Reality* (1968) and *Democracy and Economic Power* (1986). To provide financing counsel to employees seeking to set up such plans, he founded his own consulting and financing organizations in 1970. He was survived by his second wife and co-author, Patricia Hetter, and two daughters. (d. San Francisco; February 17, 1991)

FURTHER READING

Obituary. *New York Times,* Feb. 21, 1991.

Kemp, Jack French (1935–) Secretary of Housing and Urban Development Kemp was in 1988 a highly visible candidate for the Republican presidential nomination. But by 1991 he was far less visible, heading a department that was very lightly funded during a continuing federal financial crisis and a major recession. In March 1991, funds for three of his department's projects were left out of the supplemental federal funding bill, and in June the 1992 spending bill cut subsidized housing further, although funds amounting to less than the cuts were provided for additional projects involving public housing. Kemp did join other Republicans in urging credit easing, which to some extent began to happen in the latter half of 1991. Within his department, some of the huge problems inherited from the scandals of the late Reagan years continued to surface, and in June 1991 the General Accounting Office criticized the department for continuing management and financial control problems. Kemp suffered a blow to his personal prestige in May 1991, when the State Department objected to his plans to greet officially Ariel Sharon, the highly controversial Israeli housing minister. Instead, Kemp met Sharon unofficially at Washington's Israeli embassy.

California-born Kemp is a former star football player, who moved into politics after a 13-year professional football career. He was a Republican congressman from western New York (1971–89), made an unsuccessful run for his party's 1988 presidential nomination, and became a member of the Bush cabinet in 1989. He spent much of 1989 and 1990 on internal department cleanup matters as the full size and scope of the huge HUD scandals emerged, though he was able to help develop the modest 1990 housing bill. Kemp's B.A. was from Occidental College in 1957. He is married to the former Joanne Main; the couple have four children.

FURTHER READING

"An enterprising war on poverty." *New Perspectives,* Summer 1991.
"Party politics." GLORIA BORGER. *U.S. News & World Report,* Dec. 24, 1990.
"Sure, he'd rather be president. . . ." JAMES S. KUNEN. *People,* June 18, 1990.
"Bleeding-heart conservative. . . ." ROBERT KUTTNER. *New Republic,* June 11, 1990.
"Prince of poverty." FRED BARNES. *New Republic,* Oct. 8, 1990.

Kempff, Wilhelm (1895–1991) A leading pianist, German-born Kempff made his Berlin debut in 1915 and first appeared with the Berlin Philharmonic in 1918. During the interwar period, he toured widely, taught at the Stuttgart Music Academy from 1924 to 1929, and taught summer courses at Potsdam from 1931 to 1941. He made his British debut in 1951. Kempff was also a prolific recording artist, especially of the works of Beethoven, Schubert, Schumann, Chopin, and Liszt. Beginning in 1957, he taught Beethoven courses at his summer home in Positano. He also composed several works, which did not find their way into the classical repertoire. He was survived by seven children. (d. Positano, Italy; May 23, 1991)

FURTHER READING

Obituary. *The Times* (of London), May 25, 1991.
Obituary. *New York Times,* May 25, 1991.

Kemptner, Thomas: See **Lebanon Hostages**

Kennedy, Anthony McLeod (1936–) Justice Kennedy was part of the increasingly conservative majority of the Supreme Court during the 1990–91 Court term, though he did write the majority opinion in the key *Edmonson v. Leesville Concrete Co.* case, which barred the exclusion of jurors in civil cases because of race, following earlier bans on exclusion because of race in criminal cases. He also wrote the majority opinion in *Mason v. New Yorker Magazine,* which ruled that invented or materially altered quotes attributed to a public figure could be libelous.

Kennedy was part of the conservative majority in *Rust v. Sullivan,* which upheld federal regulations banning federally funded family planning clinics from offering abortion counseling; *Board of Education of Oklahoma City v. Dowell,* which eased conditions for the lifting of court supervision of segregated school districts; and *Arizona v. Fulminante,* which ruled that a coerced or involuntary confession in a criminal case could be a "harmless error" if conviction would have resulted without it. The last case overturned *Chapman v. California* (1967), which had established that such a confession was always grounds for acquittal. In *Barnes vs. Glen Theater,* upholding an Indiana state law banning nude dancing, he joined the conservative majority in opening the way to local censorship of the arts. *Payne v. Tennessee* allowed "victim impact" evidence to be presented by the prosecution during the sentencing phase of criminal cases, thereby reversing 1987 and 1989 cases that had decided the opposite. He also joined the majority in such cases as *County of Riverside, California v. McLaughlin,* ruling that those arrested without warrants could be held up to 48 hours while a judge decided whether there was probable cause for the arrest; *Florida v. Bostick,* ruling that police could board buses and search passengers' luggage, with their permission; and *Coleman v. Thompson,* restricting the use of habeas corpus writs by state prisoners who have exhausted state appeals.

Two key dissents were in *United Automobile Workers v. Johnson Controls Inc.,* a landmark women's rights case ruling that according to the 1978 Pregnancy Discrimination Act employers could not ban pregnant women from jobs potentially dangerous to their unborn children; and *Chison v. Roemer* and *Houston Lawyers v. Texas Attorney General,* a ruling that the federal Voting Rights Act, which prohibited discriminatory voting practices or election district abuses, applied to elected judges, who were "representatives" within the meaning of the law.

California-born Kennedy was appointed to the Sacramento-based 9th Circuit U.S. Court of Appeals in 1975; he had been recommended for the post by then-California governor Ronald Reagan. Thirteen years later, in 1988, President Reagan appointed him to the Supreme Court, after his nomination of Robert Bork was rejected by the Senate. Kennedy's B.A. was from Stanford in 1958, his LL.B. from Harvard in 1961. He is married to Mary Davis; the couple have three children.

FURTHER READING

"A new day in court." LAUREN TARSHIS and JAMES EARL HARDY. *Scholastic Update,* Nov. 1, 1991.

Reshaping the Supreme Court: New Justices, New Directions. ANNE B. RIERDEN. Watts, 1988.

Packing the Courts: The Conservatives' Campaign to Rewrite the Constitution. HERMAN SCHWARTZ. Macmillan, 1988.

"Kennedy, Anthony McLeod." *Current Biography,* July 1988.

"Far more judicious." GEORGE J. CHURCH and AMY WILENTZ. *Time,* Nov. 23, 1987.

"A conservative's conservative?" *U.S. News & World Report,* Nov. 23, 1987.

Kennedy, Ted (Edward Moore Kennedy, 1932–) It was not a terribly good year for Senator Kennedy. In 1991 there were serious personal problems, including highly publicized alcohol-related incidents involving his oldest son and his former wife, and the rape accusation made against his nephew, William Kennedy Smith; the media coverage heavily featured Senator Kennedy, although he was in no way accused of direct involvement in the alleged rape said to have occurred at Senator Kennedy's Palm Beach home. Added to the long-standing Chappaquidick incident charges, which had never been fully resolved, the net result was to compromise Senator Kennedy seriously in the public's perception—and to all but silence him during the Anita Hill–Clarence Thomas confrontation in the Senate Judiciary Committee hearings on Thomas's Supreme Court nomination in October. When Kennedy did speak, on the Senate floor, he was mocked by other senators, including Senator Orrin Hatch, previously reported in the media to have been a personal friend.

He acknowledged the effect of these events in an extraordinary October 25, 1991, speech at the John F. Kennedy School of Government at Harvard University, saying, "I am painfully aware that the criticism directed at me in recent months involves far more than honest disagreements with my positions, or the usual criticism from the far right. It also involves the disappointment of friends and many others who rely on me to fight the good fight. To them I say: I recognize my own shortcomings—the faults in the conduct of my private life. I realize that I alone am responsible for them, and I am the one who must confront them. . . . I believe that each of us as individuals must not only struggle to make a better world, but to make ourselves better, too."

As chairman of the Senate Labor and Human Resources Committee, and a key Democratic voice in the Senate, Kennedy continued during 1991 to speak on a wide range of issues. Major matters included his strong opposition to the Persian Gulf War; opposition to the Bush administration's education plan, as attacking the nation's public school system; co-sponsorship of a major revision of the nation's health care system; and, with his Democratic colleagues, a sustained and increasingly effective attack on Bush administration economic policies as the year wore on and the deepening 1990–91 recession refused to be wished away.

Boston-born Kennedy is the fourth son of Joseph and Rose Fitzgerald Kennedy, and the brother of President John Fitzgerald Kennedy, assassinated in 1963, and Senator Robert Francis Kennedy, assassinated while a presidential candidate in 1968. He has represented Massachusetts in the Senate since 1963. He probably would have been his party's presidential candidate in 1972 and in later elections, as well, but for the Chappaquidick incident of 1969, in which he left the scene of a fatal accident. Kennedy's B.A. was from Harvard in 1956, his LL.B. from the University of Virginia in 1959. He married Virginia Joan Bennett in 1958 and has three children.

FURTHER READING

"Sobering times." Evan Thomas and Mark Starr. *Newsweek,* Dec. 9, 1991.
"The two faces of Ted." Lester David. *Ladies Home Journal,* Sep. 1991.
"The end of the line. . . ." Elizabeth Kaye. *Esquire,* Aug. 1991.
"The end of the dream. . . ." James Carroll. *New Republic,* June 24, 1991.
"A question of survival. . . ." Gloria Borger and Missy Daniel. *U.S. News & World Report,* May 27, 1991.
"Boys' night out. . . ." Michelle Green. *People,* Apr. 22, 1991.
"Ted Kennedy. . . ." Michael Kelly. *GQ–Gentlemen's Quarterly,* Feb. 1990.
Chappaquidick Revealed. Kenneth R. Kappel and John H. Davis. Shapolsky, 1989.
Senatorial Privilege: The Chappaquidick Coverup. Leo Damore. Regnery, 1988; Dell, 1989.

Kerrey, Bob (Joseph Robert Kerrey, 1943–) The junior senator from Nebraska entered the Democratic presidential nomination race on September 30, 1991, running as a liberal, and very strongly stressing the need for a national health care system, which he proposed to fund with a new payroll tax and increased taxes on the rich. He also supported a tougher stand on unequal international trade, and particularly on Japanese restrictions on American imports. While at year's end still lacking a very specific set of proposals on many key domestic and international issues, he stressed his business experience and war record in putting himself forward for the presidency.

Nebraska-born Kerrey went into the U.S. Navy right out of college. He served as a commando during the Vietnam War and was wounded in action in 1969, spending many months in a naval hospital, an experience he has often alluded to during his political career. He was awarded the Congressional Medal of Honor. After the war, Kerrey went into business, developing the Grandmother's restaurant chain and several other enterprises until he entered politics. He was governor of Nebraska (1983–87) and has been a first-term U.S. senator since 1989. He was formerly married and has two children. He has also been in the news because of his highly publicized friendship with actress Debra Winger.

FURTHER READING

"Is he ready for the big leagues?" Jon D. Hull. *Time,* Dec. 9, 1991.
"Primed for combat." Kim Hubbard and Linda Kramer. *People,* Nov. 25, 1991.
"The no bull campaign." Howard Fineman. *Newsweek,* Oct. 14, 1991.
"Introducing 'present man.' " Gloria Borger. *U.S. News & World Report,* Oct. 7, 1991.
"Looking back at Vietnam. . . ." Joseph L. Galloway. *U.S. News & World Report,* July 15, 1991.
"The unfinished politician." Robin Toner. *New York Times Magazine,* Apr. 14, 1991.
"Kerrey, Bob." *Current Biography,* Feb. 1991.
"A senator of candor most rare." Hays Gorey. *Time,* Oct. 29, 1990.

Kerry, John Forbes (1943–) The junior Democratic senator from Massachusetts saw four years of hard, tenacious work on the Bank of Credit and Commerce International (BCCI) scandal bear fruit in 1991, as the bank became the center of one of the most highly publicized bank scandals of the century. Kerry encountered BCCI in 1987 while investigating international drug trading as chairman of the Senate Foreign Relations Subcommittee on Terrorism, Narcotics, and International Operations. In 1988, he discovered the $20 million BCCI account of Panama General Manuel Noriega, and in 1990, discovered ties between BCCI and its secretly owned Washington-area First American Bankshares, chaired by longtime Washington insider Clark Clifford since 1982. Ultimately, the $20 billion international bank became the center of an enormous worldwide scandal, with regulators in several countries simultaneously moving against it. On July 5, 1991, BCCI operations in seven countries were closed down, with losses to depositors and investors estimated at more than $5 billion. Kerry reappeared as a principal in the story in August 1991, to reveal through the declassification of government documents that the Central Intelligence Agency (CIA) had investigated BCCI five years before, in 1986, and that several U.S. agencies had since then known about BCCI and its illegal activities, but none had moved against the bank.

Kerry was also highly visible as a Vietnam veterans' advocate, and on the Vietnam prisoners-of-war missing-in-action issue (POW-MIA). On April 16, he sponsored a benefit performance of the play *Miss Saigon* for two Vietnam veterans' organizations. In August, he went to Vietnam, and in September reported significant progress in seeking information about POW-MIAs.

Denver-born Kerry served as a young, front-line naval lieutenant in Vietnam (1966–69), winning a Silver Star and a Bronze Star with an Oak Leaf Cluster, and was wounded three times. On his return home, he became in 1969 a founder and national coordinator of Vietnam Veterans Against the War. He was an assistant county district attorney (1976–79), practiced law in Boston (1979–82), and was state lieutenant governor (1983–85). Kerry won election to the Senate in 1985. He is the author of *The New Soldier* (1971). Kerry's B.A. was from Yale University, and his J.D. from Boston College. He is married to the former Julia Stimson Thorne; they have two children.

FURTHER READING

"Kerry, John Forbes." *Current Biography,* June 1988.

Kert, Larry (Frederick Lawrence Kert, 1931–91) Los Angeles–born Kert studied acting with Sanford Meisner in New York, made his debut in cabaret, and worked in the New York theater during the 1950s. In 1957, he became a star as Tony, leader of the Jets, opposite Carol Lawrence in *West Side Story* (1957–60), introducing such songs as "Maria," "Tonight," and "Something's Coming." During the 1960s, he played in a wide range of theater roles, including several replacement leads. He was nominated for a Tony after he replaced Dean Jones in *Company* (1970), and later starred in the play in London. On screen, his first substantial role was in *New York, New York* (1977). He also guest starred in a large number of television shows, as well as developing a career in cabaret. Kert died of AIDS (acquired immune deficiency syndrome); he was survived by his companion, Ron Pullen, two sisters and a brother. (d. New York City, June 5, 1991)

FURTHER READING

Obituary. *The Times* (of London), June 18, 1991.
Obituary. *Variety,* June 10, 1991.
Obituary. *New York Times,* June 7, 1991.

Kessler, David Aaron (1952–) Dr. Kessler became chairman of the then seriously troubled Food and Drug Administration (FDA) on February 15, 1991, and quickly moved to revitalize the agency. On April 24, he began a major, long-term campaign against false and misleading food labeling, starting by forcing Proctor and Gamble to remove the word *fresh* from its processed Citrus Hill orange juice labels. Other companies followed Proctor and Gamble's lead, and massive national publicity resulted from this first of Kessler's campaigns against highly visible companies and products. By June, he had instituted a reorganization at the FDA and initiated a speed-up of FDA evaluation and approval procedures. He also initiated a powerful assault on some pharmaceutical company practices and products, starting with retin-A, an acne drug that was being used as an "anti-aging" drug, and on the unapproved use of collagen and silicone injections and implants for cosmetic purposes. The FDA also attacked such misleading practices as labeling products "no cholesterol" when that was in the very nature of the product, as with vegetable oil. In November, Kessler announced a full-scale FDA review of food labeling, aimed at producing a whole new set of regulations late in 1992.

Kessler was highly qualified to take on the massive task of turning around the FDA. A magna cum laude graduate of Amherst College, his 1978 LL.B. was from the University of Chicago and his 1979 medical degree from Harvard University Medical School. He also took courses at the New York University Graduate School of Business Administration. His residency was in pediatrics at Johns Hopkins, while in the same period he was a consultant to the Senate Labor and Human Resources Committee (1981–84). He was attached to New York's Montefiore Medical Center (1984–91), the last six years as director of the Jack D. Weiler Hospital, part of the Montefiore–Albert Einstein Hospital complex. He also taught food and drug law at Columbia Law School (1986–90) and served on a Health and Human Services commission set up to review the operation of the FDA before taking over as its chairman. He is married to lawyer Paulette Steinberg; they have two children.

FURTHER READING

"Kessler, David Aaron." *Current Biography,* Sep. 1991.
"A shot in the arm. . . ." HERBERT BURKHOLZ. *New York Times Magazine,* June 30, 1991.
"Food fight! . . ." DAVID GROGAN. *People,* June 24, 1991.
"The enforcer. . . ." *Newsweek,* May 27, 1991.

Kevorkian, Jack (1928–) Some call him Dr. Death. An advocate of physician-assisted suicide, which he terms *medicide,* Kevorkian has invented a so-called suicide machine, which

gives lethal doses of drugs intravenously, and by which people can opt for death at the time and place of their choosing. Kevorkian first came to public attention in April 1990 when he appeared on the *Donahue* show describing his suicide machine. In June 1990, Janet Adkins, a 54-year-old English professor who had seen the show and was suffering from early stages of Alzheimer's disease, used his machine to kill herself. First-degree murder charges were brought against Kevorkian, but then dropped because the law was unclear; however, in January 1991, the court ordered him not to assist further suicides.

In October 1991, Kevorkian was present when two other women committed suicide, using other devices he created. In November, Michigan suspended Kevorkian's medical license over his assisted-suicide activities, and as 1991 closed, a Michigan grand jury was weighing possible murder charges over the October deaths. Notably, none of the three women had a terminal illness, the usual situation for euthanasia; all made videotapes discussing their reasons for and feelings about committing suicide. Kevorkian put forward his ideas and defended his actions in a 1991 book, *Prescription Medicine: The Goodness of Planned Death,* which received considerable public attention as part of the continuing "right-to-die" debate.

Born and educated in Michigan, Kevorkian was licensed as a physician in 1953, interned in Michigan hospitals, and then worked as a pathologist at the Pacific Hospital in Long Beach, California, until 1982. An advocate of euthanasia throughout his medical career, Kevorkian has published various books and articles on the subject, generally abroad, and has been unemployed since 1982, he believes because of his upsetting ideas.

FURTHER READING

"The odd odyssey of 'Dr. Death.' . . ." GLORIA BORGER. *U.S. News & World Report,* Aug. 27, 1990.
"The right to die. . . ." D'ARCY JENISH. *Maclean's,* June 25, 1990.
"A vital woman. . . ." BONNIE JOHNSON et al. *People,* June 25, 1990.
"The doctor's suicide van. . . ." MELINDA BECK. *Newsweek,* June 18, 1990.

Khamenei, Mohammed Ali (1940–)

In the wake of the Persian Gulf War and with Iranian economic and political problems mounting, the relatively moderate forces led by Iranian President Ali Rafsanjani gained ascendancy in the continuing struggle for Iranian state power. On June 2, Rafsanjani's most powerful fundamentalist opponent, Ayatollah Khamenei, reversed position to state his support of Rafsanjani's new economic and political policies, which called for much stronger economic ties with the West and other Gulf nations. Khamenei also acquiesced to Rafsanjani's autumn 1991 moves to release American and other hostages held in Lebanon by the Iranian-controlled Hezbollah (Party of God).

Khamenei was a disciple and political ally of Ayatollah Ruhollah Khomeini; he was imprisoned in Iran on several occasions during the 1960s and 1970s, and exiled in 1978, returning to Iran when Khomeini came to power in 1979. He was president of Iran (1981–89), and became supreme Iranian Shiite Muslim religious leader and a competitor in the internal struggle for state power after Khomeini's death in 1989. He is married and has five children.

FURTHER READING

"Iran without Khomeini." MICHAEL LEDEEN. *American Spectator,* Aug. 1989.
"Change in Teheran. . . ." *National Review,* June 30, 1989.
"Burying the passions. . . ." BILL HEWITT. *Newsweek,* June 19, 1989.

"Khamenei, Hojatolislam (Sayed) Ali." *Current Biography,* Nov. 1987.

Kiker, Douglas (Ralph Douglas Kiker, Jr., 1930–91) Georgia-born Kiker began his long career in journalism in 1950 as a reporter for the Spartanburg, South Carolina, *Herald.* After naval service during the Korean War, he was a reporter for the *Atlanta Journal* (1959–62), served as director of information for the Peace Corps (1962–1963), and emerged on the national scene as the probing, highly regarded White House correspondent for the New York *Herald Tribune* (1963–66). Kiker joined NBC television in 1966 and became one of the best-respected television correspondents of the next quarter century; among his honors was a 1971 Peabody Award. He was also a novelist, with two 1950s novels and a series of mystery novels set on Cape Cod, beginning with *Murder on Clam Pond* (1986). He was survived by his wife, the former Diana Knight, a daughter, and four sons. (d. Chatham, Massachusetts; August 15, 1991)

FURTHER READING

Obituary. *Variety,* Aug. 19, 1991.
Obituary. *New York Times,* Aug. 15, 1991.

Kilburn, Peter: See **Lebanon Hostages**

King, Stephen (1947–) Prolific and enormously popular novelist Stephen King had two new books for his fans in 1991. One was *Needful Things: The Last Castle Rock Story* (1991), involving the demise of the spooky fictional setting for many King stories. The other was the third installment of King's "Dark Tower" fantasy series, *The Waste Lands: The Dark Tower Book III* (1992), featuring gunslinger-knight Roland of Mid-World and other characters from previous installments—*The Dark Tower: The Gunslinger* (1982) and *The Dark Tower: The Drawing of the Three* (1987)—as they seek the Dark Tower, source of the degradation of Roland's planet. During 1991, King was also working on a new novel, *Delores Claiborne.*

King also ventured into television in summer 1991, as creator and writer of a seven-episode "novel for television," *Stephen King's Golden Years,* focusing on a laboratory janitor (Keith Szarabajka) who becomes younger after a chemical accident; King made a cameo appearance as a bus driver in the fifth episode. In May, television viewers were treated to an adaptation of a King short story, *Sometimes They Come Back.* Rob Reiner's 1990 film *Misery,* based on King's 1974 novel, starring Kathy Bates (in an Oscar-winning performance) and James Caan, was released on video in mid-1991. In a bizarre twist, in May 1991, a disturbed man carrying a phony bomb was arrested and charged with terrorizing King's wife, claiming that the female character in *Misery* was based on his aunt, convicted as a baby killer. During 1991, King's *The Dark Half* (1989) was being filmed in Pittsburgh, with Timothy Hutton and Amy Madigan.

Maine-born King received his B.S. from the University of Maine in 1970, then taught English at the Hampden Academy (1971–73), before embarking on his writing career. Among his many novels, in addition to the *Dark Tower* series, are *Carrie* (1974), *Salem's Lot* (1975), *The Shining* (1976), *The Stand* (1978; republished uncut, 1990), *Firestarter* (1980), *Dance Macabre* (1981), *Cujo* (1981), *Pet Sematary* (1983), *The Talisman, Cycle of the Werewolf* (1985), *Skeleton Crew* (1986), *The Eyes of the Dragon* (1987), *Misery* (1987), *The Tommyknockers* (1987), *The Dark Half* (1989), and *Four Past Midnight*

(1990). He has also published many short stories and short screenplays as well as novels under the name of Richard Bachman, including *Rage* (1977), *The Long Walk* (1979), *Roadwork* (1981), *The Running Man* (1982), and *Thinner* (1984). Many of King's works have been adapted for the screen, among them *Carrie* (1976), *The Shining* (1980), *Christine* (1983), *The Dead Zone* (1983), *Stand By Me* (1986; based on *The Body*), *The Running Man* (1987), *Pet Sematary* (1989), and *Misery* (1990). King himself directed from his own scripts *Children of the Corn* (1984) and *Maximum Overdrive* (1986). King married Tabitha Jane Spruce in 1971; they have three children.

FURTHER READING

"Stephen King." MARK MARVEL. *Interview,* Oct. 1991.
The Shape Under the Sheet: The Complete Stephen King Encyclopedia. STEPHEN SPIGNESI. Popular Culture, 1991.
Stephen King: Man and Artist, rev. ed. CARROL F. TERRELL. North Lights, 1991.
The Stephen King Story. GEORGE BEAHM. Andrews & McMeel, 1991.
King Stephen, 3rd ed. R. H. DAVIS. Longman, 1990.
The Stephen King Companion. GEORGE BEAHM, ed. Andrews & McMeel, 1989.
Feast of Fear: Conversations with Stephen King. TIM UNDERWOOD and CHUCK MILLER, eds. Underwood-Miller, 1989; McGraw-Hill, 1989.
The Moral Voyages of Stephen King. ANTHONY MAGISTRALE. Starmont House, 1989.
Stephen King: The First Decade, Carrie to Pet Sematary. JOSEPH REINO. Macmillan, 1988.
Bare Bones: Conversations on Terror with Stephen King. TIM UNDERWOOD and CHUCK MILLER, eds. McGraw-Hill, 1988; Warner, 1989.
Landscape of Fear: Stephen King's American Gothic. TONY MAGISTRALE. Bowling Green University, 1988.
Reign of Fear: Fiction and Film of Stephen King. DON HERRON, ed. Underwood-Miller, 1988.
The Gothic World of Stephen King: Landscape of Nightmares. GARRY HOPPENSTAND and RAY B. BROWNE, eds. Bowling Green University, 1987.
Kingdom of Fear: The World of Stephen King. TIM UNDERWOOD and CHUCK MILLER. NAL-Dutton, 1987.
The Stephen King Phenomenon. MICHAEL R. COLLINGS. Starmont House, 1987; Borgo Press, 1987.
The Stephen King Concordance. MICHAEL R. COLLINGS. Borgo Press, 1987.
Stephen King Goes to Hollywood. CHUCK MILLER and TIM UNDERWOOD. NAL-Dutton, 1987.
Stephen King: The Art of Darkness. DOUGLAS E. WINTER. NAL-Dutton, 1986.
The Annotated Guide to Stephen King: A Primary and Secondary Bibliography of the Works of America's Premier Horror Writer. MICHAEL R. COLLINGS. Starmont House, 1986; Borgo Press, 1986.

Kinnock, Neil Gordon (1942–) Head of the British Labour Party and of the parliamentary opposition, Kinnock continued to gain strength during 1991 as he moved even further toward the center of British politics, as part of his preparation for a strong run against Prime Minister John Major in the coming British general elections, to be held no later than July 1992. Early in 1991, and against considerable opposition within his own party, he supported the use of force in the Persian Gulf, and also supported the Allied ground offensive when it came.

At the September 29–October 3 annual Labour Party Conference, he attacked the left socialist Militant Tendency within the party, suspending two members of Parliament from the party as prelude to a wider attack. Simultaneously, he put Labour forward as moderate rather than radical in its domestic policies, calling for rather modest National Health Service and other welfare improvements while sharply attacking Major's ability to cope with Britain's deepening recession. Abroad, Kinnock favored substantial aid to the post-coup Soviet Union and attacked Major as being indecisive on European Community matters.

Kinnock began his political career in the mid-1960s in Labour Party educational work, became a Labour Member of Parliament in 1970, and has remained in Parliament for two decades, while steadily moving up in his party. He became party leader and leader of the parliamentary opposition in 1983. In 1987 he published *Making Our Way: Investing in Britain's Future.* Kinnock attended the University College of Cardiff. He married Glenys Elizabeth Parry in 1967; the couple have two children.

FURTHER READING

"The rewards of Labour. . . ." HUGO YOUNG. *New Republic,* May 27, 1991.
"A coal miner's son." MARY NEMETH. *Maclean's,* May 14, 1990.
Neil Kinnock: The Path to Leadership. G. M. DROWER. Weidenfeld & Nicolson, 1984.

Kinski, Klaus (Nikolaus Gunther Nakszynski, 1926–91) Polish-born German actor Kinski began his career on stage and film in post–World War II Berlin. He spent almost two decades in a wide range of small film roles, in the 1960s making some impact in *Dr. Zhivago* (1965) and several spaghetti westerns. His breakthrough came in the Spanish conquistador's role in Werner Herzog's *Aguirre: The Wrath of God* (1972), and it is for this and several other roles in Herzog films that he is best known by far. These included the vampire's role in Herzog's remake of *Nosferatu, The Vampyre* (1979) and the title role in *Fitzcarraldo* (1982). His later work was far less rewarding. His autobiography, *All I Need Is Love: A Memoir* (1988), created some controversy for its explicit sexual passages and attacks on some of those he had known and worked with; it was described by many of those mentioned in it as libelous. He was survived by his third wife, Minhoi Wiggers, a son, and two daughters, one of them the actress Nastassia Kinski. (d. Lagunitas, California; November 23, 1991)

FURTHER READING

Obituary. *Variety,* Dec. 2, 1991.
Obituary. *New York Times,* Nov. 27, 1991.
Obituary. *The Times* (of London), Nov. 27, 1991.

Kline, Kevin Delaney (1947–) In May 1991, Kline starred as television soap opera actor Jeffrey Anderson in Michael Hoffman's film comedy *Soapdish,* opposite Sally Field as a soap opera star and Whoopi Goldberg as the producer of the show, "The Sun Also Sets." In December, he starred as Mack in Lawrence Kasdan's *Grand Canyon,* set in contemporary and rather dangerous Los Angeles; the cast included Danny Glover, Steve Martin, Mary McDonnell, and Mary-Louise Parker. Forthcoming was a role in Richard Attenborough's *Charlie,* the biography of Charles Chaplin, starring Robert Downey, Jr., in the title role, in a cast that includes Geraldine Chaplin, Dan Aykroyd, and Penelope Ann Miller. Also forthcoming was a starring role in the Robert Zemeckis film comedy *Death Becomes Her,* with Meryl Streep, Goldie Hawn, and Bruce Willis.

St. Louis–born Kline became a star on Broadway in the late 1970s, winning a Tony for *On the Twentieth Century* (1978), starring in *Loose Ends* (1979), and winning a second Tony for *Pirates of Penzance* (1980), a role he repeated in the 1983 film version. He also appeared off-Broadway in the early 1970s, and as *Richard III* (1983), *Henry V* (1984), and *Hamlet* (1986). On screen, he played in such films as *Sophie's Choice* (1982), *The Big Chill* (1983), *Silverado* (1985), *A Fish Called Wanda* (1988; he won a Best Supporting Actor Oscar), and *I Love You to Death* (1990). In 1990 he also starred in and directed *Hamlet* for the Public Broadcasting System's "Great Performances" series. Kline's B.A. was from Indiana University, and he also attended the Juilliard School. He married Phoebe Cates in 1989; they have one son, born in 1991.

FURTHER READING

"Kevin Kline. . . ." SHARI ROMAN. *Video,* Dec. 1991.
"Kevin's choice." JOE MORGENSTERN. *Connoisseur,* July 1991.

Knight, Jonathan: See **New Kids on the Block**

Knight, Jordan: See **New Kids on the Block**

Kohl, Helmut (1930–) German Prime Minister and Christian Democratic Party leader Kohl, elected chancellor of newly united Germany in December 1990, found his political position at home weakening during much of 1991

as his party lost a series of state elections; unemployment and resurgent Naziism grew in the east; Eastern Europeans seeking a better life flooded into Germany; and the threat of inflation grew. Yet his personal position was still strong; his popularity and political standing had become enormous in Germany after he played a central role in reuniting the country. On August 7, he announced his candidacy in the 1994 elections, while continuing to invest in the economic redevelopment of the former East Germany and to pay for it by raising taxes and cutting government expenditures in the former West Germany. Simultaneously, he moved to appease anti-foreign feeling by limiting asylum while at the same time speaking out sharply against the Neo-Nazi movement.

Kohl also continued to play a major role on the international scene. He offered massive aid to the Soviet government after the aborted August coup and sought to develop relations with newly emerging Russia and Boris Yeltsin as the year progressed. He was also the beneficiary of the new American resolve to withdraw large military forces from Europe. Germany supported the Allied side but played little role in the Persian Gulf War, sending money rather than military forces.

Kohl began his political career in the Rhineland, becoming Christian Democratic Party chairman in the Rhineland (1966–73) and deputy national chairman of his party in 1969; he has been national chairman since 1973. He was opposition leader in the West German parliament (1976–82), and then succeeded Chancellor Helmut Schmidt. He has throughout his career been a rather careful centrist, much concerned with the development of the European Community and pursuing a Western-oriented but also independent course. Kohl attended the University of Frankfurt and the University of Heidelberg. He married Hannelore Renner in 1960; the couple have two children.

FURTHER READING

"King Kohl." T. S. Allman. *Reader's Digest.* (Canadian), May 1991.

"Who's sitting pretty. . . ." *Business Week,* Mar. 11, 1991.

"Helmut Kohl. . . ." Bruce W. Nelan. *Time,* Jan. 7, 1991.

"Herr Klutz. . . ." Anne McElvoy. *New Republic,* Dec. 10, 1990.

"Kohl power." Edward M. Steen. *Inc.,* Nov. 1990.

"Helmut Kohl. . . ." David Gow. *World Press Review,* Oct. 1990.

"Driving toward. . . ." Henry Muller and Karsten Prager. *Time,* June 25, 1990.

Koppel, Ted (1940–) In his eleventh year as host of ABC's nightly news-interview program "Nightline," broadcast journalist Koppel continued to have the inside track on some of the year's hottest stories. After the failed August 1991 Soviet coup, Koppel was in Moscow doing a live interview with then-foreign minister Alexander Bessmertnykh, who announced his resignation to the television audience, and only then picked up the telephone (still on camera) to break the news to U.S. Secretary of State James Baker. When Oliver North went public with his belief that ex-President Reagan "knew it all," he gave Koppel two nights of exclusive interviews before launching the publicity campaign for his book, *Under Fire*. It was "Nightline" that broke the story of a possible connection (witting or unwitting) between just-released hostage Terry Waite and Oliver North's Iran-Contra activities. And when Soviet President Mikhail Gorbachev bowed to the inevitable and resigned his post in December 1991, Koppel was there to record the event, which aired on television on a special "PrimeTime Live" program, *The Final Days*.

During the Persian Gulf War, Koppel reported from the Allied base at Dhahran, Saudi Arabia, with field reports from journalists like his frequent substitute, Forrest Sawyer. In February 1991, his colleagues at the Friars Club honored Koppel as having the best national news program. During 1991, Koppel signed a new contract with ABC for an estimated $5 million.

British-born Koppel emigrated to the United States with his German refugee family in 1953. He began his broadcasting career at New York's WMCA in 1963, in that year moving to ABC, where he has spent his entire career since. He went to Vietnam as an ABC correspondent, worked in Hong Kong and Miami as an ABC bureau chief, and anchored the "ABC Saturday Night News" in the late 1970s. In March 1980, he emerged as a leading figure in American broadcast journalism, as ABC turned its nightly reports on the Iran hostage crisis into the Koppel-anchored Monday-to-Friday "Nightline," identified with him ever since. Koppel's B.A. in journalism was from Syracuse University, his M.A. in journalism from Stanford. He is married to Grace Anne Dorney; the couple have four children, one of whom—Andrea—is also a television journalist.

FURTHER READING

"Anchor monster. . . ." JOHN KATZ. *Rolling Stone,* Jan. 10, 1991.
"Ted Koppel." RICHARD M. COHEN. *Life,* Oct. 1988.
"Ted Koppel's edge." MARSHALL BLONSKY. *New York Times Magazine,* Aug. 14, 1988.

Kosinski, Jerzy Nikodem (1933–91) Lodz-born Kosinski, a novelist, became well known after publication of his first novel, *The Painted Bird* (1965), which he described as based on his experiences as a six-year-old Jewish child wandering the countryside of his native Poland during the early years of World War II. Using the pseudonym Joseph Novak, he had previously published two books of essays on political themes: *The Future Is Ours, Comrade* (1960) and *No Third Path* (1962). His further works, most of which were not nearly so well received, included *Steps* (1968), *The Art of the Self* (1968), *Being There* (1971), *The Devil Tree* (1971), *Blind Date* (1977), *Passion Play* (1979), *Pinball* (1982), and *The Hermit of 69th Street* (1988). *Being There* was made into the 1979 film starring Peter Sellers. Kosinski himself played the small but key role of Grigori Zinoviev in Warren Beatty's film *Reds* (1981). Kosinski was president of the American branch of PEN, the organization of poets, playwrights, essayists, editors, novelists (1973–75). He was a suicide. He was survived by his second wife, Katherina von Fraunhofer-Kosinski, and a stepbrother. (d. New York City; May 3, 1991)

FURTHER READING

"Kosinski's masque. . . ." ANTHONY HADEN-GUEST. *Vanity Fair,* Oct. 1991.
"The haunted bird." JOHN TAYLOR. *New York,* July 15, 1991.
"The most considerate of men." JOHN CORRY. *American Spectator,* July 1991.
Obituary. *Current Biography,* July 1991.
"The death of a mythmaker. . . ." JACK KROLL. *Newsweek,* May 13, 1991.
Obituary. *Variety,* May 13, 1991.
Obituary. *The Times* (of London), May 6, 1991.
Obituary. *New York Times,* May 4, 1991.
Jerzy Kosinski: An Annotated Bibliography. GLORIA L. CRONIN and BLAINE H. HALL. Greenwood, 1991.
Jerzy Kosinski. NORMAN LAVERS. Macmillan, 1982.
Jerzy Kosinski: Literary Alarm Clock. BYRON L. SHERWIN. Spertus, 1981.

Kozol, Jonathan (1936–) Educator and social critic Kozol once again "hammered out danger, hammered out warning" in his extraordinarily moving and influential 1991 book *Savage Inequalities: Children in America's Schools.* His book took its readers deep into the American

educational system, to overcrowded, decaying schools in poor communities all over the country, and to children who had no books, no heat, no science equipment, no computers, no safety, far too few teachers, and little or no hope. He compared those schools and children with those in affluent communities, often nearby, and demanded for poor children some of the equality that has always been such an important part of the American dream. His main proposal for accomplishing this was a complete revision of the way American schools were funded, and replacement of the property tax approach that guaranteed unequal funding with equal funding for all schools. His powerful book made an immediate impact. Very notably, *Publishers Weekly* took the unprecedented step of devoting its cover and first two pages to an open letter to President George Bush, recommending that he read the book and take action on its recommendations. While not arguing with his goals, some critics felt that the practical implementation of his plans would be a long time in coming, given American political realities and within the context of a long-term recession and the even longer-term financial crisis faced by all public authorities. Even so, his searing look at the way poor American children were being short-changed and damaged in their schools was taken very seriously indeed.

Boston-born Kozol taught in the Boston public school system (1964–65) and in the Newton system (1966–68). His experience was the basis for his highly acclaimed book, *Death at an Early Age; The Destruction of the Hearts and Minds of Negro Children in the Boston Public Schools,* which won a 1968 National Book Award. He went on to become a leading educator and education writer, lecturing widely, writing many essays, and publishing such books as *Free Schools* (1972), *The Night Is Dark and I Am Far from Home: A Political Indictment of the U.S. Public Schools* (1975), *Children of the Revolution: A Yankee Teacher in the Cuban Schools* (1978), *Prisoners of Silence: Breaking the Bonds of Adult Illiteracy in the United States* (1980), *On Being a Teacher* (1981), *Alternative Schools: A Survivor's Guide* (1982), *Illiterate America* (1985), and *Rachel and Her Children: Homeless Families in America* (1988). His B.A. was from Harvard in 1958; he was a Rhodes Scholar at Oxford from 1958 to 1959.

FURTHER READING

"Savage inequalities. . . ." PETER SCHRAG. *New Republic,* Dec. 16, 1991.
"Jonathan Kozol." GORDON W. E. NORE. *Progressive,* Dec. 1991.
"Save the children." WILLIAM PLUMMER and MARIA SPEIDEL. *People,* Oct. 7, 1991.
"Jonathan Kozol on. . . ." *Publishers Weekly,* Sep. 27, 1991.

Kravchuk, Leonid Makarovich

(1934–) On Sunday, December 1, 1991, almost 90 percent of those Ukrainians voting approved of full independence for Ukraine. On December 2, Leonid Kravchuk, formerly the communist president of the Ukrainian Soviet republic, was elected president of noncommunist Ukraine. The new country, with 52 million people and approximately one quarter of the economic strength of the Soviet Union, was immediately recognized by Russia, and President George Bush quickly sent Secretary of State James F. Baker to Ukraine to talk with Kravchuk about the future of Soviet nuclear weapons sited there.

The new Ukrainian president then turned to what were for him far more immediate questions, including how to get through the winter with a very badly damaged distribution system; economic and political relations with the other sections of what had until very recently been the monolithic Soviet state; and the development of new institutions for a new nation, including a new army. Independence had come very quickly, in a fast-changing situation; as recently as late August, Kravchuk had only very cautiously opposed the failed right-wing coup, resigning his Communist Party positions on August 27, later than many other leaders.

In a quick and major development, Kravchuk, Russian president Boris Yeltsin, and Belarus president Stanislav Shushkevich on December 8, 1991, founded a new "Commonwealth of Independent States," invited all the other former Soviet republics into the commonwealth, and declared the Soviet Union at an end. Then began the long, complex process of developing the new nation and many new sets of relationships, with disputes among Commonwealth members over military and other major matters emerging almost immediately.

Ukraine-born Kravchuk began his career as a political economy teacher at the city of Chernovtsy, then moving into Communist Party work; he joined that party in 1958. Most of his career was spent as a party ideology secretary in a series of minor posts. With the rise of Mikhail Gorbachev, and the wholly new situation Gorbachev created in the Soviet Union, Kravchuk in the late 1980s became a reform leader, and in due course, a leader of the powerful movement to secede from the Soviet Union. He was elected President of Ukraine by its parliament on July 23, 1990. Kravchuk attended Kiev University. He is married to political economist Antonina Kravchuk; they have one son.

FURTHER READING

"Divided they fall. . . ." DOUGLAS STANGLIN. *U.S. News & World Report,* Dec. 30, 1991.
"The end of the U.S.S.R." GEORGE J. CHURCH. *Time,* Dec. 23, 1991.
"A house of cards." MALCOLM GRAY. *Maclean's,* Dec. 16, 1991.
"Europe's new state: Ukraine." *Economist,* Dec. 7, 1991.
"Your pace or mine?" *Economist,* June 22, 1991

Kristofferson, Kris (1936–) Country music artist and actor Kristofferson continued to pursue both sides of his career in 1991. On screen, he and Willie Nelson starred in the sequel to their 1990 television movie, *Pair of Aces,* in *Another Pair of Aces: Three of a Kind,* which aired in April 1991. Nelson was once again the safecracker, Kristofferson the Texas Ranger, in a cast that included Joan Severance as the FBI agent and love interest, and Rip Torn. For the Christmas season, Kristofferson and Kim Cattrall starred as a frontier couple opposite Sheldon Peters Wolfchild as Blackfoot chief Many Horses in the television film *Miracle in the Wilderness,* a modern, multicultural drama on Christmas religious themes. Forthcoming was a starring role as a detective opposite Drew Barrymore in the feature film *No Place to Hide.*

On the country music side, the Christmas season saw a release of a two-disc Sony Music CD set presenting Kristofferson as a singer of his own songs and as a songwriter. The first disc contains his own recordings of 17 of his own songs, the second the same songs sung by such music headliners as Willie Nelson, Waylon Jennings, Janis Joplin, Johnny Cash, and Bob Dylan.

Texas-born Kristofferson has appeared in such films as *Cisco Pike* (1972), *Alice Doesn't Live Here Anymore* (1974), *The Sailor Who Fell from Grace with the Sea* (1976), *Heaven's Gate,* (1981) *Rollover,* (1981), and *Welcome Home* (1990). He has also appeared in such telefilms as *Stagecoach* (1986), *Amerika* (1987), and *Pair of Aces* (1989). He is also a well-known country and western singer and songwriter, who went on the road again in 1990, touring with his friends Johnny Cash, Waylon Jennings, and Willie Nelson, as the Highwaymen. Kristofferson attended Pomona College and Oxford University. He has been married three times and has three children.

FURTHER READING

"Kristofferson." ROSA JORDAN. *Progressive,* Sep. 1991.
"Kris Kristofferson. . . ." PATRICK CARR. *Country Music,* Jan.–Feb. 1988.
Written in My Soul: Rock's Great Songwriters . . . Talk About Creating Their Music. BILL FLANAGAN. Contemporary, 1986.

Kurosawa, Akira (1910–) *Rhapsody in August* was the 30th film of celebrated Japanese director Kurosawa; because it was his, the film's opening at the 1991 Cannes Film Festival was one of the major cultural events of the year. Far from being in the epic style of so much of his work, the film is done on a small scale, perhaps as counterpoint to the massive, tragic event at its heart, the atom bombing of Nagasaki on August 9, 1945. The film, set in Nagasaki now, focuses on the visit of four Japanese teenagers to their grandmother (Sachiko Murase), who tells them the story of the Nagasaki bombing, hidden in large part from their generation, and of their grandfather, her husband, killed in the bombing. A few days later, their Japanese-American cousin, played by Richard Gere, arrives—to apologize for the bombing. The film created some controversy in the United States, some Americans feeling that Kurosawa should have had his Japanese characters also apologize for Pearl Harbor and other Japanese wartime actions. In 1991 Kurosawa received the lifetime achievement award of the Association of Asian Pacific American Artists, although some in the same group criticized him for casting Gere in the film rather than an Asian-American.

Kurosawa was an assistant director from 1936 to 1943; his first film as a director was *Sugata Sanshiro* (1943). He emerged as a major figure during the postwar period, bringing Japanese films to a world audience in the 1950s, with such films as *Rashomon* (1950), which won a Best Foreign Film Oscar; *The Seven Samurai* (1954); and *Throne of Blood* (1957), his adaptation of *Macbeth.* His later films included such classics as *Yojimbo* (1961), *Redbeard* (1964), *Derzu Uzala* (1976), *Kagemusha* (1980), *Ran* (1984), his adaptation of *King Lear,* and *Akira Kurosawa's Dreams,* which opened the 1990 Cannes Film Festival. In 1982 he published *Something like an Autobiography.* He attended the Doshusha School of Western Painting.

FURTHER READING

"Kurosawa, Akira." *Current Biography,* July 1991.
The Warrior's Camera: The Cinema of Akira Kurosawa. Stephen Prince. Princeton University Press, 1991.
"A. Kurosawa." Ralph Rugoff. *Interview,* Sep. 1990.
"Akira Kurosawa." John Clark. *Premiere,* Aug. 1990.
"Japan's emperor. . . ." Ian Buruma. *New York Times Magazine,* Oct. 29, 1989.
"Akira Kurosawa." Gerald Peary. *American Film,* Apr. 1989.

L

Lancaster, Burt (Burton Stephen Lancaster, 1913–) Lancaster starred as lawyer and former presidential candidate John W. Davis, lawyer for the losing side, opposite Sidney Poitier as Thurgood Marshall in *Separate But Equal,* which aired in April 1991. Written and directed by George Stevens, Jr., the four-hour television miniseries was about the course of the dispute that ultimately led to the landmark 1954 U.S. Supreme Court school desegregation decision in the case of *Brown v. Board of Education of Topeka,* Marshall's greatest victory. Lancaster, a major figure in world cinema for over four decades, spent 1991 recuperating from the stroke he suffered in November 1990. He was as always highly visible on world screens in many of his classic roles, including a restored version of Luchino Visconti's 1963 *Il Gattopardo* (*The Leopard*), which was shown in September at the Venice International Film Festival, and Bernardo Bertolucci's *1900,* restored to its originally intended length and re-released into theaters and on cable. Lancaster was the 28th recipient of the Screen Actors Guild Lifetime Achievement Award for "fostering the finest ideals of the acting profession."

New York-born Lancaster was an acrobat (1932–39), half of the team of Lang and Cravat. After World War II, he very quickly became a leading film star with his extraordinary debut in *The Killers* (1946). A few of his many notable films were *All My Sons* (1948), *From Here to Eternity* (1953), *The Rose Tattoo,* (1955), *Gunfight at the O.K. Corral* (1957), *Separate Tables* (1958), *The Devil's Disciple* (1959), *Elmer Gantry* (1960), for which he won a Best Actor Oscar, *Judgment at Nuremberg* (1961), *Bird Man of Alcatraz* (1962), *The Leopard* (1963), *Seven Days in May* (1964), *The Swimmer* (1968), *Conversation Piece* (1975), *Atlantic City* (1980), and *Field of Dreams* (1989). Lancaster attended New York University. In 1990 he was married for the third time, to Susan Scherer; he has five children.

FURTHER READING

The Cinema History of Burt Lancaster. David Fury. Artists Press, 1989.

Shooting Stars: Heroes and Heroines of Western Film. Archie P. McDonald. Indiana University Press, 1987.

"Lancaster, Burt." *Current Biography,* Apr. 1986.

Burt Lancaster. Minty Clinch. Scarborough House, 1985.

Burt Lancaster. Robert Windeler. St. Martin's, 1984; Jove, 1985.

Burt Lancaster: The Man and His Movies. Allan Hunter. St. Martin's, 1984.

Land, Edwin Herbert (1909–91) Connecticut-born Land, a leading 20th-century inventor, in the late 1920s worked with tiny crystals to create his first light-polarizing device, and in the early 1930s he discovered how to use such crystals embedded in plastic to polarize light, as in safety glass. In 1937, he founded the Polaroid Corporation to market his invention. In 1947, he invented the Polaroid Land Camera, which produces photographs within the camera and quickly turns out prints, inaugurating the era of instant photography. In 1963, his company developed the first instant color photography process. Land built his company into a major industrial corporation before retiring in 1982. A prolific inventor, he was credited with over 500 patents. He was survived by his wife, Helen Maislen, and two daughters. (d. Cambridge, Massachusetts; March 1, 1991)

FURTHER READING

Obituary. *Current Biography,* May 1991.
Obituary. *The Times* (of London), Mar. 4, 1991.
Obituary. *New York Times,* Mar. 2, 1991.
"Edwin Land. . . ." *Life,* Fall 1990.
"Pioneers: Three Men of Genius. . . ." *Life,* Fall 1988.
Land's Polaroid: A Company and the Man Who Invented It. PETER C. WENSBERG. Houghton Mifflin, 1987.
The Instant Image: Edwin Land and the Polaroid Experience. MARK OLSHAKER. Scarborough House, 1980.

Landon, Michael (Eugene Maurice Orowitz, 1936–91) New York City–born Landon became a major television figure in the long-running hit western series "Bonanza" (1959–73), and it is as Little Joe Cartwright that he is still seen in innumerable reruns in his own country and around the world. He also wrote and directed some episodes of "Bonanza." From 1974 to 1983, he starred as Charles Ingalls in a second worldwide television hit series, "Little House on the Prairie," based on the autobiographical Laura Ingalls Wilder children's book. He wrote and directed most of the episodes of that series, and of his third series, "Highway to Heaven" (1984–88). He also appeared in several films and telefilms, including *I Was a Teenage Werewolf* (1975) and *Sam's Son* (1976), and directed and produced the television series "Father Murphy" (1981–84). He died of cancer; two months before his death, he publicly announced that he was fighting the disease. Landon was survived by his third wife, Cindy, five sons, and four daughters (d. Malibu, California; July 1, 1991)

FURTHER READING

Obituary. *Variety,* July 8, 1991.
Obituary. *The Times* (of London), July 5, 1991.
Obituary. *New York Times,* July 2, 1991.
Michael Landon: A Biography. MARSHA DALY. St. Martin's, 1987.

Landsbergis, Vyatautas (1932–) President of Lithuania, Landsbergis led his country to full independence in 1991, after a year that began with Soviet army attacks in Vilnius and included a good deal of Soviet-Baltic skirmishing. Although Iceland and Czechoslovakia recognized Lithuania in February, and Boris Yeltsin reaffirmed Russian support for Lithuanian independence, attacks from Soviet hardliners continued in Lithuania, most notably the murders of six border guards by Soviet Black Beret commandos on July 31.

With the attempted right-wing Soviet coup of August 19, some Soviet troops and tanks moved into Vilnius and other Baltic cities; fighting broke out between Lithuanian militia and Soviet forces in Vilnius. But most Soviet commanders and troops refused to move against the Baltic governments, and there was no major armed clash. With the failure of thc coup, the Landsbergis government reaffirmed Lithuanian independence on August 21, and neighboring Latvia and Estonia also declared themselves independent. The new nations were recognized by many of the world's countries within a week, and by the United States on September 2. On September 6, the Soviet government recognized the three new countries.

Then, for Landsbergis, the business of government really began. A major early issue was the accusation that Lithuania was planning to exonerate many Nazi war criminals. Landsbergis denied the accusation; his government quickly changed the new policies that would have done just that. Another major issue was a fast-developing dispute with Poland over the fate of ethnic Poles in Lithuania—it was an early example of the kinds of ethnic disputes that had by then started to develop throughout the former Soviet empire.

Landsbergis is a very recent politician, who has spent most of his working life as a distinguished Soviet musicologist, teaching at the Vilnius Conservatory. He began to emerge as a major Lithuanian and Soviet political figure in 1989, at the head of Sajudis, the leading non-communist Lithuanian nationalist organization. In May 1989, he was a highly visible Lithuanian nationalist delegate to the first session of the

Soviet Congress of People's Deputies. On March 11, 1990, the Lithuanian parliament scored a historic "first," seceding from the Soviet Union; it elected Landsbergis the first president of independent Lithuania. Divorced, then remarried, Landsbergis has three children.

FURTHER READING

"Landsbergis talks tough. . . ." *U.S. News & World Report,* Dec. 17, 1990.
"Orchestrating freedom." JOHN BUDRIS. *World Monitor,* Dec. 1991.
"Landsbergis, Vytautas." *Current Biography,* July 1990.
"The meddlesome musicologist. . . ." JEFF TRIMBLE. *U.S. News & World Report,* May 14, 1990.

Lange, Jessica (1949–) Lange's major 1991 film was Martin Scorsese's remake of *Cape Fear,* the 1962 Gregory Peck–Robert Mitchum vehicle; she starred as Leigh Bowden, in the role created by Polly Bergen, opposite Nick Nolte as Sam Bowden (the Gregory Peck role) and Robert De Niro as Sam Cady (the Robert Mitchum role). She and De Niro are also co-starring in another Scorsese presentation, the Irwin Winkler remake of Jules Dassin's 1950 film *Night and the City,* forthcoming in 1992. A second forthcoming 1992 film was *Blue Sky;* she stars opposite Tommy Lee Jones in the story of a nuclear engineer and his family enmeshed in a military cover-up situation. Also due for 1992 was a starring role on Broadway in a revival of Tennessee Williams's *A Streetcar Named Desire,* with Alec Baldwin, Amy Madigan, and Timothy Carhart; an April opening was scheduled. Lange's very busy 1992 schedule also includes a starring role on television, in the "Hallmark Hall of Fame" production of *O Pioneers!,* based on the 1913 Willa Cather novel.

Minnesota-born Lange became one of the leading movie stars of the late 1970s and 1980s, with such films as *All That Jazz* (1979), *The Postman Always Rings Twice* (1981), *Frances* (1982), *Tootsie* (1982), *Crimes of the Heart* (1986), *Music Box* (1989), and *Men Don't Leave* (1990). She attended the University of Minnesota. She was formerly married to Paco Grande and has three children, one from a former relationship with ballet star Mikhail Baryshnikov, two from her relationship with actor-playwright Sam Shepard.

FURTHER READING

"Full-tilt Jessica." NANCY COLLINS. *Vanity Fair,* Oct. 1991.
"Jessica." VALERIE MONROE. *Harper's Bazaar,* Jan. 1991.
"Jessica Lange." *American Film,* Aug. 1990.
"The enigmatic allure. . . ." LINDA BIRD FRANCKE. *Cosmopolitan,* Feb. 1990.
Jessica Lange. J. T. JEFFRIES. St. Martin's, 1986.

Lansbury, Angela Brigid (1925–) The star of "Murder, She Wrote" changed course in the hit show's eighth season. In 1990, she had seemed to be easing out of the show, starring in only 13 of its 22 episodes. But her very large audience demanded nothing less than her mystery writer/sleuth Jessica Fletcher, and the show began to decline. In 1991, Lansbury decided to star in all 22 episodes, her audience returned, and the show was a major hit once again. While still talking about wanting more time to do character leads in the theater and some feature films as well, Lansbury seemed set to stay at the top of American television for as long as she wished. She did, however, find time to star as the voice of Mrs. Potts, the teapot with a heart of gold, in the animated film *Beauty and the Beast,* one of the hits of the 1991 Christmas season. On May 15, Lansbury received a lifetime achievement award from the British Academy of Film and Television Arts (BAFTA). In 1991 she also published a book of advice and thoughts on living: *Angela Lansbury's Positive Moves.*

British-born Lansbury began her long film and theater career with a supporting role in *Gaslight* (1944) and played competently in over a score of substantial film roles during the following 24 years. But it was on Broadway and in television, both much later, that she became a major star. She won four Tony Awards on Broadway, for *Mame* (1966), *Dear World* (1969), *Gypsy* (1973), and *Sweeney Todd* (1979). Then, quite late in her career, she became a major television star with "Murder, She Wrote" (1984–), also starring in such telefilms as *The Shell Seekers* (1989) and *The Love She Sought* (1989). Lansbury married Peter Shaw in 1949; the couple have two children.

FURTHER READING

"She's conquered movies. . . ." RICHARD ALLEMAN. *Vogue,* Dec. 1991.
"Angela Lansbury has. . . ." SUZANNE ADELSON. *People,* Nov. 7, 1988.
"Solving the case of. . . ." PHYLLIS BATTELLE. *Woman's Day,* Sep. 13, 1988.
Angela Lansbury: A Biography. MARGARET W. BONNANO. St. Martin's, 1987.

Lean, David (1908–91) London-born Lean began his long film career at the age of 19 as an all-purpose "tea boy" at Gaumont British, beginning to work as a newsreel editor in 1930 and a feature film editor in 1934. He soon became a leading film editor, most notably of *Pygmalion* (1938), *Major Barbara* (1941), *49th Parallel* (1941), and *One of Our Aircraft Is Missing* (1942). With Noel Coward, he co-directed the classic *In Which We Serve* (1942), and went on to become a leading director of his time, with such films as *This Happy Breed* (1944); *Blithe Spirit* (1944); the classic *Brief Encounter* (1945); the equally classic adaptations of Dickens's *Great Expectations* (1946) and *Oliver Twist* (1948); *Hobson's Choice* (1954); *Summertime* (1955); the epic *The Bridge on the River Kwai* (1957), for which he won a Best Director Oscar; the epic *Lawrence of Arabia* (1962), and another Best Director Oscar; the epic *Doctor Zhivago* (1965); and the failed epic *Ryan's Daughter* (1970), which was treated savagely by many critics—so savagely that his career was abruptly derailed. He made a massive comeback with *A Passage to India* (1984), and at his death was planning a film version of Joseph Conrad's novel *Nostromo.* He was survived by his sixth wife, Sandra. (d. London, England; April 16, 1991)

FURTHER READING

Obituary. *Current Biography,* June 1991.
"Master of spectacle. . . ." PAMELA YOUNG. *Maclean's,* Apr. 29, 1991.
Obituary. *U.S. News & World Report,* Apr. 29, 1991.
Obituary. *Variety,* Apr. 22, 1991.
Obituary. *The Times* (of London), Apr. 17, 1991.
Obituary. *New York Times,* Apr. 17, 1991.
David Lean and His Films. ALAIN SILVER and JAMES URSINI. Silman James Press, 1991.
"David Lean." DAVID EHRENSTEIN. *American Film,* Mar. 1990.
"David Lean is back." THOMAS SOTINEL. *World Press Review,* Aug. 1989.
"Lean, Sir David." *Current Biography,* June 1989.
David Lean. STEPHEN SILVERMAN. Abrams, 1989.
David Lean. MICHAEL A. ANDEREGG. Macmillan, 1984.

Lebanon Hostages From early 1984 through 1991, over two score Western hostages were kidnapped by Muslim extremists operating in Lebanon. Most of the extremist groups involved were affiliated with the Hezbollah, or Hizb-Allah, the Party of God, an Iranian-controlled or strongly influenced Shiite Muslim militia that became a major force in the Lebanese civil war. There were also hundreds of other hostages in the Middle East, some of them war prisoners and some political prisoners, in the hands of half a dozen nations; but Western media and national attentions were focused on the Western hostages.

With the end of the Cold War and the success of the United States and its allies in the Persian Gulf War, a set of new balances and forces emerged in the Middle East. One of the results was a new willingness—even an eagerness—on the part of Muslim terrorists and their governmental sponsors and protectors to release the remaining Lebanon Western hostages, with whatever guarantees of their own future safety they might gain. Seizing the opportunity, United Nations General Secretary Javier Pérez de Cuéllar entered into direct negotiations—primarily through his deputy, Giandomenico Picco—with the Iranian government and several terrorist groups, ultimately playing a major role in the 1991 release of 9 of the remaining 11 Western hostages, and of the bodies of some of those who had been murdered in captivity.

As of the end of 1991, two Western hostages remained in Lebanon. They were **Heinrich Struebig** and **Thomas Kemptner,** both Palestinian refugee relief workers kidnapped in 1989. Born in Germany, they were being held as hostages for the release of two terrorists, Mohammed Ali Hamadi and Abbas Hamadi, who were imprisoned in Germany. At year's end, Picco was reportedly negotiating for the release of the hostages.

The last of the hostages released in 1991 was **Terry Anderson,** who was freed on December 4. He had been chief Middle Eastern Associated Press correspondent when kidnapped in 1985. His was the longest hostage imprisonment, lasting almost seven years, or 2,454 days.

The 1991 hostage releases began with that of British journalist **John McCarthy,** released on August 8; he had been kidnapped in 1986. American writer **Edward Tracy,** kidnapped in 1986, was released on August 11. British flyer **Jack Mann,** kidnapped in 1989, was released on September 24. **Jesse Turner,** American University of Beirut faculty member, kidnapped in 1987, was released on October 21. Church of England hostage negotiator **Terry Waite,** kidnapped in 1987 while attempting to obtain release of previously taken hostages, and American University of Beirut faculty member **Thomas Sutherland,** kidnapped in 1985, were both released on November 18. American University of Beirut controller **Joseph Cicippio,** kidnapped

Terry Anderson.

Terry Waite.

in 1986, was released on December 2, and American University of Beirut faculty member **Alann Steen,** kidnapped in 1987, was released on December 3. All the hostages had been held under inhumane conditions and several had been beaten during their captivity, with permanent damage to some, including Joseph Cicippio and Alann Steen.

Some hostages had not survived. **William Higgins,** head of the UN truce supervision team and a U.S. lieutenant colonel, was kidnapped in 1988 and later murdered by his captors, probably in 1989; his body was recovered in late 1991. **William Buckley,** U.S. Central Intelligence Agency station chief in Beirut, was kidnapped in 1984 and murdered in 1985; his body was recovered in 1991. **Peter Kilburn,** a librarian at the American University of Beirut, was kidnapped in 1984 and murdered in 1986. British teachers **John Leigh Douglas** and **Philip Padfield** were kidnapped and murdered in 1986. British journalist **Alec Collett,** kidnapped in 1984, was murdered in 1984 or 1985. French scientist **Michel Seurat,** kidnapped in 1985, died in captivity of unknown causes, as did Italian businessman **Alberto Molinari,** kidnapped in 1985.

FURTHER READING

"Terry Anderson. . . ." *People,* Dec. 30, 1991.

"The faces. . . ." Carla Anne Robbins. *U.S. News & World Report,* Dec. 2, 1991.

"Hostages to terror." *Maclean's,* Apr. 30, 1991.

Forgotten: A Sister's Struggle to Save Her Brother, America's Longest Held Hostage. PEGGY SAY and PETER KNOBLER. Simon & Schuster, 1991.
Pity the Nation: The Abduction of Lebanon. ROBERT FISK. Simon & Schuster, 1991.
Holding On. SUNNIE MANN. Trafalgar Square, 1991.
America Held Hostage: From the Teheran Embassy Takeover to the Iran-Contra Affair. DON LAWSON. Watts, 1991.
"God in the chaos." SANDRA P. ALDRICH. *Christian Herald,* Nov.–Dec. 1989.
"Not again. . . ." RICHARD LACAYO. *Time,* Aug. 14, 1989.
"The lost life of Terry Anderson." SCOTT MACLEOD. *Time,* Mar. 20, 1989.
"Waite, Terence (Hardy)." *Current Biography,* Sep. 1986.
"Inciting the. . . ." *Maclean's,* May 19, 1986.
"Waite's secret mission. . . ." WILLIAM E. SMITH. *Time,* Dec. 2, 1985.
"Screen test. . . ." *Time,* Feb. 11, 1985.

Lee, Spike (Shelton Jackson Lee, 1957–) Lee continued to generate controversy in 1991. After winning a fight to remove White director Norman Jewison from the upcoming Malcolm X biofilm, on the grounds that an African-American had to do the film, Lee became the film's director. He then was himself criticized by Amiri Baraka and others as someone who would do an "exploitation" film, although they had not seen the script, written by James Baldwin and Arnold Perl in 1969. Director, co-producer, and co-scriptwriter Lee began filming *Malcolm X* in the autumn of 1991; it was scheduled for 1992 release. The film, based on Alex Haley's book *The Autobiography of Malcolm X,* stars Denzel Washington in the title role, in a cast that includes Lee, Angela Bassett, Kate Vernon, Al Freeman, Jr., Theresa Randle, Delroy Lindo, and Albert Hall.

Lee also wrote, directed, and produced *Jungle Fever,* an interracial love story starring Wesley Snipes and Annabella Sciorra as the lovers, in a cast that included Lee, Ossie Davis, Ruby Dee, Samuel L. Jackson, Lonette McKee, John Turturro, Frank Vincent, and Anthony Quinn; Stevie Wonder and Terence Blanchard wrote the music for the film, which opened in June 1991.

Atlanta-born Lee is a very recent professional filmmaker, making early films such as *She's Gotta Have It* (1986) and *School Daze* (1988); with Lisa Jones, he wrote books about the making of both films. He became a notable and very controversial filmmaker in 1989, with release of his film *Do the Right Thing,* a fictional story that sharply explored racial tensions in his home area of Bedford-Stuyvesant in Brooklyn. Denzel Washington starred in Lee's equally controversial 1990 film *Mo' Better Blues,* attacked by many as anti-Semitic for its story of the exploitation of Black artists, in this instance by two Jewish club owners. Lee's 1979 B.A. was from Morehouse College and his 1983 M.A. in filmmaking from New York University.

FURTHER READING

"Spike Lee. . . ." DAVID BRESKIN. *Rolling Stone,* July 11, 1991.
"Spike Lee. . . ." ELVIS MITCHELL. *Playboy,* July 1991.
"Spiking a fever. . . ." JACK KROLL. *Newsweek,* June 10, 1991.
"Spike's peak. . . ." GERRI HIRSHEY. *Vanity Fair,* June 1991.
Five for Five: The Films of Spike Lee. TERRY MCMILLAN. Stewart Tabori & Chang, 1991.
"Lee, Spike." *Current Biography,* Mar. 1989.

Lefebvre, Marcel Francois (1905–91) Born at Tourcoing, in northern France, Archbishop Lefebvre was ordained a Catholic priest in 1929. He then joined the Holy Ghost Fathers, a missionary order, and from 1932 to 1960 was in Africa; he was archbishop of Dakar from 1955 to 1962. Lefebvre emerged as a leading Catholic conservative after being named to the preparatory commission for the Second Vatican Council by Pope John XXIII. This council, the most liberal in the modern history of his church, almost entirely rejected his proposals, instead introducing such departures as the modern non-Latin Mass, to him entirely unacceptable. He then went into sharp and highly visible opposition, denouncing the new Mass and other liberalizing moves, and in 1969 founding the conservative Fraternity of St. Pius X. Lefebvre was suspended in 1976 and reinstated in 1978. He decisively rejected a compromise solution offered by conservative Pope John Paul II in 1988. He then ordained four bishops, without the required approval of the Pope, triggering a threat of excommunication and beginning a major split in his church. A highly political figure, Lefebvre supported several figures on the Right, including Jean-Marie Le Pen, and was a monarchist. (d. Martigny, Switzerland; March 25, 1991)

FURTHER READING

Obituary. *Current Biography,* May 1991.
"Lefebvre was. . . ." PETER HEBBLETHWAITE. *National Catholic Reporter,* Apr. 5, 1991.
Obituary. *New York Times,* Mar. 26, 1991.
"By fielding four new bishops. . . ." WILLIAM PLUMMER. *People,* July 18, 1988.
"Quo Vadis. . . ?" WILLIAM D. DINGES. *America,* June 11, 1988.

Le Gallienne, Eva (1899–1991) London-born Le Gallienne made her London stage debut in *Monna Vanna* in 1914 and her Broadway debut in *Mrs. Botany's Daughters* in 1917. Her breakthrough role was on Broadway, as Julie in *Liliom* (1921), followed by a second starring role, in *The Swan* (1923). She made a special place for herself in American theater history with her pioneering noncommercial Civic Repertory Theater; from 1926 to 1933, at the 14th Street Theater, she presented a wide range of classic and new plays in repertory and at very low ticket prices, and starred in such roles as her memorable *Peter Pan* and *Alice in Wonderland.* Ultimately, lack of money forced her to close the theater and she returned to Broadway, playing largely in the classics during the balance of the 1930s and into the 1940s. She co-founded the American Repertory Theater (1946–48) and later directed and acted in the National Repertory Company (1961–66). She continued to appear on stage through the 1970s, most notably as *Mary Stuart,* on tour often in the years 1957–62, and on Broadway in *The Royal Family* (1975). In 1982, at the age of 83, she directed a revival of *Alice in Wonderland,* appearing as the White Queen. Her films include *Prince of Players* (1955), *The Devil's Disciple* (1959), and *Resurrection* (1980), for which she won a Best Supporting Actress Oscar nomination. Her *With a Quiet Heart: An Autobiography* was published in 1953. (d. Weston, Connecticut; June 3, 1991)

FURTHER READING

Obituary. *Current Biography,* Aug. 1991.
Obituary. *Variety,* June 10, 1991.
Obituary. *The Times* (of London), June 10, 1991.
Obituary. *New York Times,* June 5, 1991.
Eva Le Gallienne: A Bio-Bibliography. ROBERT A. SCHANKE. Greenwood, 1989.

Lemmon, Jack (John Lemmon III, 1925–) Oscar-winning actor Lemmon played in several new and forthcoming films during 1991. Starring roles late in his career were somewhat further apart, but he drew audience and critical attention in anything he did. One such was his cameo as Jack Martin in Oliver Stone's *JFK,* playing side by side with Ed Asner as Guy Bannister. Forthcoming was a starring role in the James Foley film *Glengarry Glen Ross,* in a cast that includes Al Pacino, Alec Baldwin, Alan Arkin, Jonathan Pryce, Kevin Spacy, and Ed Harris. David Mamet wrote the screen adaptation of his play. Also forthcoming was an appearance in the Robert Altman film *The Player,* in a cast that includes a good many Hollywood luminaries. Lemmon also issued a new album in 1991, his first in a quarter-century: *Jack Lemmon: Piano and Vocals,* with four new compositions by Lemmon; he also sang four of the songs in the album.

Boston-born Lemmon played in early television and began his long film career by winning a Best Supporting Actor Oscar for his Ensign Pulver in *Mister Roberts* (1954). Nineteen years later, he won a Best Actor Oscar for *Save The Tiger* (1973). Among his other films, a few of the most notable were *Bell Book and Candle* (1958), *Some Like It Hot* (1959), *The Apartment* (1960), *Days of Wine and Roses* (1962), *Irma La Douce* (1963), *The Odd Couple* (1968), *The Prisoner of Second Avenue* (1975), *The China Syndrome* (1978), *Missing* (1981), *Mass Appeal* (1984), and *Dad* (1989). Lemmon's B.A. and B.S. are from Harvard. He was formerly married to Cynthia Boyd Stone, married Felicia Farr in 1962, and has two children.

FURTHER READING

"Lemmon, Jack." *Current Biography,* Aug. 1988.
"Jack of all trades." BURT PRELUTSKI. *American Film,* Mar. 1988.
Actors: A Celebration. RITA GAM. St. Martin's, 1988.
The Films of Jack Lemmon. JOE BALTAKE. State Mutual, 1987.
Jack Lemmon. MICHAEL FREEDLAND. St. Martin's, 1985.

LeMond, Greg (1961–) American bicyclist LeMond was in the unusual position of also-ran in cycling's most important race, the Tour de France, in July 1991. In his six previous appearances in the three-week, 22-stage race, he had won three times and never finished lower than third. But in the 2,462-mile 1991 race, hampered by a viral infection, the defending champion acknowledged days before the end that he could not win, though with an extraordinary effort in the last stage he pulled ahead of Andy Hampsten into seventh place, to finish as the top American in the race.

In February 1991, LeMond was awarded the Jesse Owens International Trophy in New York City. In May—racing as usual with France's famed Z team—he also cycled the Tour Du Pont (formerly the Tour de Trump), a 1,125-mile, 12-day, 11-stage ride through Virginia, Delaware, Maryland, and Pennsylvania, coming in second in the final stage and twelfth overall. In late 1990 and early 1991, he encountered some health problems and was forced to cancel or pull out of several races.

California-born, Nevada-raised LeMond was a leading amateur cyclist before turning professional in 1980, then quickly beginning to win the series of races that established him as one of the world's top cyclists. He first won the Tour de France in 1986; then, after a 1987 hunting accident that almost killed him and kept him out of racing for two years, made an extraordinary comeback to win it again in 1989 and 1990. LeMond married Kathy Morris in 1981; they have three children.

FURTHER READING

"Greg LeMond. . . ." HAL HIGDON. *Boys' Life,* June 1990.
Greg LeMond: Premier Cyclist. A. P. PORTER. Lerner, 1990.
LeMond: The Incredible Comeback of an American Hero. SAMUEL ABT. Random House, 1990.
"Struggling back." SAMUEL ABT. *New York Times Magazine,* June 5, 1988.
"No more Mr. Nice Guy. . . ." DAVID WALSH. *Bicycling,* Apr. 1988.

Leonard, Sugar Ray (Ray Charles Leonard, 1956–) A great boxer retired in February 1991—for the fifth time; this time, he says, for good. While still in the ring at Madison Square

Garden, after losing a contest for the World Boxing Council superwelterweight title, Leonard crossed to the opposite corner to congratulate opponent Terry Norris, and then announced "This is my last fight." Onlookers were not surprised, for Leonard had been thrashed as never before by his younger, faster opponent, who said of Leonard after the fight, "He's still my idol."

Leonard then turned to face the challenge of shaping the rest of his life, acknowledging that the task would not be easy. In March 1991, responding publicly to leaked stories about charges made by his ex-wife, Juanita, during 1990 divorce proceedings, Leonard admitted to using cocaine and drinking alcohol heavily from 1983 to 1986, when surgery for a detached retina left him in a deep depression, with his career in question. He said that his marriage had failed because of his behavior in that period and that he had halted his drug use (on his own, without a treatment program) because he wanted to be a better father to his two sons. He will not have to worry about money. Leonard has been one of sports' highest-paid athletes, with earnings estimated at over $90 million in his professional career, over half of that coming since 1987 when his fights have been shown on television on a highly profitable pay-per-view basis.

After winning the Olympic gold medal at Montreal in 1976, North Carolina-born Leonard turned professional in 1977 and won the World Boxing Council welterweight title in 1979, the World Boxing Association middleweight title in 1981, and the combined welterweight title in 1981. He then retired, after 1982 eye surgery, but returned to win the World Boxing Council middleweight title in 1987 and the World Boxing Council light heavyweight title in 1988. He fought Thomas Hearns to a draw in June 1989, and then in December 1989 decisively beat Roberto Duran in Las Vegas, though it took 60 stitches to close up his cuts. He married Juanita Wilkinson in 1980; they divorced in 1990. They had two children; Ray Leonard, Jr., at age eight, became a Junior Golden Gloves champion.

FURTHER READING

"So long, Sugar. . . ." PAT PUTNAM. *Sports Illustrated,* Feb. 18, 1991.

"The world according to Ray." GARY SMITH. *Sports Illustrated,* Dec. 4, 1989.

"Leonard bashing." DAVID MILLER. *Sport,* Dec. 1989.

Sugar Ray Leonard: And Other Noble Warriors. SAM TOPEROFF. McGraw-Hill, 1987.

Sugar Ray Leonard. CAROLYN GLOECKNER. Crestwood House, 1985.

Sports Star: Sugar Ray Leonard. S. H. BURCHARD. Harcourt Brace, 1983.

Sugar Ray Leonard. JAMES HASKINS. Lothrop, 1982.

Sugar Ray Leonard: The Baby-Faced Boxer. BERT ROSENTHAL. Childrens, 1982.

A Fistful of Sugar: The Sugar Ray Leonard Story. ALAN GOLDSTEIN. Putnam, 1981.

Levinson, Barry L. (1932–) Hollywood director Levinson scored another major success in 1991, with *Bugsy,* a Christmas season release. Written by James Toback, the film starred Warren Beatty in the title role, as the New York Gangster, Bugsy Siegel, who went west and ultimately founded the gambling complex at Las Vegas, in a cast that included several other Hollywood stars as characters from life—among them Annette Bening as Virginia Hill, Ben Kingsley as Meyer Lansky, Joe Mantegna as George Raft, and Bill Graham as Lucky Luciano. The film was critically acclaimed, and at year's end seemed also headed for commercial success, although there was still some question as to how much. By then, Levinson had been voted best director by the Los Angeles Film Critics and the National Board of Review, and nominated for best director at the Golden Globe awards. The Los Angeles critics had voted *Bugsy* best film, and honored Toback for the best screenplay. The film and those associated with it had been voted eight Golden Globe nominations. Forthcoming for Levinson as producer was the film *Wilder Napalm,* scheduled for 1992 release.

Baltimore-born Levinson worked as a writer and comedian in television, and as a screenplay writer, before turning to directing feature films. His early screenplays include *Silent Movie* (1976) and *High Anxiety* (both co-written with Mel Brooks), *And Justice for All* (1979), *Inside Moves* (1980), and *Best Friends* (1982). He made his directorial debut with the well-received *Diner* (1982), and went on to direct and in some instances co-write such films as *The Natural* (1984), *Good Morning Vietnam* (1987), *Tin Men* (1987), *Rain Man* (1988), for which he won a Best Director Oscar, and *Avalon* (1990). In 1990 he published *Avalon, Tin Men, and Diner: Three Screenplays.* Levinson attended American University.

FURTHER READING

"Storyteller." GAVIN SMITH. *Film Comment,* Nov.–Dec. 1990.
"Baltimore, my Baltimore. . . ." BEN YAGODA. *American Film,* Nov. 1990.
"Levinson, Barry." *Current Biography,* July 1990.
"Barry in Baltimore." ALEX WARD. *New York Times Magazine,* Mar. 11, 1990.

Li Peng (1928–) Chinese Premier Li Peng, officially China's first leader but in fact second to Deng Xiaoping, continued to encounter massive economic and political problems during 1991. As leader of the Communist Party's conservative faction in the late 1980s and early 1990s, he had been the central figure in the triumph of the conservatives in 1989, with the accompanying Tiananmen Square massacre of student demonstrators on June 4, 1989. But afterward, as premier, he encountered the same kinds of severe economic problems that had caused Deng in the 1980s to move away from the unworkable centralized command economy now being reestablished. In his report to the March National Peoples Congress, Li listed a series of problems—low productivity, low quality, waste, and poor morale—that the 1980s move toward a more market-oriented economy had started to correct. And so Li—and Deng—once again faced the impossible question of how to develop a competitive modern economy and still entirely repress the Chinese people.

Li also faced the new freedom of the peoples of the Soviet Union—for the Chinese leadership a frightening development occurring immediately to the north, along the whole long border between the two countries—and with it a possible new infusion into China of the virus of democracy. Li held the line, though, making no serious democratic concessions and reacting very adversely to Western attempts to raise human rights abuse questions. He sharply rejected the comments of British Prime Minister John Major during his September visit to China, and of U.S. Secretary of State James Baker during his November visit, while at the same time trying to restore badly damaged trade links with the West.

Li Peng began his long, steady rise in the Chinese Communist bureaucracy as a young protegé of Premier Zhou En-lai. He emerged as a major figure in the 1980s, as minister of Power in 1981 and as a Politburo member in 1985. In the late 1980s, as great tension developed between the liberal and conservative wings of the Chinese leadership, he became a conservative faction leader. Li attended the Moscow Power Institute. He married Zhu Lin in 1958; the couple have three children.

FURTHER READING

Tiananmen Square. SCOTT SIMMIE and BOB NIXON. University of Washington Press, 1989.
"Li Peng." *Current Biography,* Nov. 1988.

Lithgow, John Arthur (1945–) Further displaying his very wide range, Lithgow appeared in a diverse group of films during 1991. In February he starred as badman Earl Talbot Blake, opposite Denzel Washington as police officer Nick Styles in Russell Mulcahy's thriller *Ricochet.* In December, he starred as fundamentalist missionary Leslie Huben in Hector Babenco's *At Play in the Fields of the Lord,* set in a South American jungle, in a cast that included Tom Berenger, Daryl Hannah, Aidan Quinn, Kathy Bates, and Tom Waits. On television, he starred opposite James Woods in the television film *The Boys,* about two long-term friends who face a terminal illness together. Forthcoming was a starring role opposite Lolita Davidovich in Brian De Palma's *Raising Cain.*

Rochester-born Lithgow began playing substantial roles on the New York stage in the early 1970s, in such plays as *The Changing Room* (1972), *Beyond Therapy* (1982), *Requiem for a Heavyweight* (1985), and *M. Butterfly* (1988). His most notable films include *The World According to Garp* (1982; he received an Oscar nomination), *Terms of Endearment* (1983; a second Oscar nomination), *The Manhattan Project* (1986), and *Memphis Belle* (1990). He has also appeared in several television films, including *The Day After* (1983) and *Amazing Stories* (1987; he won an Emmy). Lithgow is a 1967 Harvard graduate and also attended the London Academy of Music and Dramatic Art. He has been married twice, last to Mary Yeager in 1981, and has two children.

FURTHER READING

"John Lithgow. . . ." MEGAN ROSENFELD. *American Baby,* Aug. 1988.

Lloyd Webber, Andrew (1948–) Very successful composer and producer Lloyd Webber sold 30 percent of his Really Useful Holdings company to Polygram, a Dutch record company in August 1991, in a transaction reportedly worth at least $132 million, in the process extending his own contract with the company until the year 2003 and expanding it to cover his film and television work. Although most of his many productions, including *Cats, Starlight Express,* and *Phantom of the Opera,* continued to play and tour very successfully, the worldwide recession caught up with him, as with so may others. In February, he closed his New York production of *Aspects of Love,* starring his former wife, Sarah Brightman, after 377 performances, shorter than any other Lloyd Webber Broadway run. He also closed the failed, very expensive comedy *La Bete* after 24 performances, with a reported loss of $2 million. Forthcoming were the film version of *Evita,* with Madonna in the title role; an as-yet-unnamed movie musical; and a new night-time water spectacular, *Noah's Ark,* for Disney World, in Orlando, Florida, with an original symphonic score for the pageant.

Lloyd Webber emerged as a leading musical theater composer in 1968, with *Joseph and the Amazing Technicolor Dreamcoat,* lyrics by Tim Rice; he then wrote the trailblazing rock opera *Jesus Christ Superstar* (1970), with lyrics again by Rice. Lloyd Webber won Tonys for the musicals *Evita* and *Cats.* His compositions also include a *Requiem Mass* (1975) and *Variations on a Theme by Paganini* (1977), as well as the film scores for *Gumshoe* (1971), *Jesus Christ Superstar* (1973), and *The Odessa File* (1974). Lloyd Webber attended Oxford University and the Royal Academy of Music. He married fashion entrepreneur Madeleine Gurdon in 1991. He has been married twice before, until 1990 to singer-actress Sarah Brightman, and has two children. He is the brother of cellist Julian Lloyd Webber.

FURTHER READING

"Andrew Lloyd Webber leaves. . . ." Tom Gliatto. *People,* July 23, 1990.
Andrew Lloyd Webber: His Life and Works. Michael Walsh. Abrams, 1989.
"The changing face of Broadway. . . ." Marilyn Stasio. *Life,* Feb. 1988.
"Magician of the musical. . . ." Michael Walsh. *Time,* Jan. 18, 1988.
"Andrew Lloyd Webber. . . ." John Rockwell. *New York Times Magazine,* Dec. 20, 1987.

Lourié, Eugené (1901–91) Kharkov-born Lourié left his native Russia for France in 1921, and in the early 1920s began his six-decades-long career as a film set designer and art director; in the early years, he also worked with the Ballets Russes, painted, and did costuming for films. In the 1930s, he emerged as a leading French film art director and set designer, working most notably with Jean Renoir on such classic films as *Grand Illusion* (1937) and *The Rules of the Game* (1939). Emigrating to the United States in 1941, he continued to work in Hollywood with Renoir, on such films as *The Southerner* (1945), *The Diary of a Chambermaid* (1946), and *The River* (1951), with Charles Chaplin on *Limelight* (1952), and in a wide range of other films, though later in his career he found fewer opportunities to work on major films. His memoir was the book *My Work in Films* (1985). He was survived by his wife, Laure, and a daughter (d. Woodland Hills, California; May 26, 1991)

FURTHER READING

Obituary. *Variety,* June 19, 1991.
Obituary. *The Times* (of London), June 16, 1991.

Lu Gwei-Djen (1904–91) A Chinese biochemist who became one of the world's leading historians of science, Lu was educated in China, at Ginling College and as a clinical pathologist at Peking Union Medical College. She taught and was a research fellow at St. Johns University in Shanghai until the mid-1930s, leaving China in 1937 to take her doctorate at Cambridge. After working in nutritional biochemistry in the United States, she returned to China in 1946, worked with Joseph Needham and taught nutritional biochemistry at Ginling, and then left China to work with UNESCO in Paris. She then joined Needham at Cambridge in the great work of both their lives, the massive multivolume series *Science and Civilization in China,* and in several smaller related works. She also was largely responsible for the development of the East Asian History of Science Library and Research Centre at Cambridge, and was associate director of the center. She and Dr. Needham married in 1990, after the death of his first wife, with whom Lu had been associated since their student days together at Cambridge in the 1930s. She is survived by Dr. Needham.

FURTHER READING

Obituary. *The Times* (of London), Dec. 3, 1991.

Luke, Keye (1904–91) Canton-born Luke grew up in Seattle and worked as a visual artist in the film industry before making his 1934 acting debut in *The Painted Veil.* He played Chan's Number 1 son in the long series of 1930s and 1940s *Charlie Chan* films, and also played in such films as *Oil for the Lamps of China* (1935) and *The Good Earth* (1937), appearing in more than 100 films, often in stereotypical "Chinese" roles. Later in his career, he appeared in the far more satisfying role of the teacher in the television series "Kung Fu" (1972–75) and in a wide range of other television roles. Most recently, he played Dr. Yang in Woody Allen's *Alice* (1990). He was survived by a daughter. (d. Whittier, California; January 12, 1991)

FURTHER READING

Obituary. *Variety,* Jan. 21, 1991.
Obituary. *New York Times,* Jan. 16, 1991.

Luria, Salvador Edward (1912–91) Born in Turin, Luria, who was Jewish, fled fascist Italy for Paris in 1938, and emigrated to the United States in 1940. Trained in radiology, he became a leading research biologist. He shared a 1969 Nobel Prize for his work in genetics, which was central to the development of molecular biology. He taught at Indiana University from 1943 to 1959, and at the Massachusetts Institute of Technology (M.I.T.) from 1959 until his death. Luria was a founder and from 1972 to 1985 director of the M.I.T. Center for Cancer Research. He wrote several works, some technical, others for general audiences; these included *Life: The Unfinished Experiment* (1973), which won a National Book Award, and *A Slot Machine, a Broken Test Tube: An Autobiography* (1985). Luria was committed to several social causes, including the control of nuclear power, and was publicly opposed to the Vietnam War and later to several other American military involvements. In 1969, he was blacklisted by the U.S. National Institutes of Health. He was survived by his wife, Zella Hurwitz Luria, and a son. (d. Lexington, Massachusetts; February 6, 1991)

FURTHER READING

Obituary. *Current Biography,* Apr. 1991
Obituary. *New York Times,* Feb. 7, 1991.

Lynch, David (1946–) Lynch's offbeat television series "Twin Peaks" was canceled and then briefly revived in the spring of 1991. It did poorly in the ratings, though, and was once again canceled, this time permanently. But the highly regarded director was not daunted; after a series of negotiations and rumors, he struck a three-picture deal with French entrepreneur Francis Bouygues, whose CIBY 2000 was set to co-produce and finance a full-length theatrical film, *Twin Peaks—Fire Walk with Me* as a sequel to the television series, with most of the original cast in place, including Kyle MacLachlan as Agent Dale Cooper. Filming began in early September. The second Lynch–CIBY 2000 project was scheduled to begin in the spring of 1992. Lynch's earlier work was very much on view in 1991, as *Wild at Heart* moved from theatrical release to the home screen. In addition, *Eraserhead* was scheduled for re-release by Miramar Pictures.

Montana-born Lynch directed four films before 1990: *Eraserhead* (1977); *The Elephant Man* (1980), adapted from the stage play; the science fiction *Dune* (1984); and *Blue Velvet* (1986), a film about American small-town life that is widely regarded as an earlier approach to the themes of his recent works. With the April 1990 premiere of his offbeat nighttime soap opera television series "Twin Peaks," Lynch suddenly emerged as a major director and also as a highly publicized media figure. Lynch's next large work was the film *Wild at Heart* (1990), which starred Nicolas Cage and Laura Dern; the film won the grand prize at the Cannes Film Festival, although it was not as well received in the United States. Lynch attended the Corcoran School of Art, the Boston Museum School of Fine Arts, and the Pennsylvania Academy of Fine Arts. He has been married twice and has two children.

FURTHER READING

"You are now leaving. . . ." STEVE POND and MARCIA COBURN. *Playboy,* Feb. 1991.
"Weird America." JOSEPH SOBRAN. *National Review,* Oct. 1, 1990.
"Czar of Bizarre. . . ." RICHARD CORLISS. *Time,* Oct. 1, 1990.
"The Rolling Stone interview. . . ." DAVID BRESKIN. *Rolling Stone,* Sep. 6, 1990.
"David Lynch." JIM JEROME. *People,* Sep. 3, 1990.
"David Lynch." JOHN CLARK. *Premiere,* Sep. 1990.
"Lynch-time." BART BILL. *Vogue,* Feb. 1990.

Lynes, Joseph Russell, Jr. (1910–91) Massachusetts-born Lynes, a writer and editor who in the 1950s became known as a leading American tastemaker, began the publishing aspect of his career soon after his 1932 graduation from Yale, as an assistant at Harper Brothers from 1932 to 1936, and publications director at Vassar from 1936 to 1937. He taught from 1937 to 1944, then joined Harper's Magazine as an assistant editor. From 1947 to 1967, he was managing editor at Harper's. This was the period of his greatest popularity, in which he wrote such widely circulated books as *Highbrow, Middlebrow* (1949), *Snobs* (1950), *Guests* (1951), *The Tastemakers* (1954), and the essays published as *A Surfeit of Honey* (1957). Among his later publications were *The Lively Audience: A Social History of the Visual & Performing Arts in America, 1890–1950* (1985), and *Life in the Slow Lane: Observations on Art, Architecture, Manners, and Other Such Spectator Sports* (1991). He was survived by his wife, the former Mildred Akin, a daughter, and a son. (d. New York City; September 14, 1991)

FURTHER READING

Obituary. *New York Times,* Sep. 16, 1991.

M

McCain, John Sidney, III (1936–) Arizona Republican Senator McCain, himself a six-year North Vietnamese prisoner-of-war (POW), continued his long campaign for a Vietnam War POW accounting in 1991; his efforts included a January trip to Hanoi. A strong supporter of the Bush administration during the Persian Gulf War, he voted for the January 12 war resolution and went on to defend U.S. war prisoners who appeared on Iraqi broadcasts, stating that anything they said against the United States was surely due to "physical beatings and other abuse."

On February 27, 1991, after 14 months of hearings, the Senate Ethics Committee dropped the charges of wrongdoing against McCain in the case of the "Keating Five," which had clouded his career for several years. The committee stated that McCain had been guilty of nothing worse than "exercising poor judgment." In early March, McCain announced that he would pay into the Treasury the $112,000 in campaign contributions he had received from Charles H. Keating, Jr. The combination of dropped charges and repayment of contributions seemed to go far to rehabilitate McCain in the eyes of his constituents as he faced his 1992 reelection campaign.

McCain is a much-decorated career naval officer, who fought in Vietnam and was a North Vietnamese prisoner of war (1967–73). He was later based in Washington (1977–81), leaving the Navy as a captain. Turning to politics, he became a two-term Arizona Republican congressman (1982–86), and began his senatorial term in 1987. He graduated from the Naval Academy in 1958 and attended the National War College (1973–74). He married Cindy Hensley in 1980; the couple have six children.

FURTHER READING

"Seven sorry senators. . . ." MARGARET CARLSON. *Times,* Jan. 8, 1990.

"McCain, John Sidney 3d." *Current Biography,* Feb. 1989.

McCarthy, John: See **Lebanon Hostages**

McCartney, Paul (1942–) One of the highlights of 1991 was the premiere of McCartney's first classical work, the 97-minute *Liverpool Oratorio,* presented on June 28, 1991, by the Royal Liverpool Philharmonic at the Liverpool Anglican Cathedral. The orchestra had commissioned the work, a collaboration between McCartney and U.S. conductor and composer Carl Davis. Davis conducted the orchestra, its chorus, the cathedral boys' choir, and group of soloists that included soprano Kiri Te Kanawa and tenor Jerry Hadley, before an audience of 2,500 in the cathedral. A record of the work was done for autumn release, and a documentary was filmed. The *Oratorio* opened in the United States at Carnegie Hall on November 18, 1991.

In a more popular vein, *Get Back,* a concert film drawn from his 1989–90 concert tour, opened in New York City in October; it was directed by Richard Lester. Another concert film, this one of a charity show in Liverpool, was televised as *Paul McCartney: Going Home.* He also issued *Unplugged–The Official Bootleg Album,* as a limited-edition album of performances on "MTV Unplugged" in an attempt to pre-empt unauthorized copying. Another 1991 release was *Choba b CCCP: The Russian Album,* a collection of off-the-cuff performances of rock classics that had been recorded in 1987; 14 cuts had been released in the Soviet Union in 1988. In May, he also recorded "Mary Had a Little Lamb" on the benefit album *For Our Children* for the Pediatric AIDS Foundation.

Linda and Paul McCartney continued to act on environmental issues during 1991, as in their purchase of 80 acres in Somerset, England, as a gift to the League Against Cruel Sports, to add to the League's 2,300 acres of sanctuaries for deer and other hunted animals. They also took their vegetarian beliefs into the marketplace, in May introducing a line of frozen vegetarian products as an alternative to meat dishes.

Liverpool native McCartney is a major figure in popular music; from 1960 to 1970, with John Lennon, George Harrison, and Ringo Starr, he was a member of the Beatles, as rhythm guitarist and then bass guitarist. He and John Lennon wrote a great many of the Beatles' songs, and he was often the group's lead singer. In 1970, he went on his own, and in 1971 formed Wings; for the next two decades he continued to compose, perform, and record for worldwide audiences. In 1989, he went on the road for the first time in 13 years, playing to record-setting audiences on a world tour, which also produced a live album, *Tripping the Live Fantastic,* released in November 1990. In 1984, McCartney published *Give My Regards to Broad Street.* He married Linda Eastman in 1969; they have four children.

FURTHER READING

"Paul McCartney." Tom Mulhern. *Guitar Player,* July 1991.
Blackbird: The Life and Times of Paul McCartney. Geoffrey Giuliano. NAL-Dutton, 1991.
Strange Days: The Music of John, Paul, George and Ringo Twenty Years On. Walter Podrazik. Popular Culture, 1991.
Yesterday: The Biography of a Beatle. Chet Flippo. Doubleday, 1988.
It Was Twenty Years Ago Today. Derek Taylor. Simon & Schuster, 1987.
McCartney: The Definitive Biography. Chris Salewicz. St. Martin's, 1986.
The Beatles, 2nd ed. Hunter Davies. McGraw-Hill, 1985.
Yesterday . . . Came Suddenly: The Definitive History of the Beatles. Bob Cepican and Waleed Ali. Morrow, 1984.
Paul McCartney: In His Own Words. Paul Gambaccini. Putnam, 1983.
Paul McCartney. Alan Hamilton. Trafalgar Square, 1983.

McCone, John Alex (1902–91) San Francisco-born McCone, an engineer, became a steel company executive in the late 1920s, and in 1937 was a founder of what by the early 1940s was the large international engineering firm Bechtel-McCone. During World War II, he also became president of the California Ship Building Company, and after the war was also owner and president of Hendy International. His government service began as a Truman administration Air Policy Board appointee in 1947; in 1948, he became a special deputy to James V. Forrestal, the secretary of defense, in that position helping to create the Central Intelligence Agency (CIA); and in 1950–51 he was an Air Force under secretary. He undertook several special missions during the 1950s. He was head of the Atomic Energy Commission from 1958 to 1960, leaving that body at the end of the Eisenhower administration, but he was brought back to Washington in 1961 by President John F. Kennedy, replacing Allan Dulles as head of the CIA after the disastrous Bay of Pigs invasion.

McCone played a major intelligence role during the 1962 Cuban Missile Crisis. He resigned from the CIA and left government service in 1965. During the 1970s, congressional investigating committees developed testimony alleging that during his CIA tenure the agency had engaged in large-scale illegal wiretapping of American citizens and had developed assassination plots against Fidel Castro and Patrice Lumumba, among others. McCone denied any knowledge of such acts, and also denied charges that he had as a corporate director during the 1970s offered money to help bring down Chile's Allende government. He was married twice, and is survived by a sister, three stepdaughters, and two stepsons. (d. Pebble Beach, California; February 14, 1991)

FURTHER READING

Obituary. *Current Biography,* Apr. 1991.
Obituary. *The Times* (of London), Feb. 8, 1991.
Obituary. *New York Times,* Feb. 6, 1991.
Friends in High Places: The Bechtel Story. LATON McCARTNEY. Simon & Schuster, 1988.

McIntyre, John (1907–91) Spokane-born McIntyre, a leading character actor who appeared in hundreds of radio, movie, and television roles, began his acting career in radio, and emerged as a substantial character actor in films and television from the early 1950s. He was best known for his long run in television's "Wagon Train" series, playing wagonmaster Chris Hale from 1961 to 1965. On screen, he played major character roles in such films as *The Asphalt Jungle* (1950), *Winchester '73* (1950), *The Far Country* (1955), *The Tin Star* (1957), *Psycho* (1960), *Elmer Gantry* (1960), *Summer and Smoke* (1962), and *Rooster Cogburn* (1975). He also appeared on television in the series "Naked City" (1959) and "The Virginian" (1967–69), in the latter appearing with his wife, Jeannette Nolan, who survives him, along with a daughter. (d. Pasadena, California; January 30, 1991)

FURTHER READING

Obituary. *New York Times,* Feb. 1, 1991.

McIntyre, Joseph: See **New Kids on the Block**

McKellen, Ian (1939–) British actor McKellen won his country's highest acting honor—the Olivier Award or "Larry"—for the fifth time in 1991, for his performance in the title role of Shakespeare's *Richard III.* With the Royal National Theatre, he had taken the production and *King Lear* on a six-month world tour, including Japan and Eastern Europe, during mid-1991, before returning to perform in London. In November 1991, McKellen and director Richard Eyre visited New York City to prepare for their U.S. tour, starting in June at the Brooklyn Academy of Music (BAM).

Earlier in 1991, McKellen had been offered a knighthood and decided to accept it, becoming Sir Ian. The honor was especially notable because he had been openly working on behalf of gay rights in Britain since announcing his own homosexuality on a BBC program three years earlier. Some fellow gay activists criticized him for accepting the honor from a Conservative government they felt was anti-gay. But he was defended by many other gay artists, who felt that the honor "was a significant landmark in the history of the British gay movement," as 18 of them, including John Schlesinger, Cameron Mackintosh, Simon Callow, Ned Sherrin, and Alec McCowen stated in an open letter to *The Guardian.*

Also in 1991 McKellen was Cameron Mackintosh professor of contemporary theatre at Oxford University. The chair was endowed in 1989 by Mackintosh, producer of hits such as *Cats, Les Miserables,* and *Phantom of the Opera;* his successor in the post is Alan Ayckbourn, starting in 1992.

A leading British actor since the early 1960s, McKellen has played on stage in a wide range of leading roles. He made his stage debut in 1961, joined the National Theatre Company in 1965, made his Broadway debut in 1966 in *The Promise,* and was a founder of the Actor's Company in 1972. His debut with the Royal Shakespeare Company came in 1974, with his *Dr. Faustus.* He further developed his international reputation with *Bent* (1979) and with *Amadeus* (1980), for which he won a Tony on Broadway. He toured in his one-man show *Acting Shakespeare* in 1984, played in a series of major roles with the National Theatre during the 1980s, and was an associate director of the National Theatre (1984–86). His films include *Alfred the Great* (1965), *Plenty* (1985), and *Scandal* (1988). He has also appeared often on television.

FURTHER READING

"McKellen. . . ." JACK PITMAN. *Variety,* Jan. 7, 1991.

McKissick, Floyd (1922–91) A leading civil rights activist of the 1950s and 1960s, McKissick began his civil rights work with a nonviolent integrated bus journey through the then-segregated South, led by James Farmer, founder of the Congress of Racial Equality (CORE). In 1951, McKissick applied for admission to the then all-White University of North Carolina Law School, and was refused admission because of his race. Thurgood Marshall, at that time head of the legal staff of the National Association for the Advancement of Colored People (NAACP), won his admission at the Court of Appeals stage. Later, as a lawyer, McKissick handled many desegregation cases. McKissick moved away from nonviolence in the mid-1960s; in 1966, when he succeeded James Farmer as director of CORE, he called for Black Power, rather than a Black-White civil rights alliance, and fostered the tactics of violent confrontation. During the 1972 presidential election, he supported Richard M. Nixon and changed his party affiliation to Republican. For the balance of the 1970s, he devoted much of his time to the unsuccessful Soul City project in North Carolina. In June 1990, he was appointed a North Carolina state district judge. He was survived by his wife, the former Evelyn Williams; his son and law partner Floyd McKissick, Jr.; three daughters, and three sisters. (d. Durham, North Carolina; April 28, 1991)

FURTHER READING

Obituary. *Current Biography,* June 1991.
"Judge Floyd McKissick. . . ." *Jet,* May 13, 1991.
Obituary. *New York Times,* Apr. 30, 1991

MacLaine, Shirley (Shirley MacLean Beaty, 1934–) MacLaine won yet another Golden Globe nomination, for 1991's best supporting actress, for her role as a Hollywood mother to Meryl Streep's actress daughter in the film *Postcards from the Edge* (1990). The MacLaine nomination and Streep's Best Actress Os-

car nomination helped to build the film's successful theatrical run, followed by an even more successful home video run. In November 1991, MacLaine published another autobiographical work, *Dance While You Can,* which focused less than some of her other works on spiritual questions and such matters as reincarnation, and more on her life, motives, and family relationships, with her daughter, mother, father, and brother. Forthcoming were a starring role in the film *Used People,* with Jessica Tandy, Kathy Bates, Marcello Mastroianni, and Marcia Gay Harden; and possibly a film based on the life of Louise Brooks.

Virginia-born MacLaine, the sister of actor Warren Beatty, became a Hollywood star in the 1960s, with such light films as *The Apartment* (1960), *Two for the Seesaw* (1962), *Irma La Douce* (1963), and *Sweet Charity* (1969). Later in her career, she became a leading dramatic actress, in such films as *The Turning Point* (1977), *Being There* (1979), *Terms of Endearment* (1983), for which she won a Best Actress Oscar, *Madame Souszatska* (1988), *Steel Magnolias* (1989), *Waiting for the Light* (1990), and *Postcards from the Edge* (1990). She also produced, co-directed, and appeared in the documentary film *The Other Half of the Sky: A China Memoir* (1975), and has written several very popular books, including *Many Happy Returns* (1984), *Dancing in the Light* (1985), and *Don't Fall off the Mountain* (1987). She was previously married and has one child.

FURTHER READING

"Write while you can. . . ." BILL GOLDSTEIN. *Publishers Weekly,* Aug. 8, 1991.
"The real MacLaine." NANCY COLLINS and ANNIE LEIBOVITZ. *Vanity Fair,* Mar. 1991.
"Shirley MacLaine lives." PAT DOWELL. *Washingtonian,* Oct. 1988.
Shirley MacLaine and the New Age of Movement. JAMES W. SIRE. Inter-Varsity, 1988.
Shirley MacLaine. MICHAEL FREEDLAND. Salem House, 1986.
Shirley MacLaine. ROY PICKARD. Hippocrene, 1985.
The Films of Shirley MacLaine. CHRISTOPHER DENIS. Carol, 1982.

McMillan, Edwin Mattison (1907–91) California-born McMillan, a leading U.S. physicist, was a pioneer researcher in atomic physics, from 1932 working with Dr. Ernest O. Lawrence and his newly invented cyclotron at the University of California at Berkeley. McMillan taught physics at the university (1935–73), then becoming an emeritus professor. But his main work was in research. He was co-discoverer of oxygen-15 in 1934, and he and Philip Abelson in 1940 discovered neptunium, the 93rd element and the first element beyond those in the naturally occurring 92-element periodic table. His work led directly to Glenn Seaborg's 1941 discovery of plutonium, the essential component of the atomic bomb. McMillan and Seaborg shared the 1951 Nobel Prize in chemistry for this work. McMillan was also a key developer of the U.S. atomic bomb, dropped on Hiroshima and Nagasaki in 1945, and ushering in the fear-filled period then called the Nuclear Age. He was later to express grave concerns about the use of his discoveries.

After World War II, McMillan focused on the development of accelerators as tools of research in physics and invented the Synchrotron, his work parallel with that of Russian physicist Vladimir I. Vekslov, with whom he shared the 1963 Atoms for Peace Prize. He later was awarded the National Medal of Science. McMillan was head of the Lawrence Laboratory (1958–73). He was survived by his wife, Elsie, a daughter, and two sons. (d. El Cerrito, California; September 7, 1991)

FURTHER READING

Obituary. *The Times* (of London), Sep. 10, 1991.
Obituary. *New York Times,* Sep. 10, 1991

MacMurray, Fred (Frederick Martin MacMurray, 1908–91) Versatile film and television star MacMurray began his career as a musician, in the late 1920s, and went on to appear in several musical theater roles before beginning his long Hollywood career in 1934. He quickly became one of the leading stars of Hollywood's Golden Age, playing comedy and drama equally well, in his breakthrough film, *Gilded Lady* (1935), such films as *Alice Adams* (1935), and *The Trail of the Lonesome Pine* (1936), and in his two most notable dramatic roles, as the murderer in *Double Indemnity* (1944) and as Lieutenant Kiefer in *The Caine Mutiny* (1954). Late in his career, he became a very familiar face on home screens as the star of the long-running series "My Three Sons" (1960–72), and in movie theaters as the star of a series of Disney films. He was survived by his wife, the actress June Haver, three daughters, and a son. (d. Santa Monica, California; November 5, 1991)

FURTHER READING

Obituary. MARK GOODMAN. *People,* Nov. 18, 1991.
Obituary. *Variety,* Nov. 11, 1991.
Obituary. *The Times* (of London), Nov. 7, 1991.
Obituary. *New York Times,* Nov. 6, 1991.

McPartland, Jimmy (James Dugald McPartland, 1907–91) Chicago-born McPartland, a cornetist and trumpeter, began his seven-decades-long musical career in 1922, a founder of Chicago's Austin High School Gang, a group of high school friends that included tenor saxophonist Bud Freeman. Resident at Friars Inn and working with Eddie Condon and other jazz musicians, the group played a key role in modifying New Orleans jazz, creating the new Chicago style. From the mid-1920s, McPartland played with the Wolverines and the Ben Pollack orchestra, recorded with Benny Goodman, and played in several Broadway pit bands. He led his own group (1936–41), briefly played with Jack Teagarden, and then served in the army during World War II. He met jazz pianist Marian Turner in 1944 while she was touring in Belgium; they married in 1945, and she then built her career as Marian McPartland, working with him until forming her own group in 1951. Beginning in the 1950s, McPartland also appeared as an actor in several musicals. He continued to play into his 80s. He was survived by his wife, Marian; they had been divorced in 1967, and remarried two weeks before his death. (d. Port Washington, New York; March 13, 1991)

FURTHER READING

Obituary. JOHN McDONOUGH. *Down Beat,* May 1991.
Obituary. *The Times* (of London), Mar. 20, 1991.
Obituary. *New York Times,* Mar. 14, 1991.
Voices of the Jazz Age: Profiles of Eight Vintage Jazzmen. CHIP DEFFAA. University of Illinois Press, 1990.

Madonna with Kathleen Turner (left) and Martha Graham (right).

Madonna (Madonna Louise Ciccone, 1958–) Highly visible entertainer Madonna continued to generate enormous media coverage throughout the year, perhaps most notably as the star of the exhibitionist documentary film *Truth or Dare,* filmed during her 1990 "Blond Ambition" concert tour. The film, which did well at the box office, emphasized her dominance of her company and entourage while on tour, along with her apparently much-desired lack of privacy. Along similar lines, her attendance at the Cannes Film Festival became one of the media events of the year. Madonna worked in two forthcoming films during the year: *Shadows and Fog,* which finished filming in July, but was not released until March 1992 because of Orion Pictures' financial problems; and Penny Marshall's *A League of Their Own,* scheduled for summer 1992 release. She was also reportedly set to star as *Evita* in the film version of the Andrew Lloyd Webber work, though her celebrity was such that she was also said to be interested in half a dozen other roles.

Michigan-born Madonna is one of the best-known celebrities of her time, in concert and with such albums as *Madonna* (1983), *Like a Virgin* (1983), *True Blue* (1986), *You Can Dance* (1987), and *Like A Prayer* (1989). She is also a competent actress, as demonstrated in such films as *Desperately Seeking Susan* (1985) and *Who's That Girl?* (1987) and her Broadway stage debut in *Speed-the-Plow* (1988). In 1990, she played Breathless Mahoney in Warren Beatty's *Dick Tracy,* which sparked her "Blond Ambition" international concert tour and the album *I'm Breathless* (1990); she also released a collection of her previous work, *The Immaculate Collection* (1990). Both albums spawned best-selling singles. Her video of "Justify My Love" was judged so steamy that MTV refused to air it; the single became an immediate best-seller. Madonna was formerly married to actor Sean Penn (1985–89). She attended the University of Michigan (1976–78).

FURTHER READING

Madonna: The Book. NORMAN KING. Morrow, 1992.
"The companies they keep." FRED GOODMAN. *Working Woman,* Dec. 1991.
"Madonna on TV." KURT LODER. *TV Guide,* Nov. 23, 1991.
"Madonna revealed." DOUGLAS THOMPSON. *Cosmopolitan,* Nov. 1991.
"Single sex and the girl. . . ." JOSEPH SOBRAN. *National Review,* Aug. 12, 1991.
"True confessions. . . ." CARRIE FISHER and STEVEN MEISEL. *Rolling Stone,* June 13 and 27, 1991. (Two parts)
"Madonna in bloom. . . ." CARL WAYNE ARRINGTON. *Time,* May 20, 1991.
"Unmasking. . . ." BRIAN D. JOHNSON. *Maclean's,* May 13, 1991.
"Madonna & Michael." STEVE DOUGHERTY. *People,* Apr. 15, 1991.
"The misfit." LYNN HIRSCHBERG and STEVEN MEISEL. *Vanity Fair,* Apr. 1991.
"Playgirl of the western world." MICHAEL KELLY. *Playboy,* Mar. 1991.
"Madonna. . . ." DONALD BRADBURN. *Dance,* Feb. 1991.
Madonna Revealed. DOUGLAS THOMPSON. Carol, 1991.
Madonna, Unauthorized. CHRISTOPHER ANDERSEN. Simon & Schuster, 1991.

Madonna: Her Complete Story. NAL-Dutton, 1991.
Madonna Superstar: Photographs. KAEL LAGERFELD. Norton, 1991.
Madonna. WILLIAM RUHLMANN. Smithmark, 1991.
Icons: Intimate Portraits. DENISE WORRELL. Atlantic Monthly, 1989.
Madonna, Spirit and Flesh. SHARON STARBOOKS. NAL-Dutton, 1985.
Madonna: Lucky Star. MICHAEL MCKENZIE. Contemporary, 1985.
Madonna. GORDON MATTHEWS. Simon & Schuster, 1985.
Madonna. PHILIP KAMIN. H. Leonard, 1985.

Mailer, Norman (1923–) The year 1991 saw the publication of *Harlot's Ghost,* Mailer's massive new 1,310-page novel, the fictional memoir of CIA agent Harry Hubbard, focusing on CIA plots, counterplots, and a considerable array of illegal and legal actions from 1948 to 1964, at the height of the Cold War. The book, which received mixed reviews, was the first of at least two; Mailer planned to begin work on a sequel in the summer of 1992, after finishing a brief biography of Pablo Picasso. During the book publicity period, Mailer strongly objected to an adverse review of the work by John Simon in the *New York Times;* he demanded and won the right to a highly publicized rebuttal, which was also printed by the *Times*.

New Jersey-born Mailer's World War II military service was the basis for his first published novel *The Naked and the Dead,* which launched him as a major writer. The book was later adapted into the 1958 Raoul Walsh film. Some of his best-known later novels included *Barbary Shore* (1951), *The Deer Park* (1955), *The American Dream* (1965), *The Executioner's Song* (1979; he was awarded a 1980 Pulitzer Prize), *Ancient Evenings* (1983), and *Tough Guys Don't Dance* (1983), which he adapted into the 1983 film and directed. An essayist and short story writer, his *Armies of the Night* (1968) won a Pulitzer Prize for nonfiction. He also won a 1969 National Book Award. Mailer was a co-founder of *The Village Voice* (1954), an editorial board member of the magazine *Dissent* (1953–69), and president of the American branch of PEN (1984–86). Mailer attended Harvard University. He has been married six times, most recently to Norris Church, and has six daughters and three sons.

FURTHER READING

"Patriarchs don't pummel." HELLE BERING-JENSEN. *Insight,* Oct. 18, 1991.
"Mailer's alpha and omega." TOBY THOMPSON. *Vanity Fair,* Oct. 1991.
"Stormin' Norman." CHRISTOPHER HITCHENS. *Vogue,* Oct. 1991.
"His punch is better. . . ." BONNIE ANGELO and PAUL GRAY. *Time,* Sep. 30, 1991.
"The old man and the novel." SCOTT SPENCER. *New York Times Magazine*. Sep. 22, 1991.
"Mailer and Vidal. . . ." CAROLE MALLORY. *Esquire,* May 1991.
The Lives of Norman Mailer: A Biography. CARL ROLLYSON. Paragon, 1991.
Radical Fictions and the Novels of Norman Mailer. NIGEL LEIGH. St. Martin's, 1990.
"Moonraker." TOM PIAZZA. *Omni,* July 1989.
Conversations with Norman Mailer. J. MICHAEL LENNON, ed. University Press of Mississippi, 1988.
Mailer's America. JOSEPH WENKE. University Press of New England, 1987.
Norman Mailer. HAROLD BLOOM, ed. Chelsea House, 1986.
Critical Essays on Norman Mailer. J. MICHAEL LENNON. G. K. Hall, 1986.
Mailer: His Life and Times. PETER MANSO. Simon & Schuster, 1985; Viking Penguin, 1985.
Norman Mailer Bibliography. B. A. SOKOLOFF. Bern Porter, 1985.

Major, John (1943–) British Prime Minister Major faced several critical questions during his first full year in office. Succeeding Margaret Thatcher on November 27, 1990, he

immediately found himself plunged into the Persian Gulf crisis, and in the run-up to the Persian Gulf War ground offensive. Major strongly supported the war, sending British heavy armor into the ground offensive when it came, to join the air and sea forces already in place. Virtually unknown on taking office, his popularity at home rose sharply with the victory in the Gulf. He also hosted the July Group of Seven London meeting, and spoke quickly and strongly against the aborted August Soviet coup, both actions helping to build his strength at home. He also very strongly supported European financial and political union, but ran into powerful opposition within his own party, led by Margaret Thatcher, and was forced to compromise his position somewhat.

At home, Major quickly canceled the enormously unpopular poll tax, in late autumn introducing a far more popular graduated set of property taxes. During 1991, Britain experienced a deepening and very serious recession, part of a worldwide economic slowdown. Autumn bank interest rate cuts, which came even earlier than expected, helped Major's popularity, but did little to restart the lagging British economy. With business leaders joining Labour in sharp criticism of government inaction, and powerful opposition also developing within his own party, Major faced substantial economic and political problems at home. Playing for time, he decided not to hold a general election until 1992.

London-born Major's first career was with Standard Chartered Bank (1965–79). He joined the Conservative Party in 1960, was a Lambeth Borough Councillor (1968–71), and became a member of Parliament in 1979, after two unsuccessful tries. His rise in the Thatcher government was very rapid; by 1985, he was a junior minister at the Department of Health, and by 1986 social security minister. He became treasury chief secretary in 1987, foreign secretary in July 1989, chancellor of the exchequer in October 1989, and then at 47 the youngest British prime minister of the 20th century. He married Norma Johnson in 1970; the couple have two children.

FURTHER READING

"Who's sitting pretty. . . ." *Business Week,* Mar. 11, 1991.
"Major player. . . ." Edward Pearce. *New Republic,* Jan. 21, 1991.
"After Thatcher. . . ." Joe Rogaly. *World Press Review,* Jan. 1991.
John Major: Prime Minister. Press Association Staff and John Jenkins. Trafalgar Square, 1991.
"A quiet dropout. . . ." Bill Hewitt. *People,* Dec. 10, 1990.
"Thatcher's favorite." Andrew Bilski. *Maclean's,* Dec. 3, 1990.
"John Major." *Economist,* Nov. 24, 1990.
"Major, John." *Current Biography,* Oct. 1990.

Malkovich, John (1953–) A very busy actor, Malkovich in 1991 starred in movies made on both sides of the Atlantic. April saw release of a British film, *The Object of Beauty,* directed by Michael Lindsay-Hogg; Malkovich starred as Jake, along with Andie MacDowell, Lolita Davidovich, Rudi Davies, Joss Ackland, and Victor Swayle. He also appeared in the film *Queens Logic* (1991). Forthcoming were the Woody Allen film *Shadows and Fog,* its scheduled 1991 release delayed by Orion Pictures' financial troubles; a starring role as Lenny in the film remake of John Steinbeck's *Of Mice and Men:* and the Bruce Robinson film *Jennifer Eight.* Always active in the theater, Malkovich also starred off-Broadway at New York's American Place Theater, in a new Sam Shepard one-act play, *States of Shock.*

Before becoming a New York stage player, Illinois-born Malkovich was from 1976 a leading member of Chicago's Steppenwolf theater company. He won an Obie off-Broadway for his role in *True West* (1982), appeared as Biff to Dustin Hoffman's Willy Loman in the 1984 Broadway revival of *Death of a Salesman,* and took his highly praised stage performance in Lanford Wilson's *Burn This* from New York to London late in 1990, making his British stage debut. He began his film career in 1984, with *Places in the Heart,* and went on to strong dramatic roles in such films as *The Killing Fields* (1984), *Eleni* (1985), *The Glass Menagerie* (1987), *Empire of the Sun* (1987), *Dangerous Liaisons* (1988), and *The Sheltering Sky* (1990). He has also appeared and directed in regional theater, and appeared on television. He is married to actress Glenne Headly.

FURTHER READING

"Life, art and Malkovich." JOE MORGENSTERN. *Playboy,* May 1990.

"Wild card." BECKY JOHNSON and BRIGITTE LACOMBE. *Interview,* Mar. 1989.

"Malkovich, John." *Current Biography,* May 1988.

"Mind over Malkovich." MARGY ROCHLIN. *Interview,* Oct. 1987.

"Acting's burning talent." *Harper's Bazaar,* Nov. 1987.

Mamet, David Alan (1948–) Playwright Mamet's work was primarily for the screen in 1991. In a double-barreled effort, he wrote and directed the police melodrama *Homicide,* starring one of his favorite actors, Joe Mantegna, which opened at the Cannes Film Festival in May. February 1991 brought Mamet's adaptation of a translation of Anton Chekhov's *Uncle Vanya* to the Public Broadcasting Service's "Great Performances" series; it was directed by Gregory Mosher, with a cast including David Warner, Ian Holm, Mary Elizabeth Mastrantonio, Ian Bannen, Rebecca Pigeon, and Rachel Kempson. Mamet had previously done an adaptation of two other Chekhov plays, *The Cherry Orchard* and *Three Sisters,* which opened on stage in New York in April 1991. Mamet also wrote the screen adaptation of his own play *Glengarry Glen Ross,* about cut-throat real estate salesmen hustling worthless Florida land. Shot in 1991 for 1992 release and directed by James Foley, the film attracted a high-powered cast, including Al Pacino, Jack Lemmon, Alec Baldwin, Alan Arkin, Jonathan Pryce, and Ed Harris.

Chicago-born Mamet emerged as a substantial playwright in the 1970s, with such works as *Sexual Perversity in Chicago* (1973), *American Buffalo* (1976), *A Life in the Theatre* (1976), *The Woods* (1977), *Edmond* (1983), *Glengarry Glen Ross,* (1984; he won a Pulitzer Prize for drama), and *Speed-the-Plow* (1987). His screenplays include *The Postman Always Rings Twice* (1981), *The Verdict* (1982), *The Untouchables* (1987), and *We're No Angels* (1989). He co-wrote and directed the films *House of Games* (1987), and wrote and directed *Things Change* (1988). Among his nonfiction works are *Writing in Restaurants: Essays and Prose* (1986) and *On Directing Film* (1990). Mamet's B.A. was from Goddard College. He was previously married to actress Lindsay Crouse.

FURTHER READING

David Mamet: Language as Dramatic Action. ANNE DEAN. Fairleigh Dickinson, 1990.

"The prophet of Broadway." JONATHAN LIEBERSON. *New York Review of Books,* July 21, 1988.

"Mamet on the make." BOB DAILY. *Chicago,* May 1988.

American Voices: Five Contemporary Playwrights in Essays and Interviews. ESTHER HARRIOTT. McFarland, 1988.

David Mamet. DENNIS CARROLL. St. Martin's, 1987.

David Mamet. C. W. BIGSBY. Routledge Chapman & Hall, 1985.

Mandela, Nelson Rolihiahia (1918–) In the largest sense, 1991 was a year of triumph for Mandela as his lifelong fight against South African racism continued to bring impressive results. As the African National Congress (ANC) leader continued to negotiate the future shape of South Africa with Prime Minister Frederik Willem De Klerk, many of the main legal instruments of White domination began to disappear, among them the 1913 and 1936 Land Acts, which reserved nearly 90 percent of the land for Whites; the hated 1950 segregated Population Registration; and the 1966 Group Areas Act. Limited school desegregation also came, though here as in many areas much remained to be done. De Klerk and Mandela also began to move toward a wholly new shaping of the South African government, with De Klerk's new constitution proposals in September; although rejected by Mandela and the ANC, De Klerk's proposals served as a real basis for negotiation.

However, the Inkatha-ANC civil war escalated even further in 1991, claiming thousands of lives, and costing the ANC much of its momentum. The ANC had long claimed that government security forces were arming and aiding Inkatha, and a national scandal erupted when De Klerk on July 19 admitted that the government had made substantial payments to Inkatha. But the admission did not topple the De Klerk government or stop the war. Mandela met with Inkatha leader Gatsha Buthelezi several times, and De Klerk attempted to mediate the conflict, but with little success. Although De Klerk, Buthelezi, and Mandela signed a peace pact in September, Buthelezi immediately expressed doubt that the pact would work, clashes continued, and the war seemed far from over.

Mandela was elected president of the ANC on July 5 at the groups' national congress in Durban. He succeeded Oliver Tambo, who for health reasons could not go on and was elected to the largely honorary national chairman's post. On the personal side, Mandela stood by his wife, Winnie Mandela, who was tried and convicted of kidnapping and accessory-to-assault charges in connection with the 1989 beatings of several young boys in Soweto by her bodyguards. She is free while her case is on appeal, a process that is expected to take some years.

Mandela was early a leading advocate of nonviolence (1944–60), but both he and the previously nonviolent ANC changed their peaceful stances after the Sharpeville Massacre of 1960. He was imprisoned in 1962, sentenced to a life term for sabotage. During his 28-year-long imprisonment, he became a worldwide symbol of the long fight against South African racism. On February 11, 1990, his release by De Klerk's new South African government ushered in a new period in South African history, leading to a full cease-fire after 30 years of guerrilla warfare. Mandela attended the University College at Fort Hare and the University of the Witwatersrand, and practiced law in Johannesburg in the early 1950s. He married Winnie Mandela, his second wife, in 1958. Among his autobiographical writings are *No Easy Walk to Freedom* (1986) and *Nelson Mandela: The Struggle Is My Life* (rev. ed., 1986). With Fidel Castro, he also wrote *How Far We Slaves Have Come!* (1991).

FURTHER READING

Nelson Mandela: Voice of Freedom. LIBBY HUGHES. Macmillan, 1992.
Nelson Mandela: The Man, the Struggle, the Triumph. DOROTHY HOOBLER and THOMAS HOOBLER. Watts, 1992.
"Mandela. . . ." SCOTT MACLEOD. *Time,* Jan. 7, 1991.
Nelson Mandela: Strength and Spirit of a Free South Africa. BENJAMIN PROUND. Gareth Stevens, 1991.
Nelson Mandela: Symbol of Resistance and Hope for a Free South Africa. E. S. REDDY, ed. Apt Books, 1991.
Nelson Mandela. BRIAN FEINBERG. Chelsea House, 1991.
Nelson Mandela. RICHARD TAMES. Watts, 1991.
Mandela, Tambo, and the African National Congress: The Struggle Against Apartheid, a Documentary Study, 1948–1990. SHERIDAN JOHNS and R. HUNT DAVIS, JR., eds. Oxford University Press, 1991.
Nelson Mandela: "No Easy Walk to Freedom." BARRY DENENBERG. Scholastic, 1991.
Nelson Mandela. BRIAN FEINBERG. Chelsea House, 1991.
Nelson Mandela. RICHARD TAMES. Watts, 1991.
"Mandela in America." JOSHUA MURAVCHIK. *Commentary,* Oct. 1990.
"An interview with. . . ." SCOTT MACLEOD. *Time,* June 25, 1990.
"Nelson Mandela. . . ." D. MICHAEL CHEERS. *Ebony,* May 1990.
"No easy walk. . . ." DAVID OLIVER RELIN. *Scholastic Update,* Mar. 23, 1990.
"Nelson Mandela." BILL HEWITT. *People,* Feb. 26, 1990.
Nelson Mandela: A Voice Set Free. REBECCA STEFFOF. Fawcett, 1990.

Mandela: Echoes of Era. ALF KUMALO and MPHAHLELE ES'KIA. Viking Penguin, 1990.
The Struggle: A History of the African National Congress. HEIDI HOLLAND. Braziller, 1990.
Higher than Hope: The Authorized Biography of Nelson Mandela. FATIMA MEER. HarperCollins, 1989.
Nelson Mandela: South Africa's Silent Voice of Protest. J. HARGROVE. Childrens, 1989.

Mandela, Winnie (Winnie Nomzano, 1934–) Long one of the world's most respected women, as a leader of the South African freedom movement and as the wife of imprisoned South African leader Nelson Mandela, Winnie Mandela's reputation has suffered greatly in recent years. In early 1989, her bodyguards were charged with the beating and murder of a young boy and the beatings of several other young boys in Soweto, and she was said to have been involved in the initial beating. In February 1989, she was publicly censured by the leadership of the African National Congress (ANC) and other leaders. In May 1990 two of her bodyguards were convicted of murder; she was not charged, but the judge in the case accused her of involvement. In September 1990, she was formally charged with kidnapping and assault. After a 14-week trial, she was on May 13, 1991, found guilty on four counts of kidnapping and one of accessory to assault, and on May 14 was sentenced to six years' imprisonment. She was set free while her case was on appeal, a process that is likely to take some years. In April, Mandela also was defeated in her bid for the presidency of the ANC Women's League, and in July lost her position as head of the ANC's social welfare department; both setbacks were reportedly connected with widespread dismay in ANC ranks over the beating case, although Mandela continued to be a leading ANC activist and a member of the ANC executive committee.

Winnie Mandela was a social worker before becoming active in the ANC in 1956. She married Nelson Mandela in 1958; the couple then joined their work in the South African freedom movement. She, too, became a worldwide symbol of resistance to racism, as she pressed for his release during his 28 years in prison and at the same time continued her anti-apartheid work. She was forced into silence for long periods by the South African government and internally exiled in 1977, but from 1985 she was able to defy the government, due to growing worldwide condemnation of apartheid and of the imprisonment of Nelson Mandela. Among her writings is *A Part of My Soul Went with Him* (1985).

FURTHER READING

"Blood soccer. . . ." JOHN CARLIN. *New Republic,* Feb. 18, 1991.
"The ordeal and. . . ." D. MICHAEL CHEERS and JESSE JACKSON. *Ebony,* May 1990.
"Mother of the nation." ANDREW BILSKI. *Maclean's,* Feb. 12, 1990.
Nelson and Winnie Mandela. JOHN VAIL. Chelsea House, 1989.
Winnie Mandela: Life of Struggle. JAMES HASKINS. Putnam, 1988.
Nelson and Winnie Mandela. DOROTHY HOOBLER and THOMAS HOOBLER. Watts, 1987.
Winnie Mandela. NANCY HARRISON, Braziller, 1986.
Winnie Mandela: The Soul of South Africa. MILTON MELTZER. Viking, 1986.

Mann, Daniel (Daniel Chugerman, 1912–91) Best known for several of his 1950s and 1960s films, Mann began his career as a musician and comedian working in cabaret in and around New York City in the 1930s. His major breakthrough came on Broadway, with his direction of *Come Back, Little Sheba* (1950), followed by Tennessee Williams's *The Rose Tattoo* (1951). *Sheba* took him to Hollywood; his directorial debut was the film version of the play, with Shirley Booth, who had starred on Broadway, in an Oscar-winning film role. He went on to direct the film version of *The Rose Tattoo* (1955), with Anna Magnani winning an Oscar. Other notable films were *The Teahouse of the August Moon* (1956), *The Last Angry Man* (1959), and *Butterfield 8* (1960). His later films were considerably less interesting, although his television film, *Playing for Time* (1980), was a major success.

FURTHER READING

Obituary. *Variety,* Dec. 2, 1991.
Obituary. *The Times* (of London), Nov. 26, 1991.
Obituary. *New York Times,* Nov. 23, 1991.

Mann, Jack: See **Lebanon Hostages**

Manzù, Giacomo (1908–91) A leading 20th-century sculptor, born in Bergamo, Manzù began showing his work while living in Milan (1929–33). He created the first of his many versions of *Girl in a Chair* in 1933, and had his first solo show in Rome in 1937. He did the first of his more than 50 sculptures of cardinals in 1936, showing it in 1938. Among his most notable works were the doors of the Salzburg Cathedral (1958); his portrait bust of his friend, Pope John XXIII (1963); the doors for Rome's St. Peters Basilica, dedicated as the *Portal of Death* (1964); and the *Door of Peace and War* at St. Laurents Church in Rotterdam (1968). His work of seven decades covered a very wide range of subjects and included many smaller sculptures of young women, children, and domestic objects. Though very close to Pope John, Manzù was also a communist, who designed a monument to Lenin on Capri, and in 1968 was awarded a Lenin Peace Prize. He was survived by his second wife, Inge, and two children. (d. Rome; January 17, 1991)

FURTHER READING

Obituary. *Current Biography,* Mar. 1991.
Obituary. *The Times* (of London), Jan. 21, 1991.
Obituary. *New York Times,* Jan. 19, 1991.
Homage to Manzù. L. Amiel, 1985.
Giacomo Manzù: Catalogue of the Graphic Work. Alfonso Ciranna. Wofsy Fine Arts, 1982.

Maradona, Diego Armando (1961–) There was crying in the streets of Argentina in 1991 as soccer fans watched the career of their idol Dieguito—Little Diego—unravel before their eyes. In January he was fined $70,000 for missing practices and games with his Italian team, Napoli, which also sued him for damaging its image. Though his more than $2-million-a-year contract extended to 1993, he announced that he might retire at the end of 1991. In March 1991, after rumors of drug use, Maradona tested positive for cocaine after a match and was suspended by the Italian league for 15 months, a suspension made international through June 30, 1992, by the International Soccer Federation.

Returning to Argentina, Maradona trained with the national team but in April was arrested on drug possession charges; he was able to escape a possible jail term by entering a drug treatment program. Argentinian President Carlos Menem removed his title of "sporting ambassador," and his $4-million-a-year endorsements contracts were in jeopardy. In September, he received (in absentia) a 14-month suspended sentence for cocaine possession from a Naples court, a plea-bargained arrangement. By October, Maradona—expressing unhappiness with intense media discussion, pro and con, about his situation—announced that he was considering moving to the United States to play indoor soccer.

A child soccer prodigy, Maradona turned professional in 1976, with the Buenos Aires Argentinos Juniors team, later switching to the Boca Juniors and appearing on the national team. To his great disappointment, he did not make the 1978 World Cup national team, though he did play in 1982, a year his team did not make the finals. His contract was sold to Barcelona in 1982, and in 1984 to Naples, where he led the club to Italian league titles in 1987 and 1990, and to a European Soccer Cup win in 1989. In an extraordinary triumph, he led the Argentine national team to victory in the World Cup in 1986. He married longtime companion Claudia Villafanes in a strikingly lavish ceremony in 1989; they have two daughters.

FURTHER READING

"Maradona, Diego." *Current Biography,* Nov. 1990.
"The biggest little athlete alive. . . ." Ron Arias. *People,* June 18, 1990.
"Soccer's little. . . ." George Vecsey. *New York Times Magazine,* May 27, 1990.
"Prima Dona." Rick Telander. *Sports Illustrated,* May 14, 1990.

Marcos, Imelda Romualdez (1930–) Philippine President Corazon Aquino had previously banned any return to the Philippine Republic by Imelda Marcos, but reversed her position in March 1991, allowing Marcos to return to face trial, beginning a long set of negotiations over how, where, and under what conditions Marcos and the body of former dictator Ferdinand Marcos might return home. Ultimately, on November 4, 1991 Imelda Marcos returned to Manila to face a wide range of charges, but without her husband's body; it remained unburied in a Honolulu mausoleum, awaiting resolution of the dispute over whether it would be buried in Manila, as demanded by

Imelda Marcos, or in northern Luzon, as directed by the Philippine government.

Imelda Marcos, who had been notable during her husband's long reign only for the extravagance of her life-style, was on her return home hailed by Marcos loyalists as a national heroine and a possible candidate for the Philippine presidency. She was also charged by the government on 80 civil and criminal counts, on December 9 pleading not guilty on seven counts of tax evasion, the first of the charges to move toward trial. Soon afterward, she confirmed her presidential candidacy.

Imelda Marcos went into exile with her husband, former Philippine dictator Ferdinand Marcos, in February 1986; for the next five years, the Philippine government attempted to recover large sums of money allegedly stolen and secreted abroad by Marcos during his two decades in office. The Philippine government estimated the funds and properties abroad to be worth $5-10 billion, but no such sums were ever found, and recoveries by 1990 had been in the far lower $200-250 million range. A former beauty queen, Imelda Romualdez married Ferdinand Marcos in 1954, and then became the Philippines' First Lady when he won the presidency in 1965; the couple had three children.

FURTHER READING

"War of the widows." STEPHEN BROOKES. *Insight,* May 13, 1991.

"Shopping a plea. . . ." JOSEPH TREEN. *New Republic,* May 28, 1990.

Imelda: Steel Butterfly of the Philippines. KATHERINE ELLISON. McGraw-Hill, 1989.

"Imelda and. . . ." KEN KELLEY and PHIL BRONSTEIN. *Playboy,* Aug. 1987.

Imelda Marcos: The Rise and Fall of One of the World's Most Powerful Women. CARMEN N. PEDROSA. St. Martin's, 1987.

Inside the Palace: The Rise and Fall of Ferdinand and Imelda Marcos. BETH D. ROMULO. Putnam, 1987.

The Marcos Dynasty: The Incredible Inside Story Behind the Rise of Imelda and Ferdinand Marcos. . . ." STERLING SEAGRAVE. Harper, 1987.

Marsalis, Wynton (1961–) Jazz musician Marsalis, in a highly productive year, issued a critically praised third album in his "Standard Time" series, called *The Resolution of Romance,* playing trumpet to the piano of his father, Ellis Marsalis. In the summer of 1991, he also released a three-CD set, titled *Soul Gestures in Southern Blue,* a very well received series of compositions, all but three of them by Marsalis. In *Down Beat*'s annual poll, Marsalis was named Musician of the Year.

Wynton Marsalis was artistic consultant to the fifth year-long season of the Classical Jazz series at Lincoln Center's Alice Tully Hall, starting in August, and performed in all series concerts during the season. Alice Tully Hall also played host to a very notable May 3 one-night performance of *The Reincarnation of Mozart;* Marsalis played trumpeter Aloysius Louis Weber, who plays jazz improvisations of Mozart themes in this musical fantasy for children.

New Orleans-born Marsalis is the son of pianist and teacher Ellis Marsalis, younger brother of saxophonist Branford Marsalis, and older brother of trombonist Delfeayo Marsalis. After briefly playing with Art Blakey's Jazz Messengers, Wynton Marsalis emerged as one of the leading trumpet soloists of his time, functioning equally well in the classics and in jazz, though he has focused on jazz in the late 1980s and early 1990s. A few of his many notable albums are *Fathers and Sons* (1982), *Wynton Marsalis* (1982), *Trumpet Concertos* (1983), *Black Codes from the Underground* (1985), *Standard Time* (Vol. 1, 1987; Vol. 2, 1990), *Majesty of the Blues* (1989), and *The Resolution of Romance* (1990). He studied at the Juilliard School of Music (1979–81).

FURTHER READING

"Horns of plenty. . . ." THOMAS SANCTON. *Time,* Oct. 22, 1990.

"Wynton. . . ." DAVE HELLAND. *Down Beat,* Sep. 1990.

Outcats: Jazz Composers, Instrumentalists, and Singers. FRANCIS DAVIS. Oxford University Press, 1990.

"Wynton and Branford Marsalis. . . ." A. JAMES LISKA. *Down Beat,* Sep. 1989.

Marshall, Armina (1895–1991) An actress and playwright, Marshall was born on Oklahoma's Cherokee Strip and spent her youth in California; she went to New York in 1922 to study at the American Academy of Dramatic Arts. Her acting career included several Theater Guild plays. She married Lawrence Langner in 1925, and with him and Theresa Helburn became a key figure in the Guild. As co-administrator, she helped to build it into a major force in the American theater, introducing major American works by such playwrights as Eugene O'Neill and Maxwell Anderson and works from abroad by George Bernard Shaw, Anton Chekhov, and Noel Coward. In 1943, the Guild introduced *Oklahoma!*, beginning a new day for the American musical theater. Marshall and Langner also founded the Westport Country Playhouse in 1931. They cowrote seven plays, including *The Pursuit of Happiness,* which made its way to Broadway in 1933. She was also active in many other theatrical institutions. She was survived by her son, Philip Langner. (d. New York City; July 20, 1991)

FURTHER READING

Obituary. *Variety,* July 29, 1991.
Obituary. *New York Times,* July 22, 1991.

Marshall, Thurgood (1908–) Justice Marshall announced his retirement from the U.S. Supreme Court on June 27, 1991, at the end of the 1990–91 term, effective upon the appointment of his successor. He left the Court a historic figure, in practical and symbolic terms. Earlier in his career, he was the most celebrated civil rights lawyer of his time, and was then a leading liberal member of the Court for 24 years (1967–91) and also its first Black member.

By his final term one of the few remaining Supreme Court liberals, Marshall wrote no majority opinions, although he did concur with his liberal colleagues in several cases. Among the most notable of these were *United Automobile Workers v. Johnson Controls Inc.,* a landmark women's rights case which held that employers could not ban pregnant women from jobs potentially dangerous to their unborn children; *Edmonson v. Leesville Concrete Co.,* barring exclusion of jurors in civil cases because of race, following earlier bans on exclusion because of race in criminal cases; *Pacific Mutual Life Insurance Co. v. Haslip,* holding that it was unconstitutional for courts to restrict punitive damages awarded by juries in civil cases, although states could do so by law; *Masson v. New Yorker Magazine Inc.,* holding that invented or materially altered quotes attributed to a public figure could be libelous; and two cases holding that the federal Voting Rights Act, prohibiting discriminatory voting practices or election district abuses, applied to elected judges, who were "representatives" within the meaning of the law.

But he was on the minority side far more often in his last term, in such decisions as *Rust v. Sullivan,* upholding federal regulations banning federally funded family planning clinics from offering abortion counseling; *Board of Education of Oklahoma City v. Dowell,* which eased conditions for the lifting of court supervision of segregated school districts, even when the net results of all efforts to desegregate schools had been the re-creation of single-race schools, reflecting local housing patterns, and *Arizona v. Fulminante,* holding that coerced or involuntary confession in a criminal case could be a "harmless error" if conviction would have resulted without it. He was also on the losing side in *County of Riverside, California v. McLaughlin,* holding that those arrested without warrants could be held up to 48 hours while a judge decided if there was probable cause for the arrest; *Cohen v. Cowles Media,* establishing that a breach of a promise of confidentiality made to a news source was not protected by the First Amendment as against a suit for damages caused by the breach; *Barnes v. Glen Theater,* which upheld an Indiana state law banning nude dancing and was widely viewed as opening the way to local censorship of the arts; *Florida v. Bostick,* holding that police could board buses and search passengers' luggage, with their permission; and *Coleman v. Thompson,* greatly restricting the use of habeas corpus writs by state prisoners who have exhausted state appeals to challenge the constitutionality of their convictions, reversing the 1963 *Fay v. Noia* decision. On June 27, his last day on the Court, he was outraged by the conservative majority's decisions in *Harmelin v. Michigan,* which held that a Michigan law requiring a life sentence without the possibility of parole for possession of 650 grams (1.5 pounds) of cocaine did not violate the cruel and unusual punishment prohibition of the Eighth Amendment, although the federal law was much less stringent; and in *Payne v. Tennessee,* which allowed "victim impact" evidence to be presented by the prosecution during the sentencing phase of criminal cases, thereby reversing 1987 and 1989 cases that had decided the opposite.

As top lawyer for the National Association for the Advancement of Colored People (NAACP) from 1940 to 1962, Baltimore-born Marshall was at the center of the long struggle for civil rights. His most important case as a lawyer was *Brown v. Board of Education of Topeka, Kansas* (1954), which destroyed the basis of school segregation and paved the way for the civil rights revolution that soon came. The story of that fight was retold in the telefilm *Separate But Equal* (1991); he was portrayed by Sidney Poitier. President John F. Kennedy, Jr., appointed Justice Marshall to the Second Circuit Court of Appeals in 1962. Three years later, in 1965, President Lyndon B. Johnson appointed him United States Solicitor-General, and then in 1967 to the Supreme Court. He was succeeded by Clarence Thomas, after a long, damaging confrontation fight that ultimately became the Anita Faye Hill–Clarence Thomas sexual harassment confrontation. Marshall was married to Vivian Burey from 1929 to her death in 1955, married Cecilia Suyat in 1955, and has two children. He attended Lincoln University and the Howard University Law School.

FURTHER READING

"Thurgood Marshall. . . ." MELISSA ETLIN. *NEA Today,* Oct. 1991.
"The best I could. . . ." *Ebony,* Sep. 1991.
"Thurgood Marshall. . . ." FRANK MCCOY. *Black Enterprise,* Sep. 1991.
"Personal and other mysteries. . . ." ROBERT F. DRINAN. *National Catholic Reporter,* July 19, 1991.
"A justice comes in. . . ." CHARLOTTE ALLEN. *Insight,* July 15, 1991.
"Thurgood Marshall's. . . ." *Jet,* July 15, 1991.
"A warrior retires. . . ." KAREN S. SCHNEIDER, *People,* July 15, 1991.
"A great original's lives. . . ." TOM MATHEWS. *Newsweek,* July 8, 1991.
"A lawyer who changed America. . . ." RICHARD LACAYO. *Time,* July 8, 1991.
"Embracing a great man's. . . ." DONALD BAER. *U.S. News & World Report,* July 8, 1991.
Thurgood Marshall: First Black Supreme Court Justice. CAROL GREENE. Childrens, 1991.
"Ebony interview with. . . ." *Ebony,* Nov. 1990.
"The Thurgood Marshall. . . ." JUAN WILLIAMS. *Ebony,* May 1990.
Thurgood Marshall: The Fight for Equal Justice. DEBRA HESS. Silver Burdett, 1990.
Thurgood Marshall. LISA ALDRED. Chelsea House, 1990.
Eight Men and a Lady. HERMAN SCHWARTZ, ANDREA NEAL, and DAVID SAVAGE. National Press, 1990.
"Marshall, Thurgood." *Current Biography,* Sep. 1989.
Marshall: Hero for our Times. LEONARD MOSLEY. Hearst, 1982.

Martin, Steve (1945–) In February 1991, Martin opened in the well-received Mick Jackson film *L.A. Story,* starring as a weatherman opposite his real-life wife, Victoria Tennant, as a London *Times* reporter. The film was a moderate box-office success, and a great success later in the year on home video. Martin also starred in what had been the Spencer Tracy role in the commercially successful Charles Shyer remake of the classic *Father of the Bride,* opposite Diane Keaton, with Kimberly Williams as the bride, in the Elizabeth Taylor role. Further 1991 starring roles were in Lawrence Kasdan's well-received *Grand Canyon,* as a gross movie producer, and opposite Goldie Hawn in *Housesitter.*

Texas-born Martin was a television comedy writer and comedian in cabaret before emerging as a leading comedian in television, on records, and in films in the late 1970s, most notably as a prominent guest and sometimes host on "Saturday Night Live" and with his Grammy-winning albums *Let's Get Small* (1977) and *A Wild and Crazy Guy* (1978). He became a leading comedy film star with *The Jerk* (1979), and went on to such films as *Pennies from Heaven* (1981), *Dead*

Men Don't Wear Plaid (1982), *The Man with Two Brains* (1983), *The Lonely Guy* (1984), *All of Me* (1984), *Three Amigos* (1986), *Little Shop of Horrors* (1986), *Planes, Trains and Automobiles* (1987), *Roxanne* (1987; he also wrote and produced), *Dirty Rotten Scoundrels* (1988), *Parenthood* (1989), and *My Blue Heaven* (1990). On stage in 1989, he and Robin Williams starred in an acclaimed New York revival of *Waiting for Godot*. Martin attended the University of California. He married Victoria Tennant in 1986.

FURTHER READING

"The king of. . . ." ELVIS MITCHELL. *GQ—Gentlemen's Quarterly,* July 1990.
"Steve Martin. . . ." CORK MILLNER. *Saturday Evening Post,* Nov.–Dec. 1989.
Icons: Intimate Portraits. DENISE WORRELL. *Atlantic Monthly,* 1989.
"I'm just a White guy. . . ." ELVIS MITCHELL. *American Film,* Nov. 1988.
Steve Martin—A Wild and Crazy Guy: An Unauthorized Biography—Well Excuuuse Us! MARSHA DALY. NAL-Dutton, 1980.
Steve Martin: The Unauthorized Biography. GREG LENBURG, RANDY SKREVEDT, and JEFF LENBURG. St. Martin's, 1980.

Mason, Belinda (1958–91) An immensely courageous AIDS victim and advocate, reporter, and short story writer, Belinda Mason contracted AIDS (acquired immune deficiency syndrome) in 1987 during the birth of her second child, when health care workers gave her a contaminated blood transfusion that had not been tested for AIDS. After learning of her infection, she became an advocate for those stricken with the disease, founded Kentuckian People with AIDS, and then became president of the National Association of People with AIDS. In 1988, she was appointed by President Ronald Reagan to the National Commission on AIDS.

A powerful advocate for humane treatment for AIDS victims, Mason opposed Bush administration moves to bar those with AIDS from entering the United States, and such measures as compulsory testing of all health workers for the disease, feeling that the question of social stigma outweighed what she felt were the small benefits to be gained by such moves; in August 1991, shortly before her death, she wrote a public letter to President George Bush on these matters. She was survived by her husband, Steven Carden, and two young children. (d. Nashville; September 9, 1991)

FURTHER READING

Obituary. *New York Times,* Sep. 10, 1991.
"AIDS commissioner. . . ." LINDA KRAMER. *People,* Dec. 11, 1989.

Mason, Jackie (Yacov Moshe Maza, 1930–) In late January 1991, Mason canceled three days of his one-man Broadway show, *Jackie Mason: Brand New,* to visit Israel, then under Iraqi missile attack during the Persian Gulf War. He later reported that his first Tel Aviv news conference was interrupted by an Iraqi missile bombardment. Mason appeared in Jerusalem and Tel Aviv; in November, he was honored by Israel in a London ceremony.

On November 12, Mason sponsored and starred in a New York Paramount Theater benefit performance for the widows and orphans of New York City police killed in the line of duty. He was making a comeback in New York and once again becoming identified with the city after his highly publicized 1989 problems. In a very damaging incident, Mason was in 1989 asked to leave the New York mayoralty campaign of Republican candidate Rudolf Giuliani after having been accused of using a racial epithet against Democratic candidate David Dinkins, although Mason denied the charge; Mason was also charged with having made other racial insults. ABC later canceled the new and rather popular series *Chicken Soup,* starring Mason and Lynn Redgrave, after only seven episodes had been run.

Mason, the child of a rabbinical family, became an ordained rabbi at 24, but in the mid-1950s moved into show business, playing Catskill resorts and soon changing his stage name to Jackie Mason. The comic became a hit guest on television and in cabaret in the early 1960s, but his career went downhill from the mid-1960s through the mid-1980s, though he continued to appear in cabaret and television. He scored a comeback in his one-man Broadway show *The World According to Me!* (1986–87), releasing a 1987 book of the same title and telling of his resurrection in *Jackie, Oy!: The Birth and Rebirth of Jackie Mason* (1988), written with Ken Gross. Another book is *How to Talk Jewish* (1991), written with Ira Berkow. Mason has also appeared in several films.

FURTHER READING

"Enough with the. . . ." MARK JACOBSON. *Esquire,* Sep. 1990.
"Jackie Mason's racial remarks. . . ." *Jet,* Oct. 16, 1989.
"The world according to Mason." HAP ERSTEIN. *Insight,* July 10, 1989.
"The Yiddish. . . ." JOHN McCOLLISTER. *Saturday Evening Post,* Mar. 1989.
"The casualness of it." WHITNEY BALLIETT. *New Yorker,* Sep. 19, 1988.
"Mason, Jackie." *Current Biography,* July 1987.
Jackie Mason's America. JACKIE MASON. Carol, 1983.

Mastroianni, Marcello (1923–) The great Italian star Mastroianni found a vehicle worthy of his talents in 1991: the Theo Angelopoulos film *The Suspended Step of the Stork.* It tells of Albanian, Kurdish, and Iranian refugees arriving in Greece, fearful and destitute, their families and lives broken—conditions long a part of European life, and still so. Mastroianni starred opposite Jeanne Moreau, in a cast that included Gregory Karr, Chrysikou, and Ilias Logothetis. While the film was being shot on location in Greece, the local Greek Orthodox bishop charged that the film contained erotic scenes and unpatriotically proposed abolition of national borders; local clerics threatened to burn the film set and excommunicate any local inhabitants who helped make the film, but the national government openly supported the filmmakers. Also in 1991 Mastroianni starred opposite Julie Andrews in Gene Saks's romantic comedy *Tchin-Tchin,* which opened at Cannes to less than enthusiastic reviews. Forthcoming were roles in Christian de Chalonge's *The Colonel's Children* and in *Used People.*

Mastroianni began his film career in 1947 and emerged to world prominence in the late 1950s in such films as *White Nights* (1957), *La Dolce Vita* (1960), *The Night* (1961), *Divorce Italian Style* (1961), *8½* (1963), *Yesterday, Today, and Tomorrow* (1963), and *Marriage Italian Style* (1964). His later work includes such films as *Down the Ancient Stairs* (1974), *City of Women* (1980), *Dark Eyes* (1987), *Splendor* (1989), *What Time Is It?* (1989), and *Everything's Fine* (1990). Mastroianni attended the University of Rome. He was formerly married and has one child.

FURTHER READING

"Marcello? Marcello? . . ." MARCELLE CLEMENTS. *Premiere,* June 1991.
"The 35-second seduction. . . ." GEORGINA HOWELL. *M Inc.,* Apr. 1991.

Masur, Kurt (1927–) The new music director of the New York Philharmonic made his debut at Lincoln Center's Avery Fisher Hall on September 11, 1991, a year earlier than had been planned. He also announced that he would be staying on indefinitely with the Leipzig Gewandhaus Orchestra, living in New York City and Leipzig more than five months each every year. Well received as a conductor, Masur also took two highly popular steps to make classical music accessible to young people and to a wide public: He quickly began a young people's series and in November, the Philharmonic Forums, a series of free open discussions with the public, at Avery Fisher Hall.

Masur is one of Germany's leading conductors, developing the bulk of his career in East Germany before unification. He was an opera company director in Erfurt and Leipzig and conductor of the Dresden Philharmonic (1955–58). He directed the Mecklenburg State Opera

(1958–60), was music director of Berlin's Komische Opera (1960–64), went back to Dresden as music director of the Philharmonic (1967–72), and directed the Leipzig Gewandhaus from 1972 to 1990. He has also toured widely and is principal guest conductor of the London Philharmonic. In April 1990, he was named to succeed Zubin Mehta as music director of the New York Philharmonic, one of the most prestigious posts in the world of classical music.

Masur was also a major figure in the events that led up to the peaceful East German revolution of 1990, intervening on several occasions to avert civil war and bring a peaceful revolution. Afterward, his prestige was so great that there was talk of making him head of the new government, much like the writer Vaclav Havel in Czechoslovakia—but Masur chose to stay with his musical career.

Masur attended the National Musical School as Breslau and the Leipzig Conservatory. He is married to singer Tomoko Sakurai and has five children.

FURTHER READING

"New York's new maestro." ROBERT ANGUS. *Audio,* Dec. 1991.
"New Philharmonic maestro. . . ." PETER G. DAVIS. *New York,* Sep. 23, 1991.
"Maestro of the moment." JOHN ROCKWELL. *New York Times Magazine,* Sep. 8, 1991.
"From Leipzig. . . ." WILLIAM H. YOUNGREN. *World Monitor,* Apr. 1991.
"Masur, Kurt." *Current Biography,* Sep. 1990.

Maxwell, Robert (Jan Ludwig Hoch; Ian Robert Maxwell, 1923–91) On November 5, 1991, the body of financier Robert Maxwell was found in the ocean off the Canary Islands after an apparent fall from his yacht, the *Lady Ghislaine.* Spanish authorities ultimately ruled that his death was from natural causes, although a worldwide media-fed controversy immediately emerged, fanned by prior reports of his financial problems, which proved far more severe than most observers had realized during his lifetime.

Maxwell emerged as a major communications industry figure during the post–World War II period. He founded Pergamon Press in 1949, and during the next four decades expanded his areas of control to include such companies as Great Britain's Mirror Group of newspapers, New

York's Macmillan Publishing Company, and a wide range of other publishing, printing, broadcast media, and related companies. Maxwell overexpanded and overpaid for acquisitions in the fevered 1980s, and continued to expand in some directions even after it was clear that his financial difficulties were mounting, as with his purchase of the New York *Daily News,* the launch of *The European,* the purchase of several U.S. tabloids, and his investments in German and Eastern European publishing companies. What was not understood before his death was that he was using the supposedly protected pension funds of his employees and former employees to meet his current cash needs, in amounts that ultimately may prove to be in the $500 million to $1 billion range—or even more; and that at the time of his death the total assets of his companies may have been worth less than their debts. At the end of 1991, the long process of assessment and ultimate disposition had barely begun, with investigations also proceeding on both sides of the Atlantic.

Maxwell was also a Labour Member of Parliament (1964–70). He married Elisabeth Meynard in 1945; the couple had nine children, of whom seven survive. (d. off the Canary Islands; November 5, 1991)

FURTHER READING

Obituary. ANDREWS PHILLIPS. *Maclean's,* Nov. 18, 1991.
"Death of a tycoon." BARBARA RUDOLPH. *Time,* Nov. 18, 1991.

"A tycoon's final days." JOSHUA HAMMER. *Newsweek,* November 18, 1991.
"Tycoon's mysterious death." KEN GROSS. *People,* Nov. 18, 1991.
Obituary. *Variety,* Nov. 11, 1991.
Obituary. *New York Times,* Nov. 6, 1991.
Obituary. *The Times* (of London), Nov. 6, 1991.
"Playboy interview. . . ." DAVID SHEFF. *Playboy,* Oct. 1991.
"Maxwell's silver hammer. . . ." PETER J. BOYER. *Vanity Fair,* June 1991.
"Maxwell's house. . . ." TOM BOWER. *New Republic,* Apr. 8, 1991.
"As big and tough as King Kong. . . ." KEN GROSS. *People,* Apr. 1, 1991.
"Maxwell, Ian Robert." *Current Biography,* Sep. 1988.
Maxwell. JOE HAINES. Houghton Mifflin, 1988.

Mazowiecki, Tadeusz (1927–) After his 1990 presidential campaign loss to Lech Walesa, former Polish premier Mazowiecki remained a considerable force in his country's political life. In May 1991, he was the key figure in the organization of the new Democratic Union party and became the party's first president. No party came close to winning a parliamentary majority in the October elections, but Mazowiecki's party, with approximately 12 percent of the vote, was one of the two leading parties. The party of his successor, Premier Jan Krzystztof Bielecki, received only approximately 7 percent of the vote. Mazowiecki offered to form a new government; though Walesa rejected his offer, it was clear that Mazowiecki was still a major figure in Polish politics.

Mazowiecki, a lawyer and journalist, worked as a journalist for the Catholic association PAX in the early post–World War II period. Fired in 1955, he in 1958 founded the reformist Catholic monthly *Wiez* (*Bond*), which he edited until 1981. He was elected to the Polish parliament in 1961 and was a member until being barred in 1972, having embraced even sharper opposition to the government in the late 1960s. He became a key Solidarity adviser and ally in 1980, and in 1981 he organized and was first chief editor of the Solidarity newspaper. He was imprisoned during 1981–82, then continuing to be a Solidarity leader and close co-worker of Lech Walesa throughout the 1980s. He participated in the 1989 Solidarity–government talks that led to the establishment of Polish democracy. On August 4, 1989, he became a historic figure, as the first noncommunist head of a Soviet-bloc country, as the first democratically elected noncommunist to replace a communist leadership, and as Poland's first democratically elected premier since 1948. Mazowiecki has been married and widowed twice, and has three sons.

FURTHER READING

"What's left. . . ." ALMA GUILLERMOPRIETO. *Mother Jones,* Sep.–Oct. 1990.
"Mazowiecki, Tadeusz." *Current Biography,* Feb. 1990.
"The transition to. . . ." SYLVIE KAUFFMANN. *World Press Review,* Oct. 1989.
" 'People are impatient.'. . ." JOHN BORRELL and TADEUSZ KUCHARSKI. *Time,* Sep. 11, 1989.
"The new man at the top." HOLGER JENSEN. *Maclean's,* Aug. 28, 1989.
"An epochal shift. . . ." MARGUERITE JOHNSON. *Time,* Aug. 28, 1989.

Mazursky, Paul (1930–) In *Scenes from a Mall,* starring Woody Allen as Nick and Bette Midler as Deborah, Mazursky returned to his favorite Los Angeles locale (although Allen insisted that the film be shot in the New York area, and it was) to explore the married life of two rather mature "yuppies," he a highly successful lawyer, she a highly successful author and psychologist, as they spend a day at the Beverly Centre, telling secrets, fighting, making love, moving on. The film was moderately well reviewed, but weak at the box office, and weak later in the year in home video rentals. Mazursky's second 1991 film was a comedy about a film director directing a teenage movie about a flying cucumber, titled *The Pickle;* Danny Aiello starred, in a cast that included Shelley Winters and Dyan Cannon. Forthcoming was *Moscow on the Moscow,* a sequel to his *Moscow on the Hudson.*

Brooklyn-born Mazursky worked as a New York-based actor and comedian during the 1950s, moving to Los Angeles in 1959. He became a writer for television in the 1960s, most notably with the "Danny Kaye Show" (1963–67), and wrote his first film *I Love You, Alice B. Toklas* (1968) with Larry Tucker. His breakthrough film was *Bob & Carol & Ted & Alice* (1970), which he wrote and directed, setting the pattern of his work of the next two decades. Some of his most notable films were *Blume in Love* (1973), *Harry and Tonto* (1974), *An Unmarried Woman* (1978), and *Moscow on the Hudson* (1985), all of which he wrote and directed; *Down and Out in Beverly Hills* (1985) and *Moon Over Parador* (1988), which he also produced; and *Enemies, A Love Story* (1989), which he co-wrote, directed, produced, and appeared in. Mazursky's B.A. was from Brooklyn College. He married Betsy Purdy in 1953; the couple have two children.

FURTHER READING

"Paul Mazursky." *American Film,* Jan. 1990.
"Paul Mazursky. . . ." DIGBY DIEHL. *People,* June 16, 1986.

Menem, Carlos Saul (1935–) President of Argentina and of its Justicialist Nationalist Movement (Peronist party), Menem survived an army revolt, immense unpopularity due to his economic policies, and a major governmental scandal that touched him personally, to emerge stronger in late 1991 than he had been going into the year. In December 1990, forces loyal to the government suppressed an army revolt led by Colonel Mohamed Ali Seineldin. During January 1991, Menem faced a major financial crisis, reshuffled his cabinet twice, and moved his foreign minister, Domingo Cavallo, into the job of economy minister. Cavallo declared a January 29–30 bank holiday and made a series of stabilizing and austerity moves that enraged large sections of the trade union movement, traditionally the Peronist support base, generating countrywide wildcat strikes in early February. Menem's popularity plummeted still further when his government seized control of the national railroad and fired hundreds of strikers after a March strike had stopped service.

During the summer of 1991, Menem faced a different kind of problem in the form of a drug money laundering scandal involving accusations against the family of his estranged wife Zulema, his appointments secretary and sister-in-law Amira Yoma, her former husband, her brother, and some of his other closest advisers.

Yet Cavallo's drastic measures to some extent, however temporarily, brought a measure of stability to the Argentine economy and currency. The September mid-term election brought Menem's party a surprising victory. He publicly declared the election a "vote of confidence"; his departure from power no longer seemed quite as imminent.

Menem has spent almost all of his long career in law and politics in his home province of Rioja, beginning with his Peronist youth group activities of the mid-1950s and association with the provincial labor confederation. He became president of the Rioja Justicialist party in 1963 and was three times elected provincial governor (1973, 1983, 1987). He was elected president of Argentina in May 1989 and succeeded President Raul Foulkes Alfonsin on July 8, four months before his scheduled December inauguration, because of Argentina's economic problems. He took office following food riots and the declaration of a state of siege, soon losing his early popularity as the economic crisis continued. Menem attended Cordoba University. He was married to Zulema Fatima Yoma Menem in 1966; the highly publicized breakup of their marriage ultimately resulted in her June 1990 eviction from the presidential mansion by an army contingent. They have two children.

FURTHER READING

"A talk with. . . ." LINDA ROBINSON. *U.S. News & World Report,* May 7, 1990.
"Menem, Carlos Saul." *Current Biography,* Nov. 1989.

Mengistu, Haile Miriam (1937–) Ethiopian dictator Mengistu resigned and fled Ethiopia to Zimbabwe on May 21, 1991, as the rebel army of the Tigre People's Liberation Front, in alliance with five other rebel groups, approached Addis Ababa, routing collapsing Ethiopian Second and Third Army forces. At the same time, Eritrean rebel forces were completing the defeat of Ethiopian army forces in Eritrea. The war ended a week later, when rebel forces took Addis Ababa. Mengistu had ruled Ethiopia for 14 years, at a cost to the country of an estimated 1–2 million civilian deaths, mostly from disease and famine, and many of them because one or both sides blocked the shipment of emergency relief supplies.

Mengistu, then an army major, emerged as one of the leaders of the 1974 military coup that deposed emperor Haile Selassie. He became dictator of the one-party Ethiopian state in 1977. In

1984, he established the Worker's Party, and in 1987 the Democratic Republic of Ethiopia. With a great deal of material help from the Soviet Union, and with Cuban troops fighting on the Ethiopian side in the field, he continued and deepened the long Eritrean–Ethiopian civil war, with neither side able to win. His forces in the Ogaden region of Ethiopia also fought and drove back the invading Somalis in 1977–78 but were unable to win against rebel forces in that area.

In 1987, Eritrean rebel forces won decisive victories; it was the beginning of the end for Mengistu. New insurgency also developed in Tigre province, which by late 1988 was largely in rebel hands. In 1990, with the end of the Cold War, the Soviet Union cut off arms shipments; it was the final blow in a war that had begun to wind down. In 1991 his time ran out.

Mengistu attended the Holeta Military Academy. He is married to Wubanchi Bishaw.

FURTHER READING

"The fall of the black Stalin." Alex Shoumatoff. *Vanity Fair,* Nov. 1991.
Ethiopia. Dennis B. Fradin. Childrens, 1988.
"The famine next time." *New Republic,* Dec. 15, 1986.

Mercury, Freddie (Frederick Bulsara, 1946–91) Mercury was a songwriter, pianist, and lead singer of the rock group Queen, formed in 1971, which also included guitarist Brian May, drummer Roger Taylor, and bassist John Deacon. Their breakthrough album was *Sheer Heart Attack* (1974), with its hit singer "Killer Queen." Their next major hit came a year later, with the album *A Night at the Opera* (1975), which contained their hit single "Bohemian Rhapsody," written by Mercury. In the mid-1970s, they also became a major touring attraction, with Mercury as a flamboyant, crowd-pleasing lead singer drawing great attention on stage and in the media, as did Mercury's announced and highly publicized bisexuality. They remained a popular recording and touring group through the mid-1980s, though Mercury's developing illness apparently forced them to greatly curtail their activities in the late 1980s and the early 1990s. The day before he died, Mercury announced that he had AIDS (acquired immune deficiency syndrome), ending long speculation that this was the case; his final bronchopneumonia was AIDS-related. (d. London; November 24, 1991)

FURTHER READING

Obituary. *People,* Dec. 9. 1991.
Obituary. *Variety,* Dec. 2, 1991.
Obituary. *The Times* (of London), Nov. 26, 1991.
Obituary. *New York Times,* Nov. 25, 1991.

Michener, James Albert (1907–) Although he had announced a year earlier that he would write no more "big" novels because of the long research involved, the prolific novelist in his 84th year continued to publish at a rate that was envied by many much younger writers. In April 1991 he published *The Novel,* a fictional story set in the publishing world. In early 1992, he published an autobiographical work: *The World Is My Home: A Memoir.* Forthcoming was another "big" novel, this one *Mexico,* written in the 1960s, but abandoned when two-thirds done. Michener's agent, Owen Laster, had found the book contract in the late 1960s but not the mislaid manuscript; it was finally found in a box in Michener's Bucks County, Pennsylvania home, and was then completed.

In September, Michener gave $5 million to Swarthmore College—$3 million immediately and $2 million more promised; he was a scholarship student at Swarthmore in the late 1920s, graduating in 1929, and had previously given $2 million to his alma mater.

Michener was a teacher and editor during the late 1930s and 1940s. He emerged as a major U.S. popular author in 1947, with his Pulitzer Prize-winning first novel *Tales of the South Pacific;* the book was adapted into the musical *South Pacific* in 1949. He went on to write many best-sellers, many of them historical novels and several of them adapted into hit movies. Some of his best-known novels are *The Bridges at Toko-ri* (1953), *Sayonara* (1954), *The Bridge at Andau* (1957), *Hawaii* (1959), *The Source* (1965), *Iberia* (1968), *Centennial* (1974), *Chesapeake* (1978), *The Covenant* (1980), *Space* (1982), *Texas* (1985), *Alaska* (1988), and *Caribbean* (1989). He has also written several volumes of essays and edited several art books. Michener attended Swarthmore College. He has been married three times, since 1955 to Mari Yoriko Sabusawa.

FURTHER READING

"The man who. . . ." LYNN ROSELLINI. *U.S. News & World Report,* June 17, 1991.
"The continuing sagas of. . . ." JIM SHAHIN. *Saturday Evening Post,* Mar. 1990.
"What makes love last. . . ." SUSAN ARNOUT. *McCall's,* Feb. 1987.
James A. Michener: A Biography. JOHN P. HAYES. Macmillan, 1984.

Midler, Bette (1945–) For her work in the fight against AIDS (acquired immune deficiency syndrome), actress and singer Bette Midler on September 15, 1991, received Hollywood's fifth annual Commitment to Life award. She capped the two-hour benefit show with her signature song "Friends," in mourning and celebration of those who had become victims of the disease.

Midler opened in two films during 1991. In Paul Mazursky's *Scenes from a Mall,* she starred as a highly successful Los Angeles author and psychologist opposite Woody Allen, as her equally successful lawyer husband, the two "yuppies" revealing some of their marital problems during a day spent telling secrets, fighting, and making love at the Beverly Centre. Though reasonably well received, the film encountered box-office problems. In November, Midler produced and starred as Dixie Rydell opposite James Caan as Eddie Sparks in *For the Boys,* the show business story of two USO performers going through three wars. Though Midler's performance was praised, the film was not very well received, and also ran into immediate box-office problems.

Hawaii-born Midler, on stage and screen from 1965, was in the early 1970s the long-running lead singer at New York's Continental Baths, a gay men's health club. She began her recording career with the album *The Divine Miss M* (1973), also recording such albums as *Bette Midler* (1973), *Thighs and Whispers* (1979), *Divine Madness* (1980), and *Some People's Lives* (1990), as well as the soundtrack album from *The Rose* (1980), her first starring film role. Her single "Wind Beneath My Wings" won a 1990 Grammy award for best song. Midler went on to play in such films as *Jinxed* (1982), *Down and Out in Beverly Hills* (1986), *Ruthless People* (1986), *Outrageous Fortune* (1987), *Beaches* (1989), and *Stella* (1990), and has also appeared in television. She published *A View from a Broad* (1980). Midler attended the University of Hawaii. She married Martin von Haselberg in 1984; the couple have one child.

FURTHER READING

"La belle Bette." KEVIN SESSUMS. *Vanity Fair,* Dec. 1991.
"A fashion fairy tale extravaganza." JONATHAN VAN METER. *Vogue,* Dec. 1991.
"Bette Midler and 'The Boys.' " EMILY YOFFE. *Newsweek,* Nov. 25, 1991.
"Bette." VERNON SCOTT. *Good Housekeeping,* Mar. 1991.
"The best Bette yet." CLIFF JAHR. *Ladies Home Journal,* Jan. 1990.
Bette Midler. ACE COLLINS. St. Martin's, 1989.
Bette Midler: Outrageously Divine. MARK BEGO. NAL-Dutton, 1987.

Miles, Bernard James (1907–91) Born in Uxbridge, England, Miles was an actor who developed London's Mermaid Theater. He made his theatrical debut in 1930 in Shakespeare's *Richard III,* and went on to play in a wide range of stage roles during the 1930s and 1940s, including several roles at the Old Vic. In 1950, he founded the Mermaid, presenting *The Tempest* (1951) and playing in *Macbeth* (1952) and several other plays. He then spent six years developing a permanent Mermaid stage at Puddle Dock, on the Thames; it opened in May 1959 and has been in operation ever since, although an expensive reconstruction in the late 1970s, followed by large deficits in the early 1980s, forced sale of the theater. Miles resigned as artistic director; he and his wife, actress Josephine Wilson, also lost most of their money in the venture. Miles also had a long film career, in such movies as *Channel Crossing* (1933), *One of Our Aircraft Is Missing* (1942), *In Which We Serve* (1942), *Great Expectations* (1946), *Nicholas Nickleby* (1947), *Fame Is the Spur* (1947), *Moby Dick* (1956), and *Saint Joan* (1957). His books included *The British Theatre* (1947) and *Curtain Calls* (1981). He was survived by a son and a daughter. (d. Knaresborough, England; June 14, 1991)

FURTHER READING

Obituary. *The Times* (of London), June 15, 1991.
Obituary. *New York Times,* June 15, 1991.

Milken, Michael (1946–) Milken began serving his 10-year prison term on March 4, 1991, with the possibility that he would serve as little as two years. He was the central figure in the massive Drexel Burnham Lambert stock scandals of the late 1980s, which brought multiple indictments of the Drexel firm in 1988 after a two-year investigation, aided by convicted stock market manipulator Ivan Boesky. Drexel pleaded guilty to six felony counts in 1988 and agreed to pay $650 million. Milken was indicted on 98 counts in March 1989, resigned from Drexel in June 1989, and in April 1990 pleaded guilty to six felony counts and agreed to pay $600 million. On November 21, 1990, he was sentenced to 10 years in prison, 3 years on probation, and 1,800 hours of community service.

The fallout from the Drexel Burnham Lambert and Milken cases was far from over, however. In January, the federal government sued Milken and others for a total of $6 billion dollars, charging junk bond market manipulation. In September, Drexel Burnham Lambert sued Milken. And in a rather spectacular move, noted attorney Alan M. Dershowitz in October joined the Milken defense, immediately going on the offensive with a series of newspaper advertisements and other public statements in defense of his new client.

Milken's entire career had been with Drexel Burnham Lambert. He worked part-time with the firm while in college and joined its bond department in 1970. During the 1970s, he began his long career as a high-yield bond trader, developing the "junk bond" concept. He moved the firm's bond department to Beverly Hills, California, in 1978, and vastly expanded junk bond operations throughout the 1980s, using it as a financing technique that raised tens of billions of dollars and earned billions in fees for the firm. He personally earned over $1 billion. But in the mid-1980s, allegations of insider trading and other securities frauds began to surface, and a long series of federal investigations and prosecutions began. Milken's B.B.A. was from the University of California, and his M.B.A. from the Wharton School of the University of Pennsylvania. He is married to Lori Anne Hackett.

FURTHER READING

"Insider reporting." JUDE WANNISKI. *National Review,* Dec. 2, 1991.
"A reversal of misfortune? . . ." MICHELE GALEN. *Business Week,* Nov. 11, 1991.
"Michael Milken. . . ." TAD FRIEND. *Esquire,* May 1991.
Den of Thieves: The Untold Story of the Men Who Plundered Wall Street and the Chase That Brought Them Down. JAMES B. STEWART. Simon & Schuster, 1991.
"Junk bonding." JOE M. DOMANICK. *Inc.,* Oct. 1990.
New Crowd: The Changing of the Jewish Guard on Wall Street. JUDITH R. EHRLICH and BARRY J. REHFELD. Little, Brown, 1989.

Miller, Arthur (1915–) Celebrated playwright Arthur Miller provided two of the theater highlights of 1991, one on each side of the Atlantic. The first was the early November London premier of his comedy, *The Ride Down Mt. Morgan,* his first full-length new play in seven years. Directed by Michael Blakemore, the work starred Tom Conti as a bigamist, and Gemma Jones and Clare Higgins as the two wives who meet in his hospital room after he has suffered an automobile accident. The work opened to very mixed reviews.

December 10 saw the Broadway opening of a revival of Miller's classic *The Crucible,* set during the 17th-century Salem witch-hunts, directly aimed at the political witch-hunts of the McCarthy period of the 1950s and thought by many to be equally relevant to the 1990s. It was the first offering of the new National Actors Theatre and starred Martin Sheen and Maryann Plunkett as John and Elizabeth Proctor; Plunkett's extraordinary portrayal was critically acclaimed. The play also starred Fritz Weaver and Michael York, and was directed by Yossi Yzraely. Forthcoming was a screen version of the work, adapted for film by Miller and produced by his son, Bob Miller. Miller's new one-act play, *Clara,* was presented on television in February on the "General Motors Playhouse Theater;" directed by Burt Brinckerhoff, it starred Darren McGavin and William Daniels.

Miller has been a leading American playwright since the 1947 production of *All My Sons,* which won a New York Drama Critic Award. He became a world figure with his Pulitzer Prize-winning *Death of a Salesman* (1949), in which Lee J. Cobb created the memorable Willy Loman. His most notable further work included the Tony-winning *The Crucible* (1953), the Pulitzer-winning *A View from the Bridge* (1955), *After the Fall* (1963), *Incident at Vichy* (1965), *The Price* (1968), and *The American Clock* (1979). He wrote the screenplay for *The Misfits* (1961), which starred his second wife Marilyn Monroe, who committed suicide in 1962. His second screenplay was for Karel Reisz's *Everybody Wins* (1990), starring Nick Nolte and Debra Winger. Miller's recent work also includes an Americanized adaptation of Ibsen's *An Enemy of the People* (1990), done in a televised production for PBS's "American Playhouse." In 1987 he published *Timebends: A Life.* Miller attended the University of Michigan. He has been married three times, since 1962 to photographer Inge Morath, with whom he has collaborated on two travel books, and has two children.

FURTHER READING

"Miller's crossing." James Kaplan. *Vanity Fair,* Nov. 1991.

"The theater. . . ." Alvin P. Sanoff. *U.S. News & World Report,* Jan. 11, 1988.

Miller the Playwright. Dennis Welland. Heinemann, 1988.

Conversations with Arthur Miller. Matthew C. Roudane, ed. University Press of Mississippi, 1987.

Minnelli, Liza (1946–) Multi-talented actress, singer, and dancer Liza Minnelli continued to work live before a wide range of audiences in cabaret and concert during 1991. At New York's Radio City Music Hall, her April 23–May 12 run set a new house record, an indication of her enduring popularity. On screen, she starred in the musical *Stepping Out,* as a professional dancer turned small town tap-dance school teacher. She and Lewis Gilbert co-produced the poorly received film, adapted by Richard Harris from his long-running London stage play, with music by Peter Matz. The cast included Luke Reilly as her musician husband, Shelley Winters, Ellen Greene, Bill Irwin, Jane Krakowski, and Andrea Martin.

Minnelli, the daughter of actress-singer Judy Garland and director Vincente Minnelli, began her stage and recording careers in 1963. In 1964, she appeared at the London Palladium with Garland and went on to become one of the leading popular entertainers of her time. She won a Best Actress Oscar in *Cabaret* (1972) and also appeared in such films as *Charlie Bubbles* (1967), *The Sterile Cuckoo* (1969), *Tell Me That You Love Me, Junie Moon* (1970), *Lucky Lady* (1975), *Silent Movie* (1976), *New York, New York* (1977), *Arthur* (1981; and the 1988 sequel), and *Rent-a-Cop* (1988). On stage, she has appeared in *Flora, the Red Menace* (1965), *The Act* (1977), and *The Rink* (1984), and has also often appeared on television. Minnelli has been married three times.

FURTHER READING

"Lisa Minnelli." John Clark. *Premiere,* May 1991.

"Liza Minnelli." K. D. Lang. *Interview,* Mar. 1991.

"Minnelli, Liza." *Current Biography,* July 1988.

Liza! Liza!: An Unauthorized Biography of Liza Minnelli. Alan W. Petrucelli. Karz-Cohl, 1983.

Mitchell, George John (1933–) Although Senate majority leader Mitchell ruled himself out of the 1992 presidential race on March 31, as one of his party's chief spokespersons he remains a highly visible possible future candidate. Early in 1991, Mitchell opposed the January Persian Gulf War resolution but fully supported the decision to go to war once it had been made by President Bush. But throughout the year, he sharply criticized Bush as a do-

nothing president on such issues as the deepening recession and the growing health care and financial crises, seeing his message take hold and electoral prospects change as the recession deepened. Mitchell co-sponsored the June Democratic health care bill and successfully fought for extension of unemployment benefits. On the foreign policy side, he unsuccessfully tried to set human rights conditions for renewal of China's most favored nation trade status; backed resistance to requested Israeli loan guarantees on the eve of the Middle East peace talks; and in November introduced a proposal to cut foreign aid and use the money saved to fund an unemployment insurance extension. In 1991, Mitchell published *World on Fire: Saving an Endangered Earth,* a very well-received book on environmental issues in which he discussed many of the main ecological crises facing humanity, was highly critical of Bush administration ecological policies, and outlined a program for U.S. government action to help save the environment from further damage.

Maine-born Mitchell began his career in Washington as a Justice Department attorney (1960–62) and was an assistant to Maine Democratic Senator Edmund Muskie (1962–65). He went home to practice law and politics in Maine, became a U.S. attorney and then U.S. district judge in the late 1970s, and became a Maine Democratic senator in 1981, succeeding Muskie. Mitchell rose quickly in the Senate and in his party; he became majority leader of the Senate in 1988. With fellow Maine senator William S. Cohen, a Republican, Mitchell wrote *Men of Zeal: A Candid Story of the Iran-Contra Hearings* (1988). His B.A. was from Bowdoin College in 1954, his LL.B. from Georgetown University in 1960. He has one child.

FURTHER READING

"Hill potatoes. . . ." FRED BARNES. *New Republic,* May 20, 1991.
"Mitchell, George John." *Current Biography,* Apr. 1989.
"A hardball player. . . ." HAYS GOREY. *Time,* Dec. 12, 1988.

Mitchum, Robert (Robert Charles Duran Mitchum, 1917–) It was a year of continuing great celebrity for Mitchum, now a revered figure in world films. In a major ceremonial appearance, he opened the 44th Cannes Film Festival and was called on to make several other such appearances during the year. On screen, he and Gregory Peck appeared in small roles in one of the major films of 1991, the Martin Scorsese remake of the 1962 film *Cape Fear,* starring Robert De Niro in the original Mitchum role, Nick Nolte in the Peck role, and Jessica Lange. Another of his films was remade, as well—the 1955 *Night of the Hunter,* as a television film starring perennial hero Richard Chamberlain as villainous "Preacher" Harry Powell, in the role Mitchum had so memorably created.

Connecticut-born Mitchum has been on screen for over four decades, from his very promising Oscar-nominated role in *The Story of G.I. Joe* (1945), through his massive Pug Henry role in television's miniseries *The Winds of War* (1983) and its sequel *War and Remembrance* (1987). He has played leads and strong character roles in dozens of films, such as *Out of the Past* (1947), *The Night of the Hunter* (1955), *The Wonderful Country* (1959), *The Sundowners* (1960), *El Dorado* (1967), *Ryan's Daughter* (1971), *Farewell, My Lovely* (1975), *The Big Sleep* (1977), *The Ambassador* (1984), and *Mr. North* (1988). He has also played in many other television roles, including his lead in the series, "A Family for Joe" (1990). Mitchum married Dorothy Spencer in 1940; the couple have three children, including the actors James and Christopher Mitchum.

FURTHER READING

"Robert Mitchum." GRAHAM FULLER. *Interview,* Dec. 1991.

"Robert Mitchum. . . ." FRANK THOMPSON. *American Film,* May 1991.
Them Ornery Mitchum Boys: The Adventures of Robert and John Mitchum. JOHN MITCHUM. Creatures at Large, 1989.
Robert Mitchum: A Biography. GEORGE EELLS. Watts, 1984; Jove, 1985.
Robert Mitchum. DEREK MALCOM. Hippocrene, 1984.

Mitterrand, François (François Maurice Marie Mitterrand, 1916–) As French President Mitterrand celebrated his tenth year in office, he encountered major economic, social, and political problems at home that threatened his ability to govern. Mitterrand's experience was much like that of George Bush in the United States, who came out of the Persian Gulf War victory with enormous popularity, only to find domestic problems reversing his popularity. After initial hesitation, Mitterrand fully supported the Gulf War, sending substantial French air, sea, and land forces to fight in the Gulf, and came out of it with a reported record 85 percent French electorate approval rating. But late in the year, his popularity hovered near the 50 percent level as unemployment grew, pay raises were strongly resisted, and major unemployment demonstrations and strikes developed.

There were also serious farm problems, some of them highly political. As farm prices declined, French farmers resisted European Community demands that farm price supports be cut, even though demanded by other nations, including the United States. As Eastern Europe became free, the French government also weakened its opposition to Eastern European meat imports, further enraging French farmers. By late autumn, massive farmer protests were in progress, and Mitterrand's Socialist Party was blamed for growing farm problems.

In the spring of 1990, violence against Muslims and Jews flared; in mid-May, after several Jewish graves had been desecrated, Mitterrand once again stated his deep opposition to racism and anti-Semitism, and on May 14 marched with an estimated 80,000–100,000 Parisians to protest the resurgence of fascism and racism in France; he was joined by the leaders of the other major French political parties. But in 1991, opposition to African and other immigration grew, late-spring riots in several immigrant ghettos developed, and immigration became a major issue, at the political expense of the Mitterrand government.

In foreign affairs, Mitterrand continued to support the movement of France into the developing European economic and political union, though resisting entry of the newly free Eastern European nations into the group. He also continued to encourage the development of Soviet democracy, although his initial silence and seeming acceptance of the August Soviet coup was politically embarrassing.

Mitterrand was a soldier captured early during World War II, but he escaped from the Germans and became an active Resistance fighter. He entered politics after the war and was a Socialist Deputy in the national assembly (1946–58; 1962–81), holding many cabinet positions in the early years, when his party held power. At the same time, he rose within the Socialist Party and was its First Secretary (1971–81), while also becoming a vice president of the Socialist International (1972–81). In 1981, he was elected president of France, and was re-elected to a second seven-year term in 1988. Mitterrand attended the University of Paris. He married Danielle Gouze in 1944; the couple have two children. His brother is general Jacques Mitterrand.

FURTHER READING

Seven Years in France: François Mitterrand and Unintended Revolution, 1981–1988. JULIUS W. FRIEND. Westview, 1988.
The Black and the Red: François Mitterrand and the Story of an Ambition. CATHERINE NAY. Harcourt Brace, 1987.

Mitterrand's France. SONIA MAZEY and MICHAEL NEWMAN, eds. Routledge Chapman & Hall, 1987.
François Mitterrand: A Political Odyssey. DENIS MACSHANE. Phaidon, 1983.

Miyazawa, Kiichi (1919–) Powerful Japanese politician Kiichi Miyazawa, leader of the strongest faction of the ruling Liberal Democratic Party (LDP), was chosen prime minister by his party on October 27, 1991, and took office on November 6, succeeding Toshiki Kaifu, who had declined to seek re-election. Kaifu had been elected as one of the few "clean" candidates available after the 1988 Recruit stock scandal had forced the resignation of Prime Minister Noburo Takeshita and many others in his government, including Miyazawa. Kaifu's decision not to seek re-election as LDP head came after Miyazawa and other LDP leaders had refused to pass his proposed reform program, aimed at preventing further corrupt political practices. On November 6, the day he took office, Miyazawa named a new cabinet that included many politicians earlier forced from power after their involvement in major scandals, including the Recruit stock scandal; among them was former Prime Minister Nakasone, named a senior adviser to the Miyazawa government. Often an outspoken critic of the United States, Miyazawa began his term of office at a time of considerable U.S.-Japanese abrasion over Japanese trade policies, which American trade officials were very openly calling discriminatory, aimed at protecting Japanese business and the very favorable Japanese balance of trade.

Tokyo-born Miyazawa, the child of a prominent Japanese political family, is a graduate of Tokyo Imperial University. He began his five-decade-long political career during World War II and was with the Finance Ministry (1942–52) through the war and the postwar American occupation of Japan; he became secretary to the minister of Finance in 1949. A powerful leader of the ruling Liberal Democratic Party (LDP), he became an elected official in 1953, and then vice minister of Education (1959–69), holding a series of cabinet-level posts for the following three decades. He was chairman of the Executive Council of the LDP (1984–86), and became a key leader of the most powerful of the three LDP factions in that period. He is married to Yoko Miyazawa; they have two children. He also has two brothers, both active in government.

FURTHER READING

"Miyazawa unravels." *Economist,* Dec. 14, 1991.
"Raw and fishy. . . ." JOANNA PITMAN. *New Republic,* Nov. 4, 1991.

Molinari, Alberto: See **Lebanon Hostages**

Mollenhoff, Clark Raymond (1921–91) Iowa-born Mollenhoff, a journalist and author, was a reporter for Cowles Publications for most of four decades. He began his career as a reporter for the *Des Moines Register* in 1941, was in the U.S. Navy for two years during World War II, and went back to the newspaper after the war. In 1950, he became a Washington correspondent for Cowles and was for the following two decades a leading American investigative reporter, winning a 1958 Pulitzer Prize for national reporting for his exposé of labor racketeering, especially in James Hoffa's Teamsters Union. He was a personal investigator for President Richard M. Nixon for nine months in 1969 and 1970, in that brief period becoming involved in the Clement Haynesworth Supreme Court matter and several other highly publicized controversies. From 1970 to 1978, he was with

Cowles again and was a syndicated columnist. Mollenhoff also wrote several books, mostly on political matters, including a book of poetry, *Ballad to an Iowa Farmer & Other Reflections* (1991). He was survived by his second wife, the former Jane Schurz, a daughter, a son, two brothers, a stepdaughter, and three stepsons. (d. Lexington, Virginia; March 2, 1991)

FURTHER READING

Obituary. *Current Biography,* May 1991.
Obituary. *New York Times,* Mar. 3, 1991.

Montand, Yves (Ivo Levi, 1921–91) Italian-born French actor and singer Montand, a major international film star for more than four decades, began his career in cabaret, in pre–World War II Marseilles, his home town. He fought with the Resistance during World War II. In the mid-1940s, he became the lover and protegé of the French singer Edith Piaf. As a singer, he is best known for such early songs as "Autumn Leaves" and "Urchins of Paris." His breakthrough film role came in *The Wages of Fear* (1947). He married the actress Simone Signoret in 1950; together they starred in a 1956 French film version of Arthur Miller's *The Crucible.* The first of his few English-language films was *Let's Make Love* (1960), most notable for his off-camera but highly publicized affair with co-star Marilyn Monroe. He also starred in *On a Clear Day You Can See Forever* (1970). But his major political films made a far greater international impact, including *La Guerre Est Finis* (1966), *Z* (1969), and *State of Siege* (1973). Late in his career, he was highly acclaimed in the films *Jean de Florette* (1986) and *Manon of the Spring* (1986). Always involved in political and social causes, he was early in his life a person of the "left," who strongly criticized the French war in Algeria and the United States early in the Cold War. He broke with communism in 1956, however, strongly criticizing the Soviet Union, and later remained an independent. He was married to Signoret until her death in 1985. He was survived by his companion, Carole Amiel, and one child. (d. Paris; November 9, 1991)

FURTHER READING

Obituary. Marjorie Rosen et al. *People,* Nov. 25, 1991.
Obituary. *Variety,* Nov. 18, 1991.
Obituary. *New York Times,* Nov. 10, 1991.
"Architectural Digest visits. . . ." Charlotte Aillaud and Daniel H. Minassian. *Architectural Digest,* Jan. 1989.
"Yves Montand. . . ." Brad Darrach. *People,* May 16, 1988.
"Montand, Yves." *Current Biography,* Sep. 1988.
"Montand." Harland Jacobson. *Film Comment,* Sep.–Oct. 1987.

Moore, Demi (Demi Guynes, 1962–) Propelled into stardom by her 1990 role in *Ghost,* Moore had a very busy year. Perhaps more spectacularly, she appeared nude and in an advanced state of pregnancy on the August cover of the magazine *Vanity Fair,* igniting a storm of publicity. The baby, her second daughter, was born on July 20. On screen, Moore co-produced and starred in *Mortal Thoughts,* directed by Alan Rudolph, in a cast that included her husband Bruce Willis, and Glenne Headly, John Pankow, Harvey Keitel, and Billie Neal. Moore also starred as clairvoyant Marina in *The Butcher's Wife,* opposite George Dzundza as her husband and Jeff Daniels as a psychiatrist who initially disbelieves in her powers. She was teamed with Chevy Chase as a pair of city-types lost in a small Atlantic-coast town dominated by a bizarre local bigwig, played by Dan Aykroyd, who also wrote and directed the film, *Nothing But Trouble.*

New Mexico-born Moore was reporter Jackie Templeton in television's "General Hospital," and played in such 1980s films as *Choices* (1981), *Parasite* (1982), *St. Elmo's Fire* (1985), *Wisdom* (1986), and *We're No Angels* (1989). Her breakthrough came in 1990, with a starring role opposite Patrick Swayze and Whoopi Goldberg in the fantasy *Ghost,* which became the surprise top-grossing film of the year and therefore made her a bankable star. She married Bruce Willis in 1987; they have two children.

FURTHER READING

"Demi's big moment." Nancy Collins and Annie Leibovitz. *Vanity Fair,* Aug. 1991.
"The haunting magic of. . . ." Tom Burke. *Cosmopolitan,* Dec. 1990.
"They heard it through. . . ." Jeannie Park. *People,* Nov. 12, 1990.
"Bruce, Demi, and baby. . . ." Nancy Anderson. *Good Housekeeping.* Nov. 1988.

Moreau, Jeanne (1928–) French actress Moreau was seen in an extraordinary range of international settings in 1991. In what *Variety* hailed as the "performance of a lifetime," she starred as con artist Lady M in Laurent Heynemann's *La Vieille Qui Marchait Dans La Mer* (*The Old Lady Who Wades in the Sea*), who not only is caught stealing jewels but also must face her protegé's love for a younger woman. At the Cannes Film Festival, she appeared opposite Marcello Mastroianni in Theo Angelopoulos's *The Suspended Step of the Stork,* a film about Albanian, Kurdish, and Iranian refugees arriving in Greece, and the broken families, fear, and human debris of European life that they represent. Also at Cannes, in Rustam Khamdamov's Soviet film *Anna Karamazova,* she was a newly freed prisoner moving through the Stalinist Soviet Union of the 1940s. Moreau was also notable as Amande, a courtesan tutoring an assassin in feminine wiles, in Luc Besson's *La Femme Nikita,* the French box-office hit of 1990, which appeared in the United States in 1991. She also appeared in Wim Wenders's *Until the End of the World,* a futuristic thriller shot in 20 cities in 7 countries, with an international cast including William Hurt, Solveig Dommartin, Sam Neill, and Max von Sydow; and *Map of the Human Heart,* a World War II tale directed by Vincent Ward, with Jason Scott Lee, Patrick Bergin, Anne Parillaud, and John Cusack.

Paris-born Moreau has been a leading actress on the French stage and screen since 1948. She became an international film star in the 1950s, and has appeared in such films as *Frantic* (1957), *The Lovers* (1958), *Les Liaisons Dangereuses* (1959), *Jules and Jim* (1961), *Diary of a Chambermaid* (1964), *Viva Maria* (1965), *The Bride Wore Black* (1967), and *Lumiere* (1976; she also directed). Moreau attended the National Conservatory of Dramatic Art. She has been married twice and has one son.

FURTHER READING

"La lumiere." MOLLY HASKELL and ANDREA R. VAUCHER. *Film Comment,* Mar.–Apr. 1990.
"Moreau." FRANCOISE SAGAN. *Vogue,* Nov. 1985.

Motherwell, Robert (1915–91) A leading abstract impressionist, Motherwell began his career as a painter and teacher in the late 1930s; his first solo show was in Paris, in 1939. He taught art briefly at the University of Oregon in 1939, went to New York to study with art historian Meyer Shapiro at Columbia University in 1940, and there developed his thinking and career. His first American solo show was in 1944 at Peggy Guggenheim's "Art of This Century" gallery. In 1948, Motherwell, with William Baziotes, Mark Rothko, Barnett Newman, and David Hare, became a founder of the "Subjects of the Artist" art school, on Eighth Street in Greenwich Village. The group, which later became the Eighth Street Club, was a center of the developing abstract expressionist movement, later to be called the New York School. Motherwell taught at Hunter College from 1950 to 1958.

In 1949, Motherwell began the long series of over 150 paintings, all called *Elegy to the Spanish Republic,* that are his best-known work; the last was *Elegy to the Spanish Republic No. 172* (*With Blood*) (1990). Another major series was *Open,* begun in the late 1960s. He was also a prolific collagist and printmaker. After 1969, when he parted from his third wife, the artist Helen Frankenthaler, his studios were at Greenwich, Connecticut, with summer quarters at Provincetown, Massachusetts. He was survived by his fourth wife, photographer Renate Ponsold, two daughters, and a sister. (d. Provincetown, Massachusetts; January 24, 1991)

FURTHER READING

"Remembering Motherwell." ARTHUR C. DANTO. *ARTnews,* Sep. 1991.
Obituary. *Current Biography,* Sep. 1991.
Obituary. *The Times* (of London), June 19, 1991.
Obituary. *New York Times,* June 18, 1991.
Robert Motherwell: The Formative Years. ROBERT S. MATTISON. UMI, 1989.
Robert Motherwell. DORE ASHTON and JACK FLAM. Abbeville, 1983.
Robert Motherwell, rev. ed. H. H. ARNASON and BARBARALEE DIAMONSTEIN. Abrams, 1982.
Robert Motherwell and Black. STEPHANIE TERENZIO. Petersburg Press, 1980.

Moynihan, Daniel Patrick (1927–) In 1991, Moynihan, who is chairman of the Senate Finance Committee's subcommittee on Social Security, once again took his proposal to cut Social Security taxes to the Senate floor. He had

spent most of 1990 fighting for the same proposal, arguing that rising Social Security surpluses were being used to mask mounting deficits, and that the surpluses were an unnecessary drain on those least able to pay. In April, the Senate once again rejected the tax cut, fearing that the cuts might harm the financial integrity of the critically important Social Security fund. He was considerably more successful on transportation issues, as sponsor of the Senate version of the omnibus five-year transportation bill, passed by the Senate on June 19.

Oklahoma-born Moynihan, a Democrat, served in appointive positions in New York State government in the early 1960s, in that period also co-authoring the influential and controversial *Beyond the Melting Pot* (1963). He was based at Harvard University (1966–77) while also holding a series of appointive federal positions, notably as ambassador to India (1973–75) and American United Nations representative (1975–76). Moving into electoral politics, he began the first of his three senatorial terms in 1977. In the Senate, he has been a member of the influential rules, taxation, foreign relations, and finance committees, in finance becoming head of the Social Security subcommittee. Among his more recent written works are *Counting Our Blessings: Reflections on the Future of America* (1980), *Loyalties* (1984), *Family and Nation* (1986), and *Came the Revolution: Argument in the Reagan Era* (1988). Moynihan's B.A. was from New York's City College in 1943, and his M.A. and Ph.D. from Tufts University in 1948 and 1949; he also attended the London School of Economics. He married Elizabeth Brennan in 1955; the couple have four children.

FURTHER READING

"Liberal? Conservative? . . ." JAMES TRAUB. *New York Times Magazine,* Sep. 16, 1990.
" 'A true capacity for governance.' " MAURA MOYNIHAN. *American Heritage,* Oct.–Nov. 1986.
"Moynihan, Daniel Patrick." *Current Biography,* Feb. 1986.

Mubarak, Hosni (Mohammed Hosni Mubarak, 1928–) As the Persian Gulf crisis developed into the Persian Gulf War, Egyptian President Mubarak became a key member of the Gulf Alliance. Egypt sent approximately 45,000 troops into the conflict, including divisional strength frontline troops that participated in the successful frontal assault on Iraqi positions in Kuwait and southern Iraq.

Early in the crisis, Egypt suffered severe economic dislocation, as more than one million Egyptian nationals in Iraq and Kuwait were forced to flee those countries. In the aftermath of the war, however, Egypt received massive debt relief and new foreign aid that more than made up for any direct and indirect war costs. Western lenders, led by the United States, forgave approximately $25 billion of Egypt's $50 billion in outstanding foreign debt, also providing interest rate reductions, payment stretchouts, and probably future forgiveness of more debt. Additionally, they also guaranteed at least $8 billion more in foreign aid. In return, Mubarak moderated his resistance to the introduction of austerity measures and other economic reforms, though still concerned about their possible impact on unemployment and social unrest. With Egypt's massive population growth and weak economy, and with Islamic fundamentalist unrest seriously threatening Egyptian democracy, Mubarak's problems continued to multiply, even with temporary economic relief.

Mubarak was a career air force officer who moved up to direct the Air Academy (1967–69), became Air Force chief of staff (1969–72) and later commander in chief (1972–75). He became Anwar Sadat's vice president in 1975 and moved into the presidency in 1981 after Sadat's assassination. He won a second term in the 1987 elections. In 1988, the Mubarak government moved against the fundamentalists, beginning a period of widespread arrests under emergency decrees in effect since the Sadat assassination. Mubarak has been a moderate within the Arab world throughout his presidency and a considerable force in the search for Middle East and Arab-Israeli peace. As president of the Organization of African Unity (1989–90), he tried to help settle such regional conflicts as those in Ethiopia, Chad, and Namibia. After the August 1990 Iraqi attack on Kuwait, he led moderate Arab response, convening an Arab summit meeting on August 8 and attempting to convince Saddam Hussein to withdraw. When the Iraqis would not do so, Mubarak led in the formation of the multinational Arab army sent to Saudi Arabia. He attended the Egyptian military and air academies. Little is known of his private life, except that he is married, to Suzanne Mubarak, and has at least two children.

FURTHER READING

"Who's sitting pretty. . . ." *Business Week,* Mar. 11, 1991.
Hosni Mubarak. John Solecki. Chelsea House, 1991.
"A call to negotiate. . . ." Dean Fisher. *Time,* Sep. 10, 1990.
"The view from Cairo." Mortimer B. Zuckerman. *U.S. News & World Report,* Apr. 16, 1990.
Egypt after Nasser: Sadat, Peace and the Mirage of Prosperity. Thomas W. Lippman. *Paragon,* 1989.

Mulroney, Brian (Martin Brian Mulroney, 1939–) For Canadian Prime Minister Mulroney, 1991 was a very bad year, with the two unresolved issues at the heart of Canadian political and economic life continuing to threaten his political career. The first was the country's deeply depressed economy and the widespread popular perception that federal government cutbacks in such areas as education, health, and welfare programs were causing great hardship and deepening the long Canadian recession. Mulroney's attempts to stimulate the lagging economy included such moves as increased farm subsidies and tax relief for Canadian lumber exporters, but by year's end no upturn was in sight.

The second and extraordinarily upsetting issue—as it threatened the existence of the nation—was the question of whether Quebec was to remain part of Canada, and if so on what terms. Mulroney had been the prime mover in negotiating the Meech Lake Accords of June 1987 and had lost much of his support after the 1990 failure of the agreements. Facing a deadline imposed by a Quebec law mandating a sovereignty referendum by the end of 1992 if there was no satisfactory proposal by then, Mulroney tried again. On September 24, 1991, he proposed major constitutional changes aimed at replacing the failed Meech Lake Accords, with the aim of keeping Quebec in Canada. His main proposal was recognition of a "distinct" Quebec identity within Canada, with additional proposals that included Quebec power to override Canada's 1982 Bill of Rights and other elements of special status. His restructuring proposal also included a 10-year plan for Eskimo and Indian self-government, revised economic arrangements among the provinces, and a shift of several economic powers to the provinces. His proposals were received rather cautiously by all concerned, and a new national debate began. His popularity continued to decline, one late autumn poll showing it as under 10 percent.

Mulroney practiced law in Montreal (1965–76), and then moved into industry, as executive vice president and then president of the Iron Ore Company of Canada (1976–83). He became Progressive Party leader and a member of parliament in 1983, and prime minister in 1984. He was returned to power in the general election of November 1988 after having made the election a virtual referendum on the recently concluded 1988 Canada-U.S. trade pact. Mulroney attended St. Francis Xavier and Laval Universities. He married Mila Pivnicki in 1973; the couple have four children.

FURTHER READING

"Life of Brian. . . ." JOHN SAWATSKY. *Saturday Night,* Oct. 1991.
"Mulroney revealed. . . ." ANTHONY WILSON-SMITH. *Maclean's,* Oct. 1991.
"Mulroney vs. the unions." ANTHONY WILSON-SMITH. *Maclean's,* Sep. 23, 1991.
"Mulroney up close. . . ." ANTHONY WILSON-SMITH, *Maclean's,* June 10, 1991.
"Under the gun. . . ." BRUCE WALLACE. *Maclean's,* Sep. 24, 1990.
" 'Off to the races.' " KEVIN DOYLE and ANTHONY WILSON-SMITH. *Maclean's,* June 25, 1990.
Sacred Trust: Brian Mulroney and the Conservative Party in Power. DAVID BERCUSON. Doubleday, 1987.

Murdoch, Rupert (Keith Rupert Murdoch, 1931–) Media baron Murdoch maintained his highly defensive position in 1991, as he had in 1990, and managed to survive without encountering the kind of financial catastrophe that seemed imminent at the beginning of the year. In early 1991, Murdoch was involved in long, complex negotiations with his bank creditors, in an attempt to restructure and stretch out loan repayments. In this, he was successful, although being forced by creditors to pay bonuses and higher interest rates for the privilege. Having bought some time, he made a series of substantial moves. During 1991, he sold nine major U.S. consumer magazines, including *New York, Seventeen,* the *Daily Racing Form,* and *Premiere;* sold much of his share of the Enquirer/Star group; closed down or consolidated newspaper properties in Australia; and cut staff worldwide. By late in 1991, his News Corporation stock had considerably rebounded, and a stock offering to raise much-needed cash with which to meet further huge debt payments became possible. On November 24, 1991, his News Corporation announced bank agreement to delay large principal repayments and also announced plans for new stock and bond issues.

Australian-American publisher Murdoch started with a small Australian family newspaper in 1952, and by 1990 had built a large worldwide communications company, controlling such publications and companies as Fox Television, 20th Century Fox Films, *The Times* of London, HarperCollins Publishers, Sky Television, *The Australian* and many other publications in Australia, *New York* magazine, and Triangle Publications, purchased for $3 billion in 1988, until then the largest acquisition in publishing history. He became dangerously overextended in 1990, as worldwide advertising revenues fell in a growing recession, existing assets realized less money on sale, and interest rates remained high for a time. His debts exceeded $8 billion by late 1990, and in the changed atmosphere of the early 1990s, he quickly ran into major problems. Murdoch attended Oxford University. He married Anna Maria Torv in 1976; the couple have two children.

FURTHER READING

"Uppers and downers." HELEN KAY. *Management Today,* Oct. 9, 1991.
"Murdoch's map maker." *Economist,* Jan. 26, 1991.
"A chastened man." *Economist,* Jan. 19, 1991.
Outfoxed: Marvin Davis, Barry Diller, Rupert Murdoch and the Inside Story of America's Fourth Television Network. ALEX B. BLOCK. St. Martin's, 1990.
Rupert Murdoch. JEROME TUCCILLE. Donald I. Fine, 1989.
Citizen Murdoch: The Unexpurgated Story of Rupert Murdoch—The World's Most Powerful and Controversial Media Lord. THOMAS KIERNAN. Dodd, Mead, 1986.

Arrogant Aussie: The Rupert Murdoch Story. MICHAEL LEAPMAN. Carol, 1985.

Murphy, Eddie (1961–) It was a year of deals and plans for popular movie star Eddie Murphy. In late September, after many months of negotiation, he and Paramount Pictures announced an extension of their long-standing relationship, going back to his 1982 film debut in *48 Hrs.* Murphy agreed to star in the two Paramount films still owed under his old contract, plus two more, with Murphy continuing to produce for films and television and free to make one outside film. The first project, a film based on a Murphy story, was *Boomerang,* which began shooting in November 1991. He quickly followed up with a Disney film agreement, to do *The Distinguished Gentleman,* scheduled to shoot in the spring of 1992, after *Boomerang.* Negotiations also proceeded toward production of another *Beverly Hills Cop* film, although it was proving difficult for Paramount to reach agreement with Don Simpson and Jerry Bruckenheimer, who had produced the first two films in the series. Murphy, though formally committed to the film, seemed hesitant to proceed without them.

Brooklyn-born Murphy was one of the leading entertainment celebrities of the 1980s, beginning with his regular featured role on television's "Saturday Night Live" (1980–84). His recording career began with the album *Eddie Murphy* (1982), and included *Eddie Murphy Comedian* (1983), and *So Happy* (1989). He began a spectacular film career with *48 Hrs.* (1982), and went on to such other films as *Trading Places* (1983), *Beverly Hills Cop* (1983; *II,* 1986; *III,* 1989), *Harlem Nights* (1989), and *Another 48 Hrs.* (1990). Murphy and model Nicole Mitchell have one child.

FURTHER READING

"Eddie Murphy. . . ." WALTER LEAVY. *Ebony,* Jan. 1990.
Films of Eddie Murphy. EDWARD GROSS. Movie Publications, 1990.
"Eddie Murphy. . . ." BILL ZEHME. *Rolling Stone,* Aug, 24, 1989.
"Eddie Murphy. . . ." BONNIE ALLEN. *Essence,* Dec. 1988.
"Eddie Murphy. . . ." JAMES MCBRIDE. *People,* Aug. 8, 1988.
Eddie Murphy. TERESA KOENIG and RIVIAN BELL. Lerner, 1985.
Eddie: Eddie Murphy from A to Z. MARIANNE RUTH. Holloway, 1985.
The Unofficial Eddie Murphy Scrapbook. JUDITH DAVIS. NAL-Dutton, 1984.

Murray, Arthur (Arthur Murray Teichman, 1895–1991) Born in New York City, Murray began his career as a ballroom dance teacher at Castle Hall, the dancing school run by Vernon and Irene Castle. He later taught at a resort in Asheville, North Carolina, and established his first studio in Atlanta, Georgia, in the early 1920s. He moved to New York City in 1924, during the 1920s built a nationwide mail order dance instruction business, and in the 1930s began to develop a national web of franchised dance studios that ultimately numbered over 300. He and his wife and partner, Kathryn, also became radio celebrities, in the weekly "Arthur Murray's Dance Party." Murray's "hard sell" promotion methods were often criticized by state and federal regulators; in 1960, the Federal Trade Commission ordered his company to cease employing several selling techniques, and in particular the false contests he had been successfully promoting for many years. Murray sold his business in 1964, staying on as a consultant. He was survived by his wife, the former Kathryn Kohnfelder, two daughters, and a brother. (d. Honolulu; March 3, 1991)

FURTHER READING

Obituary. ROBERT C. ROMAN. *Dance,* July 1991.
Obituary. *Current Biography,* May 1991.
Obituary. *The Times* (of London), Mar. 25, 1991.
Obituary. *Variety,* Mar. 11, 1991.
Obituary. *New York Times,* Mar. 4, 1991.
My Husband, Arthur Murray. KATHRYN MURRAY. Revisionist Press, 1985.

Murray, Bill (1950–) Gifted actor and comedian Murray scored a success in the spring of 1991, as Bob Wiley in the title role of the Frank Oz film comedy *What About Bob?*. Bob is a psychiatric patient who follows his psychiatrist, played by Richard Dreyfuss, on holiday; the interplay between the two and between Bob and the psychiatrist's family supplies both situation and comedy. The rather well-received film was a "sleeper," doing unexpectedly well at the box office and even better later in the year in home video rental grosses. Forthcoming was a starring role in *Mad Dog and Glory,* produced by Martin Scorsese and directed by John MacNaughton, with a cast that includes Robert De Niro, Uma Thurman, Kathy Baker, David Caruseo, and Mike Starr.

Illinois-born Murray began his career with Chicago's Second City Troupe, and emerged as a television star in the late 1970s, as a regular on "Saturday Night Live." He has appeared in such films as *Meatballs* (1977), *Caddyshack* (1980), *Stripes* (1981), *Ghostbusters* (1984), *Little Shop of Horrors* (1986), *Scrooged* (1988), *Ghostbusters II* (1989), and *Quick Change* (1990; he co-produced, co-directed and starred). Murray attended Regis College. He married Margaret Kelly in 1980; the couple have two children.

FURTHER READING

The Rolling Stone Interviews: The 1980s. St. Martin's, 1989.
"The rumpled anarchy. . . ." TIMOTHY WHITE. *New York Times Magazine,* Nov. 20, 1988.
The Second City. DONNA MCCROHAN. Putnam, 1987.

Musaveni, Yoweri (1944–) Uganda's President Musaveni faced severe economic problems and a continuing low-level insurgency during 1991, as well as growing support for a return to democracy. At the same time, he was able to further stabilize Uganda and to bring in much needed ecotourist revenue from abroad, from those who came to see the country's magnificent, restored, though still-endangered national park system, such an important part of the world's heritage. But the problems were great: Civil war, though diminished, continued in the north and east. Coffee and other commodity prices continued low in the worldwide 1990–91 recession; international aid was not enough to fill the gap, and the aid that arrived did not always find its way through corrupt government officials into the country's depressed economy. A failed invasion of neighboring Rwanda by Uganda-based Rwandan exiles, which was reportedly assisted by Ugandan army officers, embittered relations between the countries, while tension continued on the Sudanese and Kenyan borders. Musaveni again barred a return to multiparty democracy, postponing presidential and parliamentary elections until 1995—so far away as to make the promise meaningless. Musaveni was 1990–91 president of the Organization of African Unity (OAU); his term ended at the annual meeting of the OAU, held June 3–5 at Abuja, Nigeria.

The Ugandan leader was a very young research assistant in the government of Milton Obote (1971–72) and went into exile when dictator Idi Amin took over his country, spending the years 1971–79 in Tanzania. He returned to Uganda with the Tanzanian troops that toppled Amin in 1979. He was defense minister in 1980, and then went into opposition, leading the National Resistance Army (NRA) in a guerrilla insurrection (1981–86). After the victory of his forces, he in 1986 became president of Uganda and the country's defense minister. Musaveni attended the University College of Dar es Salaam. He is married and has four children.

FURTHER READING

"Uganda enjoys. . . ." CHARLES T. POWERS. *Los Angeles Times,* June 8, 1986.

Navratilova, Martina (1956–) In a year of personal turmoil, veteran superstar Navratilova tried to re-center her life around tennis, with partial success. With wins at Birmingham, Eastbourne, and Oakland, Navratilova tied Chris Evert's record of 157 singles victories. But at Wimbledon, where she was the defending champion going for an unprecedented tenth title, she was cut down in straight sets in the quarterfinals by 15-year-old Jennifer Capriati, losing not even on a contested point but on her own double-fault. It was the first time since 1981 that she was not in the Wimbledon finals. At the U.S. Open in September, she was not even ranked in the top four, but was seeded sixth; she did reach the final, only to be knocked off by 17-year-old Monica Seles.

But as she faced such rising stars, some less than half her age, she found new support from tennis fans, who came to perceive her as an underdog and to cheer her efforts, as seen by the thundering ovation she received after her hard-fought loss to Monica Seles in the Virginia Slims final in November 1991. In the same tournament, she and longtime doubles partner Pam Shriver won a dramatic doubles final over Gigi Fernandez and Jana Novotna; after accepting the trophy, Navratilova announced she was donating $5,000 of her winnings to AIDS research. Personal distractions were considerable; they included a palimony suit brought by former companion Judy Nelson, and a related suit brought by Navratilova against her former attorney, Jerry Loftin, now representing Nelson.

Prague-born Navratilova emerged as a leading Czech tennis player while still in her early teens and was Czech national champion (1972–75). She was a notable defector to the West in 1975, and then went on to become the top-ranked woman tennis player in the world for four years in a row (1982–85) as well as having a Grand Slam (1983–84). She continued to win major tournaments throughout the latter 1980s as well, and in all has won the U.S. Open four times (1983–84, 1986–87) and Wimbledon an unprecedented nine times (1978–79, 1982–87, 1990), with a record six consecutive titles. Navratilova has also been a notable doubles player; she and Pam Shriver won three doubles Grand Slams (1983–84; 1984–85; 1986–87) and a record 109 consecutive doubles matches (April 24, 1983–July 6, 1985). Navratilova and Gigi Fernandez won the U.S. Open doubles championships in 1990, sweeping the main doubles championships for the year. In 1985 she published *Martina: Autobiography,* written with George Vecsey. Navratilova became a U.S. citizen in 1981.

FURTHER READING

"Ten living legends. . . ." Steve Wulf. *Sports Illustrated,* Dec. 23, 1991.

"Not obsessed about. . . ." Jim Martz. *Sporting News,* July 2, 1990."

"Postscript to. . . ." Ann Smith and Lewis Rothlein. *Women's Sports and Fitness,* Mar. 1990.

Martina Navratilova: Tennis Power. R. R. Knudson. Viking, 1986; Puffin, 1987.

Martina Navratilova. JANE M. LEDER. Crestwood House, 1985.

Nazarbayev, Nursultan Abishevich

(1940–) Kazakh leader Nazarbayev, elected by his parliament to the new post of president in April 1990, became a major figure in Soviet politics during 1991. As the Soviet Union began to splinter, he played the role of a political moderate, trying to mediate differences between Mikhail Gorbachev and Boris Yeltsin and aiming to keep an economic union of the former Soviet republics, while at the same time developing direct ties between Kazakhstan and the other republics, especially Russia. Until the Soviet breakup, he strongly advocated maintenance of some sort of central Soviet political authority, feeling that Kazakhstan, a poor country, might find total independence very difficult. He sharply opposed the attempted August right-wing coup, and August 22 resigned all his Communist Party positions. Nazarbayev was also an economic radical, quickly moving Kazakhstan toward a market economy, with help from advisers brought in from abroad.

Nazarbayev played a particularly important role in nuclear arms and weapons reduction questions, very strongly supporting U.S. and Soviet weapons cuts, closing a nuclear testing range, and demanding that Kazakhstan be made a nuclear-free zone. But in late September, he changed his views somewhat, demanding joint control of large stocks of nuclear weapons. The question was one of great importance to humanity, for Kazakhstan holds major nuclear weapons installations.

Kazakhstan-born Nazarbayev, who joined the Communist Party in 1962, worked as an economist at the Karaganda Metallurgical Combine (1960–69), and then moved into party work. After holding a series of local posts, he emerged as Kazakh central committee secretary (1979–84), was leader of his party in Kazakhstan from 1984, and was a member of the Soviet Communist Party central committee from 1986.

FURTHER READING

"The end of the U.S.S.R." GEORGE J. CHURCH. *Time,* Dec. 23, 1991.

"Warily seeking sovereignty." ROBIN KNIGHT. *U.S. News & World Report,* Sep. 23, 1991.

"The khan of Kazakhstan. . . ." CARROLL BOGERT. *Newsweek,* July 8, 1991.

"The war within the corridors. . . ." MARY NEMETH. *Maclean's,* Apr. 1, 1991.

Nelson, Willie

(1933–) Financial problems continued to plague the great country singer Willie Nelson in 1991. In 1990, the Internal Revenue Service, claiming that he owed $16.7 million in back taxes, had placed liens on and then auctioned off Nelson's real estate and personal property. The process continued in 1991, with auctions of his Colorado and Texas homes, golf course, country club, and several other properties. In an attempt to raise money, Nelson in June released the album *Who'll Buy My Memories (The I.R.S. Tapes)*. The album featured just Willie Nelson and his guitar, singing many of his classic songs, and immediately became itself something of a classic. On screen, Nelson appeared opposite Kris Kristofferson in the television movie *Another Pair of Aces: Three of a Kind,* which aired to mixed reviews in April; it was a sequel to their telefilm *Pair of Aces* (1990), with Nelson a safecracker and Kristofferson a Texas Ranger.

Whatever his own troubles, Nelson continued to lend his name and art to a wide range of social causes, as in his appearance on the San Diego Children's Hospital Foundation benefit album, the proceeds to go to many children's hospitals. Early in the year, before the Persian Gulf crisis turned into a hot war, he offered to send his anti-Vietnam War song "Jimmy's Road" and his reading of Mark Twain's "The War Prayer" to anyone who would send him a blank tape.

Texas-born Nelson began composing and recording in the early 1960s, emerging as a country music star in the mid-1970s, then crossing over to become a major popular music star as well, on records, in concert, and on screen. His first national hit was the song "Blue Eyes Cryin' in the Rain," from his *Redheaded Stranger* album (1975). He went on to become one of the most popular musicians of the 1970s and 1980s, with such songs as "Georgia on My Mind," "Stardust," "On the Road Again," "Always on My Mind," and "Blue Skies," and such albums as *Waylon and Willie* (1978), *Stardust* (1978), and *Honeysuckle Rose,* the soundtrack album of his 1980 film of that name. He has also appeared in such films as *Barbarossa* (1982), *Red-Headed Stranger* (1986), and *Pair of Aces* (1990). In 1990, he went on the road again with his friends Johnny Cash, Waylon Jennings, and Kris Kristofferson as the Highwaymen. In 1988 he published his autobiographical *Willie.* Nelson attended Baylor University. He has been married three times and has five children.

FURTHER READING

"The ballad of. . . ." RON ROSENBAUM. *Vanity Fair,* Nov. 1991.
"Willie the actor. . . ." GARY CARTWRIGHT. *Texas,* May 1991.
"Poor Willie. . . ." ROBERT DRAPER. *Texas,* May 1991.
Country Musicians . . . Other Great American Artists—Their Music and How They Made It. JUDIE EREMO, ed. Grove-Weidenfeld, 1987.
Heart Worn Memories: A Daughter's Personal Biography of Willie Nelson. SUSIE NELSON. Eakin Press, 1987.
Willie: A Biography of Willie Nelson. MICHAEL BANE. Dell, 1984.
Willie Nelson: Country Outlaw. LOLA SCOBEY. Zebra, 1982.

Nemerov, Howard (1920–91) New York City-born Nemerov, a leading American poet, won a Pulitzer Prize for poetry in 1978, shared a 1979–80 Bollingen Prize, and was U.S. Poet Laureate (1988–90). His volumes of poetry include *Image and the Law* (1947), *Guide to the Ruins* (1950), *The Salt Garden* (1955), *Mirrors and Windows* (1958), *The Next Room of the Dream* (1964), *The Blue Swallow* (1967), *Gnomes and Occasions* (1973), *The Western Approaches* (1977), *Collected Poems* (1977), *Sentences* (1983), and *Inside the Onion* (1984). His novels include *Federigo, or the Power of Love* (1954) and *The Homecoming Game* (1957). He also published several volumes of essays. He was survived by his wife, the former Margaret Russell, three sons, his mother, and a sister. Another sister was the photographer Diane Arbus (1923–71). (d. St. Louis; July 5, 1991)

FURTHER READING

Obituary. *Current Biography,* Sep. 1991.
Obituary. *The Times* (of London), July 9, 1991.
Obituary. *New York Times,* July 7, 1991.
Elizabeth Bishop and Howard Nemerov: A Reference Guide. DIANA E. WYLLIE. G. K. Hall, 1983.
Howard Nemerov. ROSS LABRIE. Macmillan, 1980.

New Kids on the Block (clockwise from left): Jonathan Knight, Jordan Knight, Donnie Wahlberg, Joe McIntyre, and Danny Wood.

New Kids on the Block (Jonathan Knight, 1968– ; Jordan Knight, 1971– ; Joseph McIntyre, 1972– ; Donnie Wahlberg, 1969– ; Daniel Wood, 1969–) Perhaps no longer so new, the New Kids are definitely the richest kids on the block. In September 1991, *Forbes* magazine announced that the New Kids had dethroned Bill Cosby to top their list of highest-earning entertainers, with estimated 1990–91 earnings of about $115 million. Oddly, the report came at a time when the New Kids seemed to be not *quite* the sensation that they had been. Their new record, *No More Games/The Remix Album* (1991), received less-than-glowing reviews for the vocals, though lauded as dance mixes. An ABC-TV Saturday morning based on the New Kids was dropped after the 1990–91 season. The New Kids have had little respect from reviewers and have been criticized for not writing their own songs—though they note that Frank Sinatra never wrote *his*—but they have an enormous following, especially among teens and pre-teens, and tour widely, often with sold-out concerts, projecting a clean-cut, upbeat, anti-drug message.

The singing group was formed in 1985 by composer-promoter Maurice Starr, who selected the members after a Boston-wide talent search. Starr not only writes their music but also shapes their style and routines and orchestrates the marketing of associated merchandise. Donnie Wahlberg and Jordan Knight sing lead vocals, with his brother Jon Knight and Joe McIntyre on backup vocals, along with Danny Wood, who doubles on the keyboard. By 1986, the group had signed with Columbia Records; their first record *New Kids on the Block* (1986) was only a moderate success, though it became number one in England. Then a hit single, "Please Don't Go Girl" (1988), was followed by their phenomenally successful second album, *Hangin' Tough* (1988), which sold over 8 million copies and spun off five hit singles. After that came *Merry, Merry Christmas* (1989) and *Step by Step* (1990), and a string of videos and concerts. In 1990 they published *Our Story: The New Kids on the Block.* All the New Kids come from the Dorchester neighborhood of Boston.

FURTHER READING

New Kids on the Block. KEITH E. GREENBERG. Lerner, 1991.
Block Party. SETH MCEVOY and LAURE SMITH. Pocketbooks, 1991.
"Donnie Wahlberg takes a poke. . . ." *People,* Sept. 24, 1990.
"New kids on the block. . . ." *Teen,* Jan. 1990.
On the Road with New Kids on the Block. NANCY KRULIK. Scholastic, 1990.
New Kids on the Block: The Whole Story by Their Friends. ROBIN MCGIBBON. Avon, 1990.
Meet the New Kids on the Block. NAL-Dutton, 1990.
Lives and Loves of the New Kids on the Block. JILL MATTHEWS. Pocketbooks. 1990.
New Kids on the Block Handbook. Modern Publications (NYC), 1990.
New Kids on the Block. CHARLOTTE SINCLAIR. Outlet, 1990.
New Kids on the Block. LYNN GOLDSMITH. Rizzoli International, 1990.
New Kids on the Block. GRACE CATALANO. Bantam, 1989.

Newman, Paul (1925–) Quite aside from his long, enormously successful film career and always current worldwide celebrity, Newman has become a major philanthropist. In January, his Newman's Own food company gave $8 million in 1990 profits to more than 400 charities throughout the world; total donations were then approximately $36 million, with more coming every year. On October 11, he and Joanne Woodward shared the 40th annual Freedom from Want Award of the Franklin and Eleanor Roosevelt Institute. On television, Newman, who is president of the Actors Studio, hosted *Miracle on 44th Street: A Portrait of the Actors Studio.* Forthcoming was the film comedy *Stark Truth,* based on a John Guare filmscript, with Newman reportedly set to star and direct.

Cleveland-born Newman has been a film star for 35 years, breaking through in *Somebody up There Likes Me* (1956) and *Cat on a Hot Tin Roof* (1958). A few of his many major films are *Exodus* (1960), *The Hustler* (1961), *Sweet Bird of Youth* (1962; he had starred in the Broadway play in 1959), *Hud* (1963), *Harper* (1966), *Cool Hand Luke* (1967), *Butch Cassidy and the Sundance Kid* (1969), *The Sting* (1973), *Absence of Malice* (1981), *Harry and Son* (1984; he also wrote and directed), and *The Color of Money* (1986, for which he won a Best Actor Oscar), *Fat Man and Little Boy* (1989), *Blaze* (1990), and *Mr. and Mrs. Bridge* (1990; he co-starred with Woodward). Newman's B.A. was from Kenyon College in 1949; he also attended Yale Drama School. He was previously married to Jacqueline Witte, married Joanne Woodward in 1958, and has had six children. Newman has also been a racing car driver.

FURTHER READING

"Paul Newman and. . . ." MAUREEN DOWD. *McCall's,* Jan. 1991.
"Mr. and Mrs. Bridge." GRAHAM FULLER. *Interview,* Nov. 1990.
"Joanne Woodward. . . ." BETH WEINHOUSE. *Redbook,* Jan. 1990.
Paul Newman. ELENA OUMANO. St. Martin's, 1989.
Icons: Intimate Portraits. DENISE WORRELL. Atlantic Monthly, 1989.
No Tricks in My Pocket: Paul Newman Directs. STEWART STERN. Grove-Weidenfeld, 1989.
Paul and Joanne: A Biography of Paul Newman and Joanne Woodward. JOE MORELLA and EDWARD Z. EPSTEIN. Delacorte, 1988.
Paul Newman: An Illustrated Biography. J. LANDRY. McGraw-Hill, 1983.
The Films of Paul Newman. LAWRENCE J. QUIRK. Carol, 1981.

Nichols, Mike (Michael Igor Pechowsky, 1931–) As director and co-producer, Nichols was for much of 1991 deeply involved in the film *Regarding Henry,* the story of a high-powered, ruthless New York attorney who is seriously injured by a bullet to the head, and who during rehabilitation entirely changes his outlook on life. Harrison Ford starred as lawyer Henry Turner, opposite Annette Bening as his wife, Sarah, in a cast that included Bill Nunn, Mikki Allen, and Donald Moffat. The film was not very well received by critics or the public. Forthcoming was a New York production of the play *Death and the Maiden,* a thriller by Chilean writer Ariel Dorfman that was a hit at London's Royal Court Theater in late 1991, with Juliet Stevenson in the central role. Scheduled for early 1992, it was to star Gene Hackman, Richard Dreyfuss, and Glenn Close.

Berlin-born Nichols appeared in cabaret during the late 1950s and was partnered with Elaine May on Broadway in 1960 in *An Evening with Mike Nichols and Elaine May.* He received a Best Director Tony for *The Odd Couple* (1965), and has directed five Tony-winning plays: *Barefoot in the Park* (1963), *Luv* (1964), *Plaza Suite* (1968), *The Prisoner of Second Avenue* (1971), and *The Real Thing* (1984). In 1989, he directed a notable revival of Samuel Beckett's *Waiting for Godot,* starring Robin Williams and Steve Martin. He has also directed such films as *Who's Afraid of Virginia Woolf* (1966), the Oscar-winning *The Graduate* (1967), *Carnal Knowledge* (1971), *Silkwood* (1983), *Biloxi Blues* (1987), *Working Girl* (1988), and *Postcards from the Edge* (1990). In 1988 he published *Life, and Other Ways to Kill Time.* Nichols attended the University of Chicago (1950–53). He was formerly married to Patricia Scott and Margot Callas, and married Diane Sawyer in 1988.

FURTHER READING

"Waiting for Mike." STEPHEN FARBER. *Connoisseur,* June 1991.
"Without cutaways. . . ." GAVIN SMITH. *Film Comment,* May–June 1991.
"Mr. Success." ALICE ARLEN. *Interview,* Dec. 1988.
"The happiest couple. . . ." LISA GRUNWALD. *Esquire,* Dec. 1988.
"Genius of Broadway." RHODA KOENIG. *New York,* Dec. 24, 1984.

Nicholson, Jack (1938–) As always, film star Nicholson was highly visible on television during 1991—as the most prominent of all the courtside Los Angeles Lakers basketball fans. His Los Angeles detective Jake Gittes, older in *The Two Jakes* than he was in the earlier *Chinatown,* was also highly visible on television; the film, although a box office disaster, was a 1991 home video hit. Forthcoming was *Man Trouble,* filmed in the summer and fall of 1991; Nicholson stars as an attack dog trainer, opposite Ellen Barkin. Bob Rafelson directed and Carole Eastman write the filmscript; both had worked with Nicholson on the classic *Five Easy Pieces.* Also forthcoming were the title role in the high-budget biofilm *Hoffa,* directed by Danny DeVito, which was scheduled to start shooting in February 1992, and Rob Reiner's *A Few Good Men,* with Tom Cruise and Demi Moore.

New Jersey-born Nicholson played strong supporting roles from the late 1950s, most notably in *Easy Rider* (1969), and then moved into the powerful dramatic roles that made him a major figure for the next two decades, in such films as *Five Easy Pieces* (1970), *Chinatown* (1974), *One Flew over the Cuckoo's Nest* (1975; he won a Best Actor Oscar), *The Postman Always Rings Twice* (1981), *Reds* (1981), *Terms of Endearment* (1983; he won a Best Supporting Actor Oscar), *Prizzi's Honor* (1985), *Heartburn* (1986), *Ironweed* (1987), and *Batman* (1989). In 1990, he directed and starred in *The Two Jakes,* a sequel to *Chinatown.* He was formerly married to Sandra Knight; they had one daughter. He had a 17-year relationship with actress Anjelica Huston that ended in 1990. He and actress Rebecca Broussard have two children, a daughter born in 1990 and a son born in 1992.

FURTHER READING

Jack Nicholson: An Unauthorized Biography. DONALD SHEPERD. St. Martin's, 1991.
Jack Nicholson: An Unauthorized Biography. BARBARA SIEGEL and SCOTT SIEGEL. Avon, 1991.
"The myth that Jack built." STEVE ERICKSON. *Esquire,* Sep. 1990.
"Hollywood's wild card." BRIAN D. JOHNSON *Maclean's,* Aug. 20, 1990.
"Jake Jake. . . ." JULIAN SCHNABEL. *Interview,* Aug. 1990.
"Forget it, Jack. . . ." JAMES GREENBERG. *American Film,* Feb. 1990.
The Films of Jack Nicholson. DOUGLAS BRODE. Carol, 1990.
Jack Nicholson: A Biography. DAVID DOWNING. Scarborough House, 1984.

Nixon, Richard Milhous (1913–) Former President Nixon, although still carrying the disgrace of Watergate, seemed no longer a political liability to other Republican Party leaders in 1991. He visited the Soviet Union for two weeks in March–April 1991, and on April 2 met separately with Mikhail Gorbachev and Boris Yeltsin. On April 24, he lunched with President George Bush and other political figures at the White House and reported on his Soviet trip and meetings. Nixon also publicly joined ex-president Ronald Reagan in supporting the Brady gun control bill. On the ceremonial side, he and Patricia Nixon were present at the November 4 opening of the Reagan presidential library at Simi Valley, California, joining all the other living ex-presidents and their wives.

Yet, although apparently rehabilitated almost two decades later, Nixon was still pursued by Watergate. On June 5, 1991, the National Archives released transcripts of the remaining 60 hours of Watergate-related and other White House conversations not previously made public; these final tapes became the subject of national, generally very adverse media comments, and Watergate once again emerged to haunt Richard Nixon, if only for a little while.

California-born Nixon became the 37th president of the United States in 1969 and resigned to avoid impeachment in 1974 after his complicity in the Watergate scandal was exposed. He had previously been a leading member of the House Un-American Activities Committee while a California congressman (1947–51), senator from California in the early 1950s, and Dwight D. Eisenhower's vice president (1953–61). He was defeated for the presidency by John F. Kennedy in 1960 and came back to defeat Hubert Humphrey in 1968 and George McGovern in 1972. He presided over the last stages of his country's defeat in Vietnam and played a key role in reestablishing U.S.-Chinese relations, but in the long run he is chiefly notable for his multiple illegal attacks on domestic political opponents, which climaxed with the Watergate Democratic National Committee break-ins of his "plumbers," which ultimately destroyed his career and reputation.

His written works include *RN: Memoirs of Richard Nixon* (1978); *The Memoirs of Richard Nixon* (2 vols.; 1978–79); *1999: Victory Without War* (1988); and *In the Arena: A Memoir of Victory, Defeat, and Renewal* (1990). Nixon's B.A. was from Whittier College in 1934, his LL.B. from Duke in 1937. Nixon married Thelma Patricia Ryan in 1940, nicknamed Pat. The couple have two children.

FURTHER READING

"The two Dicks." DICK TUCK. *Los Angeles,* Aug. 1991.
"Forgiving an enemy." HENRIK BERING-JENSEN. *Insight,* July 8, 1991.
"Richard Milhous Nixon." DOUGLAS A. FULMER. *Ad Astra,* July–Aug. 1991.
Nixon: Ruin and Recovery, 1973–1990, 1991. *Nixon: The Triumph of a Politician, 1962–1972,* 1989. *Nixon: The Education of a Politician, 1913–1962,* 1987. STEPHEN E. AMBROSE. Simon & Schuster.
Silent Coup: The Removal of Richard Nixon. LEN COLODNY and ROBERT GETTLIN. St. Martin's, 1991.
Watergate and Afterward: The Legacy of Richard M. Nixon. LEON FRIEDMAN and WILLIAM F. LEVANTROSSER, eds. Greenwood, 1991.
Richard M. Nixon: Politician, President, Administrator. LEON FRIEDMAN and WILLIAM F. LEVANTROSSER, eds. Greenwood, 1991.
One of Us: Richard Nixon and the American Dream. TOM WICKER. Random House, 1991.
Richard Nixon. RICHARD M. PIOUS. Silver Burdett, 1991.
The Great Stream of History: A Biography of Richard M. Nixon. LAURIE NADEL. Macmillan, 1991.
Richard Nixon: The Making and Unmaking of a President. REBECCA LARSEN. Watts, 1991.
Richard Nixon and His America. HERBERT S. PARMET. Little, Brown, 1990.
Richard M. Nixon, President. SALLIE RANDOLPH. Walker, 1989.
Richard Milhous Nixon: The Rise of an American Politician. ROGER MORRIS. Holt, 1989.

Nolte, Nick (1942–) In November 1991, Nolte opened as Sam Bowden in Martin Scorsese's *Cape Fear,* a remake of J. Lee Thompson's 1962 classic, which starred Gregory Peck as Bowden; he and his family are stalked by evil ex-con Max Cady, in 1962 played by Robert Mitchum and in 1991 by Robert De Niro. Jessica Lange also starred as Leigh Bowden, in the role created by Polly Bergen. Nolte was well received, playing Sam Bowden in Scorsese's far more complex post-heroic 1991 style. A month later, Nolte opened as dissipated Southern teacher and coach Tom Wingo in *The Prince of Tides,* produced and directed by Barbra Streisand, who also starred as

Nolte's lover, psychiatrist Susan Lowenstein. Nolte's performance was widely hailed, as was Streisand's direction, with its focus on Nolte and on their relationship, rather than on what might easily have become a Streisand star vehicle and a far less effective film. Forthcoming were *Lorenzo's Oil,* in which Nolte plays a father seeking a cure for his young son's fatal disease, opposite Susan Sarandon as his wife; and an appearance in Robert Altman's *The Player,* along with many other leading film figures.

Nebraska-born Nolte spent years in regional theater before emerging as a film star in the mid-1970s, in *The Deep* (1977), and went on to star in such films as *Who'll Stop the Rain* (1978), *North Dallas Forty* (1979), *Cannery Row* (1982), *48 Hrs.* (1982), *Under Fire* (1983), *Down and Out in Beverly Hills* (1986), *Three Fugitives* (1989), *Everybody Wins* (1990), *Another 48 Hrs.* (1990), and *Q&A* (1990). He has also appeared in television, most notably in *Rich Man, Poor Man* (1976). Nolte attended Pasadena College. He has been married three times, since 1984 to Rebecca Linger; they have one child.

FURTHER READING

"Off-balance heroes." PETER DE JONGE. *New York Times Magazine,* Oct. 27, 1991.
"Nick Nolte. . . ." STEPHANIE MANSFIELD. *GQ—Gentlemen's Quarterly,* Oct. 1991.
"Prince of Hollywood." MEREDITH BRODY. *Connoisseur,* Sep. 1991.
"Nick Nolte." PETER BECKER. *M Inc.,* Sep. 1991.
"The passions of. . . ." ERIC GOODMAN. *McCall's,* Sep. 1991.

Noriega, Manuel (Manuel Antonio Noriega Morena, 1938–) On September 5, 1991, after 20 months of imprisonment, the trial of Panama's former government head Noriega began, in a U.S. District Court in Miami. In 1988, while still in power, Noriega had been indicted in Florida on drug trafficking charges. After the November 20, 1989, U.S. invasion of Panama, a period in hiding, and a period of asylum in the Vatican's Panama City diplomatic mission, Noriega surrendered to U.S. forces. On January 3, 1990, he was flown to Miami and arraigned on drug trade-related charges, although he claimed the status of a political prisoner. Then began a very long set of pre-trial preparations, jury selection processes, and many months of hearings on disputed pre-trial matters. Ultimately, in August 1991, Judge William V. Hoeveler acceded to defense requests for previously withheld government documents, clearing the way for the trial to begin. Noriega was charged with ten counts of cocaine distribution, cocaine manufacturing, and money laundering. During the next three months, the prosecution presented its case. In December, the trial was further delayed by Judge Hoeveler's heart surgery, and was at year's end scheduled to reopen in late January 1992.

Noriega was a career Panamanian military intelligence officer. As head of Panamanian intelligence (1970–82) and dictator (1982—89), he was deeply involved with U.S. military and intelligence activities in Latin America and was on the CIA payroll for many years. He was also even more profitably associated with one or more drug cartels in the same period. Both arrangements were upset by his February 1988 Florida drug indictment, the same charges on which he was to be tried in 1991. Noriega attended Panama University. He is married to Felicidad Sieiro and has three children.

FURTHER READING

Our Man in Panama: The Shrewd Rise and Brutal Fall of Manuel Noriega. JOHN DINGES. Random House, 1991.
"Our man in Panama. . . ." SEYMOUR M. HERSH. *Life,* Mar. 1990.
"Noriega on ice. . . ." RICHARD LACAYO. *Time,* Jan. 15, 1990.
"The Noriega files." FREDERICK KEMPE. *Newsweek,* Jan. 15, 1990.
"Lifestyle of a dictator." RAE CORELLI. *Maclean's,* Jan. 1, 1990.
Divorcing the Dictator: America's Bungled Affair with Noriega. FREDERICK KEMPE. Putnam, 1990.
"Noriega Morena, Manuel Antonio." *Current Biography,* Mar. 1988.

North, Alex (1910–91) Pennsylvania-born North studied at Philadelphia's Curtis Institute, with Aaron Copland in New York in the early 1930s, and at the Moscow Conservatory from 1933 to 1935. He emerged in the mid-1930s as a social activist composer, writing scores for Federal Theater Project plays, and for such documentaries as *China Strikes Back* (1936), *Heart of Spain* (1937), and *People of the Cumberland*

(1937), as well as several ballets. After working on propaganda and morale-building musical assignments during World War II, he returned to New York, composing such works as *Revue for Clarinet and Orchestra*. He continued to write for the concert hall and theater after his move to Hollywood in the early 1950s, beginning with his score for *Death of a Salesman* (1951; he had written the 1948 theater score).

From the 1950s on, North became best known as a prolific film score composer, who won 15 Academy Award nominations, but received his first Oscar in 1986—an honorary award for a lifetime of achievement. He scored such films as *A Streetcar Named Desire* (1951), *Viva Zapata* (1952), *The Misfits* (1961), and *Cheyenne Autumn* (1964), and also worked extensively for television, winning an Emmy for *Rich Man, Poor Man* (1976). He was survived by his wife, Annemarie, a daughter, two sons, and two brothers. (d. Los Angeles; September 8, 1991)

FURTHER READING

Obituary. *Variety,* Sep. 16, 1991.
Obituary. *The Times* (of London), Sep. 13, 1991.
Obituary. *New York Times,* Sept. 11, 1991.
The Composer in Hollywood. CHRISTOPHER PALMER. M. Boyars, 1990.

North, Oliver (1943–) Oliver North's Iran-Contra case ended as sharply and dramatically as it had begun. On September 16, 1991, federal judge Gerhart A. Gesell dropped all charges against North. A week earlier, former National Security Advisor Robert C. McFarlane, a key possible witness for the prosecution, had declared that he had been greatly affected by watching North's televised testimony before a congressional investigating committee, making it impossible for his testimony in the forthcoming North trial to be unbiased. The case was doomed; prosecutor Lawrence E. Walsh declared that he would no longer seek to prosecute North, as the congressional hearings had fatally tainted his case.

North very quickly followed up his court victory with the book *Under Fire: An American Story* (written with William Novak), which became a best-seller. In the book and in a major publicity tour, North charged that Ronald Reagan knew and approved of the actions of those around him in the Iran-Contra scandals. However, North produced little in the way of evidence to support his assertion, and former President Reagan continued to deny all knowledge of diversion of funds to the Contras.

North, a career Marine officer, was on active service in Vietnam in 1968–69. From 1981 to 1986, he was deputy director of the military affairs bureau of the U.S. National Security Council, working directly out of the White House; he became a Marine lieutenant colonel in 1983. North was involved in developing several covert operations during his White House years; one of them blew up in late 1986, becoming the Iran-Contra affair, a set of scandals that resulted in North's dismissal from his White House post, though not from the Marines, in November 1986. North then became an international figure, as he testified on television before congressional committees. North is a graduate of the United States Naval Academy at Annapolis. He is married to Betsy (Frances Elizabeth) Stuart; they have three children.

FURTHER READING

"Oliver North. . . ." *Christianity Today,* Nov. 25, 1991.
"The unsinkable. . . ." BARRETT SEAMAN. *Time,* Oct. 28, 1991.
Opening Arguments: A Young Lawyer's First Case: United States v. Oliver L. North. JEFFREY TOOBIN. Viking Penguin, 1991.
Guts and Glory: The Oliver North Story. BEN BRADLEE, JR. Donald I. Fine, 1988.
The Secret Government. BILL MOYERS. Seven Locks, 1988.

Men of Zeal: A Candid Story of the Iran-Contra Hearings. WILLIAM S. COHEN and GEORGE J. MITCHELL. Viking Penguin, 1988.
Defiant Patriot: The Life and Exploits of Lieutenant Colonel Oliver North. PETER MEYER. St. Martin's, 1987.
Taking the Stand: The Testimony of Lieutenant Colonel Oliver L. North. DANIEL SCHORR, ed. Pocket Books, 1987.

Norville, Deborah (1958–) Cast as the "bad guy" in the 1990 break-up of television's successful "Today" show partnership of Bryant Gumbel and Jane Pauley, Norville and the show's ratings were not able to overcome the negative publicity surrounding her assumption of Pauley's position. In February 1991, she went on what was scheduled to be a two-month maternity leave, with Katie Couric as her temporary replacement. "Today's" ratings immediately improved, and in April NBC announced that Norville would not return, being replaced permanently by Couric. Norville said that she would be spending the next year at home with her infant son, Karl Nikolai, born February 27, though the media carried considerable discussion of a "did she jump or was she pushed" nature. Norville's contract, with several years left to run at an estimated $1 million per year, was reportedly bought out for a handsome sum. In September she took over Sally Jessy Raphael's network radio nightly talk show for ABC, broadcasting from her homes in Manhattan and Long Island.

After graduating summa cum laude from the University of Georgia's broadcasting journalism program, Georgia-born Norville broke into television in 1978 at Atlanta's WAGA and in 1981 moved on to Chicago's WMAQ (once also Pauley's professional home), where she won an Emmy for local news reporting. Moving to New York in early 1987, she joined "NBC News at Sunrise," became news reader on "Today" in August 1989, and then replaced Pauley as coanchor at the end of 1989. She is married to fine arts auction executive Karl Wellner; they have one son.

FURTHER READING

"Norville, Deborah." *Current Biography,* Apr. 1990.
"Deborah Norville. . . ." LARRY B. DENDY. *Saturday Evening Post,* Mar. 1990.
"TV's new golden girl." JAN HOFFMAN. *GQ—Gentlemen's Quarterly,* June 1989.

Nujoma, Sam Daniel (1929–) As the long, complex set of wars and civil wars in southern Africa receded, President Nujoma led his new country of Namibia in what during 1991 was a remarkably peaceful transition toward multiparty and multiracial democracy. Not without major problems, certainly; 22 years of civil war had left the very poor former colony even poorer and with some ethnic unrest, as well. And the South African-Namibian relationship was far from cordial: In March, Namibia asked for return of the Walvis Bay, the country's only deep-water Atlantic port, and received a quick South African refusal; and in July, South Africa admitted that it had supplied $35 million to opposition parties before the 1989 Namibian elections, a charge long denied by the South Africans. But the May 1991 end of the Angolan civil war, with its concurrent withdrawal of Cuban troops, removed a major source of unrest in the north, and South Africa was preoccupied with its own problems, both developments enhancing the possibility of aid and investment for Namibia from abroad.

Nujoma was a co-founder of SWAPO in 1959. He was imprisoned in that year, went into exile in 1960, and until 1966 led the campaign to gain independence by peaceful means. After being expelled by the occupying South Africans in 1966, he led the Namibian independence movement in the 22-year-long guerrilla war that ended with South African withdrawal from Namibia, ending 75 years of South African domination of the last European colony on the continent. Nujoma returned to Namibia on September 14, 1989, and on February 16, 1990, was elected the first president of Namibia by the new constituent assembly. He was inaugurated on March 21, 1990; United Nations Secretary-General Pérez de Cuéllar administered the oath of office, and South African president F. W. De Klerk attended the ceremony. Nujoma is married to Kowambo Theoplidine Katjimuina; the couple have four children.

FURTHER READING

"Nujoma, Samuel Daniel." *Current Biography,* Feb. 1990.

Namibia: Struggle for Independence. Y. Gorbunov and S. Nujoma. Imported Publications, 1988.

Nunn, Sam (Samuel Nunn, Jr., 1938–) Georgia Democrat Nunn, head of the powerful Senate Armed Services Committee, continued to press for defense budget cuts in 1991, though during and after the Persian Gulf War somewhat moderating his position, particularly after the success of Patriot missiles in destroying Iraqi missiles. Nunn also played a considerable role in the developing Soviet-American relationship, as when he in June urged that the United States use its skills to help the Soviet Union to convert from military to civilian goods. Nunn has often been discussed as a possible Democratic presidential candidate. However, in March 1991, he took himself out of the 1992 presidential race stating, "I am not running. I am not planning to run."

Georgia-born Nunn was a Georgia state legislator (1968–72) and began his long career in the Senate in 1973. He became chairman of the Senate Armed Services Committee in 1986 and was regarded as a possible 1988 Democratic presidential and then vice presidential candidate during the run-up to the Dukakis nomination, but he refused the vice presidential nomination when it was offered. During the late 1980s, as the Cold War wound down, Nunn moved from general support of military spending plans toward a call for large cuts in spending, armaments, and force levels. In late July 1990, his committee reported out the first large Senate defense-cut bills in decades. Nunn's B.A. and LL.B. were from Atlanta's Emory University. He married Colleen O'Brien in 1964; the couple have two children.

FURTHER READING

"The mystique of. . . ." Sidney Blumenthal. *New Republic,* Mar. 4, 1991.

"Wanted. . . ." Douglas Harbrecht. *Business Week,* Nov. 19, 1990.

"Born to be mild. . . ." Timothy Noah. *Washington Monthly,* Dec. 1989.

"Smart, dull and very powerful." Michael Kramer. *Time,* Mar. 13, 1989.

Nureyev, Rudolf (Rudolf Hametovich Nureyev, 1938–) The great dancer Nureyev made what may have been his last set of appearances in 1991; at 52, he announced another "final" tour. Yet he still danced well, if to less critical acclaim. In June, at Verona, Italy, he appeared as Gustav von Aschenbach in Flemming Flindt's ballet *Death in Venice,* adapted from the Thomas Mann novel, in a role that called for both acting and dancing skills. In spring 1991, he toured the United States and Western Europe, appearing in Maurice Béjart's *Songs of a Wayfarer,* José Limon's *Moor's Pavane,* and Flemming Flindt's *The Overcoat,* based on the Gogol story, a role created for him by Flindt in 1989. Nureyev also began a new career, as a conductor, in July leading a chamber orchestra in Vienna. His dancing career coming to a close, he declared himself quite serious about embarking on his new career.

Nureyev joined the Leningrad-based Kirov Ballet as a soloist in 1958 and quickly became a leading Soviet dancer. Three years later, in 1961, he defected to the West and within a year was a world figure in the ballet, very notably as Margot Fonteyn's partner at London's Royal Ballet. During the next quarter-century, he danced as a guest artist in many countries and became a leading choreographer as well, of such works as *Tancredi* (1966), *Romeo and Juliet*

(1977), and *Washington Square* (1985). He was artistic director of the Paris Opera Ballet (1983–89) and its principal choreographer (1989–90), while continuing to dance throughout the world. In 1989–90, he starred on stage in musical theater for the first time, in a U.S. tour of *The King and I*. He has also appeared in several films, including *Valentino* (1977) and *Exposed* (1982).

FURTHER READING

"And now, superstar?" IRIS M. FANGER. *World Monitor,* June 1991.
"Nureyev. . . ." ELIZABETH KAYE. *Esquire,* Mar. 1991.
"Nureyev now!" PAUL H. LEMAY. *Dance,* May 1990.
"Nureyev resigns. . . ." ROBERT JOHNSON. *Dance,* Feb. 1990.

O'Connor, Cardinal John J. (1920–)

Cardinal O'Connor, the Roman Catholic archbishop of New York, found himself again a center of controversy in 1991, most notably over the continuing issue of his views on AIDS (acquired immune deficiency syndrome) and how to deal with the disease. During the late 1980s, his running battle with New York's gay community had featured scores of demonstrations outside St. Patrick's Cathedral; the largest of these, on December 10, 1989, drew 4,000–5,000 demonstrators. Forty demonstrators were arrested inside St. Patrick's Cathedral. In 1991, the short film *Stop the Church,* a documentary made about that demonstration, scheduled to be aired on August 27, was pulled by the Public Broadcasting Service (PBS) as anti-Catholic. The documentary included the 1960s Tom Lehrer song "The Vatican Rag," and many sharply personal and derogatory statements made about the prelate by some of the protesters. The PBS withdrawal of the film was widely attacked as censorship.

On another quite different kind of controversial matter, O'Connor was widely quoted as not opposing the practice of exorcism, viewed as a medieval survival by many inside and outside the Catholic Church. The controversy was spurred by an April 4 telecast in which an exorcism ritual was actually performed by two Catholic priests, operating with the approval of a consultant to Cardinal O'Connor, and by implication with his consent.

Philadelphia-born O'Connor was ordained in 1945. He became a U.S. Navy chaplain in 1952 and ultimately chief Navy Chaplain, a rear admiral, and in 1979 an auxiliary bishop. He became bishop of Scranton, Pennsylvania, in 1983, archbishop of the New York archdiocese in 1984, and a cardinal in 1985. Always notable for his frankly expressed conservative views, he became a highly controversial figure in 1989 and 1990, as he spoke out on such matters as his opposition to abortion, to homosexuality, to the use of condoms to combat AIDS, and to heavy-metal music, seeing it as aiding demonic possession. On June 14, 1990, he made an implied threat to excommunicate Catholic political leaders who favored abortion, a threat widely thought aimed at New York governor Mario Cuomo, but withdrew it three days later. O'Connor recently published two books involving encounters with others of often-differing views, *His Eminence and Hizzoner: A Candid Exchange* (1989), with former New York mayor Ed Koch, and *A Journey of Faith: A Dialogue Between Elie Wiesel and John Cardinal O'Connor* (1990). His degrees include an M.A. from St. Charles College in 1949, an M.A. from the Catholic University of America in 1954, a Ph.D. from Georgetown University in 1970, and a D.R.E. from Villanova University in 1976.

FURTHER READING

"Cardinal. . . ." JEFFERY L. SHELER. *U.S. News & World Report,* Dec. 31, 1990.

"New York's new power brokers. . . ." *Manhattan, Inc.,* Sep. 1989.

"Quizzing the men. . . ." ARTHUR JONES. *National Catholic Reporter,* Feb. 26, 1988.

John Cardinal O'Connor: At the Storm Center of a Changing American Catholic Church. NAT HENTOFF. Macmillan/Scribner, 1988.

O'Connor, Sandra Day (1930–) Justice O'Connor was largely identified with the increasingly conservative majority in the Supreme Court during the 1990–91 term. She wrote the majority opinions in three key cases: In *Country of Riverside, California v. McLaughlin,* she ruled that those arrested without warrants could be held up to 48 hours while a judge decided if there was probable cause for the arrest; in *Florida v. Bostick,* she ruled that police could board buses and search passengers' luggage, with their permission; and in *Coleman v. Thompson,* she sharply restricted the use of habeas corpus writs by state prisoners who have exhausted state appeals, to challenge the constitutionality of their convictions, reversing the far wider use of habeas corpus established by *Fay v. Noia* (1963). She also joined the conservative majority in several other major rulings, including *Barnes v. Glen Theater; Board of Education of Oklahoma City v. Dowell; Arizona v. Fulminante; Harmelin v. Michigan,* and *Payne v. Tennessee.* But in *United Automobile Workers v. Johnson Controls Inc.,* a landmark women's rights case, she took the liberal position, finding with the majority that according to the 1978 Pregnancy Discrimination Act employers could not ban pregnant women from jobs potentially dangerous to their unborn children. She also differed from her most conservative colleagues in *Rust v. Sullivan,* which upheld federal regulations banning federally funded family planning clinics from offering abortion counseling, writing a separate dissent. On December 19, 1991, O'Connor wrote the majority opinion in *Simon & Schuster v. Members of the New York Crime Victims Board,* striking down the New York State "Son of Sam" law.

El Paso-born O'Connor made history in 1981 when she became the first woman Supreme Court justice, the climax of long careers in law and politics. She had moved from private practice to become Arizona assistant attorney general (1965–69), into politics as an Arizona state senator (1969–75), and then back into a series of Arizona judicial posts, ultimately becoming a state court of appeals judge (1979–81). O'Connor's B.A. and LL.B. were from Stanford, in 1950 and 1952. She married John Jay O'Connor in 1952; the couple have one child.

FURTHER READING

Sandra Day O'Connor. NORMAN L. MACHT. Chelsea House, 1992.

"A new day in court." LAUREN TARSHIS and JAMES EARL HARDY. *Scholastic Update,* Nov. 1, 1991.
Sandra Day O'Connor: A New Justice, a New Voice. BEVERLY BERWALD. Fawcett, 1991.
Sandra Day O'Connor. BEVERLY GHERMAN. Viking Penguin, 1991.
Sandra Day O'Connor. PETER HUBER. Chelsea House, 1990.
Eight Men and a Lady. HERMAN SCHWARTZ, ANDREA NEAL, and DAVID SAVAGE. National Press, 1990.
"Sandra Day O'Connor. . . ." MERRILL MCLOUGHLIN. *Ladies Home Journal,* Nov. 1989.
Equal Justice: A Biography of Sandra Day O'Connor. HAROLD WOODS and GERALDINE WOODS. Dillon, 1985.
Justice Sandra Day O'Connor. JUDITH BENTLEY. Messner, 1985.
Justice Sandra Day O'Connor. MARY V. FOX. Enslow, 1983.

O'Faolain, Sean (John Whelan, 1900–91) A leading Irish writer, born in Cork, O'Faolain became an active revolutionary while a student, fought with the Irish Republican Army during the Irish war of independence (1919–21), and refused to accept the partition of Ireland, fighting again on the losing side of the brief Irish civil war that followed. He left Ireland to study at Harvard in 1928, and then taught and studied in England, returning to Ireland in 1933. O'Faolain was recognized as a major writer with the publication of his first short story collection, *Midsummer Night Madness and Other Stories* (1932), and for his first novels, *A Nest of Simple Folk* (1933) and *Bird Alone* (1936). He also wrote several biographies of Irish historical figures, including Daniel O'Connell, Hugh O'Neill, Constance Markievicz, and Eamon de Valera. He founded the literary magazine *The Bell* in 1940, and edited it until 1946. His later work also included a play, travel books, a wide range of essays, such novels as *Come Back to Erin* (1940), and an autobiography, *Vive Moi* (1964). His collected short stories were published in three volumes (1980–82; and in a one-volume U.S. edition in 1983). He was survived by a son, and by a daughter, the novelist Julia O'Faolain (d. Dublin; April 20, 1991)

FURTHER READING

Obituary. *Current Biography,* June 1991.
Obituary. *The Times* (of London), Apr. 22, 1991.
Obituary. *New York Times,* Apr. 22, 1991.
"O'Faolain, Sean." *Current Biography,* Apr. 1990.
Sean O'Faolain's Irish Vision. RICHARD BONACCORSO. State University of New York Press, 1987.

Olav V (1903–91) Born in England, Olav was educated in Norway and at Balliol College, Oxford. He married Princess Martha of Sweden in 1925. Olav was the Norwegian Crown Prince until 1954, succeeding to the throne after the death of his father, Haakon VII. In 1940, with the German invasion of Norway, he and his father fled north before the advancing Nazis, and after two months of fighting retreat were ultimately evacuated from Tromsö. Olav had offered to stay in Norway, as a focus for the Resistance; instead, he spent the war in British exile, working with Free Norwegian forces. He returned to Norway on May 13, 1945. Olav was a well-loved figure for many in his country. As the constitutional monarch of a democracy, his power was negligible, and he and his father made no attempt to increase the power or status of the monarchy, both being committed to a simple and rather inexpensive life style. He was survived by a son, Crown Prince Harald, heir to the throne, and by two daughters. (d. Oslo; January 17, 1991)

FURTHER READING

Obituary. *The Times* (of London), Jan. 19, 1991.
Obituary. *New York Times,* Jan. 18, 1991.
"King Olav. . . ." BOB BAVIER. *Yachting,* June 1991.
Obituary. *Current Biography,* Mar. 1991.

Ortega Saavedra, Daniel (1945–) Although voted out of power in 1990, Ortega remained leader of Nicaragua's Sandinista movement, as president of the Sandinista National Liberation Front (FSLN), and also remained a substantial figure in Latin American politics. During the balance of 1990 and 1991, he and his party remained in opposition, sometimes cooperative, often sharply uncooperative with Violeta Chamorro's government, but at no point going over into a renewal of the civil war. However, many armed clashes flared throughout the country between Sandinistas holding property confiscated while they were in power and former Contras and others from whom the property had been confiscated.

Ortega became active in the movement to overthrow the Anastasio Somoza dictatorship while a teenager, became a Sandinista guerrilla fighter in 1963, and was a national leader of the Sandinista movement in 1966–67. He was imprisoned (1967–74) and in the late 1970s became a major leader of the successful rebellion against Somoza. In 1979, he and Violeta Chamorro were two of the five leaders of the coalition that ruled Nicaragua after Somoza fled. Ortega became the Marxist leader of Sandinista-ruled Nicaragua (1981–90) and its president (1985–90). After the cease-fire of March 1988 effectively ended the eight-year-long Nicaraguan Civil War, he negotiated a series of agreements with the Contras that paved the way for the transition to democracy. Ortega's then-surprising agreement to allow free elections was one of the notable features of the period.

Ortega attended Managua's Centralamerican University. He is married to Rosario Murillo; the couple have seven children.

FURTHER READING

Daniel Ortega. JOHN STOCKWELL. Chelsea House, 1991.

"Crisis of the clams. . . ." ARTURO CRUZ, JR., and CONSUELO CRUZ SEQUEIRA. *New Republic,* May 21, 1990.

Life Stories of the Nicaraguan Revolution. DENIS L. HEYCK. Routledge Chapman and Hall, 1990.

Daniel Ortega. JOHN STOCKWELL. Chelsea House, 1989.

O'Toole, Peter (Peter Seamus O'Toole, 1932–) Veteran star O'Toole worked a good deal in 1991. On screen, he appeared as a royal etiquette adviser in David S. Ward's film *King Ralph,* which starred John Goodman as a Las Vegas entertainer who becomes King of England. O'Toole also returned to the London stage in the title role of the long-running Keith Waterhouse play *Jeffrey Bernard is Unwell;* he had starred in the role in 1989. Forthcoming films included Alexandro Jodorowsky's *The Rainbow Thief;* Ian Pringle's *Isabelle Eberhardt;* and as Lord Sarn in *Rebecca's Daughters,* a comedy-love story set in 19th-century Wales at the time of the "Rebecca riots" of farmers against oppressive English road tolls. The latter is based on a Dylan Thomas screenplay written in 1945 and never produced, and also stars Joely Richardson and Paul Rhys. O'Toole was to star in *Déjà Vu,* John Osborne's sequel to *Look Back in Anger,* scheduled to open at the Liverpool Playhouse in November 1991, but instead pulled out of the production before rehearsals were due to begin in late October. O'Toole was also working on his autobiography, to be published by Macmillan of Britain in 1992.

Galway-born O'Toole began his long theater career in the mid-1950s, in repertory with the Bristol Old Vic Theatre, and went on to play in a wide range of stage roles for the next three decades, with such companies as the Old Vic, the National Theatre, and Dublin's Abbey Theatre. He is best known by far for his films, quickly emerging as a major international star in the title role of *Lawrence of Arabia* (1960), and going on to such films as *Becket* (1964), *The Lion in Winter* (1968), *Man of La Mancha* (1972), *Zulu Dawn* (1978), *My Favorite Year* (1982), and *The Last Emperor* (1986). In 1990, he starred in the telefilm *Crossing to Freedom.* O'Toole attended the Royal Academy of Dramatic Art. He was formerly married, to actress Sian Phillips, and has three children.

FURTHER READING

Peter O'Toole: A Biography. NICHOLAS WAPSHOTT. Beaufort, 1984.

Peter O'Toole. MICHAEL FREEDLAND. St. Martin's, 1983.

P

Pacino, Al (Alfred Pacino, 1940–) After his return to the massive Michael Corleone role in *The Godfather, Part III,* Pacino's 1991 film was a real change of pace. He started shooting early in the year as short-order cook Johnny, opposite Michelle Pfeiffer as waitress Frankie in Garry Marshall's romantic comedy *Frankie and Johnny,* adapted by Terrence McNally from his play *Frankie and Johnny in the Clair De Lune.* The film, originally a two-character play set in a bedroom, was greatly "opened out," with all but the Pacino and Pfeiffer roles added, though the growing love affair between Frankie and Johnny remained at the center of the generally highly regarded film. Forthcoming was another major work, the film version of David Mamet's Pulitzer Prize-winning play, *Glengarry Glen Ross,* adapted for the screen by Mamet, directed by James Foley, and starring Pacino, Jack Lemmon, Alec Baldwin, Alan Arkin, Jonathan Pryce, Kevin Spacey, and Ed Harris. The film, shot in the late summer and fall of 1991, was scheduled for fall 1992 release. Also forthcoming was a starring role in Martin Brest's *Scent of a Woman.*

New York-born Pacino is one of the leading alumni of the Actor's Studio, beginning his long association with the group in 1966 and becoming one of its artistic directors (1982–84). He worked in the theater through the 1960s, and in the early 1970s emerged as a major film star, breaking through as Michael Corleone in *The Godfather* (1972). He went on to star in such films as *Serpico* (1973), *The Godfather, Part II* (1974), *Dog Day Afternoon* (1975), *Cruising* (1980), *Scarface* (1983), *Sea of Love* (1989), *Dick Tracy* (1990), and *The Godfather, Part III* (1990). He also continued to work in the theater, in such plays as *Camino Real* (1973), *Richard III* (1973), and *American Buffalo* (1981).

FURTHER READING

"Al Pacino." JULIAN SCHNABEL. *Interview,* Feb. 1991.
"Pacino powers . . ." JOHN PODHORETZ. *Insight,* Jan. 14, 1991.
Life on the Wire: The Life and Art of Al Pacino. ANDREW YULE. Donald I. Fine, 1991.

Paldfield, Philip: See **Lebanon Hostages**

Page, Ruth (1899–1991). A leading American ballet dancer and choreographer, born in Indianpolis, Page made her professional debut with Anna Pavlova's company, touring South America with Pavlova in 1918. She then danced with Adolph Bolm's Ballet Intime in Chicago, appearing in *The Birthday of the Infanta* (1919), and during the 1920s appeared with Bolm as prima ballerina of the *Music Box Revue* (1923–24), with Diaghilev's Ballets Russes in 1925, and the Metropolitan Opera Ballet (1926–28). In 1928, she danced Terpsichore in Bolm's world premier of Stravinsky's *Apollo,* in Washington, D.C. In the early 1930s, she studied in Germany with Mary Wigman and toured with Harold Kreutzberg, though her main work was in Chicago, in several of her own companies and as ballet mistress of the Chicago Opera. She founded the Chicago Opera Ballet in 1956; as Ruth Page's International Ballet, it continued until 1970. As a choreographer, some of her best-known ballets were *Frankie and Johnny* (1938; for the Chicago Federal Theater), *Revanche* (1951; based on the opera *Il Trovatore*), and *Vilia* (for *The Merry Widow,* 1953). She also staged many ballets based on operas. She was survived by her second husband, French stage designer and artist André Delfau, and by a brother. (d. Chicago; April 7, 1991)

FURTHER READING

Obituary. *Current Biography.* July 1991.
Obituary. *Variety,* Apr. 22, 1991.
Obituary. *The Times* (of London), Apr. 12, 1991.
Obituary. *New York Times,* Apr. 9, 1991.

Panufnik, Andrzej (1914–91) Polish-born composer and conductor Panufnik was at the beginning of his career when the Germans invaded Poland in 1939. He spent the war in the Polish resistance, performing undergound and composing forbidden patriotic songs. All of his work, save for a few pieces he reconstructed from memory, were destroyed during the 1944 Warsaw uprising against the Germans. A prolific composer, Panufnik was also a highly regarded conductor; he became director of the Crakow Philharmonic in 1945 and director of the Warsaw Philharmonic in 1946. But although highly honored, he ultimately rejected life in communist Poland, defecting to Britain in 1954; there he was director of the Birmingham Symphony (1957–59), thereafter devoting his time to composing and occasional guest directing. His compositions include ten symphonies and a wide range of other works. He returned to Poland for the first time in 36 years in 1990, conducting his *Tenth Symphony* at the Warsaw Philharmonic Hall. His autobiography was *Composing Myself* (1987). He was survived by his wife, Camilla Jessel, a daughter, and a son. (d. London; October 27, 1991)

FURTHER READING

Obituary. *New York Times,* Oct. 29, 1991.
Obituary. *The Times* (of London), Oct. 28, 1991.

Papp, Joseph (Joseph Papirovsky, 1921–91) Papp was a key figure in the American theater for three decades. He founded New York's Shakespeare Workshop in 1954, which he developed into the landmark New York Shakespeare Festival, housing it in the Off-Broadway Public Theater complex and Central Park's Delacorte Theater; it became the leading American theater company, in the classics and in the introduction of new plays. Many new plays and productions of the classics went on to Broadway, as did *Hair* (1967) and *A Chorus Line,* which originated at the Public Theater, moved to Broadway in 1975 and became the longest-running Broadway show in history, closing in 1990 after 6,137 performances. From 1973 to 1977, the Shakespeare Festival was the theater portion of New York's Lincoln Center. Papp also produced for films and television. Always an advocate of artistic freedom, he in 1990 became the first major cultural figure to stand up against "anti-obscenity" pledges imposed by the National Endowment of the Arts in its attempt to introduce censorship. In August 1991, losing his fight against cancer, he named JoAnne Akalaitis to succeed him. He was survived by his fourth wife, Gail Bovard Merrifield, three daughters, and two sons. (d. New York City; October 31, 1991)

FURTHER READING

Obituary. Margaret Spillane. *Nation,* Nov. 25, 1991.
"A curtain falls." Michelle Green. *People,* Nov. 18, 1991.

"A showman of the people." WILLIAM A. HENRY. *Time,* Nov. 11, 1991.
Obituary. JACK KROLL. *Newsweek,* Nov. 11, 1991.
"Singular sensation. . . ." MIRIAM HORN. *U.S. News & World Report,* Nov. 11, 1991.
Obituary. *Variety,* Nov. 4, 1991.
Obituary. *The Times* (of London), Nov. 2, 1991.
Obituary. *New York Times,* Nov. 1, 1991.
"Joe Papp." VANCE MUSE. *Life,* Apr. 1989.
Joseph Papp and the New York State Shakespeare Festival: An Annotated Bibliography. CHRISTINE E. KING and BRENDA COVEN. Garland, 1988.

Parr, Albert E. (1901–91) A marine biologist, oceanographer, and museum director, Parr began his career in his native Norway, as a zoologist at the Bergen Museum. He joined the staff of the New York Aquarium in 1926. In 1931, he joined the staff of the Peabody Museum, worked in oceanography at Yale University, and was Yale's director of marine research from 1937 to 1942; in that period he conducted a wide range of field research, especially in the Gulf of Mexico and the Caribbean. He became director of the Peabody in 1938, and was from 1942 to 1959 director of New York's American Museum of Natural History, presiding over a period of great growth for that institution. He retired from administration in 1959 but continued as a senior scientist with the museum; he became its director emeritus in 1968. Parr was a prolific writer and editor in marine research. He was survived by two daughters, two sons, a sister, and a brother. (d. Wilder, Vermont; July 17, 1991)

FURTHER READING

Obituary. *New York Times,* July 20, 1991.

Pasternak, Joseph (1901–91) Hungarian-born Pasternak emigrated to the United States after World War I. He worked as a busboy and then in a succession of jobs at Paramount Studios in the early 1920s, beginning his long career in 1923 as an assistant director. He moved to Universal in 1926, becoming head of their Berlin-based European operations in 1928. He made his name in Europe, as a producer of light, entertaining musicals; when Universal closed its Berlin office in 1935, he moved back to Hollywood and spent the next three decades as a leading film musical producer. With 14-year-old Deanna Durbin's first film, the hit *Three Smart Girls* (1936), Pasternak supplied Universal a much-needed financial boost, following up with nine more Durbin films before moving to MGM in the mid-1940s. He also revived Marlene Dietrich's film fortunes with *Destry Rides Again* (1939), *Seven Sinners* (1940), and *Flame of New Orleans* (1941). His later films included *Anchors Aweigh* (1945) and *In the Good Old Summertme* (1949). He was survived by his wife, Dorothy, and three sons. (d. Los Angeles; September 13, 1991)

FURTHER READING

Obituary. *The Times* (of London), Sep. 20, 1991.
Obituary. *New York Times,* Sep. 18, 1991.

Pauley, Jane (1950–) Still personally popular, NBC newscaster Pauley was not as successful on her own show as she had been as co-anchor on the "Today" show with Bryant Gumbel. Ratings for her prime-time half-hour magazine series, "Real Life with Jane Pauley" (and for Tom Brokaw's "Exposé" which followed it on Sunday night) were disappointing; sometimes NBC fell behind not only CBS and ABC but also the Fox network in these time slots. Both series were ended in November, and NBC announced plans to take the best elements of the two programs and meld them into a single hour-long show, to be co-anchored by Pauley and someone else to be named later, with its debut scheduled for March 1992. During 1991, Pauley was also a regular substitute for Tom Brokaw on the "NBC Nightly News."

Indianapolis-born Pauley began her television career in 1972 as a reporter for WISH, Indianapolis, and moved to anchor Chicago's WMAQ. In 1976, she became a national figure as co-anchor of the "Today" show, also working as a reporter for the "NBC Nightly News" in the early 1980s. After 13 years as co-anchor, she departed to anchor her own prime-time news program for NBC, "Real Life With Jane Pauley," also hosting several news specials. Pauley's B.A. was from Indiana University in 1978. She is married to cartoonist Garry Trudeau; the couple have three children.

FURTHER READING

"See Jane run. . . ." ILEANE RUDOLPH. *TV Guide,* Jan. 5, 1991.

"Surviving nicely, thanks. . . ." RICHARD ZOGLIN. *Time,* Aug. 20, 1990.
"The loved one." PHOEBE HOBAN. *New York,* July 23, 1990.
"Jane's search for tomorrow." JEFF ROVIN. *Ladies Home Journal,* July 1990.
"Yesterday, today and tomorrow." GLENN PLASKIN. *American Health,* Mar. 1990.
The Imperfect Mirror: Inside Stories of Television Newscasters. DANIEL PAISNER. Morrow, 1989.

Peck, Gregory (Eldred Gregory Peck, 1916–) At 75 a historic figure in world film, actor Peck was still going strong. The hero of *To Kill a Mockingbird, Gentlemen's Agreement, The Man in the Grey Flannel Suit,* and *On the Beach* played a powerful new lead as New England mill owner Andrew (Jorgy) Jorgenson, opposite Danny DeVito as a corporate predator Lawrence Garfield (Larry the Liquidator) and Penelope Ann Miller as lawyer Kate Sullivan, in Norman Jewison's *Other People's Money.* It was what has come to be seen as a classic Peck portrayal of a strong, honest, compassionate American prototype—but in the 1980s one who loses to a despicable financier and the world he typifies. Peck also revisited an earlier film, playing a cameo as lawyer Lee Heller in Martin Scorsese's 1991 remake of *Cape Fear;* Nick Nolte this time played lawyer Sam Bowden, Peck's 1962 role, and was stalked by Robert De Niro as ex-con Max Cady, the role originated by Robert Mitchum. It was also another year of awards and presentations for film industry elder statesman Peck; perhaps most notably, he was in December awarded Kennedy Center honors for lifetime cultural achievement. Scheduled for early 1992 was a major Lincoln Center retrospective.

California-born Peck is one of the leading American actors of the 20th century; for the past 46 years, he has been a massive, incorruptible presence on the American film scene. He made his New York theater debut in 1942, and emerged as a Hollywood star in 1945, with *The Keys of the Kingdom,* then going on to star in such films as *The Yearling* (1946), *Duel in the Sun* (1947), *Gentlemen's Agreement* (1947), *Twelve O'Clock High* (1949), *The Gunfighter* (1950), *Captain Horatio Hornblower* (1951), *The Snows of Kilimanjaro* (1952), *Roman Holiday* (1953), *Moby Dick* (1954), *The Man in the Grey Flannel Suit* (1956), *The Big Country* (1958), *Pork Chop Hill* (1959), *On the Beach* (1959), *The Guns of Navrone* (1961), *To Kill a Mockingbird* (1962; he won a Best Actor Oscar), *Cape Fear* (1962), *Behold a Pale Horse* (1964), *Mirage* (1965), *Arabesque* (1966), *The Stalking Moon* (1968), *I Walk the Line* (1970), *The Omen* (1976), *MacArthur* (1977), *The Boys from Brazil* (1978), and very late in his career as Ambrose Bierce, opposite Jane Fonda in *Old Gringo* (1989). Peck studied at the University of California and New York's Neighborhood Playhouse. He has been married twice, last in 1955 to Veronique Passani, and has had five children, two of whom—Anthony and Cecilia—pursue acting careers.

FURTHER READING

"Gregory Peck. . . ." RON HAVER. *American Film,* Mar. 1989.
"Impeccable. . . ." ROSEMARY HOLUSHA. *Saturday Evening Post,* Jan–Feb. 1989.
"Gregory Peck. . . ." JENNY CULLEN. *Ladies Home Journal,* Nov. 1988.
The Films of Gregory Peck. JOHN GRIGGS. Carol, 1987.
Gregory Peck. MICHAEL FREEDLAND. Morrow, 1980.

Penn, Sean (1960–) Beginning a new stage in his career, Penn in 1991 wrote, directed, and produced the relatively low-budget film *The Indian Runner,* about two brothers in a farm family, one the local sheriff, the other a Vietnam veteran finding the transition to civilian life enormously difficult. Inspired by the Bruce Springsteen song "Indian Runner," the film featured David Morse, Viggio Mortensen, Valeria Golino, Patricia Arquette, Charles Bronson, Dennis Hopper, and Sandy Dennis. The film opened in autumn 1991, to somewhat mixed reviews, but most agreed that Penn had a future as a director if he chose to pursue it.

California-born Penn, son of director Leo Penn, emerged as one of the leading young film stars of the 1980s in such films as *Taps* (1981), *Fast Times at Ridgemont High* (1982), *Bad Boys* (1983), *Racing with the Moon* (1984), *The Falcon and the Snowman* (1985), *At Close Range* (1986) with his brother Christopher Penn, *Colors* (1988), *Judgment in Berlin* (1988), *Casualties of War* (1989), *We're No Angels* (1989), and *State of Grace* (1990). On stage, he has appeared in such plays as *Heartland* (1981) and *Hurlyburly* (1988). He was married to Madonna (1985–89). Penn and actress Robin Wright, costars in *State of Grace,* have one daughter.

FURTHER READING

"Playboy interview. . . ." DAVID RENSIN. *Playboy,* Nov. 1991.
"Sean Penn at close range." GAVIN SMITH. *Film Comment,* Sep.–Oct. 1991.
"Sean Penn." JULIAN SCHNABEL and DENNIS HOPPER. *Interview,* Sep. 1991.

Penney, William George (1909–91) A leading British nuclear physicist and atomic weapons expert, Penney is known as the father of the British atomic bomb and hydrogen bomb. He began his career in 1936 as a mathematics instructor at London's Imperial College. He was engaged in weapons research during World War II and in 1944 was sent by his government to Los Alamos, where he worked on the development of the atomic bomb, helping to build the first one, exploded at Alamagordo, New Mexico, on July 6, 1945. He was in the plane that dropped the second atomic bomb used in warfare, on Nagasaki, at 9:30 A.M. on August 9, 1945; Penney had helped to build that bomb as well. He was also present at the 1946 U.S. atomic bomb tests at Bikini Atoll. In 1946, he became a key figure in the British effort to build an atomic bomb and in 1952 directed the first test explosion of a British bomb, at the Monte Bello Islands off Australia, later continuing to test at the Maralinga Test Range on the Australian mainland. He was head of the British Atomic Research Establishment at Aldermaston (1953–59) and supervised testing of hydrogen bombs at Christmas Island in 1957 and 1958. He also played a role in the conclusion of the 1963 atmospheric test ban treaty. He left government service to become director of the Imperial College of Science in 1963, retiring in 1973.

The nuclear establishment Penney helped to create and the weapons tests he conducted have long been attacked by opponents as extraordinarily "dirty," involving massive nuclear fallout, radioactive waste, and long-term health problems; although late in his life he expressed some concerns about nuclear weapons and about the safety of some of the tests conducted, Penney generally defended the weapons, their production facilities, and the tests as necessary and right. He was survived by his second wife, formerly Eleanor Jean Quennell, and by two sons. (d. East Hendred, England; March 3, 1991)

FURTHER READING

Obituary. RUDOLF PEIERLS. *Physics Today,* Oct. 1991.
Obituary. *Current Biography,* May 1991.
Obituary. *New York Times,* Mar. 7, 1991.
Obituary. *The Times* (of London), Mar. 6, 1991.

Pérez de Cuéllar, Javier (1920–) During his final year in office, United Nations Secretary-General Pérez de Cuéllar saw substantial progress toward the settlement of several conflicts and disputes in which he had played a mediator's role, as in the end of the long war in Angola and the settlements in Cambodia and El Salvador. Most of these came with the end of superpower sponsorship of warring factions after U.S.-Soviet agreement to end the Cold War. He also played a significant role in the long negotiations to free the Lebanon hostages, going to Tehran to meet with Iranian President Ali Rafsanjani September 10–13, as the final hostage agreements took shape. He also tried to play a peacemaker's role as the Persian Gulf crisis moved toward war, but without success; ultimately, the UN became the vehicle through which collective action was taken against Iraq.

Pérez de Cuéllar joined the UN after a long Peruvian diplomatic career, which included ambassadorships to Switzerland and the Soviet Union. He was Peruvian permanent representative to the UN (1971–75), a member of the Security Council (1973–74), and UN president

(1974). He was a UN mediator and troubleshooter in the late 1970s and early 1980s, and became its fifth secretary-general in 1982. In 1988, he played a substantial role in mediating the end of the long Iran-Iraq war. He was succeeded by Egyptian diplomat Boutros Boutros Ghali. Pérez de Cuéllar attended Lima's Catholic University. He is married to Marcela Temple; they have two children.

FURTHER READING

"Javier of the U.N. . . . ." MORTON KONDRACKE. *New Republic,* Aug. 13, 1990.
"Negotiating peace. . . ." HUGO SADA. *World Press Review,* May 1989.

Pfeiffer, Michelle (1959–) Film star Pfeiffer was highly visible throughout 1991, as *Russia House,* last year's co-starring vehicle with Sean Connery, became a hit on home screens. In 1991, she starred opposite Al Pacino in Garry Marshall's romantic comedy *Frankie and Johnny,* adapted by Terrence McNally from his play *Frankie and Johnny in the Clair De Lune.* The film, the story of a developing love affair between waitress Frankie and short-order cook Johnny, started shooting early in 1991 and was one of the hits of the fall season. Pfeiffer also starred in the *Love Field,* one of a dozen films temporarily shelved by troubled Orion Pictures in October 1991 for lack of promotion money; at year's end its release date was still uncertain. Far more definitely forthcoming was the *Batman* sequel, *Batman Returns,* which started shooting in August 1991, in which Pfeiffer stars as Catwoman opposite Michael Keaton and Danny DeVito.

California-born Pfeiffer very quickly emerged as one of the leading film players of the 1980s, starring in such films as *Grease 2* (1982), *Scarface* (1983), *Into the Night* (1984), *Ladyhawke* (1985), *Sweet Liberty* (1986), *The Witches of Eastwick* (1987), *Married to the Mob* (1988), *Tequila Sunrise* (1988), *Dangerous Liaisons* (1989), and *The Fabulous Baker Boys* (1989; she won an Oscar nomination). In the summer of 1989, she appeared as Olivia in *Twelfth Night* at the New York Shakespeare Festival. She was formerly married, to actor Peter Horton.

FURTHER READING

"Tough guise." JONATHAN VAN METER. *Vogue,* Oct. 1991.
"Queen for a decade." MARC ELIOT. *California,* Sep. 1991.
"The fabulous Pfeiffer girl." ROBERT SEIDENBERG. *American Film,* Jan. 1991.
"Michelle Pfeiffer as. . . ." HAL HINSON. *Esquire,* Dec. 1990.
"Pfeiffer, Michelle." *Current Biography,* Mar. 1990.

Phillips, Lou Diamond (1962–) Phillips spent a good part of 1991 shooting a new movie, *The Dark Wind,* portraying Navajo tribal policeman Jim Chee in a murder mystery set in an Arizona Native American reservation. The film, adapted from the Tony Hillerman novel, was directed by Errol Morris and co-produced by Robert Redford. The American Indian Registry for the Performing Arts had initially criticized the casting of part-Cherokee Phillips as a Navajo in *The Dark Wind,* but his involvement was supported by Navajo groups, and the film went forward. Unfortunately the film fell afoul of Carolco Pictures' financial problems and its original January 1992 release date passed with the film still on the shelf. For Scott Goldstein's *Ambition,* Phillips wrote the screenplay and starred as a mystery writer who manipulates a serial killer for literary purposes; the low-budget thriller was generally not well received. Also released in 1991 was *Harley,* a film originally shot in 1984, in which Phillips plays a juvenile delinquent sent to a Texas ranch. Forthcoming was another ethnic starring role, this one as the young Eskimo in the Jacques Dorfman film *Agaguk,* with Toshiro Mifune and Jennifer Tilly.

After playing in cabaret as a comedian, and in small roles in theater and television, Phillips suddenly emerged as one of the leading young film stars of the late 1980s, beginning with his role as Mexican-American rock star Richie Valens in the Luis Valdez film *La Bamba* (1987). He went on to appear in such films as *Stand and Deliver* (1987), *Young Guns* (1988; and the 1990 sequel *Young Guns II*), *Disorganized Crime* (1989), *Renegades* (1989), *First Power* (1989), and *Show of Force* (1989). Texas-born Phillips attended the University of Texas. He is married to actress Julie Cypher.

FURTHER READING

"Does Lou Diamond Phillips. . . ." ALICE LANE. *Mademoiselle,* Feb. 1990.
"Lou Diamond Phillips. . . ." *Teen,* Sep. 1989.

Pickering, Thomas Reeve (1931–) U.S. permanent representative to the United Nations Pickering continued to use his long diplomatic experience in the Middle East to great advantage in the aftermath of the Persian Gulf War and the Cold War, as the United Nations took over inspection and peacekeeping functions in Iraq, Kuwait began to heal its war wounds, and new relationships began to develop among several of the countries in the area, climaxed by the autumn Middle East Peace Conference in Madrid. Similarly, Pickering's experience in Africa and Central America came into play as the UN began to play a substantial role in attempting to resolve long-running regional conflicts that had earlier been fanned by U.S.-Soviet Cold War rivalries and were now beginning to be solved with the participation of the former superpower enemies.

New Jersey-born Pickering is a career diplomat, who joined the foreign service in 1959, after serving in the navy. His long career took him to posts in Sub-Saharan Africa in the late 1960s, and to a series of very "hot spot" ambassador's posts from the mid-1970s, in Jordan, Nigeria, and El Salvador, in Israel (1985–88), and in 1989 to the United Nations, in a non-cabinet-level position. Pickering's B.A. was from Bowdoin in 1953, his M.A. from the Fletcher School in 1954. He married Alice Stover in 1955; the couple have two children.

FURTHER READING

"Cosmo talks to. . . ." Michele Willens. *Cosmopolitan,* Sep. 1989.

Pilpel, Harriet Frleischl (1912–91) A leading civil liberties, family law, women's rights, and literary lawyer, Pilpel was long associated with the American Civil Liberties Union; she was general counsel from 1979 to 1986 and was first chairwoman of the organization's national advisory council at the time of her death. She had also been general counsel of the Planned Parenthood Federation of America and served on its International Law Panel. She also served the federal government in several advisory capacities, including membership in the federal Commission on the Status of Women during the Kennedy and Johnson administrations and from 1965 to 1976 was a consultant to the Women's Bureau of the Labor Department. Pilpel lectured frequently and made many television appearances as an advocate of women's rights and a wider range of civil liberties. She was survived by her second husband, Irvin B. Schwartz, a daughter, a son, and two sisters. (d. New York City; April 23, 1991)

FURTHER READING

Obituary. *New York Times,* Apr. 24, 1991.

Pinter, Harold (1930–) For celebrated modern British playwright Harold Pinter, 1991 was an unusually productive year on stage and screen. His first new full-length play in 13 years, the one-hour-long *Party Time,* premiered in London, as did his eight-minute-long *The New World Order,* described as a "short, satirical response to the gulf war." Pinter also directed a revival of his classic *The Caretaker* in London, with Donald Pleasance again as Davies in the role he had so memorably created in 1960. Pinter wrote the screenplay of the Jerry Schatzberg film *Reunion,* based on the Fred Uhlman book, which starred Jason Robards as an American, once German, going back to revisit Germany for the first time since his youth. He also wrote the screenplay of Paul Schrader's horror-thriller *The Comfort of Strangers,* based on the Ian McEwan novel; the film starred Christopher Walken, Natasha Richardson, Rupert Everett, and Helen Mirren.

London-born Pinter began his career as an actor, from 1949 working largely in repertory. He moved into playwriting in the late 1950s, scoring his first major success with *The Caretaker* (1960; he also adapted it into the 1964 film), and went on to such works as *The Homecoming* (1965; and the 1973 film), *Old Times* (1970), *No Man's Land* (1975), and *Family Voices* (1980). He has also directed such plays as *Exiles* (1970), *Butley* (1971; and the 1973 film), *Otherwise Engaged* (1975), and *The Common Pursuit* (1984), and has written many screenplays, including *The Servant* (1962), *The Quiller Memorandum* (1965), *The Go-Between* (1969), *The French Lieutenant's Woman* (1980), *The Turtle Diary* (1984), *The Handmaid's Tale* (1990), and *The Heat of the Day* (1990). Pinter has been married twice, to actress Vivien Merchant and since 1980 to the writer Antonia Fraser, and has one child.

FURTHER READING

"The Pinter principle." DONALD CHASE. *American Film,* Oct. 1990.
Harold Pinter, 2nd ed. BERNARD F. DUKORE. St. Martin's, 1990.
Harold Pinter. LOIS GORDON, ed. Garland, 1990.
Pinter the Playwright, 4th ed. MARTIN ESSLIN. Heinemann, 1988.
Harold Pinter. HAROLD BLOOM, ed. Chelsea House, 1987.
Pinter: The Player's Playwright. DAVID T. THOMPSON. Schocken, 1985.
Harold Pinter. GUIDO ALMANSI and SIMON HENDERSON. Routledge Chapman & Hall, 1983.

Pochin, Edward (1909–91) A research endocrinologist, born in Cheshire, England, Pochin was one of the world's leading radiological protection scientists. He was one of those who brought home the huge new dangers generated by the atomic era; as understanding grew, so did his importance to humanity. Pochin studied medicine at Cambridge, joined Britain's Medical Research Council in 1941, and from 1946 to 1974 was director of the Medical Research Council's clinical research department at London's University Hospital medical school. During the postwar period, as atomic weapons and energy development began to create radiation exposure problems, his work on the thryoid gland led him to examine the hazards created by iodine-131 release, and from there into the entire spectrum of radiation hazards, as a member of the Medical Research Council's committee on protection against ionizing radiation. He was one of those who dealt with the aftermath of the catastrophic 1957 fire at Britain's Windscale nuclear facility. He became a member of the International Commission on Radiological Protection (ICRP) in 1959, and was commission chairman from 1962 to 1969, as well as holding several other key British and international radiation protection posts. His landmark 1987 "Pochin Report" on radiological hazards at Britain's Aldermaston nuclear establishment raised major worldwide questions. Pochin wrote prolifically on radiation hazards, evaluation, and standard setting. He was survived by a daughter and a son. (d. January 29, 1991)

FURTHER READING

Obituary. *The Times* (of London), Jan. 31, 1991.

Poindexter, John Marlan (1936–) Naval officer and former National Security Advisor Poindexter was indicted on seven Iran-Contra-related charges on March 14, 1988, after a long grand jury investigation directed by special prosecutor Lawrence E. Walsh. On April 7, 1990, after six days of deliberation, a federal jury convicted him on five felony counts. On June 11, 1990, he received a six-month jail term, becoming the first Iran-Contra scandal figure to be sentenced to prison. But on November 15, 1991, a 2–1 decision of the U.S. Court of Appeals for the District of Columbia reversed all five of Poindexter's felony convictions outright, without sending them back to the lower courts for review. The court ruled, as had the court in the Oliver North case, that the Poindexter conviction had been fatally tainted by the public congressional Iran-Contra hearings, in that testimony by Oliver North had been admitted, and that North's testimony had been "prejudicially influenced" by his having been exposed to Poindexter's public testimony at the hearings. The court based its decision on the North testimony alone, although implying that several other witnesses may have been similarly tainted.

Rear Admiral Poindexter, a career naval officer, joined the White House-based national security staff in 1981. He became deputy national security advisor in 1983 and national security advisor in 1985, resigning on November 25, 1986, with the eruption of the Iran-Contra scandal, the most highly visible of the many covert operations developed during his White House years. Poindexter then refused to testify before congressional committees without a grant of immunity, and ultimately did testify with limited immunity. He retired from the Navy in December 1987. Poindexter attended the U.S. Naval Academy at Annapolis and the California Institute of Technology. He is married and has four children.

FURTHER READING

Perilous Statecraft. MICHAEL LEDEEN. Macmillan, 1989.
Inside the National Security Council: The True Story of the Making and Unmaking of Reagan's Foreign Policy. CONSTANTINE C. MENGES. Simon & Schuster, 1988.
Men of Zeal: A Candid Story of the Iran-Contra Hearings. WILLIAM S. COHEN and GEORGE J. MITCHELL. Viking Penguin, 1988.
"Poindexter, John M(arlan)." *Current Biography,* Nov. 1987.

Poitier, Sidney (1924–) In a very welcome return to major dramatic work, Poitier in April 1991 starred as Thurgood Marshall in *Separate But Equal,* the four-hour television miniseries written and directed by George Stevens, Jr., about the course of the dispute that ultimately led to the landmark 1954 U.S. Supreme Court school desegration decision in the case of *Brown v. Board of Education of Topeka, Kansas,* Marshall's greatest victory. Burt Lancaster played former presidential candidate John W. Davis, lawyer for the losing side. In October 1991, Poitier was named to receive the 1992 Life Achievement Award of the American Film Institute, the 20th person to be so honored. Forthcoming were starring roles in the film comedy *Sneakers,* opposite Robert Redford, which began shooting in October 1991, and reportedly in the film *Summer Knowledge.*

Miami-born Poitier grew up in the Bahamas, retaining his West Indian accent in a 45-year-long stage and screen career that has included appearances in such plays as *Anna Lucasta* (1948) and *A Raisin in the Sun* (1959). He became Hollywood's first major Black movie star in the late 1950s; his most notable films were *The Defiant Ones* (1958), *Porgy and Bess* (1959), the film version of *A Raisin in the Sun* (1961), *Lilies of the Field* (1963; he was the first Black actor to win a Best Actor Academy Award), *In the Heat of the Night* (1967), and *Guess Who's Coming to Dinner* (1967). Poitier also became a director, of such films as *Buck and the Preacher* (1972; he also starred), *Uptown Saturday Night* (1982), *Hanky Panky* (1984), and *Ghost Dad* (1990). In 1980 he published the autobiographical *This Life.* He has been married twice and has six children.

FURTHER READING

"Sidney Poitier." FRANK SPOTNITZ. *American Film,* Sep.–Oct. 1991.
"Poitier's stellar career. . . ." *Jet,* Mar. 20, 1989.
"Poitier thanks. . . ." RALPH TYLER. *Variety,* Mar. 8, 1989.
Sidney Poitier. CAROL BERGMAN. Chelsea House, 1989.
Long Journey: A Biography of Sidney Poitier. CAROLYN EWERS. NAL-Dutton, 1981.

Pol Pot (Tol Saut; Saloh Sar, 1928–) The world hailed the October 23, 1991, Treaty of Paris, which provided for an immediate cease-fire in the long Cambodian Civil War, the return home of an estimated 350,000 refugees, and the posting of thousands of United Nations (UN) troops and civilian personnel to keep the peace, help set up a new government, and prepare for free elections to be held in 1993. But there was great worldwide concern, as well, for the strongest single force in Cambodia, and seemingly an essential part of the new government, was the Khmer Rouge (Red Khmer) organization, which under Pol Pot's leadership was directly responsible for the Cambodian Holocaust (1975–78), a series of mass murders in which an estimated one to three million Cambodians died, until the 1978 Vietnamese invasion of Cambodia took the country.

Pol Pot had officially stepped down as head of Khmer Rouge in 1985 but was widely thought still to be the undisputed leader of the movement. After the September 1989 Vietnamese withdrawal, Pol Pot's forces fought the Cambodian government, at first in coalition with U.S.-backed and Soviet-backed rebel forces and then as an increasingly powerful single organization, which by midsummer 1990 was threatening to take the capital city, Phnom Penh. With the Cambodian Holocaust very much in mind, and as Pol Pot continued to gain strength, the United States stopped its aid to Cambodian rebel forces in July 1990, while Norodom Sihanouk, under United Nations and great power auspices, moved forward to develop the Paris peace treaty. After adoption of the treaty, Sihanouk and his allies quickly moved to take operational control of the country and to exclude the Khmer Rouge from the new government. Sihanouk, who was named president on November 20, 1991, called for genocide trials of the Khmer Rouge leadership, especially singling out Pol Pot for attack.

Pol Pot has spent his whole life as a communist activist, beginning as a teenager in the Indochinese Communist Party in the 1940s. After World War II, he moved up in the Cambodian communist party, and in 1963 emerged as party general secretary and organizer of the Khmer Rouge army. He became prime minister of Cambodia, then renamed Kampuchea, in 1976, after the 1975 Khmer Rouge victory, but resumed his career as a guerrilla leader after the successful Vietnamese invasion of Cambodia in 1978. His wife is Khieu Ponnary.

FURTHER READING

Cambodia, Pol Pot, and the United States: The Faustian Pact. MICHAEL HAAS. Greenwood, 1991.
Pol Pot: A Political Biography. DAVID P. CHANDLER. Westview, 1991.
"Skeletons in the closet. . . ." STEPHEN J. MORRIS. *New Republic,* June 4, 1990.
Leftism: From de Sade and Marx to Hitler and Pol Pot. ERIK LEDDIHN. Regnery Gateway, 1990.
Pol Pot. REBECCA STEFOFF. Chelsea House, 1989.
Pol Pot Plans the Future: Confidential Leadership Documents from Democratic Kampuchea, 1976–1977. DAVID P. CHANDLER, ed. Yale University, Southeast Asia, 1989.
Beyond the Horizon: Five Years with the Khmer Rouge. LAURENCE PICQ. St. Martin's, 1989.
How Pol Pot Came to Power. BEN KIERNAN. Schocken, 1985.

Porter, Sylvia Field (1913–91) Long Island-born Porter, a leading financial writer for more than five decades, began her writing career in the early 1930s, with freelance financial articles, and by 1934 had a weekly column in *The American Banker.* In 1935, she began her long association with the *New York Post* (1935–77), starting with an irregularly published column and by 1936 becoming the newpaper's financial editor, with a daily column that was syndicated in 1947. She moved to the New York *Daily News* in 1978. Her first book was *How to Make Money in Government Bonds* (1939). It was followed by several more books, including her tax guide, published annually from 1960, and her very popular *Sylvia Porter's Money Book* (1975). Her last book was *Sylvia Porter's Your Finances in the 1990s* (1990). She also published the magazine *Sylvia Porter's Personal Finance* (1984–87). She was married twice, and was survived by a daughter, a stepson, and a brother. (d. Pound Ridge, New York; June 5, 1991)

FURTHER READING

Obituary. *Current Biography,* Aug. 1991.
Obituary. *New York Times,* June 7, 1991.

Powell, Colin Luther (1937–) In August 1990, Lieutenant General Powell began the huge American buildup in the Persian Gulf, soon becoming a key figure in the Persian Gulf War. Powell was highly visible, traveling often to the Persian Gulf and holding a series of press conferences—jointly with Defense Secretary Richard Cheney and sometimes also including General Norman Schwarzkopf—aimed at building popular support for the war. Cheney and Powell conducted the first wartime press conference on January 17 and continued to appear together throughout the war and into the postwar period; for example, both welcomed home American POWs after the war. Powell was widely reported to have urged a go-slow policy during the run-up to the Gulf War, favoring containment rather than direct military action; but he never publicly opposed that action and carried the war through fully once the decision had been made.

New York-born Powell began his long military career in 1958; he has held a series of line and staff posts in Europe and the United States, including command posts in the 101st Airborne and 4th Infantry divisions. He was National Security Affairs assistant to President Reagan (1987–89). Powell was appointed chairman of the Joint Chiefs of Staff by President George Bush on August 10, 1989; it was a historic "first," as he was the first African-American to hold the post. One of his earliest major tasks was the organization of the December 1989 Panama invasion. He has also sent American forces into El Salvador, Liberia, and the Philippines. Powell's B.S. was from the City University of New York in 1958, his M.B.A. from George Washington University in 1971. Most unusual for one who has gone so far in the U.S. Army, he is not a West Point graduate, instead having become an officer through the Reserve Officer Training Corps (ROTC). He married Alma Johnson in 1962; the couple have three children.

FURTHER READING

Colin Powell: A Biography. JAMES HASKINS. Scholastic, 1992.
Colin Powell. WARREN BROWN. Chelsea House, 1992.
Story of Colin Powell and Benjamin Davis. KATHERINE APPLEGATE. Dell, 1992.
"Colin Powell." *People,* Summer 1991.
"Five who fit the bill." *Time,* May 20, 1991.
" 'Nobody knows my politics.' " TOM MATHEWS. *Newsweek,* May 13, 1991.
"The reluctant warrior. . . ." EVAN THOMAS. *Newsweek,* May 13, 1991.
"America's Black Eisenhower. . . ." JOHN RANELAGH. *National Review,* Apr. 1, 1991.
"Another Ike?" VICTOR GOLD. *Washingtonian,* Apr. 1991.
"What next. . . ." STEVEN V. ROBERTS. *U.S. News & World Report,* Mar. 18, 1991.
"In the footsteps of two Georges." BRUCE B. AUSTER. *U.S. News & World Report,* Feb. 4, 1991.
Colin Powell. JONATHAN EVERSTON. Bantam, 1991.
Colin Powell: Four Star General. ELAINE LANDAU. Watts, 1991.
Colin Powell: Straight to the Top. ROSE BLUE and CORINNE J. NADEN. Millbrook, 1991.

Pryce, Jonathan (1947–) Celebrated British actor Jonathan Pryce won a 1991 Tony for leading actor in a musical for his starring role as the Eurasian pimp in *Miss Saigon.* He created the role on the London stage in 1989 and took it to Broadway in 1990, after initial U.S. Actors' Equity objections to a White actor in the role had been overcome. During 1991, Pryce also starred as William Wallace in the film *The Man from the Pru,* based on a real-life 1930s Liverpool murder, in a cast that included Anna Massey and Susannah York. He also starred in the British television miniseries *Selling Hitler,* about a set of faked Hitler diaries, the center of a major 1983 scandal. Forthcoming was a role in a James Foley's film version of David Mamet's play and screenplay *Glengarry Glen Ross,* playing with Al Pacino, Jack Lemmon, Alec Baldwin, Alan Arkin, Kevin Spacey, and Ed Harris.

A leading British actor, Pryce has played in a series of major stage roles from the mid-1970s. He won a Tony for *The Comedians* (1986), a production originating in England that transferred to New York. His 1980 *Hamlet* won Britain's Olivier Award. Pryce's other plays include *The Caretaker* (1981), *Accidental Death of an Anarchist* (1984), *The Seagull* (1985), *Macbeth* (1986; title role), and *Uncle Vanya* (1988). He has also appeared in such films as *The Ploughman's Lunch* (1983), *Brazil* (1985), *The Doctor and the*

Devils (1986), *Consuming Passions* (1988), *The Adventures of Baron Munchausen* (1988), and *The Rachel Papers* (1989); in several television films; and in the television series "Roger Doesn't Live Here Any More" (1981). He attended the Royal Academy of Dramatic Art.

FURTHER READING

"Mr. Saigon." MICHAEL BILLINGTON. *Interview,* Apr. 1991.
"Mr. Saigon. . . ." CHRIS SMITH. *New York,* Mar. 11, 1991.

Pugo, Boris Karlovich (1937–91) A Latvian, Pugo was born in Kver (then Kalinin), northwest of Moscow, and was educated as an engineer, graduating from Riga Polytechnical Institute in 1960. His career, however, was almost entirely within the Communist Party apparatus, from early days in the party's youth affiliate, the Konsomol. He was a KGB (Committee of State Security) secret police official from 1976 to 1984, from 1980 to 1984 as head of KGB Latvian operations, working under KGB head Yuri Andropov, who from 1982 to 1984 led the Soviet Union. A conservative, Pugo was often seen by others as one of the moderate new Soviet leaders who were nurtured by Andropov; he worked with reformer Mikhail Gorbachev from Gorbachev's accession to power in 1985. Pugo was Communist Party head in Latvia (1984–88); he became a member of the party Central Committee in 1986 and later of the party Control Committee.

In December 1990, under attack by conservatives and attempting to save his government in a worsening economic and political situation, Gorbachev replaced his liberal Interior minister, Vadim V. Bakatin, with conservative Pugo. But Gorbachev had miscalculated; Pugo quickly became a leader of the hard line opposition and initiated several armed attacks against democratic protesters. He became a key leader of the failed coup in August 1991; on August 22nd, he committed suicide, shooting himself as he was about to be arrested.

FURTHER READING

"Prelude to a putsch." STROBE TALBOTT. *Time,* Sep. 2, 1991.
Obituary. *The Times* (of London), Aug. 24, 1991.
"Skillful party climber." *New York Times,* Aug. 21, 1991.

Qaddafi, Muammar Muhammed al- (1942–) For three days in August 1991 the Libyan head of state had reason to believe that his situation might be greatly transformed, as he hailed the "magnificent" Soviet right wing coup. But it was not to be. Increasingly isolated on the world stage, Qaddafi had earlier in the year even offered to send troops to Saudi Arabia in the early stages of the Persian Gulf Crisis, though later verbally supporting the Iraqis. Qaddafi continued to try to attract Western investment and repair relations with his neighbors as he faced economic problems and Muslim fundamentalist challenges to his rule.

The United States attitude toward Libya in no way softened, although Qaddafi cut back his aid to terrorists during 1990 and 1991. In November 1991, the investigation of the 1988 Lockerbie airplane bombing resulted in charges that two Libyans, allegedly government secret service operatives, were responsible for the bombing; their extradition to the United States to stand trial was demanded. Qaddafi refused, and the stage was set for yet another U.S.-Libya confrontation.

Qaddafi is a career military officer; he led the 1969 military coup in Libya and quickly seized power for himself, holding it as a dictator ever since; he had himself named president in 1977. He has made repeated, largely unsuccessful, attempts to establish himself as a major radical leader of the Arab world, fanning anti-western Islamic fundamentalism, supporting terrorist activities, and siding with Iraq during the Persian Gulf Crisis. His long direct intervention in the Chadian civil war (1975–87) was no more successful; he was finally forced to sue for peace after defeat on the battlefield, the loss of large air bases, and Chadian invasion of southern Libya. He has stopped just short of going to war with Egypt on several occasions. There have also been several armed clashes with the United States; in the most serious of these, U.S. warplanes and ships bombarded Libya in April 1986. Qaddafi attended Libya University. He is married and has five children.

FURTHER READING

Qaddafi on the Edge. Camelia Sadat. HarperCollins, 1991.

Qaddafi, Terrorism, and the Origins of the U.S. Attack on Libya. Brian L. Davis. Greenwood, 1990.

Muammar El-Qaddafi. Ted Gottfried. Chelsea House, 1987.

Qaddafi and the Libyan Revolution. David Blundy and Andrew Lycett. Little, Brown, 1987.

The Making of a Pariah State: The Adventurist Politics of Mummar Quaddafi, Martin Sicker. Greenwood, 1987.

Qaddafi: His Ideology in Theory and Practice. Mohamed El-Khawas. Gordon, 1987.

Libya: Qadhafi's Revolution and the Modern State. Lillian C. Harris. Westview, 1986.

Qin Benli (1917–91) Born in Zhejiang, Qin was one of China's leading journalists, whose commitment to truth and reform cost him heavily throughout his career. In 1957, on the eve of Mao Zedong's "Great Leap Forward" campaign, he was fired from his position as deputy editor of *Wen Hui Bao,* a major Shanghai daily newspaper, for his alleged "rightist" tendencies, later becoming an editor at a minor magazine. In 1966, during the massive attack on China's intellectuals and artists that accompanied the Cultural Revolution, he was forced out of journalism and internally exiled, returning to his career a decade later, in 1976. In 1980, Qin founded the weekly *World Economic Herald,* sponsored by the Shanghai Academy of Social Sciences, which quickly became one of China's leading reform publications. He strongly supported reformer Hu Yaobang, who was deposed in 1986; Qin then supported reformer Zhao Ziyang. In April 1989, Qin sponsored a seminar on Hu Yaobang, and published statements calling for a re-evaluation of Hu's contributions to China. For this, the *World Economic Herald* was closed by the Chinese government. After the June 1989 Tienanmen Square massacare of dissenting Chinese students, Hu, by then ill with the cancer that eventually killed him, was placed under "unofficial" house arrest; several members of his former staff were more openly imprisoned. He was survived by his wife. (d. Shanghai; April 15, 1991)

FURTHER READING

Obituary. *The Times* (of London), Apr. 18, 1991.
Obituary. *New York Times,* Apr. 16, 1991.
" 'The final days of the Herald.' " ANDREW GIARELLI. *World Press Review,* May 1990.
"International Editor of the Year." *World Press Review,* May 1990.

Quaid, Dennis (Dennis William Quaid, 1954–) As *Postcards from the Edge* (1990), in which he starred with Meryl Streep and Shirley MacLaine, moved successfully from the theatrical release into home video, Quaid was set to star opposite Isabella Rossellini in David Lean's *Nostromo,* based on the Joseph Conrad novel. But the film was postponed because of Lean's illness, and ultimately canceled due to his death. Forthcoming for Quaid was a starring role opposite Debra Winger in Glen Gordon's *Wilder Napalm,* in a cast that includes Arliss Howard, Jim Varney, and M. Emmet Walsh. Also forthcoming were three projects in development with Cathleen Summers: an environmental-theme movie, *Troppo,* about nuclear testing in the South Pacific during the 1950s; *Two-Bit Romance;* and *Hideaway,* based on the Dean Koontz suspense novel.

Houston-born Quaid played a lead as one of the four young men in *Breaking Away* (1979), and went on to roles in such 1980s films as *Longriders* (1979), *The Right Stuff* (1983), *Dreamscape* (1984), *Enemy Mine* (1985), and *The Big Easy* (1987). He starred as singer Jerry Lee Lewis in the film biography *Great Balls of Fire* (1989), and began the 1990s with *Come and See the Paradise* (1990) and *Postcards from the Edge* (1990). Quaid attended the University of Houston. He married actress Meg Ryan in 1991. He is the brother of actor Randy Quaid.

FURTHER READING

"The devil and. . . ." JAN HOFFMAN. *Premiere,* Aug. 1989.
"Playing the killer." NICK TOSCHES. *Vogue,* July 1989.
"Simmer down, son." ROBERT PALMER. *American Film,* June 1989.
"Goodness gracious." JOHN ED BRADLEY. *Esquire,* Mar. 1989.
"Whole lotta shakin'." HERB RITTS and KEVIN SESSUMS. *Interview,* June 1989.
Dennis Quaid. GAIL BIRNBAUM. St. Martin's, 1988.

Quayle, Dan (James Danforth Quayle, III, 1947–) For a few days in May 1991, the possibility of a Quayle presidency came alive—and with it all the old doubts about whether he would be a good president. President George Bush was hospitalized on May 4 with atrial fibrillation, which was ultimately diagnosed as being caused by easily treatable Grave's Disease. But in the few days that Bush's health might have seriously been in question, the prospect of a possible Quayle presidency generated a great deal of negative comment, including polls that showed a majority of Americans believed he was unqualified to succeed to the presidency.

During 1991, Quayle's vice presidency continued to be largely a stand-by matter, featuring many trips and ceremonial speeches. Although he was often at the president's side, he did not fulfill any seriously important functions, as has been the case since his taking office in 1989. But he continued to be haunted by the extremely adverse image that had been developed during

the 1988 presidential campaign, as very unfavorable media attention had focused on a series of quite unfortunate statements he had made. During much of 1990 and 1991, Quayle seemed better able to withstand and survive media attack and played his administration role without great public abrasion. As both major parties began the long run-up to the 1992 presidential election, the main question seemed to be whether George Bush would pick him once again as his running mate.

Indiana-born Quayle worked in his family's newspaper business for several years before becoming an Indiana state employee in 1971. He became a congressman in 1977, was a U.S. senator from Indiana (1981–89), and was chosen by George Bush to be his running mate in the 1988 presidential campaign. Quayle's B.S. was from DePauw University in 1969, his J.D. from Indiana University in 1974. He married Marilyn Tucker in 1972; they have three children.

FURTHER READING

"Qualye alert." FRED BARNES. *New Republic,* May 27, 1991.

Newsweek, May 20, 1991. "The right's point man." TOM MORGANTHAU. "Why Quayle is doomed." JONATHAN ALTER. "The Quayle handicap. . . ." EVAN THOMAS. "Rx for the veep."

Time, May 20, 1991. "Why not the best? . . ." DAN GOODGAME. "Is he really that bad?" MICHAEL DUFFY.

"A talk with. . . ." LEE WALCZAK and DOUGLAS HARBRECHT. *Business Week,* Apr. 1, 1991.

"Quayle so far." DAVID BROCK. *Commentary,* Jan. 1991.

The Official Unauthorized Biography of J. Danforth Quayle. Electric Strawberry, 1991.

"Roasting Quayle. . . ." MARCI McDONALD. *Maclean's,* Nov. 19, 1990.

"Quayle etches national profile. . . ." BILL WHALEN. *Insight,* Nov. 5, 1990.

"Late bloomer." GARRY WILLS. *Time,* Apr. 23, 1990.

"Quayle, (James) Dan(forth)." *Current Biography,* June 1989.

Quayle Droppings: The Politics of J. Danforth Quayle. ARTHUR F. IDE. Liberal Press, 1988.

Quill, Timothy E. (1949–) A doctor from upstate New York, Quill made a major contribution to the world-wide discussion and debate over doctor-assisted suicide when he wrote in the March 7, 1991, issue of the *New England Journal of Medicine* of how he had thought through and ultimately decided to help one of his patients commit suicide, at her request. Quill reported that the 45-year-old woman, known only as Diane, had leukemia and killed herself in 1990 by ingesting lethal amounts of barbiturates. He published the story with her family's permission, as part of the continuing consideration of the question of suicide.

Under great pressure from anti-euthanasia forces, the Rochester District Attorney took the matter to a grand jury on July 19, 1991. The grand jury refused to prosecute Dr. Quill, reflecting very widely held American views on the right to suicide, which go quite against the main body of state laws on the matter. In August, the Board for Professional Medical Conduct of the New York State Health Department refused to bring charges of professional misconduct against Dr. Quill. While opposed to assisted suicides, the Board pointed out that Quill and his patient had a long-standing medical relationship, that Quill had not directly taken the patient's life, and that the decision as to how much of the prescribed medication to take is the patient's own decision.

Quill is a primary care internist at the Genesee Hospital in Rochester, New York. He had previously been director of a hospice program. He was married in 1991.

FURTHER READING

"Mercy mission? . . ." AMY BERNSTEIN. *U.S. News & World Report,* Mar. 18, 1991.

Quinn, Anthony (Anthony Rudolph Oaxaca Quinn, 1915–) For veteran actor Quinn, as for so many other stars, a career that began with strong character roles was later in life moving back to just such roles, the actor enriching each work with his presence. In 1991, Quinn appeared as Lou Carbone in *Jungle Fever,* an interracial love story, written, directed, and produced by Spike Lee, in a cast that includes Lee, Wesley Snipes, Annabelle Sciorra, Ossie Davis, Ruby Dee, Samuel L. Jackson, Lonette McKee, John Turturro, and Frank Vincent. Quinn also appeared as Nick in the romantic comedy *Only the Lonely,* written and directed by Chris Columbus; John Candy starred, in a cast that included Maureen O'Hara, Ally Sheedy, and Macaulay Culkin. Reportedly forthcoming was a starring role in Jeff Angelucci's *The Actor,* along with Lauren Bacall.

Chihuahua-born Quinn appeared in a wide range of supporting roles in action films early in his career, as in *The Plainsman* (1937), *Blood and Sand* (1941), and *Viva Zapata* (1952; he won a Best Supporting Actor Oscar), and then was able to broaden his work greatly, appearing as Zampanó opposite Giulietta Masina's Gelsomina in Federico Fellini's classic film *La Strada* (1954); in *Lust for Life* (1956), for which he won a second Best Supporting Actor Oscar; and in such further films as *The Guns of Navarone* (1961), *Lawrence of Arabia* (1962), *Zorba the Greek* (1964), *The Shoes of the Fisherman* (1968), and *Lion of the Desert* (1980). His recent screen work includes *Onassis: The Richest Man in the World* (1988), *The Old Man and the Sea* (1990), and *Revenge* (1990). He starred on Broadway in the title role of the musical *Zorba* (1983–86). His autobiography is *The Original Sin: A Self-Portrait* (1972). Quinn has been married twice, most recently to Iolanda Addolori in 1966, and has eight children, including the actors Francesco, Valentina, and Danielle.

FURTHER READING

"Anthony Quinn." VERONICA WEBB. *Interview,* May 1991.

" 'It's not very hard work. . . .' " JOANNA ELM. *TV Guide,* Mar. 24, 1990.

R

Rafsanjani, Ali Akbar Hashemi

(1934–) As Iran's isolation increased in the aftermath of the Persian Gulf War and as the country's economic crisis deepened, the relatively moderate forces led by Iranian President Rafsanjani gained strength and the Iranian government began to take a far more conciliatory line. On January 17, as the air war began, Rafsanjani was sharply critical of the United States and its allies. By early March, after the Iraqi defeat, Iran was widely reported to be arming Iraqi rebel Shiites and Kurds, and urging the ouster of Saddam Hussein. On May 27, in a major departure from previous policy, Rafsanjani called for economic ties with the West and with other Gulf nations—and on June 2 was backed in this by his most powerful Islamic fundamentalist opponent, Ayatollah Ali Khamenei.

The change of policy also extended to the American and other European hostages held in Lebanon by the Iranian-controlled Hezbollah (Party of God). In the autumn of 1991, following a September 10–13 Tehran meeting between United Nations Secretary-General Javiér Perez de Cuéllar and Rafsanjani, 9 of the 11 Western hostages remaining in Lebanon were released.

Iran's human rights record continued to be wholly unacceptable to international human rights organizations, and internal repression continued, most notably with the September jailing of nine members of the only legal opposition party, for daring to criticize the Iranian government publicly. Rafsanjani also denied reports that his government had organized the August 8, 1991, Paris murder of former Iranian premier Shahpur Bakhtiar.

Rafsanjani was long associated with Ayatollah Ruhollah Khomeini. He became a key figure in Iranian politics, as speaker of the national assembly during the 1980s. As speaker, he sometimes played the role of hard-line Iranian politician, as when he called for the assassination of the author Salman Rushdie for writing the book *The Satanic Verses,* but sometimes he functioned as a relative moderate, who made very tentative overtures to the West in a bid to re-establish broken relationships. He became president of Iran in August 1989 during the period of maneuvering following the death of Ayatollah Khomeini. Rafsanjani's personal life has been kept very private, but it is known that he is married and has several children.

FURTHER READING

"Who's sitting pretty. . . ." *Business Week,* Mar. 11, 1991.

"Rafsanjani, Ali Akbar Hashemi." *Current Biography,* Nov. 1989.

" 'Rafsanjani would have. . . .' " ALFRED BALK. *World Press Review,* Aug. 1989.

"Iran without Khomeini." MICHAEL LEDEEN. *American Spectator,* Aug. 1989.

"Burying the passions. . . ." BILL HEWITT. *Newsweek,* June 19, 1989.

"Santa satan? . . ." MAGGIE MAHAR. *Barron's,* Jan. 16, 1989.

Ragni, Gerome (1943–91) Pittsburgh-born Ragni was best known by far for the musical *Hair,* one of the key works of the counterculture of the 1960s; he and James Rado collaborated on the book and lyrics, with music by Galt MacDermot. The work premiered at the New York Shakespeare Festival in 1967 and was then rewritten and restaged, beginning its long run on Broadway in 1968. He and Rado also appeared in the play, which featured such songs as "Aquarius" and "Good Morning, Starshine." Ragni had previously appeared on Broadway with Richard Burton in *Hamlet* (1964), and also in several off-Broadway plays. He and McDermot wrote the musical *Dude* (1972). He also collaborated with Steve Margoshes on *Jack Sound and his Dog Star Blowing His Final Trumpet on the Day of Doom* (1977), and again with Rado and McDermot on the musical *Sun,* unproduced at the time of his death. He was survived by his wife, the former Stephanie Williams, a son, his mother, five sisters, and two brothers. (d. New York City; July 10, 1991)

FURTHER READING

Obituary. *Variety,* July 22, 1991.
Obituary. *New York Times,* July 13, 1991.

Raitt, Bonnie (Bonnie Lynn Raitt, 1949–) Popular singer and composer Bonnie Raitt continued to build on the comeback that began with her *Nick of Time* (1989) album. Her big 1991 album was *Luck of the Draw,* a collection of blues, soul, and rock songs. Four of the songs were her own: "All At Once," "Tangled and Dark," "Come to Me," and "One Part Be My Lover," the lyrics of the latter song by her husband, actor Michael O'Keefe; the title song was written by Paul Brady. Don Was (*Nick of Time*) once again produced the record, which immediately headed for the top five on the record best-seller charts. Raitt also had a popular single: "Something to Talk About." She continued to tour, as she had for two decades, but now with far greater audience appeal than ever before. Raitt and O'Keefe were married on April 28, 1991.

California-born Raitt, the daughter of singer John Raitt, became a popular folk and blues figure in the early 1970s, with such albums as *Bonnie Raitt* (1971), *Give It Up* (1972), *Streetlights* (1974), and *Sweet Forgiveness* (1977). She was far less popular in the late 1970s and throughout the 1980s, and was dropped by her old record company, Warner. She scored a phenomenal success in February 1990, with a sweep of the Grammy awards, winning best album, best female pop vocal, and best female rock vocal for her *Nick of Time* album and its title song, and best traditional blues recording, for "I'm in the Mood," a duet with John Lee Hooker on Hooker's album, *The Healer.* Raitt attended Radcliffe College.

FURTHER READING

"Raitt, Bonnie." *Current Biography,* Aug. 1990.
"Bonnie Raitt. . . ." James Henke. *Rolling Stone,* May 3, 1990.
"20 questions. . . ." Paul Engleman and John Rezek. *Playboy,* Nov. 1989.
"Veteran rocker. . . ." Kim Hubbard. *People,* Apr. 24, 1989.

Randall, Tony (Leonard Rosenberg, 1920–) The year 1991 saw the realization of Randall's long-deferred dream, the establishment of a National Actors Theatre, at the Belasco Theatre on Broadway. Randall had discussed the idea for half a century and had actively promoted the theater for several years, going through the enormous effort of raising the necessary millions of dollars to establish the company. His effort included a highly successful

benefit performance opposite Jack Klugman of Neil Simon's *The Odd Couple,* the basis of their long-running television series. The company's first season began on November 21, with Arthur Miller's *The Crucible,* staring Martin Sheen, Maryann Plunkett, Fritz Weaver, and Michael York. With Weaver out with laryngitis, Randall stepped in as his understudy for a few preview performances. Forthcoming at year's end were two more plays to round out the company's first season: Georges Feydeau's farce *A Little Hotel on the Side,* starring Maryann Plunkett, Lynn Redgrave, Rob Lowe, and Randall; and Henrik Ibsen's *The Master Builder,* starring Earle Hyman, directed by Randall.

Tulsa-born Randall has played in a wide variety of stage and screen roles during his five-decade career. He is best known by far for his role as Felix opposite Jack Klugman in the long-running television series (1970–74) developed from Neil Simon's 1965 play *The Odd Couple;* Randall won a 1975 Emmy award. He also starred in "Mr. Peepers" (1952–55), "The Tony Randall Show" (1976–77), and "Love, Sydney" (1981–83). Much of his work on stage was in the 1940s and early 1950s. His many films include *Oh Men Oh Women* (1957), *Pillow Talk* (1959), *Send Me No Flowers* (1964), and *The Alphabet Murders* (1966). His autobiographical reminiscences were published in *Which Reminds Me* (1989). Randall attended Northwestern University, Columbia University, and the Neighborhood Playhouse. He is married to Florence Mitchell.

FURTHER READING

"A bargain on Broadway. . . ." *U.S. News & World Report,* Dec. 16, 1991.

Rao, P. V. Narasimha (Pamulaparti Venkate Narasimha Rao, 1921–) Rao was named Indian prime minister on June 20, 1991, after Indian prime minister Rajiv Gandhi was assassinated at Sriperumbudur, Tamil Nada, in southern India, on May 26, while on a campaign swing. Gandhi's death shocked India; the forthcoming election was indefinitely postponed, and Rao's administration was widely viewed as a caretaker government, his task to stabilize the country until new general elections were held.

Rao took office calling for spending cuts and free market solutions to India's massive economic problems. But he also inherited the huge ethnic and religious problems that had plagued Gandhi and his successors, Vishwanath Pratap Singh and Chandra Shekhar. Fighting intensified in the Punjab and in Kashmir, and Hindu-Muslim fighting continued to spread throughout the country, as what amounted to an undeclared border war flared between India and Pakistan.

Uttar Pradesh-born Rao is a longtime Congress Party leader who supported Indira Gandhi during her rise to power and went with her faction when the party split in 1969. He was chief minister of the state of Andra Pradesh (1971–73), and held several cabinet positions thereafter, including four years (1980–84) as Indian foreign minister. He is also a well-known translator and writer. Rao attended the universities of Bombay and Nagpur. He has eight children.

FURTHER READING

"India's premier. . . ." EDWARD A. GARGAN. *New York Times.* Aug. 6, 1991.
"For India's new leader. . . ." BERNARD WEINRAUB. *New York Times,* June 23, 1991.
"Congress Party's calculating. . . ." BERNARD WEINRAUB. *New York Times,* June 22, 1991.

Rather, Dan (1931–) News anchor Rather and the "CBS Evening News" fell on hard times in 1991, sometimes even falling to third place behind NBC in the nightly news ratings race, with ABC pulling farther into the lead, especially during the Persian Gulf War, when CBS was criticized for getting a slow start in its coverage. Many observers noted that, with its deep staff cuts, CBS had far fewer resources in the field than did ABC, NBC, or even CNN. Even so, Rather took the heat, and for a time rumors circulated that he might be replaced or given a co-anchor.

In late February, with Rather anchoring out of Dhahran, Saudi Arabia, CBS scored a coup when correspondent Bob MacKeown slipped away from censors and into Kuwait City to send out the first video reports from the city, then in the process of being liberated. By April, the "CBS Evening News" had added a nightly issues-oriented feature called "Eye on America," akin to ABC's "American Agenda," and had also begun some cosmetic changes, such as more sophisticated graphics and varied pacing of stories. Like his ABC and NBC counterparts, Rather journeyed to Moscow in July for the Bush-Gorbachev summit, and like ABC (but not NBC) he took his nightly news program to Madrid in late October, reporting live from the start of the Middle East Peace Conference. Rather also appeared on CBS's series "48 Hours," anchoring the two-hour fifth-season premiere in September, a series of vignettes about city life, called "Street Stories."

Personally, Rather returned to his roots in his new book, *I Remember: Fifty Years Ago in America* (1991), memoirs of growing up in Texas in the 1930s and early 1940s, written with Peter Wyden. Some reviewers noted that this book seemed to strike a deep "down-home" persona in Rather, in contrast to the superstar image cultivated in recent years.

Texas-born Rather became CBS news anchor in 1981, climaxing a long career that began in Houston in the early 1950s. His breakthrough came when, as a young CBS correspondent in Dallas, he reported live to the nation on the November 22, 1963, assassination of President John F. Kennedy. After working as a CBS White House correspondent in 1964, and then abroad, he returned to Washington as CBS White House correspondent (1966–74) and played a substantial role as an investigative reporter during the unfolding Watergate affair and through the resignation of Richard Nixon. With Peter Jennings at ABC and Tom Brokaw at NBC, he has for a decade been one of the three chief American reporters and interpreters of the news. Earlier written works include *The Palace Guard* (1974), with Gary Gates, and *The Camera Never Blinks* (1977), with Mickey Herskowitz. Rather's B.A. was from Sam Houston State College in 1951. He is married to Jean Goebel; the couple have two children.

FURTHER READING

"Dan Rather is. . . ." ROBERT DRAPER. *Texas,* Nov. 1991.
Anchors: Brokaw, Jennings, Rather and the Evening News. ROBERT GOLDBERG and GERALD J. GOLDBERG. Carol, 1990.
Dan Rather and Other Rough Drafts. MARTHA A. TURNER. Eakin, 1987.

Ray, Aldo (Aldo DaRe, 1926–91) Pennsylvania-born Ray made his film debut as a football player in *Saturday's Hero* (1951). In 1952, he starred opposite Judy Holliday in *The Marrying Kind,* and in the same year played a key supporting role in *Pat and Mike,* starring Spencer Tracy and Katharine Hepburn. He also starred opposite Humphrey Bogart and Peter Ustinov in the comedy hit *We're No Angels* (1955), and opposite Robert Ryan and Tina Louise in *God's Little Acre* (1958). Much of the rest of his career was spent in military roles, in such films as *Miss Sadie Thompson* (1953), *Battle Cry* (1955), *Men in War* (1957), and most notably as Sergeant Croft in Raoul Walsh's *The Naked and the Dead* (1958; adapted from the Norman Mailer novel). He also played a tough soldier in John Wayne's *The Green Berets* (1968). After the 1960s, most of his roles were less rewarding. He was survived by a daughter, two sons, his mother, a sister, and three brothers. (d. Martinez, California; March 27, 1991)

FURTHER READING

Obituary. *The Times* (of London), Apr. 2, 1991.
Obituary. *Variety,* Apr. 1, 1991.
Obituary. *New York Times,* Mar. 28, 1991.

Reagan, Ronald Wilson (1911–) Three years after the end of his second term, echoes of the Reagan presidency continued to make headline news. Perhaps the most striking were an echo from near the beginning of his presidency and one from late in his second term.

In his autobiography, published in May 1991, exiled Iranian President Abolhassan Bani-Sadr charged that during the 1980 presidential campaign Ronald Reagan had made a deal with the Iranian government to stall the release of the Iranian hostages until after the presidential election; others made similar accusations. Calling the charges "nauseating," former president Jimmy Carter joined the former hostages in calling for investigation of their veracity; Reagan denied them and Congress in early August set up an investigation of the claims.

In his book *Under Fire,* published in October 1991, Iran-Contra figure Oliver North charged that Reagan "knew everything" about the 1986 Iran-contra scandal, early and in great detail, and that the White House had covered up the extent of Reagan's knowledge. North's allegations stirred interest but little more, as he produced no hard evidence to back up his claims.

Ronald Reagan continued to campaign for Republican candidates during his retirement and to take public positions on the issues of the day, most notably reversing his position to support the Brady Bill, a handgun control law. On the personal side, November 4, 1991, saw the opening of the Reagan presidential library at Simi Valley, California; the Reagans were joined by all the other living ex-presidents and their wives at the ceremonial opening of the $60 million privately funded facility. Also on the personal side, Reagan denounced as "patently untrue" the charges made in Kitty Kelley's best-selling book *Nancy Reagan: The Unauthorized Biography.*

For Illinois-born Ronald Reagan, the presidency was the culmination of his second major career; after briefly working as a sportscaster in the midwest, he had become a film actor, in the late 1930s and early 1940s playing in such movies as *Knute Rockne—All American* (1940) and *King's Row* (1942). He headed the Screen Actors Guild (1947–52). He was governor of California (1967–75), and after two unsuccessful runs for the Republican nomination was ultimately nominated and defeated Jimmy Carter in the 1980 election. During his presidency, he notably began with the hard-line anti-communism of his "evil empire" speech and ended with the series of treaties and Reagan-Gorbachev meetings that, under his successor George Bush, brought the long Cold War to a close. Reagan also presided over the buildup of a national debt that approached two trillion dollars by the time he left office.

After leaving office, Reagan was largely able to put the Iran-Contra affair behind him, successfully claiming executive privilege as to his diaries during the Poindexter trial and limiting his involvement to videotape testimony at that trial. November 1990 saw publication of his bestselling autobiography *An American Life;* his wife had published her view in 1989 in *My Turn: The Memoirs of Nancy Reagan.* Reagan's B.A. was from Eureka College in 1932. He was previously married to actress Jane Wyman (1940–48); the couple had two children. He married Nancy Davis Reagan in 1952; they had two more children.

FURTHER READING

Ronald Reagan: The Great Communicator. KURT RITTER and DAVID HENRY. Greenwood, 1992.
"Ronald Wilson Reagan." A. ROYCE DALBY. *Ad Astra,* July–Aug. 1991.
"Ronald and. . . ." DANIEL WATTENBERG. *Insight,* July 22, 1991.
Prelsident Reagan: A Role of a Lifetime. LOU CANNON. Simon & Schuster, 1991.
A Shining City on a Hill: Ronald Reagan's Economic Rhetoric, 1951–1989. AMOS KIEWE and DAVIS W. HOUCK. Greenwood, 1991.
Ronald Reagan. RENEE SCHWARTZBERG. Chelsea House, 1991.
Reagan and Thatcher. GEOFFREY SMITH. Norton, 1991.
Ronald Reagan. JOHN DEVANEY. Walker, 1990.
Reagan as President: Contemporary Views of the Man, His Politics, and His Policies. PAUL BOYER, ed. I. R. Dee, 1990.
The Reagan Years. HODDING CARTER. Braziller, 1988.
Early Reagan: The Rise to Power. ANNE EDWARDS. Morrow, 1987.
Mister President: The Story of Ronald Reagan, rev. ed. MARY V. FOX. Enslow, 1986.
Make-Believe: The Story of Nancy and Ronald Reagan. LAURENCE LEAMER. Dell, 1984.
Hollywood on Ronald Reagan: Friends and Enemies Discuss Our President, the Actor. DOUG McCLELLAND. Faber & Faber, 1983.

Reasoner, Harry (1923–91) Iowa-born Reasoner began his long career in journalism with the *Minneapolis Times* in 1942, rejoining the newspaper after World War II. After acquiring experience in local television, he joined CBS in New York in 1956, and as a reporter, host, and news anchor covered a very wide range of network assignments during the next 14 years, perhaps most notably as a key member of the "60 Minutes" interviewing team. He succeeded Dan Rather as CBS White House correspondent in 1965. After a shift from CBS to ABC (1970–78), he became an anchor and then co-anchor of the flagship "Evening News" show. He then returned to CBS, and to the long-running "60 Minutes" show, retiring in May 1991. Reasoner was one of the most highly respected broadcast journalists of his generation, with a long series of awards that included two Emmys and a Peabody. He wrote of his experiences in *Before the Colors Fade* (1981). Reasoner was survived by his second wife, Lois, five daughters, and two sons. (d. Norwalk, Connecticut; August 5, 1991)

FURTHER READING

Obituary. *Current Biography,* Oct. 1991.
"Good night, Harry. . . ." MARK GOODMAN. *People,* Aug. 19, 1991.
Obituary. *The Times* (of London), Aug. 13, 1991.
Obituary. *Variety,* Aug. 12, 1991.
Obituary. *New York Times,* Aug. 7, 1991.

Redford, Robert (Charles Robert Redford, Jr., 1937–) Multi-faceted film figure and environmentalist Redford displayed many of his interests during 1991. Redford co-produced *The Dark Wind,* a murder mystery set on an Arizona Native American reservation. Adapted from the Tony Hillerman novel, the film starred Lou Diamond Phillips as Navajo tribal police officer Jim Chee. Redford also directed the forthcoming film *A River Runs Through It,* a Richard Friedenberg adaptation of the 1976 Norman Maclean novel, based on the Maclean family's life in Montana (1910–35). And actor Redford appears in two forthcoming films: the Phil Alden Robinson comedy *Sneakers,* along with Sidney Poitier, River Phoenix, and Ben Kingsley; and the romantic comedy *The President Elopes.* Longtime environmentalist Redford was the guest of honor at the Environmental Media Association's first annual awards ceremony, held at Sony (formerly Columbia) Studios in Culver City on October 1, 1991. He also wrote the introduction to the Jonathan Porritt book *Save the Earth* (1991).

California-born Redford began his spectacular film career in the late 1960s; his first starring role was in *Barefoot in the Park* (1967), a role he had played on Broadway in 1963. He went on to star in such classics as *Butch Cassidy and the Sundance Kid* (1969), *Jeremiah Johnson* (1972), *The Way We Were* (1973), *The Sting* (1973), and *All the President's Men* (1976). He later directed the Oscar-winning *Ordinary People* (1980), directed and starred in *The Natural* (1984), starred in *Out of Africa* (1985), directed and produced *The Milagro Beanfield War* (1988), and starred in *Havana* (1990). During the 1980s and early 1990s, his film institute at Sundance, Colorado, became a mecca for moviemakers from all over the world. Redford attended the University of Colorado, Pratt Institute, and the American Academy of Dramatic Arts. He married Lola Jean Van Wagenen in 1958; they later separated. They have two children.

FURTHER READING

"Redford talks. . . ." NEIL GABLER. *New York,* Dec. 10, 1990.
"Hollywood goes. . . ." MERLE LINDA WOLIN. *New Republic,* Apr. 16, 1990.
Robert Redford. BRUCE CROWTHER. Hippocrene, 1985.
Robert Redford. DAVID DOWNING. St. Martin's, 1983.

Redgrave, Lynn (1943–) For British actress Lynn Redgrave, 1991 opened on a controversial note. While she and her sister, Vanessa Redgrave, were appearing together on the London stage in Chekhov's *The Three Sisters* (1990–91), in February 1991, Vanessa publicly called for "the withdrawal of U.S., British, and all imperialist troops from the Persian Gulf." During the uproar that followed, Lynn Redgrave publicly distanced herself from her sister. In the same month the sisters also appeared together in a telefilm revival of *What Ever Happened to Baby Jane?,* Lynn as Baby Jane (the Bette Davis role in the 1962 original film) and Vanessa as Blanche (the Joan Crawford role). The two productions were the first time the sisters had acted together.

In September, Lynn Redgrave appeared as Dona Ana in a concert reading of George Bernard Shaw's *Don Juan in Hell,* opposite David Carradine, Stewart Granger, and Ricardo Montalban. Forthcoming in early 1992 was a starring Broadway role in the National Actors Theatre production of Georges Feydeau's *A Little Hotel on the Side,* alongside Tony Randall, Maryann Plunkett, and Rob Lowe. Also in 1991 Redgrave published the semi-autobiographical potpourri *This Is Living: How I Found Health and Happiness.*

London-born Redgrave quickly emerged as a star in the film *Georgy Girl* (1966; she was nominated for an Oscar), and went on to a very diverse career on both sides of the Atlantic, in theater, films, and television, which included everything from *Tom Jones* (1963) to *The Happy Hooker* (1975) on screen; *St. Joan* (1977) to *Sweet Sue* (1987) on stage; and *Centennial* (1978) to the series "House Calls" (1984) and "Chicken Soup" (1989) on television. Redgrave attended London's Central School of Speech and Drama. She married director John Clark in 1967; the couple have three children. She is the daughter of actress Rachel Kempson and actor Michael Redgrave, the sister of actress Vanessa Redgrave and actor-director Corin Redgrave, and the aunt of actresses Natasha Richardson, Joely Richardson, and Jemma Redgrave.

FURTHER READING

"Fuming over. . . ." KAREN S. SCHNEIDER. *People,* Mar. 11, 1991.
"The Redgrave sisters." RODDY MCDOWALL. *Interview,* Feb. 1991.
"Catching up with. . . ." LEE RANDALL. *Weight Watchers Magazine.* Aug. 1990.
Life Among the Redgraves. RACHEL KEMPSON. NAL-Dutton, 1988.

Redgrave, Vanessa (1937–) British actress Vanessa Redgrave once again found herself embroiled in a political controversy during 1991. In February, while appearing in London opposite her sister and niece, Lynn Redgrave and Jemma Redgrave, in Chekhov's *The Three Sisters,* she publicly called for "the withdrawal of U.S., British, and all imperialist troops from the Persian Gulf." During the storm that followed, she was dropped by the producers from the U.S. national tour of *Lettice and Lovage.* Actors' Equity filed a grievance on her behalf in March, on the basis of political discrimination, but in August an arbitrator ruled that the producers had barred Redgrave for economic reasons, because of public reaction to her criticism of the Persian Gulf War, rather than because of their own opposition to her political views. Her career proceeded. In February, the sisters also appeared together in a telefilm revival of *What Ever Happened to Baby Jane?,* Lynn as Baby Jane (the Bette Davis role in the original 1962 film) and Vanessa as ex-film star Blanche (the Joan Crawford role). The two productions were the first times the sisters had ever worked together.

Vanessa Redgrave also starred as Catherine the Great of Russia in the TNT television miniseries *Young Catherine,* in a cast that included Christopher Plummer, Maximilian Schell, and Julia Ormond; the role won her a 1991 Emmy for best supporting actress in a movie or series. She starred opposite Keith Carradine in a less-praised work, *Ballad of the Sad Cafe* (1991), Simon Callow's film based on Edward Albee's stage adaptation of the Carson McCullers novel. On stage, she starred as Isadora Duncan in the Martin Sherman play *When She Danced* (1991) at London's Globe Theatre. Forthcoming was a starring role in James Ivory's *Howard's End,* adapted from the E. M. Forster novel for film by Ruth Prawer Jhabvala, with a cast that also includes Anthony Hopkins, Emma Thompson, James Wilby, Helena Bonham Carter, Joseph Bennett, Adrian Ross Magenty, Prunella Scales, Sam West, and Jemma Redgrave. Her book, *Vanessa Redgrave: An Autobiography,* was published in the autumn of 1991.

Vanessa Redgrave is one of the most celebrated stage and screen actresses of her time, emerging in the early 1960s in the classics and then in her very notable starring role in the stage version of Muriel Spark's *The Prime of Miss Jean Brodie* (1966). She reached world audiences on screen in such films as *Isadora* (1968), *Julia* (1977), *Agatha* (1978), television's *Playing for Time* (1979), *The Bostonians* (1983), and *Comrades* (1986). Her recent work includes Peter Hall's acclaimed revival of Tennessee Williams's *Orpheus Descending* (1989; on Broadway and on television in 1990); and a London stage version of *The Three Sisters* (1990–91). Active in far left politics for many years, and notably a supporter of the Palestine Liberation Organization, she also produced and narrated *The Palestinians* (1977). Vanessa Redgrave attended the Central School of Speech and Drama (1955–57). She was formerly married to director Tony Richardson, and has a son and two daughters, the actresses Natasha Richardson and Joely Richardson. She is the daughter of actor Michael Redgrave and actress Rachel Kempson, and the sister of Lynn Redgrave and actor-director Corin Redgrave, father of Jemma Redgrave.

FURTHER READING

"A woman of conscience." NICHOLAS WROE. *New Statesman and Society,* Oct. 4, 1991.
"Who's afraid of. . . ." STEPHEN SCHIFF. *Vanity Fair,* July 1991.
"Fuming over. . . ." KAREN S. SCHNEIDER. *People,* Mar. 11, 1991.
"The Redgrave sisters." RODDY McDOWALL. *Interview,* Feb. 1991.
"Vanessa ascending. . . ." WILLIAM A. HENRY III. *Time,* Oct. 9, 1989.
Life among the Redgraves. RACHEL KEMPSON. NAL-Dutton, 1988.

Reeve, Christopher (1952–) To the world's moviegoers, Reeve is still Superman, the star of the four Superman films, all worldwide hits, with a fifth Superman movie still promised. Reeve, however, has insisted on playing a far wider range of roles, and in 1989 and 1990 focused largely on the theater. In 1991, he returned to some screen roles, perhaps most notably in a far-out-of-type role as the pedophile and child molester in the January telefilm *Bump in the Night,* opposite Meredith Baxter-Birney. He also starred opposite Marge Helgenburger in the television film *Death Dreams,* on supernatural themes. Forthcoming were starring roles in Peter Bogdanovich's screen version of Michael Frayn's play *Noises Off,* in a cast that includes Michael Caine, Carol Burnett, John Ritter, and

Denholm Elliott; and in the film *Change of Heart* opposite Deborah Raffin.

New York City-born Reeve has appeared on Broadway in *A Matter of Gravity* (1978) and *Fifth of July* (1980), has played a wide range of roles in regional theater, and has worked in London opposite Vanessa Redgrave and Wendy Hiller in *The Aspern Papers* (1984). His recent appearances in the theater include a New York Shakespeare Festival production of Shakespeare's *Winter's Tale* (1989) and a London stage production of Chekhov's *The Three Sisters* (1990–91), with Lynn and Vanessa Redgrave and their niece, Jemma Redgrave. He has also appeared in such films as *Somewhere in Time* (1980), *Deathtrap* (1982), *Monsignor* (1982), *The Bostonians* (1984), and *Switching Channels* (1988), as well as in several television films, including *The Great Escape* (1988). Reeve attended the Juillard School; his B.A. is from Cornell University. He has two children.

FURTHER READING

"Christopher Reeve. . . ." MICHAEL J. BANDLER. *McCall's,* Sep. 1987.

Caught in the Act: New York Actors Face to Face. DON SHEWEY and SUSAN SHACTER. NAL-Dutton, 1986.

The Christopher Reeve Scrapbook. MARGERY STEINBERG. Putnam, 1981.

Rehnquist, William Hubbs (1924–) Chief Justice Rehnquist, bolstered by the addition of conservative Associate Justice David Souter to replace liberal William Brennan, continued to lead an increasingly conservative U.S. Supreme Court during the 1990–91 Court term.

Rehnquist once again wrote several of the majority's key opinions during the term. His opinion in *Rust v. Sullivan,* which upheld federal regulations banning federally funded family planning clinics from offering abortion counseling, was widely viewed as part of a planned run-up to a direct attack on *Roe v. Wade.* In *Board of Education of Oklahoma City v. Dowell,* his majority opinion eased conditions for the lifting of court supervision of segregated school districts, even when the net result of all efforts to desegregate schools had been the re-creation of single race schools, reflecting local housing patterns. *Arizona v. Fulminante* ruled that coerced or involuntary confession in a criminal case

could be a "harmless error" if conviction would have resulted without it; this overturned *Chapman v. California* (1967), which had established that such a confession was always grounds for acquittal. His opinion in *Barnes v. Glen Theater,* upholding an Indiana state law banning nude dancing, was widely viewed as opening the way to local censorship of the arts. In *Payne v. Tennessee,* he allowed "victim impact" evidence to be presented by the prosecution during the sentencing phase of criminal cases, thereby reversing 1987 and 1989 cases that had decided the opposite. Rehnquist also joined the majority in such cases as *Pacific Mutual Life Insurance Co. v. Haslip,* which ruled it unconstitutional for courts to restrict punitive damages awarded by juries in civil cases, although states could do so by law; *County of Riverside, California v. McLaughlin,* ruling that those arrested without warrants could be held up to 48 hours while a judge decided if there was probable cause for the arrest; *Cohen v. Cowles Media,* ruling that a breach of a promise of confidentiality made to a news source was not protected by the First Amendment as against a suit for damages caused by the breach; *Florida v. Bostick,* ruling that police could board buses and search passengers' luggage, with their permission; *Coleman v. Thompson,* restricting the use of habeas corpus writs by state prisoners who have exhausted state appeals, to challenge the constitutionality of their convictions, which reversed *Fay v. Noia* (1963); and *Harmelin v. Michigan,* ruling that a

Michigan law requiring a life sentence without possibility of parole for possession of 650 grams (1.5 pounds) of cocaine did not violate the cruel and unusual punishment prohibition of the Eighth Amendment, although the federal law was much less stringent.

Rehnquist joined the minority in *United Automobile Workers v. Johnson Controls, Inc.,* a landmark women's rights case ruling that according to the 1978 Pregnancy Discrimination Act employers could not ban pregnant women from jobs potentially dangerous to their unborn children. He also dissented in *Edmonson v. Leesville Concrete Co.,* which barred exclusion of jurors in civil cases because of race, following earlier bans on exclusion because of race in criminal cases; in *Chison v. Roemer* and *Houston Lawyers v. Texas Attorney General,* ruling that the federal Voting Rights Act, prohibiting discriminatory voting practices or election district abuses, applied to elected judges, who were "representatives" within the meaning of the law; and in *Masson v. New Yorker Magazine,* which ruled that invented or materially altered quotes attributed to a public figure could be libelous.

Milwaukee-born Rehnquist clerked with Supreme Court Justice Robert Jackson (1952–53), and then practiced law in Phoenix until 1969. He was a Washington-based assistant attorney general (1969–71), was named to the Supreme Court by then-president Nixon in 1971, and was confirmed only after a sharp Senate battle over his allegedly extremely conservative views. President Reagan appointed him Chief Justice in 1986; he was confirmed after another Senate battle. Rehnquist's B.A. was from Stanford in 1958, his M.A. from Harvard in 1949, and his L.L.B. from Stanford in 1952. He married Natalie Cornell in 1953; the couple have two children.

FURTHER READING

"A new day in court." LAUREN TARSHIS and JAMES EARL HARDY. *Scholastic Update,* Nov. 1, 1991.

Original Intent: Chief Justice Rehnquist and the Course of American Church-State Relations. DEREK DAVIS. Prometheus, 1991.

Eight Men and a Lady. HERMAN SCHWARTZ, ANDREA NEAL, and DAVID SAVAGE. National Press, 1990.

Packing the Courts: The Conservatives' Campaign to Rewrite the Constitution. HERMAN SCHWARTZ. Scribner/Macmillan, 1988.

The Supreme Court: The Way It Was—the Way It Is. WILLIAM H. REHNQUIST. Morrow, 1987.

Reilly, William Kane (1940–) Environmental Protection Agency (EPA) Administrator Reilly continued to deal with critical issues in 1991, many of them centrally important to future generations. A leading environmentalist before his 1989 appointment, in office he found himself often hampered by disagreements with other Bush administration figures, most notably John Sununu. One area of contention was wetlands protection; the August 1, 1991, redefinition of U.S. wetlands functioned to open up millions of previously protected acres to private development, although Reilly had argued for a definition that would open up far less.

Reilly criticized administrative expenses of Superfund contractors in June, and even more sharply, toxic waste cleanup contracting costs in October. The EPA also continued to press for atomic plant cleanup, and in May took the unusual step of fining the Energy Department for slowness in carrying through its planned cleanup at the Fernald, Ohio, nuclear plant. A major accomplishment was the May 7 issuance of new regulations limiting the amount of lead permissible in drinking water; another was the August 1 nationwide series of prosecutions of lead polluters. At the same time, Reilly found very much still to be done: For example, he called existing pesticide regulations "anachronistic" when, after the catastrophic July 14 Sacramento River pesticide spill, the chemical spilled was found not to have been listed as a regulated substance by the Department of Transportation.

Illinois-born Reilly has held a series of key environmental posts, including the presidency of the Conservation Fund from 1973, presidency of the World Wildlife Fund (1985–89), and several federal government positions. Reilly's B.A. was from Yale in 1962, his 1965 J.D. was from Harvard, and his 1971 M.S. in urban planning was from Columbia. He is married to Elizabeth Bennett Buxton; they have two children.

FURTHER READING

"Voice in the wilderness." KEN GROSS and JANE SIMS. *People,* Dec. 23, 1991.
"Preventing pollution won't hurt. . . ." *Design News,* Sep. 17, 1990.
"Reilly, William Kane." *Current Biography,* July 1989.

Reiner, Rob (1945–) While actor-writer-director Reiner's film *Misery* (1990) was in successful early-1991 theatrical release, he was focusing on his next project, which became the six-part television series *Morton and Hayes.* The series, written by co-star Phil Mishkin, premiered in July 1991. Eddie Hayes, played by Bob Amaral, and Chick Morton, played by Kevin Pollak, were a 1940s comedy team, much like the then-popular Abbott and Costello; their adventures were the stuff of the series. Reiner introduced each episode. Though moderately well received, the series did not "take off" with either critics or audience. In the summer of 1991, CBS announced reruns of a very successful series, and viewers were able to see Reiner once again in his early role as "Meathead" in the classic "All in the Family." Forthcoming was his feature film *A Few Good Men,* starring Tom Cruise, Jack Nicholson, and Demi Moore.

New York City-born Reiner became a television scriptwriter in the late 1960s and played "Meathead" in the long-running television series "All in the Family" (1971–78), for which he won 1974 and 1978 Emmys. He moved into film direction in the mid-1980s, with the pseudo-documentary film *This Is Spinal Tap* (1984), and then directed several other well-received feature films, including *The Sure Thing* (1985), *Stand by Me* (1986), and *The Princess Bride* (1987). His breakthrough film was *When Harry Met Sally. . . .* (1989), which he directed and co-produced; the film starred Billy Crystal, Meg Ryan, and Carrie Fisher. He also directed *Misery* (1990). Reiner attended the University of California at Los Angeles. He has been married twice, first to actress-director Penny Marshall, then to Michele Singer in 1989. He is the son of actor, writer, and director Carl Reiner.

FURTHER READING

"Pals." ROBERT LLOYD. *American Film,* July–Aug. 1989.
"Reiner's reason." APRIL BERNARD and MICHELLE SINGER. *Interview,* July 1989.
"Reiner, Rob." *Current Biography,* May 1988.

Remick, Lee (1935–91) Massachusetts-born Remick made her stage debut in summer stock in 1952 and her Broadway debut in *Be Your Age* (1953); during the early 1950s she appeared in several other plays and in many television productions. Her film debut was in 1957, in *A Face in the Crowd,* and she went on to be a leading dramatic star in such films as *The Long Hot Summer* (1958); *Anatomy of a Murder* (1959); *Days of Wine and Roses* (1962), which won her an Academy Award nomination; *Baby the Rain Must Fall* (1965), *A Delicate Balance* (1973), *The Omen* (1976), and *The Europeans* (1979). On Broadway, her most notable work was as the blind woman in *Wait Until Dark* (1966). Remick also played major roles in such televison films as *Summer and Smoke* (1972), *Jennie* (1975; as Winston Churchill's mother, Lady Randolph Churchill), *Ike* (1979; as Kay Sommersby), and *Haywire* (1980; as Margaret Sullavan). She was survived by her second husband, producer Kip Gowans, a daughter, a son, two stepdaughters, and her mother. (d. Los Angeles; July 2, 1991)

FURTHER READING

Obituary. *Current Biography,* Sep. 1991.
"The face of courage. . . ." *People,* July 22, 1991.
Obituary. *The Times* (of London), July 8, 1991.
Obituary. *Variety,* July 8, 1991.
Obituary. *New York Times,* July 3, 1991.

Revelle, Roger (1909–91) Seattle-born Revelle, a leading oceanographer and environmental scientist, joined the staff of the Scripps Institution of Oceanography at La Jolla, California, after completing his doctorate at Scripps in 1936. During World War II, he was chief oceanographer in the U.S. Navy's Bureau of Ships, and from 1946 to 1948 headed the geophysics branch of the Office of Naval Research. He returned to Scripps in 1948 and was its director from 1951 to 1964. In that very fruitful period, he planned the oceanographic aspects of the 1957–58 International Geophysical Year and generated and carried through the extraordinarily important 1964 International Deep Sea Drilling Project, which proved the continental drift theory, opened the way to the theory of plate tectonics, and greatly increased human understanding of earth history. In this period, he also began to explore carbon dioxide emissions and to develop a theory of environmentally dangerous global warming, today a massive international concern. In 1964, by then deeply concerned about population increases, poverty, and worldwide environmental threats, he founded and became director of Harvard's Center for Population Studies. He returned to San Diego in 1975 to teach at the San Diego campus of the University of California, which by then also included Scripps. He was survived by his wife, Ellen, three daughters, and a son. (d. San Diego, California; July 15, 1991)

FURTHER READING

Obituary. *Current Biography,* Sep. 1991.
Obituary. *The Times* (of London), July 18, 1991.
Obituary. *New York Times,* July 17, 1991.

Reynolds, Burt (1936–) Veteran actor and sometime director Burt Reynolds starred in the 1991–92 season of the very successful television series "Evening Shade," set in a semi-rural Arkansas town. The unusually effective cast of the series included a number of well-known theater people—Elizabeth Ashley, Ossie Davis, Charles Durning, Jay R. Ferguson, Marilu Henner, and Hal Holbrook. For his role as high school football coach Wood Newton in "Evening Shade," Reynolds won an Emmy as lead actor in a comedy series. Reynolds also seized a chance to return to the theater, in late spring directing the play *Eleemosynary* at the Flat Rock Playhouse in Hendersonville, North Carolina; the cast included Ashley. Forthcoming was an appearance in the Robert Altman film *The Player,* along with a wide range of stage, screen, and television stars.

Georgia-born Reynolds became a very popular film star in the 1970s, with such films as *Deliverance* (1972), *The Man Who Loved Cat Dancing* (1973), *White Lightning* (1973), *The Longest Yard* (1974), *W. W. and the Dixie Dance Kings* (1975), *Nickelodeon* (1976), the two *Smokey and the Bandit* films (1977, 1980), *Hooper* (1978), *Sharkey's Machine* (1981), the two *Cannonball Run* films (1981, 1984), *Physical Evidence* (1989), and *Breaking In* (1989). On television, he appeared in many episodes of "Gunsmoke" (1965), and starred in the series "Hawk" (1966), "Dan August" (1970–71), "ABC Mystery Movie" (1988–89; as B. L. Stryker), and "Evening Shade" (1990–). Reynolds attended Palm Beach Junior College and Florida State University. Formerly married to Judy Carne, he married Loni Anderson in 1988; they have one child.

FURTHER READING

"What's hot. . . ." DAVID WALLACE. *Ladies Home Journal,* Sep. 1991.
"Talking with Loni Anderson. . . ." LAWRENCE EISENBERG. *Redbook,* Dec. 1988.
Burt Reynolds: Superstar. CAROLINE LATHAM. Putnam, 1986.
Burt!: The Unauthorized Biography. MARC ELIOT. Dell, 1982.
Burt Reynolds: An Unauathorized Biography. SYLVIA RESNICK. St. Martin's, 1982.
The Films of Burt Reynolds. NANCY STREEBECK. Carol, 1982.

Richards, Ann (1933–) New Texas Democratic Governor Richards early in her term saw the opposition party provide a boost to Texas's ailing economy; on January 8, the Republican Party decided to hold its 1992 national convention in Houston, from August 17 to 20. But it was a relatively minor boost; on taking office, Richards faced an estimated $5 billion deficit in a $53 billion two-year state budget. One very special problem was that of school financing, as the Texas Supreme Court had in 1990 declared the current state school financing method, based on property taxes, to be unconstitutional. The Texas legislature responded on April 11, 1991, by enacting a bill that set up a new statewide funding equalization system, the net effect of

which was to transfer funds from richer to poorer school districts. Richards signed the bill into law on April 15, and a massive shift began in the school system, most visibly with large teacher layoffs and mass student-parent protests in Dallas and other Texas cities.

The new Richards administration was notable for its appointment of women and minority group members to high state government posts, including naming national figure Barbara Jordan to the new post of State of Texas Special Counsel on Ethics; Zan Holmes, an African-American minister, to the University of Texas Board of Regents; and Hispanic-American leader Lena Guerrero to the Texas Railroad Commission. Many of her other key advisers were also women, including chief of staff Mary Beth Rogers.

Waco-born Richards began her political career in 1972 as a campaign worker for and then administrative assistant to Austin state representative Sarah Weddington. In 1976, Richards won election as a county commissioner, was elected state treasurer in 1982, and was re-elected in 1986. She drew national attention as keynote speaker at the 1988 Democratic National Convention, in a mudslinging address featuring sharp personal attacks on Republican presidential candidate George Bush. Richards became Texas governor-elect on November 6, 1990, winning by a very small margin (51%–49%) over first-time Republican Clayton W. Williams, Jr., in an unusually dirty campaign marked by its negative advertising and name-calling; the campaign followed an equally dirty three-way Democratic primary campaign. Richards, a recovered alcoholic, attended Baylor University. She has four children.

FURTHER READING

Storming the Statehouse: Running for Governor with Ann Richards and Dianne Feinstein. CELIA MORRIS. Macmillan, 1992.
"Uncandid camera." PAUL BURKA. *Texas Monthly,* Dec. 1991.
"The titan of Texas." AL REINERT. *Vogue,* Aug. 1991.
"Ann of a hundred days. . . ." PAUL BURKA. *Texas,* May 1991.
"Cosmos talks to. . . ." MARK DONALD. *Cosmopolitan,* Apr. 1991.
"Richards, Dorothy Ann Willis." *Current Biography,* Feb. 1991.
"Ann Richards. . . ." MIMI SWARTZ. *Texas Monthly,* October 1990.
Straight from the Heart—My Life. ANN RICHARDS. Simon & Schuster, 1990.

Richardson, Tony (Cecil Antonio Richardson, 1928–91) British director and producer Richardson made his major breakthrough on stage, with his direction of John Osborne's landmark play *Look Back in Anger* (1956), and became a major figure in world cinema in the 1960s, with a series of classic films that began with the 1959 film version of the Osborne play. His major films included *The Entertainer* (1960), a Laurence Olivier vehicle he had directed on stage in 1957; *A Taste of Honey* (1961); *The Loneliness of the Long Distance Runner* (1962); and *Tom Jones* (1963), for which he won a Best Director Oscar. He continued to work in theater and films during the following two decades, with emphasis on the theater, although his later films included *The Border* (1982), *The Hotel New Hampshire* (1984), and *Blue Skies,* made in 1990 but not yet released at his death. He had been married to Vanessa Redgrave (1960–67). He was survived by three daughters, the actresses Natasha Richardson and Joely Richardson, and Katherine Grimond. (d. Los Angeles; November 14, 1991)

FURTHER READING

Obituary. *New York Times,* Nov. 18, 1991.
Obituary. *Variety,* Nov. 18, 1991.

Riding, Laura (Laura Reichenthal, 1901–91) New York City-born Riding, a poet and essayist, was educated in the United States; in the mid-1920s, she was part of the group of mostly southern poets called "the fugitives," led by John Crowe Ransom, who introduced her work to English poet Robert Graves. Riding went to England in 1926, and by 1927 was Graves's collaborator and lover; their work together included *A Survey of Modernist Poetry* (1927) and *A Pamphlet Against Anthologies* (1928).

Riding and Graves left England for the Island of Majorca in 1929, after Graves's wife had left him for another of Riding's lovers, and lived on Majorca until 1936, then returning to Britain. Riding's work in this period included the poems published in her *Collected Poems* (1938), such essays as those published in *Anarchism Is Not Enough* (1927), and the novel *A Trojan Ending* (1937). Riding and Graves parted in 1939; she later married Schuyler B. Jackson and stopped writing poetry. Her most notable later work was *The Telling* (1972). (d. Wabasso, Florida; September 2, 1991)

FURTHER READING

Obituary. *The Times* (of London), Sep. 4, 1991.
Obituary. *New York Times,* Sep. 4, 1991.
Robert Graves: The Years with Laura, 1926–1940. Richard P. Graves. Viking Penguin, 1990.
Laura Riding: A Bibliography. Joyce Wexler. Garland, 1981.

Riegle, Donald Wayne, Jr. (1938–) Senator Riegle, the very influential chairman of the Senate's Banking, Housing, and Urban Affairs Committee, was one of the "Keating Five," a group of senators charged with having unethically intervened with federal bank regulators on behalf of the Lincoln Savings and Loan Association of Irvine, California, controlled by Charles H. Keating, Jr. The bank was in 1989 taken over by federal banking authorities, in a bailout carrying an estimated cost of at least $2 billion. On February 27, 1991, after 14 months of hearings, the Senate Ethics Committee dropped the case against Riegle with a mild rebuke concerning his appearance of misconduct. He expressed great relief and resumed his role as a major critic of Bush administration financial policy, continuing with his Democratic colleagues to sharpen his criticism as President Bush's political vulnerability on economic issues became even more apparent. At the same time, Riegle and other leading Democrats called for new commitments on such matters as health insurance and unemployment benefit extension.

Flint-born Riegle worked at IBM and was a college teacher in the early 1960s, then turning toward a political career. He was a four-term Michigan Democratic congressman before his 1977 entry into the Senate. His 1960 B.A. was from the University of Michigan, his 1961 M.B.A. from Michigan State, and his 1970 LL.D. from St. Benedict's College. He married Lori Hansen in 1978; the couple have four children.

FURTHER READING

"Seven sorry senators. . . ." Margaret Carlson. *Time,* Jan. 8, 1990.
"Riegle, Donald W(ayne), Jr." *Current Biography,* Oct. 1986.

Riley, Pat (Patrick James Riley, 1945–) Pat Riley left the studio booth to go back to the sidelines in 1991. After spending a season as pre-game and half-time commentator for NBC television's basketball games, Riley accepted the challenge of coaching basketball's New York Knicks back to the premier status they once enjoyed. In the process, he got a raise from $400,000 a year to an estimated $1.2 million, with incentives up to $1.5 million. Early indications were that the Knicks' gamble in hiring Riley was paying off. Despite the summer uncertainty over center Patrick Ewing's status, when the season started the recently lackluster Knicks became winners; by January 1992, nearly halfway through the season, they were leading their division, though it was admittedly the league's weakest. And with those wins, Riley was giving the coach's best answer to those who said his previous success was due, not to his own skills, but to his having Earvin (Magic) Johnson and Kareem Abdul-Jabbar on his championship Los Angeles Lakers team.

Riley has spent his whole career in and around basketball. During his eight years as a professional basketball player, he was a guard with the San Diego Rockets (1967–70), the Los Angeles Lakers (1970–75), and the Phoenix Suns (1975–76). He was an assistant coach with the Lakers (1979–81), and then began his extraordinarily successful nine-year run as Laker head coach (1981–90). Under Riley, the Lakers had a won-lost record of 533–194, and won four National Basketball Association (NBA) championships (1982, 1985, 1987, and 1988). In 1990 he was for the first time named NBA Coach of the Year. In June 1990, after a winning season but an early elimination in the playoffs, Riley resigned from the Lakers. At that point, he led all coaches in NBA history, including the legendary Red Auerbach, in percentage of regular-season games won, at .733, and total number of playoff victories, at 102. Riley had broadcast Laker games (1977–79), and returned to broadcasting, at NBC television, after resigning his coaching job. In 1988 he published *Show Time: Inside the Lakers' Breakthrough Season.* He is married to Chris Riley; the couple have two children.

FURTHER READING

"A whole new ball game. . . . MICHAEL STONE. *New York,* Nov. 25, 1991.
"Coach Pat Riley brings. . . ." ERIC POOLEY. *New York,* Sep. 23, 1991.
" 'Call me Mister Riley.' " AL STUMP. *Los Angeles Magazine,* Oct. 1989.
"The transformation. . . ." DIANE K. SHAH. *GQ—Gentlemen's Quarterly,* Jan. 1989.

Rizzo, Frank (Francis Lazzaro Rizzo, 1920–91) Philadelphia-born Rizzo, a highly controversial former police chief and mayor of his home city, began his career in 1943, following his father into the police force. During the next 28 years, he rose through the ranks to become police commissioner, in the 1960s becoming a national symbol of law and order to conservatives and a national symbol of police violence and racism to many Blacks, Hispanics, and members of other minority groups, and to those on the liberal side of the political spectrum. In 1971, running as a Democrat on a law-and-order platform, he was elected to his first term as Philadelphia mayor, and was re-elected in 1975. He left office after two terms, as required by local law, let a term go by, and ran again; this time he was defeated by W. Wilson Goode in the Democratic primary. Rizzo changed parties in 1986, won an upset victory in the 1991 Philadelphia Republican mayorality primary, and was engaged in his mayoral campaign at the time of his death. He was survived by his wife, Carmella, and two children. (d. Philadelphia; July 16, 1991)

FURTHER READING

Obituary. *Current Biography,* Sep. 1991.
"Last rites. . . ." THERESA CONROY. *Philadelphia,* Sep. 1991.
"Back on the mayor go-round. . . ." STEPHEN GOODE. *Insight,* July 22, 1991.
Obituary. *New York Times,* July 17, 1991.
"Some frank talk. . . ." *Philadelphia,* Apr. 1987.

Robards, Jason, Jr. (Jason Nelson Robards, Jr., 1922–) For distinguished U.S. actor Robards, 1991 was a year of great variety and accomplishment. In April, he starred as Armand Hammer in the television documentary on the Soviet nuclear disaster, *Chernobyl: The Final Warning,* a production that was done with much Soviet participation and had great impact in both the United States and what was then the Soviet Union. He also narrated a new Public Broadcasting System documentary *Pearl Harbor: Surprise and Remembrance,* which debuted in November as part of the "American Experience" series. Still on television, Robards starred as Abraham Lincoln in the fiction film *The Perfect Tribute;* as financier Jules Mendelson opposite Rebecca De Mornay as his mistress, Flo March, in the miniseries *An Inconvenient Woman;* and as Mark Twain in the Disney telefilm *Mark Twain and Me,* about the relationship between the author and an 11-year-old admirer,

Dorothy Quick (played by Amy Stewart), whose autobiography sparked the movie.

On screen, in Jerry Schatzberg's powerful dramatic film *Reunion,* Robards starred as an American, once German, going back to revisit Germany for the first time since his youth. The screenplay by Harold Pinter was based on the Fred Uhlman book. On Broadway, Robards starred opposite Judith Ivey in the new Israel Horovitz play *Park Your Car in Harvard Yard,* a two-character work; unfortunately, the work was not very well received. Forthcoming was a starring role in the film *Storyville,* written and directed by Mark Frost, along with James Spader and Joanne Whalley-Kilmer.

Chicago-born Robards became a leading player on the American stage in 1956 as Hickey in Eugene O'Neill's *The Iceman Cometh,* a role he repeated in 1976 and 1988. His work in O'Neill included *Long Day's Journey into Night* (1956, 1976, 1986), *A Moon for the Misbegotten* (1973), and *A Touch of the Poet* (1977). He won a Tony in *The Disenchanted* (1958), and also starred in such plays as *A Thousand Clowns* (1962; and the 1965 film), *After the Fall* (1964), and *The Country Girl* (1972). On screen, he appeared in many films, largely in strong supporting roles; his most notable films include *The Love of Isadora* (1969), *All the President's Men* (1976; he won a Best Supporting Actor Oscar), *Julia* (1977; and a second Best Supporting Actor Oscar), and *Melvin and Howard* (1979), as well as many telefilms, most notably in *The Iceman Cometh* (1961), *One Day in the Life of Ivan Denisovitch* (1963), *Haywire* (1980), *The Day After* (1983), *Sakharov* (1984), and *Inherit the Wind* (1988). His recent work includes the films *Parenthood* (1989) and *Black Rainbow* (1990). Robards attended the American Academy of Dramatic Arts. He has been married four times and has seven children. He is the son of actor Jason Robards.

FURTHER READING

"Jason Robards, Jr. . . ." Eirik Knutzen. *Dynamic Years,* Sep.–Oct. 1982.
"The one great scorer. . . ." *People,* Dec. 28, 1981.

Julia Roberts and Kiefer Sutherland.

Roberts, Julia (Julie Roberts, 1967–) In 1990–91 Julia Roberts emerged as a top film star and one of Hollywood's most sought-after actresses. Her role as the prostitute, opposite Richard Gere, in *Pretty Woman* (1990) won her a 1991 Academy Award nomination and a Golden Globe Award as best actress. But Roberts's success is based on more than Pretty-Woman-style fairy tales. In Joel Schumacher's *Flatliners*

(1990)—where she met Kiefer Sutherland, later her fiancé—she played one of a group of medical students experimenting with death. Following that, in *Sleeping with the Enemy* (1991), she played a young wife trying to escape her psychotically abusive husband (Patrick Bergin). Then came Joel Schumacher's *Dying Young* (1991), with Roberts as nurse Hilary O'Neil, who falls in love with a dying cancer patient (Campbell Scott). Only then did she return to fairy tales, changing her hair to strawberry blond as Tinker Bell in Steven Spielberg's Peter Pan film, *Hook* (1991). She was also one of many stars appearing briefly in Robert Altman's forthcoming Hollywood satire, *The Player*.

Drained by making several films without a break, Roberts scheduled a year off from moviemaking after finishing *Hook*. As of late 1991, she was set to go back before the cameras in June 1992 in a western, *Renegades*. On the personal side, Roberts and Sutherland parted in June 1991, calling off a highly publicized wedding.

Georgia-born Roberts began her acting career with a small role as sister to her real-life brother, actor Eric Roberts, in the western *Blood Red* (1986; released in 1989). After a single 1986 guest role on the television series "Crime Story," followed by a role in the HBO telefilm *Baja, Oklahoma* (1987), she very quickly moved into feature films, in *Satisfaction* (1988), playing guitar in an all-female rock band; in her breakthrough role as the socially constrained waitress in *Mystic Pizza* (1988); and in *Steel Magnolias* (1989), as diabetic Shelby, winning a Golden Globe award and an Oscar nomination for best supporting actress. She is the sister of actor Eric Roberts and actress Lisa Roberts.

FURTHER READING

"Julia Roberts." John Clark. *Premiere,* Dec. 1991.
"Hooked on Julia!" *Teen,* Nov. 1991.
"20 questions. . . ." *Playboy,* Nov. 1991.
"Queen for a decade." Marc Eliot. *California,* Sep. 1991.
"Miss Roberts regrets." Louise Lague. *People,* July 1, 1991.
"Julia Roberts. . . ." Sally Ogle Davis. *Ladies Home Journal,* July 1991.
"Roberts, Julia." *Current Biography,* May 1991.
"Bare-foot girl. . . ." Johanna Schneller. *GQ—Gentlemen's Quarterly,* Feb. 1991.
"The jewel who's Julia." Susan Schindehette. *People,* Sep. 17. 1990.
"Suddenly, Julia." Robert Palmer. *American Film,* July 1990.
"The barefoot principessa. . . ." Michael Reese. *Newsweek,* Mar. 26, 1990.
"Julia Roberts." Catherine Seipp. *Harper's Bazaar,* Sep. 1989.
"Family ties. . . ." Doug Garr. *Harper's Bazaar,* Feb. 1989.

Robinson, Earl Hawley (1910–91)
Seattle-born Robinson, a composer and singer, studied music at the University of Washington and privately with Aaron Copland in the mid-1930s. From 1936 to 1939, he worked with the Federal Theater Project on several shows, including *Sing for Your Supper,* which included "The Ballad of Uncle Sam," revised in 1940 to become his best-known longer work, the cantata "Ballad for Americans" (words by Lewis Allen). Another well-known work was the labor song "Joe Hill," in memory of Joseph Hillstrom, the Industrial Workers of the World (IWW) activist executed on a murder charge in Utah in 1915, a song notably revived by Joan Baez at the 1969 Woodstock Festival. A third popular work was the song "The House I Live In" (words by Lewis Allen), a Frank Sinatra hit record in 1942 and in 1945 an Oscar-winning short film starring Sinatra. Robinson also composed such works as the cantata *The Lonesome Train* (1944), the songs for the film *A Walk in the Sun* (1945), and the documentary *Muscle Beach* (1948), as well as a considerable number of other songs, longer musical works, and film- and television-related music. He also was the author of several songbooks. Robinson's career was considerably damaged when he was blacklisted for alleged communist affiliations during the McCarthy period. He later taught at the University of California at Santa Barbara. He was twice married. (d. Seattle; July 20, 1991)

FURTHER READING

Obituary. *The Times* (of London), Aug. 6, 1991.
Obituary. *Variety,* July 29, 1991.
Obituary. *New York Times,* July 23, 1991.

Robinson, Mary (Mary Bourke, 1944–)
Ireland's first woman president, Mary Robinson has for two decades been a leading Irish liberal and human rights lawyer. She received her B.A. and LL.B. from Trinity College, Dublin, and her

LL. M. from Harvard Law School. Returning to Ireland from the United States in 1968, she became the youngest-ever law professor at Trinity. A year later, in 1969, she ran as a Labour candidate, won election to the Irish Senate, and went on to serve for 20 years in that body, until 1989.

Robinson quickly emerged as a spokesperson for change in Ireland, particularly in the areas of women's rights and the rights of minorities. She has strongly supported the legalization of divorce, equal employment, the legalization of contraceptives, day care for the children of working mothers, repeal of laws discriminating against homosexuals and making homosexuality a criminal offense, increased abortion information, and other liberal objectives. She has also strongly supported efforts to find a peaceful solution to the continuing crisis in Northern Ireland and is seen by many as very well positioned to do so, as a Catholic who is married to a Protestant, and the product of a largely Protestant college. Robinson scored an upset victory in the 1990 Irish presidential election, winning by a narrow margin what has so far been a powerless ceremonial post. She is married to lawyer Nicholas Robinson; they have three children.

FURTHER READING

"Robinson, Mary Bourke." *Current Biography,* Apr. 1991.

Mary Robinson: A President with a Purpose. FERGUS FINLAY. Dufour, 1991.

"Here's to you Mrs. Robinson. . . ." RON ARIAS. *People,* Nov. 26, 1990.

Roddenberry, Gene (Eugene Wesley Roddenberry, 1921–91) After winning a Distinguished Flying Cross and an Air Medal for his World War II service as a flyer, Roddenberry became a civilian flyer and then a Los Angeles policeman. His writing career began with a considerable range of television series scripts in the 1950s and early 1960s. In 1966, he created the "Star Trek" series; his humane vision of a future galaxy-wide body of utterly diverse peoples living together in peace struck a chord that produced large numbers of devoted fans—so devoted that the "Trekkies" forced network reconsideration of a decision to cancel the show after two years, winning a third and final 1968–69 season. The series turned out to have a life of its own, beyond cancellation, and has since been shown uninterruptedly in worldwide reruns, inspired a sequel series, and generated six feature films, the most recent opening in late 1991. Roddenberry continued to work in television afterward, but it is "Star Trek" that was his major work and the springboard of several books, most recently *Star Trek: The First Twenty-five Years* (1991; with Susan Sackett). He was survived by his wife, the actress Majel Leigh Hudec, two daughters, a son, a sister, a brother, and his mother. (d. Santa Monica, California; October 24, 1991)

FURTHER READING

"Master of the universe. . . ." TOM GLIATTO et al. *People,* Nov. 11, 1991.

"Wagon train to the stars. . . ." DAVID GATES. *Newweek,* Nov. 4, 1991.

Obituary. *Variety,* Oct. 28, 1991.

Obituary. *New York Times,* Oct. 26, 1991.

Obituary. *The Times* (of London), Oct. 26, 1991.

"Eugene Wesley Roddenberry. . . ." KAREN BOEHLER. *Ad Astra,* July–Aug. 1991.

Interview. DAVID ALEXANDER. *Humanist,* Mar.–Apr. 1991.

Roh Tae Woo (1932–) South Korean President Roh Tae Woo in 1991 again faced the twin questions that had dominated South Korean life since the late 1940s: the ever-present danger posed by North Korea and the question

of democracy in South Korea, always at risk from the anti-democratic practices of many successive South Korean governments. Amnesty International had in 1990 verified many of the charges of human rights abuse leveled against the Roh Tae Woo government, including the arrest and torture of dissidents.

Both Koreas were admitted to the United Nations on September 17, 1991. One week later, on September 24, Roh Tae Woo used that forum to present a unification plan, which included a peace treaty formally ending the Korean War; a period of free trade and free access for the citizens of both Koreas; and an end to the North Korean atomic arms program. Three days later, as part of his historic unilateral reduction of U.S. nuclear arms, President Bush announced plans to remove tactical nuclear weapons from South Korea, and later announced plans to reduce the number of American troops stationed there. But by November, the United States was calling attention to the North Korean nuclear program, demanding that it be stopped, and postponing planned troop cuts.

April and May saw massive South Korean demonstrations with the involvment of an estimated 400,000–500,000 people, sparked by the April 26 riot police murder of a student demonstrator. Roh Tae Woo quickly fired his interior minister to try to defuse the demonstrations, but without succcess; after another month of demonstrations, Premier Ro Jai Bong on May 18 resigned, to be replaced on May 24 by Chung Won Shik, while arrested demonstators were freed and charges against opposition leader Kim Dae Young were dropped. On September 10, the two main South Korean opposition parties merged—the New Democratic Party led by Kim Dae Jung, and the smaller Democratic Party led by Lee Ki Taek—in a move to create a unified opposition for general elections, expected in 1992.

Roh Tae Woo was a career military officer; he fought in the Korean War, in the late 1970s rose to divisional command, and retired in 1981 as a four-star general. He held several appointive cabinet level posts in the early 1980s, then entering electoral politics as a national assemblyman and chairman of the National Justice Party in 1985. He became president of the Republic of Korea in February 1988. He attended the Korean Military Academy. He is married to Kim Ok Sook; the couple have two children.

FURTHER READING

"Roh. . . ." BRADLEY MARTIN. *Newsweek,* June 18, 1990.

"Roh faces. . . ." LAXMI NAKARMI. *Business Week,* Dec. 19, 1988.

"Roh Tae Woo." *Current Biography,* Feb. 1988.

Ronstadt, Linda (Linda Marie Ronstadt, 1946–) Highly regarded singer Linda Ronstadt once again worked with Aaron Neville in 1991, this time co-producing the album *Warm Your Heart;* the 1989 Ronstadt-Neville single, "Don't Know Much," had won a Grammy as best duo or group pop vocal. She also continued to accentuate her Hispanic musical heritage, in concert and on records. For the forthcoming film *The Mambo Kings,* she recorded the 1950s hits "Perfidia" and "Quierme Mucho." The film, adapted from Oscar Hijuelos's Pulitzer Prize-winning novel, *The Mambo Kings Play Songs of Love,* stars Armand Assante and Antonio Banderas, and includes peformances by Tito Puente and Celia Cruz. During the Christmas season, Ronstadt appeared on television in the Luis Valdez adaptation of the Mexican Christmas play *La Pastorela.*

Tucson-born Ronstadt began her recording and tour career in the late 1960s and emerged in the mid-1970s as a very versatile and popular country star. Her first hit album was *Heart Like a Wheel* (1974), containing two of her most popular songs: "You're No Good" and "I Can't Help

It if I'm Still in Love with You." She went on to record such albums as *Different Drum* (1974), *Prisoner in Disguse* (1975), *Hasten Down the Wind* (1976), *Blue Bayou* (1977), *Living in the U.S.A.* (1978), *Mad Love* (1980), *Lush Life* (1984), *Trio* (1986; with Dolly Parton and Emmylou Harris), *'Round Midnight* (1987), *Canciones de Mi Padre* (1987), and *Cry Like a Rainstorm—Howl Like the Wind* (1989). On stage, she starred in *The Pirates of Penzance* (1981; on film, 1983), and off-Broadway in *La Boheme* (1984).

FURTHER READING

"Skylark." JONATHAN SCHWARTZ. *GQ—Gentlemen's Quarterly,* Feb. 1990.
Linda Ronstadt. MARK BEGO. Eakin, 1990.

Roosevelt, James (1907–91) New York City-born Roosevelt was the oldest son of Franklin Delano Roosevelt and Anna Eleanor Roosevelt. He began his long and varied career in the early 1930s, leaving Boston University law school for insurance sales. He campaigned for his father in 1932 and 1936, leaving business to work as a presidential aide (1936–38). In the late 1930s, he went into the film business, and in 1941 produced the comedy *Pot O' Gold,* starring James Stewart. Roosevelt served with the Marines in the Pacific during World War II, winning a Navy Cross and Silver Star. He lived in California after the war, was a California Democratic national committeeman (1948–52), and served in Congress (1954–65), resigning to take a United Nations post. He left the UN in 1966 to become an executive of Bernard Cornfeld's Investors Overseas Services, which later collapsed spectacularly. In 1972, he participated in the Democrats for Nixon organization. Roosevelt founded the National Committee to Preserve Social Security and Medicare in 1983. He was survived by his fourth wife, Mary Lena Winskill, four daughters, and three sons. (d. Newport Beach, California; August 13, 1991)

FURTHER READING

Obituary. *Variety,* Aug. 19, 1991.
Obituary. *The Times* (of London), Aug. 15, 1991.
Obituary. *New York Times,* Aug. 14, 1991.

Rose, Pete (Peter Edward Rose, 1941–) Celebrated player and manager Pete Rose has the unhappy distinction of being the only qualified player alive who is banned from eligibility for the Baseball Hall of Fame in Cooperstown, New York. During early 1991, he completed his five months in federal prison in Marion, Illinois; spent three months in a halfway house in Cincinnati, Ohio; and then spent the rest of the year doing community service, all stemming from his conviction for income tax evasion. His ineligibility, however, results from charges that he bet on baseball games while manager of the Cincinnati Reds; Rose admitted an "addiction to gambling," though he was never convicted in court of these specific transgressions. And therein lies the continuing controversy surrounding Rose—the conflict between those who agree with the action of late commissioner A. Bartlett Giamatti in placing Rose on the permanently ineligible list in August 1989, and those who feel that Rose deserves to be honored for his achievements, whatever mistakes he might later have made.

In any case, Rose continues to be news. His appearance at a baseball card show—his first public outing after his release in April 1991—was covered by the major networks, ESPN, CNN, and many newspapers. If and when he will apply for reinstatement to official baseball's good graces and therefore to Hall-of-Fame eligibility—and if so, how baseball commissioner Fay Vincent will rule—is an open question. Meanwhile Rose continues his lucrative round of card shows, speaking engagements, and other personal appearances.

Cincinnati-born Rose was one of the leading baseball players of his time. He started his career as 1963 National League Rookie of the Year and went on to achieve more hits than any other player in the history of the game, (4,256), become the Most Valuable Player in the league in 1973, and play on 15 All-Star teams. He led the Cincinnati Reds as a player (1963–78), as player-manager (1984–87), and as manager (1987–89) until his time of troubles came. Rose has co-authored *Countdown to Cobb: My Diary of the Record-Breaking 1985 Season* (1985), *Ballplayer: The Headfirst Life of Peter Edward Rose* (1988), and *My Story* (1989), the latter two with Roger Kahn. He was formerly married to Karolyn Ann Englehardt, married Carol Woliung in 1984, and has two children.

FURTHER READING

Hustle: The Myth, Life, and Lies of Pete Rose. Michael Y. Sokolove. Simon & Schuster, 1992.
Baseball Babylon: From the Black Sox to Pete Rose, the Real Stories Behind the Scandals that Rocked the Game. Dan Gutman. Viking Penguin, 1992.
"Collision at. . . ." George F. Will. *New York Review of Books,* June 27, 1991.
"Welcome to hardball city." Mike Lupica. *Esquire,* June 1991.
Collision at Home Plate: The Lives of Pete Rose and Bart Giamatti. James Reston, Jr. HarperCollins, 1991.
Hustle: The Myth and Life of Pete Rose. Michael Y. Sorolove. Simon & Schuster, 1990.
"Fields of. . . ." George V. Higgins. *American Scholar,* Spring 1990.
Pete Rose: "Charlie Hustle." Ray Buck. Childrens, 1983.
Pete Rose: Baseball's Charlie Hustle. Nathan Aaseng. Lerner, 1981.

Ross, Diana (1944–) Veteran singer Diana Ross's 1991 album was Motown's *The Force Behind the Power.* The cover song, written by Stevie Wonder, was reasonably well received, but the song that drew by far the most attention was the ballad "When You Tell Me That You Love Me," with favorable comments also on the Terry Britten-Graham Lyle song "Change of Heart." Ross took the album's songs on tour in the autumn of 1991. Still forthcoming, but somewhat less sure than it had earlier seemed, was the projected television film biography of the late international entertainer Josephine Baker for Ted Turner's TNT. The film was reportedly encountering "script problems" and had not been cast by late in the year. If it is ultimately produced, it will be Ross's first film since *The Wiz,* in 1978.

In 1960, then-teenager Ross and her friends Mary Wilson and Florence Ballard formed the Supremes, with Ross as lead singer. The trio became one of the leading vocal groups of the 1960s. Ross left to go solo in 1969 and has been a popular music superstar ever since, with such albums as *Diana Ross* (1970), *Lady Sings the Blues* (1972; and the film, with Ross in an Oscar-nominated performance as Billie Holiday), *Touch Me in the Morning* (1973), *The Wiz* (1978; in the film version of the play), *Diana* (1981), *Why Do Fools Fall in Love?* (1981), and *Ain't No Mountain High Enough* (1989). Detroit-born Ross has been married twice and has five children.

FURTHER READING

Call Her Miss Ross: The Unauthorized Biography of Diana Ross. J. Randy Taraborrelli. Ballantine, 1991.
All That Glittered: My Life with the Supremes. Tony Turner and Barbara Aria. NAL-Dutton, 1990.
Diana. J. Randy Taraborrelli and Reggie Wilson. Doubleday, 1985.
Diana Ross: Star Supreme. James Haskins. Viking Penguin, 1985.
Diana Ross. Geoff Brown. St. Martin's, 1983.
Reach Out: Diana Ross Story. Leonard Pitts, Jr., Sharon, 1983.
I'm Gonna Make You Love Me: The Story of Diana Ross. James S. Haskins. Dial, 1980; Dell, 1982.

Rostropovich, Mstislav (Mstislav Lepoldovich Rostropovich, 1927–) "For me, those three days spent in my country with my people at the most critical time were the best days of my life." So said celebrated cellist Mstislav Rostropovich. On hearing of the attempted August 1991 right-wing Soviet coup, he immediately flew from Paris to Moscow, went directly to the Russian parliament building, and joined the resistance. There he stayed, with one three-hour break, until the coup collapsed. On September 17, 1991, Rostropovich and his wife, singer Galina Vishnevskaya, announced plans to create a foundation for the purpose of building a modern children's hospital in Moscow. To start the fund-raising process, they announced three concerts in 1992, the first in Washington on February 10, the others at locations to be announced. Previously, they had sent large quantities of medical supplies to the Soviet Union.

Born in Baku, cellist, pianist, and conductor Rostropovich was a child prodigy, who made his debut as a cellist at the age of 13. During the 1950s, he was generally recognized as one of the world's leading cellists and was a greatly honored Soviet musician, winner of two Stalin Prizes and a Lenin Prize. Disillusioned with the Soviet system of the time, after incurring official displeasure for aiding dissident Alexander Solzhenitsyn, he and Vishnevskaya left for the West in 1974. He became music director of Washington, D.C.'s National Symphony Orchestra in 1977. Both he and his wife were stripped of their Soviet citizenships in 1978. In the Gorbachev era, their citizenship was restored, as were their medals and honors, and Rostropovich made a triumphant return to Moscow in February 1990 with the Washington National Symphony Orchestra. Rostropovich studied at the Moscow Conservatory, graduating in 1948, and taught at the Moscow and Leningrad Conservatories. He and Vishnevskaya have two children.

FURTHER READING

The Great Cellists. MARGARET CAMPBELL. Trafalgar Square, 1989.

"Rostropovich, Mstislav." *Current Biography,* Nov. 1988.

Ruffin, David (David Eli Ruffin, 1941–91) Mississippi-born Ruffin was the lead singer of the Temptations from 1964 to 1968, a period that brought the group enormous popularity, with such hit songs as "The Way You Do the Things You Do" (1964); "My Girl" (1965, the group's first number one hit); "Ain't Too Proud to Beg" and "Beauty's Only Skin Deep" (both in 1966); and "I Wish It Could Rain" and "All I Need," both in 1967. The group then consisted of Ruffin, Eddie Kendricks, Otis Williams, Paul Williams, and Mel Franklin. Ruffin left the group to go solo in 1968; although he began with the hits "My Whole World Ended" and "Walk Away from Love" (1975), his later career sagged, to a large extent because of his continuing drug abuse problems. He and Eddie Kendricks rejoined the Temptations in 1982, but only to make the album *Reunion.* He reportedly died of a drug overdose. He was survived by three daughters, two sons, two brothers, and his stepmother. (d. Philadelphia; June 1, 1991)

FURTHER READING

"Former Temptation. . . ." MICHAEL GOLDBERG. *Rolling Stone,* July 11, 1991.

"Death of ex-Temptation. . . ." *Jet,* June 17, 1991.

"David Ruffin's sad finale." VERN E. SMITH. *Newsweek,* June 17, 1991.

"A death in the night. . . ." *People,* June 17, 1991.

Obituary. *The Times* (of London), June 6, 1991.

Obituary. *New York Times,* June 3, 1991.

Rushdie, Salman (Ahmed Salman Rushdie, 1947–) "Free speech is life itself." Salman Rushdie spoke those striking words at a surprise appearance at Columbia University, on December 11, 1991. For yet another year, the British writer had remained in hiding, under Scotland Yard protection, as Islamic fundamentalist assassins continued to hunt him. He hid with good reason: On July 3, Ettore Caprioli, the Italian translator of *The Satanic Verses,* was knifed in Rome by an attacker who claimed to be an Iranian seeking Rushdie. On July 12, Hitoshi Igarashi, the Japanese translator of the book, was stabbed to death near Tokyo. On September 16, 1991, Rushdie's *Haroun and the Sea of Stories* was named best children's novel of 1990 by the Writer's Guild of Great Britain. Rushdie made a rare, unannounced public appearance to accept the award, then went back into hiding, with no change in sight. As the extraordinary situation moved into its fourth year, the U.S. and British governments remained silent, as did the United Nations. In her December 9 Stockholm acceptance speech, Nobel laureate Nadine Gordimer defended Rushdie, urging UN action on his behalf, aimed at securing Iranian withdrawal of the Rushdie death sentence. During 1991, Rushdie published a new work, *Imaginary Homelands: Essays and Criticisms 1981–1991.*

Rushdie's 1988 novel *The Satanic Verses* became a worldwide best-seller after many fundamentalist Muslims protested its publication, rioting, publicly burning the book, and threat-

ening the life of its author and publishers. In February 1989, Iran's Ayatollah Khomeini publicly sentenced him to death and offered $1 million to anyone who would murder Rushdie, a threat since repeated by others and taken very seriously indeed, then and now. Ayatollah Khamenei repeated the death threat in February 1990. Rushdie continued to deny any intent to insult those of the Muslim faith, while calling for free speech for those who would murder him; he also publicly apologized to any who may have been offended by his book, for a time opposing its issuance in paperback, and affirming his allegiance to Islam, all to no immediate avail.

Bombay-born Rushdie is a leading novelist whose works also include *Midnight's Children* (1981), which won a Booker Prize, and *Shame* (1983). He attended King's College, Cambridge. He has been married twice, and has one child.

FURTHER READING

" 'Free speech is life itself.' " KARSTEN PRAGER. *Time,* Dec. 23, 1991.
"The fugitive. . . ." MARK ABLEY. *Saturday Night,* May 1991.
"Keeping up with. . . ." JAMES FENTON. *New York Review of Books.* Mar. 28, 1991.
Salman Rushdie. JAMES HARRISON. Macmillan, 1991.
A Satanic Affair: Salman Rushdie and the Rage of Islam. MALISE RUTHVEN. Trafalgar Square, 1991.
The Novels of Salman Rushdie. R. K. DHAWAN and G. R. TANEJA, eds. Advent (NY), 1991.
Salman Rushdie: Sentenced to Death. W. J. WEATHERBY. Carroll & Graf, 1990.
The Rushdie Affair: The Novel, the Ayatollah, and the West. DANIEL PIPES. Carol, 1990.
The Rushdie File. SARA MAITLAND, ed. Syracuse University Press, 1990.
The Salman Rushdie Controversy in Inter-Religious Perspective. DAN COHN-SHERBOK, ed. E. Mellen, 1990.
Salman Rushdie and the Third World: Myths of the Nation. TIMOTHY BRENNAN. ST. MARTIN'S, 1989.

Russell, Paul (1947–91) Texas-born Russell was a leading dancer, choreographer, and teacher for two decades, and a trailblazing Black artist in European ballet. He studied at New York City's School of American Ballet and the Dance Theater of Harlem School, making his debut with the Hartford Ballet in 1970. He joined the Dance Theater of Harlem in 1971 and quickly became a leading dancer with the company, especially notable for his performances in *Corsair* and *Forces of Rhythm.* After studying at Leningrad's Kirov School in 1978, he danced with the Scottish National Ballet from 1978 to 1980, memorably as "Siegfried." He danced with the San Francisco Ballet from 1981 to 1986, until an injury ended his dancing career, then turned to choreography and more fully to teaching. He was a victim of acquired immune deficiency syndrome (AIDS). He was survived by his companion, Randy Griffin. (d. San Francisco; February 15, 1991)

FURTHER READING

Obituary. *Dance,* July 1991.
Obituary. *The Times* (of London), Feb. 27, 1991.
Obituary. *New York Times,* Feb. 19, 1991.

Ryan, Nolan (1947–) On May 3, 1991, Ryan broke his own extraordinary record, pitching his seventh no-hitter against a powerful Toronto Blue Jays team at Arlington Stadium. The 44-year-old Ryan, one of the most notable pitchers in baseball history, struck out 16 batters (some of whom had not even been born when Ryan entered the league), adding to his record as the leading strikeout pitcher in the history of baseball. As news of the potential no-hitter spread, area fans converged on the Texas Rangers' Arlington Stadium for the late innings, and baseball lovers around the country crowded around television sets, especially after ESPN tuned in during the eighth inning. A month earlier, Ryan had pitched in an exhibition game opposite his son Reid, a freshman pitcher for the University of Texas Longhorns. During 1991, he published *Nolan Ryan: The Authorized Pictorial History,* and *Nolan Ryan's Pitcher's Bible: The Ultimate Guide to Power, Precision, and Long-Term Performance,* written with Tom House. *King of the Hill: An Irreverent Look at the Men on the Mound* with Mickey Herskowitz, is scheduled for 1992 publication.

Texas-born Ryan is far and away the leading strikeout artist in the history of baseball, with over 5,300 strikeouts to his credit; has pitched a record seven no-hitters; and holds numerous other records. He pitched for the New York Mets (1966–71), the California Angels (1972–79), and the Houston Astros (1979–88) before moving to the Texas Rangers. He scored his 300th career victory on August 1, 1990, becoming the 19th pitcher to reach that milestone, and bringing his career record at that point to 300–267. He has been a member of seven All-Star teams. In 1988 he published *Throwing Heat: The Autobiography of Nolan Ryan,* written with Harvey Frommer. He attended Alvin Junior College (1966–69). He married Ruth Elsie Holdruff in 1967; they have three children.

FURTHER READING

"Ten living legends. . . ." Steve Wulf. *Sports Illustrated,* Dec. 23, 1991.
"Sales pitcher." John Anderson. *Texas,* Sep. 1991.
Interview. *Sporting News,* May 13, 1991.
"Nolan Ryan. . . ." Sam Blair. *Boys' Life,* Apr. 1991.
"Citizen Ryan. . . ." Leigh Montville. *Sports Illustrated,* Apr. 15, 1991.
"Man of the Year." Dave Nightingale. *Sporting News,* Jan. 7, 1991.
"Ryan's song. . . ." Phil Rogers. *Sporting News,* Aug. 13, 1990.

Ryder, Winona (Winona Laura Horowitz, 1971–) The very new film star Winona Ryder opened in two well-received films late in 1990, both of which became hits early in 1991 and then went on to success on the home screen. In *Mermaids,* she starred opposite Cher, as the very religious and sexually repressed teenage daughter of a thoroughly liberated woman. In the fantasy *Edward Scissorhands,* she starred as the conventional daughter of a suburban family who falls in love with a boy (Johnny Depp) who literally has scissors instead of hands, having been left unfinished by the scientist who created him. Forthcoming was a starring role in Francis Ford Coppola's *Bram Stoker's "Dracula",* in a cast that includes Gary Oldman, Anthony Hopkins, and Keanu Reeves.

Minnesota-born Ryder became a teenage film star in the late 1980s, making her debut in *Lucas* (1986). She appeared in *Beetlejuice* (1988), and played a breakthrough role as Veronica in *Heathers* (1989), in the same year also starring in *Great Balls of Fire.* In 1990, she was in *Welcome Home Roxy Carmichael.* She studied at San Francisco's American Conservatory Theater.

FURTHER READING

"Winona." *Harper's Bazaar,* Jan. 1991.
"Winona Ryder. . . ." Julia Reed. *Vogue,* Dec. 1990.
"Winona." Claire Connors. *Seventeen,* Dec. 1990
"Winona Ryder. . . ." Jeff Giles and Michel Haddi. *Interview,* Dec. 1990.
"Wise child." Phoebe Hoban. *Premier,* June 1989.
Hot actress. . . ." David Handelman. *Rolling stone,* May 18, 1989.

Sabah, Jabir al-Ahmed al-Jabir al- (1928–) On February 26, 1991, Allied ground forces took Kuwait City, held by Iraq since August 2, 1990, and Kuwaiti Emir Sabah was free to return home—to a country looted by the Iraqis, who had set more than 500 of Kuwait's oil wells ablaze before leaving, creating an enormous ecological disaster. The Emir was returning to a people who were in many instances unwilling to settle for a return to authoritarian rule. There was also strong sentiment for taking revenge on Palestinian and Jordanian nationals living in Kuwait, some of whom had served the conquering Iraquis.

The Emir returned to Kuwait City on March 14, after some utilities had been restored, and he and his family then proceeded to take control of the country again. But there was popular protest, and the Emir on June 2, 1991, promised that parliamentary elections would be held in October 1992; democratic forces protested and demonstrated against the long election delay. Human rights organizations and Western reporters cited many instances of human rights abuses in the months that followed as revenge was taken on alleged collaborators. After an initial period of bureaucratic fumbling, the massive oil well fires were attacked, the last of them extinguished in November 1991. Meanwhile, the Emir and his family ruled much as before, his long-dominant family having abolished the beginnings of Kuwaiti democracy in 1976.

Sabah is the head of the Kuwaiti royal family, in a government that includes many members of the ruling family. One of them is his son, Saad, who is both prime minister and crown prince. He was educated primarily through private tutoring.

FURTHER READING

"After the liberation." Milton Viorst. *New Yorker,* Sep. 30, 1991.
"Rolls-Royce revolutionaries." Michael Kelly. *New Republic,* Apr. 8, 1991.
"Who's sitting pretty. . . ." *Business Week,* Mar. 11, 1991.

Salinas de Gortari, Carlos (1948–) The gravity of the enormous human and economic problems facing Mexican President Salinas, his Institutional Revolutionary Party (PRI), and his country was underscored by two related developments in 1991. First, on March 18, Salinas ordered the closing of Mexico's largest oil refinery, located in Mexico City, 11 days after Mexican environmental authorities had declared a second-stage air pollution alert, indicating severely dangerous ozone levels. Mexico City has become one of the world's most dangerous places to live, with more than 20 million people crowded into a small area of near-permanent air inversion, most of them living in wholly unsanitary, barely livable conditions in the shantytowns surrounding the city itself. The danger increases every year, as millions more

crowd into a limited area, with respiratory diseases a major killer and epidemic disease always in immediate prospect. And so the second related development: The massive cholera epidemic that began in Peru in January 1991 reached Central America that summer, and by mid-September was reported to have reached Mexico, with incalculable consequences yet to be reported. On June 5, 1991, the United Earth Prize, awarded for leadership in protecting the environment, was given to Mexican President Carlos Salinas de Gortari. Environmentalists in many countries demonstrated a wide range of adverse reactions to his selection.

During 1990 and 1991, Salinas strongly urged adoption of U.S.-Mexican free trade proposals, with Canada also becoming involved in continuing talks. He also sought improved Latin American economic cooperation, hosting the multinational first Ibero-American summit meeting at Guadalajara, Mexico, on July 18 and 19. In an effort to restore the sagging public image of his party, Salinas in September 1990 forced through a series of new party rules aimed at cutting the power of the party bureaucracy and bringing internal democracy, and simultaneously developed a public works program aimed at softening the impact of the recession. His efforts bore electoral fruit in the form of a sweeping victory in the August 1991 midterm elections; however, although he denied opposition charges of widespread electoral fraud, his party later admitted fraud in two of the six state gubernatorial races and gave up the governorships.

Salinas has spent his whole career in a series of increasingly responsible Mexican federal government financial planning posts, beginning with his term as assistant director of public finance in the finance ministry (1971–74). Before his 1987 presidential nomination, he was minister of planning and the federal budget (1982–87). Salinas attended the National University of Mexico and Harvard. He is married to Yolanda Cecilia Occelli González; they have three children.

FURTHER READING

"President Salinas. . . ." Stephen B. Shepard. *Business Week,* Aug. 12, 1991.
"Mexico according to. . . ." Mortimer B. Zuckerman. *U.S. News & World Report,* July 8, 1991.
"North American. . . ." Nathan Gardels. *New Perspectives,* Winter 1991.
"The man behind the mask. . . ." John Moody. *Time,* Nov. 19, 1990.
"Salinas takes a gamble. . . ." Robert A. Pastor. *New Republic,* Sep. 10, 1990.
"How do you say. . . ." Dick J. Reavis. *Texas Monthly,* Oct. 1989.
"Salinas de Gortari, Carlos. *Current Biography,* Mar. 1989.
"A Gorbo for Mexico. . . ." Morton Kondracke. *New Republic,* Feb. 20, 1989.

Sampras, Pete (1971–) "A monkey on my back" was Sampras's phrase for the weight of being defending champion of the U.S. Open. He had been the surprise winner of the Grand Slam tennis event in September 1990, and did not feel free until a year later, when Jim Courier defeated him in the quarterfinals of the 1991 Open. Though the 1990 win brought him fame and fortune, the pressure was enormous for the 19-year-old, as he moved up in the rankings from 81st to 6th. Though he won the Grand Slam Cup in Munich in December 1990, his performance after the U.S. Open was far from stellar, partly because he was hampered by injuries, including a pulled hamstring, a sprained ankle, a tender Achilles tendon, and shin splints; these kept him out of the Australian Open while he bowed out early at Wimbledon and the French Open. Not until he was relieved of the U.S. Open title could Sampras, as he put it, "go back to my normal lifestyle"—or so he hoped. In October 1991, Sampras won the Lyons Grand Prix, and in Novem-

ber the Association of Tennis Professionals (ATP) Tour World Cup in Frankfurt, Germany. In his Davis Cup debut in December 1991, he lost twice, in the United States loss of the cup to France.

Maryland-born Sampras grew up in Palos Verdes, California, where he was groomed for tennis stardom from second grade. He dropped out of Palos Verdes High School after his junior year to turn professional, at 19 becoming the youngest male ever to win the U.S. Open.

FURTHER READING

"Sampras: King of Aces." HAL HIGDON. *Boys' Life,* Sep. 1991.
"The Sampras stakes." PETER M. COAN. *World Tennis,* July 1991.
"Pete Sampras. . . ." DAVID HIGDON. *World Tennis,* Nov. 1990.
"Calm, cool and collecting." CINDY SHMERLER, *World Tennis,* Nov. 1990.
"Open for debate." STEVE FLINK. *World Tennis,* Nov. 1990.
"Focused. . . ." BRUCE NEWMAN. *Sports Illustrated,* Oct 22, 1990.
"Clean-cut Sampras. . . ." JOE GERGEN. *Sporting News,* Sep. 24, 1990.
"Float like a butterfly. . . ." ANDREW ABRAHAMS. *People,* Sep. 24, 1990.
"Now playing. . . ." TOM CALLAHAN. U.S. *News & World Report,* Sep 24, 1990.
"Upset time. . . ." ALEXANDER WOLFF. *Sports Illustrated,* Sep. 17, 1990.
"Sampras. . . ." JIM MARTZ. *Sporting News,* Sep. 17, 1990.

Sarandon, Susan (Susan Abigail Tomaling, 1946–) The year 1991 saw the greatest film success so far in Sarandon's career: her co-starring role with Geena Davis in *Thelma and Louise,* the "sleeper" of the year. Sarandon starred as Louise, out for some excitement, and Davis as Thelma, her wild, dangerous partner. Critics likened the film to earlier male-buddy road outlaw films, feminists debated their portrayals, and large audiences came to see it. Ridley Scott directed and co-produced. Forthcoming were a starring role in Paul Schrader's film *Light Sleeper,* and an appearance in Robert Altman's film *The Player,* along with a good many other screen, stage, and television stars. Active in several political causes, Sarandon was sharply critical of some U.S. actions in the Persian Gulf War, particularly criticizing the U.S. media for accepting Pentagon restrictions on their coverage of the war.

New York City-born Sarandon began her film career with *Joe* (1970), and went on to play a wide variety of roles in the next two decades in such films as *The Rocky Horror Picture Show* (1974), *Pretty Baby* (1978), *Loving Couples* (1980), *Atlantic City* (1981), *The Hunger* (1983), *Compromising Positions* (1985), *The Witches of Eastwick* (1987), *Bull Durham* (1988), *The Dry White Season* (1989), and *White Palace* (1990). She has also appeared in several plays and on television. Her B.A. was from the Catholic University of America. She was formerly married to actor Chris Sarandon. She has two children, the second one from her relationship with actor Tim Robbins; another child was expected in May 1992.

FURTHER READING

"Susan Sarandon bashes back. . . ." DONNA MINKOWITZ. *Advocate,* June 4, 1991.
"Susan Sarandon." GRAHAM FULLER. *Interview,* June 1991.
"The prime of. . . ." BEN YAGODA. *American Film,* May 1991.
"Susan Sarandon." ROD LURIE. *Los Angeles,* May 1991.
"Sarandon, Susan." *Current Biography,* Sep. 1989.

Savimbi, Jonas (1934–) A quarter century of armed revolution and civil war ended for Savimbi in 1991. On May 1 the National Union for the Total Independence of Angola (UNITA), led by Savimbi, and the Angolan government, led by President José Eduardo Dos Santos, chairman of the Popular Movement for the Liberation of Angola (MPLA), signed an agreement to end the 16-year-old civil war, with fighting to end by May 15. The agreement provided for multiparty free elections, to take place in 1992, and a merger of ground forces. Contrary to some expectations, the truce held. On May 25, Cuban forces completed their pullout from Angola. On May 31, Savimbi and Dos Santos formally signed the peace agreement, which had been achieved with the help of the Soviet Union and the United States, formerly key suppliers and sponsors of the two sides in the long civil war.

Savimbi became active in the anti-Portuguese Angolan revolutionary movement in the early 1960s. In 1966, he founded the UNITA, and has led it through 25 years of revolution and civil war. From 1975, he led a guerrilla war against the Soviet and Cuban-backed Angolan government of the MPLA, while being substantially helped by Portuguese exiles from Angola and by the South African government. Savimbi attended the University of Lausanne. Though his personal life has been kept very private, he has been married and has several children.

FURTHER READING

The Cold War Guerilla: Jonas Savimbi, the U.S. Media and the Angolan War. ELAINE WINDRICH. Greenwood, 1992.

"Can this man save Africa?" DAVID REED. *Reader's Digest,* May 1987.

Jonas Savimbi: A Key to Africa. FRED BRIDGLAND. Paragon House, 1987.

Scalia, Antonin (1936–) Justice Scalia continued to be part of the Supreme Court's new conservative majority during the 1990–91 Court term. He wrote the majority opinion in *Harmelin V. Michigan,* ruling that a Michigan law requiring a life sentence without possibility of parole for possession of 650 grams (1.5 pounds) of cocaine did not violate the cruel and unusual punishment prohibition of the Eighth Amendment, although the federal law was much less stringent. He also voted with the majority in such cases as *Payne v. Tennessee,* which allowed "victim impact" evidence to be presented by the prosecution during the sentencing phase of criminal cases; *Barnes v. Glen Theater,* upholding an

Indiana state law banning nude dancing; *Florida v. Bostick,* ruling that police could board buses and search passengers' luggage, with their permission; *Coleman v. Thompson,* restricting the use of habeas corpus writs by state prisoners who have exhausted state appeals, *Rust v. Sullivan,* which upheld federal regulations banning federally funded family planning clinics from offering abortion counseling; *Board of Education of Oklahoma City v. Dowell,* which eased conditions for lifting court supervision of segregated school districts; and *Arizona v. Fulminante,* ruling that coerced or involuntary confession in a criminal case could be a "harmless error" if conviction would have resulted without it.

Scalia wrote a dissent in *County of Riverside, California v. McLaughlin,* which ruled that those arrested without warrants could be held up to 48 hours while a judge decided if there was probable cause for the arrest, arguing that 24 hours should be the maximum time allowed. His other dissents included *United Automobile Workers v. Johnson Controls Inc.,* a landmark women's rights case ruling that according to the 1978 Pregnancy Discrimination Act employers could not ban pregnant women from jobs potentially dangerous to their unborn children; *Edmonson v. Leesville Concrete Co,* which barred exclusion of jurors in civil cases because of race, following earlier bans on exclusion because of race in criminal cases; *Chison v. Roemer* and *Houston Lawyers v. Texas Attorney General,* which ruled that the federal Voting Rights Act, prohibiting discriminatory voting practices or election district abuses, applied to elected judges; and *Masson v. New Yorker Magazine,* which ruled that invented or materially altered quotes attributed to a public figure could be libelous.

New Jersey-born Scalia taught law at the University of Virginia (1967–74), was an assistant attorney general (1974–77), and taught law again, at the University of Chicago (1977–82). He was appointed to the District of Columbia U.S. Court of Appeals by President Ronald Reagan in 1982, and to the Supreme Court by Reagan in 1986. Scalia's B.A. was from Georgetown University in 1957, his LL.B. from Harvard in 1960. He married Maureen McCarthy in 1960; the couple have nine children.

FURTHER READING

"A new day in court." LAUREN TARSHIS and JAMES EARL HARDY. *Scholastic Update,* Nov. 1, 1991.
"Top gun on the high court." FRED BARNES. *Reader's Digest,* July 1991.
Eight Men and a Lady. HERMAN SCHWARTZ, ANDREA NEAL, and DAVID SAVAGE. National Press, 1990.
Packing the Courts; The Conservatives' Campaign to Rewrite the Constitution. HERMAN SCHWARTZ. Scribner/Macmillan, 1988.
"What they say it is. . . ." *Time,* July 6, 1987.

Scelba, Mario (1901–91) Sicilian-born Scelba, a former Italian prime minister, began his career in pre-fascist Italy, as the protegé of Don Luigi Sturzo, founder of the Popular Party, a Catholic party that preceded the Christian Democratic Party, Scelba's party throughout his political career. Scelba was inactive politically during the fascist period and was one of the organizers of the Christian Democratic Party after the fall of Mussolini. He served at the cabinet level in several postwar governments, emerging in five De Gasperi governments as a strongly conservative Interior minister, who during the 1950s used police and paramilitary forces to forcibly smash strikes and other demonstrations by the organizations of the left, with special attention to the Communist Party, which had come out of the war a very powerful force in Italian political life. Scelba was prime minister (1954–55), served as Interior minister again (1960–62), and throughout his later career continued to speak for the conservative elements of his party. He became party chairman in 1965, spent his later years in the Senate, and retired in 1983. He was survived by a daughter. (d. October 29, 1991)

FURTHER READING

Obituary. *The Times* (of London), Nov. 1, 1991.

Schaefer, Jack Warner (1907–91) Cleveland-born Schaefer was a journalist for two decades before publication of his first novel, for which he is best known by far: It was *Shane* (1949). A. B. Guthrie and Jack Sher adapted his work into the classic 1953 western film, directed by George Stevens, with Alan Ladd in the title role as the retired gunfighter who takes on one more fight, this time in defense of a family of homesteaders, leading a cast that included Jean Arthur, Van Heflin, Brandon de Wilde, and Jack Palance. Schaefer went on to write many more novels and stories on western themes, including the novels *First Blood* (1953), *The Plainsmen* (1963), and *Monte Walsh* (1963); his short stories are collected in several volumes. He was survived by his second wife, the former Louise Deans, a daughter, three sons, two sisters, and a brother. (d. Santa Fe, New Mexico; January 24, 1991)

FURTHER READING

Obituary. *New York Times,* Jan. 27, 1991.

Scheider, Roy (1935–) As *The Russia House* became a much-viewed 1991 home video release, Scheider became even more visible than he had been on theatrical release of the film in 1991. His 1990 *Somebody Has to Shoot the Picture* also found cable audiences. On the home screen, Scheider also narrated portions of the baseball celebration *When It Was a Game,* with James Earl Jones and Jason Robards, Jr. In late December, Scheider starred in the much-anticipated screen adaption of the William Burroughs novel *Naked Lunch,* a complex, difficult work to create on film. David Cronenberg wrote and directed; the cast also included Peter Weller, Judy Davis, and Julian Sands. Forthcoming was a starring role in a major vehicle; Michaelangelo Antonioni's *The Crew,* with a cast that included

Yves Montand, Giancarlo Giannini, Matt Dillon, and Greta Scacchi.

Scheider emerged as a film star in the 1970s, in strong supporting roles in such movies as *The French Connection* (1971), *Klute,* (1971), and then as the star of the worldwide hit *Jaws* (1975; and the 1978 sequel), as well as *Marathon Man* (1976), *Sorcerer* (1977), *All that Jazz* (1979), *The Men's Club* (1986), *Night Game* (1989), *Listen to Me* (1989), *The Fourth War* (1990), *Russia House* (1990), and *Somebody Has to Shoot the Picture* (1990). He has also appeared in such plays as *The Chinese Prime Minister* (1963), *The Alchemist* (1964), and *Stephen D* (1968), for which he won an Obie Award. Scheider's B.A. was from Franklin and Marshall College in 1955. He has been married twice and has two children.

FURTHER READING

"Blue Thunder's. . . ." CHET FLIPPO. *People,* May 23, 1983.

"Recognizing Roy Scheider." PETE HAMMILL. *New York,* May 23, 1983.

Schrader, Paul Joseph (1946–) The highly regarded writer of such screen classics as *Raging Bull* and *Taxi Driver,* whose directorial efforts have sometimes seemed uneven, Schrader opened the artistically successful horror-thriller *The Comfort of Strangers* in 1991. He directed a cast that included Christopher Walken, Natasha Richardson, Rupert Everett, and Helen Mirren; the screenplay, by Harold Pinter, was based on the Ian McEwan novel. Forthcoming was the film *Light Sleeper,* starring Willem Dafoe as the kind of near-psychopathic, highly moral outsider—though in this case a drug dealer—that Schrader has created in several earlier films. Schrader wrote and directed the film; the cast includes Susan Sarandon, Dana Delany, and David Clennon.

Michigan-born Schrader emerged as a leading screenwriter with such films as *Taxi Driver* (1976), *Obsession* (1976), the classic *Raging Bull* (1981), *The Mosquito Coast* (1986), and the highly controversial *The Last Temptation of Christ* (1988). He co-wrote the screenplays of *The Yakuza* (1974), *Rolling Thunder* (1977), and *Old Boyfriends* (1979), and wrote and directed *Hardcore* (1978) and *American Gigolo* (1979). He also co-wrote and directed *Blue Collar* (1978) and *Mishima* (1985), and directed such films as *Cat People* (1982), *Light of Day* (1987), and *Patty Hearst* (1988). Early in his career, he was an editor of the magazine *Cinema* (1970), and in the same period wrote the book *Transcendental Style in Film: Ozu, Bresson and Dreyer* (1972). He also published *Schrader on Schrader* (1990), written by Kevin Jackson. Schrader's B.A. was from Calvin College, his M.A. from the Unviersity of California at Los Angeles. He is married to actress Mary Beth Hurt.

FURTHER READING

"Paul Schrader. . . ." *American Film,* July–Aug. 1989.

"Citizen Paul." RICHARD GEHR. *American Film,* Sep. 1988.

Schuyler, James Marcus (1923–91) Chicago-born Schuyler was a poet long identified with what some critics called the New York School, a group of largely New York-based poets that included John Ashbery and Kenneth Koch, whose work is often expressed in ordinary, colloquial speech and is usually accompanied by artwork that is meant to be part of the total poetic work, rather than only illustrative of it. Schuyler and other New York School poets have been much influenced by the ideas of surrealism and those post–World War II action painters also described as a New York School. Schuyler's poetry collections include *Salute* (1960), *May 24th or So* (1966), *Freely Espousing* (1969), *The Crystal Lithium* (1972), *Hymn to Life* (1974), *The Morning of the Poem* (1980; it won a 1981 Pulitzer Prize), and *A Few Days* (1985). His *Selected Poems* were published in 1988. He also wrote several novels and plays. (d. New York City; April 12, 1991)

FURTHER READING

Obituary. *New York Times,* Apr. 13, 1991.

Schwarzenegger, Arnold Alois (1947–) Film star and worldwide celebrity, Schwarzenegger in 1991 appeared in one of the most commercially successful films ever made: *Terminator 2: Judgment Day.* The film, directed and produced by James Cameron, was written by Cameron and William Wisher; the cast included Linda Hamilton, who had appeared in the earlier *Terminator* film, as well as Joe Morton, Edward Furlong, Earl Boen, and S. Epatha Merkerson. With its massive special effects, it cost an estimated $100 million but by January 1992 had grossed more than $400 million worldwide, and ultimate grosses were estimated at $450–500 million. An extraordinarily profitable film, it was also extraordinarily violent and was much prized by its viewers for its violence, as had been several earlier Schwarzenegger films. This film also tried for redeeming social significance, as his earlier films had not, including a strong female character (Hamilton), a sympathetic and heroic African-American (Morton), and an anti-war statement in the form of an extremely violent nuclear catastrophe.

Schwarzenegger came out of 1991 probably the world's most bankable movie star. He is also a multi-faceted entrepreneur, a friend of President George Bush, and a substantial contributor to many causes, including the Simon Wiesenthal Center, which honored him with its 1991 Leadership Award at a dinner on June 16, 1991, attended by President Bush. During 1991, Schwarzenegger, who also wants to be a director, directed "The Switch," an episode of television's "Tales from the Crypt." Schwarzenegger and his wife, Maria Shriver, had a second daughter in July 1991.

Austrian-born Schwarzenegger was a champion bodybuilder (1969–75), turning later to films. He played in such films as *Stay Hungry* (1976) and *Pumping Iron* (1977), and emerged as an action film star in *Conan, the Barbarian* (1982; and the 1983 sequel), then went on to such very popular films as *The Terminator* (1984), *Commando* (1985), *Raw Deal* (1986), *Predator* (1987), *Red Heat* (1988), *Total Recall* (1990), and *Kindergarten Cop* (1990). He has also written several bodybuilding books. He attended the University of Wisconsin. He married newscaster Maria Owings Shriver in 1986; the couple have two children.

FURTHER READING

"Schwarzenegger, Arnold." *Curent Biography,* Oct. 1991.
"Mr. Big Shot." Bill Zehme. *Rolling Stone,* Aug. 22, 1991.
"Arnold Schwarzenegger. . . ." Jeff Rovin. *Ladies Home Journal,* Aug. 1991.
"Rnld Schwzngr." Pat H. Broeske and Herb Ritts. July 1991.
Schwarzenegger. NAL-Dutton, 1991.
"Box-office brawn. . . ." Richard Corliss. *Time,* Dec. 24, 1990.
"Pumping. . . ." Lynn Rosellini. *U.S. News & World Report,* Nov. 26, 1990.
"Brand loyalty." Suzanne Moore. *New Statesman & Society,* Aug. 3, 1990.
Arnold Schwarzenegger: A Portrait. George Butler. Simon & Schuster, 1990.
Arnold: The Unauthorized Biography. Wendy Leigh. Congdon & Weed, 1990.

Schwarzkopf, H. Norman (1934–) Four-star general Schwarzkopf emerged from the Persian Gulf War an American military hero, acclaimed at home and abroad as no one since Dwight Eisenhower at the end of World War II. In early August 1990, when Saddam Hussein's Iraqi forces invaded Kuwait, Schwarzkopf commanded the U.S. Rapid Deployment Force, later renamed the U.S. Central Command. He commanded all U.S. and Allied forces in the Gulf during the huge build-up that began on August 3, ultimately commanding the massive forces that went into action in January, 1991. During the build-up period, his strategy began to unfold, with feints and amphibious exercises in the Gulf. The air war, which began on January 17, quickly grounded the Iraqi air force, and with it the eyes of the Iraqi military; Schwarzkopf then began the massive armored deployment west that constituted the critical Allied thrust around the main Iraqi defenses and into northern Kuwait and southern Iraq when the ground war began, on February 24. Three days later, the war was over. Iraq's reserve Republican Guard divisions, always Schwarzkopf's main concern, had been decisively defeated by Allied armor and aircraft, and even the Iraqi frontline defenses had been destroyed, with Allied armor moving into Kuwait City far more quickly than many had expected. Schwarzkopf himself detailed the entire operation in a historic conference at Riyadh, Saudi Arabia, on February 27, as much of the world watched. The general, tagged "Stormin' Norman" (an old nickname) by some media people in the early days of the build-up, had by then emerged as a world figure, and one to be reckoned with in the years to come if he were to desire a political career. After the war, Schwarzkopf came home to tumultuous celebrations. In the autumn of 1991, he retired from the Army. He also signed a contract to write his autobiography, for a reported $5 million advance.

New Jersey-born Schwarzkopf is a career military officer. He is a 1956 graduate of West Point, who later studied guided missile engineering at the University of Southern California. An infantry officer for much of his career, he joined the Army as a second lieutenant, was a paratroop adviser during his first Vietnam tour of duty, and was an infantry battalion commander during his second tour of duty. He was wounded twice in Vietnam and won three Silver Stars. He commanded mechanized infantry divisions at home and in Germany during the 1970s and early 1980s, and was deputy commander of American forces during the 1983 Granada invasion, becoming a leading field commander in the late 1980s. He married Brenda Holsinger in 1968; they have three children.

FURTHER READING

Norman Schwarzkopf. Rebecca Stefoff. Chelsea House, 1992.
"Desert Norm." C. D. B. Bryan. *Reader's Digest* (Canadian), July 1991.
"Schwarzkopf, H. Norman." *Current Biography,* May 1991
"Fierce loyalty and affection. . . ." Richard Mackenzie. *Insight.* Mar. 18, 1991.
"A general's cunning. . . ." Richard Mackenzie and Eric Felten. *Insight,* Mar. 18, 1991.
"Operation Desert Norm. . . ." C. D. B. Bryan. *New Republic,* Mar. 11, 1991.
"Stormin' Norman. . . ." *People,* Mar. 11, 1991.
"A bear leads the invasion." *Maclean's,* Mar. 4, 1991.
"A soldier of conscience. . . ." Tom Mathews and C. S. Manegold. *Newsweek,* Mar. 11, 1991.
"Sayings of Stormin' Norman." *Time,* Mar. 11, 1991.
"Stormin' Norman. . . ." Jesse Birnbaum and Dan Fischer. *Time,* Feb. 4, 1991.
"The Gulf. . . ." Linda Rocawich. *Progressive,* Jan. 1991.
In the Eye of the Storm: The Life of General H. Norman Schwarzkopf. Roger Cohen and Claudio Gatti. Farrar, Straus & Giroux, 1991.
H. Norman Schwarzkopf. E. J. Valentine. Bantam, 1991.
H. Norman Schwarzkopf: Road to Triumph. M. E. Morris. St. Martin's, 1991.
Schwarzkopf: An Insider's View of the Commander and his Victory. Robert D. Parrish. Bantam, 1991.
Schwarzkopf in His Own Words. Richard Pyle. NAL-Dutton, 1991.
In the Eye of Desert Storm. C. D. Bryan. Abrams, 1991.

Scorsese, Martin (1942–) *GoodFellas* and its director continued to win major awards in 1991: best film, best director, and best screenplay from the British Academy of Film and Television Arts (BAFTA), and best director and best picture from the U.S. National Society of Film Critics.

Scorsese's major 1991 film was his well-received version of *Cape Fear,* the 1962 Gregory Peck-Robert Mitchum vehicle, remade with much darker tones. Scorsese's version starred Nick Nolte in the Sam Bowden role created by Peck in 1962, and Robert De Niro in the Sam Cady role created by Mitchum. Jessica Lange and Juilette Lewis co-starred, in a cast that included Peck and Mitchum in cameo roles. In 1991 Scorsese also appeared in a rare acting role, as a director in Irwin Winkler's McCarthy-era film *Guilty by Suspicion;* De Niro and Annette Bening starred. Scorsese is producing the forthcoming *Mad Dog and Glory,* directed by John MacNaughton and starring De Niro. Another forthcoming production is a remake of Jules Dassin's 1950 *Night and the City,* to be directed by Irwin Winkler and starring De Niro and Jessica Lange. In April, Scorsese and Universal Pictures announced a six-year producing and directing agreement. Increasingly a worldwide film industry figure, Scorsese was decorated in 1991 by the French government for his efforts on behalf of film preservation; he also donated his personal motion picture collection to the International Museum of Photography at the George Eastman House in Rochester, N.Y.

New York-born Scorsese scored his first major success with *Mean Streets* (1973), which explored the underside of New York life. He went on to become one of the major directors of the modern period, which such other films as *Alice Doesn't Live Here Anymore* (1974), *Taxi Driver* (1976), *New York, New York* (1977), the classic *Raging Bull* (1980), *The Color of Money* (1986), the highly controversial *The Last Temptation of Christ* (1988), and *GoodFellas* (1990). He also appeared as an actor in a small but key role as Van Gogh in *Akira Kurosawa's Dreams* (1990). Scorsese's 1964 B.S. and 1966 M.A. in film communications were both from New York University. He has been married four times and has two children.

FURTHER READING

"Martin Scorsese." GRAHAM FULLER. *Interview,* Nov. 1991.
"Slouching toward Hollywood. . . ." PETER BISKIND. *Premiere,* Nov. 1991.
"Playboy interview. . . ." DAVID RENSIN. *Playboy,* Apr. 1991.
Martin Scorsese: A Journey. MARY P. KELLY. Thunder's Mouth, 1991.
The Future of the Movies: Interviews with Martin Scorsese, George Lucas, and Steven Spielberg. ROGER EBERT and GENE SISKEL. Andrews & McMeel, 1991.
"Martin Scorsese." ANTHONY DECURTIS. *Rolling Stone,* Nov. 1, 1990.
"Blood and pasta." AMY TAUBIN. *New Statesman & Society,* Nov. 9, 1990.
"Made men." KATHLEEN MURPHY and GAVIN SMITH. *Film Comment,* Sep.–Oct. 1990.
"God's lonely man. . . ." RICHARD GEHR. *Video Magazine,* Mar. 1990.
Martin Scorsese; A Guide to References & Resources. MARION WEISS. G. K. Hall, 1987.
Martin Scorsese and Michael Cimino. MICHAEL BLISS. Scarecrow, 1985.

Scott, George C. (George Campbell Scott, 1927–) Veteran stage, screen, and television star George C. Scott continued to appear in all three media during 1991. On the New York stage, he directed and starred as Gramps in the Circle in the Square revival of Paul Osborn's 1938 fantasy *On Borrowed Time,* in a cast that included Teresa Wright, Matthew Porac, Bette Henritze, Nathan Lane, and Alice Haining. He also starred in the television film *Finding the Way Home,* as a temporary amnesiac; and in *Mittleman's Hardware,* as hardware store owner Max Mittelman, who finds a new life in a Hispanic farm workers' community, produced by James Garner and co-starring Hector Elizondo. Scott also hosted and narrated "Brute Force," an Arts & Entertainment series on the development of modern arms. Forthcoming was the film version of Sam Shepard's play *Curse of the Starving Class,* with Olympia Dukakis.

Virginia-born Scott suddenly emerged as a star with his 1957 *Richard III* at the New York Shakespeare Festival. He went on to appear in Shakespeare, Chekhov, O'Neill, Coward, and several contemporary works as well, very notably as Willy Loman in the 1975 Broadway revival of *Death of a Salesman,* and a year later in *Sly Fox;* he directed both plays. He later appeared in *Present Laughter* (1982), which he also directed, and *The Boys of Autumn* (1988). He played strong supporting roles in such films as *The Hanging Tree* (1959) and *Dr. Strangelove* (1964), moving into leads with his Best Actor Oscar-winning role as *Patton* (1969; he refused the award as a matter of principle), and leads in such other films as *Jane Eyre* (1971), *The Hospital* (1971), *The Day of the Dolphin* (1973), *Movie, Movie* (1978), *Firestarter* (1984), *Exorcist III: Legion* (1990), and *Descending Angel* (1990). He has also appeared in many telefilms, and in the series "East Side, West Side" (1963–64) and "Mr. President" (1989). Scott attended the University of Missouri. He has been married four times, twice to Colleen Dewhurst, and from 1972 to Trish Van Devere. He has six children, one of them actor Campbell Scott.

FURTHER READING

"This time. . . ." BILL DAVIDSON. *TV Guide,* Sep. 6, 1986.
"George C. Scott. . . ." JEFF DEROME. *American West,* Nov.–Dec. 1985.

Scowcroft, Brent (1925–) Lieutenant General Scowcroft, the U.S. National Security Advisor, played a major role in developing worldwide Bush administration foreign policy and military strategy and tactics. During 1991, much of his focus was on what became the collapse of the Soviet Union, the Persian Gulf War, and the emergence of a new set of power relations throughout the world, resulting in the end of many regional conflicts and moves toward the resolution of many others. He is also a key behind-the-scenes troubleshooter. It was Scowcroft, for example, who went to China secretly in July 1989 and openly in December 1989 to re-establish working relations with a Chinese government that had not long before shocked the world with its Tienanmen Square student massacres. Similarly, he played a substantial role in Mideast affairs after the Gulf War, as when he flew unannounced to Saudi Arabia in early April to meet with King Fahd.

Scowcroft is an old "Washington hand," a career military officer and strategic planner who was President Ford's national security assistant, was out of power during the Carter and Reagan administrations, and came back to the White House with President Bush. Scowcroft graduated from West Point in 1947 and went to Washington as an Air Force strategic planner in the mid-1960s after teaching at West Point and at the Air Force Academy, as well as serving in Belgrade as an Air Force attache. He was a White House-based military assistant to President Nixon (1971–72), was deputy national security assistant (1973–75), and became President Ford's national security assistant (1975–77). During the Carter and Reagan administrations, he served on several advisory committees, most notably as a member of the Tower Commission, joining its adverse report on Reagan administration behavior during the Iran-Contra affair. Utah-born Scowcroft was a West Point graduate in 1947; his M.A. and Ph.D were from Columbia (1953, 1967). He married Marian Horner in 1951; the couple have one child.

FURTHER READING

"Brent Scowcroft. . . ." PRISCILLA PAINTON. *Time,* Oct. 7, 1991.
"We won't let. . . ." KENNETH T. WALSH. *U.S. News & World Report,* Dec. 24, 1990.
"Even Saddam. . . ." DOUGLAS HARBRECHT. *Business Week,* Sep. 10, 1990.
"Distrust, but verify. . . ." FRED BARNES. *New Republic,* Mar. 6, 1989.

Seles, Monica (1974–) Puzzled tennis fans looked on as Monica Seles passed up a chance to win a Grand Slam in 1991 and instead embroiled herself in a public relations nightmare. She won the Australian, French, and U.S. Opens with her remarkable power; compiled a 74–6 won-lost record for the year; and earned over $2,450,000, breaking a one-year earnings record set in 1984 by Martina Navratilova. In the process, she wrested the number one world tennis ranking from Steffi Graf, who had held it for a record-breaking 186 weeks; Seles lost it again briefly in August after her loss to 15-year-old Jennifer Capriati in the Mazda Classic, but by year's end she was back in the top spot. The hard-hitting Seles reached the finals of all 16 tournaments she entered in 1991, winning 10 of them. In December, she was named player of the year by the International Tennis Federation, at 17 the youngest woman to be named world champion.

The trouble was two key "no-shows." After winning the Australian and French Opens, Seles abruptly dropped out of Wimbledon in June, at first not disclosing the reason or even her whereabouts, then giving the cause as a "minor accident." (She had been troubled by shin splints earlier in the year.) For her late and insufficiently explained and documented withdrawal she was fined $6,000 by the Women's Tennis Association—and received a great deal of negative publicity, for she had been the youngest player to be top-seeded at Wimbledon and the first top seed ever to withdraw from competition. Then in July, she failed to appear at the Federation Cup competition, at Nottingham, England, which she had been informed was a necessary qualifying step for the Olympics, appearing instead at a lucrative but unauthorized exhibition match at Mahwah, New Jersey, where she was defeated by Jennifer Capriati—and was then fined $20,000 more and banned from the 1992 Olympics by the International Tennis Federation. She had previously feuded with the Yugoslav national federation, for whom she would have played at Nottingham, unhappy about the way she and her family were treated before they left Yugoslavia.

A leading amateur tennis player in her native Yugoslavia and throughout Europe, Seles came to America with her family at age 11 to train at the Bradenton Tennis Academy in Florida under Nick Bollettieri; she was also coached by her father, cartoonist and documentary filmmaker

Xarolj. Seles turned professional in 1989 and emerged in 1990 as a dominating presence on the women's tennis scene, winning the Italian and German Opens, and defeating then number one player Steffi Graf at the French Open, becoming the youngest player since 1887 to win a Grand Slam event.

FURTHER READING

"Mystery woman or material girl?" PETER BODO. *Tennis,* Nov. 1991.
"Madonna is the model." PETER NEWCOMB. *Forbes,* Aug. 19, 1991.
"Monica Seles. . . ." PETER BODO. *Tennis,* Jan. 1991.
"Grunts, giggles. . . ." JIM MARTZ. *Sporting News,* Aug. 27, 1990.
"Hitting out in all directions." CINDY SHMERLER. *World Tennis,* Aug. 1990.
"Yiii! Can this be. . . ." SUSAN REED. *People,* July 2, 1990.

Selleck, Tom (1945–) Television and film star Selleck, previously noted for action films and comedy, became the center of a highly controversial situation in 1991. He had contracted with Universal Pictures to play the leading role in *Tokyo Diamond,* later renamed *Mr. Baseball,* before Universal's parent company, MCA, was bought by Matsushita Electric, a giant Japanese industrial company. The film was to be a comedy about an aging, sloppy American baseball player nearing the end of his career who signs to play in Japan and encounters an alien baseball culture, which includes anti-foreign bias and an emphasis on warlike spirit, group over individual dominance, and brutal workout practices. During 1991, after the Matsushita takeover, the still-forthcoming film's director was replaced and the script was greatly reworked, to show the Selleck character making great personal changes to conform to the "superior" Japanese ways, while such questions as Japanese anti-foreign and specifically anti-American bias were greatly soft-pedaled; anti-Black bias in Japanese baseball was reportedly not even taken up. All the parties concerned denied any undue influence on the filmmakers by Matsushita and also denied any trace of self-censorship. Selleck is also starring in the forthcoming Ted Kotcheff film *Folks.* Selleck also was one of the hosts of the notable television environmental-issues documentary *A User's Guide to Planet Earth,* which aired in April on ABC; other stars who appeared included Roseanne Barr, Jeff Bridges, and Richard Chamberlain. On the personal side, Selleck won an apology and the financial settlement of his $20 million libel suit against the tabloid *The Globe,* which carried a July 2 article seeming to imply that he was gay.

Detroit-born Selleck appeared on stage and screen during the 1970s, and emerged as a major star in the title role of "Magnum P.I." (1980–88). His films include *High Road to China* (1983), *Lassiter* (1984), *Runaway* (1985), *Three Men and a Baby* (1987), *Her Alibi* (1989), *Three Men and a Little Lady* (1990), and *Quigley Down Under* (1990). Selleck attended the University of Southern California. He has been married twice, last to actress Jillie Mack in 1987, and has two children.

FURTHER READING

"Three men and. . . ." JEFF ROVIN. *Ladies Home Journal,* Dec. 1990.
"Magnum, P(retty) I(ndecisive)." PAT JORDAN. *GQ—Gentlemen's Quarterly,* Oct. 1989.
"Tom Selleck." MERRILL SHINDLER. Los Angeles Magazine, Feb. 1989.
Tom Selleck: An Unauthorized Biography. JASON BONDEROFF. NAL-Dutton, 1983.

Serkin, Rudolf (1903–91) A child prodigy in his native Austria, Serkin made his debut as a pianist with the Vienna Symphony at 12. Five years later, he met the celebrated German violinist Ernst Busch; Serkin and Busch made a historic alliance, playing together throughout Europe and in the Busch Chamber Players; Serkin also appeared as a soloist. In 1927, Serkin and Busch left Germany for Switzerland, and after the rise of Hitler left Germany permanently, becoming Swiss citizens; in Switzerland, Serkin and Busch's daughter Irene married. Busch and Serkin appeared together in the United States in 1933; in 1936, Serkin made his solo debut with Arturo Toscanini's New York Philharmonic and quickly became a major figure in the United States. He moved to the United States in 1939, beginning his long affiliation with Philadelphia's Curtis Institute of Music (1939–75); he later directed the Institute (1968–1975). In 1948 Busch and Serkin founded the Marlboro Festival, and after Busch's death in

1950 Serkin became festival director. Serkin was for six decades one of the world's leading pianists and an especially notable interpreter of such central figures as Beethoven, Schubert, Brahms, Mozart, and Schumann. He was survived by his wife, Irene, four daughters, and two sons, one of whom is the pianist Peter Serkin. (d. Marlboro, Vermont; May 8, 1991)

FURTHER READING

Obituary. *Current Biography,* July 1991.
Obituary. *The Times* (of London), May 11, 1991.
Obituary. *New York Times,* May 10, 1991.
"Serkin, Rudolf." *Current Biography,* June 1990.
"The maestro's still a student. . . ." JOSEPH RODDY. *Yankee,* Aug. 1985.

Seurat, Michel: See **Lebanon Hostages**

Seuss, Dr. (Theodor Seuss Geisel, 1904–91) Massachusetts-born Geisel, an extraordinarily gifted author, artist, and filmmaker, was as Dr. Seuss the treasured companion of three generations of the world's children. An English major at Dartmouth in the mid-1920s, he was a cartoonist and editor of the campus humor magazine and later studied literature at Lincoln College of Oxford University, there meeting Helen Marion Palmer, who later became a children's author, and his collaborator and first wife. He was an illustrator and editorial cartoonist in the late 1920s and during the 1930s, and began his long career as Dr. Seuss in 1937 with *And to Think That I Saw It on Mulberry Street,* the first of many of the most popular children's books ever published; an estimated 200 million of his books were ultimately to circulate in many languages throughout the world. His books include such classics as *Horton Hatches the Egg* (1940), *Horton Hears a Who!* (1954), *How the Grinch Stole Christmas* (1957), *The Cat in the Hat* (1957), *Yertle the Turtle* (1958), *Green Eggs and Ham* (1960), *The Lorax* (1971), and *The Butter Battle Book* (1984). He also created such animated cartoons as the Oscar-winning *Gerald McBoing Boing* (1950), and several "Grinch" and "Cat in the Hat" cartoons. On a far more serious note, he created two Oscar-winning documentaries: *Hitler Lives* (1946; with Don Siegel) and *Design for Death* (1947; with Helen Palmer Geisel). He continued to write as long as he lived; in 1990, he wrote a book designed for children, that became a best-seller for people of all ages: *Oh, the Places You'll Go!* and wrote the script and 12 songs for a forthcoming feature film based on the book. He is survived by his wife, the former Audrey Stone Diamond. (d. La Jolla, California; September 24, 1991)

FURTHER READING

Obituary. *School Library Journal,* Nov. 1991.
"Dr. Seuss remembered." GERALD HARRISON et al. *Publishers Weekly,* Oct 25, 1991.
"The doctor beloved by all. . . ." STEFAN KANFER. *Time,* Oct. 7, 1991.
"Oh, the places he'll go!" JERRY ADLER. *Newsweek,* Oct. 7, 1991.
"Even the grinch must be blue." *People,* Oct. 7, 1991.
"Green eggs and me." PETER W. BERNSTEIN. *U.S. News & World Report,* Oct. 7, 1991.
Obituary. *Variety,* Sep. 30, 1991.
Obituary. *The Times* (of London), Sep. 27, 1991.
Obituary. *New York Times,* Sep. 26, 1991.
"Dr. Seuss." *Life,* July 1989.
Dr. Seuss (Theodore Seuss Geisel). RUTH K. MACDONALD. G. K. Hall; Macmillan, 1988.
Dr. Seuss from Then to Now. SAN DIEGO MUSEUM OF ART STAFF, ed. Random House, 1987.
Dr. Seuss: We Love You. PATRICIA S. MARTIN. Rourke, 1987.

Shamir, Yitzhak (Yitzhak Yzernitsky, 1915–) Israeli Prime Minister Shamir received an enormous political gift in 1990 and 1991, as the Palestine Liberation Organization (PLO) applauded Saddam Hussein's invasion of Kuwait and then supported the Iraqi side in the Persian Gulf War. Yasir Arafat and the PLO came out of the war greatly discredited and in much weakened condition, rejected by most of their former Arab allies and with Saudi, Kuwaiti, and other oil-rich Gulf state contributions cut off. In the aftermath of the war, the PLO was also driven out of its key Lebanese base at Sidon, losing most of its heavy weapons, as Syrian-backed Lebanese troops attacked and disarmed PLO forces. On the other hand, in 1991 as in previous years, the right-wing Shamir government dissipated much of its advantage by continuing to encourage Israeli settlement on formerly Arab Palestinian lands in the Occupied Territories, strongly resisting world criticism. In September, the Israelis went so far as to attack the Bush administration's withholding of $10 billion in U.S. loan guarantees by bringing pressure to bear inside the U.S. Congress, receiving instead only intense administration displeasure and further damaging U.S.-Israeli relations. In late October, after considerable hesitation and delay, Shamir led the Israeli delegation into the Madrid Middle East peace conference and later agreed to the continuance of the talks in Washington, but at year's end the talks had bogged down over procedural issues, raising serious questions as to the commitment of several of the parties, including Israel, to the Middle East peace process.

Shamir became a Zionist in his native Poland and emigrated to Israel in 1935. In 1937, he became a member of the terrorist Irgun Zvai Leumi, and in 1940 he left the Irgun with Abraham Stern to become a founder of the terrorist Lehi, better known as the Stern Gang. In 1942, he became chief of operations of the Stern Gang, which was responsible for a great many terrorist operations, most notably the assassinations of Lord Moyne in 1944 and of UN mediator Folke Bernadotte in 1948. He was a member of Israeli intelligence (1955–65). Shamir moved into politics with the Herut Party in 1970, was elected to the Israeli parliament in 1973, was foreign minister in the Menachim Begin government (1980–83), and succeeded Begin as prime minister in 1983. He was foreign minister (1984–86), and again became prime minister in 1986. Shamir attended Warsaw University and the Hebrew University of Jerusalem. He is married and has two children.

FURTHER READING

"When Shamir blinked. . . ." Eliahu Salpeter. *New Leader,* Aug. 12, 1991.
"Who's sitting pretty. . . ." *Business Week,* Mar. 11, 1991.
"The view from Jerusalem." *U.S. News & World Report,* Apr. 16, 1990.
"A talk with. . . ." J. Robert Moskin. *Present Tense,* May–June 1989.
"A talk with Dr. No." Jacques Amalric and Alain Frachon. *World Press Review,* Apr. 1989.
"Saying no to Arafat. . . ." Scott Macleod. *Time,* Jan. 2, 1989.
"Shamir stands his ground. . . ." *Newsweek,* Jan. 2, 1989.

Sharon, Ariel (1928–) Israeli Housing Minister Sharon pushed hard for an acceleration of Israeli settlement on occupied Arab lands during 1991 and spoke out against any peace agreements that might include land-for-peace arrangements. He continued to be a highly controversial figure, opening settlement after settlement on occupied lands to mounting international criticism, some of the sharpest criticism coming from U.S. Secretary of State James F. Baker and other Bush administration figures. Sharon-U.S. relations hit a new low in May 1991 when State Department objections forced U.S. Secretary of Housing and Urban Development Jack Kemp to cancel his plans to greet Sharon officially in Washington; instead, the two men met unofficially at the Israeli Embassy. Sharon was the only member of the Israeli cabinet to vote against participating in Middle East peace talks, further staking out his position as Shamir's chief conservative opponent in Israeli political life. On October 10, Sharon announced that he would run against Shamir in the 1992 elections.

A career military officer, Sharon was active in the main Israeli fighting force, the Haganah, from the mid-1940s, and fought in the 1948 Israeli War of Independence and accompanying First Arab-Israeli War. He conducted anti-guerilla actions in the low-level border war that followed and rose to divisional command during the 1967 and 1972 Arab-Israeli wars. He went into politics in 1973 and held several cabinet-level posts during the 1970s. He was appointed defense minister by Menachem Begin in 1981 and was a chief architect of the 1982 Lebanon invasion, being forced to resign that post after the Sabra and Shatilla massacres, though remaining in the cabinet through the 1980s. In 1986 he was involved in a notable libel suit with *Time* magazine. In 1990, he published *Warrior: An Autobiography*. Sharon attended Hebrew University. He is married and has two children.

FURTHER READING

"A place to call home." DANIELLE PLETKA. *Insight,* Oct. 28,1991.

"Destroy Iraq's military. . . ." NATHAN GARDELS. *New Perspectives,* Winter 1991.

"Never! Never! Never!" MURRAY J. GART. *Time,* Apr. 17, 1989.

Blood Libel: The Inside Story of General Ariel Sharon's History-Making Suit Against Time Magazine. URI DAN. Simon & Schuster, 1987.

Reckless Disregard: Westmoreland v. CBS et al; Sharon v. Time. RENATA ADLER. Knopf, 1986.

Shawcross, Arthur (1946—) Serial murderer Shawcross was called the Genesee River Killer. On December 13, 1990, after a three-month trial that generated massive national media coverage, Shawcross was convicted by a Rochester, New York, jury on ten counts of second-degree murder, for killing ten Rochester-area women between March 1988 and January 1990. After hearing conflicting psychiatric testimony, the jury had rejected his insanity defense. On February 1, 1991, Judge Donald Wisner sentenced Shawcross to life imprisonment without the possibility of parole; his maximum sentences of 25 years to life for each of the murders added up to a minimum of 250 years in prison. Shawcross reportedly confessed to an 11th killing and may be again brought to trial.

At the time of the killings, Shawcross was on parole; he had previously strangled two children in Watertown, New York, in 1972, been convicted of the crimes, and been released in June 1987 after serving 15 years of his term. He was arrested in January 1990 after police spotted him near the frozen body of one of his victims. A food-service worker, Shawcross had been abused as a child and was a Vietnam veteran, experiences he cited unsuccessfully in his insanity defense.

FURTHER READING

Arthur Shawcross: The Genesee River Killer. JOEL NORRIS. Windsor (NY), 1992.

Sheen, Martin (Ramon Estevez, 1940—) On December 10, 1991, Sheen opened in the first production of the new National Actors Theatre, at Broadway's Belasco Theatre, playing John

Proctor opposite Maryann Plunkett as Elizabeth Proctor in a revival of Arthur Miller's *The Crucible.* Sheen's portrayal won mixed responses from the reviewers, though Plunkett won rave reviews and the play was a hit. On screen, Sheen starred opposite Jacqueline Bisset in the Ian Toynton film *The Maid,* made in France. Sheen also directed his first film, the Vietnam War-based *Cadence,* starring in the film with his sons Charlie Sheen and Ramon Estevez. Sheen also starred in the television true-life drama *Guilty Until Proven Innocent,* as the father of a young New York State man falsely convicted of murder and freed seven years later, who ultimately won almost $2 million in damages from the state in a landmark case. Forthcoming was a starring role in the film *Limited Time.*

Ohio-born Sheen played on stage with the Living Theater from 1959, on Broadway in *The Subject Was Roses* (1964; and in the 1968 film version) and at the New York Shakespeare Festival in the late 1960s. On screen, he appeared in such films as *Catch-22* (1970), *Apocalypse Now* (1979), *Gandhi* (1982), and *Wall Street* (1987), and such telefilms as *The Execution of Private Slovik* (1974), *The Missiles of October* (1974) as Robert Kennedy, *Blind Ambition* (1979) as John Dean, *Kennedy* (1982) as John F. Kennedy, and *Samaritan: The Mitch Snyder Story* (1986), as AIDS activist Snyder. He married Janet Sheen in 1961; they have four children, two of them the actors Charlie Sheen and Emilio Estevez.

FURTHER READING

Martin Sheen: Actor and Activist. PATRICIA MCKISSACK. Childrens, 1991.

Shevardnadze, Eduard (Eduard Amvroslyevich Shevardnadze, 1928–) Long a trusted aide of Soviet president Mikhail Gorbachev, former foreign minister Shevardnadze greatly changed his stance on December 20, 1990, breaking with Gorbachev and resigning his position because of the too-slow pace of reform and Gorbachev's appointment of hard-line conservative communists to key positions. On resigning, Shevardnadze warned very strongly of the possibility of an attempt to restore a right-wing dictatorship, raising the prospect of a disastrous Soviet civil war should that happen. On February 20, 1991, Shevardnadze emerged as the leader of a new organization, the Soviet Foreign Policy Association, and once again repeated his warnings. On July 1, he moved back into active political life as a founder of the Democratic Reform Movement, which was not fully a political party on formation but was clearly oriented in that direction. Hard-line communists then began an investigation of his loyalty to the Communist Party; Shevardnadze responded on July 3 by resigning from the party.

The August 19 coup fully justified Shevardnadze's warnings. When it came, he spoke out quickly, and joined the Russian resistance at the White House, with Boris Yeltsin speaking to an estimated 150,000–200,000 people on August 20. In the aftermath of the coup, he remained an independent force and did not rejoin Gorbachev and the central government. Only in December, as the Soviet Union began to fragment, did he once again become Soviet foreign minister. During 1991, he published *The Future Belongs to Freedom: World Peace and Democracy in the U.S.S.R.*.

Until his spectacular resignation Shevardnadze had spent his whole life in the Communist Party and Soviet government work, starting in the late 1940s and rising through a series of Communist Party positions in his native Georgia through the early 1970s. His first major move came in 1972, when he led an anticorruption campaign in Georgia and replaced the Republic's party leader. He was first secretary of the Georgian communist party (1972–85), becoming a Soviet Central Committee member in 1976. Long associated with Mikhail Gorbachev, Shevardnadze replaced Andrei Gromyko as Soviet foreign minister in 1985 and remained so throughout the extraordinary Gorbachev era. He attended the Kutaisi Pedagogical Institute.

FURTHER READING

"Mikhail Gorbachev has. . . ." *U.S. News & World Report,* Sep. 2, 1991.
"A growing momentum. . . ." PIERRE BOCEV. *World Press Review,* Sep. 1991.
"Shevardnadze. . . ." *Fortune,* May 20, 1991.
"Shevardnadze. . . ." *Time,* May 13, 1991.
"The alternative is dictatorship." *Time,* Apr. 16, 1990.
"Falcon of the Kremlin." E. KAYE FULTON. *Maclean's,* Feb. 26, 1990.

Siegel, Don (Donald Siegel, 1912–91) Film director and producer Siegel was born in Chicago but educated in Britain, and studied acting at the Royal Academy of Dramatic Art. He began his film career in 1933 as a film librarian at Warners, moved into editing and montage, directed several short films in the early 1940s, and won two Academy Awards in 1945 for the shorts *Star in the Night* and *Hitler Lives,* the latter made with Theodore Geisel (Dr. Seuss). His first feature film was *The Verdict* (1946); he went on to direct many other low-budget films in the next quarter-century, most of them such crime or science fiction films as *Riot in Cell Block 11* (1954) and *Invasion of the Body Snatchers* (1956). His work was far more highly regarded in Europe than in Hollywood; in France, he was seen as an American version of the New Wave directors of the 1950s and early 1960s, and was studied accordingly. His later work included several major action films, including *Coogan's Bluff* (1968), *Dirty Harry* (1971), and *The Shootist* (1976). Siegel was married three times and is survived by his wife, Carol, two daughters, and three sons. (d. Nipoma, California; April 20, 1991)

FURTHER READING

Obituary. *The Times* (of London), Apr. 29, 1991.
Obituary. *Variety,* Apr. 29, 1991.
Obituary. *New York Times,* Apr. 24, 1991.

Siegmeister, Elie (1909–91) A leading U.S. composer, born in New York City, Siegmeister studied with Nadia Boulanger in Paris from 1927 to 1931, returning home to the America of the Great Depression. He worked in classical forms and often in American folk themes, during the 1930s focusing on the collection of folk and popular music; in 1939, he founded the American Ballad Singers, and in 1941 he and Olin Downes published *A Treasury of American Song*. Siegmeister's major work was in classical music. His wide range of works included six symphonies (1947–83); such operas as *Darling Corie* (1952), *Miranda and the Dark Young Man* (1955), *The Mermaid in Lock No. 7* (1958), *The Plough and the Stars* (1969), *Night of the Moonspell* (1976), and *The Lady of the Lake* (1985); a considerable body of songs and other choral music; and several string quartets. He also published a number of books. Siegmeister was a music professor and composer in residence at Hofstra University from 1966 to 1976. Deeply committed to a series of social causes throughout his life, Siegmeister was blacklisted in the 1950s, during the McCarthy period. He was survived by his wife, Hannah, and two daughters. (d. Manhasset, New York; March 10, 1991)

FURTHER READING

Obituary. *Opera News,* July 1991.
Obituary. *Variety,* Apr. 15, 1991.
Obituary. *New York Times,* Mar. 11, 1991.

Sihanouk, Norodom (1922–) On October 23, 1991, Prince Norodom Sihanouk once again emerged as the Cambodian head of government, becoming president of the new Cambodian Supreme National Council by the terms of the treaty of Paris, sponsored by the United States, the Soviet Union, and China, under United Nations auspices. The treaty, which ended—at least for a time—the long Cambodian Civil War, provided for an immediate cease-fire, the return home of an estimated 350,000 refugees, and the posting of thousands of UN troops and civilian personnel to keep the peace, help set up a new government, and prepare for free elections to be held in 1993. The treaty was the result of many years of negotiations among the three main Cambodian guerrilla factions, and between Cambodia and Vietnam as well. It was a great triumph for Sihanouk, who since 1941, in and out of power, has been his country's leading politician on the world stage and has again and again returned for yet another attempt to create an independent and democratic Cambodia.

Although the treaty was hailed as a step forward, there was worldwide concern about Khmer Rouge participation in the new government: The Khmer Rouge and its leader, Pol Pot, in its years of power (1975–78) had been directly responsible for the Cambodian Holocaust, in which an estimated 1–3 million Cambodians died. Pol Pot had officially stepped down as Khmer Rouge leader in 1985, but was widely thought still to be the undisputed leader of the movement.

Sihanouk returned to Cambodia on November 14 and immediately dropped his neutralist role, sharply attacking the Khmer Rouge and its leader, Pol Pot, and calling for genocide trials of the Khmer Rouge leaders. He embraced Hun Sen, the leader of the Vietnamese-installed Cambodian government as his "son" and quickly moved to exclude the Khmer Rouge from the new Cambodian government. On November 20, Sihanouk was declared president of Cambodia. A week later, Khmer Rouge leaders arriving in Phnom Penh were stoned by angry crowds and forced to flee the city.

Prince Sihanouk was named King of Cambodia by the French colonial occupiers of his country in 1941 when he was 18 years old. He remained nominal ruler during Vichy French collaborationist rule during much of the Japanese World War II occupation. Late in the war, the Japanese openly took control of Cambodia; Sihanouk then declared Cambodian independence and led the national independence movement from then until Cambodian independence was won in 1953. He quit the throne in 1955, was prime minister of democratic Cambodia in the mid-1950s, and was the elected head of his country (1960–70). In 1970, his government was deposed by the Lon Nol military dictatorship, and Cambodia endured the civil war that ended with the 1975 victory of the Khmer Rouge. Sihanouk, under Khmer Rouge house arrest, then cooperated with the murderous new government and its Chinese allies, going into Chinese exile. He remained in exile through the balance of the Cambodian Holocaust and the 1979 Vietnamese invasion. In 1982, he became head of a new coalition government in exile (1987–88), resigning after Khmer Rouge attacks on other Cambodian guerilla groups. He returned to coalition leadership in 1988 and in 1989 started the long process of negotiation that led to the Vietnamese troop withdrawals beginning in 1989. The off-and-on negotiations continued during 1990 and 1991, leading to the 1991 peace treaty.

Sihanouk is married and has 14 children. In 1980 he published *War and Hope: The Case for Cambodia.*

FURTHER READING

"The man who would be king again." *Economist,* Sep. 29, 1990.

"The prince presses on." *Time,* Dec. 11, 1989.

"Sihanouk on the high wire . . . ." ADAM PLATT. *Newsweek,* May 15, 1989.

"An exiled leader. . . ." *Insight,* Jan. 20, 1989.

Prince Sihanouk. MADHARI KUCKREJA. Chelsea House, 1989.

"Bonnie Prince Norodom." *Economist,* Nov. 5, 1988.

"Now you see him. . . ." *Time,* July 25, 1988.

"Sihanouk's political circus. . . ." RUTH MARSHALL. *Newsweek,* Feb. 15, 1988.

Simon, Neil (Marvin Neil Simon, 1927–) The very popular playwright Neil Simon won his first Pulitzer Prize in 1991 for his hit play *Lost in Yonkers* (1990). There were several Tony awards as well: It was best play, Mercedes Ruehl was best actress in a drama, Kevin Spacey was best featured actor, and Irene Worth was best featured actress. Simon also decided to try again, after having suffered a different kind of "first." His play *Jake's Women* was the first of his 24 plays to close on the road, before reaching Broadway, after its engagement at San Diego's Old Globe Theater. During 1991, he rewrote the play, which was scheduled for a March 1992 Broadway opening, with Alan Alda starring. On screen, his script for *The Marrying Man,* starring Kim Basinger and Alec Baldwin, was far from enough to save the film, which opened in April to very poor reviews and by year's end survived only in home video.

New York City-born Simon worked as a radio and television comedy writer in the 1950s, most notably for Phil Silvers and Sid Caesar, and began his long career as a leading playwright with *Come Blow Your Horn* (1961). That was followed by almost a score of other plays, including such hits as *Barefoot in the Park* (1963; and the 1967 film adaptation), *The Odd Couple* (1965 and the 1968 film), *The Star-Spangled Girl* (1966), *Plaza Suite* (1968; and the 1971 film), *Last of the Red Hot Lovers* (1969), *The Prisoner of Second Avenue* (1971; and the 1975 film), *The Sunshine Boys* (1972; and the 1975 film), and *California Suite* (1976; and the 1978 film). Much of Simon's work is to some extent autobiographical, and five plays are directly so: *Chapter Two* (1977; and the 1979 film), *I Ought to Be in Pictures* (1980; and the 1982 film), *Brighton Beach Memoirs* (1983; and the 1986 film), the Tony-winning *Biloxi Blues* (1985; and the 1988 film), and *Broadway Bound* (1986). He has also written the books for several musicals, including *Little Me* (1962), *Sweet Charity* (1966), and *Promises, Promises* (1968); and has written several filmscripts, most notably *The Goodbye Girl*

(1977), which starred his second wife, Marsha Mason. Simon attended New York University. He has been married three times and has two children.

FURTHER READING

"King of comedy's serious work." HAP EPSTEIN. *Insight,* Mar. 18, 1991.
"The last of the. . . ." DAVID RICHARDS. *New York Times Magazine,* Feb. 17, 1991.
"Simon, Marvin Neil." *Current Biography,* Mar. 1989.
Neil Simon. ROBERT K. JOHNSON. G. K. Hall, 1983.

Simon, Paul (1941–) Throughout 1991, singer and songwriter Paul Simon built on the worldwide success of his October 1990 album *The Rhythm of the Saints,* taking its songs and Brazilian beat to live audiences numbered in the millions. On January 4, in Tacoma, Washington, he began what amounted to a triumphal year-long concert tour, titled "Born at the Right Time," with a 17-member band and ensemble that included musicians from Africa, Brazil, and the United States. Some of the tour's most-performed songs were "Bridge over Troubled Water," "Cecilia," "The Boxer," "Mother and Child Reunion," "Graceland," and "Hearts and Bones." Simon played Madison Square Garden in March and in Britain in May. In August, the group gave a free concert in New York City's Central Park before an audience of 750,000; Simon later issued a record and videocassette of the event. In January 1992, he took "Born at the Right Time" on a three-nation African tour, in South Africa marking the end of a 10-year artists' boycott recently lifted by Nelson Mandela's African National Congress. He was backed by three Black South Africans: guitarist Ray Phiri, saxophonist Barney Rachabane, and pianist Tony Cedras, as well as the a cappella group Ladysmith Black Mambazo. Although some radical Black South Africans opposed the tour, Mandela and other Black African leaders welcomed it, as did masses of South Africans of all races. On a quite different note, Simon wrote his first children's book in 1991: It was *At the Zoo,* with illustrations by Valérie Michaut, after his hit song of that title. The book was published by Doubleday on August 15, 1991, the day of his Central Park concert.

Newark-born Simon and Art Garfunkel were one of the leading folk-rock groups of the 1960s, beginning with their album *Wednesday Morning 3 A.M.* (1965), with Simon's hit song "Sounds of Silence," and ending with the extraordinarily popular Grammy-winning album *Bridge over Troubled Water* (1970), its title song still a worldwide favorite. Their work together included the albums *Parsley, Sage, Rosemary and Thyme* (1967), *Bookends* (1968), and the score of the film *The Graduate* (1968), with its Grammy-winning song "Mrs. Robinson." After 1971, Simon went on alone, creating such albums as *Paul Simon* (1972), *Still Crazy After All These Years* (1975), *Hearts and Bones* (1983), the Grammy-winning *Graceland* (1986), and *The Rhythm of the Saints* (1990). He also wrote, scored, and starred in the film *One Trick Pony* (1980). Simon attended Queens College. He has been married twice, last to actress and writer Carrie Fisher.

FURTHER READING

"Profile. . ." JESSE NASH and GEORGE FLOWERS. *Guitar Player,* Feb. 1991.
"In praise of midlife crisis. . . ." DAVID GATES. *Newsweek,* Jan. 14, 1991.
"Songs of a thinking man. . . ." JAY COCKS. *Time,* Nov. 12, 1990.
"Flying down to Rio. . . ." BRIAN D. JOHNSON. *Maclean's,* Nov. 12, 1990.
Paul Simon: Still Crazy After All These Years. PATRICK HUMPHRIES. Doubleday, 1989.
Written in My Soul: Rock's Great Songwriters. . . . Talk About Creating Their Music. BILL FLANAGAN. Contemporary, 1986.

Sinatra, Frank (Francis Albert Sinatra, 1915–) In his 76th year, the ever-popular Sinatra embarked on a world tour, everywhere playing to sold-out houses. He even sang at Pompeii, in Italy, with the local tourist board providing security to allay the fears of nervous archeologists, who feared that the crowds of Sinatra fans might damage the precious site. In 1991 Sinatra also made his first recording in seven years, singing "Silent Night" as his contribution to a Christmas song album issued by the Children's Hospital Foundation to benefit children's hospitals around the country. The year also saw re-release of an album containing 16 Cole Porter songs he had recorded from 1953

to 1960. Still winning awards, Sinatra was in 1991 elected Friars Club entertainer of the year for the eighth straight time. He was also re-elected executive director of the club.

Sinatra began his singing career in cabaret in 1935. He became a popular singer and recording artist in 1940, while appearing with Tommy Dorsey's band. In January 1943, at a four-week engagement at New York's Paramount Theatre, he became the first of the modern teenage idols, whose fans "swooned" and rioted over him. He also became a radio and film star, in "Your Hit Parade," and in such musicals as *Anchors Aweigh* (1945) and *On the Town* (1949), and won a special Oscar for his role in *The House I Live In* (1945), a plea for tolerance. But he ran into serious throat problems in 1952, and his career all but vanished. He then made an extraordinary comeback as a dramatic actor, winning a Best Supporting Actor Oscar as Maggio in *From Here to Eternity* (1953), and then went on to such films as *Guys and Dolls* (1955), *The Joker Is Wild* (1957), *The Manchurian Candidate* (1962), and *The Detective* (1968). His vocal problems eased as well; he re-emerged as one of the leading song stylists of his time, continuing to tour in concert into his mid-70s. He celebrated his 75th birthday in performance on television in December 1990 before a nationwide audience, and began his yearlong world tour in the same month. He has also written a book about his other vocation: *A Man and His Art* (1990), in 1991 retitled *Paintings: A Man and His Art*. Sinatra has been married four times and has three children, including singers Nancy Sinatra and Frank Sinatra, Jr. His second and third wives were the actresses Ava Gardner and Mia Farrow.

FURTHER READING

Frank Sinatra. JESSICA HODGE. Outlet, 1992.
"Frank Sinatra. . . ." WALTER THOMAS. *Interview,* July 1991.
"Sinatra 101." CHRISTIAN LOGAN WRIGHT. *Mademoiselle,* Apr. 1991.
Frank Sinatra: A Complete Recording History of Techniques, Songs, Composers, Lyricists, Arrangers, Sessions and First-Issue Albums, 1939–1984. RICHARD W. ACKELSON. McFarland, 1991.
"Still good and saucy. . . ." CHARLES LEERHSEN. *Newsweek,* Dec. 17, 1990.
"Under my skin." WILLIAM KENNEDY. *New York Times Magazine,* Oct. 7, 1990.
His Way: The Unauthorized Biography of Frank Sinatra. Kitty Kelley. Bantam, 1987.
Sinatra: The Man and the Myth (An Unauthorized Biography). B. ADLER. NAL-Dutton, 1987.
Frank Sinatra, My Father. NANCY SINATRA. Pocket Books, 1986.
Frank Sinatra, Ol' Blue Eyes. ASSOCIATED PRESS STAFF and NORM GOLDSTEIN. Holt, 1982.

Singer, Isaac Bashevis (1904–91) An emigrant to the United States from his native Poland in 1935, Singer began writing in Hebrew in Poland, there switched to Yiddish, and although he mastered English, continued to write in Yiddish for the rest of his career. Much of his early work focused on Jewish life in Poland; later he wrote of American locations and themes, often focusing on the immigrant experience.

Singer published his first novel *Satan in Goray* (1932) in installments in the Warsaw magazine *Globus* while he was an editor there. In 1935, he joined the staff of New York's *Jewish Daily Forward,* which published many of his short stories and serialized his novels before they appeared in book form. His novels include *The Family Moscat* (1950), *The Magician of Lublin* (1960), and *Old Love* (1979). He is most popular for such short story collections as *Gimpel the Fool* (1957), *The Spinoza of Market Street* (1961), *Zlatah the Goat* (1966), and *The Image* (1985). He also wrote many children's books and won a 1970 National Book Award for *A Day of Pleasure*. Singer won a Nobel Prize for literature in 1978. Among his autobiographical works are *A Young*

Man in Search of Love (1978), *Lost in America* (1981), *Love and Exile* (1984) and *A Day of Pleasure: Stories of a Boy Growing Up in Warsaw* (1986). He was twice married and was survived by his wife, Alma, and a son. (d. Miami; July 24, 1991)

FURTHER READING

"Our debt to I. B. Singer." JOSEPH EPSTEIN. *Commentary,* Nov. 1991.
Obituary. *Current Biography,* Sep. 1991.
"The man who. . . ." ISRAEL SHENKER. *New York Times Book Review,* Aug. 11, 1991.
"The century's storyteller. . . ." MALCOLM JONES, JR. *Newsweek,* Aug. 5, 1991.
"The last teller of tales. . . ." STEFAN KANFER. *U.S. News & World Report,* Aug. 5, 1991.
"Dream maker. . . ." CHARLES FENYVESI. *U.S. News & World Report,* Aug. 5, 1991.
Obituary. *Variety,* July 29, 1991.
Obituary. *The Times* (of London), July 26, 1991.
Obituary. *New York Times,* July 26, 1991.
Conversations with Isaac Bashevis Singer. ISAAC BASHEVIS SINGER and RICHARD BURGIN. Doubleday, 1985.
Bibliography of Isaac Bashevis Singer 1924–1949. DAVID N. MILLER. Peter Lang, 1984.
Isaac Bashevis Singer. EDWARD ALEXANDER. Macmillan, 1980.

Siskind, Aaron (1903–91) New York City-born Siskind became a documentary photographer in the 1930s, taking Depression-era pictures throughout New York City, especially in Harlem; much of his work of that period is expressed in his *Harlem Document.* But in the 1940s, his work changed dramatically; he became a leading abstractionist in art photography, seeking essentially the same kinds of results achieved by the abstract expressionist painters of the postwar period, later known as the New York School. Nor was the only parallel in the work; many of the leading abstract expressionists were also his friends and colleagues. What Siskind found for the next four decades were the abstract forms in everyday things. His work was widely exhibited throughout his later period and also collected in several books. Siskind taught high school English (1926–49), as well as photography. He later taught photography at the Illinois Institute of Technology School of Design and at the Rhode Island School of Design. He was survived by a daughter and two sisters. (d. Providence, Rhode Island; February 8, 1991)

FURTHER READING

Obituary. *The Times* (of London), Feb. 13, 1991.
Obituary. *New York Times,* Feb. 9, 1991.
"A great age. . . ." *Life,* Fall 1988.
Aaron Siskind: Pleasures and Terrors. CARL CHIARENZA. Bullfinch, 1982.

Sisulu, Walter Max Ulyate (1912–) and **Notsikelelo Albertina Sisulu** (1919–) At the July 2–7, 1991, African National Congress (ANC) Conference, and in his 51st year as a leader of the South African freedom movement, Walter Sisulu was elected deputy president of the ANC, succeeding Nelson Mandela, who moved up to the presidency. During 1991, Sisulu continued to be a strong force within the ANC for the development of a united freedom movement, rather than allowing the ANC-Inkatha civil war to lead to further fragmentation of the freedom movement. In this, he had considerable success, playing a major role in the October 27, 1991, establishment of a "patriotic united front" coalition of 90 freedom organizations, which for the first time featured an ANC–Pan-Africanist Congress alliance. In early October, Walter and Albertina Sisulu visited the United States for a series of meetings with allies and supporters. In Washington, they met with Secretary of State James Baker, House Speaker Thomas Foley, Washington Mayor Sharon Pratt Dixon, and Jesse Jackson.

Sisulu became a leader of the then-nonviolent African National Congress soon after joining it in 1940. He defied the developing system of apartheid during the 1940s and 1950s, was tried for treason in 1956, and was acquitted in 1961. He was sentenced to six years' imprisonment in 1963, jumped bail while his case was on appeal, was rearrested, and was then sentenced to life imprisonment. Walter Sisulu ended his 27-year imprisonment on October 15, 1989, as the new F. W. DeKlerk government took its first substantial steps toward peace and the end of apartheid in South Africa. He quickly returned to leadership of the ANC, from February 1990 leading the ANC group planning the move back to legal activity in South Africa.

Notsikelelo Albertina Sisulu became a leader

of the South African freedom movement in her own right. She was restricted and in some periods under house arrest from the early 1960s through the mid-1980s, was sentenced to four years in prison in 1984, but was freed on appeal. She has been Transvaal president of the United Democratic Front since 1983 and was president of the Federation of South African Women in 1984.

Walter Sisulu married Notsikelelo Albertina in 1944; the couple had five children.

FURTHER READING

The Struggle: A History of the African National Congress. HEIDI HOLLAND. Braziller, 1990.
"Sisulu freed. . . ." FRANK DEXTER BROWN. *Black Enterprise,* Jan. 1990.
"Ex-ANC leader talks. . . ." *Jet,* Nov. 6, 1989.
"Freedom at last. . . ." MARY NEMETH. *Maclean's,* Oct. 23, 1989.
"Free at last. . . ." *Economist,* Oct. 21, 1989.
"Sisulu. . . ." SCOTT MACLEOD. *Time,* Oct. 30, 1989.

Skinner, Samuel Knox (1938–) As Transportation Secretary, Samuel Skinner played a major role in the development of the Bush administration's five-year road-building plan introduced in mid-February 1991, which focused mainly on repair of existing roads. His main accomplishment during 1991 was the 1992 transportation appropriations bill, passed by both houses in October and signed by President Bush on October 28, 1991; it included increases of $500 million in mass transit funds and authorization for increases in Highway Trust Fund debt limits. There were few specific new programs proposed. As a practical matter, much of Skinner's focus during 1991 seemed to be on airline merger matters, with an easing of restrictions on foreign investment in U.S. airlines, extensive British-American negotiations over trans-Atlantic routes, and intra-airline negotiations involving TWA, Pan Am, United, American, and Delta. Skinner also played a major role in developing the March 1991 settlement of the *Exxon Valdez* claims, which was then upset by the courts; a second settlement was reached in September 1991. Skinner resigned as Transportation secretary on December 5, 1991, to become White House chief of staff, replacing John H. Sununu.

Chicago-born Skinner was an Illinois assistant U.S. attorney (1968–74). He has long been closely associated with former federal prosecutor and then Illinois governor James R. Thompson. He practiced law in Chicago (1978–84) and then moved into transportation, in 1984 becoming chairman of the regional transport authority. He became secretary of Transportation in 1989. Skinner's 1930 B.S. was from the University of Illinois, and his 1966 J.D. from DePaul University. He is married and has three children.

FURTHER READING

"Samuel Knox prepares for takeoff." ANN GRIMES. *Chicago,* Oct. 1991.
"On the move. . . ." ANNA MARIA and TONYA ARIAS. *Hispanic,* Aug. 1991.
"Skinner, Samuel Knox." *Current Biography,* Aug. 1989.

Smallwood, Joey (Joseph Roberts Smallwood, 1900–91) Newfoundland's "father of confederation," Smallwood began his career as a journalist, worked in Newfoundland and the United States, and then returned to Newfoundland as a labor organizer. A socialist, he became leader of Newfoundland's Liberal Party and in 1948 led the successful battle to take Newfoundland, including Labrador, into Canada, as the country's tenth province, ending four centuries as a British colony. Smallwood served for 22 years as the new province's first premier and was also minister of industrial development (1955–71). He was finally defeated by the Conservative opposition in 1971 and ultimately retired from politics after several unsuccessful reelection attempts. He then returned to writing, working on an encyclopedia of Newfoundland, which had been partly published at his death. He was survived by his wife, Clara, a daughter, and two sons. (d. St. Johns, Newfoundland; December 17, 1991)

FURTHER READING

"A titan passes." JOHN DE MONT. *Maclean's,* Dec. 30, 1991.
Obituary. *New York Times,* Dec. 11, 1991.
Obituary. *Variety,* Nov. 11, 1991.
Obituary. *The Times* (of London), Nov. 4, 1991.

Smart, Pamela Wojas (1967–) On March 22, 1991, an Exeter, New Hampshire, jury found 23-year-old Pamela Smart guilty of conspiring to murder her husband, Gregg Smart, concluding a bizarre murder case that had drawn international attention, with daily proceedings televised live in New Hampshire and run whole or in part throughout the country. She was sentenced to life imprisonment, without parole.

On the night of May 1, 1990, six days before his first wedding anniversary, 24-year-old insurance agent, Gregg Smart was shot and killed at their home in Derry, New Hampshire; he was found dead by Pamela Smart, a high school media services specialist, on her return from a school board meeting. The police investigation that followed yielded evidence that Pamela Smart had conspired with her lover, then-15-year-old William Flynn, and with his schoolmates Patrick Randall and Vance Lattime, to kill her husband, at least partly for the $140,000 insurance on his life. All three of her co-conspirators later confessed, and Flynn admitted to pulling the trigger. The three had implicated themselves by bragging about the murder to other teenagers.

FURTHER READING

"The temptress bride." ROSALINE WRIGHT. *Ladies Home Journal,* July 1991.
"School aide Pam Smart. . . ." STEPHEN SAWICKI. *People,* Apr. 8, 1991.
"The teacher gets detention. . . ." CHARLES LEERHSEN. *Newsweek,* Apr. 1, 1991.
"Murders they wrote. . . ." NANCY GIBBS. *Time,* Apr. 1, 1991.
"Grieving spouse or. . . ." WILLIAM PLUMMER. *People,* Feb. 4, 1991.

Smith, Maggie (Margaret Natalie Smith, 1934–) Celebrated actress Maggie Smith made one of her rare appearances in a Hollywood film late in 1991, in Steven Spielberg's updated version of J. M. Barrie's classic children's story *Peter Pan,* titled *Hook.* Smith played Granny Wendy, in a cast led by Robin Williams as Peter Banning and Peter Pan, Dustin Hoffman as Captain Hook, Julia Roberts as Tinkerbell, and Bob Hoskins as Smee. Forthcoming was a starring role in Lindsay Anderson's film adaptation of Anton Chekhov's *The Cherry Orchard,* opposite Alan Bates and Bob Hoskins; Anderson and Frank Grimes wrote the screenplay. Reportedly also forthcoming was a starring role in a film adaptation of the Muriel Spark novel *Momento Mori.*

Smith has been one of the leading actresses of the English-language theater since the mid-1960s. She was Desdemona to Laurence Olivier's Othello at the National Theatre in 1964, and went on to a long series of classic and modern roles, as in *Miss Julie* (1965), *Hedda Gabler* (1970), and *Private Lives* (1972). She won the 1990 Tony for best actress in a Broadway play, in Peter Shaffer's *Lettice and Lovage,* a role she had earlier created on the London stage. She won a Best Actress Oscar in the title role of *The Prime of Miss Jean Brodie* (1969) and starred in the telefilm *The Lonely Passion of Judith Hearne* (1987), as well as appearing in many key character roles on screen, such as *Travels With My Aunt* (1972) and *California Suite* (1978; she won a Best Supporting Actress Oscar). She has been married twice and has two children.

FURTHER READING

"There's nothing. . . ." GEORGINA HOWELL. *Vogue,* Apr. 1990.
"English accents. . . ." MARK MATOUSEK. *Harper's Bazaar,* Apr. 1990.
"There is nothing. . . ." MATT WOLF. *New York Times Magazine,* Mar. 18, 1990.

Smith, William Kennedy (1960–) A medical student, the son of Kennedy family adviser Steven Smith and the nephew of Senator Edward Kennedy, William Kennedy Smith received massive media attention when he was accused of raping Patricia Bowman at the Kennedy family estate at Palm Beach, Florida, on March 30, 1991. Although there was no charge that Edward Kennedy was in any way involved in the alleged rape, the case was widely used as an opportunity to attack Kennedy, with reviews of the 1969 Chappaquiddick incident, stories referring to alleged public drunkenness, and hints that he somehow might have been involved, at least to the extent of drinking with the alleged victim and her alleged attacker before she had been invited out to the estate. A related dispute over whether Ms. Bowman should have been publicly named in the media was also a source of much public debate, as was a continuing debate as to whether Smith and Kennedy had been treated too considerately by the local police.

The trial, when it came, was almost an anticlimax, although it received enormous media attention. After a ten-day trial, which included testimony by Smith, Bowman, Kennedy, several other witnesses and non-witnesses, and several experts, the jury took 77 minutes to acquit Smith on all counts. Ms. Bowman, who had testified with her face shielded from the television cameras, later identified herself in a nationally televised interview with Diane Sawyer on "Prime Time Live." In a related development, possible charges of obstruction of justice against Kennedy family friend William Barry, said by Palm Beach police to have misled them in the early stages of Smith investigation, were later dropped.

William Smith is the son of Jean Kennedy and Steven E. Smith. His bachelor's degree is from Duke University and his M.D. from Georgetown University.

FURTHER READING

"The trial you won't see. . . ." DAVID KAPLAN. *Newsweek,* Dec. 16, 1991.
"The end of the line. . . ." ELIZABETH KAYE. *Esquire,* Aug. 1991.
"Boys' night out. . . ." MICHELLE GREEN. *People,* Apr. 22, 1991.

Snelling, Richard Arkwright (1927–1991) Pennsylvania-born Snelling graduated from Harvard University in 1948 and moved to Shelburne, Vermont in 1953, there founding the ski equipment company Shelburne Industries. A Republican, he served in the state legislature in 1959–60 and again in 1973–76, then winning election as state governor. He served four two-year terms as governor (1977–85), in that period becoming known as a moderate conservative who was deeply concerned about environmental matters and sharply opposed to his own party's cuts of federal funding for many kinds of state and local programs. He was president of the National Governors' Conference in 1981 and 1982.

Snelling began his fifth term as Vermont Governor in 1991; he died of a heart attack while in office and was succeeded by Lieutenant Governor Howard Dean. He was survived by his wife, Barbara, two daughters, and two sons. (d. Shelburne, Vermont; August 14, 1991)

FURTHER READING

Obituary. *New York Times,* Aug. 14, 1991.

Solzhenitsyn, Alexander (Alexander Isayevich Solzhenitsyn, 1918–) On September 17, 1991, chief Soviet prosecutor Nicolai Trubin dropped the treason charges that had been outstanding against Solzhenitsyn since 1974; the expatriate Soviet writer responded by declaring that he was then ready to return home, but only after he finished his work in progress. Solzhenitsyn had been offered a Soviet literary prize in 1990, along with restoration of his Soviet citizenship, which had been stripped from him at the time of his expulsion, but he had refused to return to the Soviet Union until it ended communism.

Solzhenitsyn wrote a highly influential essay in September 1990, titled "Rebuilding Russia," in which he argued for a go-it-alone policy on the part of the Soviet Union's Slavic peoples, those of Russia, Ukraine, and Belarus; his thinking was widely thought to have influenced that of Boris Yeltsin and other Russian leaders. The work was published in book form as *Rebuilding Russia: Toward Some Formulations* (1991).

Solzhenitsyn was one of the great Soviet dissenters. He survived imprisonment and exile to create a body of powerful work that strongly affected Soviet and world thinking and helped pave the way for the reforms of the Gorbachev era and the dissolution of the former Soviet Union. He was imprisoned in a labor camp (1948–53) and then internally exiled to Siberia (1953–57), but he used these experiences to create his novel *One Day in the Life of Ivan Denisovich* (1962), a trailblazing exposé of the Soviet penal system. Denied publication in the Soviet Union, he published his major works abroad; these included the novels *The First Circle* (1968), *The Cancer Ward* (1968), *August 1914* (1971; republished in expanded form in 1989), and *The Gulag Archipelago* (1973–75). Some of his nonfictional reflections have been published in works such as *The Oak and the Calf: A Memoir* (1980) and *Solzhenitsyn at Harvard: The Address, Twelve Early Responses, and Six Later Reflections* (1980). Solzhenitsyn won the Nobel Prize for literature in 1970. He attended Rostov University. He has been married twice and has three children.

FURTHER READING

The Great Reversal: Politics and Art in Sozhenitsyn. PAUL N. SIEGEL. Walnut, 1991.
"Writers. . . ." PETER HEBBLETHWAITE. *National Catholic Reporter,* Oct. 5, 1990.
Solzhenitsyn's Political Thought. JAMES F. PONTUSO. University Press of Virginia, 1990.
"Russia's prophet in exile. . . ." PAUL GRAY. *Time,* July 24, 1989.
"Solzhenitsyn, Aleksandr Isayevich." *Current Biography,* July 1988.
Solzhenitsyn: A Biography. MICHAEL SCAMMELL. Norton, 1986.
Solzhenitsyn in Exile: Critical Essays and Documentary Materials. JOHN B. DUNLOP, RICHARD S. HAUGH, and MICHAEL NICHOLSON, eds. Hoover Institute Press, 1985.
The Solzhenitsyn-Sakharov Dialogue: Politics, Society, and the Future. DONALD R. KELLEY. Greenwood, 1982.
Solzhenitsyn: The Moral Vision. EDWARD E. ERICSON, JR. Eerdmans, 1982.

Sondheim, Stephen Joshua (1930–) A new Sondheim musical is something of an event in the theater world. In that sense, the opening of his 90-minute, 9-song *Assassins* at New York's Playwrights' Horizons in January 1991 was an event—but, as it turned out, rather a small one, for the show was very dimly received by critics. The show, about the American presidential assassins, had a limited three-week run and was not picked up for Broadway. However, the songs were permanently saved in the original cast album. It was Sondheim's first musical since *Into the Woods.* There was another honor for Sondheim, though. In 1991, he won a Best Original Song Oscar for "Sooner or Later," from the film *Dick Tracy* (1990). And his previous musicals continued to be revived all over the world.

New York City-born Sondheim emerged as a leading American musical theater lyricist in the late 1950s with the lyrics for *West Side Story* (1957) and *Gypsy* (1959), and then as a leading composer, as well, with both words and music for

A Funny Thing Happened on the Way to the Forum (1962). As composer and lyricist, he has won five Tonys, for *Company* (1970), *Follies* (1971), *A Little Night Music* (1973), *Sweeney Todd* (1979), and *Into the Woods* (1988), and a Pulitzer Prize for *Sunday in the Park with George* (1984). During 1990, he was Oxford University's first visiting professor of drama and musical theatre, resident at St. Catherine's College, a position funded by producer Cameron Mackintosh. Sondheim's B.A. was from Williams College in 1950.

FURTHER READING

Art Isn't Easy: The Theatre of Stephen Sondheim, rev. ed. JOANNE GORDON. Southern Illinois University Press, 1992.

"Exploring Along with Sondheim." HAP ERSTEIN. *Insight*, Aug. 28, 1989.

"Broadway's age. . . ." MIRIAM HORN. *U.S. News & World Report*, Feb. 1, 1988.

Sondheim & Co., 2nd ed. CRAIG ZADAN. Harper, 1988.

Souter, David Hackett (1939–) Having declined to take a position on abortion and a wide range of other matters during his 1990 confirmation hearing, and as he had expressed his views very seldom during his previous professional life, Justice Souter began his Supreme Court career very much a question mark on most of the main issues of the day.

During the 1990–91 term, his first, many of those questions began to be answered, as he lined up in most instances solidly with the increasingly conservative majority of the Court, although in a few cases taking a different course. In the key *Rust v. Sullivan* case, Souter upheld federal regulations banning federally funded family planning clinics from offering abortion counseling. He also held with the conservative majority on several other key cases: *Arizona v. Fulminante* ruled that coerced or involuntary confession in a criminal case could be a "harmless error" if conviction would have resulted without it; *Barnes v. Glen Theater* upheld an Indiana state law banning nude dancing; *County of Riverside, California v. McLaughlin*, ruled that those arrested without warrants could be held up to 48 hours while a judge decided if there was probable cause for the arrest; *Florida v. Bostick* ruled that police could board buses and search passengers' luggage, with their permission; *Coleman v. Thompson* greatly restricted the use of habeas corpus writs by state prisoners who have exhausted state appeals; *Harmelin v. Michigan* ruled that a Michigan law requiring a life sentence without possibility of parole for possession of 650 grams (1.5 pounds) of cocaine did not violate the cruel and unusual punishment prohibition of the Eighth Amendment; and *Payne v. Tennesee* allowed "victim impact" evidence to be presented by the prosecution during the sentencing phase of criminal cases, thereby reversing 1987 and 1989 cases that had decided the opposite.

On the other hand, Souter concurred with Justice Blackmun's majority opinion in *United Automobile Workers v. Johnson Controls Inc.*, holding that employers could not ban pregnant women from jobs potentially dangerous to their unborn children, according to the 1978 Pregnancy Discrimination Act. He also joined Justice Stevens in *Chison v. Roemer* and *Houston Lawyers v. Texas Attorney General*, ruling that the federal Voting Rights Act, prohibiting discriminatory voting practices or election district abuses, applied to elected judges, who were "representatives" within the meaning of the law; and found with the majority in *Edmonson v. Leesville Concrete Co.*, which barred exclusion of jurors in civil cases because of race, following earlier bans on exclusion because of race in criminal cases.

Massachusetts-born Souter moved up in the New Hampshire attorney general's office (1968–76), and was then state attorney general (1976–78). He was a state court judge (1978–83) and a state Supreme Court justice from 1983 until his 1989 appointment by George Bush to the U.S. Supreme Court. Souter's B.A. and LL.B. were from Harvard; he was also a Rhodes scholar.

FURTHER READING

"A new day in court." LAUREN TARSHIS and JAMES EARL HARDY. *Scholastic Update,* Nov. 1, 1991.
"Souter, David Hackett." *Current Biography,* Jan. 1991.
"Naturally right. . . ." JEFF ROSEN. *New Republic,* Sep. 24, 1990.
"A retiring Yankee judge. . . ." BILL HEWITT. *People,* Aug. 6, 1990.
"An 18th century man. . . ." MARGARET CARLSON. *Time,* Aug. 6, 1990.
"In search of Souter." DONALD BAER. *U.S. News & World Report,* Aug. 6, 1990.
"An old-fashioned judge." *Economist,* July 28, 1990.

Spacek, Sissy (Mary Elizabeth Spacek, 1949–) In late 1991, Spacek starred as Liz Garrison opposite Kevin Costner as New Orleans district attorney Jim Garrison in Oliver Stone's *JFK,* his film on the assassination of President John F. Kennedy, in a cast that included Jay O. Sanders, Joe Pesci, Tommy Lee Jones, Gary Oldman, Michael Rooker, and Laurie Metcalf, with key smaller roles played by stars Jack Lemmon, Ed Asner, Walter Matthau, Donald Sutherland, and John Candy. Forthcoming was a starring role in Martin Davidson's film *Hard Promises,* as a woman caught between her ex-husband, who does not know they have been divorced, and the man she is about to marry. Also forthcoming was a starring role in the television film *Miss Sherri,* as a thalidomide-damaged woman who seeks an abortion.

Texas-born Spacek emerged as a star in the mid-1970s, in such films as *Prime Cut* (1972), *Badlands* (1974), and in her breakthrough role in *Carrie* (1976), for which she won a Best Actress Oscar nomination. She went on to star in such films as *Three Women* (1977), *Coal Miner's Daughter* (1980) for which she won a Best Actress Oscar, *Raggedy Man* (1981), *Missing* (1982), *The River* (1984), *'Night Mother* (1986), *Crimes of the Heart* (1986), and *The Long Walk Home* (1989). Spacek attended the Lee Strasberg Theatrical Institute. She is married to art director Jack Fisk and has two children.

FURTHER READING

"Mettle of the belle." PAT DOWELL. *American Film,* Mar. 1991.
"Sissy Spacek's long walk home. . . ." JAN JARBOE. *Texas Monthly,* Feb. 1991.
"I've kinda found my rhythm." MICHAEL J. BANDLER. *McCall's,* Feb. 1991.
Country Girl: The Life of Sissy Spacek. MARK EMERSON and EUGENE E. PFAFF, JR. St. Martin's, 1988.

Spader, James (1960–) As his earlier *White Palace* became a hit video rental, Spader opened in a rather straightforward modern corruption-in-Washington film, wrapped around an equally standard theme, that of two buddies, in this case two law students who go their separate ways, one clean and the other crooked. The film was *True Colors* (1991), directed by Herbert Ross, with a cast that included John Cusack, Imogen Stubbs, Richard Widmark, and Mandy Patinkin. Forthcoming was the Mark Frost film *Storyville,* another political corruption story, this one set in Louisiana; Spader stars as Cray Fowler, heir to a rich, powerful political dynasty, in a cast that includes Joanne Whalley-Kilmer, Charlotte Lewis, and George Kee Cheung. Also forthcoming was a starring role opposite Theresa

Russell in Nicolas Roeg's *Chicago Loop;* Paul Theroux adapted his own novel for the screen.

Boston-born Spader made his film debut in *Endless Love* (1981) and went on to play in such popular films as *Tuff Turf* (1985), *The New Kids* (1985), *Pretty in Pink* (1986), *Mannequin* (1987), *Baby Boom* (1987), *Wall Street* (1987), *Less than Zero* (1987), *sex, lies, and videotape* (1989), *Bad Influence* (1990), and *White Palace* (1990). Spader studied at the Michael Chekhov Studio. He and his wife, Victoria, have one son.

FURTHER READING

"James Spader. . . ." SUSAN SPILLMAN. *Cosmopolitan,* Aug. 1988.
"James Spader." *Seventeen,* Nov. 1987.

Speck, Richard (1941–91) On July 14, 1966, Speck became a mass murderer. At approximately 11 P.M. that night, he entered a town house at 2319 East 100th Street in Chicago, occupied by nine women students at the South Chicago Community Hospital School of Nursing, bound all of them at gunpoint, and during the next several hours systematically raped and murdered eight of them. Only Corazon Amurao escaped, by slipping out of her bonds and hiding from him; she lived to identify him after he had two days later attempted suicide and was tentatively identified by a doctor at Cook County Hospital. The apparently unmotivated murders generated worldwide media attention. Speck was convicted of murder and sentenced to death, but was resentenced to eight consecutive terms of life imprisonment after the Supreme Court had outlawed the death penalty. He spent the rest of his life in prison. He was survived by a son, a sister, and a brother. (d. Joliet, Illinois; December 5, 1991)

FURTHER READING

Obituary. *New York Times,* Dec. 6, 1991

Spessivtseva, Olga Alexandrovna (1895–1991) Rostov-born, classical ballerina Spessivtseva graduated from St. Petersburg's Imperial Ballet Academy in 1913, then joined the Maryinsky Theatre company. She became a soloist at the Maryinsky in 1916, soon becoming a leading dancer with the company, and went to the United States with Diaghilev's Ballets Russes company during World War I. She became prima ballerina at the Maryinsky in 1918, there dancing her extraordinary *Giselle* and becoming one of the leading interpreters of the role. In 1921, she danced with the Ballets Russes again, in the London production of *The Sleeping Beauty.* She emigrated from the Soviet Union in 1924 and was a leading dancer at the Paris Opera from 1924 to 1932, in that period also creating several roles, including Balanchine's *Le Chatte* (1927). She danced less from the mid-1930s, and went to the United States as an adviser to the Ballet Theater in 1939. Spessivtseva suffered a nervous breakdown in 1943 and was institutionalized for the balance of her life, from 1963 in the open country environment of the Tolstoy Farm at Valley Cottage, New York. (d. September 16, 1991)

FURTHER READING

Obituary. *The Times* (of London), Sep. 19, 1991.
Obituary. *New York Times,* Sep. 18, 1991.

Spielberg, Steven (1947–) Director, writer, and producer Spielberg created yet another massive film in 1991, directing the $60–80 million *Hook,* a modern version of J. M. Barrie's Peter Pan tale, about a grown-up Peter (a workaholic corporate attorney) who returns to Neverland to rescue his own children from the wicked Captain Hook. The film, which opened for the Christmas season with considerable success, starred Robin Wiliams as Peter Banning/Peter Pan, Dustin Hoffman as Captain Hook, Julia Roberts as Tinkerbell, Bob Hoskins as Smee, and Maggie Smith as Granny Wendy, with Phil Collins and Glenn Close in cameos. Forthcoming was another special effects blockbuster: *Jurassic Park,* based on the Michael Crichton novel, scheduled for summer 1993 release. Several other major projects were also planned, including a feature-length documentary on the life of physicist Stephen W. Hawking, author of *A Brief History of Time;* an animated film version of Andrew Lloyd Webber's *Cats;* and the production of six television films for Turner Network Television (TNT). On the personal side, Spielberg and actress Kate Capshaw were married on October 14, 1991, at East Hampton, New York. They have three children, the third one born in March 1992.

Spielberg directed and in several instances also produced many of the most successful action-adventure and science fiction spectacles of the 1970s and 1980s, including *Jaws* (1975), *Close Encounters of a Third Kind* (1977; and co-authored), *1941* (1979), *Raiders of the Lost Ark* (1981), *E.T.* (1982; and produced), *Indiana Jones and the Temple of Doom* (1984), *The Color Purple* (1985; and produced), *Indiana Jones and the Last Crusade* (1989; the third in the series), and *Always* (1989, a remake of *A Guy Named Joe*). He also wrote and produced *Poltergeist* (1982) and co-produced *Back to the Future* (1985). Spielberg attended California State College. He was formerly married to actress Amy Irving. He has five children.

FURTHER READING

"Peter pandemonium." FRED SCHRUERS. *Premiere,* Dec. 1991.
"Steven Spielberg." MAURA J. MACKOWSKI. *Ad Astra,* July–Aug. 1991.
The Future of the Movies: Interviews with Martin Scorcese, George Lucas, and Steven Spielberg. ROGER EBERT and GENE SISKEL. Andrews & McMeel, 1991.
Icons: Intimate Portraits. DENISE WORRELL. Atlantic Monthly, 1989.
The Picture Life of Steven Spielberg. MICHAEL LEATHER. Watts, 1988.
Steven Spielberg: Amazing Filmmaker. JIM HARGROVE. Childrens, 1988.
The Fantastic Films of Steven Spielberg—Master Filmmaker. ROBERT G. MARRERO. RGM Publications, 1987.
Steven Spielberg. DONALD R. MOTT and CHERYL M. SAUNDERS. G. K. Hall, 1986.
Steven Spielberg. D. L. MABERY. Lerner, 1986.
Steven Spielberg's Amazing Stories. STEVEN BAUER. Berkley, 1986.
Steven Spielberg: Creator of E.T. TOM COLLINS. Dillon, 1983.
The Steven Spielberg Story. TONY CRAWLEY. Morrow, 1983.

Stallone, Sylvester Enzio (1946–) The worldwide hero of the *Rocky* and *Rambo* films tried his hand at comedy in 1991, as Angelo (Snaps) Provolone in the John Landis film *Oscar,* in a cast that included Ornella Muti, Peter Riegert, Vincent Spano, and Kirk Douglas in a cameo appearance. The film opened to mixed reviews, yet its appearance was thought to have helped the home video appeal of *Rocky V,* which appeared soon after. Forthcoming was the Renny Harlin film *Cliffhanger,* scheduled for 1992 release, although promised Carolco funding seemed at risk near the end of 1991. Also forthcoming was the Roger Spottiswoode film comedy *Stop! or My Mom Will Shoot,* with a cast that included JoBeth Williams and Estelle Getty.

In July, Stallone won an apology and a financial settlement of his lawsuit against *The Spectator,* a British magazine; it had accused him of evading armed forces service during the Vietnam War. In September, he also sued a supermarket tabloid for libel; a story had charged that he was impotent because of steroid use.

In 1976, New York City-born Stallone starred in *Rocky;* he also wrote the screenplay. The movie won a Best Film Oscar, was a worldwide hit, and Stallone was immediately a worldwide star. He has since done four sequels: *Rocky II* (1979; he wrote the screenplay and directed), *Rocky III* (1982), *Rocky IV* (1985; he directed), and *Rocky V* (1990). He also starred as Rambo in *First Blood* (1982), *Rambo: First Blood Part II* (1985), and *Rambo III* (1988), and in such other action films as *F.I.S.T.* (1978), *Paradise Alley* (1978), *Nighthawks* (1981), *Rhinestone* (1984), *Cobra* (1986), *Over the Top* (1987), *Lock Up* (1989), and *Tango and Cash* (1989). Stallone attended the American College of Switzerland and Miami University. He has been married twice and has two children.

FURTHER READING

"Stallone on the range." GRAYDON CARTER. *Vogue,* Dec. 1991.
"The shaping of an icon. . . ." DAVID KLINGHOFFER. *Insight,* May 20, 1991.
"Rocky: The article. . . ." FRANZ LIDZ. *Sports Illustrated,* Nov. 12, 1990.
"Move over, Rambo. . . ." LAURA MORICE. *Mademoiselle,* Feb. 1990.
"Sly Stallone's rocky road. . . ." LEO JANOS. *Cosmopolitan,* Jan. 1990.
"Requiem for a heavyweight. . . ." CAMERON STAUTH. *American Film,* Jan. 1990.
Rocky and the Films of Sylvester Stallone. ED GROSS. Movie Publications Services, 1990.
Sylvester. A. C. CRISPIN. Tor, 1985.
Stallone! JEFF ROVIN. Pocket Books, 1985.
Sylvester Stallone: An Illustrated Life. MARSHA DALY. St. Martin's, 1984.

Steenburgen, Mary (1953–) With the home video success of *Parenthood* and *Back to the Future Part III,* Steenburgen became an even more familiar on-screen face. During 1991, she was seen in theatrical release as Stella in *The Butcher's Wife,* opposite George Dzundza as her secret lover, Leo; Demi Moore as Marina; and Jeff Daniels as Alex. Forthcoming was a starring role in *Clifford,* opposite Martin Short and Charles Grodin.

Arizona-born Steenburgen made her film debut in *Goin' South* (1978), and went on to such films as *Ragtime* (1981), *Time After Time* (1979), *Melvin and Howard* (1980), for which she won a Best Supporting Actress Oscar, *Cross Creek* (1983), *Dead of Winter* (1987), *End of the Line* (1987), *Parenthood* (1989), and *Back to the Future Part III* (1990). She also produced and played a bit role in *The Whales of August* (1987). In addition, she appeared in such telefilms as *Tender Is the Night* (1985) and *The Attic: The Hiding of Anne Frank* (1988). Steenburgen attended Hendricks College and studied at New York's Neighborhood Playhouse. She married actor Malcolm McDowell in 1980; the couple have two children.

FURTHER READING

"After years on the mommy track. . . ." Mary H. J. Farrell. *People,* Aug. 28, 1989.
"Mary, Mary, quite contrary." Tim Appelo. *Savvy Woman,* May 1989.

Steinbrenner, George Michael III (1930–) Will Steinbrenner be back? That was one of the most-asked questions of baseball in 1991. In July 1990, he had been "permanently" barred from day-to-day management of his once-great New York Yankees baseball team, after investigation showed that he had paid $40,000 to gambler Howard Spira for information derogatory to then-Yankee Dave Winfield, attempting to interfere with a Winfield trade. He had also been ordered to bring his controlling interest in the Yankees to below 50 percent. Late in 1991, persistent rumors of a Steinbrenner rehabilitation began to fly faster with the resignation of theatrical producer and interim manager Robert Nederlander. He was quickly replaced by Daniel McCarthy, but by year's end baseball commissioner Fay Vincent was saying that he would be prepared to consider reinstating Steinbrenner if two related lawsuits were dropped—one against the baseball commission by the Yankees organization, the other by Steinbrenner against the company that transcribed his mid-1990 hearings. As 1992 began, it seemed that Steinbrenner might indeed be coming back, but when and under what conditions were still unclear.

Because of his baseball troubles, Steinbrenner had dropped off the U.S. Olympic Committee for five months, then returned to the committee as vice president in late December 1990; but in the autumn of 1991 he lost his seat on the board of the Atlanta Committee for the 1996 Olympics and later declined to accept designation as an alternate to that board. He was also writing his autobiography, scheduled to be delivered in late 1992.

Ohio-born Steinbrenner is a leading shipbuilding company executive; he has run the American Ship Building Company since 1967. He bought a controlling interest in the New York Yankees in 1973 and quickly became a highly controversial figure, who hired and fired managers again and again, and engaged in widely publicized feuds with key players. Steinbrenner's B.A. was from Williams College in 1952. He married Elizabeth Joan Zieg in 1956; the couple have four children.

FURTHER READING

"Welcome to hardball city." Mike Lupica. *Esquire,* June 1991.
"George Steinbrenner. . . ." Jeffrey Kluger. *Playboy,* May 1991
"The many woes. . . ." Tom Callahan. *U.S. News & World Report,* Aug. 6, 1990.
Steinbrenner! Dick Schaap. Putnam, 1982; Avon, 1983.
The Boss: George Steinbrenner's Story. Peter Golenbock. Crown, 1982.
Damned Yankees: A No-Holds-Barred Account of Life with "Boss" Steinbrenner. Bill Madden and Moss Klein. Warner, 1990.

Stern, David (1942–) It was Earvin (Magic) Johnson and Larry Bird, and later Michael Jordan, who sparked basketball's enormous popularity from the early 1980s, but many observers credit David Stern, commissioner of the National Basketball Association (NBA), with

creating the environment in which basketball thrived. They cite particularly innovative arrangements that encourage parity among the league's teams; groundbreaking approaches to collective bargaining, under which players get 53 percent of the NBA's gross revenues; the building of wide audiences through network and cable television contracts, at home and abroad, rather than limited pay-per-view arrangements; and a vision of basketball as a worldwide sport. In 1991 Stern continued to cooperate and consult with basketball organizations around the world but rejected the idea of the NBA playing regular-season games in Europe, focusing instead on broadcasting, sponsorship, licensing, exhibition games, coaching clinics, and international tournaments, such as the McDonald's Open, the Olympics (with NBA players for the first time in 1992), and a possible future world championship. Though several cities would like to have NBA basketball teams, Stern said the league needs time to absorb the four teams recently added. One indication of Stern's value to the league is his five-year contract signed in 1990, worth $3.5 million, with bonuses up to $10 million.

In November 1991, Stern was by the side of Magic Johnson when he announced his retirement from basketball due to contracting the human immunodeficiency virus (HIV), the virus that causes AIDS (acquired immune deficiency syndrome). Stern was working with other sports figures to formulate an appropriate response to the dangers posed to athletes by the AIDS virus. With other sports commissioners, Stern was also working on plans for student athletes to retain their college eligibility if they failed to sign with a professional team; and in June he testified to Congress against sports lotteries.

New York-born Stern was associated with Proskauer Rose Goetz & Mendelsohn (1966–78), the NBA's law firm, before being named NBA general counsel in 1978. He became executive vice president for business and legal affairs in 1980, and NBA commissioner in 1984. From 1983 he also served as adjunct professor of law at New York's Cardozo Law School. Stern received his B.A. from Rutgers Unviersity in 1963 and his LL.B. from Columbia University. He married Dianne Bock in 1963; they have two sons.

FURTHER READING

"Stern, David Joel." *Current Biography,* Apr. 1991.

Stevens, John Paul (1920–) Justice Stevens continued to be aligned generally with the diminishing liberal minority of the Supreme Court during the 1990–91 session, though in some instances helping to swing the Court to more liberal positions. He wrote the majority opinion in two related cases, *Chison v. Roemer* and *Houston Lawyers v. Texas Attorney General,* holding that the federal Voting Rights Act, prohibiting discriminatory voting practices or election district abuses, applied to elected judges, who were "representatives" within the meaning of the law. He also found with the majority in the landmark *United Automobile Workers v. Johnson Controls Inc.* which held that employers could not ban pregnant women from jobs potentially dangerous to their unborn children; *Edmonson v. Leesville Concrete Co.,* barring exclusion of jurors in civil cases because of race, following earlier bans on exclusion because of race in criminal cases, and *Pacific Mutual Life Insurance Co. v. Haslip,* holding that it was unconstitutional for courts to restrict punitive damages awarded by juries in civil cases, although states could do so by law.

Stevens wrote dissenting opinions in such key cases as *Rust v. Sullivan,* upholding federal regulations banning federally funded family planning clinics from offering abortion counseling; *Payne v. Tennessee,* which allowed "victim impact" evidence to be presented by the prosecution during the sentencing phase of criminal cases; and *County of Riverside, California v. McLaughlin,* holding that those arrested without warrants could be held up to 48 hours while a judge decided if there was probable cause for the arrest. He also dissented on decisions easing conditions for lifting court supervision of segregated school districts, in *Board of Education of Oklahoma City v. Dowell;* and holding that coerced or involuntary confession in a criminal case could be a "harmless error" if conviction would have resulted without it, in *Arizona v. Fulminante.* Further key dissents were in *Barnes v. Glen Theater,* which upheld an Indiana state law banning nude dancing; *Florida v. Bostick,* holding that police could board buses and search passengers' luggage, with their permission; *Coleman v. Thompson,* greatly restricting the use of habeas corpus writs by state prisoners who have exhausted state appeals to challenge the constitutionality of their convictions; and *Harmelin v. Michigan,* which held that a Michigan law requiring a life sentence without the possibility of parole for possession of 650 grams (1.5 pounds) of cocaine did not violate the cruel and unusual punishment prohibition of the Eighth Amendment, although the federal law was much less stringent.

Chicago-born Stevens practiced law for two decades before being appointed to the Seventh Circuit U.S. Court of Appeals in 1970. President Gerald Ford appointed him to the Supreme Court in 1975. Stevens was thought to be a moderate conservative at the time of his appointment, as was Ford; the estimate was right, for Stevens often functioned as a middle force between the conservative and liberal wings of the court in the years that followed. But in later years, as the court turned sharply to the right, he was more often seen as a moderate liberal, in most instances agreeing with Justices Blackmun, Marshall, and Brennan, the latter two since retired. Stevens's B.A. was from the University of Chicago in 1941, his LL.B. from Northwestern, in 1947. He has been married twice, last to Maryan Mulholland Simon in 1979, and has four children.

FURTHER READING

"A new day in court." LAUREN TARSHIS and JAMES EARL HARDY. *Scholastic Update,* Nov. 1, 1991.

"A voice of reason. . . ." *American Legion Magazine,* June 1990.

Eight Men and a Lady. HERMAN SCHWARTZ, ANDREA NEAL, and DAVID SAVAGE. National Press, 1990.

John Paul Stevens and the Constitution: The Search for Balance. ROBERT J. SICKELS. Pennsylvania State University Press, 1988.

"What they say it is. . . ." *Time,* July 6, 1987.

Stigler, George (1911–91) A leading free market economist and a major figure in the "Chicago School" of economics, Stigler won the 1982 Nobel Prize for economics. His Ph.D. was from the University of Chicago, in 1938; after two decades in several teaching positions elsewhere, he returned there in 1958 as a professor and then professor emeritus. With his close friend, Milton Friedman, he became a key developer of "Chicago School" thinking, so influential in the economic theory and practice of conservative political leaders in many countries in the 1980s and 1990s, and most notably by Ronald Reagan, Margaret Thatcher, and George Bush. Stigler, however, did not regard himself as a politician and rejected efforts to bring him into the Reagan administration, stating that he was not a "supply-sider," calling supply-side economics a "gimmick" and sharply criticizing Reaganomics. He was survived by three sons. (d. Chicago; December 1, 1991)

FURTHER READING

Obituary. *The Times* (of London), Dec. 5, 1991.

Obituary. *New York Times,* Dec. 3, 1991.

Memoirs of an Unregulated Economist. GEORGE J. STIGLER. Basic, 1988.

Sting (Gordon Matthew Sumner, 1951–) The musician, songwriter, and actor Sting, who had forayed into the theater in 1989 and 1990, spent 1991 back in popular music. In January, he issued his third album, *The Soul Cages,* with such songs as the title song, "Island of Souls," "The Wild, Wild Sea," "Why Should I Cry for You," "Jackie," and "All This Time." The album received mixed reviews, many critics feeling that as an attempt to create a major work in the form of a song cycle, it did not quite come off. Sting toured widely for the balance of the year, his touring group including Dominic Miller, Vinnie Colaiuta, and David Sancious. His repertoire included songs from the new album and also reached deep into his personal history for songs from his days leading The Police. He also recorded further, in 1991 cutting a disc that contained his 1990 narration of Prokofiev's *Peter and the Wolf,* joined to the 1988 Chamber Orchestra of Europe recording of the work; and also recording "Cushie Butterfield" on the benefit album *For Our Children* for the Pediatric AIDS Foundation.

Sting, a former grade school teacher, became a major rock star of the early 1980s, as lead singer of The Police, formed in 1977 with Andy Summers and Stewart Copeland. Although the group continued, he largely went on his own in the late 1980s, with such albums as *The Dream of the Blue Turtles* (1985) and *Nothing Like the Sun* (1987). He also developed a substantial film and stage career; his films include *Quadrophenia* (1978), *Brimstone and Treacle* (1982), *Dune* (1984), *Plenty* (1985), and *Rosencranz and Guildenstern Are Dead* (1989). In November 1989, he made his Broadway debut as Mack the Knife in a revival of *The Threepenny Opera.* He was formerly married and has four children.

FURTHER READING

Sting: The Illustrated Lyrics. ROBERTO GILGROV. IRS Books, 1991.
"Twisting Mack the Knife. . . ." JOHN ISTEL. *Mother Jones,* Nov. 1989.
"Sting." RUDY MAXA. *Washingtonian,* Sep. 1989.
"Sting speaks." ART LANGE. *Down Beat,* Sep. 1989.
Written in My Soul: Rock's Great Songwriters. . . . Talk About Creating Their Music. BILL FLANAGAN. Contemporary, 1986.
Sting: Every Breath He Takes. BARNEY COHEN. Berkley, 1984.
Sting and the Police. RAY NIKART. Ballantine, 1984.

Stone, Oliver (1946–) Increasingly seen as one of the major film directors of the period, Stone followed his great success with *Born on the Fourth of July* with two 1991 films. The first was *The Doors,* about the legendary 1960s rock group; Stone directed and co-wrote the screenplay, with a cast that included Val Kilmer as Jim Morrison, the group's late lead guitarist; Meg Ryan; and rock star Billy Idol. Stone's second film opened on December 20; it was the highly controversial *JFK,* his work on the assassination of President John F. Kennedy. Stone wrote the screenplay, co-produced, and directed a large, very highly regarded cast that included Kevin Costner, Sissy Spacek, Jay O. Sanders, Joe Pesci, Tommy Lee Jones, Gary Oldman, Michael Rooker, and Laurie Metcalf, with key smaller roles played by stars Jack Lemmon, Ed Asner, Walter Matthau, Donald Sutherland, and John Candy. The film was preceded by months of attacks on Stone by those who disagreed with the film's version of the assassination; but the work itself, once released, was immediately recognized by the overwhelming majority of film critics as one of the classic American movies of its time, although it continued to generate massive controversy.

New York-born Stone fought in Vietnam (1965–66), an experience that deeply affected some of his most notable work. He has won three Oscars. His first was for his *Midnight Express* (1978) screenplay; the second for his direction of *Platoon* (1986), which he also wrote and which won a Best Picture Oscar. His third was as best director for *Born on the Fourth of July* (1989), filmed from the Oscar-nominated screenplay by Stone and Ron Kovic based on Kovic's autobiography; Stone himself appeared in a small role in the film, which won several other awards. Stone also co-wrote and directed such films as *Scarface* (1983), *Wall Street* (1987), and *Talk Radio* (1988). He attended Yale University; his B.F.A. was from the New York University Film School in 1971. He has been twice married, first to Najwa Sarkis, with whom he had a son; then in 1981 to former nurse Elizabeth Cox. Their son Sean, at age six, played the young Jim Morrison in *The Doors.*

FURTHER READING

"Plunging into the labyrinth." *Time,* Dec. 23, 1991.
"What does. . . ." David Ansen. *Newsweek,* Dec. 23, 1991.
"Can Hollywood solve. . . ." Mark Seal. *Texas,* Dec. 1991.
"The shooting of JFK." Robert Sam Anson. *Esquire,* Nov. 1991.
"Riders on the storm." Robert Horton. *Film Comment,* May–June 1991.
"60s something. . . ." Stephen Talbot. *Mother Jones,* Mar.–Apr. 1991.
"Oliver Stone. . . ." David Breskin. *Rolling Stone,* Apr. 4, 1991.
"Unorthodox behaviour. . . ." *Economist,* Mar. 16, 1991.
"Stone unturned." Mark Rowland. *American Film,* Mar. 1991.
"Oliver Stone." John Clark. *Premiere,* Feb. 1990.
Icons: Intimate Portraits. Denise Worrell. Atlantic Monthly, 1989.

Streep, Meryl (Mary Louise Streep, 1949–) Continuing to play in film comedies after the success of *Postcards from the Edge,* Streep starred in the spring of 1991 in Albert Brooks's *Defending Your Life;* Brooks wrote, directed, and co-starred in a cast including Rip Torn, Lee Grant, and Buck Henry. The film was moderately well received, but some of those in Streep's worldwide audience hoped that she would turn again to the dramatic roles that had made her a major figure. In a change of pace, she narrated the documentary film *Age 7 in America* at the September 25–26 Margaret Mead Film Festival at the American Museum of Natural History. Along similar lines, she recorded "Gartan Mother's Lullaby" on the benefit album *For Our Children* for the Pediatric AIDS Foundation. Forthcoming was a starring role in another screen comedy, *Death Becomes Her,* a marital infidelity, lovers' triangle piece with Bruce Willis, Goldie Hawn, and Kevin Kline. In June 1991, Streep and her husband had a fourth child, a daughter.

New Jersey-born Streep was quickly recognized as a major dramatic star in the late 1970s; her work includes such films as *The Deer Hunter* (1978), *Manhattan* (1979), *Kramer v. Kramer* (1980; she won a Best Supporting Actress Oscar), *Sophie's Choice* (1982; she won a Best Actress Oscar), *Silkwood* (1983), *Out of Africa* (1985), *Ironweed* (1987), *She-Devil* (1989), and *Postcards from the Edge* (1990). Streep's B.A. was from Vassar in 1971, her M.F.A. from Yale in 1975. She married sculptor Donald J. Gummer in 1978; the couple have four children.

FURTHER READING

"Queen for a decade." Marc Eliot. *California,* Sep. 1991.
"Getting the skinny on Streep." Michael Segell. *Cosmopolitan,* May 1991.
"Meryl Streep. . . ." Wendy Wasserstein. *Saturday Evening Post,* July–Aug. 1989.
"Ms. Streep goes. . . ." Bonnie Johnson. *People,* Mar. 20, 1989.
Meryl Streep: A Critical Biography. Eugene E. Pfaff, Jr., and Mark Emerson. McFarland, 1987.
Meryl Streep: The Reluctant Superstar. Diana Maychick. St. Martin's, 1984.
The Meryl Streep Story. Nick Smurthwaite. Beaufort, 1984.

Streisand, Barbra (Barbara Joan Streisand, 1942–) Multi-talented singer, actress, director, and producer Barbra Streisand scored a major success late in 1991, with the opening of her film *The Prince of Tides,* the story of dissipated Southern teacher and coach Tom Wingo, played by Nick Nolte, and psychiatrist Susan Lowenstein, who falls in love with him, played by Streisand, with a cast that included Blythe Danner and Kate Nelligan. Streisand also produced and directed the film, which was based on the Pat Conroy novel. She was highly praised for her direction by most critics, who especially appreciated her focus on Nolte and their relationship, rather than on what might easily have become a Streisand star turn and a far less effective movie. The film was also a substantial commercial success. For Streisand the singer it was a good year, too, with the issuance of a four-CD boxed set, *Just for the Record . . .*, which once again presented many of her hit songs—and much more, for over 50 percent of the material in the set had never before been released.

Brooklyn-born Streisand is one of the great popular music stars of the modern period, whose work also includes several very notable film, stage, and television credits. Her breakthrough roles came on stage in musical theater, in *I Can Get It for You Wholesale* (1962) and as Fanny Brice in *Funny Girl* (1964), a role for which she won a Best Actress Oscar in the 1968 film version. She became a worldwide recording star in the mid-1960s, for such Grammy-winning songs as "People" (1964) and "Evergreen" (1977; also an Oscar winner), and such Grammy-winning albums as *The Barbra Streisand Album* (1963) and *My Name is Barbra* (1965). She is a six-time Best Vocalist Grammy-winner. She also starred in such films as *Hello, Dolly* (1969), *On a Clear Day You Can See Forever* (1970), *The Owl and the Pussycat* (1971), *The Way We Were* (1973), *Funny Lady* (1975) and *Nuts* (1987). She produced and starred in *A Star Is Born* (1976) and directed, produced, and starred in *Yentl* (1983). Her 1965 television special *My Name Is Barbra* won five Emmys. She was formerly married, to the actor Elliot Gould, and has one child.

FURTHER READING

"Barbra Streisand." JOHN CLARK. *Premiere,* Dec. 1991.

"The triumph of Barbra Streisand." JOE MORGENSTERN. *Cosmopolitan,* Oct. 1991.

"Queen of Tides." KEVIN SESSUMS. *Vanity Fair,* Sep. 1991.

Barbra—An Actress Who Sings: The Unauthorized Biography of Barbra Streisand. JAMES KIMBRELL. Branden, Vol. I, 1989, Vol. II, 1992.

Barbra, the Second Decade: The Films and Career of Barbra Streisand. KAREN SWENSON. Carol, 1986.

Barbra Streisand: The Woman, the Myth, the Music. SHAUN CONSIDINE. Delacorte, 1985.

Struebig, Heinrich: See **Lebanon Hostages**

Sullivan, Louis Wade (1933–) Health and Human Services Secretary Sullivan continued to be linked to a wide range of highly controversial and centrally important issues during 1991. Some of the most highly visible of these were abortion, acquired immune deficiency syndrome (AIDS), national health insurance, sex education, Medicaid costs, food labeling, and tobacco advertising. Perhaps most permanently, his name was attached to one of the most significant and highly controversial cases in recent history, the Supreme Court May 23, 1991, ruling in *Rust v. Sullivan,* which upheld his department's 1988 regulations prohibiting federally funded family planning clinics from providing any information about abortion.

In January 1991, in a major change of policy hailed by most of those dealing with the disease, Sullivan decided to remove infection with the AIDS virus from a list of medical conditions for which immigrants can be excluded from the United States. The change was due to go into effect on June 1, but in late May the Bush administration reversed his policy, after great pressure from conservative groups. Similarly, Sullivan canceled a government-funded survey of teenage sexual activity under pressure from conservatives who felt that the questions asked were too explicit. But it seemed far more his own set of convictions that caused him sharply and steadfastly to oppose national health insurance.

Less controversial were such actions as his continuing sharp attacks on tobacco advertising, in which he called on tobacco companies to stop sponsoring sports events and suggested boycotting events that accepted such advertising. He also strongly supported new Food and Drug Administration (FDA) chairman David Kessler on such issues as truthful food labeling, a position Sullivan has long held.

Atlanta-born Sullivan, a leading doctor and educator, went to Washington after a long and distinguished career that included teaching positions at Harvard Medical School, the New Jersey College of Medicine, and Boston University; he is an internist and hematologist. He was dean of the Morehouse College Medical School from 1975 until his cabinet appointment in 1989. Sullivan's B.S. was from Morehouse College, his M.D. from Boston University. He married Eve Williamson in 1955; the couple have two children.

FURTHER READING

"The CEO of health." Marjorie Whigham. *Black Enterprise,* Sep. 1991.
"How to keep America healthy." *American Legion Magazine,* July 1990.
"Louis Sullivan finds. . . ." Maria Wilhelm. *People,* Mar. 26, 1990.
"Sullivan, Louis Wade." *Current Biography,* July 1989.

Sununu, John H. (1939–) As White House chief of staff, Sununu ran into problems in the spring of 1991, when accusations surfaced that he had improperly used government aircraft for personal and political purposes, and had also accepted expenses from industry on such occasions as his highly publicized December 1990 ski trip to Aspen, Colorado, to speak at a ski industry meeting. The criticism grew so intense that the White House was ultimately forced to issue a list of Sununu's travels, and then went even further to have President Bush instruct Sununu to get clearance from White House counsel C. Boyden Gray before taking any corporate-related trips. Pressure to drop Sununu continued throughout the year, fueled by such actions as his highly publicized—and uncleared—personal trip by government limousine

from Washington to New York City in mid-June, reportedly on the theory that he had not been required to clear surface travel.

Anti-Sununu pressure intensified in late November, after a remark contained in a speech by President Bush, favoring cuts in bank credit card interest rates, caused a 120-point drop in the Dow Jones Industrial Average. Sununu, blamed for inserting the remark in the speech, instead turned the blame back on the President, calling it an "ad lib." The extraordinary spectacle of a White House staff member defending himself by making his president look bad before the country excited a great deal of adverse comment. Sununu resigned as White House chief of staff on December 3, 1991. He was replaced by former Transportation Secretary Samuel K. Skinner.

Havana-born Sununu began his career as an engineer and educator, founding the Astro Dynamics company in 1960, teaching mechanical engineering, and then becoming associate engineering dean at Tufts University (1966–82). He moved into politics as a member of the New Hampshire legislature in 1973, ultimately becoming governor of his state (1983–89). He was a key member of the Bush presidential campaign staff in 1988, and after the election became the president-elect's chief of staff. Sununu's 1961 B.S. was from the Massachusetts Institute of Technology, as were his 1962 M.S. and his 1966 Ph.D. He married Nancy Hayes in 1958; the couple have four children.

FURTHER READING

"Sununu speaks. . . ." LEE WALCZAK and DOUGLAS HARBRECHT. *Business Week,* Dec. 2, 1991.
"The grounding of. . . ." BRIT HUME. *American Spectator,* Sep. 1991.
"The genius. . . ." SIDNEY BLUMENTHAL. *New Republic,* July 29, 1991.
"John Sununu's. . . ." KENNETH T. WALSH and STEPHEN J. HEDGES. *U.S. News & World Report,* May 13, 1991.
"Profile. . . ." TIM BEARDSLEY. *Scientific American,* Apr. 1991.
"Beasts of the beltway. . . ." FRED BARNES. *New Republic,* Dec. 24, 1990.
"John Sununu. . . ." ROWLAND EVANS and ROBERT NOVAK. *Reader's Digest,* Nov. 1990.
"Big bad John Sununu. . . ." DAN GOODGAME. *Time,* May 21, 1990.
"Big bad John." MICHAEL KELLY. *Playboy,* Nov. 1990.
"John Sununu." CRAIG UNGER. *People,* Mar. 12, 1990.
"A talk with. . . ." LEE WALCZAK et al. *Business Week,* Feb. 5, 1990.
"Sununu, John Henry." *Current Biography,* May 1989.

Sutherland, Donald McNichol (1934–) Veteran Canadian film star Donald Sutherland saw three of his films released in the spring of 1991. Perhaps most notable was his starring role as bureaucrat and Politburo member Jozef Burski in John Irving's film *Eminent Domain,* opposite Anne Archer as his wife. He also starred in Rebecca Horn's *Buster's Bedroom,* with Geraldine Chaplin and Valentina Cortese; and as the arsonist in Ron Howard's fire disaster movie *Backdraft,* a Hollywood commercial blockbuster. On television, he starred in the Canadian miniseries *Bethune: The Making of a Hero,* about Canadian physician Dr. Norman Bethune, who became a frontline red army doctor during the Chinese Civil War. He also narrated the Hugo Lawick documentary *People of the Forest: The Chimps of Gombe.* Late in 1991, Sutherland also played the small, key role of Colonel X, a James Garrison informant in *JFK,* the Oliver Stone Kennedy-assassination film. Forthcoming was a starring role in Werner Herzog's *Scream of Stone,* about a mountain-climbing team in Argentina.

Sutherland began his film career in the mid-1960s, and emerged as a star playing Korean War surgeon Benjamin Franklin "Hawkeye" Pierce in *M*A*S*H* (1970). He went on to a wide variety of dramatic roles, many of them chosen primarily for their quality, in such films as *Klute* (1971), *The Day of the Locusts* (1975), *1900* (1976), *Casanova* (1976), *Ordinary People* (1980), *Eye of the Needle* (1981), *Gauguin* (1986), *A Dry White Season* (1989), and *Lock Up* (1989). Sutherland attended the University of Toronto. He has been married three times and has five children, including actor Kiefer Sutherland.

FURTHER READING

"Donald Sutherland and. . . ." GERMANO CELAND and BRIGITTE LACOMBE. *Interview,* Sep. 1990.

Sutherland, Thomas: See **Lebanon Hostages**

Sutton, Denys Miller (1917–91) An author, editor, and major figure in the art world, London-born Sutton served in the British Foreign Office (1940–45), with the International Commission for the Restitution of Cultural Material after World War II, and with the United Nations Educational, Scientific, and Cultural Organization (UNESCO) in 1948. He began his prolific writing career in 1949, with such books as *French Drawings of the 18th Century* (1949), *American Painting* (1949), and *Flemish Painting* (1950), and went on to write a considerable body of work, including his two books on Whistler and the massive *Degas: The Man and His Work* (1986). Very active in the international museum world, he organized many notable exhibitions, on such figures as Bonnard, Whistler, Boucher, Constable, and Sargent, and on such themes as "France in the 18th Century" (1968) and "Venice Rediscovered" (1972). He was the editor of the magazine *Apollo* from 1962 to 1987. He was survived by his third wife, Cynthia Sassoon, a daughter, and a son. (d. London; January 25, 1991)

FURTHER READING

Obituary. *New York Times,* Feb. 1, 1991.
Obituary. *The Times* (of London), Jan 29,1991.

Swayze, Patrick (1954–) As *Ghost* continued to break box-office records abroad, it moved into the top spot in U.S. home video. Swayze, who had in 1990 become a major film star in the title role, playing opposite Demi Moore and Whoopi Goldberg, became a very familiar face throughout the world—especially after *People* magazine named him the "sexiest man alive" on the cover of an August 1991 issue. In 1991, Swayze starred in Kathryn Bigelow's action film *Point Break,* which opened in July, with a cast that included Keanu Reeves, Gary Busey, and Lori Petty. The bank robbery/car chase/sex-and-violence film was rather unfavorably received. Forthcoming was a quite different kind of film, Roland Joffe's *City of Joy,* based on the Dominique La Pierre book as adapted for film by Mark Medoff. Shot in Calcutta, it is the story of an American doctor (Swayze), a British woman who runs a clinic in one of the poorest sections of the impoverished city (Pauline Collins), and an Indian couple (Art Malik and Shabana Azmi).

Trained for ballet, Swayze began his career as a dancer, and danced and acted a lead in *Grease* for two years on Broadway before emerging as a leading film player late in the 1980s. His breakthrough role was as Johnny Castle in *Dirty Dancing* (1987). It was followed by a starring role opposite his wife, Lisa Niemi, in the fantasy-action film *Steel Dawn* (1987); the bouncer's role in the action film *Road House* (1989); and the police drama *Next of Kin* (1989). Swayze also appeared in the television miniseries *North and South* (1990) and several other television films.

FURTHER READING

"Body and soul." JEANNIE PARK. *People,* Aug. 26, 1991.
"From here to maturity. . . ." *Seventeen,* July 1991.
"Patrick Swayze." *People,* Dec. 31, 1990.
"Patrick Swayze. . . ." KATHRYN CASEY. *Ladies Home Journal,* Aug 1990.
"A wild and Swayze guy." BILL ZEHME. *Cosmopolitan,* Aug. 1989.
"Going Swayze." LAURA MORICE. *Mademoiselle,* June 1989.
Patrick Swayze. MITCHELL KRUGEL. St. Martin's, 1988.
The New Breed: Actors Coming of Age. KAREN HARDY and KEVIN J. KOFFLER. Holt, 1988.

Sydow, Max von (Carl Adolf von Sydow, 1929–) The celebrated Swedish actor Max von Sydow was active in films made on both sides of the Atlantic during 1991. In the spring he appeared in James Dearden's remake of the 1956 thriller *A Kiss Before Dying,* based on the Ira Levin novel, as Thor Carlsson, the rich father of twin daughters at risk from psychopath Jonathan Corliss (Matt Dillon). In the autumn, he starred in Wim Wenders's *Until the End of the World,* a futuristic thriller shot in 20 cities in seven countries, in an international cast that included William Hurt, Jeanne Moreau, Solveig Dommartin, and Sam Neill. He also appeared in the Roberto Faenza film *The Bachelor,* in a cast that included Keith Carradine and Miranda Richardson.

Forthcoming were several more films, perhaps most notably the first directorial effort of noted cinematographer Sven Nykvist, *The Ox,* also starring Liv Ullmann and Erland Josephson; and also Polish director Krsystof Zanussi's *The Touch,* an English-Polish-Danish-Swedish co-production; Dan Petrie's *A Dog in Flanders;* and John Irving's adaption of his own novel, *Cider House Rules,* starring Matthew Broderick and directed by Philip Borsos.

The classic Ingmar Bergman films in which von Sydow made his greatest impact include *The Seventh Seal* (1957), *The Magician* (1958), *The Virgin Spring* (1960), *Through a Glass Darkly* (1961), and *Winter Light* (1962). He also starred on television and in later theatrical release in two linked sagas of 19th-century Scandinavian-American immigration: *The Emigrants* (1969) and *The New Land* (1969). His later work included such films as *Three Days of the Condor*

(1975), *Hannah and Her Sisters* (1985), and *Pelle the Conqueror* (1986). He played a Catholic priest working in Hiroshima in the television film *Hiroshima: Out of the Ashes,* which premiered on August 7, 1990, the 45th anniversary of the atom bombing of the city.

Von Sydow has long been recognized as one of Sweden's leading stage actors. He attended Stockholm's Royal Dramatic Theater School, and has been associated with that theater since 1960. He married Christina Olin in 1951 and has two children.

FURTHER READING

"Scandinavia-hopping Von Sydow. . . ." Lawrence Cohn. *Variety,* Dec. 21, 1988.

T

Tagliabue, Paul John (1940–) Right at the beginning of 1991, National Football League (NFL) commissioner Tagliabue was faced with a difficult "go-or-no-go" decision: Super Bowl XXV, between the New York Giants and the Buffalo Bills, was scheduled for January 26th at Tampa Stadium—but the Persian Gulf War had started on the 17th. In the end, the game was held as planned, with the approval of President Bush and other federal officials, though with stringent security, much patriotic panoply, time out for television news updates, and scaled-back social events. The 1994 Super Bowl, originally intended for Phoenix, is to be moved, since Arizona voters rejected a holiday honoring Martin Luther King, Jr.

In his mid-season report to owners in October, Tagliabue noted that professional football had remained economically healthy despite the recession, with ticket sales at or near the record attendance levels set in the previous two seasons. Tagliabue headed the NFL committee that recommended the addition of two new teams for the 1994 season and a possible realignment into six divisions of five teams each; after the NFL in May voted for expansion, Tagliabue began reviewing applications for possible sites.

With other sport commissioners, Tagliabue was working on plans for student athletes to retain their college eligibility if they failed to sign with a professional team and in June he testified to Congress against sports lotteries. After basketball star Earvin (Magic) Johnson announced in November 1991 that he had contracted the human immunovirus (HIV), the virus that causes AIDS (acquired immune deficiency syndrome), Tagliabue initially responded that testing should be up to the individual clubs; however, he and other sports leaders began to work more earnestly on formulating a policy addressing AIDS testing.

After graduating from law school in 1965, Tagliabue worked at the Defense Department in Washington until 1969, and then for 20 years as a lawyer at Covington and Burling, becoming a partner in 1974. He became commissioner of the National Football League in 1989. Tagliabue's B.A. was from Georgetown University in 1962;

his J.D. is from New York University in 1965. He is married and has two children.

FURTHER READING

"The face of. . . ." RICK TELANDER. *Sports Illustrated,* Sep. 10, 1990.
"NFL commish's torch passed. . . ." *Sporting News,* Feb. 18, 1990.
"Tagliabue. . . ." PAUL ATTNER. *Sporting News,* Feb. 12, 1990.
"Tagliabue plans. . . ." STEVE HUBBARD. *Sporting News,* Dec. 4, 1989.
"A new quarterback. . . ." *U.S. News & World Report,* Nov. 6, 1989.
"In a blink. . . ." VITO STELLINO. *Sporting News,* Nov. 6, 1989.
"The NFL's new boss." PETER KING. *Sports Illustrated,* Nov. 6, 1989.

Tamayo, Rufino (1899–1991) The last of the four artists who after the 1910 Mexican Revolution created the "Mexican Renaissance," Tamayo was primarily a painter, unlike Clemente Orozco, Diego Rivera, and David Alfaro Siquieros, who were primarily muralists. All four shared the same commitment to Mexican culture, although Tamayo, the youngest of the four, created by far less directly political work. Child of a Zapotec family, his work merged pre-Columbian and modern influences, pursuing Mexican themes, light and color, and subjects, while at the same time being considerably abstracted. Tamayo directed the department of ethnographic drawing at Mexico City's National Museum of Archeology from 1921 to 1925 and had his first solo exhibitions in Mexico City and New York City in 1926. He lived in the United States from 1926 to 1928, taught art at New York's Dalton School from 1936 through the mid-1940s, and also taught at the Brooklyn Museum of Art, in this period creating such paintings as *Women of Tehuantepec* (1939) and *Animals* (1941). He became a major figure in Mexico in the late 1940s and a world figure during the 1950s. Tamayo's murals include those at the Palacio de Bellas Artes in Mexico City (1952) and the Paris UNESCO headquarters (1958). His artistic career was reviewed in his book *Rufino Tamayo: Fifty Years of His Painting* (1981). He was survived by his wife, pianist Olga Flores Rivas. (d. Mexico City, June 24, 1991)

FURTHER READING

Obituary. *Current Biography,* Aug. 1991.
Obituary. *The Times* (of London), June 26, 1991.
Obituary. *New York Times,* June 25, 1991.
"The poet of Mexican realism. . . ." ANNICK SANJURJO CASCIERO. *Americas,* July–Aug. 1990.
"Rufino Tamayo. . . ." IRENE BORGER. *Architectural Digest,* Sep. 1987.
Tamayo. JOSE CORREDOR-MATHEOS. Rizzoli International, 1987.
Rufino Tamayo. JACQUES LASSAIGNE. Rizzoli International, 1982.

Tandy, Jessica (1909–) Following her 1990 Best Actress Oscar for *Driving Miss Daisy,* celebrated actress Jessica Tandy starred in another film set in the small-town South: Jon Avnet's *Fried Green Tomatoes,* which opened in late December 1991. The cast of the feminist-oriented film included Kathy Bates (1991 Best Actress Oscar-winner), Mary Stuart Masterson, Mary-Louise Parker, Cicely Tyson, and Stan Shaw. Also in December, Tandy starred in the television film *The Story Lady,* as the amateur producer of a successful children's story hour on public access television who signs on with a commercial network only to see her show turned into a "product." Forthcoming was a starring role as Shirley MacLaine's mother in *Used People,* in a cast that includes Bates, Marcello Mastroianni, and Marcia Gay Harden. On June 13, Women in Film presented Tandy with a 15th Annual Women in Film Crystal Award for those who have helped expand the role of women in the entertainment industry.

London-born Tandy appeared in London and New York during the 1930s, though mainly in London and in the classics, most notably as Ophelia to John Gielgud's *Hamlet* (1934). On the Broadway stage, she created the Blanche Du Bois role in Tennessee Williams's *A Streetcar Named Desire* (1947). After she and Hume Cronyn married in 1942, they created a lasting theater partnership, appearing together in such plays as *The Fourposter* (1951), *A Delicate Balance* (1966), and *Foxfire* (1982; and the 1987 television version). She has also appeared in strong character roles in several other films. Tandy and Cronyn were awarded the 1990 National Medal of the Arts. Cronyn wrote about their life and work together in his *A Terrible Liar: A Memoir* (1991). Tandy attended the Ben Greet Academy of Acting (1924–27). Her first husband was British actor Jack Hawkins, with whom she had a daughter. She and Cronyn have two children, one of them the actress Tandy Cronyn.

FURTHER READING

"He drives Miss Daisy. . . ." EVE DROBOT. *Saturday Night,* Oct. 1991.
"Jessica Tandy. . . ." CINDY ADAMS. *Ladies Home Journal,* Apr. 1991.
Jessica Tandy: A Bio-Bibliography. MILLY S. BARRANGER. Greenwood, 1991.
"Two lives, one ambition. . . ." GERALD CLARKE. *Time,* Apr. 2. 1990.
"Happily ever after." JEANNE MARIE LASKAS. *Life,* Apr. 1990.
"She oughta be in pictures. . . ." NINA DARNTON. *Newsweek,* Jan. 1, 1990.
"Driving Miss Daisy. . . ." ROBERT SEIDENBERG. *American Film,* Jan. 1990.
"Two for the road." MARK MATOUSEK. *Harper's Bazaar,* Jan. 1990.
Actress to Actress. RITA GAM. Lyons & Burford, 1986.

Taylor, Elizabeth (1932–) For almost five decades one of the great celebrities of her time, Taylor provided one of the major media events of 1991 when on October 6 she married construction worker Larry Fortensky; the couple had met while both were being treated for substance abuse at the Betty Ford Center. The event occurred at the California ranch of singer Michael Jackson and attracted a large number of other celebrities, many media people, approximately one dozen helicopter-borne photographers, and one parachutist photographer.

During 1991, Elizabeth Taylor continued to make a massive contribution to research and treatment of AIDS (acquired immune deficiency syndrome) channeling her fund-raising activities, which by late 1991 had raised a reported $40 million, through the American Foundation for AIDS Research (AmFar). In October, she also set up her own AIDS foundation as well, funding it initially with a reported $1 million in proceeds from the sale of photographs of her wedding. The decision to set up her own foundation reportedly stemmed from a dispute within AmFar, which was largely resolved in late October.

In May 1991, Taylor settled a $20 million lawsuit against the *National Enquirer* out of court; the periodical had published stories that she had fatal lupus and was drinking while hospitalized. The publication apologized and paid Taylor an undisclosed sum.

London-born Taylor began her film career in *Lassie Come Home* and *Jane Eyre,* both in 1943, and became a star at the age of 12, in *National Velvet* (1944). She went on to star in such films as *A Place in the Sun* (1951), *Giant* (1956), *Raintree Country* (1957), *Cat on a Hot Tin Roof* (1958), *Suddenly Last Summer* (1959), *Butterfield 8* (1960; she won a Best Actress Oscar), *Cleopatra* (1962), *Who's Afraid of Virginia Woolf?* (1966, and a second Best Actress Oscar), *Under Milk Wood* (1971), and *The Blue Bird* (1975). She has starred on Broadway in revivals of *The Little Foxes* (1979) and *Private Lives* (1983). She has been married eight times, twice to actor Richard Burton, and has four children. Her other husbands were socialite Nicky Hilton, actor Michael Wilding, producer Mike Todd, singer Eddie Fisher, and Senator John Warner.

FURTHER READING

"Elizabeth Taylor. . . ." SALLY OGLE DAVIS. *Ladies Home Journal,* Nov. 1991.
"He does, she does. . . ." JEANNIE PARK. *People,* Oct. 21, 1991.
"Liz: She's survived. . . ." GEORGINA HOWELL. *Vogue,* June 1991.
"Elizabeth." ALEXANDER WALKER. *Cosmopolitan,* Jan. 1991.
All About Elizabeth: Elizabeth Taylor, Public and Private. CAROLINE LATHAM and JEANNIE SAKOL. NAL-Dutton, 1991.

Elizabeth: The Life of Elizabeth Taylor. ALEXANDER WALKER. Grove-Weidenfeld, 1991.
Five for Hollywood: Their Friendship, Their Fame, Their Tragedies. JOHN PARKER. Carol, 1991.
Elizabeth Taylor: A Celebration. SHERIDAN MORLEY. Viking Penguin, 1990.
The Films of Elizabeth Taylor. JERRY VERMILYE and MARK RICCI. Carol, 1989.
The New Elizabeth. MARIANNE ROBIN-TANI. St. Martin's, 1988.

Taylor, Lawrence (1959–) The old cliché "the joy of victory, the agony of defeat" took on special meaning for Lawrence Taylor in 1991. In January, the great defensive linebacker led the Giants to victory over the San Francisco 49ers in the conference championships, and over the Buffalo Bills in Super Bowl XXV. But when the new season rolled around, with a new coach, several player changes, and some key injuries—including a sprained left ankle for Taylor himself—the Giants floundered. At one point Taylor called a rare players' meeting to try to regroup, and after at least one loss, he criticized his teammates' intensity and questioned the motivational abilities of new coach, Ray Handley. In the end the Giants failed even to make the 1990–91 season playoffs. Privately, in September interviews, Taylor spoke out against racism, especially in the New York area, reporting that he had been denied membership by several New Jersey country clubs, including some at which he had played as a guest in celebrity tournaments.

Virginia-born Taylor was a star football player at the University of North Carolina, an All-American who was the first pick of the New York Giants in the 1981 draft. That year, he was both Rookie of the Year and Best Defensive Player of the Year. He went on to become the only player in National Football League history to be named to the Pro Bowl for nine consecutive seasons (1982–90). In the 1986–87 season he was named the Most Valuable Player in the National Football League. Along the way, in 1986, he triumphed over a serious drug problem that threatened both family and career. In 1987 he published *LT: Living on the Edge,* written with David Falkner. He married Linda Cooley in 1981; the couple have three children.

FURTHER READING

"Taylor, Lawrence." *Current Biography,* July 1990.

Tharp, Twyla (1941–) One of the world's leading choreographers, the always innovative and often controversial Tharp undertook a wide and varied range of projects during 1991. Chief among them was the further development of "The Tharp Project," a 16-dancer group that had a four-week residency at the Wexner Center for the Performing Arts at Ohio State University at Columbus, and then a brief New York season, to be followed by a February 1992 Japanese tour. Tharp also continued to work with the Boston Ballet and planned to create a new work for the company, to be introduced in the autumn of 1992. Forthcoming screen projects included two films scheduled for French television and a portion of a Public Broadcasting System dance series. Her autobiography was scheduled for publication late in 1992. Tharp was awarded a 1991 Laurence Olivier Award for special achievement.

Indiana-born Tharp was a member of the Paul Taylor dance company (1963–65), and then developed her own company, also choreographing for other companies. Much of her work is developed around jazz and other contemporary themes, as in her *Tank Dive* (1965), *Re-Moves* (1966), *Forevermore* (1967), *The Bix Pieces* (1972), *As Time Goes By* (1974), *Eight Jelly Rolls* (1971), and *Push Comes to Shove* (1976). She also choreographed the films *Hair* (1979), *Amadeus* (1984), and *White Nights* (1985). Tharp attended Pomona College, Barnard College, and the American Ballet Theater School, and studied with many leading dancers. She was formerly married and has one child.

FURTHER READING

The Tail of the Dragon: New Dance, 1976–1982. MARCIA B. SIEGEL. Duke, 1991.
"Tharp's new shtick." JOAN ACOCELLA. *Connoisseur,* Feb. 1989.
"Twyla Tharp Dance." MINDY ALOFF. *Nation,* Mar. 28, 1987.
"Twyla Tharp's return." HOLLY BRUBACH. *Atlantic,* Mar. 1987.
"The world according to Tharp." LOIS DRAEGIN. *Savvy,* Feb. 1987.

Thatcher, Margaret (Margaret Hilda Roberts, 1925–) Former Prime Minister Thatcher, who after leaving office seemed to be moving toward a much less visible role in British politics, rather sharply reversed course during 1991. She

and her handpicked successor, Prime Minister John Major, sharply disagreed on the pace and content of the proposed European single currency and political union, and by May Thatcher had taken the split public and widened her attack on Major to include other, unrelated issues as well. Near year's end, even her previously announced decision to leave the House of Commons after the next general election seemed to be in some question. At the same time, however, her retirement plans were going forward; these included formation of the Thatcher Foundation and a contract with HarperCollins to do her autobiography, to be published in two volumes, the first in 1993.

Thatcher was a chemist and then barrister before her 1959 election as Conservative Member of Parliament. She became Conservative education spokesperson in 1969, and when her party came to power again was education and science minister (1970–74). In 1975, she succeeded Edward Heath as Conservative leader, becoming the first woman to lead any major British political party, and in 1979 became Britain's first woman prime minister; she was ultimately Britain's longest-serving prime minister of the 20th century. Her era was marked by wide-scale privatization, the 1982 Falklands War, and the continuing civil war in Northern Ireland; she personally survived several assassination attempts by the Irish Republican Army (IRA). She attended Somerville College, Oxford. She married Denis Thatcher in 1951; the couple have two children.

FURTHER READING

Margaret Thatcher's Last Hurrah. E. Bruce Geelhoed. Greenwood, 1992.
Margaret Thatcher: A Bibliography. Faysal H. Mikdadi. Meckler, 1992.
" 'That woman.' . . ." Geoffrey Wheatcraft. *Atlantic,* Dec. 1991.
"Maggie's big problem." Maureen Orth. *Vanity Fair,* June, 1991.
"A Woman for Four Seasons." Owen Harries. *National Review,* Apr. 15, 1991.
Margaret Thatcher: The Woman Within. Andrew Thomson. Isis (NY), 1991.
Reagan and Thatcher. Geoffrey Smith. Norton, 1991.
"She gave Britain. . . ." Danielle Pletka. *Insight,* Dec. 17, 1990.
"Life at the top. . . ." *Maclean's,* Dec. 3, 1990.
"A legacy of revolution. . . ." Bruce W. Nelan. *Time,* Dec. 3, 1990.
Maggie: An Intimate Portrait of a Woman in Power. Chris Ogden. L. J. Kaplan, 1990.
Margaret Thatcher: Britain's Prime Minister. Dorothy Hole. Enslow, 1990.
Margaret Thatcher: First Woman Prime Minister of Great Britain. Leila M. Foster. Childrens, 1990.
Margaret, Daughter of Beatrice: A Politician's Psychobiography of Margaret Thatcher. Leo Abse. Random House, 1990.
Margaret Thatcher. Marietta D. Moskin. Mesner, 1990.
Madam Prime Minister: A Biography of Margaret Thatcher. Libby Hughes. Dillon, 1989.
The Iron Lady. Hugo Young. Farrar, Straus & Giroux, 1989.
Margaret Thatcher. Kenneth Harris. Little, Brown, 1988.

Thomas, Clarence (1948–) On July 1, 1991, President George Bush nominated U.S. Court of Appeals Judge Clarence Thomas, a conservative African-American, to the Supreme Court vacancy created by the resignation of Justice Thurgood Marshall. The appointment was highly controversial: The National Organization for Women (NOW) quickly opposed him, especially on the abortion issue; so did the National Association for the Advancement of Colored People, the A.F.L.-C.I.O., the Leadership Conference for Civil Rights, and the Congressional Black Caucus. The American Bar Association voted him a lukewarm "qualified."

Judge Thomas testified before the Judiciary Committee September 10–13, and again on September 16, stressing his personal history, largely

Clarence Thomas and Virginia Lamp Thomas (left rear).

avoiding substantive questions, and flatly refusing to discuss abortion. Although he was pressed fairly hard by some Democratic senators, the hearings were rather low key. On September 27, after a long confirmation process, the Senate Judiciary Committee deadlocked 7–7; Senate confirmation was thought probable.

Then an extraordinary thing happened. On October 7, Oklahoma State University law professor Anita Faye Hill "went public" with very specific and lurid charges against Judge Thomas; she alleged that he had sexually harassed her from 1981 to 1983, while she was his assistant at the U.S. Department of Education and then at the U.S. Equal Employment Opportunity Commission, which he then headed. The nature of Profesor Hill's charges and the fact that she was a law professor and conservative African-American of utterly unblemished reputation, made an enormous impact. Judge Thomas issued a blanket denial the next day, October 8.

Professor Hill had been approached by Senate staff members on September 3, had told her story, and had requested some degree of anonymity, how much and on what terms still and probably for decades to come a matter of dispute. The committee decided not to air her charges publicly and they were not a significant factor during the long process that led to the 7–7 deadlock. But, by now at the center of the storm, the Senate on October 8 postponed its imminent vote on the nomination, and the committee rescheduled hearings, which occurred October 11–13. Professor Hill made her accusations before the committee and was sharply and immediately attacked by its Republican members, most notably by Senators Arlen Specter, Orrin Hatch, and Alan Simpson. Senator Specter even directly accused her of perjury, a charge that was never pursued. Justice Thomas also testified, denied her allegations completely, and accused the committee of "hi-tech lynching." Professor Hill was supported by several highly reputable witnesses, all of whom testified that she had made these charges to them years before. Judge Thomas was supported by several highly reputable character witnesses. All these events occurred before a transfixed worldwide television audience.

The hearings adjourned late on Sunday, October 13. Judge Thomas was confirmed by the Senate on Tuesday, October 15, by a vote of 52–48; had a ceremonial swearing-in at the White House on October 18; and was seated on the Supreme Court on November 1. Professor Hill went home to Oklahoma to resume teaching law. Tens of millions of Americans and others around the world had witnessed the extraordinarily distasteful spectacle, which greatly damaged Professor Hill, Judge Thomas, and the reputations of many senators and the Senate itself.

Savannah-born Thomas was from early in his career a protégé of John Danforth, now a U.S. senator from Missouri. Thomas was Missouri assistant attorney general (1974–77) when Danforth was state attorney general. Thomas was a corporate lawyer for the Monsanto Company (1977–79), a legislative assistant to Senator Danforth (1979–81), assistant secretary for civil rights in the federal Education Department (1981–82), chairman of the U.S. Equal Opportunity Employment Commission (1982–89), and was named by then-president Ronald Reagan to the U.S. Court of Appeals for the District of Columbia in 1989. Thomas's B.A. was from Holy Cross College, and his J.D. from Yale Law School. His second wife is the former Virginia Lamp, a lawyer at the U.S. Labor Department and formerly at the U.S. Chamber of Commerce. Thomas has one son from a former marriage.

FURTHER READING

"The lesson of. . . ." Steve Allen. *America,* Nov. 9, 1991.

"A new day in court." Lauren Tarshis and James Earl Hardy. *Scholastic Update,* Nov. 1, 1991.

"Breaking silence." VIRGINIA LAMP THOMAS. *People,* Nov. 11, 1991.
Time, Oct. 21, 1991. "A question of character." RICHARD LACAYO. "An ugly circus." NANCY GIBBS.
Newsweek, Oct. 21, 1991. "Thomas and Hill. . . ." ELOISE SALHOLZ. "Anatomy of a debacle." DAVID A. KAPLAN. "A moment of truth."
U.S. News & World Report, Oct. 21, 1991. "Judging Thomas." GLORIA BORGER. "Asking the questions. . . ." DONALD BAER.
"Thomas and Benedict. . . ." GEORGE KANNAR. *New Republic,* Oct. 14, 1991.
"The pain of being black." JACK E. WHITE. *Time,* Sep. 16, 1991.
"Supreme mystery." DAVID A. KAPLAN. *Newsweek,* Sep. 16, 1991.
"The crowning Thomas affair." STEVEN V. ROBERTS. *U.S. News & World Report,* Sep. 16, 1991.
National Catholic Reporter, Aug. 2, 1991. "If we let Thomas. . . ." RAYMOND A. SCHROTH. "The Thomas connection. . . ." RUSS BELLANT.
"The trials of. . . ." WILLIAM MCGURN. *National Review,* Aug. 12, 1991.
"Personal and other mysteries. . . ." ROBERT F. DRINAN. *National Catholic Reporter,* July 19, 1991.
"Clarence Thomas rises. . . ." *Jet,* July 22, 1991.
"The making of a judge. . . ." PAULA CHIN. *People,* July 22, 1991.
"Marching to a different drummer. . . ." MARGARET CARLSON. *Time,* July 15, 1991.
"Scouting Thomas. . . ." KENNETH T. WALSH and GLORIA BORGER. *U.S. News & World Report,* July 15, 1991.
"A question of fairness. . . ." JUAN WILLIAMS. *Atlantic,* Feb. 1987.

Thomas, Danny (Amos Jacobs, 1912–91) One of the best-loved entertainers of his generation, Lebanese-American Thomas was born in Deerfield, Michigan, and began his career in Detroit local radio, until the early 1940s making much of his career as a master of ceremonies in Chicago. He broke into national radio as a guest on the Fanny Bryce show in 1944 and then had his own radio show (1944–49). He was a major figure in early television, in his role as a night club entertainer and family man in the long-running hit series "Make Room for Daddy" (1953–64), later known as "The Danny Thomas Show"; it is still playing worldwide in reruns. He made his movie debut in *The Unfinished Dance* (1946), and went on to play in such films as *Call Me Mister* (1951), *I'll See You in My Dreams* (1951; as Gus Kahn, opposite Doris Day), and *The Jazz Singer* (1953; as Al Jolson). Later in his career, he became a television producer. During the 1970s and 1980s, he also appeared in several further television series. He continued to appear in cabaret throughout his career. Thomas was a philanthropist, as well, most notably as a founder of St. Jude Children's Research Hospital in 1962, and for three decades afterward its chief fundraiser. His autobiography was *Make Room for Danny* (1991; with Bill Davidson). He was survived by his wife, the former Rose Marie Cassaniti; a son, television producer Tony Thomas; and two daughters, one of them actress-producer Marlo Thomas. (d. Los Angeles; February 6, 1991.

FURTHER READING

Obituary. *Current Biography,* Apr. 1991.
Obituary. *People,* Feb. 18, 1991.
Obituary. *U.S. News & World Report,* Feb. 18, 1991.
Obituary. *Variety,* Feb. 11, 1991.
Obituary. *New York Times,* Feb. 7, 1991.

Thomas, Isiah Lord (1961–) In 1991, the theme for basketball star Isiah Thomas and his Detroit Pistons was "three-peat," as they tried to win a third consecutive National Basketball Association (NBA) championship. This time, however, Michael Jordan and the Chicago Bulls stood in their way, taking the Central Division title and sweeping the Pistons in four straight games in the Eastern Conference finals. For Thomas the season was especially disappointing because he missed 34 games (and was unable to play in his tenth straight All-Star game, though voted to the squad) due to wrist surgery; he returned only in April, just before the playoffs, playing with a padded brace. Thomas had another disappointment in 1991 when he was not selected for the U.S. basketball team for the 1992 Olympics, the first to allow NBA players. During the summer of 1991, Thomas continued his activities with inner-city youth, especially against drugs and for staying in school. In December 1991, Thomas took an elbow to the head from the Utah Jazz's Karl Malone; astonishingly Thomas returned to the game, after receiving 40 stitches to close the wound. Malone, who said the blow was unintentional, was fined $10,000 and suspended for one game.

Chicago-born Thomas, nicknamed Zeke,

turned professional after years as a star guard at Indiana University, after winning the NCAA championship in 1981. He has spent his whole professional career with the Pistons, ultimately leading them to five straight trips to the conference finals (1987–91) and their back-to-back NBA championships (1989–90), during both of which he led in scoring and assists; he was named most valuable player of the 1990 playoffs. A key figure in basketball throughout the 1980s, he was a nine-time All-Star (1982–90), and twice MVP at the All-Stars. With Matt Dobek, he wrote *Bad Boys! An Inside Look at the Detroit Pistons' 1988–89 Championship Season* (1989). Thomas finished his studies at Indiana University later in the 1980s, graduating in 1987. He is married to Lynn Kendall; they have two children.

FURTHER READING

"Thomas, Isiah." *Current Biography,* Aug. 1989.
"No longer a doubting. . . ." ROLAND LAZENBY. *Sporting News,* Nov. 1, 1988.
"The importance of being Isiah." DAVID BRADLEY. *Sport,* May 1988.

Thornburgh, Richard Lewis (1932–) In a major upset that had powerful national resonance for President George Bush and the Republican Party, former U.S. attorney general and Pennsylvania governor Thornburgh was on November 5, 1991, defeated by the Democratic candidate, political unknown Harrison L. Wofford, in a race for the Pennsylvania U.S. Senate seat left vacant by the death of former Republican Senator John Heinz.

The Bush administration had been very sure of winning the Senate seat. Thornburgh's resignation had been announced in June; he had left office on August 15 and was reportedly 40 percent ahead of the unknown Wofford at the beginning of the campaign. President Bush had campaigned actively for him in Pennsylvania, and Thornburgh had run as a political "insider" in the supposedly very popular Bush administration. But Pennsylvania had been terribly hard hit by the 1990–91 recession, still in full swing and with no end in sight—and to add injury to insult, Bush vetoed an unemployment insurance extension bill while the campaign was in progress. Wofford, who campaigned as a rather old-fashioned New Deal liberal, with a program to meet hard times that included national health insurance, overcame Thornburgh's hugh early lead, winning a landslide 55 percent of the vote.

Richard Thornburgh was a practicing attorney in Pittsburgh (1959–69) and was with the Department of Justice in western Pennsylvania and later in Washington (1969–77). He then moved into electoral politics, and was governor of Pennsylvania (1979–87). He went to Washington in July 1988 as Ronald Reagan's last attorney general and was reappointed by president-elect Bush. During the 1988 presidential campaign, while then-candidate George Bush was attacking the American Civil Liberties Union, Thornburgh publicly declared that he had once been a member of the ACLU, but had resigned. Pittsburgh-born Thornburgh received his engineering degree from Yale in 1954, and his L.L.B. from the University of Pittsburgh in 1957. He married Virginia Judson in 1963; the couple has four children.

FURTHER READING

"ACLU too, buddy. . . ." JAMES BENNET. *New Republic,* Oct. 17, 1988.
"Thornburgh, Richard Louis." *Current Biography,* Oct. 1988.

Tierney, Gene (1920–91) A Hollywood star of the 1940s, Tierney began her career in 1939, in bit parts on the New York stage. She was quickly picked up by Darryl Zanuck and immediately went into starring film roles, the first of them opposite Henry Fonda in *The Return of Frank James* (1940). The next seven years saw a series of starring roles, in such films as *Tobacco Road* (1940), *Belle Starr* (1941), *Heaven Can Wait* (1943), *Laura* (1944), *A Bell for Adano* (1945), *Leave Her to Heaven* (1945), *Dragonwyck* (1946), *The Razor's Edge* (1946), and *The Ghost and Mrs. Muir* (1947). Although she won an Oscar nomination for *Leave Her to Heaven,* it was her starring role opposite Dana Andrews in *Laura* that is by far best remembered. She later starred in such films as *Never Let Me Go* (1953) and *The Left Hand of God* (1955), but her career was damaged by a breakdown in 1955, followed by five years in and out of institutions. Her first husband was couturier Oleg Cassini; in 1960, she married Texas oilman W. Howard Lee, and then effectively retired, though returning occasionally to work in films and television. Her autobiography was *Self-Portrait* (1980; with Mickey Hershowitz). She was survived by two daughters and a sister. (d. Houston, Texas; November 6, 1991)

FURTHER READING

"Haunted beauty. . . ." *People,* Nov. 25, 1991.
Obituary. *Variety,* Nov. 11, 1991.
Obituary. *The Times* (of London), Nov. 9, 1991.
Obituary. *New York Times,* Nov. 8, 1991.

Tinguely, Jean (1925–91) Born in Switzerland, Tinguely attended art school and worked as an apprentice store window decorator in Basle. In the 1940s and early 1950s he began painting and creating the kinds of imaginative constructions for which he later became best known. He moved to Paris in 1952, in the mid-1950s producing mechanical sculptures, especially the "drawing machines" that became the rage of Paris and London. He then created such auto-destructive machines as his 1960 *Homage to New York,* which was intended to blow up in the garden of New York's Museum of Modern Art but instead caught fire. Some of his other auto-destructive machines suffered similar unintended fates, as when his *Study No. 1 for an End of the World* blew up prematurely, injuring bystanders. He continued to be popular for the next three decades. Two of his best-known later works were the Pompidou Centre fountain sculpture in Paris and the large junk sculpture show in Moscow in 1990. He was survived by his second wife, the artist Niki de Saint-Phaile, a daughter, and a son. His first wife was the artist Eva Aeppli. (d. Berne, Switzerland; August 30, 1991)

FURTHER READING

"The Tinguely estate. . . ." JUDD TULLY. *ARTnews,* Nov. 1991.
Obituary. *Current Biography,* Oct. 1991.
Obituary. *The Times* (of London), Sep. 7, 1991.
Obituary. *New York Times,* Sep. 1, 1991.
Jean Tinguely: A Magic Stronger than Death. PONTUS HULTEN. Abbeville, 1988.

Tower, John Goodwin (1925–91) A leading Republican conservative for three decades, Texas-born Tower taught political science before beginning his congressional career. He lost a U.S. Senate race to Lyndon Johnson in 1960 but won the seat in 1961, when Johnson became vice president. Tower served four terms in the Senate, ultimately becoming head of the Armed Services Commitee before leaving office in 1985. He was U.S. nuclear arms negotiator at Geneva in 1985–86, and then became a consultant, many of his clients being major American companies involved in defense contracting. In 1986–87, he headed the presidential commission examining the Iran-Contra Affair, and with fellow members Edmund Muskie and Brent Scowcroft issued the Tower Commission Report, which severely criticized the Reagan administration for its conduct. Tower campaigned for George Bush in 1988. He was nominated secretary of defense by president-elect Bush in December 1988, but ran into disabling confirmation problems in hearings during the confirmation process because of allegations of former drinking problems. Although Tower took a most remarkable pledge of sobriety in three February 26, 1988, national television appearances, his nomination was ultimately refused by the Senate, a defeat for the Bush administration and a personal disaster for Tower. He told his side of the story in his book *Consequences: A Political Memoir* (1991). Tower died in an airplane crash on his way to a Sea Island, Georgia, book promotion appearance. He was twice married and was survived by two daughters. (d. Brunswick, Georgia; April 5, 1991)

FURTHER READING

"Remember the Alamo." LESLIE BENNETTS. *Vanity Fair,* Sep. 1991.
Obituary. *Current Biography,* June 1991.
Obituary. WILLIAM F. BUCKLEY, JR. *National Review,* Apr. 29, 1991.
"Flying into tragedy. . . ." BOB LEVIN. *Maclean's,* Apr. 15, 1991.
"Tragedy strikes twice. . . ." *Time,* Apr. 15, 1991.
Obituary. *U.S. News & World Report,* Apr. 15, 1991.
Obituary. *The Times* (of London), Apr. 9, 1991.
Obituary. *New York Times,* Apr. 6, 1991.
"Towering inferno. . . ." MARTIN SCHRAM. *Washingtonian,* May 1989.
"Tottering Tower. . . ." FRED BARNES. *New Republic,* Dec. 19, 1988.
Two-Party Texas: The John Tower Era, 1961–1984. JOHN R. KNAGGS. Eakin Press, 1985.

Tracy, Edward: See **Lebanon Hostages**

Travolta, John (1954–) In the Jeffrey Hornaday film *Shout,* which opened in September 1991, Travolta starred as music teacher Jack Cabe, a rock 'n' roll prophet who brings the then-new music to 1955 Texas through the Benedict Texas Home for Boys band. The cast included Jamie Walters, Heather Graham, Richard Jordan, and Linda Fiorentino. The film was not well received, and Travolta, who had made a strong comeback with *Look Who's Talking* and *Look Who's Talking Too,* suffered a considerable career setback. On the other hand, he was still highly visible abroad and on home video in his two comeback films.

New Jersey-born Travolta became a well-known actor on television in "Welcome Back Kotter" (1975–79). On screen, he played minor roles until emerging as a star in the hit *Saturday Night Fever* (1977), followed by other popular starring roles in *Grease* (1978), *Urban Cowboy* (1980), and *Staying Alive* (1983). After some lean years, Travolta came back as a star of the comedy hit *Look Who's Talking* (1989), opposite Kirstie Alley and the voice of Bruce Willis as Mikey, the baby in the film. Travolta and Alley also starred in the 1990 sequel, *Look Who's Talking Too,* with the voice of Willis again as Mikey, joined by the voices of Roseanne Barr, Richard Pryor, and Damon Wayans. Travolta has also made several records. He and actress Kelly Preston were married in 1991; it was his first and her second marriage.

FURTHER READING

"Look who's talking. . .back." SUSAN SQUIRE. *Premiere,* Mar. 1990.

Tree, Marietta (1917–91) A liberal Democrat of moneyed background and strong social service convictions, Tree became a major figure in Democratic politics duringthe 1950s. She was a key Adlai Stevenson aide and campaigner during his two unsuccessful presidential campaign runs, in 1952 and 1956, and a member of the New York State Democratic Committee from 1954 to 1960. She was then appointed as U.S. representative to the United Nations Commission on Human Rights by incoming president John F. Kennedy. She served with the UN until 1967, finally on the staff of the UN Secretariat. After her UN service, she became once again deeply involved in city planning, and especially in New York affairs. She was survived by two daughters and four brothers. (d. New York City; August 15, 1991)

FURTHER READING

Obituary. *Current Biography,* Oct. 1991.
"The last grande dame. . . ." HARRY F. WATERS. *Newseeek,* Aug. 26, 1991.
Obituary. *The Times* (of London), Aug. 20, 1991.
Obituary. *New York Times,* Aug. 16, 1991.

Trump, Donald John (1946–) Trump managed to avoid personal bankruptcy once again in the spring of 1991 by agreeing with his bankers to divest himself of some of his properties to take down his debt, while holding on to several major properties. Divestments included the Trump Shuttle (formerly the Eastern Airlines shuttle), the Atlantic City Regency Hotel, his interests in the Hyatt Hotel and Alexander's retail store chains, and his yacht, *The Trump Princess.* He was to keep his three Atlantic City casinos, New York's Trump Plaza and Trump Tower, and other Manhattan realty holdings. During the balance of 1991, Trump continued to

sell remaining properties. In a presumably related development, his book *Trump: Surviving at the Top* (1990) was renamed *The Art of Survival* (1991). On the personal side, Trump in March reached a highly publicized divorce settlement with his former wife, Ivana Trump, and in July began an also highly publicized on-and-off engagement to Marla Maples.

New York-born Trump became a major real estate developer and highly visible billionaire celebrity during the 1980s. He also became a celebrity author, with the best-selling *The Art of the Deal* (1987), written with Tony Schwartz. He encountered severe financial problems in 1990 when his heavy bank and junk bond interest payments called for much more cash than his properties were generating, and he ultimately lost effective control of his properties to the bankers who had funded his expansion. Trump's B.A. was from the Wharton School in 1968. He and his former wife, Ivana, have three children.

FURTHER READING

"Trumped!. . . ." Susan Lee. *New York Times Book Review,* July 14, 1991.
"Donald Trump gets small. . . ." Harry Hurt III. *Esquire,* May 1991.
Trumped! The Inside Story of the Real Donald Trump—His Cunning Rise and Spectacular Fall. John R. O'Donnell and James Rutherford. Simon & Schuster, 1991.
"Trouble with a big T. . . ." Christine Gorman. *Time,* June 18, 1990.
"Manhattan's favorite. . . ." Richard L. Stern and John Connolly. *Forbes,* May 14, 1990.
"Playboy interview. . . ." Glenn Plaskin. *Playboy,* Mar. 1990.
Manhattan Passions: True Tales of Power, Wealth and Excess. Ron Rosenbaum. Morrow, 1987.

Tryon, Thomas (1926–91) Connecticut-born Tryon had two successful careers, as an actor and then as a novelist. He studied acting with Sanford Meisner at New York's Neighborhood Playhouse after World War II naval service and made his Broadway debut in *Wish You Were Here* (1952); he also worked in early television. Moving to Hollywood in 1955, he played in a wide range of films, most notably in the title role of Otto Preminger's 1963 film *The Cardinal,* as well as in such films as *In Harm's Way* (1965) and *The Glory Guys* (1965). He starred opposite Marilyn Monroe in *Something's Got to Give,* her final, never-completed film. In 1971, Tryon wrote his first novel, *The Other,* a suspense thriller that became a best-seller; he never returned to his acting career. He adapted the work into the 1972 Robert Mulligan film. He was survived by two brothers. (d. Los Angeles; September 2, 1991)

FURTHER READING

Obituary. *The Times* (of London), Sep. 12, 1991.
Obituary. *Variety,* Sep. 9, 1991.
Obituary. *New York Times,* Sep. 3, 1991.

Tsedenbal, Yumjaagiyn (1916–91) Former Mongolian premier Tsedenbal began his career in 1938 as a teacher at the Mongolian School of Finance, at Ulan Bator. His rise to power was very rapid: He became assistant minister of finance and then minister of finance in 1939, the year he joined the ruling Mongolian People's Revolutionary Party. In 1940, he became a central committee member and in the same year was named his party's secretary-general. From 1941 to 1945 he was deputy commander of the Mongolian army and its chief political officer. He became deputy prime minister to Mongolia's top leader, Horloogiyn Choybalsan, who died in 1952, Tsedenbal then succeeding him. Tsedenbal, always close to the Soviet Union, was out of power from 1954 to 1958, when Mongolia moved closer to China. His return to power in 1958 signaled a move back fully into the Soviet orbit. Tsedenbal led Mongolia for 26 more years, in the later years ruling more and more absolutely. In 1984, as a new day began to appear in the Soviet Union, he was removed from power and was moved to Moscow, essential in internal exile from Mongolia. By 1988, he was being officially denounced in Mongolia for fostering a "cult of personality" during his years in power and for imprisoning and murdering dissidents; he was also being blamed for 40 years of economic stagnation. He was survived by his wife, Anastasia Filatova, and a son. (d. Moscow; April 20, 1991)

FURTHER READING

Obituary. *The Times* (of London), Apr. 23, 1991.
Obituary. *New York Times,* Apr. 23, 1991.

Turner, Jesse: See **Lebanon Hostages**

Turner, Kathleen (1954–) Turner in 1991 starred as a tough Chicago private eye in the title role of Jeff Kanew's *V. I. Warshawski,* developed from the Sarah Paretsky mystery thrillers, playing opposite Jay O. Sanders as Murray, her journalist lover, in a cast that also included Charles Durning and Angela Goethals. Although Turner and Sanders received generally favorable reviews, the film itself was not well received by critics or audiences at home or abroad, though late in the year it was a highly successful video release. Forthcoming was a starring role in Michael Lessac's *House of Cards,* with Tommy Lee Jones and Esther Rolle. Also to come was another "Warshawski," this one a BBC radio dramatization of Paretsky's *Killing Orders.*

Missouri-born Turner moved from theater into films in the early 1980s and quickly emerged as a leading movie star, in such films as *Body Heat* (1981), *Romancing the Stone* (1984), *Prizzi's Honor* (1985), *The Jewel of the Nile* (1985), *Peggy Sue Got Married* (1986), *Switching Channels* (1988), *The Accidental Tourist* (1988), and *The War of the Roses* (1989). She also starred in a 1989 New York revival of Tennessee Williams's *Cat on a Hot Tin Roof,* and was the voice of the sexy cartoon figure, Jessica, in *Who Framed Roger Rabbit* (1988). Turner attended Southwest Missouri State University and received her M.F.A. from the University of Maryland. She married Jay Weiss in 1984; they have one child. (For photo, see **Madonna**.)

FURTHER READING

"Kathleen Turner. . . ." MALCOLM MACPHERSON. *Premiere,* Nov. 1989.
"A new role for. . . ." JENNY CULLEN. *Ladies Home Journal,* July 1988.
Kathleen Turner. REBECCA STEFOFF. St. Martin's, 1987.

Turner, Ted (Robert Edward Turner, III, 1938–) A major figure in the world communications industry, Turner in 1991 also pursued a growing interest in environmental matters; saw his Atlanta Braves go from the league cellar in 1990 to the league pennant in 1991, and then lose a closely contested World Series to the Minneapolis Twins; and became highly visible as half of a celebrity pair with Jane Fonda. Turner

and fiance Fonda visited Mikhail Gorbachev in Moscow; appeared everywhere together; and ran into a controversy with Native Americans at the World Series because of the Atlantic Braves "chop," thought to perpetuate anti–Native American stereotypes. In short, Turner was very highly visible during 1991, as a celebrity and as a financier whose enterprises seemed to be prospering.

It had not been so for very long. After encountering serious financial problems in the mid-1980s, Turner in the late 1980s emerged as a world communications industry leader, at the head of the Turner Broadcasting System (TBS), the Cable News Network (CNN), and the very successful new Turner Network Television (TNT). TNT began broadcasting its combination of old movies, sports, original television movies, and a potpourri of other programming in October 1988 and quickly grew into a major asset. From 1989 to 1991 CNN grew into a worldwide broadcast news network, with hundreds of millions of viewers, with its 24-hour coverage of such massive events as the Tiananmen Square demonstrations and massacre, the San Francisco earthquake, the tearing down of the Berlin Wall and the continuing events in Eastern Europe and the Soviet Union, the Palestinian uprising, and the Persian Gulf War. In this period of extraordinary news, his communications empire has become so influential that in January 1992 *Time* magazine named Turner their "Man of the Year" for 1991. Privately, Turner and Fonda were married on December 21, 1991, at the Turner ranch near Capps, Florida.

Turner began building what ultimately became a set of major enterprises in the 1960s and during the 1970s emerged as a leading American industrial and sports figure whose holdings also include the Atlanta Hawks. A leading yachtsman, he won the America's Cup in 1977. He sponsored the Goodwill Games in Moscow in 1986 and in Atlanta in 1990. Before marrying Fonda, he had been married twice previously and has five children. He attended Brown University.

FURTHER READING

"Ted Turner turns it on." BRUCE STUTZ. *Audubon,* Nov.–Dec. 1991.

"Jane and Ted's excellent adventure." JERRY ADLER. *Esquire,* Feb. 1991.

Ted Turner: Television's Triumphant Tiger. REBECCA STEFOFF. Garrett, 1991.

"Terrible Ted. . . ." IVOR DAVIS. *Los Angeles Magazine,* Aug. 1990.

"Captain planet. . . ." JOHN MOTAVALLI. *Interview,* June 1989.

"Ted Turner. . . ." GREG DAWSON. *American Film,* Jan.–Feb. 1989.

The Alexander Complex: Six Businessmen and the Empires They Built. MICHAEL MEYER. Random House, 1989.

The Corportion Warriors. DOUGLAS K. RAMSEY. Houghton Mifflin, 1987.

Turturro, John (1957–) Turturro took Cannes in 1991. At the annual international film festival in May, he won the coveted Golden Palm as best actor for his performance in the title role in Joel and Ethan Coen's comedy *Barton Fink,* playing a New York playwright-turned-scriptwriter experiencing writer's block in a surreal 1940s Hollywood. Also shown at Cannes was Spike Lee's *Jungle Fever,* with Turturro as Paulie Carbone, sensitive neighborhood friend of Angie Tucci (Annabella Sciorra). Earlier in 1991 Turturro opened in a less successful film, *Men of Respect,* playing mobster Mike Battaglia, a Macbeth in organized crime, opposite his real-life wife, Katherine Borowitz, as Ruthie Battaglia. On stage, Turturro played the Hitlerian title role in a New York production of Bertolt Brecht's *The Resistible Rise of Arturo Ui.* Forth-

coming on film was a starring role in another comedy, *Lame Ducks,* directed by Dennis Dugan. Turturro also plans to direct his first film, *Mac,* co-authored with Brandon Cole, an homage to his father, a Queens builder who died in 1988.

New Yorker Turturro first came to public notice in John Patrick Shanley's *Danny and the Deep Blue Sea* (1984), winning an Obie. On screen he is best known for his ethnic roles, tough and often twisted, as in *To Live and Die in L.A.* (1985), *Five Corners* (1987), *The Sicilian* (1987), *Do the Right Thing* (1989), *Miller's Crossing* (1990), and *Mo' Better Blues* (1990). Turturro graduated from the State University of New York's College at New Paltz in 1978 and later attended Yale University's School of Drama. He is married to actress Katherine Borowitz; they have one son. His younger brother, Nicholas Turturro, is also an actor.

FURTHER READING

"Homebody." Joseph A. Cincotti. *GQ—Gentlemen's Quarterly,* Oct. 1991.

"Not just another. . . ." Zoe F. Carter. *Premiere,* Sep. 1991.

"Honest John. . . ." Phoebe Hoban. *New York,* Aug. 12, 1991.

"John Turturro finks twice." Gavin Smith. *Interview,* Sep. 1990.

"Getting down. . . ." Marlaine Glicksman. *Film Comment,* Sep.–Oct. 1990.

"John Turturro's. . . ." Katherine Dieckmann. *Rolling Stone,* May 17, 1990.

Tutu, Desmond Mpilo (1931–) "We are pulling one another down. What has happened to us? I agree the system wants to destroy us. But do we have to cooperate with the system?" That was Archbishop Desmond Tutu, leader of the Anglican Church in South Africa, speaking on January 27, 1991, at burial services for 36 of the 42 victims of the Sebokeng massacre, a major incident in the Inkatha-African National Congress (ANC) civil war. Nobel Peace Prize winner Tutu was a major voice for peace and reconciliation throughout 1991, as the civil war continued to grow. Later in the year, he played a considerable moral role in developing the September peace pact signed by President F. W. De Klerk, Zulu leader Gatsha Buthelezi, and ANC leader Nelson Mandela. But Buthelezi immediately expressed doubt that the accord would work, and clashes quickly resumed. Tutu once again called for peace and urged the parties to give the peace agreement a chance to go into operation.

Tutu also continued to be a major figure in the worldwide struggle for equality, as in his cosponsorship of the humanitarian Committee of Blacks and Jews to Aid Ethiopia, faced with a new threat of famine. On a more directly political question, he canceled a forthcoming speech at a U.S. Episcopal Church convention to be held in Phoenix, Arizona, after Arizona voters had rejected a state holiday to honor the Reverend Martin Luther King, Jr.

Tutu has since his ordination as an Anglican minister in 1961 become South Africa's leading apostle of nonviolence within the South African freedom movement; he is an immensely respected world figure, much as was Martin Luther King, Jr., in the 1950s and 1960s. Tutu was awarded the Nobel Peace Prize in 1984. He rose steadily within his church and has been the archbishop at the head of the Anglican church in South Africa since 1986. He was secretary of the South African Council of Churches (1979–84) and since 1987 has been president of the All-Africa Council of Churches. Among his published works are *Hope and Suffering: Sermons and Speeches* (1984), *The Words of Desmond Tutu* (1989; edited by his daughter, Naomi Tutu), and *Crying in the Wilderness: The Struggle for Justice in South Africa* (1990). Tutu attended St. Peter's Theological College and the University of London. He married Leah Nomalizo Tutu in 1955; the couple have four children.

FURTHER READING

Desmond Tutu: Religious Leader devoted to Freedom. PATRICIA LANTER. Gareth Stevens, 1991.
" 'No one will stop us. . . .' " *UNESCO Courier,* June 1990.
"South Africa. . . ." TICHARD BAUTCH. *America,* May 13, 1989.
"A skeptical view." JOHN BIERMAN. *Maclean's,* Mar. 13, 1989.
Desmond Tutu: The Courageous and Eloquent Archbishop Struggling Against Apartheid in South Africa. DAVID WINNER. Gareth Stevens, 1989.
Desmond Tutu. DENNIS WEPMAN. Watts, 1989.
The Rolling Stone Interviews: The 1980s. St. Martin's, 1989.
Archbishop Tutu of South Africa. JUDITH BENTLEY. Enslow, 1988.
Tutu: Voice of the Voiceless. SHIRLEY DU BOULAY. Eerdmans, 1988.
Desmond Tutu: Bishop of Peace. CAROL GREENE. Childrens, 1986.

Tyson, Mike (1966–) Out-of-the-ring events overshadowed boxing for Mike Tyson in 1991. Most prominent and most serious was a charge of rape, filed by a contestant at the summer 1991 Miss Black America pageant; a trial for that and three other sex-related counts was set for late January 1992 in Indianapolis, with Tyson facing a maximum of 63 years in prison if convicted on all charges, to which he pleaded not guilty. In addition, the pageant's organizer filed a $21 million lawsuit, charging that Tyson had fondled the buttocks of 10 of 23 contestants; Miss Black America of 1990, Rosie Jones, filed a $100 million lawsuit charging him with doing the same. Earlier, in March 1991 in Manhattan Family Court, Tyson had acknowledged paternity of an eight-month-old daughter and had reached a support agreement with the child's mother, Kimberly Scarborough. At year's end, at least two other lawsuits were pending.

In the ring, Tyson defeated challenger Donovan "Razor" Ruddock in March, a match that the referee ended controversially in the seventh round. In a June rematch, a punishing 12-round contest, Tyson won more decisively, breaking Ruddock's jaw. As a result, Tyson remained boxing's number two heavyweight contender, but his attempt to regain the world heavyweight championship from Evander Holyfield was derailed when a scheduled November 1991 match had to be postponed because of a rib-cage injury Tyson suffered during a workout. The match was to be rescheduled in early 1992, depending on the timing and outcome of Tyson's trial.

Brooklyn-born Tyson turned professional in 1985 and quickly became a leading heavyweight title contender. From 1986 to 1988, he successively defeated several other boxers, the last of them Michael Spinks, in June 1988, to become sole world heavyweight champion, the youngest ever. He held the title until his unexpected defeat, his first as a professional, by James "Buster" Douglas in February 1990. Tyson was formerly married to actress Robin Givens.

FURTHER READING

Mike Tyson: Money Myth Betrayal. MONTEIL ILLINGWORTH. Carol, 1991.
"Is he back?" DAVID MILLER. *Sport,* Oct. 1990.
"Mike Tyson. . . ." ROBERT E. JOHNSON. *Jet,* June 25, 1990.
"Mike Tyson. . . ." RICHARD REGEN and MICHEL CONTE. *Interview,* Oct. 1990.
Mike Tyson. JOHN HENNESSEY. Smith, 1990.
Bad Intentions: The Mike Tyson Story. PETER HELLER. NAL-Dutton, 1990.
"Fire and fear. . . ." JOSE TORRES. *Playboy,* Aug. 1989.
Blood Season: Tyson and the World of Boxing. PHIL BERGER. Morrow, 1989.
Fire and Fear: The Inside Story of Mike Tyson. JOSE TORRES. Warner, 1989.
Serenity: A Book About Fighters: Why They Fight and How It Feels to Be One. RALPH WILEY. Holt, 1989.
"Tyson, Mike." *Current Biography,* Apr. 1988.

U

Ullman, Tracey (1959–) The Emmy-winning star did not immediately return to television after cancellation of her series, "The Tracy Ullman Show." Long a theater performer, with experience on both sides of the Atlantic, she instead did a one-woman play, *The Big Love*, playing Hollywood stage mother Florence Aadland, reminiscing about her daughter's alleged rape by a deteriorating Errol Flynn in 1957. Based on Aadland's 1961 book, the play was written by Brooke Allen and Jay Presson Allen, with the latter directing. Ullman opened the show in Miami in early March; it folded after 41 performances. Forthcoming was an appearance in the Robert Zemeckis film *Death Becomes Her,* along with Meryl Streep, Goldie Hawn, Bruce Willis, and Isabella Rosellini. Ullman continued to win recognition of her comic talents, on March 11 receiving an American Comedy Award as best female television performer for "The Tracy Ullman Show." Her return to television was awaited.

On the purely business side, Ullman in April sued 20th Century Fox Film Corp., alleging that the company had failed to honor a 1987 agreement that would have yielded millions of dollars in profits and royalties from "The Simpsons," long part of the Ullman show. The company denied all charges.

Ullman has been on stage since the mid-1970s and emerged as a star in British television comedy in the early 1980s. She became a comedy star in American television in her own "The Tracey Ullman Show" (1987–90); the series won a Best Comedy Series Emmy in 1989. She also won a 1990 Emmy, for best individual performance in a variety or musical program, in *The Best of the Tracey Ullman Show;* the show won a total of 13 Emmy nominations. Ullman also appeared in supporting roles in several films, including *Plenty* (1985), and starred opposite Kevin Kline in Lawrence Kasdan's film *I Love You to Death* (1990). She also played Kate to Morgan Freeman's Petruchio in a 1990 New York stage production of *The Taming of the Shrew;* and recorded the album *You Broke My Heart in Several Places,* with its hit single "They Don't Know." Ullman is married to Allan McKeown; the couple have two children, the second a son born in August 1991.

FURTHER READING

"Tracey Ullman. . . ." Jerry Lazar. *New York Times Magazine,* Oct. 15, 1989.
"Tracking Tracey." Michael Dare and Matthew Rolston. *Interview,* Jan. 1989.
"Ullman, Tracey." *Current Biography,* Oct. 1988.
"Tracey Ullman." Bill Zehme. *Playboy,* Sep. 1988.
"Enter Tracey Ullman. . . ." Louise Farr. *TV Guide,* Feb. 20, 1988.

Updike, John (John Hoyer Updike, 1932–) It was a year of prizes for Updike's *Rabbit at Rest* (1990), the fourth and final volume of the Harry Angstrom series. On February 16, he was awarded the 1990 National Book Critics Circle award for fiction. On April 9, he was awarded the Pulitzer Prize for fiction. Up-

dike was only the second author to win a fiction Pulitzer twice; Booth Tarkington had done so for *The Magnificent Ambersons* (1919) and for *Alice Adams* (1922).

In *Rabbit at Rest,* Updike killed off his most famous character, Harry "Rabbit" Angstrom. After three decades of chronicling American civilization through the life of his White Anglo-Saxon Protestant (WASP) anti-hero, Updike decided that Rabbit was "tired of everything" and had to go. It was *Rabbit Run* (1960)—the first book in the series and his second published novel—that established Updike as a major writer; it was made into a not-very-successful film in 1970. This was followed by *Rabbit Redux* (1977) and the Pulitzer Prize-winning *Rabbit Is Rich* (1981). Early 1990 also saw the publication of Updike's personal memoir, *Self-Consciousness: Memoirs.* In late 1991, Updike also published *Odd Jobs: Essays and Criticism,* a work of many short nonfiction pieces, including many book reviews and literary essays as well as some memoirs.

Pennsyvania-born Updike has also written several other highly regarded novels, including the National Book Award-winning *The Centaur* (1963), *Couples* (1968), *Bech: A Book* (1970, and its 1972 sequel), and *The Witches of Eastwick* (1984), made into the 1987 film. He has also written short stories, many of them published in *The New Yorker,* as well as essays, poetry, and a play. Updike's B.A. was from Harvard in 1954. Formerly married to Mary Pennington, he married Martha Bernhard in 1977 and has four children.

FURTHER READING

Something and Nothingness: The Fiction of John Updike and John Fowles. JOHN NEARY. Southern Illinois University Press, 1991.
John Updike. JUDIE NEWMAN. St. Martin's, 1988.
John Updike. HAROLD BLOOM, ed. Chelsea House, 1987.
John Updike Bibliography. E. A. GEARHART. Bern Porter, 1985.
"Updike, John (Hoyer)." *Current Biography,* Oct. 1984.
John Updike. ROBERT DETWEILER. G. K. Hall, 1984.
John Updike. SUZANNE H. UPHAUS. Ungar, 1980.

Vercors (Jean Marcel Bruller, 1902–91) A writer who helped to mobilize French resistance to the German invaders of his country during World War II, Bruller studied as an electrical engineer and worked as an artist and engraver from 1925 to 1939, while also publishing several minor works of fiction. He was wounded in 1940, before the French surrender, and recuperated in the Vercors region of the French Alps, from which he took his pen name and where he began his celebrated anti-Nazi novel, *The Silence of the Sea*. Vercors, who was a founder of the famous Resistance publishing house Editions de Minuit, helped publish the book himself; it was published underground in France in 1941 and abroad in 1943, becoming a worldwide best-seller. His identity as Bruller was kept secret until after the war, and as a Resistance fighter he was known as Vercors. He continued to write prolifically after the war but never with the impact of that first novel, although such works as *You Shall Know Them* (1953), *Sylvia* (1962), and *The Raft of the Medusa* (1971) were well received in France and abroad. (d. Paris; June 10, 1991)

FURTHER READING

Obituary. *The Times* (of London), June 13, 1991.
Obituary. *New York Times,* June 13, 1991.

Vincent, Fay (Francis Thomas Vincent, Jr., 1938–) In 1991, baseball commissioner Vincent was much involved in plans for expanding the National League to the same size as the American League, with two new franchises being awarded to Miami and Denver for 1993. When the owners were unable to agree on how to allocate players and the millions in expansion entry fees, Vincent made the controversial decision to share the fees among teams in both leagues rather than just the one being expanded, as in the past.

In his December 1991 state-of-the-game speech to club executives, Vincent pressed strongly for increased minority hiring, especially at the managerial level, and addressed the problems of declining television rights fees, part of a worsening economic picture for baseball that also involves spiraling players' salaries and a cumbersome salary arbitration scheme. Although at least three major league franchises were struggling economically, while other cities were eager to host a team, Vincent remained opposed to relocation. Two problems from the past remained—their names were Pete Rose and George Steinbrenner. Both had been barred from specific baseball activities but were seeking readmittance to the game's good graces. Late in 1991, Vincent announced that Steinbrenner could open the way for reinstatement by dropping two related lawsuits. Whether Rose would be allowed to return—and so to become eligible for the Hall of Fame—was left open.

On a different front, Vincent was working with the National Collegiate Athletic Association (NCAA) on a landmark plan that would allow college players to sign with major league teams and play in special summer leagues, and so to receive pay for their education without losing their college eligibility. In June 1991, with the commissioners of several other sports, Vincent spoke strongly to the Congress against the idea of sports lotteries, concerned that they would exacerbate the problem of teenage gambling and of gambling links to sports; he noted that the baseball commissioner's position was created after the Black Sox scandal of 1919, in which that team deliberately lost the World Series. In July, Vincent attended a White House ceremony honoring the 50th anniversary of a great year for baseball, and the two who made it so: Joe DiMaggio and Ted Williams; all then joined President and Mrs. Bush on Air Force One flying to the 62nd All-Star Game in Toronto.

Before joining major league baseball in 1989, Connecticut-born Vincent was a corporate lawyer and executive, a former president of Columbia Pictures and vice president of Coca-Cola. His B.A. was from Williams College in 1960 and his LL.D. from Yale in 1963. He married Valerie McMahon in 1965; the couple have three children.

FURTHER READING

"Vincent, Fay." *Current Biography,* May 1991.
"Welcome to hardball city." MIKE LUPICA. *Esquire,* June 1991.
"Baseball's unlikely. . . ." TOM CALLAHAN. *U.S. News & World Report,* Oct. 15, 1990.
"Fay Vincent. . . ." RICHARD SANDOMIR. *Manhattan, inc.,* May 1990.
"Vincent. . . ." DAVE NIGHTINGALE. *Sporting News,* Feb. 12, 1990.

Voelker, John Donaldson (1903–91)

Michigan-born Voelker, a lawyer and judge who wrote novels as Robert Traver, practiced law in his home state, was Marquette County prosecutor from 1935 to 1950, and was a justice of the Michigan Supreme Court from 1957 to 1960. By far his best-known work was the novel *Anatomy of a Murder* (1958), in which his client was accused of the 1952 murder of a man who had allegedly raped his wife. Like most of his work, the book was in large part autobiographical. James Stewart starred as the lawyer in the 1959 Otto Preminger film, in a cast that included Lee Remick as the wife, Ben Gazzara as the accused, and George C. Scott as the prosecuting attorney. Voelker's works also included such books as *Troubleshooter: The Story of a Northwoods Prosecutor* (1943), *Small Town D.A.* (1954), *Hornstein's Boy* (1962), *Fisherman* (1964), *Laughing Whitefish* (1965), and *Trout Magic* (1974). He was survived by his wife, Grace, and three daughters. (d. Marquette, Michigan, March 19, 1991)

FURTHER READING

Obituary. *The Times* (of London), Mar. 29, 1991.
Obituary. *New York Times,* Mar. 20, 1991.

Wagner, Robert Ferdinand, Jr. (1910–91) New York City-born Wagner was a three-time mayor of his native city, and for that reason, also a world figure. A moderate liberal, he was the son of New Deal Democratic senator Robert Wagner, architect of such massive pieces of social legislation as the Wagner Act and the Social Security Act. The younger Wagner, a lawyer, began his political career with his 1937 election to the New York state assembly. After World War II service in military intelligence, he returned to a series of appointive positions in New York City government. In 1949, he was elected Manhattan borough president and in 1953 won the mayoralty, serving three terms (1954–67). In 1958, Wagner made a historic break with Tammany, as part of a Democratic Party statewide reform movement led by Eleanor Roosevelt and former governor Herbert H. Lehman. After leaving office, he returned to the practice of law and was later ambassador to Spain and President Carter's personal envoy to the Vatican. He was survived by his third wife, the former Phyllis Fraser Cerf, and two sons. (d. New York City; February 12, 1991)

FURTHER READING

Obituary. *Current Biography,* Apr. 1991.
Obituary. *Variety,* Feb. 11, 1991.
Obituary. *The Times* (of London), Feb. 11, 1991.
Obituary. *New York Times,* Feb. 10, 1991.

Wahlberg, Donnie: See **New Kids on the Block**

Waite, Terry: See **Lebanon Hostages**

Walesa, Lech (1943–) Polish President Walesa encountered a wide and varied range of problems during 1991, as the enormous promise of democracy and freedom from Soviet control met the realities of fragmented Polish politics and a sagging Polish economy. While many of his allies pressed hard for reforms, his austerity program was resisted in parliament by liberals and conservatives alike and he was refused requested emergency economic powers. Walesa also battled with parliament on election law matters, ultimately on July 1 losing the fight and accepting proportional representation based on party lists of candidates rather than direct majority election of individuals. As a result, the October 27 parliamentary elections resulted in a fragmented parliament in which no party had more than 13 percent of the votes and forming any government at all proved enormously difficult. A frustrated Walesa "joked" about assuming the premier's post himself, in addition to the presidency. As Poland moved into the winter of 1991–92, it slipped deeper into the worldwide recession, with added problems as Soviet markets dried up for lack of money to pay for goods. As winter came, the jobless rate soared to 10 percent while the the trade deficit grew—as did Walesa's problems.

Walesa became an electrician at the Lenin Shipyard in Gdansk in 1966; fired after leading the 1970 strike, he continued to organize Poland's developing labor movement. In 1980, he led the successful Lenin Shipyard strike, which sparked a nationwide series of largely successful strikes, and in September 1980, he was a founder and first president of the Polish trade union confederation, Solidarity. He was imprisoned for a year after Solidarity was outlawed in 1981 but continued to be underground leader of the union and movement. As the Gorbachev era developed, he and Solidarity emerged openly once again, and Solidarity was legalized under his leadership in 1989. He led in the negotiations that resulted in the Polish turn toward democracy and to the free elections of June 1989, won by Solidarity. Walesa refused the Polish presidency at that point, but in June 1990 he decided to run. He defeated Tadeusz Mazowiecki and Stanislaw Tyminski in a three-way vote, and in the December runoff he defeated Tyminski 3–1. Walesa was awarded the 1983 Nobel Peace Prize. In 1987 he published *A Way of Hope: An Autobiography.* He married Danuta Walesa in 1969; the couple have eight children.

FURTHER READING

Lech Walesa: The Road to Democracy. Rebecca Stefoff. Fawcett, 1992.
"Lech-luster. . . ." Victoria Pope. *New Republic,* Dec. 3, 1990.
"Walesa answers. . . ." Martin Pollack. *World Press Review,* Aug. 1990.
"Walesa's war. . . ." Anna Husarska. *New Republic,* July 23, 1990.
"Walesa's drive. . . ." Peter Hebblethwaite. *National Catholic Reporter,* June 1, 1990.
Lech Walesa: The Leader of Solidarity and Campaigner for Freedom and Human Rights in Poland. Mary Craig. Gareth Stevens, 1990.
"A symbol of hope." Phil Suda. *Scholastic Update,* Oct. 20, 1989.
"The struggle for solidarity. . . ." Barry Came. *Maclean's,* Apr. 17, 1989.
Lech Walesa. Tony Kaye. Chelsea House, 1989.
Crystal Spirit: Lech Walesa and His Poland. Mary Craig. ABC-Clio, 1987.
Lech Walesa and His Poland. Mary Craig. Continuum, 1987.
The Book of Lech Walesa: A Collective Portrait. Solidarity Friends and Members. Simon & Schuster, 1982.

Walken, Christopher (1943–) Versatile actor Christopher Walken starred on theater screen, home screens, and on stage during 1991. In the James Glickenhaus action film *McBain,* Walken starred in the title role as the leader of a group of Vietnam veterans aiding a Colombian insurrection to honor a Vietnam battlefield commitment. On a far more sophisticated note, Walken played a decadent aristocrat opposite Natasha Richardson, Rupert Everett, and Helen Mirren in Paul Schrader's horror-thriller *The Comfort of Strangers;* Harold Pinter's screenplay was based on the Ian McEwan novel. And on a classic note, in the summer of 1991 Walken was Iago to Raul Julia's Othello at the New York Shakespeare Festival in Central Park. On the television screen, he starred opposite Glenn Close in a Hallmark Hall of Fame television movie, *Sarah, Plain and Tall.* Forthcoming was a villainous starring role in the *Batman* sequel, Tim Burton's *Batman Returns,* in a cast that includes Michael Keaton, Michelle Pfeiffer, Danny DeVito, Michael Gough, Pat Hingle, Michael Murphy, and Marlon Wayans.

New York City-born Walken gained his early experience in a wide range of regional theater and New York stage roles, making his 1959 Broadway debut in *J.B.* His early work also included a notable appearance in *The Lion in Winter* (1966), and his later work a New York Shakespeare Festival appearance in *Coriolanus* (1988). He made his film debut in *The Anderson Tapes* (1972), played substantial roles in *Next Stop Greenwich Village* (1976), *Roseland* (1977), and *Annie Hall* (1977), and had a breakthrough role in *The Deer Hunter* (1978), winning a Best Supporting Actor Oscar. He went on to major roles in such films as *The Dogs of War* (1980), *Heaven's Gate* (1980), *Pennies from Heaven* (1981), *The Milagro Beanfield War* (1988), *Biloxi Blues* (1988), and *Communion* (1989). Walken attended Hofstra University.

FURTHER READING

"Walken, Christopher." *Current Biography,* Oct. 1990.
"In the danger zone." Chuck Pfeifer and Mark Matousek. *Interview,* Mar. 1988.

Wang Yani (1975–) Young Chinese artist Wang Yani had another career landmark in 1991. At the age of 16, she was the subject of a biography, *A Young Painter: The Life and Paintings of Wang Yani—China's Extraordinary Young Artist,* by Zheng Zhensun and Alice Low.

The book includes numerous examples of her painting, and Wang Yani herself traveled around the United States to publicize the book, accompanied by her father. It was her fourth trip to America. In 1989, she toured the United States when her work was exhibited in several cities, as it has also been in Europe and Japan. In that year, at age 14, she was the youngest person ever to be given a solo exhibition at the Smithsonian, in their Arthur M. Sackler Gallery for Asian Art, in Washington, D.C. Her visits often include demonstrations of her spontaneous painting technique, using traditional Chinese inks, colors, and brushes, as on her 1991 trip to Manhattan's Children's Museum.

Wang Yani was born and raised in Guangxi province in rural China and began painting at age three. Her earliest paintings featured lively cats and monkeys; later works include landscapes with birds or other animals, and in recent years she has also painted people. One of her monkey paintings, "Scratching an Itch for Mother," was pictured on a Chinese postage stamp when she was only eight years old. Wang Yani is also enormously prolific, having completed over 10,000 paintings by age 16. She has never had formal art lessons and paints from her memory and imagination, expressing thoughts and feelings rather than painting realistic works. Her father, Wang Shiqiang, himself a self-taught painter and art educator, gave up his own work—he says temporarily—to let her style develop without being shaped by his; he is managing his daughter's career until she is grown. In 1987, she had published *Wang Yani: Pictures by a Young Chinese Girl.*

FURTHER READING

"The brush of innocence." SHANNON MAUGHAN. *Publishers Weekly,* Nov. 29, 1991.
"A Young Painter. . . ." FAITH MCNULTY. *New Yorker,* Nov. 25, 1991.
A Young Painter: The Life and Paintings of Wang Yani—China's Extraordinary Young Artist. ZHENG ZHENSUN and ALICE LOW. Scholastic, 1991.
"A child prodigy. . . ." CONSTANCE A. BOND. *Smithsonian,* Sep. 1989.
Yani: The Brush of Innocence. WAI-CHING HO et al. Hudson Hills, 1989.

Washington, Denzel (1954–) Building on his success in *Glory* and *Mo' Better Blues,* Washington starred in two highly contrasting film roles in 1991, again demonstrating his range and versatility. In Russell Mulcahy's thriller, *Ricochet,* he starred as police officer Nick Styles, opposite John Lithgow as badman Earl Talbot Blake. In *Mississippi Masala,* directed and co-produced by Indian director Mira Nair, he starred as an African-American in contemporary Mississippi, in love with an immigrant Indian woman, played by Sarita Choudhury, whose family fled Uganda for the United States when Idi Amin took power in 1972. Forthcoming was the title role in Spike Lee's film biography *Malcolm X,* based on the screenplay by James Baldwin and Arnold Perl. His appearance and the film were eagerly awaited, as the long-planned and often delayed film was thought to be a potential classic. Oscar-winner Washington was a presenter at the March 25 Academy Awards ceremony. On a very serious note, he was named by Earvin (Magic) Johnson to serve on the board of directors of the Magic Johnson Foundation, formed to support education and awareness programs about AIDS (acquired immune deficiency syndrome), to fund research, and to assist in caring for those suffering from the disease.

Washington emerged as a strong stage player from the mid-1970s, at the New York Shakespeare Festival and in several off-Broadway plays, one of them the Negro Ensemble Company's *A Soldiers Play,* in a role he re-created in the 1984 film *A Soldier's Story*. He starred in the title role of *Richard III* (1990) at the New York Shakespeare Festival in Central Park. Washington became a television star in the 1980s, as Dr. Otis Chandler in "St. Elsewhere" (1982–88). His films include *Cry Freedom* (1987) as South African Black leader Steve Biko, *For Queen and Country* (1989), *The Mighty Quinn* (1980), *Heart Condition* (1989), *Glory* (1989; he won a 1990 Best Supporting Actor Oscar), and *Mo' Better Blues* (1990). Washington attended Fordham University and studied at San Francisco's American Conservatory Theater. He is married to singer Paulette Pearson; they have two children.

FURTHER READING

"The glory days of. . . ." LAURA B. RANDOLPH. *Ebony,* Sep. 1990.
"The mo' better Denzel." ELVIS MITCHELL. *California,* Sep. 1990.
"Days of glory. . . ." PHOEBE HOBAN. *New York,* Aug. 13, 1990.
"Denzel delivers." SHARI ROMAN. *Video Magazine,* Aug. 1990.

"Denzel in the swing." THULANI DAVIS. *American Film,* Aug. 1990.
"Denzel Washington." VERONICA WEBB and HERB RITTS. *Interview,* July 1990.
Filming with Attenborough. DONALD WOODS. Holt, 1987.

Watkins, James David (1927–) During 1991, Watkins's Department of Energy found that nuclear industry control and effective nuclear waste disposal posed problems far greater than any but the most severe anti-nuclear critics had supposed. He also encountered increased opposition within the Bush administration, as the true cost of a full-scale national nuclear waste cleanup began to be apparent, running into the tens of billions and perhaps hundreds of billions of dollars.

Some problems seemed so far terribly difficult to solve. The New Mexico national hazardous waste respository, the first such installation to be built after half a century of nuclear waste creation, was scheduled to open in 1988, but new and ever more serious safety questions postponed its opening to beyond 1991. Similarly, the waste cleanup at the Hanford, Washington, nuclear installation was not completed on schedule; instead, Watkins announced in January 1991 that the often-delayed cleanup would take at least one to two more years, and others questioned whether Hanford would be cleaned up by the end of the century, if ever.

Watkins also raised other very serious questions about existing programs and practices. In January, the Energy Department transferred continuing studies of the health effects of radiation on hundreds of thousands of nuclear workers to the Department of Health and Human Services. In April, in congressional committee testimony, he announced that the Savannah River nuclear plant reactor had been found to have flaws that could in a nuclear accident cause a catastrophic meltdown. In July, the Energy Department charged the companies operating the complex with massive financial irregularities, while the Justice Department opened a criminal investigation. Late in the year, a leak caused a further indefinite shutdown. The Energy Department also backed away from a cleanup timetable at the Rocky Flats plant, and in May was most unusually fined by the Environmental Protection Agency (EPA) for failure to meet a cleanup timetable at the Fernald, Ohio, nuclear plant.

Watkins backed the February 1991 Bush administration national energy plan, which stressed oil, nuclear energy, and energy conservation, and proposed opening the Arctic National Wildlife Refuge to oil exploration.

Watkins was a career naval officer, who in 37 years moved up through a series of line and staff positions to become commander of the U.S. Sixth Fleet in 1978; vice chief of naval operations in 1979, the year he became an admiral; and commander in chief of the Pacific Fleet in 1981. From 1982 until his retirement in 1986, he was chief of U.S. naval operations. In 1987, he began an entirely different kind of public career when appointed head of the national AIDS advisory commission by President Ronald Reagan; he then became a prime mover in issuing the landmark 1988 commission report, which considerably helped to focus national attention on the fight against the disease, and especially on AIDS-connected discrimination. He was appointed secretary of the Department of Energy by president-elect George Bush in January 1989. California-born Watkins received his B.S. from the U.S. Naval Academy at Annapolis in 1949, and his M.S. from the Naval Postgraduate School in 1958. He married Sheila Jo McKinney in 1950; the couple have seven children.

FURTHER READING

"How to meet our energy needs." *Design News,* Mar. 11, 1991.

"Hands-on energy leader." WILLIAM LANOUETTE. *Bulletin of the Atomic Scientists,* May 1990.
"The heat is on! . . ." THOMAS A. LEWIS. *National Wildlife,* Apr.–May 1990.
"James D. Watkins. . . ." WILLIAM LANOUETTE. *Bulletin of the Atomic Scientists,* Jan.–Feb. 1990.
"The new broom." *Economist,* Dec. 23, 1989.
"Admiral Watkins's. . . ." STEPHEN J. HEDGES. *U.S. News & World Report,* Aug. 14, 1989.
"Energy czar. . . ." VICKY CAHAN et al. *Business Week,* July 24, 1989.
"Watkins, James David." *Current Biography,* Mar. 1989.
"The metamorphosis of. . . ." LYNN ROSELLINI. *U.S. News & World Report,* July 4, 1988.

Weaver, Sigourney (Susan Weaver, 1949–) Early in 1991, Weaver continued her very successful London stage run in Chekhov's *The Three Sisters,* in a cast that included Vanessa, Lynn, and Jemma Redgrave, and Christopher Reeve; the play was directed by Corin Redgrave, brother of Vanessa and Lynn, and father of Jemma.

From that classic work, she moved back into the kind of futuristic fiction film that has made her fortune. Her movie breakthrough had come in 1979, in the original *Aliens* film. Its 1986 sequel had also been enormously successful at the box office. Now to come was *Alien 3,* again starring Weaver as Warrant Officer Ripley, this time stranded on a faraway penal colony. The expensive (more than $30 million) film was shot in London in 1991, and was expected to open in late May 1992.

New York City-born Weaver was on stage from the mid-1970s, most notably in *Hurlyburly* (1984) and *The Merchant of Venice* (1987), though she is best known for the "Aliens" films, and for such films as *Eyewitness* (1981), *Deal of the Century* (1983), *The Year of Living Dangerously* (1983), *Ghostbusters* (1984; and its 1989 sequel, *Ghostbusters II*), *Gorrillas in the Mist* (1988; in the Oscar-nominated role of Dian Fossey), and *Working Girl* (1988). Weaver attended Stanford University and the Yale Drama School. She married James Simpson in 1984; the couple have one child.

FURTHER READING

"Weaver, Sigourney." *Current Biography,* Mar. 1989.
Sigourney Weaver. T. D. MAGUFFEE. St. Martin's, 1989.
"Sigourney weaves. . . ." JESSE KORNBLUTH. *Cosmopolitan,* Dec. 1988.
"Dream Weaver. . . ." CHRISTOPHER DURANG and ROBERT MAPPLETHORPE. *Interview,* July 1988.

White, Byron Raymond (1917–) Justice White, approaching his fourth decade on the Supreme Court, continued to defy classification as liberal or conservative, though perhaps moving somewhat toward the increasingly conservative majority during the 1990–91 Court term. In the key case of *Rust v. Sullivan,* he found with the conservative majority in upholding federal regulations banning federally funded family planning clinics from offering abortion counseling; and he dissented in *United Automobile Workers v. Johnson Controls Inc.,* a landmark women's rights case ruling that according to the 1978 Pregnancy Discrimination Act employers could not ban pregnant women from jobs potentially dangerous to their unborn children. But he took the liberal position in *Edmonson v. Leesville Concrete Co.,* which barred exclusion of jurors in civil cases because of race, following earlier bans on exclusion because of race in criminal cases, and wrote dissents against conservative majority opinions in such key cases as *Arizona v. Fulminante,* which ruled that coerced or involuntary confession in a criminal case could be a "harmless error" if conviction would have resulted without it; *Barnes v. Glen Theater,*

which upheld an Indiana state law banning nude dancing; and *Harmelin v. Michigan,* which ruled that a Michigan law requiring a life sentence without possibility of parole for possession of 650 grams (1.5 pounds) of cocaine did not violate the cruel and unusual punishment prohibition of Eighth Amendment.

In the same term, White went with the conservative majority in *Board of Education of Oklahoma City v. Dowell,* which eased conditions for the lifting of court supervision of segregated school districts; *County of Riverside, California v. McLaughlin,* which ruled that those arrested without warrants could be held up to 48 hours while a judge decided if there was probable cause for the arrest; *Florida v. Bostick,* which ruled that police could board buses and search passengers' luggage, with their permission; *Coleman v. Thompson,* which sharply restricted the use of habeas corpus writs by state prisoners who have exhausted state appeals; and *Payne v. Tennessee,* which allowed "victim impact" evidence to be presented by the prosecution during the sentencing phase of criminal cases, thereby reversing 1987 and 1989 cases that had decided the opposite.

White wrote the majority opinion in *Cohen v. Cowles Media,* ruling that a breach of a promise of confidentiality made to a news source was not protected by the First Amendment, as against a suit for damages caused by the breach; and wrote a dissent in *Masson v. New Yorker Magazine,* which ruled that invented or materially altered quotes attributed to a public figure could be libelous.

Colorado-born White was football star "Whizzer" White in the late 1930s. After World War II, he practiced law in Denver until 1960. He then campaigned for John F. Kennedy in 1960; as president, Kennedy appointed him a deputy attorney general in 1961 and then a Supreme Court Justice in 1962. White's B.A. was from the University of Colorado in 1938, his LL.B. from Yale in 1945. He is married to Marion Stearns; the couple have two children

FURTHER READING

"A new day in court." LAUREN TARSHIS and JAMES EARL HARDY. *Scholastic Update,* Nov. 1, 1991.
"Byron White leads. . . ." DAVID A. KAPLAN. *Newsweek,* Apr. 30, 1990.
Eight Men and a Lady. HERMAN SCHWARTZ, ANDREA NEAL, and DAVID SAVAGE. National Press, 1990.
"What they say it is. . . ." *Time,* July 6, 1987.

Wilder, L. Douglas (Lawrence Douglas Wilder, 1931–) Facing mounting budget deficits, Virginia governor Wilder in February 1991 pushed through his state legislature a budget containing a massive $2.2 billion in cuts, at the same time refusing to accept any tax increases.

Wilder was highly visible on the national scene throughout 1991, as he prepared to announce his candidacy for the 1992 Democratic presidential nomination, which he did on September 13. Quite understandably, he called it a "long shot," an evaluation underscored by the continuing difficulty his finance committee was having in raising funds, even enough to qualify for federal matching campaign funds. On January 8, 1992, he withdrew from the race, after running last in several candidate preference polls.

Wilder was also engaged in a highly visible feud with Virginia Democratic senator Charles S. Robb; ultimately, national Democratic Party leaders made it clear that the careers of both men were being damaged, and on June 18 Wilder and Robb held a highly publicized peace meeting, then claiming a peaceful end to the affair. Three Robb aides resigned in late July.

Richmond-born Wilder became governor after a long career in state government. He was a Democratic member of the Virginia Senate (1969–85), and was lieutenant governor of his state (1986–89). On November 7, 1989, he won the Virginia gubernatorial election by a razor-thin 50.1 percent to 49.9 percent, surviving a recount to become the first African-American governor in the history of the United States. Wilder's B.S. was from Virginia Union University in 1961, his J.D. from Howard University in 1959. He has three children.

FURTHER READING

"Can Doug Wilder's. . . ." RUSSELL MILLER. *Rolling Stone,* Oct. 31, 1991.
"The no bull campaign." HOWARD FINEMAN. *Newsweek,* Oct. 14, 1991.
"Terminators 2—Robb v. Wilder. . . ." FRED BARNES. *New Republic,* July 8, 1991.
"Wilder and Wilder. . . ." JOHN HOOD. *Reason,* Mar. 1991.
"Va. governor Wilder talks. . . ." *Jet,* Feb. 25, 1991.
"L. Douglas Wilder. . . ." LYNN NORMENT. *Ebony,* Feb. 1991.
Racism as a Factor in the 1989 Gubernatorial Election of Doug Wilder. DAVID R. JONES. E. Mellen, 1991.
"Mild Wilder. . . ." FRED BARNES. *New Republic,* Aug. 13, 1990.
"Wilder, Lawrence Douglas." *Current Biography,* Apr. 1990.
"The first Black elected governor. . . ." LAURA B. RANDOLPH. *Ebony.* Feb. 1990.
Wilder: Hold Fast to Dreams: A Biography of L. Douglas Wilder. DAVID P. BAKER. Seven Locks, 1990.
Claiming the Dream: The Victorious Campaign of Douglas Wilder of Virginia. MARGARET EDDS. Algonquin, 1990.

Williams, Robin (1952–) One of the "big" commercial movies of 1991 was Steven Spielberg's Christmas film *Hook,* a modern version of J. M. Barrie's *Peter Pan* tale, about a grown-up Peter (Peter Banning, a workaholic corporate attorney) who returns to Neverland to rescue his own children from the wicked Captain Hook. Williams starred as Peter, opposite Dustin Hoffman as Captain Hook, in a cast that included Julia Roberts as Tinkerbell, Bob Hoskins as Smee, and Maggie Smith as Granny Wendy. In autumn 1991 Williams starred in Terry Gilliam's *The Fisher King,* as the leader of a group of Manhattan derelicts literally seeking the Holy Grail, opposite Jeff Bridges as a troubled upper-class disc jockey seeking redemption. Earlier in 1991, Williams starred as a psychiatrist turned grocery clerk in the Kenneth Branagh thriller *Dead Again,* opposite Branagh and Emma Thompson. In a change of pace, on April 9 he narrated a Russian folk tale, *The Fool and the Flying Ship,* to kick off Showtime's new animated children's series "We All Have Tales."

Chicago-born Williams began his career as a comic in cabaret, playing many West Coast clubs, and then moved into television, in variety and later as a star in "Mork and Mindy" (1978–82). He became a leading film star of the 1980s, in such movies as *The World According to Garp* (1982), *Moscow on the Hudson* (1984), *Good Morning Vietnam* (1987), *The Adventures of Baron Munchausen* (1989), *Dead Poets Society* (1989; he won a Best Actor Oscar nomination), *Cadillac Man* (1989), and *Awakenings* (1990). With Whoopi Goldberg and Billy Crystal, Williams has been a prime mover in the *Comic Relief* benefits for the homeless. In 1989 he published *To Be Somebody.* Williams attended Claremont College, Marin College, and the Juilliard School. Formerly married to Valerie Velardi, he married Marsha Garces in 1989; he has two children.

FURTHER READING

"A Peter Pan for yuppies." KURT ANDERSEN. *Time,* Dec. 16, 1991.
"Peter pandemonium." FRED SCHRUERS. *Premiere,* Dec. 1991.
"Robin Williams. . . ." JEFF GILES and MARK SELIGER. *Rolling Stone,* Feb. 21, 1991.
"Awake and sing." FRED SCHRUERS. *Premiere,* Jan. 1991.
"Talking with. . . ." CARSON JONES. *Redbook,* Jan. 1991.
"Robin Williams. . . ." JOE MORGENSTERN. *New York Times Magazine,* Nov. 11, 1990.
"Robin Williams has. . . ." LISA GRUNWALD. *Esquire,* June 1989.
"Actor. . . ." *Life,* Spring 1989.

Willis, Bruce (Bruce Walter Willis, 1955–) After his huge popular success in the two *Die Hard* films, Willis was considered one of Hollywood's most "bankable" stars. But in 1991 he encountered an enormous career setback, after starring as a cat burglar in the title role of the ill-fated Michael Lehmann film *Hudson Hawk.* The film, very expensive to make and expected to be a commercial blockbuster, was panned by many critics, although some thought it a mildly entertaining work. It also did very badly at the box office, and therefore entered film history as a monumental disaster.

His other 1991 films were not as unfortunate. They included Alan Rudolph's *Mortal Thoughts,* in which he starred (and co-produced), opposite his wife, Demi Moore, and Glenne Headly; Robert Benton's *Billy Bathgate,* opposite Dustin Hoffman, also a box-office disappointment; and late in the year Tony Scott's *The Last Boy Scout,* opposite Damon Wayans, a box-office success, and so commercially something of a comeback film. Forthcoming was a starring role in the comedy *Death Becomes Her,* with Meryl Streep, Goldie Hawn, and Kevin Kline. On the personal side, Willis and Moore had their second child, a daughter, in July 1991.

German-born Willis worked in the New York theater from the late 1970s, and appeared in several small film roles in the early 1980s. He emerged as a television star in the long-running series "Moonlighting" (1985–89), and with *Blind Date* (1987) moved into starring roles in films. He went on to star in *Sunset* (1988), *Die Hard* (1988), its sequel *Die Hard II* (1989), *In Country* (1989), and *The Bonfire of the Vanities* (1990). He was also the featured voice of baby Mikey in *Look Who's Talking* (1989) and *Look Who's Talking Too* (1990). Willis attended Montclair State College. He and Demi Moore married in 1987; they have two daughters.

FURTHER READING

"Demi's big moment." NANCY COLLINS and ANNIE LEIBOVITZ. *Vanity Fair,* Aug. 1991.
"Bruce on the loose." ANTHONY HADEN-GUEST. *Vanity Fair,* Jan. 1991.
"Bruce Willis. . . ." FRED ROBBINS. *McCall's,* June 1989.
"Bruce Willis. . . ." *Video Review,* Feb. 1989.
"Playboy interview. . . ." LAWRENCE GROBEL. *Playboy,* Nov. 1988.
"Bruce Willis. . . ." DENNIS WATLINGTON. *Cosmopolitan,* Sep. 1988.
"Bruce Willis. . . ." AUDREY LAVIN. *Redbook,* Aug. 1988.

Wilson, Angus (1913–91) A leading British writer and critic, Wilson began writing short stories in the mid-1940s, after a career that included a position in the British Museum's Department of Printed Books and intelligence work during World War II. He emerged as a major satirist and moralist with his first published work, the short stories collected in *The Wrong Set* (1949), and in the decades that followed produced a wide range of works, including short stories, novels, plays, filmscripts, biographies, and essays. Some of his best-known novels are *Hemlock and After* (1952), *Anglo-Saxon Attitudes* (1956), *The Old Men at the Zoo* (1961), *No Laughing Matter* (1967), and *Setting the World on Fire* (1980). He also held a series of professorships from the early 1960s, and was much in demand as a visiting professor and lecturer on American campuses. At his death, there were no immediate survivors. (d. Bury St. Edmonds, England; May 31, 1991)

FURTHER READING

Obituary. *Current Biography,* Aug. 1991.
"Late call. . . ." PAUL BINDING. *New Statesman & Society,* June 14, 1991.
Obituary. *The Times* (of London), June 3, 1991.
Obituary. *New York Times,* June 2, 1991.
Angus Wilson. AVERILL GARDNER. Macmillan, 1985.
Four Contemporary Novelists: Angus Wilson, Brian Moore, John Fowles, V. S. Naipaul. KERRY McSWEENEY. University of Toronto Press, 1983.
Angus Wilson: Mimic and Moralist. PETER FAULKNER. Viking Penguin, 1980.

Wilson, August (1945–) Award-winning playwright August Wilson, whose work continues to be set in the African-American 20th-century experience, had a new play on tour in 1991: *Two Trains Running.* The play, set in a Pittsburgh restaurant in 1969, starred Al White as restaurant proprietor Memphis Lee, Cynthia Martels as Risa, Roscoe Lee Browne as Holloway, Sullivan Walker as Hambone; John Cothran, Jr., as ex-con Sterling, Anthony Chisholm as bookie Wolf, and Chuck Patterson as undertaker West; Lloyd Richards directed. After playing New Haven, Boston, Seattle, and San Diego, the play opened at Washington's John F. Kennedy Center on November 14; its Broadway opening was scheduled for April 1992. Wilson's *Fences* awaited its screen adaptation. On February 6, 1991, Wilson and Lloyd Richards received Black Filmmakers Hall of Fame Paul Robeson Awards.

Playwright and poet Wilson emerged as a major figure in the American theater during the 1980s; his plays include *Jitney* (1982); *Ma*

Rainey's Black Bottom (1984); *Fences* (1987), which won a Best Play Tony and a Pulitzer Prize, and in which James Earl Jones won a Best Actor Tony; and *The Piano Lesson,* for which he won a second Pulitzer Prize. *The Piano Lesson* was also chosen as best play of the season by the New York Drama Critics Circle. Wilson dropped out of school in the ninth grade, at age 15. He was formerly married.

FURTHER READING

"An elegant duet. . . ." RACHAEL MIGLER. *GQ—Gentlemen's Quarterly,* Apr. 1990.
"Fine-tuning. . . ." MEL GUSSOW. *New York Times Magazine,* Sep. 10, 1989.
"The light in August." CHIP BROWN. *Esquire,* Apr. 1989.
"On Broadway. . . ." CHARLAYNE HUNTER-GAULT. *Vogue,* Aug. 1988.
"Exorcising the demons. . . ." WILLIAM A. HENRY. *Time,* Apr. 11, 1988.

Winfrey, Oprah (1954–) Broadcast journalist, producer, and actress Winfrey dominated the afternoon talk-show circuit in 1991, with top ratings that translated into record contract renewal sums for as far forward as the 1994–95 season. She was third on *Forbes* magazine's 1991 list of highest-paid performers, behind New Kids on the Block and Bill Cosby. Moving in new directions, Winfrey contracted with ABC to produce all the 1992–93 season "Afterschool Specials" series programs including the usual fictional dramas, two "town meeting" talk shows, and a documentary; she will also introduce reruns of previous shows. In November 1991 she produced the off-Broadway play *From the Mississippi Delta* at New York's Circle-in-the-Square; it was the story of Dr. Endesha Ida Mae Holland, who rose from prostitution to become a university professor of women's studies.

Winfrey used her considerable celebrity on behalf of powerless children, speaking before the Senate Judiciary Committee in November 1991 on child abuse, and referring to her own experience as an abused child; she urged passage of a bill establishing a national screening program for child-case providers, including careful background checks. She also donated $100,000 to buy books for a new Chicago library, noting "Books were my path to personal freedom." Winfrey expresses unhappiness with the continuing public examination of her weight ups-and-downs, and says she wants to focus on being healthy and fit, and to appreciate herself, not judge herself because of her weight.

Mississippi-born Winfrey began her broadcasting career in 1972, as a reporter for WVOL radio while still in school and then for WTVF-TV (both in Nashville), then moved to Baltimore's WJZ-TV as co-anchor in 1976. Becoming co-host of the station's morning show, she entered a new career, scoring a major success as the host of "AM Chicago" for Chicago's WLS-TV, which was renamed "The Oprah Winfrey Show" in 1984 and became a nationally syndicated hit show. She also starred in the 1989 television miniseries *The Women of Brewster Place,* later developing the role in the short-lived television prime time series, "Brewster Place" (1990). Winfrey attended Tennessee State University. She has appeared in several films, including *The Color Purple* (1985) and *Native Son* (1986).

FURTHER READING

"Oprah's crusade." MARY H. J. FARRELL et al. *People,* Dec. 2, 1991.
"The companies they keep." FRED GOODMAN. *Working Woman,* Dec. 1991.
"Oprah Winfrey. . . ." ALAN EBERT. *Good Housekeeping,* Sep. 1991.
"Next on Oprah." BILL BRASHLER. *Ladies Home Journal,* Aug. 1991.
"Walking in the light." PEARL CLEADGE. *Essence,* June 1991.
Oprah Winfrey. GERALDINE WOODS. Dillon, 1991.
"Oprah Winfrey tells. . . ." *Jet,* Sept. 17, 1990.
"A brain for. . . ." MATTHEW SCHIFRIN and PETER NEWCOMB. *Forbes,* Oct. 1, 1990.
Oprah Winfrey: TV Talk Show Host. MARGARET BEATON. Childrens, 1990.
Oprah Winfrey: Talk Show Host and Actress. LILLIE PATTERSON and CORNELIA H. WRIGHT. Enslow, 1990.
Oprah Winfrey: Media Success Story. ANNE SAIDMAN. Lerner, 1990.
Everybody Loves Oprah!: Her Remarkable Life Story. NORMAN KING. Morrow, 1988.
Oprah! ROBERT WALDRON. St. Martin's, 1987.

Winger, Debra (1955–) During 1991, Debra Winger was seen as Kit Moresby, opposite John Malkovich's Port, in movie theaters in Bernardo Bertolucci's *The Sheltering Sky* (1990), based on Paul Bowles's best-selling novel, a post–World War II existential tale of a "caravan of horrors." Winger later reported that the experience of shooting the film in the Sahara, in what was for her the totally alien Taureg culture, changed her life and awareness of self, and strengthened her decision to seek a new personal life away from Los Angeles. The film was critically well received but did not do well at the box office or later in home video release.

Winger did not sign a contract for it, but in the summer of 1991 she was set to star in Penny Marshall's film about a women's baseball team, *A League of Their Own;* she later withdrew over "creative differences." Forthcoming was a starring role opposite Dennis Quaid in the Glenn Gordon Caron film *Wilder Napalm,* which started production in November 1991. Winger's name was also in the media in 1991 because of her highly publicized friendship with Nebraska Senator Bob Kerrey, a candidate for the 1992 Democratic presidential nomination.

Cleveland-born Winger began her career in television, most notably in the series "Wonder Woman" (1976–77), and then moved into films. She emerged as a highly regarded dramatic actress in such films as *French Postcards* (1979), *Urban Cowboy* (1980), *Cannery Row* (1982), *An Officer and a Gentleman* (1982), *Terms of Endearment* (1983), *Legal Eagles* (1986), *Black Widow* (1987), *Betrayed* (1988), and *Everybody Wins* (1990). Winger attended California State University. She was formerly married to actor Timothy Hutton; she has one child.

FURTHER READING

"Straight shooting star." LYNN HIRSCHBERG. *American Film,* July–Aug. 1988.
"The taming of Debra Winger." ARTHUR LUBOW. *Cosmopolitan,* May 1987.
Debra Winger: Hollywood's Wild Child. M. J. CAHILL. St. Martin's, 1985.

Wolfson, Isaac (1897–1991) Glasgow-born Wolfson, the child of Russian-Jewish immigrants, joined Universal Stores in 1926 (renamed Great Universal Stores—abbreviated GUS—in 1930) and built the company into a massive retail empire in the six decades that followed, maintaining close personal control of day-to-day company operations until 1986, when he resigned his chairmanship. Wolfson was a large-scale philanthropist, funding the Wolfson Foundation with 6 million pounds in 1955 and making large contributions to a wide range of institutions, including Oxford University, the Weizmann Institute of Science, Cambridge University, and many others in the United Kingdom and Israel. He was survived by a son, British financier Leonard Gordon Wolfson, and five sisters. (d. Rehevot, Israel; June 20, 1991)

FURTHER READING

Obituary. *New York Times,* June 22, 1991.
Obituary. *The Times* (of London), June 21, 1991.

Wonder, Stevie (Steveland Judkins Morris, 1950–) A new Stevie Wonder album is an event in the world of popular music. In June 1991, he issued his first new album in four years, *Music from the Movie "Jungle Fever,"* Spike Lee's interracial love story. The title song of the 11-song soundtrack album is "Jungle Fever"; other notable songs are "Chemical Love," "Each Other's Throats," "If She Breaks Your Heart," and "These Three Words." In 1991, Wonder also wrote "The Force Behind the Power," the cover song of the new Diana Ross album. He also continued to work on his forthcoming album, tentatively titled *Conversation Piece,* while as always appearing and playing at benefits for a wide range of social causes. On June 14, Wonder received the second annual Nelson Mandela Courage Award for humanitarian efforts at TransAfrica Forum's "Bridge to Freedom" dinner in Los Angeles.

Singer, composer, and instrumentalist Wonder is one of the leading popular musicians of the past three decades, his extraordinary accomplishments even more remarkable because of his lifelong blindness. Wonder was a child prodigy, a multi-talented musician who sang and played harmonica, piano, organ, and drums, and later composed much of his work for the synthesizer. His first record, for Motown, was *Little Stevie Wonder, the 12 Year Old Genius* (1967). He went on to become one of the most popular musicians of the next three decades. Many of his songs have become American and worldwide standards, such as "My Cherie Amour" (1969), the Grammy-winning "You Are the Sunshine of My Life" (1972), "Superstition" (1973), "Living for the City" (1975), and the Oscar-winning "I Just Called to Say I Love You" (1984). His many records include such works as the Grammy-winning *Innervisions* (1973), the Grammy-winning *Songs In the Key of Life* (1976), *Journey Through the Secret Life of Plants* (1979), *In Square Circle* (1986), and *Characters* (1987). He was formerly married to Syreeta Wright (1971–72), and has three children.

FURTHER READING

"Stevie's jungle adventure." JAMES T. JONES IV. *Down Beat,* Sep. 1991.
"Former child stars. . . ." MICHELLE MCCALOPE. *Jet,* Apr. 15, 1991.
"Stevie Wonder." MICHAEL GOLDBERG. *Rolling Stone,* Nov. 5, 1987.
Twenty Years of Rolling Stone. JANN S. WENNER. FRIENDLY PRESS, 1987.
Stevie Wonder. JOHN SWENSON. Harper, 1986.
Stevie Wonder. JEFFREY PEISCH. Ballantine, 1984.
Mr. Wonderful: Stevie Wonder. LEONARD PITTS, JR. Sharon, 1984.

Wood, Daniel: See **New Kids on the Block**

Woods, James (1947–) In March 1991, veteran film and television actor James Woods starred as New York detective John Moss in John Badham's comedy-thriller *The Hard Way,* co-starring Michael J. Fox as a film actor studying him for a role, in a cast that included Annabella Sciorra, Stephen Lang, and Penny Marshall. Woods also starred opposite John Lithgow in the television film *The Boys,* about two long-term friends who face a terminal illness together. Forthcoming was a starring role in Michael Ritchie's *Diggstown,* along with Louis Gossett, Jr., Oliver Platt, Heather Graham, and Bruce Dern. Woods is also set to star in *Citizen Cohn,* HBO's television film biography of highly controversial lawyer Roy Cohn. Also forthcoming was a starring role in Barnet Kellman's *Straight Talk* opposite Dolly Parton, with Griffin Dunne, Teri Hatcher, and John Sayles.

Utah-born Woods appeared on the New York stage and in films in the early 1970s, and emerged as a star in such films as *The Onion Field* (1979), *Fast Walking* (1982), *Split Image* (1982), *Videodrome* (1983), *Once upon a Time in America* (1984), *Against All Odds* (1984), *Joshua Then and Now* (1985), *Best Seller* (1987), *Cop* (1987), *True Believer* (1989), and *Immediate Family* (1989). He has also appeared in many telefilms, winning an Emmy for *Promise* (1986), and a second Emmy as Bill Wilson, a co-founder of Alcoholics Anonymous, in *My Name is Bill W* (1989). Woods attended the University of California and the Massachusetts Institute of Technology. He has been married twice.

FURTHER READING

"James Woods. . . ." *American Film,* May 1990.
"Woods, James." *Current Biography,* Nov. 1989.
"Fighting his way. . . . RICHARD B. WOODWARD. *New York Times Magazine,* Aug. 20, 1989.
"James Woods. . . ." NEIL HICKEY. *TV Guide,* Apr. 29, 1989.
"Arresting appeal.. . ." BETSY BORNS. *Harper's Bazaar,* Feb. 1989.

Ian Woosnam (foreground) and Nick Faldo (background).

Woosnam, Ian (1958–) Diminutive Welsh golfer Woosnam played big in 1991, to become number one golfer in the world rankings, replacing fellow British golfer Nick Faldo. That top position was solidified by his win on the final putt at the 55th Masters in April, over Tom

Watson (his final-round partner and teenage idol) and Jose-Maria Olazabal—all three of whom were tied at the 18th tee. The popular Woosnam was the third straight British player to win the Masters, after Sandy Lyle in 1988 and Faldo in 1989 and 1990. In December, after winning four other events worldwide, Woosnam was named World Player of the Year by *Golf Digest.*

The 5′ 4½″ Woosnam, nicknamed Woosie, grew up on the Welsh border; his local golf club had 15 holes in Wales and 3 in England. Turning professional at 18, he spent years in the shadow of better-known golfers, although he was the top money winner on the European tour in 1987, winning over $2 million. Woosnam is widely regarded as a "working class" golfer who has "paid his dues." He is married to Glendryth Woosnam; they have two children.

FURTHER READING

"Little big man." MICHAEL MCDONNELL. *Golf Magazine,* Apr. 1988.

"Wielder of a big stick." SARAH BALLARD. *Sports Illustrated,* Mar. 28, 1988.

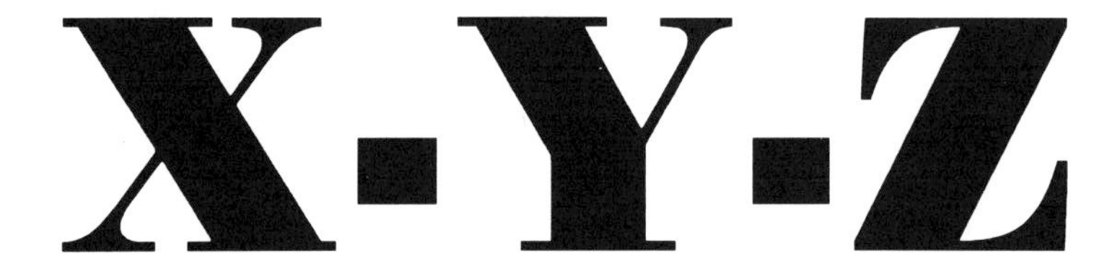

Yellen, Jack (1892–1991) A prolific songwriter, Polish-born Yellen began to sell his songs while still in high school in Buffalo. He wrote the lyrics of several of the hit songs of the 1920s, such as "Down by the O-Hi-O," for the *Ziegfeld Follies of 1920;* "I Wonder What Became of Sally" (1924); "Ain't She Sweet" (1927); and by far his best-known song, "Happy Days Are Here Again," from the film *Chasing Rainbows* (1930), which became Franklin Delano Roosevelt's campaign song in 1931 and remained the unofficial Democratic Party anthem throughout the Great Depression and World War II (Yellen was a Republican). He also wrote a considerable string of songs for Sophie Tucker, including "Hard Hearted Hannah—the Vamp of Savannah," "My Yiddishe Momme" and "The Last of the Red Hot Mommas." Yellen also wrote songs for several Broadway shows and Hollywood films. He retired in the late 1940s, and from 1951 to 1969 served on the board of the American Society of Composers, Authors, and Publishers (ASCAP), which he had joined in 1917. He became a member of the Songwriters Hall of Fame in 1976. He was survived by his wife, the former Lucille Hodgeman, a daughter, a son, and a brother. (d. Springville, New York; April 17, 1991)

FURTHER READING

Obituary. *The Times* (of London), May 3, 1991.
Obituary. *New York Times,* Apr. 19, 1991.

Yeltsin, Boris Nikolayevich (1931–) ". . . we are dealing with a rightist, reactionary, anti-constitutional coup . . . The peoples of Russia are becoming masters of their own destiny." With these words on August 19, 1991, Russian president Boris Yeltsin became the leader of mass resistance to the right-wing communist coup that for three days in August threatened all that had been accomplished by Mikhail Gorbachev, Yeltsin, and other reformist Soviet leaders during the Gorbachev era. On August 19, Gorbachev was placed under house arrest while vacationing in the Crimea; his removal from office was announced by a right-wing communist State of Emergency Committee headed by Vice President Gennadi I. Yanayev, which included such key figures as Vladimir A. Kryuchkov, the KGB chairman; Boris L. Pugo, the Interior minister; and Dimitri Yazov, the Defense minister. Gorbachev resisted the coup plotters, refusing to sign away his presidency. Yeltsin, still free, immediately went to the White House, the Russian parliament building in Moscow, and became the leader of the massive resistance that quickly developed, as huge unarmed crowds gathered to defend the building. The resistance was decisively helped by the refusal of key capital military units to move against Yeltsin; indeed, elite paratroops and Soviet armor sent against him all turned themselves to face any attacking force, guaranteeing the safety and quick victory of the resistance. Prompt support of the resistance came from U.S. President George Bush

and British Prime Minister John Major, who called Yeltsin on August 20; by then the crowd around the White House numbered a reported 150,000 and resistance was reported throughout the country.

On August 21, the aborted coup collapsed, Yeltsin was a national hero, and a second, democratic Russian revolution was in the process of sweeping away the remnants of Soviet communism and ultimately the Soviet state. Gorbachev returned to Moscow on August 22, but did not seize the moment to re-establish his leadership. After a brief period of Yeltsin-Gorbachev abrasion, followed by a brief period of coalition between the two, Yeltsin emerged as by far the stronger, in popular appeal and as leader of the Russian republic, which gained power as the old Soviet central government began to fade away. Before the aborted coup, Yeltsin and his calls for democracy and decentralization had been gaining strength; after the coup, he began to exercise power essentially as the head of a sovereign state. On November 1, the Russian parliament granted him sweeping new powers that would enable him to quickly turn Russia toward a market economy.

On December 8, Yeltsin, Ukrainian President Leonid Kravchuk, and Belarus President Stanislav Shushkevich founded a new "Commonwealth of Independent States," invited all the other former Soviet republics into the commonwealth, and declared the Soviet Union at an end. This action began a new period in the history of all the political entities involved and brought a new worldwide set of relationships and problems, chief among them the fate of the Soviet nuclear arsenal. Mikhail Gorbachev resigned on December 25, 1991. As the long, cold, hungry, bitter 1991–92 Russian winter deepened, Yeltsin began to introduce crash market economy reforms, while Russia and all the states of the new Commonwealth faced a very uncertain future.

Yeltsin worked as an engineer (1955–68), then going into Communist Party work in his home city of Sverdlovsk. During the early 1980s, he strongly supported and was close to Mikhail Gorbachev; Yeltsin moved into far higher party positions in 1985, when Gorbachev came to power. He was mayor of Moscow (1985–87) and secretary of the Communist Party central committee (1985–86). He moved into opposition in

1987, becoming a leader of those who felt that reform was not proceeding quickly enough, and was for some years a "maverick" in Soviet politics, who was not taken very seriously and whose relations with Gorbachev were often abrasive.

In 1989, Yeltsin won the Moscow elections to the Congress of People's Deputies by an overwhelming majority. He was at first denied election to the Supreme Soviet by the communist majority, but was elected after a major reformist protest and became an opposition leader in the Soviet parliament. In March 1990, Yeltsin refocused, winning election as a delegate to the Russian Federation's Supreme Soviet. On May 29, 1990, he was elected president of the Russian Federation and began a campaign to secure greater Russian autonomy from the central government. In July, he also resigned from the Communist Party. By early August 1990, Yeltsin was being taken very seriously, and he and Gorbachev made the first of many on-again-off-again agreements on radical economic reform; the issues really began to be resolved a year later, after the failed coup.

Yeltsin has published an autobiography, *Against the Grain* (1990); forthcoming was his book on the August 1991 events. He attended the Urals Polytechnic Institute. Little is known of his personal life, except that he is married to Naina Yeltsin.

FURTHER READING

Boris Yeltsin: A Political Biography. VLADIMIR SOLOVYOV. Putnam, 1992.

"The end of the U.S.S.R." GEORGE J. CHURCH. *Time,* Dec. 23, 1991.

"The man who saved the future." T. D. ALLMAN. *Vanity Fair,* Oct. 1991.

"When putsch comes to shove. . . ." TATYANA TOLSTAYA. *New Republic,* Sep. 16, 1991.

"In excelsis Yeltsin." HELLE BERING-JENSEN. *Insight,* Sep. 9, 1991.

"A chastened character. . . ." JOHN KOHAN. *Time,* Sep. 9, 1991.

"Profiles of courage." MARY NEMETH. *Maclean's,* Sep. 2, 1991.

Time, Sep. 2, 1991. "The man who rules Russia." DAVID AIKMAN. "Desperate moves." BRUCE W. NELAN.

"Yeltsin's triumph." ROSE BRADY et al. *Business Week,* Sep. 2, 1991.

"Sober statesman. . . ." BILL HEWITT. *People,* July 8, 1991.

"Is Boris Yeltsin for real?" ROWLAND EVANS and ROBERT NOVAK. *Reader's Digest,* July 1991.

"Mother Russia's freedom fighter." PAUL HOFHEINZ. *Fortune,* Apr. 8, 1991.

Time, Mar. 25, 1991. "The conductor of discord." STROBE TALBOTT. "Portrait of a populist." DAVID AIKMAN. "Boris vs. Mikhail. . . ." BRUCE W. NELAN.

"Yeltsin. . . ." JOHN KOHAN. *Time,* Jan. 7, 1991.

Boris Yeltsin: Russia's First President. JOHN MORRISON. NAL-Dutton, 1991.

"New Yeltsin. . . ." JEFF TRIMBLE. *U.S. News & World Report,* Dec. 31, 1990.

"The 'Cassandra of. . . .' " STEPAN KISELEV. *World Press Review,* Nov. 1990.

" 'Yeltsin was. . . .' " JEFF TRIMBLE. *U.S. News & World Report,* Oct. 22, 1990.

"Boris Yeltsin. . . ." BILL KELLER. *New York Times Magazine,* Sep. 23, 1990.

"What makes. . . ." MIKHAIL ZARAEV. *World Monitor,* Aug. 1990.

"Yeltsin's challenge. . . ." TOM MATTHEWS. *Newsweek,* June 11, 1990.

"Yeltsin spoils. . . ." EUGENE H. METHVIN and VLADIMIR SHLAPENTOKH. *National Review,* Mar. 19, 1990.

"Boris Yeltsin explains." VALENTIN YUMASHEV. *World Press Review,* Jan. 1990.

"Yeltsin, Boris Nikolayevich." *Current Biography,* Jan. 1989.

Zappa, Frank (Francis Vincent Zappa, 1940–) Frank Zappa's 50th birthday was celebrated in November 1991 with a four-day series of concerts titled "Zappa's Universe: A Celebration" at New York City's Ritz Theater, featuring songs from Zappa's 1990 album *Broadway the Hard Way* expanded into a theater piece, as well as modern classical French composer Erik Satie's *Socrate,* with various guest singers and instrumentalists (including three of Zappa's children: Moon Unit, Dweezil, and Ahmet) performing under the direction of Joel Thome. Zappa himself had been scheduled as host and performer, in his first live appearance in New York City since 1988. Unfortunately, the guest of honor was unable to attend. After months of rumors, denials, and "no comments," Zappa's family confirmed in a news conference before the opening concert that Zappa had prostate cancer and was suffering severe reactions to the cancer treatments.

Earlier in 1991, on his own Barking Pumpkin label, Zappa had released two new double-CD sets, *Make a Jazz Noise Here* and *The Greatest Band You Never Heard in Your Life.* Rykodisc also released *You Can't Do That on Stage Anymore, Vol 4,* a collection of Zappa's live miscellania. Turning the tables on bootleggers who have made and sold over 400 unauthorized concert recordings of Zappa works, Zappa and Rhino Records copied some of these illicit works and released their own bootleg recordings in 1991.

Zappa continued active in opening cultural and business connections in Europe, especially newly free countries. He even runs a firm called Why Not Inc., advising those who want to do business in Eastern Europe. The mayor of Budapest in 1991 invited Zappa to his city to celebrate the end of the Soviet Union's military presence in Hungary. The Frankfurt Festival was scheduled to devote a week to Zappa's music in September 1992.

In July, presumably inspired by Czechoslovakia's President Vaclav Havel—who had in 1990 named him special cultural ambassador to Czechoslovakia—Zappa had announced that he was considering running for president in 1992, going so far as to confer with Washington political consultants; long politically active, he has voter registration tables set up at his concerts and speaks out strongly on political and social issues such as censorship and abortion.

Zappa became a major rock music figure in the 1960s as founder of the group the Mothers of Invention (1964–77); the group's hit albums included *Freak Out!* (1966), *Absolutely Free* (1967), and *200 Motels* (1971; and the 1971 film). On his own, he made such records as *Hot Rats* (1969), *Apostrophe* (1974), and *Joe's Garage* (1979). His hit singles included "Don't Eat the Yellow Snow" (1974), "Dancin' Fool" (1979), and "Valley Girl" (1982), in which he teamed up with his daughter Moon Unit, then only 14. Zappa's most notable later work tries to join jazz and classical music in such albums as *Boulez Conducts Zappa* (1982, 1987) and *The Perfect Stranger and Other Works* (1985). In 1989, Zappa published *A Mother of Necessity: The Real Frank Zappa Book,* written with Peter Occhiogrosso. In 1967 Zappa married Gail Sloatman, with whom he runs several music-related businesses; they have four children. Moon Unit and Dweezil starred in the television situation comedy "Normal Life" (1990–91).

FURTHER READING

"Frank Zappa stricken. . . ." KIM NEELY. *Rolling Stone,* Jan. 9, 1992.
"Frank Zappa makes . . . ." MICHAEL DAVIS. *Down Beat.* July 1991.
"Profile: Dweezil. . . ." ALAN DIPERNA. *Guitar Player,* May 1991.
"Frank Zappa—trading partner." DAVID CORN. *Nation,* Mar. 19, 1990.
"Zappa, Frank." *Current Biography,* Feb. 1990.
"Frank Zappa. . . ." TIM SCHNECKLOTH. *Down Beat,* Sep. 1989.
"Frank Zappa. . . ." STEVE DOUGHERTY. *People,* May 22, 1989.
No Commercial Potential: The Saga of Frank Zappa Then and Now. DAVID WALLEY. NAL-Dutton, 1980.

PHOTO CREDITS

Virgin Records: Paula Abdul (photo by Alberto Tolot)

Baker-Winokur-Ryder, Public Relations: Danny Aiello

Roundabout Theatre Company: Jane Alexander (photo © Susan Shacter, 1991)

U.S. Department of Education: Lamar Alexander

Embassy of Italy, Press Office: Giulio Andreotti

British Information Service, Central Office of Information, London: Andrew, Duke of York, Sarah, Duchess of York, Prince Charles, Princess Diana (photo: Terence Donovan), Elizabeth II, Neil Kinnock, John Major, Margaret Thatcher (London Press Office)

Embassy of the Philippines: Corazon Aquino

Wide World Photos: Jean-Bertrand Aristide, Warren Beatty and Annette Bening, Bill Clinton, Jimmy Connors, Macaulay Culkin (photo © 1990 20th Century Fox), Jeffrey Dahmer, Jodie Foster and Anthony Hopkins (© 1991 Orion Pictures, photo: Ken Regan), Whoopi Goldberg, Anita Hill, Kitty Kelley, Terry Anderson, Terry Waite, Madonna, Martha Graham, and Kathleen Turner, Joseph Papp, Julia Roberts and Kiefer Sutherland, Salman Rushdie, H. Norman Schwarzkopf, Pamela Smart, William Kennedy Smith, Clarence Thomas and Virginia Lamp Thomas, Ian Woosnam and Nick Faldo, Boris Yeltsin

CNN: Peter Arnett (photo: George Bennett)

© *1989 Capital Cities/ABC, Inc.*: Roseanne Barr Arnold, Neil Patrick Harris, Peter Jennings

Republican National Committee: Lee Atwater (photo: Philip Bermingham Photography)

Doubleday: Margaret Atwood (photo: Anthony Loew)

Embassy of Chile: Patricio Aylwin

U.S. Department of State: James Baker

Public Information Office, Rockefeller Institute: David Baltimore (photo: Whitehead Institute)

D.C. Office of Communications: Marion Barry

Susan Smith & Associates: Kathy Bates

U.S. Senate: Joseph Biden, George Mitchell (photo: Maureen Keating)

U.S. Supreme Court, Public Information Office: Harry Blackmun, Anthony Kennedy, Thurgood Marshall, Sandra Day O'Connor, William Rehnquist, Antonin Scalia, David Hackett Souter, John Paul Stevens, Byron White

Addison-Wesley Publishing Co.: Robert Bly (photo: © Millicent Harvey)

United Nations: Boutros Boutros-Ghali (UN Photo 178980/M.Grant), Nelson Mandela (UN photo 176005/P. Sudhakaran), Javier Pérez de Cuéllar (UN Photo 169681/J. Isaac)

National Organization on Disability: James Brady

Office of Public Affairs, U.S. Department of the Treasury: Nicholas Brady

Library of Congress: Joseph Brodsky (photo: Reid Baker)

The White House: Barbara Bush (photo: Carol T. Powers), Richard Darman (Office of Management and Budget), Marlin Fitzwater, John Sununu

U.S. Army: George Bush

Wendy Morris/PMK: Keith Carradine (photo: Jeff Sedlik, Los Angeles, © 1991)

The Carter Center: Jimmy Carter

U.S. Department of Defense: Dick Cheney, Colin Powell (photo: Russel Roederer)

© *1990 Def American Recordings, Inc.*: Andrew Dice Clay

Brazilian Embassy: Fernando Collor de Mello

© *1990 CBS Records, Inc.*: Harry Connick, Jr. (photo: Michele Singer), New Kids on the Block (photo: Timothy White)

© *1991 The David Geffen Company*: Bill Cosby (photo: Howard Bingham)

© *1991 Warner Brothers Inc., Regency Enterprises V.O.F. and Le Studio Canal*: Kevin Costner and Jay O. Sanders, Jack Lemmon, Sissy Spacek, Oliver Stone, Donald Sutherland

Embassy of El Salvador: Alfredo Cristiani

Oden Productions: Tom Cruise

N.Y. State Governor's Office: Mario Cuomo

HarperCollins: Dalai Lama (photo: Galen Rowell), Gabriel Garcia Marquez (photo: The Douglas Brothers), Philip Glass (photo: Annie Leibovitz), Mikhail Gorbachev, Raisa Gorbachev, Oliver North

PGA Tour: John Daly

Susan Geller & Associates: Geena Davis

© 1991 Universal City Studios, Inc.: Ossie Davis, Ruby Dee, Spike Lee (photo: David Lee), Anthony Quinn, John Turturro

Embassy of South Africa: Frederik Willem De Klerk

U.S. Department of Labor: Elizabeth Hanford Dole

Dennis Davidson Associates: Michael Douglas

Columbia Records: Bob Dylan (© 1989 Ken Regan/ Camera 5)

New York Knickerbockers: Patrick Ewing, Pat Riley

Royal Embassy of Saudi Arabia: King Fahd

Gerald R. Ford Library: Gerald R. Ford

Triad Artists, Inc.: Morgan Freeman

National Endowment for the Arts: John E. Frohnmayer

Embassy of Peru: Alberto Fujimori

National Cancer Institute: Robert Gallo (photo: Bill Branson)

Embassy of Spain, Information Department: Felipe Gonzalez Márquez

Farrar, Straus and Giroux: Nadine Gordimer (photo: © 1990, Sophie Bassouls/SYGMA)

Advantage International: Steffi Graf (photo: Carol Newsom)

Capitol Records: Hammer (photo: Annie Leibovitz), Bonnie Raitt (photo: Aaron Rapoport/1989)

Embassy of the Czech and Slovak Federal Republic: Vaclav Havel

Australian Overseas Information Service: Bob Hawke

Knopf: Katharine Hepburn (photo: © 1991 John Bryson), John Updike (© Davis Freeman)

Nippy, Inc./Arista: Whitney Houston

Imagine Films: Ron Howard

Embassy of Jordan: Hussein I

Toronto Argonauts: Raghib (Rocket) Ismail

Levine/ Schneider Public Relations; Virgin Records: Janet Jackson

© 1988 MJJ Productions: Michael Jackson (photo: Sam Emerson)

Los Angeles Lakers: Earvin (Magic) Johnson

Chicago Bulls: Michael Jordan

Embassy of Japan: Toshiki Kaifu, Kiichi Miyazawa

Viking: Garrison Keillor (photo: © Carmen Quesada, 1991), Stephen King (photo: Tabitha King)

Food and Drug Administration, U.S. Department of Health and Human Services: David Kessler

Prometheus Books: Jack Kevorkian (photo: Carl Gennette)

German Information Center: Helmut Kohl

ABC News: Ted Koppel

Crown Publishers: Jonathan Kozol (photo: © Thomas Victor, 1987)

Dale C. Olson & Associates, Public Relations: Shirley MacLaine

Random House: Norman Mailer (photo: © 1991 Nancy Crampton), James Michener (photo: © Elfriede Riley), Dr. Seuss (© Czeslaw Czaplinski), Donald Trump (© 1990 Random House, photo by Michael O'Brien)

Columbia Artists Management: Kurt Masur

Maxwell Macmillan: Robert Maxwell

Embassy of France: François Mitterrand (photo: Gisele Freund)

Egyptian Embassy: Hosni Mubarak (photo: Michele Iannacci)

Canadian Embassy: Brian Mulroney

Archdiocese of New York: Cardinal O'Connor (photo: Bachrach)

Grove Weidenfeld: Harold Pinter (photo: © Nigel Parry

Miss Saigon Press Office: Jonathan Pryce

Office of the Vice President: Dan Quayle

Springer Associates: Tony Randall, Lynn Redgrave

Embassy of India: P.V. Narashima Rao

CBS News: Dan Rather

Office of Ronald Reagan: Ronald Reagan

U.S. Environmental Protection Agency: William Reilly

Office of Ann Richards: Ann Richards

Shirley Herz Associates: Jason Robards, Jr.

Embassy of Ireland: Mary Robinson

Embassy of the Republic of Korea: Roh Tae Woo

Motown/Image Equity Management Inc.: Diana Ross

Mexican Embassy, Press Division: Carlos Salinas

ProServ: Pete Sampras (photo: Michael Baz)

Embassy of Israel: Yitzhak Shamir, Ariel Sharon

Scoop Management: Frank Sinatra

U.S. Department of Transportation: Samuel Skinner

National Basketball Association: David Stern

U.S. Department of Health and Human Services: Louis Sullivan

National Football League: Paul Tagliabue

© 1990 Warner Bros. Inc.: Jessica Tandy

U.S. Attorney General's Office: Richard Thornburgh

Turner Broadcasting Service: Ted Turner

Baseball Commissioner's Office: Fay Vincent

U.S. Department of Energy: James Watkins

Office of the Governor of Virginia: L. Douglas Wilder

Rykodisc USA: Frank Zappa

Courtesy of the subject: Hume Cronyn (photo: V. Tony Hauser), David Dinkins (photo: James Hamilton),

Sharon Pratt Dixon Kelly, Bob Dole, Thomas Foley, Richard Gephardt, William H. Gray, Alan Greenspan (photo: Brooks Photography), Gene Hackman, Tom Harkin, Jesse Helms, Lee Iacocca, James Earl Jones, Ted Kennedy (photo: Dennis DeSilva), Bob Kerey, John Kerry, Angela Lansbury, Sugar Ray Leonard, John McCain, Daniel Patrick Moynihan, Sam Nunn

Cumulative Alphabetical Index

For ease of access, we have here provided a cumulative alphabetical index of all those who have appeared in either edition of **People in the News**. For each person, the index gives the year of any edition in which he or she appears, and (after the colon) the page number where the entry begins. So for Corazon Aquino, who appears in both the first and second editions, the index entry reads:

Aquino, Corazon **'92:11 / '91:11**

Note that this edition of **People in the News** also includes a cumulative index by occupation beginning on page 395.

Cumulative Index by Occupation

For ease of access, we have indexed those profiled in **People in the News** by occupation or other area of news interest. Under the appropriate headings, such as "Law and Court Cases" or "Stage and Screen," readers will find volume and page references for all who have appeared in any edition of **People in the News**.

For each person, the index gives the year of any editions in which he or she appears, and (after the colon) the page number where the entry begins. So for Corazon Aquino, who appears in both the first and second editions, the index entry is found under the heading "Politics" and reads:

Aquino, Corazon **'92:11 / '91:11**

Note that some people are listed under more than one heading, such as Willie Nelson, who appears under both "Music" and "Stage and Screen."

The main body of each edition of **People in the News** is, of course, self-indexed, with individuals listed alphabetically. This and succeeding volumes also contain a cumulative alphabetical index, beginning on page 387.

Business and Finance

Dance

Education

Journalism and Publishing

Law and Court Cases

Literature

Military

Miscellaneous

Music

Politics

Religion

Science, Technology, and Medicine

Social Activism

Social Sciences

Sports and Games

Stage and Screen

Visual Arts